The Public Relations Digest

The Public Relations Digest

A Collection of Leading Works for Students of CIPR Qualifications

Compiled from:

Public Relations: Concepts, Practice and Critique
by Jacquie L'Etang

Public Relations Theory II
Edited by Carl H. Botan and Vincent Hazleton

Exploring Public Relations Second Edition
by Ralph Tench and Liz Yeomans

Handbook of Public Relations
Edited by Robert L. Heath

Public Relations: Critical Debates and Contemporary Practice
Edited by Jacquie L'Etang and Magda Pieczka

How to Research Third Edition
by Loraine Blaxter, Christina Hughes and Malcolm Tight

PEARSON

Custom
Publishing

Pearson Education Limited
Edinburgh Gate
Harlow
Essex CM20 2JE

And associated companies throughout the world

Visit us on the World Wide Web at:
www.pearsoned.co.uk

First published 2009
This Custom Book Edition © 2009 Published by Pearson Education Limited

Compiled from:

Public Relations: Concepts, Practice and Critique
by Jacquie L'Etang
ISBN 978 1 4129 3048 2
Copyright © Jacquie L'Etang 2008

Public Relations Theory II
Edited by Carl H. Botan and Vincent Hazleton
ISBN 978 0 8058 3385 0
Copyright © 2006 by Lawrence Erlbaum Associates, Inc.

Exploring Public Relations Second Edition
by Ralph Tench and Liz Yeomans
ISBN 978 0 273 71594 8
Copyright © Pearson Education Limited 2006, 2009

Handbook of Public Relations
Edited by Robert L. Heath
ISBN 978 1 4129 0954 9
Copyright © 2001 by Sage Publications, Inc.

Public Relations: Critical Debates and Contemporary Practice
Edited by Jacquie L'Etang and Magda Pieczka
ISBN 978 0 8058 4618 8
Copyright © 2006 by Lawrence Erlbaum Associates, Inc.

How to Research Third Edition
by Loraine Blaxter, Christina Hughes and Malcolm Tight
ISBN 978 0 335 21746 5
Copyright © Loraine Blaxter, Christina Hughes and Malcolm Tight 2006

ISBN 978 1 84776 427 0

Printed and bound in Great Britain by Hobbs the Printers, Totton, Hants.

Contents

Preface

The Chartered Institute of Public Relations began offering qualifications over ten years ago. Since then, though especially from 2005, it has refined and restructured its syllabus, so that it now has a number of awards, the core ones covering Public Relations issues in general and allowing for a progression from a short, A level standard introductory course (the level 3 Foundation Award) through to its flagship qualification, the Diploma, which is set at Master's level.

This book is an element in the expansion of the Institute's activities as a professional, examining, chartered body. It is a collection of some fifteen of the leading articles or chapters published previously that we consider are among those of major relevance to CIPR Diploma students and which consequently appear at the head of that qualification's recommended reading list. It is therefore meant to be a handy resource for those who embark on study for this qualification, though naturally we hope that it will prove to be a convenient tool for others as well.

As is indicated at the outset of the Introduction, there is a growing body of literature on our subject. As a result, such a collection of works as now presented in this book can only be just a sample of what is available, and students are then encouraged to read as widely as possible. That said, considerable thought has gone into the creation of this collection, including the selection and reselection of the material to use. It will then be an excellent platform for CIPR students to begin with, and we hope, build upon by enhancing their understanding through subsequent reading.

The task of writing a preface is always made pleasurable by allowing for the opportunity to thank and so recognise those who have been instrumental in bringing the volume into being. In the CIPR these have included Jo Fawkes FCIPR, a recent Chief Examiner for the Diploma, who made the initial selection of articles and contributions for this Digest. Special tribute must be paid especially to Sue Wolstenholme FCIPR, who served as Chair of Examiners from 2005–8 and who remains Chair of the CIPR Qualifications Committee. Sue made the final selection of the book's contents and wrote the illuminating Introduction. Stephanie Seyde and Debbie Cole of Pearson Education Limited both spent many hours on this project, without which it could never have seen the light of day.

James Scott Petre
CIPR
52–53 Russell Square
London WC1B 4HP

The student's guide to reading this book

It is possible that students coming to some of the ideas expressed in this book for the first time might feel lost among the differences of opinion and the strength of fors and againsts but the way to use the book is to weigh the evidence and develop arguments using it, along with other knowledge or experience that the reader may have, as I have tried to indicate in the following introduction.

Studying public relations at post graduate level, while also holding down an often demanding job is not an easy matter and the fact that so many are choosing to do so internationally, with the CIPR, is a positive sign for the future development of the profession. As the course is studied in many different cultures and communities, it is important to note from the start that no one book or curriculum can fully prepare someone to work professionally in public relations or, as it is called in some countries and organisations, communication. The aim of the CIPR qualifications is to provide a framework for practice to be part of a personal commitment to continuing professional development. This book has been compiled to stimulate learning and critical reflection by presenting the ideas and observations of a number of academics in the field of study. It is only a small sample of the growing literature that serious students should be **exploring widely, evaluating and criticising**, as they must also the practice that they observe or experience around them.

Jacquie L'Etang gives the Digest an excellent opening in **chapter one** by setting the discipline in its historical and modern contexts through an exploration of its roles. She provides a good model for students as she encourages, challenges and questions to create the framework for a scholarly examination of public relations practice.

In the **second chapter** the Grunigs and Dozier describe their Excellence Theory study of 1992 and consider claims for public relations as an excellent practice. They make some interesting assessments of the return on investment (ROI) into PR finding it to be 186% generally but rising to 225% in those departments which they define to be most excellent and falling to 140% in the least excellent.

They are critical of organisations which fail to be as effective as those which have in their view, empowered PR to be a strategic managerial function rather than leaving its potential untapped at the technical level. The chapter provides eager scholars with much to discuss, especially around the possible contradiction in the hegemony of the dominant coalition and genuine dialogue. The issue of dialogue is considered further, from different standpoints in chapters 3, 4, 5, 7, 10, 11, 12 and 13, showing readers that there are and need to be a number of ways of discussing the subject and underlining the fact that students must always explore around and further within any issue that they undertake to consider. The findings of the Grunigs' excellence study are also challenged in chapters 3 and 12.

Grunig's 'four models', which, since their first appearance in 1984, have provided the majority of PR students with something tangible to test and criticise or less energetically to just describe, are revisited with 2-way symmetry still regarded to be the ideal. Activism is cited as often being the catalyst for excellence and in **chapter four** Heath credits it for the rise in issues management in the 60s, which could well be linked. Dejan Vercic is described as having tested the excellence model in Slovenia and as a result added ethics to the mix.

A wide range of useful theories is discussed in **chapter three**, by Lee Edwards. While acknowledging the place that is still held by systems theory in the practice directed body of PR knowledge, Edwards considers the debate on publics and presents criticism from Sriramesh, Moghan and Wei (2007) on the theories advanced by Grunig (developed from original thinking by John Dewey in 1927). Sriramesh *et al* asserted that culture is not well enough accounted for within the definitions of publics but I would argue that, as publics are formed around an issue or concern, they can be cross cultural as in defining them closely, all their standpoints must be considered. Also Hallahan as cited, might have seen that many communication strategies exist to move publics from latent or inactive to active, rather than, as he is quoted here as *'privileging only active publics'*.

Adding weight to Vercic's findings, discussed in the previous chapter on the role of ethics, Cheney and Dionisopoulos are cited as maintaining that ethics must be closely observed in the profession to moderate the considerable power of PR (see also chapter 13). Edwards also refers to a number of studies that illustrate the concern that not only are women still treated unequally in the profession, despite being 70% of the practitioners but also the balance of ethnic minorities slowly rising through the ranks does not reflect the diversity in society. Heath's discussion on the "myth" of 2-way symmetry in a business world, where power bases are unequal and self-interestedly shaped, adds further to concerns about the excellence study findings described in chapter two.

Edwards provides a different perspective using Pal and Dutta (2008) and their argument for a critical modernist theoretical view of PR being based in critical theory and postmodernism. This perspective proposes that the language and positioning of the discourses produced by PR affects the way in which power is distributed across social structures. Later in the chapter Edwards tells us that postmodernists recognize the PR challenges faced by, among other things, the fragmented audiences, more aggressive media and a greater number of active publics and builds a perspective, which *'integrates this fragmentation and diversity into approaches to PR.' (p. 61)*

Inger Jensen's work interpreting Habermas' public sphere is given due consideration and Moloney's preference for a persuasive sphere has echoes of Pfau and Wan in chapter eleven, but emphasises that the targets of persuasion have responsibilities too. Also Merton's constructivist PR discusses the power of public relations to create reality, to which students should pay attention with close reference to ethical behaviour. That created reality can be for the good, as depicted by the use of reference to McKie and Munshi (2007) and their argument for corporate social responsibility. However they do acknowledge the uncertainty and ambiguity and having to address evolving challenges such as climate change, the decline of western dominance and the need for business to be more socially and economically sustainable. (See also chapter 7.)

As I would contend, if there is going to be any level of excellence in public relations practice, there has to be issues management, which Heath asserts in the **fourth chapter** grew out of the fertile ground of the 60s and 70s when deference withdrew and criticism or activism against business grew. *'The rhetoric of IM is best conceived of as dialogue' (p. 73) 'not to shield an organisation against emerging legislation or regulation but to balance the interests of all segments of the community.' (p. 78)*. He sums issues management up as monitoring, identifying, evaluating, prioritising, creating response and implementing. Well applied issues management is most likely to lead to a company becoming more socially responsible as it endeavours to build relationships with its publics and Heath here discusses how CSR might take an organisation above reproach by engaging interlocking cultures and building coalitions, keeping the firm ethically attuned to the

community. *'People identify because they share symbolic substance that reflects their shared identity and mutual interests' (p. 80)*

Unfortunately the fact is that, as Merton – cited by Edwards in **chapter three** – wrote about the power of the practice, that power is not always used to the most ethical of purposes. Heath illustrates here that public relations can be manipulative at one end and truth seeking at the other or it can be facile impression management, all too often or engaging in the refinement of knowledge, values and truth to the mutual good of interested parties. If those are the *continua* it would be interesting to plot how far along the line the unethical or facile approaches go before the practice starts to redeem itself.

Because issues management cannot be overlooked by the serious PR practitioner Heath's consideration of the rhetorical theory approach to it provides insights and ideas that add depth and develop the value of this important discipline as *'the rhetoric of issues management entails appeals to share substance and thereby to engage in the courtship of identification' (p. 84)* He puts forward a strong challenge to those supporting the symmetrical model, which could inspire some interesting research as he says: *'Symmetry of relationships is best defined by the ability of ideas to sustain themselves under the scrutiny of public discourse' (p. 87)* Or maybe, I would add, where those ideas would be open to change under the influence of meaningful dialogue.

Chapter five is the introduction to Heath's first section of the 2001 Handbook and it provides a useful debate about his views on the position that academics take as compared with practitioners, in preferring PR to be more about conflict reduction rather than income generating. Students might ask why academics prefer to think of their chosen subject very differently from the way in which it is practised and with that question explore how far that debate might (or not) be affecting practice. Heath outlines the emerging definitions that come out of what he sees as the academic standpoint, which focus upon mutuality and all that has to be in place to be granted society's licence to operate. (This important point should be considered alongside chapter seven and the evolution of CSR). He discusses the chapters in the section and their promotion of symmetrical communication; rhetorical approaches to relationship building; new approaches to appreciate complexity and diversity and ways in which community can be a tyranny for individuality unless collectivism is genuinely accommodated; putting publics at the centre of planning (which they are in an issues management approach) and he calls for a closer examination of the role of PR in the struggle for democracy. That was written before the 2008 US election, which will almost certainly spawn many research papers citing evidence for the role that public relations might have had in rekindling democracy!

Gerard Choo, in Tench and Yeomans, gives a thoughtful and much needed discussion on audiences, stakeholders and publics in **chapter six**. Despite thought provoking discussions on reception analysis, audience activity, the linear communication model and a useful consideration of the differing views of media effects, the chapter is still slightly confusing with the assertion that publics need not be stakeholders but that stakeholders become publics. The chapter suggests that publics are always active and therefore stakeholders are latent publics *(p.106)* which will hopefully set some bright minds thinking as to why we need to refer to stakeholders at all. Chay-Nemeth's application of Foucault's concept of governmentality (1991) is cited as extending the theory of publics into new and valuable areas looking at their context historically and culturally and adding some challenges to the rest of the debate.

Staying with Tench and Yeomans as the source text, in **chapters seven** and **eight** Ralph Tench first of all outlines some debates about community and society taking the need for a relationship with society and an increasingly ethical approach to public relations as the main reasons for the growth in CSR. He offers a new tool for analysis based upon a continuum within a sphere, which runs from irresponsibility to responsibility and is set within an understanding of internal and external environmental awareness. He argues that this approach gives a more dynamic analysis than that previously given by Carroll's pyramid as it explores the *'multi-faceted layers of complexity that are shared by context.'* (p. 125) While it does bring in far more for the analyst to consider I feel that the pyramid is still needed to assess an organisation's movement from that which is regulated to that which is done for purely philanthropic reasons. In **chapter eight** Martin Langford discusses crisis management, offering a range of examples and also illustrating well that a crisis is also an opportunity to show much more about the organisation than every day running ever can and therefore, as it stresses, the communication function is of paramount importance.

Campaigning organisations and pressure groups are discussed by Sue Wolstenholme in **chapter nine**. With activists having been credited in chapters 2 and 4 as having had an important role in the development of public relations it is worth considering how they are motivated, how they function and how those who are attacked by them might defend their positions or work for consensus.

Further reflections on the dialogue that might or might not be happening in public relations are undertaken by Lynn Zoch and Juan C Molleda in **chapter ten** with a look at the various uses and interpretations of framing from sociological, message focussing and journalistic standpoints. Using information subsidies as the focus they consider the power in the holding of and the access to information.

Kopenhaver, cited on p. 173, gives an interesting viewpoint on media relations, asserting that editors who believe that those sending news releases have a similar education level in news values to their own are more likely to see the release as informational rather than promotional. There are also various findings on ways to increase the success factors in news releases. A number of writers concerned with the agenda building process in the news media and its effect upon public opinion, are compared by Zoch and Molleda in a useful table on p. 175.

Believing that persuasion is an intrinsic function of public relations, Pfau and Wan, in **chapter eleven**, present another challenge to the asymmetry/symmetry argument in the achievement of excellence, asserting that it has stunted PR scholarship in terms of goal compatibility, compromise, power and accommodation. The view, that if it is democratic it is ethical to support persuasion, demands attention but claiming that persuasion is inherently unethical is also flawed as it can be necessary in turning ignorance into knowledge as much as part of the worst aspects of propaganda. They agree that it is the means and/or the ends of persuasion where the measure of ethics has to be applied. As with many academics in Europe, Pfau and Wan promote communication theory as the core academic area to be studied rather than public relations. They consider a number of models and theories including functional theory, which although they concede is full of potential rather than answers as yet, it can be used to promote the view that communication based on value expressive attitudes is common in public relations. They illustrate the point with the assertion that spending on sponsorship in the US doubled from the late 1980s to the mid 1990s along with advocacy advertising and CSR. They add further evidence to their position on persuasion by claiming that it is vital to lobbying, fundraising and media relations.

In **chapter twelve** Weaver, Motion and Roper offer a worthwhile discussion of the concepts that swirl around and sometimes become stuck to public relations. Propaganda and spin are given a thorough investigation set within their historical context and truth (whose truth?) is also interrogated to present a good range of arguments for those seeking to critically analyse. From Bernays onwards ideas are reflected upon from an analytical standpoint to include a clear and vital consideration of Grunig and Habermas and whether strategic or communicative action can be claimed as being symmetric. As they conclude: *'that the critical discourse theory view of public relations, and indeed propaganda, provides a means of understanding the significance of the public relations contribution to the formation of hegemonic power, constructions of truth, and the public interest. Understood in these terms public relations becomes a tool of social power and change for utilization by* *not only those who hold hegemonic power but also those who seek to challenge and transform that power and reconfigure dominant perceptions of the public interest'. (p. 221)*

Anne Gregory presents a broad view of the role of ethics in the professional practice of public relations in **chapter thirteen**. Along with some useful definitions and theoretical underpinning, Gregory discusses some of the academic debate around whether or not public relations practice can cite many examples of ethical behaviour to be able to claim to act, as Grunig described the function in 1984, as the conscience of an organisation.

In **chapter fourteen** Blaxter, Hughes and Tight provide a good set of questions to focus the final research project. Although referring to the university setting as the background, the principles are very similar for all researchers. However, for most people studying the CIPR Diploma, the role of the employer or manager in deciding upon a topic will be more significant. Also, in the same vein, it is worth considering the wider profession and the type of subjects that could be used for publication, to indicate the value of research or to develop the body of knowledge.

The **final chapter** fittingly presents a thorough consideration by Theilmann and Szondi of research in many of its guises, for practice and academic study. The chapter also picks up the importance of evaluation, which is one of the most important ways that public relations can command a better share of the budget. As Dejan Vercic commented at the Euprera conference in Milan in 2008, without evaluation public relations will remain more like witchcraft rather than becoming a science.

Sue Wolstenholme

CHAPTER 1

Jacquie L'Etang

Public relations:
defining the discipline and the practice*

Chapter aims

On completion of this chapter you should be able to:

- understand aspects of the diverse nature of PR work and the complex role of PR in society
- understand the connection between the study of PR and the discipline of communications
- describe key PR processes and language used in practice to describe PR work
- critique a 'checklist' approach to PR
- apply key principles to PR evaluation
- debate the connections between PR and propaganda and issues that arise from this for the PR discipline and practice
- describe various possible reasons for the evolution of PR in a variety of cultural contexts
- describe how sociology can help us to understand the PR occupation more fully.

Before you read a single word . . .

- What do you think public relations is?
- Where have you drawn your ideas from?
- If you are thinking of pursuing a career in public relations, explain why.

Key concepts

Evaluation	Public	Professionalism	Public sphere
Linearity	Public opinion	Propaganda	Strategic PR
Othering	Public relations	Psyops	System of knowledge

* Chapter 2 in *Public Relations Concepts, Practice and Critique*, by Jacquie L'Etang (2008). Copyright © Jacquie L'Etang. Reproduced with permission.

Introduction

This chapter will give you a good understanding of the function and purpose of public relations, the key processes that are utilized in practising public relations and a broader understanding of the public relations occupation in society. The chapter combines **functional** and **critical** approaches (Table 1.1).

Public relations: its purpose, role and scope

If we think about the term 'public relations', we can understand a great deal about the activity by analyzing the term and pursuing a number of readings. On the one hand, it clearly suggests ongoing relationships that are open to view – they are 'public'. Alternatively, **public** may suggest a particular group or 'the general public' or **public opinion** – and the latter term in particular suggests that the practice of PR is partly linked to notions of democratic process and broader political arrangements. It implies the importance of the majority view and notions of consensus and dissensus. There is also the concept of **the public sphere** as a space where rational discussion among citizens can take place in resolving opinion about the current issues of the day.

Then there is the term specific to public relations, that of *publics* – this is clearly derived from the analytical work of the sociologist Park in the early twentieth century in his work distinguishing certain types of group from crowds or masses (Park, 1972). The term 'public' focuses our attention on specific groups within society who have interests in particular issues or with particular organizations. The term 'publics' is sometimes used interchangeably with that of audiences – however, the latter term implies a more passive and possibly less powerful group.

To take a more pragmatic and descriptive approach:

Public relations involves the communication and exchange of ideas to facilitate change. American PR author Banks remarked, 'Public relations literally is born and immersed in controversy – no need for change, no need for PR' (Banks, 1995: ix). Change entails the expression of opinions and discussions of ideas and policy options. Organizations need specialists to perform that function and to interface between the organization and those groups with which it has or would like to have relationships. Public relations entails the analysis of organizational actions which may impact on relationships or reputation.

However, PR is not 'customer care' or simply 'promotion' of the organizational view. It also entails anticipating the analysis of new and emerging issues that may affect an organization, not just a set of communication techniques. It is about clarity and intellectual honesty based on evidence, not sucking up to people or being likeable or liked (though that may help in any job!).

In basic descriptive functional terms, public relations involves the communication and exchange of ideas either in response to, or to facilitate change. It entails argument and case-making. It is thus intrinsically connected to policy initiatives, their promotion and responses to these by organizational actors and their representatives. Most communication is achieved through the use of various technologies (telephone, e-mail, internet, SMS), some is mediated by *public media*, and some is direct face-to-face communication (meetings, press conferences). It also requires the facilitation of individual *intra-personal communication* (reflection and reflexive thinking). Thus public relations involves *interpersonal communication*, *intra-group communication* (within groups), *inter-group communication* (between groups) and *mass communication*. But public relations practitioners need not only to understand communication processes but the social and organizational context in which

Table 1.1 Functional and critical approaches in public relations: key questions

Functional questions	Critical questions
■ How can I measure media content?	■ Does PR impede or assist democracy?
■ How can I evaluate this PR campaign?	■ Is public relations another term for propaganda?
■ Which psychological models could be used to structure a persuasive campaign?	■ Is public relations a profession?

communication takes place. Thus public relations work takes into account a very wide range of factors, some of which are relational, some of which are organizational and some of which are environmental, encompassing local, national and international issues and contexts.

Public relations exists in all sectors at many different levels. See Box 1.1 on public relations work and Box 1.2 on jobs in public relations.

You can read all sorts of stories and get up to speed with current developments in the PR industry in the UK by reading *PRWeek* or equivalent professional journals and trade magazines. However, you should bear in mind that many of the stories that you read are one-sided accounts from the perspective of the agency or client.

To sum up, contemporary PR is:

■ present in all changes – technological, economic, social, political, legal

■ issue-driven (reactive and proactive – bringing things on to the public agenda as well as responding to new developments)

■ dynamic and flexible

■ problem-solving

■ involves standing back from immediate problems to view the wider picture and the complexity of organizational relationships and overlapping networks

■ integral to complex post-industrial societies and takes place in a wide variety of contexts: politics, science, health, the arts, sport, entertainment, leisure, education, commerce.

Consequently, public relations is varied and responsive in different contexts and can entail:

■ interpreting perceptions of the organization

■ gathering intelligence from the environment to shed light on issues that might affect publics' motivations

■ identifying problems that may emerge from publics

■ understanding others' perspectives

■ assessing relationships

■ establishing contexts for discussion, debate, denial, apologia

■ being silent

■ resisting lobbying attempts

■ reaching agreement/consensus/compromise

■ advocacy – promotion

■ public service

■ rhetoric/persuasion

■ diplomacy

■ debating issues

Box 1.1

Public relations work

■ **Ideological PR: promoting democracy in Iraq**
Consultancy Bell Pottinger won a £2.3 million contract to promote democracy in Iraq (*PRWeek*, 11 March 2004)

■ **Sports tourism**
The England cricket team's 'Barmy Army' supporters' organization recruited a PR agency to promote its tours and establish a press office (*PRWeek*, 21 July 2006)

■ **Fashion PR**
Modus Publicity re-launched Selfridges, throwing a party which involved 'a transvestite in the cooking department doing cookery demonstrations with oil and chains, and a feminist poet in the beauty department strapped to a lipstick' (*PRWeek*, 15 September 2006)

■ **Promotion of science . . . intra-governmental lobbying**
The UK National Endowment for Science Technology and the Arts (NESTA), an organization created by the British government, aimed to 'improve the climate for innovation across the UK' and to influence government policy, especially the Department of Trade and Industry (DTI) and the Treasury with regard to the improvement of science teaching in schools (*PRWeek*, 9 June 2006)

■ **Behavioural change: car safety**
Liverpool City Council used a consultancy to raise awareness of the dangers of overcrowding in cars and drink and drug driving (*PRWeek*, 17 December 2006)

■ **Consumerism vs religion**
Lobby group Deregulate sought a PR agency to help it completely deregulate Sunday trading whereas their opponent, the Lord's Day Observance Society, planned to use in-house expertise and was confident it could mobilize public support (*PRWeek*, 16 June 2006 and 23 June 2006)

Box 1.2

Job opportunities in public relations: definitions, tasks, language

Communications & marketing manager: regeneration and housing, Lambeth

As part of our excellent communications team, you will help to deliver a first-class service. Motivated by success, you will use your innovation, flair and expertise to help improve and enhance the reputation of the council among residents, stakeholders and partners. If you have a positive attitude and think you can contribute to our growing success, we are looking to recruit . . . (*PRWeek*, 3 November 2006: 48)

Stakeholder & communications executives: London Underground

You'll cultivate relationships with key stakeholders, including politicians, watchdog bodies, business organizations and lobby groups. This will involve organizing events, forums and visits, and using them to engage and influence stakeholders. You'll also provide LU representatives with comprehensive briefings, speech notes and presentations. (*PRWeek*, 3 November 2006: 48)

PR managers: Compass Group

Due to the size and scale of the business we now need to hire three PR managers – skilled media specialists who can advise on a number of issues and build long-term relationships with key journalists, maximising media opportunities. These brand new roles are multi-disciplined and span three business sectors: business and industry; sport, leisure and hospitality; health, education, defence and government. The PR manager for each business group will be tasked with the development and implementation of a proactive and creative media relations-led PR programme specifically tailored to its industry sector. (*PRWeek*, 29 October 2006: 36)

Internal communications manager: British Airways

. . . we want you to design and implement our employee communications and involvement strategy. Working in line with and contributing to the formation of the business plan you'll provide communications support for all internal and face-to-face events and develop a communications plan in close conjunction with our corporate media relations team. With clear and effective communication skills that span a range of formats you'll be skilled in translating complex messages into simple and understandable language . . . you'll be an engaging and innovative communicator. . . . (*PRWeek*, 27 October 2006: 44)

Media liaison executive: Primary and Secondary National Strategies

To continue to positively impact on teaching and learning in schools. . . . You will have excellent writing and communication skills . . . [to secure] a consistent presence in a range of publications including national and industry press, academic journals and other stakeholder publications and websites. (*PRWeek*, 27 October 2006: 40)

Head of government & external affairs: AstraZeneca

We are one of the world's leading pharmaceutical companies, our business is focused on providing innovative, effective modern medicines that make a real difference in important areas of healthcare. Our success is based on a commitment to discovery, finding new ideas that are inspired by life and which in turn help to inspire the lives of our stakeholders. . . . You will be responsible for understanding and anticipating issues and opportunities arising from Government and other policymakers and delivering a business-led public affairs strategy . . . (*PRWeek*, 27 November 2006: 41)

■ democratic education

■ building coherent identity – cohesiveness/consensus

■ communication acts

Some of these raise ethical problems. For example, is consensus necessarily a desirable social goal? Do attempts to achieve organizational cohesiveness run the risk of being little more than management propaganda?

There are also other more pragmatic problems. There may simply be limits to the way in which some organizational relationships can be improved. Some writing about public relations is open to the criticism that it is over-idealistic. Some writing about public relations (usually from journalists and media sociologists who focus on the media relations aspect of public relations practice) condemns the practice out of hand as manipulative and anti-democratic.

Personal development

■ What qualities seem important to PR practitioners, and why?

■ Do you have or can you develop these qualities?

■ How can you write your CV to demonstrate that you have these qualities?

PR definitions

■ You may notice that jobs in PR carry widely different titles. Why do you think this is? (One job describes PR as 'Media manager', a term that is also used to describe those who manage media organizations.)

■ Notice that PR work is referred to as 'translation'. What skills do you think this sort of work requires and why?

■ In some cases job ads emphasize the terms 'strategy' and 'relationship' but the tasks described seem focused on media relations. Why do you think this is?

These are all important ideas, but it is only through detailed research of particular cases and historical events, or through philosophical discussion, that we can really be in a position to make judgements. It is also useful to look at the way in which practitioners go about their business.

Public relations: key processes

What processes enable public relations practitioners to get that 'wider picture', to understand relationships and to help organizations and publics change? How can the busy practitioner step back from the hustle and bustle of office life, the writing of promotional literature and the constraints of administering publications schedules and researching the detail required for annual reports?

First of all, what do we mean by 'processes'? In public relations literature these are usually defined as linear steps – a basic checklist. Typically, these are expressed as:

■ research

■ objectives

■ publics

■ messages

■ strategy and tactics

■ evaluation

Note that strategy in this context means the articulation of an overall concept or approach to a campaign, problem or a public prior to the selection of particular communication techniques that will have the potential to *reify* (realize or make real or concrete) the strategy. Shortly, I shall raise some critical questions about the concept of **strategic PR**.

You can find many such lists in public relations texts. What they have in common is their linear structure, their clarity and their rationalism. They are one way of making sense of working life and of imposing structure and order. It is, nevertheless, worth thinking about aspects which are not alluded to in such lists, which are, oddly, all the aspects of relationships with which public relations is supposed to take account. For example: emotions, feelings, relationship states.

Take one example in a popular text which includes a chapter on 'Starting the planning process'. This begins with the headline 'Getting in control' and highlights aspects of planning that benefit the individual practitioner and his or her workload. For example: 'it focuses effort . . . it improves effectiveness . . . it encourages the long-term view . . . it helps demonstrate value for money . . . it minimises mishaps . . . it reconciles conflicts of interests and priorities . . . it facilitates proactivity' (Gregory, 2000: 34–37). However, such points do not tell us whether it helps public relations practitioners achieve their aim in terms of improving organizational relationships. It only looks at public relations from the organization's perspective and not in terms of assessing relationships from a variety of perspectives. Thus it introduces a power relationship between the organization and its publics. In the qualitative paradigm of social science, this process of positioning an audience or a research subject is referred to as **Othering**.

So, while broadly useful, many checklists are somewhat formulaic and can raise lots of questions.

The following list offers a little more detail and explanation but still is linear in structure:

■ environmental scanning and research (including issues analysis)

■ situation analysis (historical review plus developing scenarios)

■ organizational/market strengths, weaknesses, opportunities, threats

■ benchmarking against competitor organizations

■ combining internal and external intelligence

- identifing key publics, researching, understanding and classifying (1) in relation to organization and current issues and (2) in relationship and emotional terms

- defining and conceptualizing stakeholder/public relationships in relation to ideal

- prioritizing

- aiming and supporting researchable objectives (including those for the state of relationships)

- messages

- technique selection (in the light of budget/time constraints)

- communication

- evaluation, review and re-analysis involving key publics (taking on board positive and negative feedback)

What is the problem with linearity and checklists?

There is a problem for those who seek to position public relations as an occupation that seeks to establish *true dialogue* between an organization and its stakeholders. Because the managerial approaches outlined above necessarily begin with the strategic aims and objectives of the organization, they set a particular agenda for change which does not necessarily involve stakeholders. In other words, although PR is seen as managing relationships, those relationships may not be suitably prioritized. An alternative approach would be to engage stakeholders in the process of defining aims, objectives and desirable outcomes at the outset (Coalter, 2006). This could help prevent ill-defined or ill-informed programmes and public relations could potentially act as a catalyst for organizational development and learning via consultative relationships. The critical point I am making here is that common models of the sort I have outlined do not fit with the normative (idealistic) dialogic models. In other words, there is a discrepancy between some of the idealistic values expressed and the mechanistic methodology. If PR practitioners (and their organizations) are really serious about establishing 'dialogue', then inviting stakeholders to define objectives and outcomes might be a first step. Useful applications of this approach might be made in employee relations and corporate social responsibility programmes. As this book went to press Ströh made some similar points when she claimed, 'Publics . . . do not want merely to be identified, described, researched and communicated to (as suggested by most models of strategic corporate communication management); instead they want to be part of strategy formulation . . .' (Ströh, 2007: 210).

There are also some more pragmatic concerns with the linearity of a checklist approach:

- Any elements of processes need to be carried out concurrently, on an ongoing basis, not consecutively.

- They create the illusion of discrete steps and a controlled process which does not reflect reality, thus being of limited assistance to the busy practitioner.

Empirical research into managerial work showed that scientific and administrative approaches to management did not reflect managerial reality and were therefore of limited assistance to managers. It can be argued that the same limitation may apply to public relations. Step-by-step approaches may provide a simplified guide and are a starting point, but do not help interpretative processes. Ultimately, more is needed than checklists. Understanding and engaging in relationships requires commitment and time. Public opinion and media processes are complex and sometimes contentious. Public relations practitioners need some specialized knowledge and a way of codifying it for those outside the field. Judgements and recommendations made by those in public relations need to be based on a system of knowledge. They need to be capable of some conceptual analysis and to be able to conduct empirical research – if they cannot do so, then they are no more than organizational witch doctors!

Knowledge and theory: research and evaluation

What is meant by **system of knowledge**? The phrase refers to frameworks of linked concepts that form theories that explain the world and help us to understand problems. For public relations, that system is necessarily complex. Public relations practitioners will need to draw on a range of communication and media theories, management and organizational theories. However, to carry out research public relations practitioners need some understanding of systems of knowledge (*epistemology*), and to carry out programmes of corporate social responsibility they need to understand *ethics* and *public policy*, they need a grasp of *philosophy* and *politics*. **Public relations**, as we shall see later, is a *cultural practice* and so it is important to understand the fundamental principles that structure society (*anthropology*). In short, one cannot have too much theoretical knowledge to practise public relations intelligently and effectively! Indeed, there is a very famous quote from the social scientist Kurt Lewin that 'there is nothing as practical as a good theory'.

Effectiveness in public relations, is, however, usually presented as a question of achieving specific relationship and organizational policy objectives. In order to assess effectiveness, public relations practitioners must use a variety of research techniques to establish if their efforts have had any impact (bearing in mind that there will have been other influences affecting the situation and publics – public relations does not happen in laboratory conditions). Designing good social research is therefore a key skill for the competent practitioner and I would go so far as to argue that this skill (and the underpinning knowledge) alone has the ability to deliver professional status to public relations. Research needs to be understood at the strategic (epistemological and paradigm) level, not purely as a technical skill. It is the deeper knowledge that empowers the practitioner to make intelligent and sophisticated choices. Checklists should be reminders and not reified to the status of a theory.

To sum up, the ability to research and evaluate:

■ has the potential to bestow credibility on the occupation and is the route to gaining professional status

■ provides some comparability with other management disciplines (though this can be a disadvantage in that these may be overly in favour of quantitative approaches)

In our evidence-based scientific culture that emphasizes rationalism, public relations needs to possess, employ and demonstrate its facility with high-level intellectual knowledge and the ability to apply such concepts to data. In the past, practitioners were criticized for their subjective 'seat of the pants' approach. Aware that the failure to evaluate caused credibility problems, **evaluation** has become and remains something of a 'holy grail' for public relations. Because of this, the Chartered Institute of Public Relations (CIPR) in the UK worked hard to draw up a standardized approach. While this has been a useful intervention, it has weaknesses simply because it *is* standardized and used as a 'bolt on'. Only when practitioners have a good facility to understand and carry out a variety of research can the occupation move forwards to professional status. As English philosopher Francis Bacon said in 1597, 'knowledge is power' (www.quotationspage.com, accessed 23 January 2007).

One important issue that remains a problem in public relations practice is over what it is that is to be evaluated. Many practitioners concentrate on media output but do not try to determine knowledge, attitude, understanding, behavioural change in key publics, relationships or networks. Media evaluation is useful in determining that a campaign has succeeded in bringing an issue to media attention, but should not be seen as evidence that media consumers have actually noticed or been influenced by media content. This often means that their objectives and

evaluation do not actually link to each other in the way they should. Box 1.3 analyzes some brief examples reported in *PRWeek*. It should of course be noted that the synoptic accounts presented in *PRWeek* may have edited out important details that were present in original campaign documents. Box 1.4 offers top tips on writing objectives and planning evaluation.

Public relations: the occupation

Public relations work is relatively unstructured and jobs are often not well defined. This has advantages and disadvantages. For the ambitious there is often the ability to develop their job into the areas of work which interest them – and maybe to achieve promotion along the way. On the other hand, it can be difficult to manage career moves. For example, the term 'Account Executive' in consultancies can include a very wide variety of tasks and require different levels of experience and seniority in small or large consultancies.

Consultancies have their own specific culture and mystique, often appearing to be 'glamorous gurus' who participate in 'beauty parades' – promotional pitches for business – which can be 'exhausting but exhilarating' (Hinrichsen, 2001: 454).

In reality, the work can be long and hard. Public relations has remained an un-unionized occupation despite the attempts of the National Union of Journalists (NUJ) in the 1970s, which worked on behalf of those journalists who had crossed over into PR. Although the NUJ won a number of cases over pay, by 1967 they had given up the quest for a minimum salary and PR became subject to the vagaries of the market (L'Etang, 2004: 129). This means that the pressures of the business can, and do, lead to excessive hours of work (Box 1.5).

'Strategic' public relations

'Strategic' PR can be seen as a Holy Grail for some PR academics and some PR practitioners. Thus it is worth reflecting on the following questions:

■ What is strategic PR?

■ Does strategic PR exist?

■ Is strategic PR interesting?

■ Does strategic PR matter?

Within general PR discourse, strategic PR is assumed to be high-status, important, desirable, intelligent, far-seeing

Box 1.3

Comparing objectives with evaluation procedures

1 London Youth Games Ltd (*PRWeek*, 10 February 2006)

Objectives: To increase awareness of competitive sporting opportunities available to young people in London and promote positive images of the city's youth. To help partner organizations such as Sport England to increase participation in sport.

Measurement and evaluation: Media coverage.

Results: Participation in games with a breakdown of figures by minority backgrounds and disability. Media coverage.

Comment: Objectives should specify how much awareness and whose, and define what is meant by 'positive images'. Media coverage should be specifically related to that objective and specific publics. Why was media coverage important? What did readers/target publics make of the coverage? Objectives should specify how much participation. Research and evaluation should attempt to identify whether the event encouraged those who did not normally participate in sport to do so.

2 Camden Council (*PRWeek*, 30 June 2006)

Objectives: To increase voter turnout and voter registration.

Measurement and evaluation: Coverage was 'balanced'.

Results: Voter turnout increased. More than 2,500 people canvassed for views on voting.

Comment: Objectives should be made quantifiable. Specific attitudes and behaviours could be spelt out in detail. Which media and why? What counts as positive and negative coverage could be specified. Did voter registration increase and if so by how much? How did turnout compare to other local elections nationally and historically? What other issues and news coverage might have influenced motivation to vote?

3 Science Museum events (*PRWeek*, 15 September 2006)

Objectives: To position the exhibition as an examination of fame, photography and image management in the Victorian age. To reach out to a new corporate audience from the engineering sector.

Measurement and evaluation: Exhibition received media coverage in trade titles.

Results: Energy firm booked exhibition for corporate event.

Comment: Objectives should specify among whom the exhibition is to be positioned and why. Why is the corporate sector important and what attitudinal/behavioural change is desired? Who reads the media in which coverage was received and how did this help towards achieving objective?

– and it is taken for granted that it is 'a good thing'. Yet strategic public relations can also be read as cunning, clever, self-interested, pompous and powerful. *Strategy* was originally conceived as rationally intended purposeful thought to guide action – and is clearly self-interested (Pettigrew et al., 2002b: 11–12). The field of *strategic management* has traditionally lacked critique or reflexivity, and only a small critical paradigm (composed largely of European scholars) has discussed strategic management as an ideological practice, focused on domination and power (Pettigrew et al., 2002b: 11). In other words, 'strategy' is not neutral, though the term may be used to disguise power and politics in public relations, especially in the fields of *issues management* and *public affairs*. Critical independent public relations students and researchers might want to ask themselves and others:

■ What sort of strategic management are PR practitioners signing up to?

■ What sort of strategic management are PR practitioners actually doing?

■ What assumptions underpin strategic public relations (theory and practice)?

Finally, and more provocatively, could we see 'strategic PR' which uses a range of research skills, social psychological and sociological concepts as a form of civilian political warfare or *psyops*?

Psyops

Psyops or *political warfare* is a research-driven effort to persuasive communication that draws upon communications theory and research, media research, analysis and tactics, planning skills, messaging, group dynamics, teamwork and spin, or 'accentuating the positive' (Cooper, 1982: 310–312). Definitions include:

Box 1.4

Writing objectives and planning evaluation: top tips

- An objective should be specific and researchable.

- Avoid generalities such as 'raise the profile', which are too broad and rather meaningless. Be as specific as possible.

- Spell out what changed knowledge, attitude or behaviour you are seeking, whose, why and by when.

- Make sure you link such desired changes to overall aims and strategic objectives which are likely to do with reputation or market position or particular important relationships.

- Do not assume that media coverage is the be-all and end-all even though media coverage may be a by-product of actions you take.

- Think about who reads the media.

- Remember the media and readers are active, not passive, recipients awaiting organizational communication and instruction.

- Focus on relationships, reputation and public opinion (of which media coverage is a part), which can be examined in terms of quality as well as quantity.

- Make sure that research and evaluation includes research besides media content analysis and that it is precisely targeted at the initial audiences you defined at the outset.

- Consider surveying or interviewing key members or experts about an important issue.

- Above all, link evaluation to your core objectives.

In short, if you set objectives that entail change-making (a relationship, an attitude, a behaviour) the research should evaluate and measure that change element directly. Assessing or counting media coverage on the assumption that this will necessarily directly influence the change item is misguided. Evaluating media explains media, not stakeholders, although media can play an important role in public opinion. Therefore, the evaluation of objectives is likely to require multi-method research to understand media coverage and change processes. Where media coverage is set as an objective, this focus should be justified, and supported by qualitative and quantitative targets.

Box 1.5

Working in a public relations consultancy

If public relations is seen as a glamorous field then public relations firms may be viewed as 'Glamour Central'. There can be prestige and excitement, and there is always a fast pace. Some other advantages are . . . variety . . . big budgets . . . the collegial atmosphere can be stimulating and motivating. . . . On the flip side, agency life can be rigorous, stressful and demanding. Some of the issues are . . . the long hours . . . people usually work late in the day and on weekends . . . pressure . . . the agency environment is like a pressure cooker . . . turnover . . . could be attributed to resignations over working conditions . . . some agencies must let people go if they lose big accounts. (Hinrichsen, 2001: 452–3)

Psychological operations . . . is a communicative act or program, since its purpose is to affect other's perceptions, attitudes, and opinions – and through that effect to influence their behavior. (McLaurin, 1982a: 2)

[Psyop programmes require] critical information about . . . targets (friendly, neutral, hostile) . . . [and] must include the following:

1. *The definition of key audiences (both friendly and enemy) within the society.*
2. *The beliefs, attitudes, opinions, and motivations of key audiences as individuals and groups.*
3. *The analysis of current vulnerabilities of specific audiences within the society.*
4. *The determination of message content and the most effective (best) communication channels to reach the target.*
5. *The impact or effect of PSYOP communication. (Katz, 1982: 123)*

While psyops is normally defined a part of the military's propaganda effort it is clear that it is methodologically linked to PR. That connection goes some way to explaining critiques of the PR function and its methods. The role of persuasive communication in a society raises questions over its sponsors and its accountability. Complex societies need to exchange ideas, develop and advocate policies without infringing media freedom and citizen rights of access to information. The occupation of public relations is necessarily ethically challenged because it is situated at centres of power; seeks to influence decision-making; and is unregulated.

Public relations: historical and social role

It is beyond the scope of this chapter to give a respectable account of PR history. Most PR textbooks give a somewhat bowdlerized account of US history plus a few references to Greeks and Romans to suggest that PR has long been connected to the promotion of cultural identity and political debate. The common notion that prevails is that Americans invented public relations and then exported it everywhere else in the world. In the case of the UK, this is patently not true and it is becoming clearer that in many countries forms of public relations were carried out at various stages (Muruli, 2001; Borghetti, 2003; Murphy, 2003; L'Etang, 2004; L'Etang and Muruli, 2004; Toledano, 2005; Puchan, 2006; Al Saqur, 2007; Ismail, 2007). Remembering that public relations arises at points of change and over issues where there is disagreement over policy and practice, we can appreciate that there are many contexts in which formal organizational communication is required. Governments have long appreciated this and have had the resources at their disposal to try to influence key groups of citizens and public opinion more widely. Governmental communication has often been accused on 'being propaganda', and so this chapter explores some of the issues that bear upon a discussion of the relationship between public relations and **propaganda**. This discussion naturally takes us into a discussion of ethics, and from thence to a consideration of the terms professionalism and professionalization.

This section does not explain how to practise public relations, but alerts readers to the importance of the occupation's development, its aspirations for professional status and the challenges its faces for social legitimacy. To some extent it looks at the nature of arguments that have been made against public relations in the past and those that exist right up to the present day. Thus this section opens up debate on public relations' social role through discussion of:

- history
- propaganda
- professionalism and professionalization
- features of the occupation

History and development of public relations

While it is not possible here to review the emergence of public relations on a global basis, it can be noted that:

- academics are still recovering PR history around the world
- understanding different paths of evolution will generate insights into practice and potentially could lead to new concepts, frameworks and theory
- in many countries PR evolved as part of nation-building and national identity processes, sometimes as part of de-colonization or freedom-fighting
- in many countries PR developed as part of political propaganda, sometimes during times of war
- there will in due time be multiple histories (corporate, political, biographical, sectoral, liberal, Marxist, etc.) and interpretations for any one nation or stateless nation
- theoretical frameworks derived from historical evolution in one country cannot be sensibly applied as interpretative models in other cultures
- PR was not invented by Americans and then exported elsewhere
- PR practice is not necessarily morally progressive

Public relations and propaganda

For some (Ewen, 1996; Schlesinger et al., 2001), PR is intrinsically about political control:

> The rise of PR as an occupation began at the turn of the [twentieth] century in the US and slightly later in the UK. Universal suffrage and other democratic reforms were a key factor in increasing the influence that could be exerted by the people on decision-making. In short, PR emerged in response to the democratization that followed increasing social unrest and the rise of organized labour. At the same time, new communications technologies were being developed and it became possible to reach a new mass market. (Schlesinger et al., 2001: 14)

The conceptual relationship between public relations and propaganda is both controversial (particularly for

Box 1.6

Definitions of propaganda

Propaganda in the broadest sense is the technique of influencing human action by the manipulation of representations. These representations may take spoken, written, pictorial or musical form. (Lasswell, 1934/1995: 13)

Propaganda is . . . the deliberate attempt by some individual or group to form, control or alter the attitudes of other groups by the use of instruments of communication, with the intention that in any given situation the reaction of those so influenced will be that desired by the propagandist. (Quarlter, cited in Hazan, 1976:11)

Propaganda is the preconceived, systematic and centrally co-ordinated process of manipulating symbols, aimed at promoting uniform behaviours of large social groups, a behaviour congruent with the specific interests and ends of the propagandist. (Hazan, 1976: 12)

Propaganda is not neutral, it aims to further the aims of the propagandist. (Wright, 1991: xiii)

For others propaganda is 'brainwashing' – akin to religious conversion, political indoctrination, the changing of delusional beliefs by mentally ill patients. (Watson, 1978: 289)

All modern societies are inundated with propaganda from every quarter. The vast bureaucracies which dominate all institutional arenas generate their own propaganda, for both internal and external consumption. Bureaucracies produce propaganda, among many other reasons, to divert attention from unpalatable hard choices; or to dress up organizational performance when soliciting appropriations or investment; or to mollify employees wary of organizational aims. (Jackall, 1995: 7)

Propaganda is a form of communication that is different from persuasion because it attempts to achieve a response that furthers the desired intent of the propagandist. Persuasion is interactive and attempts to satisfy the needs of both persuader and persuadee. (Jowett and O'Donnell, 1986: 13)

[Old propaganda] was characterized by the attempt of the few to impose a picture of reality on the many. . . . [New propaganda] underlined a process of negotiation among many participants . . . the audience has always had the power of resistance . . . as our media allow us to interact globally with others in a community of interest, we need a new way to think about reality construction. (Edelstein, 1997: xiii)

---

practitioners who fear moral opprobrium) and difficult. First of all, as has been noted by other authors, particularly Fawkes (2006: 267–287), many basic definitions of propaganda could be equally well used to describe public relations. Box 1.6 shows some of the many definitions of propaganda.

Critical reflection

Read through the quotes in Box 1.6. Once you have reflected on their meaning and implications, read them again, this time replacing the term 'propaganda' with that of 'public relations'. What is the outcome and implications of this exercise?

The definitions shown in Box 1.6 indicate some overlaps between public relations and propaganda. For some analysts, public relations *is* propaganda. And if that was

not enough, the historical evidence in the UK shows that a number of early PR practitioners graduated from careers in wartime propaganda to peacetime PR, thus suggesting shared concepts or *modus operandi* (L'Etang, 2004: 49; 2006b: 149–152).

In addition to historical evidence which shows that regimes and governments and their appointees have used their power to filter and distort information, there are also some intrinsic problems concerned with trying to make public relations activity transparent to members of society. This also raises issues of access to public relations services in the first place, and the relationship between public relations and the media. For some writers, propaganda, as compared to public relations, is a question of whether or not 'the truth' is told and propaganda equated with 'lies'. For others, propaganda is simply persuasion. Reasons why this is a difficult area include the following:

- People tend to come to the debate with fixed ideas about the relationship between public relations and propaganda.

Sponsors/types of propaganda	Propaganda media
Religious	Books
Regime	Literature
Colonial	Film
Territorial	Poetry
Royal	Articles
Bureaucratic/administrative	Architecture
Political/ideological	Symbols
Terrorist/freedom-fighter	Music
Corporate	Posters
Activists	

Table 1.2 Propaganda sponsors, type and media

■ Definitions are often relativist according to the communication act that is being debated. In other words, one person's PR is another's propaganda depending on what side you take in the debate.

■ The hierarchy between the concepts has altered over time partly as a consequence of 'propaganda' becoming a pejorative term or 'devil word'. At various stages 'public relations' has been seen as a propaganda technique and propaganda as a public relations technique. During the inter-war period, and, to some limited extent after the Second World War, British practitioners used the term interchangeably.

■ Attempts to define terms are complicated by moral judgements about 'good' and 'bad', 'right' or 'wrong' (L'Etang, 2006a: 23–40).

Box 1.7

Analytical approaches to defining propaganda

Level of analysis

■ State
■ Ideology
■ Organization
■ Individual
■ Text

Criteria

■ Intent of communicator
■ Nature of established relationships (historical review)
■ Areas of exploitation/coercion
■ Authenticity
■ Fairness

Critical reflection

Compare and contrast:

■ propaganda and psyops
■ pysops and persuasion
■ psyops and PR
■ persuasion and PR
■ propaganda and PR

Critical reflection

Can you think of an example of what you perceive to be 'propaganda'? What are your reasons for doing so? How are you making the decision? On the basis of apparent motivation? Effects? Accuracy? Manipulation? Your own views of protagonists, sponsors, rhetoric or impact?

Figure 1.7 shows some of the many levels at which propaganda can be analyzed and suggests some key criteria.

The connection with propaganda has almost certainly impacted the public relations occupation in its ability to achieve professional status. Public relations is still not 'respectable' and lacks 'social legitimacy'. In this next section, public relations' attempt to achieve professional status is briefly reviewed, along with key definitions of the term 'professional'.

Professionalism and professionalization

As an occupation public relations suffers from a lack of delineation, weak boundaries, and 'encroachment' from other disciplines such as marketing and human resources. It is not unionized so its workers are open to exploitation, and it is barely regulated since most practitioners are not members of professional organizations and there are only legal restrictions (in the UK) in relation to lobbying. However, as Magda Pieczka pointed out:

When all is said and done, above all else the industry values having the flexibility of a practice unconstrained by statutory regulation. But the price for this freedom is evidently paid in the reputation granted to the public relations industry. (Pieczka, 2006b: 317)

The *public relations of public relations* remains an issue, as Elspeth Tilley reminded readers not so long ago:

The profession's own reputation remains a major concern with serious implications for practitioners, scholars and therefore also for clients and businesses who use public relations services. Has public relations become a term misunderstood beyond redemption, its use tarnishing not only those who practise it, or study it, but also those that purchase it? (Tilley, 2005: 1)

Tilley argued that media relations specialists should not describe themselves as public relations specialists because it devalued both specialisms. She suggested that: 'We ... need to rename the public relations role in organizations as Transparency, Consistency and Responsiveness Manager ... to reflect and inspire our most important functions' (Tilley, 2005: 1).

On transparency, Julia Jahansoozi commented that:

Transparency is considered a necessity for PR practitioners interested in opening up decision-making process and ensuring accountability and in pre-empting issues and averting expensive crises. ... If the process is transparent then publics are able to view the interaction and internal behaviour and can decide whether the organization actually does what it claims to be doing. ... Transparency contributes to the organization's reputation management through numerous benefits ... increased trust, credibility, co-operation ... the transparent organization is one where both internal and external [aspects] are transparent ... the translucent is where either internal or external are transparent and the opaque is where both internal and external are hidden or secret. (Jahansoozi, 2006: 80–81)

Critical reflection

Read the quotes from Pieczka, Tilley and Jahansoozi (above) and consider:

■ Is transparency a necessary condition for professional status?

■ Is transparency achieveable without regulation and, if so, how?

■ Who could monitor transparency?

■ What might motivate the drives to (a) transparency and (b) translucency in terms of (a) the PR occupation and (b) organizational work?

Definition: Lay terms of 'professional', 'professionalism' tend to imply efficiency, effectiveness and responsibility. However, some sociologists have specialized in analyzing work and professions and this has produced new insights and understandings.

Sociology of professions is a sub-field of sociology along with the sociology of work. These areas give critical understanding and help us to question the role and scope and status and power of occupations in society and in relation to each other. This approach helps us to get behind taken-for-granted norms. 'Professional', as defined by sociologists of the professions, is a conceptually rigorous term and not just 'a jumble of meanings and values, from efficiency to wealth; from prestige through altruism to public service' (O'Sullivan, 1994: 244).

The area *sociology of the professions* seeks to understand institutional structures, such as the Chartered Institute of Public Relations (CIPR), the Public Relations Consultants' Association (PRCA), International Communication Consultancy Organization and the International Public Relations Association (IPRA), and the role they play in relation to the occupation and its societal context (Box 1.8). Sociologists are also interested in social divisions (gender, class and ethnicity) and internal class structures ('management' versus 'technician' is a popular dichotomy in public relations writing). They are also interested in seeing how work affects individuals and groups and their self-identity. Sociologists have pursued a number of lines in defining professional work and professionalization processes. These include functional, descriptive accounts that attempt to define criteria and more critical engagements which explore

Box 1.8

Professional bodies in the UK

Chartered Institute of Public Relations (CIPR) (www.ipr.org.uk)
Public Relations Consultants' Association (PRCA) (www.prca.org.uk)
International Public Relations Association (IPRA) (www.ipra.org)
Global Alliance for Public Relations and Communication Management (www.globalpr.org/new)

the way in which some occupations have successfully leveraged higher status, larger salaries, political, economic, legal and social influence.

Key approaches to analyzing professionalism and professionalization

Sociologists have analyzed the professional status of some organizations in order to identify their key characteristics (traits); the common patterns and processes of occupational development that deliver professional status; the experience of those working in such elite occupations; and the way in which professionals and professionalizing occupations acquire and use power, both in relation to related occupations and more broadly in society.

Trait

Early work on professionals (Hughes, 1958; Millerson, 1964; Vollmer and Mills, 1966) tended to assume professions were a benign and stabilizing influence in society – 'a good thing'. Key characteristics of professions were seen as:

■ specialized skill and service

■ intellectual and practical training

■ professional autonomy – independent judgements and notion of what counts as good practice – expertise

■ fiduciary relationship with client – trusteeship

■ collective responsibility for occupation – ethics

■ embargo on some methods

■ testing of competence

Process

Other sociologists tried to capture the dynamics of professionalization processes – 'the natural history' – or progression. They saw the key processes as being:

■ emergence of sufficient practitioners to form a critical mass

■ establishment of training

■ founding of professional organizations

■ protection by law – status

■ adoption of a code of practice or ethics

Ethnographic

Ethnographers are like *social anthropologists* who study the culture (rituals, values, behaviours, social practices, daily life) of an occupation with a view to providing a *rich description*.

Power

The power perspective is critical, drawn originally from Weber and Marx, and takes a less favourable view of professions, which it sees as an elite group in society who have achieved a great deal for themselves and exert considerable power and authority by controlling entry to the occupation and gaining social approval for their work.

Professional project

The 'professional project' approach observes occupations' efforts to translate specialist knowledge and skills into social and economic rewards. This perspective focuses on market control, social closure and elite status.

Systems

Occupations can be seen as a series of related systems. So for public relations, any changes in emphasis or practice in journalism or marketing are likely to be important and vice versa. The growth and formalization of public relations in the UK post-Second World War greatly affected the journalism occupation in terms of working practices and also in terms of status and career progression (PR practitioners were more highly paid than journalists in the 1950s).

A key concept which has emerged from the sociology of professions and which is very important for public relations is that of *jurisdiction*. Jurisdiction is the crucial mechanism for professional status because jurisdiction, and control over tasks that are themselves defined by knowledge systems, permits the erection of boundaries (Pieczka and L'Etang, 2001). This is a big problem for public relations, especially in relation to marketing and particularly social marketing. While the discussion about porous boundaries between public relations and marketing is often presented as an issue of power (financial resources) or historical accident, it is actually about the ability to define a unique knowledge base to public relations.

What role does education play in the professionalization process?

Education is vital to professionalization because it provides the *cognitive core* and knowledge base which underpins the specialist expertise sold in the market place. Education can build a body of knowledge and improve practice. It also provides credibility, and qualifications may be used for gatekeeping purposes to achieve social closure and limit who can and cannot practice.

At present, the main gift education can offer public relations practice is that of social scientific expertise, especially that which may be applied to the process of evaluation. The ability to evaluate PR work is the academic skill which has the most potential to deliver professional status because:

■ it is complex knowledge requiring individual design and judgement on each occasion

■ it includes quantitative as well as qualitative elements and so puts public relations on a footing with other organizational managers by enabling them to share a language

Historical models of professionalism and professionalization applied to PR

Research in Europe in 2004 showed that although PR is seen as a 'professional domain' and a 'specialized management area', it 'lacks an image of professionalism' (van Ruler et al., 2004: 3). So it seems that education has so far made a rather limited impact. Maybe an alternative framework can help to explain this.

Betteke van Ruler, Professor at the University of Amsterdam and 'at the pinnacle' of European scholars (Grunig and Grunig, 2004: xiii), laid out an alternative framework for thinking about professionalism and professionalization (see Box 1.9).

In the UK professional status is still an elusive goal for PR practitioners, since entry to the occupation is not controlled by qualification or membership of a professional body. There is also a confusing plethora of job titles, a lack of general understanding about the practice in society and considerable media criticism (ongoing in the UK since the 1960s) of public relations as persuasive communication.

Box 1.9

Van Ruler's framework of professionalism and professionalization

Knowledge model

■ Professions are organized experts who apply expert knowledge to particular cases in practice.

■ The professional group develops the profession to maturity – experts who implement knowledge.

Status model

■ A means to get status and money.

■ A professional ideology.

■ Apprenticeship culture.

■ Emphasis on professional practice.

Competition model

■ An exclusive task that meets market needs.

■ The client, not the occupational group, defines what is good.

■ Competition with other occupational groups (marketing).

Personality model

■ The client defines the individual qualities that are needed in a consultant ('they know our business', 'we can work with these people').

■ A good professional is someone who coaches his or her client in difficult times ('emotional intelligence', 'charisma', 'creativity').

Source: adapted from van Ruler (2005: 159–173)

Critical reflection

■ Which of the above models would you expect PR academics to support and why?

■ How do these ideas make you feel about your own educational experiences and career ambitions?

Thinking critically: public relations in society

Remembering that part of the agenda for this book is to challenge readers to think critically and to ask questions, here are some ideas to consider . . .

The practice of public relations is a contentious one. Historically, in some cultures, it has had links to propaganda. As a practice it does seem to entail persuasion and it is quite right and proper that such activities are challenged. Because of this it has struggled to defend itself against attacks, especially from journalists, and it is clearly important for students to be clear about the nature of the work they are engaging in and to consider their own moral stance. It may be argued that PR is a social good if it facilitates information-sharing, educates citizens and thus enhances democracy. PR can contribute testing debate to underpin decision-taking. But issues of partiality, connections to power and uneven access to PR services remain a societal as well as a PR issue. Important questions to consider at this stage are:

■ Am I comfortable working like a lawyer and working for any client to the best of my professional ability?

■ Am I comfortable working for a cause or organization in which I believe and about which I am passionate?

■ Am I comfortable working for a very rich or elite organization that has tremendous resources (power/financial) that may have the ability to effect real change?

■ Am I comfortable working for a resource-poor group and using my skills to ensure that they are better heard?

■ Am I comfortable representing an organization, cause or product which does not align with my personal views?

■ Am I content for my opponents or competitors to have access to the same PR services and expertise?

Critical thinking is not necessarily negative, although since it is drawn from critical theory it tends to draw attention to imbalances of power or representation. It is useful for public relations because it alerts us to the fact that some voices may not be heard and some relationships may be disregarded or given insufficient respect. As Paul and Elder (2004) pointed out, independent thought and analysis means sometimes going against traditional organizational practice or confronting organizational mores or values in order to:

■ raise questions and problems

■ use abstract ideas to interpret information and feed back critical insights

■ develop well-reasoned conclusions tested against clear criteria

■ think open-mindedly within alternative systems of thought, bearing in mind their assumptions, implications, and practical consequences

■ communicate effectively (Paul and Elder, 2004: 1).

Thus, critical thinking is invaluable for public relations practitioners in understanding and resolving public relations problems.

Exercise

Contrast your own views on PR education with those of some American public relations students shown in Box 1.10.

Critical reflection

The quotes in Box 1.10 are examples of students who made assumptions about public relations and had their expectations confounded. To what extent do they seem legitimate or surprising?

Box 1.11 displays quotes from senior practitioners about 'the next generation – 29 young PR professionals who have already made a major impression on the industry' (Chandiramani, 2006).

Box 1.10

'I thought it would be more glamorous': US students reflect on PR education

'I don't have the same feelings for it [public relations] now, I thought it would be more glamorous.'

'I thought it would be more fun, just working with people, but I found it to be much more stressful.'

'I thought it was mainly special events and party planning.'

'I don't like it any more. I thought it would be more planning events, taking out clients, and social aspects.'

'I did not realize the journalism aspect in PR. It's not just if you are a good people person, there are big writing responsibilities.'

'I wasn't aware of all the writing involved – I didn't think it would be part of the job.'

'I thought we would learn to do press releases, press packets, media relations, and it turned out to be much more management and research.'

'There's much more responsibility and stress, but there's a wide variety of directions to go in the PR career. It's not just image building.'

'I'm excited it offers more of a challenge, more responsibility, that I can be managing people and making big, important decisions.'

Source: Bowen (2003: 199–214)

Box 1.11

The next generation

Julia Mitchell, Director, Toast, age 29: '[Her] aim is to "become an ambassador for the industry – lecturing, speaking and writing books"'.

Liz William, Account Manager, Threepipe Communications, age 24: 'belongs to several private members' clubs. "I want to push myself beyond the realm of PR"'.

Kim Blomley, PR Shell Chemicals, age 24: 'Kim's skill in relationship building is far beyond her years'.

Louise Angel, Account Director, Geronimo, age 25: 'embraces any challenge . . . even those that stretch beyond her imagination'.

Zaki Cooper, Director of Business of New Europe, age 29: '[His] contacts book is an eclectic mix [and he] lectures to students at Brunel and City universities but also makes use of his PR skills in charity work with the Council of Christians and Jews'.

Tom Cartmale, Head of PR, Oakley, age 27: 'his networking is . . . prolific: he attends CIPR and European sponsorship association forums and breakfast meetings'.

Ben Howes, PR Morrisons, age 28: 'diligent with a keen nose for news'.

Katie Jamieson, Account Director, Lewis PR, age 27: 'no-nonsense, down-to-earth results orientated approach . . .'.

Chris Clarke, Director, Clark Mulder Purdie, age 29: 'He aims to raise the quality of PR in the UK and generate respect for it in the boardroom'.

Source: *PRWeek*, 30 June 2006

Critical reflection

- What themes emerge from the quotations in Box 1.11?
- Do any comments resonate with your own plans and ideas of your future occupation and self-identity?

Review

This chapter has reviewed a range of concepts, frameworks and debates that go some way to explaining the existence and purpose of public relations. Now is the time to return to your response of the questions asked of you at the beginning of the chapter. You might like to consider:

- To what extent have my expectations been met?
- To what extent have my expectations been confounded?
- How do I feel about this occupation?
- Has anything changed about my view of PR as my future career?

In conclusion

This chapter has offered pragmatic definitions and descriptions of PR work, its role and scope. It has offered a further critique of technocratic functionalism and highlighted the limitations of a checklist approach. It has demonstrated potential flaws in PR evaluation practices. Reflecting on the PR occupation itself, the chapter has explained definitions of professionalism and professionalization and related these to the public relations occupation. According to strict sociological criteria, PR is not a profession. The chapter's critical tone is also applied in relation to the rather reverent note sounded by many PR practitioners and academics in relation to 'strategic' PR. Here, readers have been alerted to a range of sources in critical management that have de-bunked idealistic (and ideological) ideas about strategic management. In reviewing some historical trends that have facilitated the evolution and growth of PR, this chapter has not shied away, as some texts do, from the subject of propaganda. Furthermore, it has also introduced the concept of 'psyops' into the public relations context.

Recommended reading

There are many useful standard texts that provide introductions to PR which would serve well as a complement to the ideas and approach put forward in this chapter. In particular, see Lee Edwards' reviews of PR theories in Tench and Yeomans (2006) and, in the same volume, chapters by Anne Gregory (planning), Rudiger Theilmann and Gyorgy Szondi (research and evaluation) and Johanna Fawkes (propaganda and persuasion).

Histories of public relations are available in L'Etang (2004) and in L'Etang and Pieczka (2006), where different cultural historical perspectives are presented by Puchan (Germany), Tilson (Spain), Larsson (Sweden) and L'Etang (UK). A comprehensive review of the literature on professionalism and professionalization can be found in Pieczka and L'Etang (2001) in Heath's *Handbook of Public Relations* (2001). Kevin Moloney's *Rethinking Public Relations* (2nd edition, 2006) focuses in detail on conceptual and applied aspects of propaganda and political communications.

References

Al Saqur, L.H. (2007) 'Promoting social change in the Arab Gulf: two case studies of communication programmes in Kuwait and Bahrain'. Unpublished thesis, University of Stirling, Scotland.

Banks, S.P. (1995) *Multicultural Public Relations: A Social Interpretive Approach*, London: Sage.

Borghetti, G. (2003) 'The history of Italian PR: from prehistory to innovation'. Dissertation submitted as part fulfilment of the MSc in Public Relations, University of Stirling, Scotland.

Bowen, S. (2003) '"I thought it would be more glamorous": preconceptions and misconceptions among students in the public relations principles course', *Public Relations Review*, 29: 199–214.

Chandiramani, R. (2006) 'Full Sunday trading will be tricky sell' *PRWeek*, 16 June: 19.

Chandiramani, R. (2006) 'The next generation: 29 under 29' *PRWeek*, 30 June: 19–23.

Chandiramani, R. (2006) 'Full Sunday trading will be tricky sell' *PRWeek*, 16 June: 19.

Coalter, F. (2006) *Sport in development: a monitoring and evaluation manual*, London: UK Sport.

Cooper, B.H. (1982) 'Accentuating the positive', in McLaurin, R. (ed.), *Military Propaganda: Psychological Warfare and Operations*, New York: Praegar, pp. 310–312.

Edelstein, A. (1997) *Total Propaganda: From Mass Culture to Popular Culture*, Mahwah, NJ: Lawrence Erlbaum Associates.

Ewen, S. (1996) *PR! A Social History of Spin*, New York: Basic Books.

Fawkes, J. (2006) 'Public relations, propaganda and the psychology of persuasion', in Tench, R. and Yeomans, L. (eds), *Exploring Public Relations*, Harlow: Prentice Hall, pp. 266–287.

Gregory, A. (2000) *Planning and Managing Public Relations Campaigns*, London: Kogan Page.

Grunig, J. and Grunig, L. (2004) 'Foreword', in van Ruler, B. and Vercic, D. (eds) (2004) *Public Relations and Communication Management in Europe*, Berlin: de Gruyter.

Hinrischen, C. (2001) 'Best practices in the public relations agency business', in Heath, R. (ed.), *Handbook of Public Relations*, London: Sage, pp. 451–460.

Ismail, H. (2007) 'From managing ethnic conflict to nation-building: public relations strategies in Malaysian history'. Doctoral work in progress, University of Stirling, Scotland.

Jackall, R. (ed.) (1995) *Propaganda*, Basingstoke: Macmillan.

Jahansoozi, J. (2006) 'Relationships, transparency and evaluation: the implications for public relations', In L'Etang, J. and Pieczka, M. (eds), *Public Relations: Critical Debates and Contemporary Practice*, Mahwah, NJ: Lawrence Erlbaum Associates, pp. 61–92.

Jowett, G. and O'Donnell, V. (1986) *Propaganda and Persuasion*, London: Sage.

Katz, P. (1982) 'Intelligence for psychological operations', in McLaurin, R. (ed.), *Military Propaganda: Psychological Warfare and Operations*, New York: Praegar, pp. 121–154.

Lasswell, H. (1934/1995) 'Propaganda', in Jackall, R. (ed.), (1995) *Propaganda*, Basingstoke: Macmillan.

L'Etang, J. (2004) *Public Relations in Britain: A History of Professional Practice in the 20th Century*, Mahwah, NJ: Lawrence Erlbaum Associates.

L'Etang, J. (2006a) 'Public relations and propaganda: conceptual issues and methodological problems', in L'Etang, J. and Pieczka, M. (eds), *Public Relations: Critical Debates and Contemporary Practice*, Mahwah, NJ: Lawrence Erlbaum Associates, pp. 23–40.

L'Etang, J. (2006b) 'Public relations as theatre: key players in the evolution of British public relations', in L'Etang, J. and Pieczka, M. (eds), *Public Relations: Critical Debates and Contemporary Practice*, Mahwah, NJ: Lawrence Erlbaum Associates, pp. 143–166.

L'Etang, J. and Muruli, G. (2004) 'Public relations, decolonization and democracy: the case of Kenya', in Tilson, D. and Alozie, E. (eds), *Towards the Common Good: Perspectives in International Public Relations*, London: Pearson, pp. 215–238.

McLaurin, R. (ed.) (1982a) *Military Propaganda: Psychological Warfare and Operations*, New York: Praegar.

Murphy, A. (2003) 'A study of the growth of the public relations industry in Ireland, with a focus on ethics 1900–2003'. Dissertation submitted as part fulfilment of the MSc in Public Relations, University of Stirling, Scotland.

Muruli, G.M. (2001) 'Public relations in Kenya: the missing link 1939–71'. Dissertation submitted as part fulfilment of the MSc in Public Relations, University of Stirling, Scotland.

Park, R.E. (1972) *The Crowd, the Public and Other Essays*, Chicago: University of Chicago Press.

Paul, R. and Elder, L. (2004) *The Miniature Guide to Critical Thinking: Concepts and Tools*, Foundation for Critical Thinking.

Pettigrew, A., Thomas, H. and Whittington, R. (2002) 'Strategic management: the strengths and limitations of a field', in Pettigrew, A., Thomas, H. and Whittington, R. (eds), *Handbook of Strategy and Management*, London: Sage, pp. 3–30.

Pieczka, M. (2006b) '"Chemistry" and the public relations industry: an exploration of the concept of jurisdiction and issues arising', in L'Etang, J. and Pieczka, M. (eds), *Public Relations: Critical Debates and Contemporary Practice*, Mahwah, NJ: Lawrence Erlbaum Associates, pp. 303–330.

Puchan, H. (2006) 'An intellectual history of German public relations', in L'Etang, J. and Pieczka, M. (eds), *Public Relations: Critical Debates and Contemporary Practice*, Mahwah, NJ: Lawrence Erlbaum Associates, pp. 111–122.

Ströh, U. (2007) 'An alternative postmodern approach to corporate communication strategy' in Toth, E. (ed.), *The future of excellence and communication management: challenges for the next generation, Festschrift*. Mahwah, New Jersey: Lawrence Erlbaum Associates: 199–220.

Tilley, E. (2005) 'What's in a name? Everything. The appropriateness of "public relations" needs further debate', web journal *PRism*, http://praxis.massey.ac.nz (accessed 12 December 2006).

Toledano, M. (2005) 'Challenging accounts: public relations and a tale of two revolutions', *Public Relations Review*, 31: 463–470.

van Ruler, B. (2005) 'Commentary: professionals are from Venus, scholars are from Mars', *Public Relations Review*, 31(2): 159–173.

van Ruler, B. and Vercic, D. (eds) (2004) *Public Relations and Communications Management in Europe*, Berlin: de Gruyter.

Watson, P. (1978) *War on the Mind: The Military Uses and Abuses of Psychology*, London: Hutchinsons.

Wright, J. (1991) *Terrorist Propaganda: The Red Army Faction and the Provisional IRA 1968–86*, Basingstoke: Macmillan.

CHAPTER 2
James E. Grunig, Larissa A. Grunig and David M. Dozier

The excellence theory*

* Chapter 2 in *Public Relations Theory II*, edited by Carl H. Botan and Vincent Hazleton (2006). Developed from Grunig et al. (2002). Copyright © 2006 by Lawrence Erlbaum Associates, Inc. Reproduced with permission.

Introduction

In his highly influential book *The Structure of Scientific Revolutions*, Kuhn (1970) said that mature sciences differ from immature sciences because they are dominated by a single paradigm rather than being a battleground of multiple, conflicting theories. A *paradigm*, according to Kuhn, is a set of presuppositions, theories, methods, and exemplars of solutions to research problems that produce a unified worldview for the scientists associated with the paradigm. In mature sciences, scholars generally agree on common theories. In immature sciences, however, everyone seems to have his or her own theory, and debate rages among competing camps about which theories are preferable.

Some scholars in immature sciences mistakenly have interpreted Kuhn (1970) as suggesting that the discipline can be made more mature by imposing a single paradigm on the entire discipline. If others would adopt my theory, the reasoning goes, this discipline would mature. Scholars with competing theories understandably resist such attempts at theoretical imperialism. Instead, a dominant paradigm must emerge through research, conceptualization, and broadening and integrating of many theories rather than through imposing a single, narrow theory on the discipline.

In the Excellence study, we attempted to develop a broad, general theory of public relations by integrating most of the prominent middle-level theories that were available in the discipline at the time the study began in 1985. Our goal was not to impose a single theory on public relations but to try to bring both complementary and competing theories together in a way that would answer questions and solve problems of concern to most public relations practitioners and scholars.

Public relations research began in the 1950s and 1960s as an offshoot of mass communication research. Mass communication scholars then, as now, devoted most of their energy to explaining the effects of mass communication. At the time, most people, including scholars, believed the media had a major effect on elections, strongly influenced children, might be major contributors to crime and violence, created popular culture, influenced consumer choices, and affected decisions about war and peace. Most public relations practitioners in the 1950s and 1960s saw public relations primarily as an activity to influence the all-powerful media – through both day-to-day media relations activities and planned public information campaigns. Public relations researchers, therefore, joined with mass communication scholars to document the effectiveness of public relations (media relations/public information campaigns).

Research brought an end to the view that media have strong effects on attitudes and behaviors (often known as the *hypodermic needle theory*) and replaced it with the view that the media have limited effects (see, e.g., McQuail, 2000, for a history of mass communication research). Research then discredited the limited-effects view and replaced it with a different kind of powerful effects theory – a set of theories showing that the effects of the media are cognitive more than they are attitudinal and behavioral (they affect what people think about more than what they do) and that the media both influence and are influenced by culture.[1] From the vantage point of public relations, these new theories of media effects suggested that some people do indeed learn from the media in some situations, but that the media are not the solution to every public relations problem. Rather, public relations is a process in which organizations must communicate with publics in different ways in different situations. The public relations process, that is, must be managed – practitioners have to think about and plan what they do – in order to be effective.

Beginning in the 1950s, public relations textbooks, such as Cutlip and Center's (1952) first edition began to claim that public relations is both a two-way communication process and a management function. However, ideas about the management of two-way communication processes remained vague until J. Grunig (1976) introduced organizational theory to public relations and developed the concept of symmetrical communication and Broom and Smith (1978, 1979) developed the concept of the public relations manager role. From that point on, public relations scholars began to think of public relations as both a management and a communication discipline – 'the management of communication between an organization and its publics' (J. Grunig & Hunt, 1984, p. 6).

J. Grunig (1997) elaborated on this definition of public relations as communication management by emphasizing the management of an organization's communicative processes and the role of communication in management itself:

I define communication as a behavior – of people, groups, or organizations – that consists of moving symbols to and from other people, groups, or organizations. Thus, we can say that public relations is an organization's managed communication behavior. Public relations professionals plan and execute communication tor the entire organization or help parts of the organization to communicate. They manage the movement of messages into the organization, for example, when conducting research on the knowledge, attitudes, and behaviors of publics and then using the information to counsel managers on how to make the organization's policies or actions acceptable to publics. They may manage the movement of messages out of the organization when they help management decide how to explain a policy or action to a public and then write a news story or fact sheet to explain it. (pp. 242–243)

To this day, however, many public relations practitioners continue to think of public relations as mostly publicity and media relations. Many others have broadened their vision and see public relations as the part of the strategic management function through which organizations interact with their publics both before and after management decisions are made. In the early 1980s, the management approach was only beginning to enter public relations thinking. It was a preparadigm period of public relations in which scholars and practitioners, in particular, had widely differing views of the nature and purpose of public relations. This was the setting when the Foundation of the International Association of Business Communicators issued a request for research proposals (RFP) in 1984 that gave birth to the Excellence study. The IABC's RFP called for a study that would explain 'how, why, and to what extent does communication affect the achievement of organizational objectives.'

For many years, public relations professionals have expressed great interest in the third part of this research question: To what extent does communication affect the achievement of organizational objectives? Public relations professionals generally feel underappreciated by other managers when they work inside an organization or by clients when they work in a public relations firm. Often they believe they are disadvantaged in competing for organizational resources because they cannot explain the value of their work. As a result, public relations professionals long have searched for a statistical model or other evidence that would prove that public relations has value to an organization.

The IABC Foundation included two additional questions in the critical sentence in its RFP that made it possible for us go beyond the widespread interest in proving that public relations has value to an organization. The other questions allowed us to build from the explanation of the extent to which public relations has value, to develop a general theory that also explains why it has value and how the communication function should be organized to best provide this value. We collapsed these three questions into two major research questions that guided the Excellence study:

■ First, the Effectiveness Question asked why and to what extent public relations increases organizational effectiveness: How does public relations make an organization more effective, and how much is that contribution worth economically?

■ Second, the Excellence Question asked how public relations should be organized and managed to be able to make the contribution to organizational effectiveness identified in the answer to the Effectiveness Question: What are the characteristics of a public relations function that are most likely to make an organization effective?

To answer these two research questions, we tried to use most existing public relations theories as well as theories from related management and communication disciplines to build a general theory of public relations. This chapter explains this general theory and summarizes the research conducted for the Excellence study to apply and extend the theory. Although the Excellence theory by itself has not made public relations a mature science, it has provided a comprehensive paradigm that has integrated and expanded public relations research. At the same time, the Excellence theory has served as a focal point for debate and criticism – a focus that Kuhn (1970) believed is a necessary condition for a science to be mature.

An overview of the excellence study

When the IABC Foundation (now the IABC Research Foundation) issued its RFP in 1984, project director James Grunig assembled a research team of five scholars and practitioners from the United Kingdom and the United States. The team consisted of James Grunig and Larissa Grunig of the University of Maryland and David Dozier of San Diego State University; William Ehling, then of Syracuse University and now retired; Jon White, then of the Cranfield School of Management in the United Kingdom and now an independent consultant and teacher in London; and the now-deceased Fred Repper, who had recently retired as vice president of public relations for Gulf States Utilities in Beaumont, Texas.

The six members of the team wrote a proposal that promised to review the literature on organizational effectiveness to answer the question of how and why public relations has value to an organization. Because we believed that not all public relations units have value to their organizations, however, we also promised to do an extensive review of the literature on public relations and related disciplines to isolate the characteristics that make it more likely that a communication unit will add value to an organization. We could do such a review because each member of the team had been heavily involved in research on different, but complementary, aspects of communication management – such as strategic management, practitioner roles, gender and diversity, models of public relations, operations research, employee communication, organizational culture, and activism.

Conceptualization

In 1985, the IABC Foundation awarded us a grant for $400,000 to conduct the project we had outlined. The literature review started out as a paper but expanded into a book, *Excellence in Public Relations and Communication Management* (J. Grunig, 1992a). That first book presented the results of the extensive literature review that led to the conceptual framework for the study.

A number of excellence studies had been conducted for management practices in general, the most famous of which was Peters and Waterman's (1982) study, *In Search of Excellence*. We reviewed this study and similar ones and integrated the results in the chapter 'What Is Excellence in Management?' in *Excellence in Public Relations and Communication Management* (J. Grunig, 1992c). Most previous studies of excellence, however, addressed only the *how* question of the three questions posed in the IABC Foundation's research question. Previous excellence researchers typically chose what they thought were excellent organizations using arbitrary criteria, such as six financial measures used by Peters and Waterman, and then searched for management practices that these excellent organizations shared. Generally, though, these researchers could not explain why the shared practices produced the observed financial results. That problem became especially acute when many of the excellent companies suffered financial declines or went out of business even though their management practices had not changed ('Who's Excellent Now,' 1984).

In developing our study of excellence in public relations and communication management, by contrast, we began by reviewing the literature on the nature of organizational effectiveness, the nature of public relations, and the relationship between the two (L. Grunig, J. Grunig, & Ehling, 1992). That literature allowed us to answer the why question: For what reason does public relations contribute to organizational effectiveness?

With the answer to that question in mind, we then searched literature in public relations, communication, management, organizational sociology and psychology, social and cognitive psychology, feminist studies, political science, operations research, and culture to identify characteristics of public relations programs and departments and of the organizations in which they are found that answer the *how* question: By what means do excellent public relations departments make organizations more

effective? Finally, we searched the literature for concepts that would explain the value of individual public relations programs and the value of the overall public relations function to an organization – the *to what extent* question (Ehling, 1992; L. Grunig, J. Grunig, & Ehling, 1992).

The result was a comprehensive, general theory of public relations. That general theory began with a premise of why public relations has value to an organization. We could use that premise to identify and connect attributes of the public relations function and of the organization that logically would be most likely to make the organization effective. Then we could link the outcomes of communication programs that make organizations effective to the characteristics of a public relations function that theoretically would contribute the most to organizational effectiveness.

Data collection and analysis

After completing the conceptualization, we submitted the general theory and the several middle-range theories and variables incorporated into it to empirical test – quantitative and qualitative research to look for evidence that excellent public relations programs were more valuable than less excellent functions.

The first phase of the Excellence study consisted of quantitative, survey research on 327 organizations in the United States, Canada, and the United Kingdom. Questionnaires were completed by 407 senior communication officers (some organizations had more than one public relations department), 292 CEOs or other executive managers, and 4,631 employees (an average of 14 per organization). The organizations included corporations, government agencies, nonprofit organizations, and trade and professional associations.

We analyzed the quantitative data by attempting first to reduce as much of the data as possible into a single index of excellence in communication management. We tried to reduce these variables to one index after first combining a number of indicators of variables into indices, or by using the statistical technique of factor analysis to combine related variables into broader variables. We then factor analyzed these indices and factors to isolate a single factor of excellence. Factor analysis looks for clusters of variables to which people respond with similar answers when they complete a questionnaire. In the case of communication Excellence, our theory suggested that most of the characteristics of excellence would cluster together, as would the characteristics of less excellent programs.

The factors produced by factor analysis represent underlying variables that are broader than the original variables analyzed. We expected that a factor would define an underlying variable of excellence in communication management, which would subsume the variables of the subtheories integrated into our general theory. Factor analysis allowed us to determine whether all of the characteristics of excellence clustered as we predicted so that we could use the underlying factor to identify the most and least excellent communication departments as well as average ones.

We then used this index to choose organizations for qualitative research, and the qualitative information provided insights on how excellent public relations came about in different organizations as well as detail on the outcomes produced by excellence. We also used the Excellence factor to determine whether other characteristics we measured correlated with the index – thus providing additional detail on conditions related to excellent public relations. For example, we had no theoretical reason to include the use of outside consulting firms for different purposes as a part of the theory of excellence but we could correlate the index of excellence with uses of consulting firms – thus determining whether excellent departments use outside firms differently than do less excellent departments.

We began the search for a single Excellence factor with the goal of including as much of the information from the three survey questionnaires as possible in the index. We could not include variables for which we did not have information for every organization, however. Therefore, we could not include the variables from the first part of the questionnaire completed by the senior communicator, which asked 8 1/2 pages of questions about how the organization identified publics and how it planned, executed, and evaluated communication programs for those publics. Top communicators answered this set of questions for the three publics they chose as receiving the most time and resources for public relations programs. Top communicators chose from a list of 17 stakeholder groups, but they chose only eight groups often enough to provide sufficient data for analysis.

Because top communicators chose different publics, the same data were not available for all organizations. Therefore, we could not include the data on programs for different publics in the Excellence factor without eliminating many organizations from the analysis. As a result, we built the Excellence factor from the rest of the three questionnaires. Later, we correlated the data from Part I of the public relations questionnaires with the Excellence factor public by public for organizations that had programs for each of the eight publics.

There also were several questions on the top communicator's and CEO's questionnaires that produced categorical data that could not be correlated with other variables. These questions asked about power of the public relations department; membership in the dominant coali-

tion; organizational responses to activism; relationship to marketing and other managerial functions; gender of the top communicator; and country, type, and size of organization. We analyzed these variables later by comparing mean scores on the Excellence factor and its component variables for the categories of the categorical variables.

The Excellence factor we isolated strongly confirmed the theory developed in *Excellence in Public Relations and Communication Management* (J. Grunig, 1992). We found that CEOs with excellent public relations departments valued the communication function almost twice as much as did those with less excellent departments. CEOs who valued public relations most believed it should be practiced essentially as spelled out by our theory of excellence. Heads of excellent public relations departments also reported that their units practiced public relations according to these same principles of excellence. The first analysis also showed that the organizational and environmental context nurtured, but did not guarantee, excellent public relations. Finally, comparison of the Excellence index for different descriptive characteristics of organizations and communicators showed that excellence in public relations seemed to be generic to the three countries and the four types of organizations we studied. Size of the organization also made no difference. And, heads of excellent departments came from all age groups and were equally likely to be women or men.

When the survey was completed and the data analyzed, we provided a report to each of the organizations participating in the study. The report explained the theory behind the study and provided percentile scores showing each organization where it stood relative to the other organizations on overall Excellence and each of the component variables of an Excellence scale we constructed. The last phase of the study consisted of qualitative interviews of up to three people (the CEO, the head of communication, and a lower-level public relations professional) in 25 of the organizations that had the highest and lowest scores on the scale of excellence produced by the quantitative research.

After completing the research, we wrote two additional books reporting the results. The second book, *Manager's Guide to Excellence in Public Relations and Communication Management* (Dozier with L. Grunig & J. Grunig, 1995), included user-friendly review and explanation of the theory and simplified results of both parts of the study, written mostly for public relations practitioners. A third and final book, *Excellent Public Relations and Effective Organizations: A Study of Communication Management in Three Countries* (L. Grunig, J. Grunig, & Dozier, 2002) presented the complete results of both the quantitative and qualitative segments of the study.

A theoretical benchmark of best practices

The result of 10 years of literature review, theory construction, and empirical research is a benchmarking study that identifies and describes critical success factors and best practices in public relations. We go beyond typical benchmarking studies, however, which usually are empirical but not explanatory. Typical studies identify organizations that are believed to be leaders in an area of practice and then describe how they practice public relations or some other management function. They answer the *how* question (how do the benchmarked companies practice public relations?), but not the *why* or *to what extent* questions. In his book on public affairs benchmarking, Fleisher (1995) said that it is important to measure what public relations units do, but that, 'it is just as important to discover the qualitative factors – the how's and why's behind the numbers – associated with the attainment of the numbers' (p. 15).

The Excellence study provides a theoretical profile, a theoretical benchmark that we initially constructed from past research and by theoretical logic. In addition, we gathered empirical evidence from organizations to confirm that this theoretical profile explains best actual practice as well as best practice in theory. The theoretical and empirical benchmark provided by the Excellence study makes it possible for public relations units to compare themselves with what Fleisher (1995) called 'higher performing and world-class units in order to generate knowledge and action about public affairs roles, processes, practice, products/services, or strategic issues which will lead to performance improvement' (p. 4).

In most benchmarking studies, communication units compare themselves with similar units in their industry or with similar functional units inside the organization. The Excellence study, by contrast, is an example of what Fleisher (1995) called 'generic benchmarking' – identifying critical success factors across different types of organizations. Generic benchmarking is most valuable theoretically, because it is unlikely that one organization will be 'a world-class performer across the board' (p. 29). In the Excellence study, a few organizations exemplified all of the best practices, many organizations exemplified some of them, and others exemplified few of the practices – i.e., the theoretical benchmark was normally distributed in the population of organizations.

A theoretical benchmark does not provide an exact formula or detailed description of practices that a public relations unit can copy in order to be excellent. Rather, it provides a set of principles that such units can use to generate ideas for specific practices in their own organizations. As a comprehensive model of excellence in public relations, therefore, this theoretical and empirical benchmark provides a model:

- For auditing and evaluating public relations departments;

- For explaining to the managers who make important decisions (dominant coalitions) why their organizations depend on public relations, how much value communication has to their organization, and how to organize and manage the function to achieve the greatest value from it; and

- For the teaching of public relations to both beginners and experienced practitioners.

The empirical results of the Excellence study provide strong and consistent support for the general theory that guided the study. As occurs in most research, however, the results also suggest how to improve and revise many of the middle-level theories that were incorporated into the general theory. The rest of this chapter summarizes the components of our general theory of public relations and discusses the insights provided by research for revising and improving that theory.

The value of public relations: the basic premise of the general theory

The question of the value of public relations has been of great concern to professional communicators for many years because of the belief among both communicators and other kinds of management professionals that public relations is an intangible management function in comparison with other functions whose value can be described, measured, and evaluated through systematic research. In fact, the elusive goal of determining the value of public relations was the major reason why the IABC Research Foundation requested proposals for the Excellence study. Because there has been no way to demonstrate its worth, public relations often has seemed to suffer at budget time and particularly during financial crises.

For at least 25 years, therefore, public relations professionals and researchers have struggled to develop measures that would establish that public relations is effective or adds value. Among other measures, they have attempted to determine the advertising value of press clippings; to establish the readership of publications; or to do surveys or experiments to determine whether communication campaigns or programs have had measurable effects on cognitions, attitudes, or behaviors. Many professional communicators have successfully demonstrated the effects of individual communication programs in one or more of these ways. Nevertheless, evaluation of communication programs falls short of demonstrating that the overall management function of public relations has value to an organization or to society.

Recently, public relations practitioners and firms have been on a quest to develop a single indicator of the value of organizational reputation. They believe that this indicator will establish that communication has a measurable monetary return that can be attributed to the public relations function (e.g., Jeffries-Fox Associates, 2000a; Fombrun, 1996). Many commercial research firms have developed a series of evaluative, attitudinal questions to measure reputation (Jeffries-Fox Associates, 2000b).

Levels of analysis

These many forays into estimating the value of public relations have not been successful at least in part because of confusion over the organizational level at which public relations has value. We must recognize, to begin, that the value of communication can be determined at least at four levels[2]:

Program level. Individual communication programs such as media relations, community relations, or customer relations are successful when they affect the cognitions, attitudes, and behaviors of both publics and members of the organization. The program level has been the traditional focus of evaluative research in public relations. However, effective communication programs may or may not contribute to organizational effectiveness; many operate independently of the organization's mission and goals.

Functional level. The public relations or communication function as a whole can be audited by comparing the structure and processes of the department or departments that implement the function with the best practices of the public relations function in other organizations or with theoretical principles derived from scholarly research. Evaluation at this level can be called *theoretical* or *practical benchmarking.* Although the value of public relations at the program and functional level is different, public relations departments that meet evaluative criteria at the functional level should be likely to develop communication programs that meet their objectives more often than functions that do not meet these criteria.

Organizational level. For many years, organizational scholars have debated the question of what makes an organization effective. To show that public relations

has value to the organization, we must be able to show that effective communication programs and functions contribute to organizational effectiveness.

Societal level. Organizations have an impact beyond their own bottom line. They also affect other organizations, individuals, and publics in society. As a result, organizations cannot be said to be effective unless they also are socially responsible; and public relations can be said to have value when it contributes to the social responsibility of organizations.

The initial request for proposals from the IABC Research Foundation focused on the organizational level of value. The research team added the second question, the Excellence question, because we believed that public relations functions must be organized according to certain theoretical criteria before they could contribute value at the organizational level. We must address the societal level as well if we are to determine the value of public relations.

Organizational effectiveness

In our review of relevant literature, conducted at the outset of this decade-long research, we began with the organizational level to develop a definition of organizational effectiveness. We reasoned that only by defining what we mean by an 'effective' organization could we then determine the contribution that communication makes, or could make under conditions of excellent practice. The literature on organizational effectiveness is large and contradictory (overviews can be found in Goodman & Pennings, 1977; Hall, 1991, Price, 1968; and Robbins, 1990). Robbins (1990) and Hall (1991), however, identified four main schools of thought on effectiveness, emanating primarily from organizational sociology and business management, which guided our initial conceptualization of the Excellence theory. These perspectives were systems, competing values, strategic constituencies, and goal attainment. We synthesized these approaches, culling the concepts within each one that offered the most promise in explaining the relationship between effectiveness and communication (see J. Grunig, 1997, pp. 257–258).

The *goal-attainment* approach states that organizations are effective when they meet their goals. However, the approach alone cannot explain effectiveness. Different individuals within an organization as well as different external stakeholders have different goals for the organization. Therefore, the organization might be effective with respect to some constituents but not with respect to others.

The *systems* approach recognizes the importance of the environment for an organization to be effective – the interdependence of organizations with their environments. Interdependence comes from mutual need. Presumably, organizations need resources from their environment – raw materials, a source of employees, clients or customers for the services or products they produce, and so forth. The environment, too, needs the organization for its products or services. The systems approach, however, defines the environment in vague terms and does not explain which elements of the environment are important for success.

The *strategic constituencies* approach puts meaning into the term *environment* by identifying the elements of the environment whose opposition or support can threaten the organization's goals or help to attain them. The fourth approach, *competing values*, provides a bridge between strategic constituencies and goals. It states that an organization must incorporate strategic constituencies' values into its goals so that the organization attains the goals of most value to its strategic constituencies. Thus different organizations with different strategic constituencies in their environments will have different goals, and their effectiveness will be defined in different ways.

This notion of specificity within the organization's environmental niche points to the value of public relations. As boundary spanners, managers of communication help the dominant coalition determine which elements of their domain are most important to reach. Organizational effectiveness is determined in part, then, by identifying those key publics. We also know that public relations departments can develop programs that build high-quality relationships with these strategic constituencies.

Relationships help the organization manage its interdependence with the environment. Of course, communication alone does not create and maintain these relationships; but it does play a vital role. Then, too, relationships may not be entirely beneficial to the organization. They have the capacity to both limit and enhance the organization's autonomy within its environment. Nevertheless, the notion of relationships is so central to the literature of organizational sociology, business management, and – of course – public relations that at least two scholars defined *business* as 'a connected set of relationships among stakeholders where the emphasis is on the connectedness' (Freeman & Gilbert, 1992, p. 12).

Since the completion of the Excellence study, Post, Preston, and Sachs (2002) developed essentially the same theory of organizational effectiveness as we did, defining it as the *stakeholder* approach to organizational wealth:

> *Our central proposition is that organizational wealth can be created (or destroyed) through relationships with stakeholders of all kind – resource providers, customers*

and suppliers, social and political actors. Therefore effective stakeholder management – that is managing relationships with stakeholders for mutual benefit – is a critical requirement for corporate success. (p. 1)

Post, Preston, and Sachs (2002), like many contemporary management theorists they cited, pointed out that corporations have *intangible assets* as well as physical and financial assets. The most original current approach to estimating the value of these intangible assets, they added, is that of *relational wealth* – 'relationships, both among individuals and units within an organization and between any focal entity, or organization, on one hand, and other entities, groups, and organizations, on the other' (p. 40). 'Organizational wealth,' they concluded, 'is the summary measure of the capacity of an organization to create benefits for any and all of its stakeholders over the long term' (p. 45).

The stakeholder approach to organizational effectiveness also makes it possible to integrate economic performance and the achievement of social goals into a definition of effectiveness. Freeman and Gilbert (1992) saw business 'as a connected set of relationships among stakeholders where the emphasis is on the connectedness' (p. 12). They explained:

> *We need to understand that stakeholders are in it together, rather than competing for limited and scarce resources, and that the fundamental reason that organizations as connected networks are effective is that they are built on the principles of cooperation and caring. Each stakeholder is 'adding to the value' of others, creating a good deal for all. (p. 12)*

The contribution of public relations

Our review of the literature on organizational effectiveness led to the following premise, which we used to integrate a number of middle-range theories of public relations into a general theory:

> *Public relations contributes to organizational effectiveness when it helps reconcile the organization's goals with the expectations of its strategic constituencies. This contribution has monetary value to the organization. Public relations contributes to effectiveness by building quality, long-term relationships with strategic constituencies. Public relations is most likely to contribute to effectiveness when the senior public relations manager is a member of the dominant coalition where he or she is able to shape the organization's goals and to help determine which external publics are most strategic. (L. Grunig, J. Grunig, & Dozier, 2002, p. 97)*

Each of the key middle-range theories of public relations, which we integrated into a general theory, can be seen as a way of identifying publics with which an organization needs relationships to be effective and as a way of effectively cultivating relationships with these publics.

A key phrase in the foregoing proposition is that the contribution of public relations has monetary value. Although our search of the literature suggested that this monetary value comes mostly through intangible assets, many public relations professionals still would like researchers to determine an exact monetary value for the relationships created through the work of the public relations function. We explored this possibility when we conceptualized the Excellence study and rejected it as impossible for the following reasons flowing from the literature we reviewed in the first and last *Excellence* books:

- Relationships provide a context for behavior by consumers, investors, employees, government, the community, the media, and other strategic constituencies. However, they do not determine this behavior alone. The behavior of these constituencies affects financial performance; but many other factors, such as competition and the economic environment, also affect that performance.

- Relationships save money by preventing costly issues, crises, regulation, litigation, and bad publicity. It is not possible, however, to determine the cost of something that did not happen, or even to know that the negative event or behavior would have happened in the absence of excellent public relations.

- The return on relationships is delayed. Organizations spend money on relationships for years to prevent events or behaviors such as crises, boycotts, or litigation that might happen many years down the road.

- The return on relationships usually is lumpy. Good relationships with some constituencies such as consumers may produce a continuing stream of revenue, but for the most part the return comes all at once – e.g., when crises, strikes, boycotts, regulation, litigation, or bad publicity are avoided or mitigated. Similarly, relationships with potential donors must be cultivated for years before a donor makes a major gift. As a result, it is difficult to prorate the delayed returns on public relations to the monies invested in the function each year.

As a result, we concluded that the technique of compensating variation provided the best method known to date to estimate the value of relationships cultivated by public relations to the organization. Ehling (1992) developed that rationale for using this technique in the first *Excellence* book. We entered the data-gathering phase of the Excellence project with the understanding that public relations contributes both to the organization and to society. We also understand that the value of public relations lies in the value of relationships between the organization and publics in the internal and external environment of the organization. Public relations departments contribute this value at the organizational and societal levels through excellent practice at the functional and program levels. Public relations programs, for example, are effective when they accomplish objectives that help to build successful relationships with publics that have strategic value to the organization.

In our research, then, we attempted to measure the value of relationships as a means of estimating the value of public relations. After reviewing the literature on cost-benefit analysis, we identified a method for estimating the value of public relations and comparing it with the costs. Cost-benefit analysis of public relations is difficult, however, because of the intangibility of the benefit – the value of relationships. One method we identified in the literature, 'compensating variation,' offered promise.

Compensating variation, as economists term this process, provides a way of transforming nonmonetary values, such as the benefit of good relationships to the organization and to society, into monetary values. The idea behind the method is simple. You ask people how much they would be willing to pay to have something. For public relations, you ask members of the dominant coalition or public relations managers how much public relations is worth to them on either a monetary or nonmonetary scale.

A compensating variation is:

- The amount of money a beneficiary of a program (such as the dominant coalition) would be willing to pay for a program (such as public relations) so that he or she would be equally well off with the program or the payment he or she is willing to make for it, or

- The amount an entity (such as the dominant coalition) that is worse off because of the effects of a program (such as opposition from activists) would be willing to pay to eliminate the effects, so that the entity is equally well off without the program or the payment.

Our method was limited by the fact that we asked only one party to the relationships between organizations and publics to estimate the value of the relationship – the organization's side. Ideally, we also would have asked representatives of publics, such as leaders of activist groups, to estimate the value of each relationship. With a survey sample of more than 300 organizations and a set of 25 qualitative cases, the cost in time and money of interviewing representatives of publics was prohibitive. Researchers in the future should extend our analysis by choosing a smaller number of participating organizations and interviewing both sides of relationships.

Results related to value

In the survey research, we asked both the senior public relations executives and the CEOs who completed questionnaires to answer two questions based on the method of compensating variation. One of these questions asked both the CEO and the top communicator to provide a nonmonetary value for public relations in comparison with a typical department in the same organization. They assigned a value on a scale called a *fractionation scale*, in which they were told that 100 would be the value of a typical department. In addition, the top communicator and the CEO were asked to assign a cost-benefit ratio to public relations – essentially a monetary value. The top communicators also were asked to predict how they thought members of the dominant coalition would respond to these same two questions.

Based on this method, our survey research showed that CEOs and communicators alike agree that public relations returns significantly more than it costs – and more than the typical department in their organization. CEOs estimated the average return-oninvestment for public relations to be 186%. This ROI increased to 225% under conditions of excellence. It was 140% for the least excellent public relations departments. CEOs estimated values for public relations in comparison with other management functions to be 160 (where 100 was average) for all departments, 232 for excellent departments, and 109 for less excellent departments.

These estimates, of course, cannot be considered to be hard measures of the value of public relations. They are soft, comparative measures. However, the measures provided strong statistical evidence of the value of public relations. These measures of value had strong statistical correlations with the characteristics of excellent public relations – thus showing that excellent public relations contributes more value than less excellent public relations.

Our qualitative interviews with CEOs and public relations heads also confirmed our conceptualization of the value of public relations. Most were unwilling or unable to assign an exact value to public relations. However, those with excellent public relations departments were sure of the value of public relations; and they explained that value in essentially the same way we had theorized. In addition,

we found no evidence that the financial success attributed to public relations had come at the cost of social responsibility. The most effective organizations we studied relied on public relations to help determine which stakeholder groups were strategic for it and then to help develop credible, long-term relationships with those constituencies. Such high-quality relationships only exist when the organization acknowledges the legitimacy of the public, listens to its concerns, and deals with any negative consequences it may be having on that public.

Undeniable evidence came from the chemical association. There, the head of public relations developed a program of citizen advisory panels that has changed his entire industry's way of operating and, concomitantly, its reputation. This program of social responsibility reflects the vice-president's belief in the legitimacy of the public interest. His accompanying public relations efforts have been characterized in the trade press as 'sophisticated,' 'very aggressive,' 'skilled,' 'more open,' 'responsive,' and 'more effective.' He himself believes the program is helping his industry change in ways that respond to citizens' concerns about health, safety, and the environment. As he was quoted as saying in a weekly trade publication, 'Changing one's own performance, not 'educating' the public, is the only successful strategy' (as quoted in Begley, 1993, p. 23).

The functional level: characteristics of excellent public relations departments

After answering the effectiveness question, both our theory building and research turned to the Excellence question: What are the characteristics of public relations departments and programs, and of the internal and environmental context of the organization, that increase the likelihood that the public relations function will have value for both the organization and for society? Answering this question required a number of critical middle-range theories that we integrated within the general theory of excellence in our first *Excellence* book. This section reviews the characteristics of the overall public relations department. In subsequent sections, we do the same for specific communication programs and for the environmental and organizational context of excellent public relations functions. The characteristics can be placed into four categories that represent major areas of study in public relations.

Empowerment of the public relations function

The overarching theory integrating this category of concepts was the idea that the public relations function must be empowered as a distinctive and strategic managerial function if it is to play a role in making organizations effective. The senior public relations officer must play a role in making strategic organizational decisions, must be a member of the dominant coalition or have access to this powerful group of organizational leaders, and must have relative autonomy from excessive clearance rules to play this strategic role. In addition, the growth in the number of female practitioners should not hinder this empowerment of the public relations function; indeed, the growth should be valued for the diversity it brings to public relations. In addition, excellent departments should seek more of the scarce supply of minority practitioners to add to their ability to understand the environments faced by their organizations.

Specifically, we developed and tested three theoretical propositions:

1. *The senior public relations executive is involved with the strategic management processes of the organization, and communication programs are developed for strategic publics identified as a part of this strategic management process.* Public relations contributes to strategic management by scanning the environment to identify publics affected by the consequences of decisions or who might affect the outcome of decisions. An excellent public relations department communicates with these publics to bring their voices into strategic management, thus making it possible for stakeholder publics to participate in organizational decisions that affect them.

2. *The senior public relations executive is a member of the dominant coalition of the organization, or the senior public relations executive has a direct reporting relationship to senior managers who are part of the dominant coalition.* The public relations function seldom will be involved in strategic management, nor will public relations have the power to affect key organizational decisions, unless the senior public relations executive is part of or has access to the group of senior managers with the greatest power in the organization. Public relations executives also must have a good deal of freedom to make decisions about public relations problems without excessive clearance by other managers.

The third characteristic of empowerment relates to the extent to which practitioners who are not white males are empowered in the public relations function:

3. *Diversity is embodied in all public relations roles.* The principle of requisite variety (Weick, 1979) suggests that organizations need as much diversity inside as in their environment. Excellent public departments empower both men and women in all roles as well as practitioners of diverse racial, ethnic, and cultural backgrounds.

To a great extent, the Excellence data provide sound empirical support for our overarching theory of empowerment. We found that many organizations, including some of the excellent ones, had not fully empowered their public relations professionals. But in excellent public relations departments, by and large, public relations professionals were involved in strategic management. In particular, their role is as environmental scanners, providing information needed about strategic publics affected by managerial decisions. They get this information through formal research and various informal methods of gaining information about organizational constituencies.

Although not all of the managers of excellent communication functions were in the dominant coalition, nearly two-thirds of top communicators in the top 10% of our organizations were in that powerful group, compared to about 45% in the overall sample. When public relations was in the dominant coalition, that elite group also tended to include more representatives of outside constituencies. The larger the dominant coalition, the more likely it was that the top communicator was a member. That result suggests that the more an organization empowers most of its employees and outside constituents, the more likely it is also to empower public relations.

We found that the knowledge base of public relations practitioners increased their chance of being involved in strategic management and being accepted by the dominant coalition. Public relations practitioners in excellent organizations had more expertise in public relations. They did not all have college degrees in the field, although several did. Instead, they seemed to be self-educated; at least one participant in the qualitative research alluded to enhancing his practice after reading and studying the *Excellence* theory book. Others emphasized what they had learned from mentors.

The research also showed that excellent communicators are more likely to be team players than independent operators. They cultivate relationships not only with members of their external publics but also with their counterparts inside the organization. They promote teamwork within their own departments as well, empowering middle managers there to develop and work toward achieving a vision. In particular, these effective communicators have earned a close working relationship with their CEO. This relationship is characterized by credibility. It tends to result from extensive knowledge of the business or industry; longevity plus a track record of successful performance in the organization; expertise in strategic planning and managerial decision-making that is not limited to communication; and a shared worldview of the value of two-way symmetrical public relations, in particular.

Having such an expert communicator in place tended to lead to high value for public relations, rather than having a CEO who valued public relations in the first place seeking and hiring someone with that expertise. However, there were many significant exceptions to this pattern. Several senior executives in our study seemed determined to hire and support the best communicator they could find. To them, that meant a person capable of going beyond functions typically associated with public relations. It also meant a person whose expertise in public relations extended well beyond publicity, promotion, or media relations to encompass conflict resolution, environmental scanning, and dialogue with key publics.

Most of the top communicators in our survey reported directly to the CEO or indirectly through another senior manager. Such a reporting relationship does not ensure excellence, but we found that without such a clear path to the CEO public relations cannot contribute much to organizational effectiveness. A direct relationship with the CEO provides the top communicator access to strategic management processes of the organization. A direct reporting relationship, therefore, appears to be a necessary, if not a sufficient, condition for participation in strategic management, which is one of the most critical components of excellent public relations.

The need to be team players also showed up in our data on clearance procedures. Most public relations heads in our survey cannot act unilaterally. They are required to clear their activities at times where the input of top management is needed to ensure the accuracy or involvement of management. They are not required to clear more routine activities. At the same time, we found that excellent departments are more empowered than less excellent departments, as evidenced by having somewhat more autonomy to make major decisions without interference from top management.

Finally, we found that departments are excellent as often when women are the senior communicator as when men are in that role. Likewise, increasing the number of women in the public relations department and in managerial roles had no effect on excellence. At the same time, however, we found that excellent public relations departments take active steps to include women in managerial roles and to promote them from inside rather than to bring in men from other managerial functions. Likewise, we found that excellent departments actively strive to increase racio-ethnic diversity in the public relations

function – pushing for more requisite variety in public relations.

In short, excellent public relations departments are interesting and challenging places for capable and knowledgeable professionals to work. In these departments, public relations people are empowered, they play an active strategic role, their expertise in communication and environmental scanning is valued, and they are valued when they bring gender and racio-ethnic diversity into the function.

Public relations roles

Roles are abstractions about the patterned behaviors of individuals in organizations, a way of classifying and summarizing the myriad activities that an individual might perform as a member of an organization. By playing roles, individuals mesh activities, yielding predictable outcomes. Arguably, organizations are defined as systems of roles. In public relations, the concept of practitioner role has been systematically studied for about 25 years; such research places practitioner roles at the nexus of a network of important antecedent concepts and professional consequences. In the Excellence study, new role measures were developed and used to expand this important theoretical area.

Public relations researchers have conducted extensive research on four major roles that communicators play in organizations – the manager, senior adviser (also known as a communication liaison), technician, and media relations roles (for a review, see Dozier, 1992; L. Grunig, J. Grunig, & Dozier, 2002, Chapter 6). The manager and technician roles are the most common of the four. Communication technicians are essential to carry out most of the day-to-day communication activities of public relations departments, and many practitioners play both manager and technician roles. In less excellent departments, however, all of the communication practitioners – including the senior practitioner – are technicians. If the senior communicator is not a manager, it is not possible for public relations to be empowered as a management function because there are no managers in the department.

The Excellence study examined three theoretical propositions related to roles:

1. *The public relations unit is headed by a manager rather than a technician.* Excellent public relations units must have at least one senior communication manager who conceptualizes and directs public relations programs, or this direction will be supplied by other members of the dominant coalition who have little or no knowledge of communication management or of relationship building.

2. *The senior public relations executive or others in the public relations unit must have the knowledge needed for the manager role, or the communication function will not have the potential to become a managerial function.* Excellent public relations programs are staffed by people who have gained the knowledge needed to carry out the manager role through university education, continuing education, or self-study.

3. *Both men and women must have equal opportunity to occupy the managerial role in an excellent department.* The majority of public relations professionals in the three countries studied are women. If women are excluded from the managerial role, the communication function may be diminished be cause the majority of the most knowledgeable practitioners will be excluded from that role. When that is the case, the senior position in the public relations department typically is filled by a technician or by a practitioner from another managerial function who has little knowledge of public relations.

The results of the Excellence study solidly supported our proposition that the distinction between the manager and technician roles for the senior communicator in a public relations department is a core factor distinguishing excellent from less excellent departments. However, the results also showed the vital supporting role of technical expertise to the management role. More than any other variable, the availability of knowledge to perform a managerial role distinguishes excellent departments from less excellent ones. Excellent departments also have higher levels of technical expertise than less excellent departments. Nevertheless, technical expertise has value only when it is accompanied by managerial expertise. Public relations managers are most effective when they also possess technical expertise or have it available to them – especially technical knowledge in media relations. Expert technicians who have little managerial expertise or who are not supervised by expert managers have little value to the organization.

Our data also revealed more than one kind of managerial expertise. Public relations departments can possess strategic managerial expertise, administrative managerial expertise, or both. We found that excellent departments possess both kinds of expertise. We showed that strategic managers are most essential to the functioning of an excellent public relations department. In addition, our data showed that public relations departments need administrative expertise. Like technical expertise, however, administrative expertise has little value without accompanying knowledge of how to practice strategic public relations. At the same time, our data showed that communication departments possess less strategic knowledge than knowledge needed to practice any of the other roles.

The managerial role is equally important for public relations when the perspective of the dominant coalition is taken into account. Although CEOs view public relations roles in a more splintered and confusing way than do top communicators, the CEOs of organizations with excellent public relations departments expect their top communicators to be managers. Also, the greater the importance assigned to communication with outside groups by the dominant coalition, the stronger the coalition's expectation will be that the top communicator should be a manager rather than a technician.

CEOs also expect top communicators to be expert in media relations – more strongly than do top communicators. In addition, our results suggested that CEOs often hire top communicators because of their technical expertise but then learn that technical expertise is insufficient when a crisis or major internal upheaval requires more strategic communication skills. When top communicators have managerial as well as technical knowledge, as our qualitative results showed, they can meet such a challenge. When they have only technical expertise, they cannot.

We also found that gender makes little difference in the role enacted by top communicators, in the role expectations of CEOs, and in the expertise of the public relations department. However, we found that female public relations heads are more likely to play dual manager-technician roles than are men – even in organizations with excellent public relations departments. We also found that women may have less opportunity than men to gain strategic expertise because of the time they must spend doing technical tasks. The gender of the top communicator, therefore, does not help or hinder communication Excellence, but female top communicators may have to work harder to develop strategic expertise while they must engage in technical activities that are not expected of men.

Organization of the communication function, relationship to other functions, and use of consulting firms

Many organizations have a single department devoted to all communication functions. Others have separate departments for programs aimed at different publics such as employees, consumers, investors, or donors. Still others place communication under another managerial function such as marketing, human resources, legal, or finance. Many organizations also contract with or consult with outside firms for all or some of their communication programs or for such communication techniques as annual reports or newsletters.

Starting at about the time we began work on the Excellence project in 1985, there has been extensive debate about how the communication function should be organized in organizations and what its relationship should be to other management functions, especially marketing (see, e.g., Schultz, Tannenbaum & Lauterborn, 1993; Thorson & Moore, 1996). Numerous scholars and professionals have called for the integration of all communication activities in an organization into a single department or for communication to be coordinated in some way by a 'communication czar' (Schultz et al., 1993, p. 168), 'pope' (Gronstedt, 2000, p. 189), or 'chief reputation officer' (Fombrun, 1996, p. 197).

Advertising scholars and practitioners originally advocated the integration of these communication activities through the marketing function or, on a smaller scale, through a marketing communication department or executive. Public relations scholars and practitioners largely resisted this integration, although some endorsed it as a way of empowering public relations through alignment with the more powerful marketing function. Public relations people pointed out that most communication activities other than marketing communication have long been integrated through the public relations function or through a chief public relations or communication officer. They feared that marketing encroachment or dominance of the public relations function would diminish the role of public relations in organizations.

By today, integrated marketing communication (IMC) scholars and practitioners (e.g., Duncan & Moriarty, 1997; Gronstedt, 2000) have moved away from integrated *marketing* communication to what they now call 'integrated communication' – although most still concentrate their attention on consumers and marketing communication programs. This integrated communication differs little from the principle of integration of all communication activities under the public relations function that we proposed in the first Excellence book and tested in the Excellence study. Public relations scholars and practitioners, likewise, now seem to have embraced the idea of pulling marketing communication activities under the public relations umbrella – although data reported by Hunter (1999a) show that a large proportion of marketing communication programs still report to marketing rather than public relations.

For public relations to be managed strategically and to serve a role in the overall strategic management of the organization, therefore, the Excellence theory first states the theoretical principle that organizations must have an integrated communication function. An excellent public relations function integrates all public relations programs

into a single department or provides a mechanism for coordinating programs managed by different departments. Only in an integrated system is it possible for public relations to develop new communication programs for changing strategic publics and to move resources from outdated programs designed for formerly strategic publics to the new programs.

Even though the public relations function is integrated in an excellent organization, the function should not be integrated into another department whose primary responsibility is a management function other than communication. Therefore, the Excellence theory also states that public relations should be a management function separate from other functions. Many organizations splinter the public relations function by making communication a supporting tool for other departments. When the public relations function is sublimated to other functions, it cannot be managed strategically because it cannot move communication resources from one strategic public to another – as an integrated public relations function can.

When we wrote Excellence in Public Relations and Communication Management (J. Grunig, 1992a), little research was available on the role of public relations consulting firms in excellent organizations. Therefore, the Excellence theory made no predictions about the role of outside firms, but in the quantitative study we asked questions on how organizations use these firms in the communication function.

The Excellence data and those reported by Hunter (1997, 1999a) from surveys of Fortune 500 companies showed that communication functions rapidly are being organized under the rubric of public relations or corporate communication. Organizations seem to be integrating communication activities through a central public relations department. Alternatively, they have several specialized communication departments that are coordinated both formally and informally by a chief communication officer, who usually holds the title of senior vice president or vice president of corporate communication. In addition to the coordinating role of this senior communication officer, organizations use a number of ways to coordinate their activities, such as organization-wide meetings, communication policies, and unstructured interaction of communication professionals in different departments or business units. Our data showed that this integration has occurred most often in organizations that have excellent public relations functions, as we have defined excellence.

These combinations of centralized or integrated, specialized departments also tend to have a matrix arrangement with other management functions – such as marketing, human resources, or finance. They work under an integrated philosophy of communication – a philosophy that is largely strategic and symmetrical. But the communication managers in these centralized and specialized departments work as peer professionals with their counterparts in other management functions. They collaborate with their peers. In excellent departments there is little conflict and competition with other management functions – including marketing. Inside excellent communication departments, professionals work as colleagues who are equally empowered. As the field becomes female-intensive, the implications are clear: Women must be included in the organization's power and information networks.

Excellent communication departments also seek support from outside firms. All public relations departments in our sample purchased a substantial proportion of their technical publicity activities from outside firms, as well as a large proportion of their research support. Excellent public relations departments also sought strategic counseling from outside firms when they had difficulties with their publics, although most seem to possess the knowledge themselves to deal with these problems.

Whereas the marketing function in excellent organizations seldom dominates public relations, communication departments in less excellent organizations have a strong tendency to provide little more than technical support to the marketing function – technical support that most communication departments purchase from outside firms. A few of the excellent departments do seem to have adopted marketing theory as the foundation for their communication programs – with its emphasis on customers, messages, and symbols. On the positive side, however, they also have adopted the strategic, two-way approach of modern marketing – although marketing theory has steered them toward an asymmetrical rather than a symmetrical approach to communication.

The challenge for public relations theorists and practitioners, therefore, seems to be to persuade their counterparts in marketing to adopt a more symmetrical approach to communication. Recent books by Gronstedt (2000) and Duncan and Moriarty (1997) suggest that this conversion already may be occurring.

Models of public relations

J. Grunig (1976) first introduced the concept of models of public relations as a way of understanding and explaining the behavior of public relations practitioners. At that time, public relations educators routinely advocated two-way communication; but few made a distinction in the purpose of public relations in an organization. J. Grunig (1984) conceptualized the press agentry and public information models to improve on the simple concept of one-way communication. He also did not believe that all

two-way communication was the same. Some was asymmetrical: Public relations people did research and listened to publics in an effort to determine how best to change their behavior to benefit the organization. But, he believed that public relations professionals had a calling beyond this asymmetrical approach: serving as the organizational function that attempts to balance the interests of organizations with those of their publics, an approach he called 'symmetrical' communication.

Over the years, these public relations models have been researched and debated (for reviews, see J. Grunig, 2001; J. Grunig & L. Grunig, 1989, 1992; L. Grunig, J. Grunig, & Dozier, 2002, Chapter 8). Do they really describe actual public relations practice? Is the symmetrical model only an idealized, normative model? Are critical scholars correct: Is it unlikely that a large organization with more power than its publics would ever deliberately choose to practice symmetrical public relations? Is symmetrical public relations simply a deceptive term used by educators and practitioners to cover up the damage that public relations does to the interests of publics?

In *Excellent Public Relations and Effective Organizations* (L. Grunig. J. Grunig, & Dozier, 2002), we summarized and responded to these questions. We concluded that the four models are both positive and normative and that the two-way symmetrical model still appears to be a normative ideal for public relations practice. We maintained that public relations professionals can use the power of their knowledge – if they have it, and if society recognizes the value of public relations – to advocate a symmetrical approach to public relations. They should be able to advocate symmetry in public relations for the same reason that a physician tells an overweight person to exercise – because it is good for the organization, just as exercise is good for one's health.

The Excellence theory, therefore, stated that excellent departments will design their communication programs on the two-way symmetrical model rather than the press agentry, public information, or two-way asymmetrical models. Two-way symmetrical public relations attempts to balance the interests of the organization and its publics, is based on research, and uses communication to manage conflict with strategic publics. As a result, two-way symmetrical communication produces better long-term relationships with publics than do the other models of public relations. Symmetrical programs generally are conducted more ethically than are other models and produce effects that balance the interests of organizations and the publics in society. Symmetrical practitioners, therefore, have mixed motives (they are loyal to both their employers and to the publics of their organizations).

Three specific propositions were based on the symmetrical model:

1. The public relations department and the dominant coalition share the worldview that the communication department should reflect the two-way symmetrical, or mixed-motive, model of public relations.

2. Communication programs developed for specific publics are based on the two-way symmetrical, mixed-motive model.

3. The senior public relations executive or others in the public relations unit must have the knowledge needed for the two-way symmetrical model, or the communication function will not have the potential to practice that excellent model.

The quantitative and qualitative data collected in the Excellence study provided the most comprehensive information ever collected on the models of public relations. As a result, the data suggested a significant reconceptualization of the models. We did find that the four models still provide an accurate and useful tool to describe public relations practice and worldview. Practitioners and CEOs do think about public relations in these ways, and the four models do describe the way communication programs are conducted for different types of publics. However, the differences among the two one-way and the two two-way models typically blur in the minds of CEOs and in the practice of some, but not all, programs. CEOs, in particular, view an excellent public relations function as including the two-way asymmetrical model as often as it does the two-way symmetrical model.

We found the answer to that dilemma in the two-way component of the two-way asymmetrical model. CEOs like the two-way asymmetrical model because they appreciate the systematic use of research in that model. Most do not distinguish research conducted for symmetrical purposes from research conducted for asymmetrical purposes. Most CEOs do not want asymmetrical communication programs, although we did find exceptions in our survey of cases. Organizations that define public relations as a marketing function, in particular, tend to see public relations only in asymmetrical terms – or in one-way terms.

We successfully isolated three dimensions underlying the four models – one-way versus two-way, symmetry versus asymmetry, and mediated and interpersonal techniques. We also suggested further research on a fourth dimension, the ethics of communication. The overlapping concepts and practices of the models that we had found before – such as practicing the two-way symmetrical, two-way asymmetrical, and public information models concurrently – seem to have occurred because an organization had a symmetrical public relations worldview, favored extensive research, and practiced mediated as well as interpersonal communication.

Excellent public relations, therefore, can be described better in terms of these underlying dimensions than in terms of the four discrete models themselves. Excellent public relations is research based (two-way), symmetrical (although organizations constantly struggle between symmetry and asymmetry when they make decisions), and based on either mediated or interpersonal communication (depending on the situation and public). We also believe it is more ethical, although we did not measure ethics as a component of the models in the Excellence study. Future research, we predict, will establish ethics as a crucial component of excellent public relations.

We also learned from both our quantitative and qualitative data that organizations typically turn to a symmetrical approach when activist pressure or a crisis makes an asymmetrical approach too costly. Then, the CEO tends to upgrade the communication function and hire a knowledgeable top communicator – although sometimes the top communicator comes first and convinces the CEO of the need to enhance the communication function. By and large, organizations practice symmetrical public relations when the CEO understands its value and demands it; and the senior communicator and his or her communication staff have the knowledge to supply it. Much of that knowledge comes from the ability to do research, to understand publics, and to collaborate and negotiate – skills that excellent communicators must have.

The program level: characteristics of programs to communicate with specific publics

In addition to theorizing about and researching the characteristics of excellent public relations at the functional level, the Excellence study also examined the level of ongoing programs that excellent communication departments devise to develop and maintain relationships with their key publics. In particular, we addressed two concerns that pervade current discussions of public relations – strategic origination of programs and evaluation of their outcomes.

The questionnaire for the top communicator provided a list of 17 publics that serve as the focus of public relations programs in many organizations. Top communicators were asked to provide a detailed breakdown of the origins, management, and outcomes of communication programs for their top three publics, as defined by budget allocations. We analyzed communication programs for seven specific publics that were most often mentioned by top communicators: the media,[3] employees, investors, the community, customers, government, and members.

Our theory stated simply that communication programs organized by excellent departments should be managed strategically. To be *managed strategically* means that these programs are based on research and environmental scanning, that varying rather than routine techniques are used when they are implemented, and that they are evaluated either formally or informally. In addition, we predicted that the communication professionals who participated in our research would have evidence to show that these programs had improved the relationships between the organization and its publics.

We looked for support for our theoretical prediction that organizations and public relations departments that are excellent overall also will have specific communication programs that are excellent. We believed that communication programs in excellent departments would be more likely to have strategic origins and less likely to have historicist origins than those in less excellent departments. We also believed that excellent programs will be based on environmental scanning research and more likely to use evaluation research to gather evidence that shows positive outcomes from the programs. Less excellent programs, in contrast, continue year after year with little or no research to identify new or changing publics, without setting measurable objectives, and without conducting evaluation research to determine whether these objectives have been met.

The results provide remarkably robust support for the proposition that excellent public relations programs are managed strategically. When the organization and the communication department are excellent overall, communication programs for specific publics are more likely to have strategic origins and less likely to have historicist origins. Excellent departments are more than the routine publicity mills of traditional departments. Excellent programs arise from environmental scanning research, and they are evaluated through all forms of evaluation (scientific, clip-file, and informal). Managers of excellent departments also reported the availability of evidence that their programs have positive outcomes, such as meeting their objectives, changing relationships, and avoiding conflict.

We also found that communication programs have strategic origins most often in organizations experiencing pressure from activist groups. When program origins are strategic, top communicators also report greater success in dealing with activist pressure on the organization. Programs are more likely to have strategic origins if the communication department has the expertise to enact the manager role and the top communicator enacts that role frequently. When organizations experience activist pressure, they are more likely to use both formal and informal environmental scanning research. Communication programs are more likely to be evaluated through scientific, clip file, and informal evaluation when activist pressure is high. Generally, organizations are more successful in dealing with activists when the organizations evaluate their communication programs. Formal and informal scanning and the three forms of program evaluation all increase when the communication department has higher levels of managerial expertise and the head of public relations enacts that role frequently. Positive program outcomes increase as a function of overall Excellence, manager role expertise, and manager role enactment.

Government relations programs, however, did not fit this pattern when they were compared to programs for the six other publics. The explanation, we believe, is that in many organizations, government relations programs and especially lobbying functions are directly dominated by lawyers and CEOs. Communication departments typically exert little control over these programs, even if government relations is situated in the communication department on the organizational chart. For this reason, government relations programs often operate somewhat orthogonally to communication departments, independent of both strengths and weaknesses in those departments, as indicated by various measures of communication Excellence.

Lobbyists also seem to lean heavily on personal experience and interpersonal relations with legislators or regulators as the basis for their actions. Compared to others under the public relations umbrella in organizations, these practitioners are less likely to have formal training in communication management. Since expertise (e.g., manager role and two-way symmetrical communication) in the communication function is at the core of overall Excellence, quasi-autonomous government relations programs appear to operate less directly as a function of communication Excellence.

Activism and the environmental context for excellence

A central part of most research on public relations as a management function before the Excellence study looked for reasons inside and outside the organization to explain when some public relations functions are more strategic, managerial, and symmetrical than others are. In the Excellence study, we also examined the organizational context to determine whether communication Excellence can survive more or less on its own, or whether it requires a nourishing external and internal context to flourish.

In this section, we look at the external context. The Excellence theory predicted that a turbulent, complex environment with pressure from activist groups stimulates organizations to develop an excellent public relations function.

Previous research on activist groups showed that most organizations, at least in the United States, have experienced pressure from activism (L. Grunig, 1992a). In addition, research on power in organizations suggests that organizations are most likely to empower the public relations function when pressure from activists, or crises produced by that pressure, makes public relations expertise valuable (L. Grunig, 1992b). We hypothesized, therefore, that activism would push organizations toward excellence. Organizations that face activist pressure would be more likely to assign public relations a managerial role, include public relations in strategic management, communicate more symmetrically with a powerful adversary or partner, and develop more participative cultures and organic structures that would open the organization to its environment – the key variables in our index of excellence.

Our results showed that an effective organization exists in an environment characterized more by dynamism and even hostility than by stability. We confirmed that activism pushes organizations toward excellence as they try to cope with the expectations of their strategic constituencies – although activism did not guarantee excellence. The perceived incidence of activism correlated moderately and significantly with excellence in public relations, especially when estimated by the head of public relations. According to the estimates of both CEOs and senior communicators, organizations with excellent public relations were more likely to report success in dealing with activists than organizations with less excellent departments. The success of activists, however, did not correlate significantly with excellence. Importantly, these correlations were not negative: Communication Excellence seems to mean that activists do not fail to achieve their goals when organizations achieve their goals.

The quantitative data, therefore, suggested that activism stimulates excellence. The correlations probably were moderate, however, because most of the organizations studied reported facing activism. Many, but not all, seem to have responded by developing excellent public relations departments, which make them more successful in dealing with activists. Activists probably achieve some level of success regardless of how the organization responds; the difference provided by excellence is that the organization as well as the activists can achieve success – a symmetrical outcome.

Both our quantitative and qualitative data also showed that excellent public relations departments respond to activists with two-way communication, symmetrical communication, involvement of activists in organizational decisions, and both formative and evaluative research on the activists. That pattern of results fits the Excellence theory: Excellent public relations departments scan the environment and continuously bring the voices of publics, especially activist publics, into decision making. Then, they develop programs to communicate symmetrically with activists and involve them with managers throughout the organization. Finally, they use both formative and evaluative research to manage their communication programs strategically.

In our qualitative research, we heard a great deal about symmetry in response to our questions about activism in the environment. For example, the head of public relations of an industry association scoring at the top of the Excellence scale described a community program he had developed that has won national prominence and acclaim. The program's first principle is listening and responding to the community's concerns. He emphasized that responsiveness may include change on the organization's part when pressure groups do not agree with it. Perhaps in no case was this more obvious than in the chemical corporation we studied. Crises and improving company performance both helped the corporation overcome what might have been crippling pressure from outside groups. As its vice president explained, since the catastrophe in Bhopal, his entire industry has become more willing to be open to the public.

The qualitative data also showed that crises have the potential to enhance the career opportunities of public relations practitioners. Most participants in our 25 qualitative cases discussed at least one crisis situation that had resulted in a real shift both in their organization's culture and in its practice of public relations. Often, they spoke of increased appreciation for their function on the part of others in the organization; greater access to the dominant coalition as a result; more openness in communication; a new willingness to cooperate with pressure groups and the community at large; the concomitant likelihood of learning from these strategic constituencies; and greater support for or at least understanding of the organization from the community, the clients or customers, the media, and even government regulators.

The organizational context of excellent public relations

Inside the organization, previous research both by organizational and public relations scholars has examined the extent to which the organizational characteristics of structure, culture, communication system, treatment of men and women, and power of the dominant coalition predict organizational behavior, in general, and public relations practice, in particular.

After reviewing this research in *Excellence in Public Relations and Communication Management* (J. Grunig, 1992a), we concluded that a power-control theory explains organizational and public relations behavior best. That is, organizations behave in general, and practice public relations in particular, as they do because the dominant coalition chooses to organize and manage in that way. Nevertheless, previous research also suggested that the organizational context of a public relations function could nurture or impede excellent communication management, although to a lesser extent than could the dominant coalition.

Therefore, the Excellence theory included five theoretical propositions stating that organizations with excellent public relations have the following attributes:

1. Participative rather than authoritarian organizational cultures.

2. A symmetrical system of internal communication.

3. Organic rather than mechanical structures.

4. Programs to equalize opportunities for men and women and minorities.

5. High job satisfaction among employees.

The results of our research demonstrate conclusively that excellent public relations will thrive most in an organization with an organic structure, participative culture, and a symmetrical system of communication and in which opportunities exist for women and racio-ethnic minorities. Although we found that these conditions alone cannot produce excellent public relations, they do provide a hospitable environment for excellent public relations.

Most important, these conditions provide a favorable context in which all employees work most effectively – but especially women and minorities. Within such an organization employees are empowered to participate in decision-making. As a result, they are more satisfied with the organization and are more likely to support than to oppose the goals of the organization. In addition, employees who are empowered to participate in decision-making and to engage in symmetrical internal communication are likely also to be effective symmetrical communicators with members of external publics.

We also found that the effective organization provides a hospitable environment for its increasingly diverse workforce. The CEOs and employees we surveyed seemed to agree on all 22 measured aspects of how women, in particular, are treated in their organizations. Although top management's perceptions were more optimistic, we were encouraged by the general correspondence among the responses from the CEOs, top communicators, and employees. All three groups of respondents clearly differentiated areas in which women are most and least supported. The survey data suggested that equitable treatment of women, as evidenced primarily by economic equity, and programs to foster their careers (such as policies against sexual harassment and efforts to encourage women's leadership abilities) are an integral component of excellent organizations. Programs that provide a supportive work environment correlate especially highly with the other conditions found in excellent organizations. Likewise, excellent organizations are beginning to branch out and offer some proactive mentoring and advancement programs for women.

Our data showed that when the public relations function was given the power to implement symmetrical programs of communication, the result was a more participative culture and greater employee satisfaction with the organization. However, we also found that symmetrical communication is not likely in an organization with a mechanical structure and authoritarian culture. Organic structure and symmetrical communication interact to produce a participative culture, and participative culture contributes strongly to employee satisfaction with the organization.

An organic structure seems to be the key to an effective organization – triggering changes in culture, communication, and satisfaction. Symmetrical communication has a strong role in creating and implementing organic structure, but a communicator cannot step alone into any organization and implement an organic structure or symmetrical system of communication. The top communicator must work with the dominant coalition to develop an organic structure for the organization while he or she is developing a system of symmetrical communication. Our data on the internal context of an organization, therefore, did not just support the need for symmetrical communication. They also supported the need for the public relations function to be represented in the dominant coalition, in order to create the organic structural context for participative culture and subsequent employee satisfaction.

Summarizing the excellence theory

The Excellence theory is a broad, general theory that begins with a general premise about the value of public relations to organizations and to society and uses that premise to integrate a number of middle-range theories about the organization of the public relations function, the conduct of public relations programs, and the environmental and organizational context of excellent public relations. Since completion of the study, we and other researchers have begun research to extend the theory beyond the three English-speaking countries in which it was conducted. Before introducing that research, however, it is useful to summarize this complex theory.

The Excellence study has shown that public relations is a unique management function that helps an organization interact with the social and political components of its environment. This institutional environment consists of publics that affect the ability of the organization to accomplish its goals and that expect organizations to help them accomplish their own goals. Organizations solve problems for society, but they also create problems for society. As a result, organizations are not autonomous units free to make money or to accomplish other goals they set for themselves. They have relationships with individuals and groups that help set the organization's goals, define what the organization is and does, and affect the success of its strategic decisions and behaviors.

The study showed that the value of public relations comes from the relationships that organizations develop and maintain with publics. It also showed that the quality of relationships results more from the behavior of the organization than from the messages that communicators disseminate. Public relations can affect management decisions and behavior if it is headed by a manager who is empowered to play an essential role in the strategic management of the organization. In that role, communicators have greater value when they bring information into the organization than when they disseminate information out of the organization. The study also showed how communication programs for publics such as employees, consumers, or investors can be planned and managed strategically and evaluated to demonstrate their effectiveness.

Our research showed that communicators can develop relationships more effectively when they communicate with publics symmetrically rather than asymmetrically. Symmetrical communication is especially important inside the organization, where it helps to build a participative culture that, in turn, increases employee satisfaction with the organization. Symmetrical communication inside the organization and participative culture largely result from the structure that top management chooses for the organization. Communicators cannot be successful, therefore, unless they have access to the top-management team that develops an organizational structure. Our research also demonstrated the importance of diversity in a public relations department and throughout the organization. Women and men are equally effective in top communication roles, but we also learned that women have a more

difficult time than men developing the experiences needed for a top communication role.

The study showed that excellent communication functions are integrated. However, they are not integrated through another management function, such as marketing or human resources. They are integrated through a senior communication executive – who usually has a background in public relations – or through a single public relations department. We found that integrated marketing communication (IMC) programs, which combine marketing public relations and advertising, are part of an integrated public relations function. IMC should not be the concept that integrates communication.

Finally, the Excellence study showed that activism is good, rather than bad for an organization. Activism provides the impetus for excellent public relations. Excellent public relations departments develop programs to communicate actively, and symmetrically, with activists. Organizations that collaborate with activists develop a competitive advantage over organizations that do not because they behave in a way that is acceptable to publics and, therefore, make fewer decisions that result in negative publicity and regulation, litigation, and opposition.

Globalization of the excellence theory

Most organizations are affected by publics throughout the world or by competition or collaboration with organizations in other countries. As a result, all public relations is global or international. Thus, it becomes imperative for public relations professionals to have a broad perspective that will allow them to work in many countries – or to work collaboratively with public relations professionals, employees, or customers from many countries.

In public relations as well as in related fields such as management and marketing, scholars and practitioners have asked whether the principles and practices of their profession are the same regardless of the country in which they are practiced or whether the profession must be enacted differently in each country. Although the Excellence study was conducted in only three English-speaking countries, it has generated a great deal of interest among public relations scholars and practitioners worldwide. This interest suggests that the theoretical principles we have identified are not limited to the United States and that they are applicable to public relations practice outside the three Anglo countries where the study was conducted. Although the United States, Canada, and the United Kingdom are similar in many ways, they also exhibit cultural, political, and social differences. Thus, the fact that we found no difference in excellent public relations among the three countries provides some evidence that the principles are not limited strictly to the United States.

As a result, we have begun research to determine if the Excellence theory can fulfill the need for a global theory of public relations. There is a substantial literature already on international public relations, but it consists mostly of descriptive research on and case studies of public relations practice in many countries of the world (as found, e.g., in Culbertson & Chen, 1996). Many of these studies suggest that public relations is practiced in substantially different ways in different countries – often reflecting cultural differences. At the same time, research has shown that the same four models of public relations we have used to describe U.S. practice (press agentry, public information, two-way asymmetrical, and two-way symmetrical) also describe practice in other countries (J. Grunig, L. Grunig, Sriramesh, Huang, & Lyra, 1995).

We have proposed that, rather than continuing to conduct purely positive research on how public relations is practiced in different countries, scholars should construct a normative theory of excellent global public relations. A normative theory would specify how public relations should be practiced. A good normative theory is based on sound theory; but it also is built from research to identify the most effective existing, or positive, practices of public relations. This is exactly what we have done in the Excellence study.

Before we can adopt the Excellence principles as a normative theory for global practice, we must do research to ensure that they are not an ethnocentric theory. At the same time, we do not believe that different polycentric theories are necessary for each country, region, or culture of the world. Vercic, L. Grunig, and J. Grunig (1996), L. Grunig, J. Grunig, and Vercic (1998), and Wakefield (1996) have collaborated to propose a global public relations theory of generic principles and specific applications – a middle-ground theory between an ethnocentric theory and polycentric theories.

Generic principles means that in an abstract sense, the principles of public relations are the same worldwide. *Specific applications* means that these abstract principles must be applied differently in different settings. For example, the concept of employee participation in decision-making is the same concept throughout the world. However, when Stohl (1993) asked managers in Denmark, Germany, France, England, and The Netherlands how they implemented that principle, she found that they did so differently in each country – in ways that reflected the culture of that country.

As a starting point for research, we have proposed that our principles of excellence are generic principles. We also

have proposed that public relations professionals must take six contextual conditions into account when they apply the principles:

- Culture, including language
- The political system
- The economic system
- The media system
- The level of economic development
- The extent and nature of activism

Our research to date has provided evidence supporting this theory of generic principles and specific applications. The most extensive test of the theory came in Slovenia. L. Grunig, J. Grunig, and Vercic (1998) replicated the quantitative portion of the Excellence study with 30 Slovenian firms with public relations departments. They found that the principles of excellence clustered into the same Excellence factor in Slovenia as they did in the United States, Canada, and the United Kingdom, in spite of a different cultural, political, and economic context.

At the same time, the research showed that Slovenian practitioners were less involved in strategic management and were less valued by senior management than practitioners in the English-speaking countries. We also found that privatization and political change in Slovenia had encouraged activism to the extent that activism in Slovenia is now similar to that of the other countries. However, the old Yugoslavian cultural, political, and economic context in Slovenia had left its remnants inside Slovenian organizations, which still had more authoritarian cultures, more asymmetrical communication systems, and lower levels of job satisfaction than did organizations in the Anglo countries.

To deal with these differences, public relations practitioners in Slovenia found it necessary to apply the generic principles differently than in the Anglo countries. For example, they learned that they needed to counsel CEOs to support and empower public relations managers. They also developed continuing education in public relations to deal with the lack of public relations knowledge, and they had to emphasize employee relations because of the negative context inside Slovenian organizations.

Wakefield (1997) asked a Delphi panel of 23 public relations experts in 18 countries to evaluate the extent to which they believed that the Excellence principles were generic principles that applied to their countries and whether additional principles were needed. He also asked them whether all of the six specific conditions were important for applying the generic principles. With the exception of the need for diversity in public relations departments, he found consensus that the principles are generic and that the list of specific conditions is complete. Wakefield (2000) conducted a second Delphi study, which extended the database to 54 experts in 29 countries, and again found support for the principles of excellence and the contextual variables.

Wakefield (2000, 2001) has conducted research on the implications of this theory of generic principles and specific applications for the organization of a public relations function in a multinational organization and of the implications for using public relations firms in different countries. He found that in organizations with what he called a 'world class' public relations function the generic principles provided a framework for public relations practice in all countries. However, he found that these world-class companies did not centralize the function or control it through the headquarters office. Rather, they did the following:

- International public relations officers functioned as a global team with frequent interaction among headquarters and local officers and among local officers.

- The senior public relations officer at headquarters served as a team leader for achieving mutual goals, and not as the only decision-maker in a hierarchical structure.

- Ideas and solutions came from any source in the global team.

- The global team cooperatively set public relations values and guidelines, but every unit created and carried out local strategies based on these guidelines. (p. 69)

Another test of the theory came in Korea. Rhee (1999) replicated major portions of the Excellence study and also produced an index of excellence almost identical to the Excellence factor. As was true in Slovenia, however, she found that fewer Korean professionals were involved in strategic management than in the Anglo countries, and she learned that they had less knowledge of the two-way models and managerial role. She also found that symmetrical public relations in Korea had been adapted to fit Confucian culture, with its emphasis on hierarchical relationships combined with collective responsibility.

As we search for and test generic principles of public relations, we have found it beneficial to begin with the Excellence principles. However, it is important to remain open to revision of these principles and to the addition of new ones so that the generic principles are truly global and not ethnocentric. In that regard, Vercic, L. Grunig, and J. Grunig (1996) interviewed three principals of the public relations firm Pristop in Slovenia to determine if they agreed that the Excellence principles are generic, to ask them how they adapted the principles in their country, and to suggest additional principles.

The interviews confirmed the importance of the existing principles and provided examples of context-specific applications of the principles. In addition, the Slovenian professionals suggested a new generic principle: Ethics is a necessary component of excellent public relations. They pointed out that in the postsocialist context of Slovenia, corruption was common and the suspicion of corruption even more common. Therefore, they suggested that ethical practice was a crucial element of excellent public relations in order to avoid damage to their individual reputations as well as to the reputation of the public relations profession.

Although we referred to integrity tangentially throughout the three books on the Excellence project, we did not include it as a principle of excellence or ask questions about it directly in our research. At this point, however, we have added ethical practice to our list of generic principles and consider ethics an important area that needs additional study.

Research, therefore, is well underway on a normative theory of global public relations. However, much more research is needed in many countries of the world to confirm the importance of the generic principles, to refine existing principles, to identify new principles, and to provide positive examples of how to apply the principles in the different local contexts in which global public relations professionals work.

Notes

1. The best-known of these theories of cognitive effects are the agenda-setting and framing theories. For an overview of agenda setting, see McCombs and Bell (1996) and Dearing and Rogers (1996). For an overview of framing, see Wallack, Dorfman, Jernigan, and Themba (1993), pp. 67–73.

2. It is also possible to evaluate public relations at a lower level than the four described later – the level of the individual message or publication such as an annual report or a brochure. We have not addressed the individual level of evaluation in the Excellence study because the purpose of the study was to determine how the public relations function and its component programs contribute to organizational effectiveness. In general, though, evaluation can be done at the individual level using concepts similar to those used at the program level.

3. The media cannot truly be said to be a public, because they are important only as a means of communicating with publics that interact with an organization. If a key public does not use the media for information about an organization or its decisions, the media have little importance in a communication program. However, journalists

behave like members of other publics (J. Grunig, 1983) when they seek information, so we refer to them loosely in this chapter as a public.

References

Begley, R. (1993, Dec. 8). Selling Responsible Care to a critical public: CMA takes its message to the airwaves. *Chemical Week*, p. 23.

Broom, G. M., & Smith, G. D. (1978, August). *Toward an understanding of public relations roles: An empirical test of five role models' impact on clients*, Paper presented at the meeting of the Public Relations Division, Association for Education in Journalism, Seattle.

Broom, G. M., & Smith, G. D. (1979). Testing the practitioner's impact on clients, *Public Relations Review*, 5(3), 47–59.

Culbertson, H. M., & Chen, N. (eds), (1996). *International public relations: A comparative analysis*, Mahwah NJ: Lawrence Erlbaum Associates.

Cutlip, S. M., & Center, A. H. (1952). *Effective public relations*. Englewood Cliffs, NJ: Prentice Hall.

Dearing, J. W., & Rogers, E. M. (1996). *Agenda-setting*. Thousand Oaks, CA: Sage.

Dozier, D. M. (1992). The organizational roles of communications and public relations practitioners. In J. E. Grunig (ed.), *Excellence in public relations and communication management* (pp. 327–356). Hillsdale, NJ: Lawrence Erlbaum Associates.

Dozier, D. M., with Grunig, L. A., & Grunig, J. E. (1995). *Manager's guide to excellence in public relations and communication management*. Hillsdale, NJ: Lawrence Erlbaum Associates.

Duncan, T., & Moriarty, S. (1997). *Driving brand value: Using integrated marketing to manage profitable stakeholder relationships*. New York: McGraw-Hill.

Ehling, W. P. (1992). Estimating the value of public relations and communication to an organization. In J. E. Grunig (ed.), *Excellence in public relations and communication management* (pp. 617–638). Hillsdale, NJ: Lawrence Erlbaum Associates.

Fleisher, C. S. (1995). *Public affairs benchmarking*. Washington: Public Affairs Council.

Fombrun, C. J. (1996). *Reputation: Realizing value from the corporate image*. Boston: Harvard Business School Press.

Freeman, R. E., & Gilbert, D. R. Jr. (1992, Spring), Business, ethics and society: A critical agenda. *Business and Society*, pp. 9–17.

Goodman, P. S., & Pennings, J. M. (eds), (1977). *New perspectives on organizational effectiveness*. San Francisco: Jossey-Bass.

Gronstedt, A. (2000). *The customer century: Lessons from world-class companies in integrated marketing and communication*. New York: Routledge.

Grunig, J. E. (1976). Organizations and publics relations: Testing a communication theory. *Journalism Monographs*, **46**.

Grunig, J. E. (1983). Washington reporter publics of corporate public affairs programs. *Journalism Quarterly*, **60**, 603–615.

Grunig, J. E. (1984). Organizations, environments, and models of public relations. *Public Relations Research & Education*, 1(1), 6–29.

Grunig, J. E. (ed.), (1992a). *Excellence in public relations and communication management*. Hillsdale, NJ: Lawrence Erlbaum Associates.

Grunig, J. E. (1992b). Symmetrical systems of internal communication, In J. E. Grunig (ed.), *Excellence in public relations and communication management* (pp. 531–576). Hillsdale, NJ: Lawrence Erlbaum Associates.

Grunig, J. E. (1992c). What is excellence in management? In J. E. Grunig (ed.), *Excellence in public relations and communication management* (pp. 219–250). Hillsdale, NJ: Lawrence Erlbaum Associates.

Grunig, J. E. (1997). Public relations management in government and business. In J. L. Garnett & A. Kouzmin (eds), *Handbook of administrative communication* (pp. 241–283), New York: Marcel Dekker.

Grunig, J. E. (2001). Two-way symmetrical public relations: Past, present, and future. In R. L. Heath (ed.), *Handbook of public relations* (pp. 11–30), Thousand Oaks, CA: Sage.

Grunig, J. E., & Grunig, L. A. (1989). Toward a theory of the public relations behavior of organizations: Review of a program of research. In J. E. Grunig & L. A. Grunig (eds), *Public relations research annual* (Vol. 1, pp. 27–66.). Hillsdale, NJ: Lawrence Erlbaum Associates.

Grunig, J. E., & Grunig, L. A. (1992). Models of public relations and communication. In J. E. Grunig (ed.), *Excellence in public relations and communication management* (pp. 285–326). Hillsdale, NJ: Lawrence Erlbaum Associates.

Grunig, J. E., Grunig, L. A., Sriramesh, K., Huang, Y. H., & Lyra, A. (1995). Models of public relations in an international setting. *Journal of Public Relations Research*, 7, 163–186.

Grunig, J. E., & Hunt, T. (1984). *Managing public relations*. New York: Holt, Rinehart & Winston.

Grunig, L. A. (1992a). Activism: How it limits the effectiveness of organizations and how excellent public relations departments respond. In J. E. Grunig (ed.), *Excellence in public relations and communication management* (pp. 503–530). Hillsdale, NJ: Lawrence Erlbaum Associates.

Grunig, L. A. (1992b). Power in the public relations department. In J. E. Grunig (ed.), *Excellence in public relations and communication management* (pp. 483–502). Hillsdale, NJ: Lawrence Erlbaum Associates.

Grunig, L. A., Grunig, J. E., & Dozier, D. M. (2002). *Excellent public relations and effective organizations: A study of communication management in three countries.* Mahwah, NJ: Lawrence Erlbaum Associates.

Grunig, L. A., Grunig, J. E., & Ehling, W. P. (1992). What is an effective organization? In J. E. Grunig (ed.), *Excellence in public relations and communication management* (pp. 65–90). Hillsdale, NJ: Lawrence Erlbaum Associates.

Grunig, L. A., Grunig, J. E., & Vercic, D. (1998). Are the IABC's excellence principles generic? Comparing Slovenia and the United States, the United Kingdom and Canada. *Journal of Communication Management, 2,* 335–356.

Hall, R. H. (1991). *Organizations: Structures, processes, and outcomes* (5th ed.). Englewood Cliffs, NJ: Prentice-Hall.

Hunter, T. (1997), *The relationship of public relations and marketing against the background of integrated communications: A theoretical analysis and empirical study at US-American corporations.* Unpublished master's thesis, University of Salzburg, Salzburg, Austria.

Hunter, T. (1999a). *Integrated communications: Current and future developments in integrated communications and brand management, with a focus on direct communication and new information and communication technologies, such as the Internet and stakeholder databases.* Unpublished doctoral dissertation, University of Salzburg, Salzburg, Austria.

Hunter, T. (1999b). The relationship of public relations and marketing. *Integrated Marketing Communications Research Journal, 5*(1), 41–44.

Jeffries-Fox Associates (2000a, March 3). *Toward a shared understanding of corporate reputation and related concepts: Phase I: Content analysis.* Basking Ridge, NJ: Report Prepared for the Council of Public Relations Firms.

Jeffries-Fox Associates (2000b, June 16). *Toward a shared understanding of corporate reputation and related concepts: Phase III: Interviews with client advisory committee members.* Basking Ridge, NJ: Report Prepared for the Council of Public Relations Firms.

Kuhn, T. S. (1970). *The structure of scientific revolutions* (2nd ed.). Chicago: University of Chicago Press. (A third edition of Kuhn's classic book also was published in 1996.)

McCombs, M., & Bell, T. (1996). The agenda-setting role of mass communication. In M. B. Salwen & D. Stacks (eds), *An integrated approach to communication theory and research* (pp. 93–110). Mahwah, NJ: Lawrence Erlbaum Associates.

McQuail, D. (2000). *McQuail's mass communication theory* (4th ed.). Newbury Park. CA: Sage.

Peters, T. J., & Waterman. R. H., Jr. (1982). *In search of excellence.* New York: Warner.

Post, J. E., Preston. L. E., & Sachs, S. (2002). *Redefining the corporation: Stakeholder management and organizational wealth.* Stanford, CA: Stanford Business Books.

Price, J. L. (1968). *Organizational effectiveness: An inventory of propositions.* Homewood, IL: Richard D. Irwin.

Rhee, Y. (1999). *Confucian culture and excellent public relations: A study of generic principles and specific applications in South Korean public relations practice.* Unpublished master's thesis. University of Maryland, College Park.

Robbins, S. P. (1990). *Organization theory: Structure, design, and application* (3rd ed.). Englewood Cliffs, NJ: Prentice-Hall.

Schultz, D. E., Tannenbaum, S. I., & Lauterborn, R. E. (1993). *Integrated marketing communications.* Chicago: NTC Business Books.

Stohl, C. (1993). European managers' interpretations of participation: A semantic network analysis. *Human Communication Research, 20,* 97–117.

Thorson, E., & Moore, J. (eds). (1996). *Integrated communication: Synergy of persuasive voices.* Mahwah, NJ: Lawrence Erlbaum Associates.

Vercic, D., Grunig, L. A., & Grunig, J. E. (1996). Global and specific principles of public relations: Evidence from Slovenia. In H. M. Culbertson & N. Chen (eds), *International public relations: A comparative analysis* (pp. 31–65). Mahwah NJ: Lawrence Erlbaum Associates.

Wakefield, R. I. (1996). Interdisciplinary theoretical foundations for international public relations. In H. M. Culbertson & N. Chen (eds), *International public relations: A comparative analysis* (pp. 17–30). Mahwah NJ: Lawrence Erlbaum Associates.

Wakefield, R. I. (1997). *International public relations: A theoretical approach to excellence based on a worldwide Delphi study.* Unpublished doctoral dissertation, University of Maryland, College Park.

Wakefield, R. I. (2000). World-class public relations: A model for effective public relations in the multinational. *Journal of Communication Management, 5*(1), 59–71.

Wakefield, R. I. (2001). Effective public relations in the multinational organization. In R. E. Heath (ed.), *Handbook of public relations* (pp. 639–647). Thousand Oaks, CA: Sage.

Wallack, L., Dorfman, L., Jernigan, D., & Themba, M. (1993). *Media advocacy and public health: Power for prevention.* Newbury Park, CA: Sage.

Weick, K. E. (1979). *The social psychology of organizing* (2nd ed.). Reading, MA: Addison-Wesley.

Who's excellent now? (1984, November 5). *BusinessWeek,* pp. 76–87.

CHAPTER 3

Lee Edwards

Public relations theories:
an overview*

Learning outcomes

By the end of this chapter you should be able to:

- describe and evaluate the main principles of systems theories in relation to public relations
- contrast different theoretical approaches to 'publics'
- consider different theoretical views of the role of the public relations practitioner
- describe and evaluate the main principles of relationship management theory
- compare different approaches to public relations theory, including critical, rhetorical, feminist and diversity perspectives
- evaluate the key debates within public relations research traditions.

Structure

- Systems theories: emergence of public relations research
- Extending the systemic view
- Developing theory: alternative approaches
- Feminist views of public relations
- Diversity in public relations

---

* Chapter 8 in *Exploring Public Relations* Second Edition, edited by Ralph Tench and Liz Yeomans (2009).

Introduction

Public relations (PR) research and practice have traditionally been closely linked. Systems theory, which emerged in the second half of the twentieth century as PR education was established and was initially the dominant approach to PR theory, took the view that theory development should improve practice first and foremost. However, more recently the assumptions underpinning the systems theory approach have been criticised as the technological, social and cultural environments for PR have evolved. A wider range of theoretical approaches to PR has emerged, with the growth of critical, sociological and cultural approaches in particular. As the body of knowledge about PR increases, this theoretical diversity will continue to grow and improve our understandings of the profession. This chapter examines a range of theoretical approaches to PR, beginning with a brief summary of findings in the systems tradition and continuing with an examination of alternative approaches.

Systems theories: emergence of public relations research

For systems theorists, research begins with the practitioner working for the organisation, the organisation carrying out PR or the situation in which the activity takes place. The main objective of PR is to develop and execute strategies and tactics that will benefit an organisation in a given context. In 1984, two of the earliest systems theorists, James E. Grunig and Todd Hunt, published *Managing Public Relations*, in which they presented a **typology** of PR, based on observations of practice in the United States: press agentry/publicist; public information; two-way asymmetric and two-way symmetric communications (Grunig and Hunt 1984).

Press agentry is one-way communication: no dialogue with the intended audience is required and the main objective is to put forward one particular view of the world through the media and other channels. Public information is related to press agentry in that one-way information dissemination is the purpose of the activity, but it differs from press agentry in that truth is fundamental to its purpose. The information has to be accurate, true and specific – the main aim is to inform rather than persuade. Two-way asymmetric communication is rooted in persuasive communications and aims to generate agreement between the organisation and its publics by bringing them around to the organisation's way of thinking. Feedback from publics is used to adapt communications strategies to be more persuasive, not to alter the organisation's position. Finally, in two-way symmetric communication the aim is to generate mutual understanding – the two-way communications process should lead to changes in both the public's *and* the organisation's position on an issue. Grunig and his colleagues continued the quest to understand and improve PR with a three-country, long-term study of PR practice, in conjunction with the International Association of Business Communicators (IABC), to establish what might be defined as 'excellence' in PR (Grunig 1992; Grunig et al. 2002). The 10-year study produced a four-level framework for 'excellent' PR:

- programme level (why, when and how individual communications programmes are implemented)

- departmental level (how the PR department operates and fits in with other departments and the organisation as a whole)

- organisational level (understanding of, and respect given to, communications processes and audience feedback by the organisation and its staff)

- economic level (the tangible value provided by excellent PR to the organisation, in terms of happy external and internal publics).

At the heart of the theory is the following proposition from Grunig (1992: 6) about PR effectiveness:

Public relations contributes to organisational effectiveness when it helps reconcile the organisation's goals with the expectations of its strategic constituencies. This contribution has monetary value to the organisation. Public relations contributes to effectiveness by building quality, long-term relationships with strategic constituencies. Public relations is most likely to contribute to effectiveness when the senior public relations manager is a member of the dominant coalition where he or she is able to shape the organisation's goals and to help determine which external publics are most strategic.

According to the study, two-way symmetric communication practices are a keystone for excellent PR, although the authors recognise that in practice a mix of asymmetric and symmetric approaches is often used.

Mini Case Study 3.1

Symmetric and asymmetric communication practices on the web

Symmetric communication

Non-governmental organisations have to communicate effectively with their stakeholders and take their views into account if they want to ensure long-term support for their causes. Symmetric, two-way communications are therefore particularly important for them. A good example of this in practice on the web is the Oxfam site, www.oxfam.org.uk. The site is focused on ensuring visitors receive as much information as possible about the organisation and its activities, while offering plenty of opportunity for feedback and contact. It includes:

- aims and objectives of the organisation
- annual reports and evaluations of its activities
- a summary of the different processes used by Oxfam to evaluate its activities in light of these objectives
- frequently asked questions and answers, divided into sections according to areas of most common interest
- updates and headline articles on the most current activities with which Oxfam is involved and progress reports for longer running projects
- press releases and other communications, reports and reviews released by Oxfam
- educational materials relating to Oxfam's aims and objectives

- further opportunities to contact the organisation by post, email or telephone.

Asymmetric communication

Unlike examples of symmetric communications, which are less common, multiple examples of asymmetric communication can be found in all sorts of organisations. For example, Nokia, the global mobile phone manufacturer, is focused on engaging with its community of users, but in a more limited way. The company's Code of Conduct (www.nokia.com/nokia/0,8764,1108,00.html) addresses all major areas of corporate social responsibility: the environment, human rights, ethics and legal limitations, and workplace practices including discrimination and fair trading practices. It also addresses health concerns about mobile phone use, highlighting the fact that it supports research in this area and that findings so far indicate no health risk from mobile phones.

It is clear that the company acknowledges the concerns of its community of stakeholders in the twenty-first century. However, the vast majority of its website is focused on the benefits of its products for its customers, rather than asking users what they think of the company and opening itself up for change in response to their views. The website gives the impression that the image it presents of a responsible company should be sufficient to address whatever concerns people may have. For those who do have questions to ask the company, there is little opportunity for direct dialogue. While the media can give feedback on the press section of the website using a pre-structured questionnaire, and employees benefit from internal communications, it is not immediately obvious what options other groups have to voice their opinions to the company or ask questions and get direct answers.

Critiques of 'excellence'

The symmetric and asymmetric communication models in particular have stimulated a large body of research into how PR is practised. Evidence suggests that it is associated with ethical and effective communications practices (Grunig 1992), but critics have also argued that it is an idealistic model which misrepresents the reality of communications process in reality, where vested interests dictate the nature of PR practice and rarely encourage a truly balanced communications process (L'Etang 1996a). For example, Cheney and Christensen (2001: 181) argue that the 'excellence' study is based on self-reports by managers and should therefore be treated with caution. The idea of

symmetric communications also obscures the networks of power and influence that shape these practices, as exemplified, for example, by organisations' pre-selection of target publics and topics for dialogue:

Public relations scholars no longer can pretend that dialogue, symmetry and responsiveness are values and practices that concern only the actors involved in the resolution of specific corporate issues. Not only do we need to ask, on an ongoing basis, who is representing whose interests, we also need to look at the broader implications for conflict resolutions between organisations and their stakeholders.

The sentiments of Cheney and Christensen are borne out by many critical scholars, who argue that the social

Picture 3.1 This chapter will look at the evolution of public relations theory and its application in a range of social and political environments. Mass movements (Tiananmen Square protest, the fall of the Berlin Wall and the 2004/5 Ukrainian elections) were all influenced by communication techniques (*source*: © Peter Turnley/Corbis)

and environmental context of PR can only lead to a profession that is defined by corporate interests (see page 54). Others, looking either at specific areas of PR activity such as publics or approaches, have adapted the asymmetric and symmetric models in light of what they see as incomplete or inadequate theorisation (see, for example, Sriramesh et al. 2007). Pieczka (1996) offers an in-depth analysis of the theoretical foundations for systems theories, and Grunig's excellence theory in particular. Her conclusion is that, while the theory of excellence in itself is well-constructed, it does contain some contradictions. For example, two-way communications advocates openness, dialogue and inclusion – and yet PR practitioners are assumed to be most effective when they are part of an elite, the dominant coalition. She also suggests that the excellence study's research questions, which defined effective PR in terms of organisational benefits, led to a self-fulfilling prophecy that presents two-way communications as most effective and therefore most desirable. For those that do not operate according to these principles, there is an implication of failure. Clearly, this cannot be assumed

in, for example, cross-cultural models of PR where cultural influences change the nature of PR practice to suit a particular context (Holtzhausen et al. 2003).

Evolving 'excellence'

Following these critiques, Dozier, Grunig and Grunig have reformulated the model (1995; 2001). The new 'mixed motive' model builds on concepts from **game theory**, originally developed to study situations of conflict and cooperation. Murphy (1991) argued that game theory allows us to understand how PR strategies are framed in the light of the interests of various publics balancing the interests of the organisation. In turn, this helps us understand the basic types of outcome of PR activities, in particular how compromise is reached between organisations and their publics such that their two sets of interests are balanced in the communications process.

Practitioners often develop strategies and define goals based on the need to reach a compromise with audiences – for example, persuading 18–30 year olds of the value of

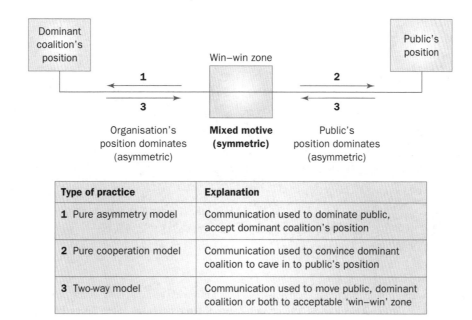

Type of practice	Explanation
1 Pure asymmetry model	Communication used to dominate public, accept dominant coalition's position
2 Pure cooperation model	Communication used to convince dominant coalition to cave in to public's position
3 Two-way model	Communication used to move public, dominant coalition or both to acceptable 'win–win' zone

Figure 3.1 New model of symmetry as two-way practices (*source:* Dozier, Grunig and Grunig 1995)

an iPod. These are non-zero-sum games, where opportunities exist for all parties to get something out of the negotiations (in this case, the seller gets the money, while the buyer gets a portable music collection). Grunig and his colleagues extended this idea of non-zero-sum situations, where organisations follow their own interests in the light of the interests of other parties, to complete their new model of communications (Figure 3.1).

While Grunig (2001) retains the term 'symmetrical' to describe the model, what is presented is a continuum. At each extreme, asymmetric communications are practised either in the interests only of the organisation or only of the public. In the centre of the continuum, called the win–win zone, mixed motive communications is practised, where the organisation and its publics enter into a dialogue of enlightened self-interest, characterised by negotiation, persuasion and compromise (Figure 3.1). This mixed motive communication is equated with symmetric communication by Grunig (2001).

Grunig argues that this continuum of two-way communication more accurately reflects the contingencies that dictate communications practices in an organisation – where, for example, asymmetric communication may be the norm for some issues, but mixed motive models may be practised for those less critical to the organisation's survival. Extending the model, Plowman (1998) further examined the specific strategies that underpinned each approach. He found seven different types of tactic:

1 contending (I win, you lose)

2 collaborating (win–win)

3 compromising (50–50 split)

4 avoiding (lose–lose)

5 accommodating (lose–win)

6 unconditionally constructive (strategic reconciliation)

7 win–win or no deal (where either both win or no deal is struck).

Contending and avoiding strategies were used for asymmetric communications in the organisation's interests, while at the other end of the continuum, the strategies used were accommodating and compromising. In the win–win window, strategies included cooperation, being unconditionally constructive, and win–win or no deal. Plowman found not only that these tactics were effective in resolving particular crises, but also that the greater the role of PR in solving organisational problems, the more likely it was to be represented at senior management level and have greater power and influence in the organisation – two of the key factors associated with excellent PR.

Publics in public relations

One of the cornerstones of systems approaches to PR is the understanding of publics that it incorporates. The basic segmentation proposed by Grunig and Repper (1992) is 'active' versus 'passive' publics. Active publics seek out information and respond to organisational initiatives. They are therefore more likely to affect the organisation. Passive publics are those that do not proactively want to engage with the organisation. Some publics may be

Think about 3.1   Negotiating an evening out

When you and your friends are discussing where to spend your Friday night, how do you decide?

■ Does one person dominate the decision and everyone else has to go along with it?

■ Do you try and meet everyone's interests, perhaps by splitting up initially and then meeting up later?

■ Does it get too complicated so you give up all trying to go out together and go your separate ways instead?

■ Do some people happily give up their ideas and go along with the others?

■ Do some people give up their ideas for now and instead do them at a later date?

■ Do you either all go out together or not go out at all?

How does the option you chose fit with Plowman's negotiation tactics? Could you negotiate it differently? What stops you doing so? Is there one person who tends to be the 'peacemaker' and finds a compromise? How much do you all rely on that person? What would happen if they were not there?

'latent', or publics-in-waiting, only becoming active when they are prompted by a particular stimulus. PR practitioners need to know what stimulus will trigger a reaction among these publics so that they can use the right communications at the right time. (This description of what practitioners should and should not do is a good example of normative theory.) In terms of identifying the types of issue that might trigger a public reaction, Grunig (1983) offered a situational theory of publics, which divides up active and passive audiences according to the types of issue that might trigger a response. He identified four basic types of public:

1 *All-issue publics* – active on all issues. Often, these types of people are very focused on injustices carried out by or through organisations. They might be equally angered by deforestation, child labour, animal testing and nuclear weapons – and take action against companies involved in any one of these things.

2 *Apathetic publics* – inattentive on all issues. These people are generally not aware of, or are unconcerned by, events in their environment. They are self-focused and they are highly unlikely to take part in any action – from petitions to demonstrations – to make their views heard.

3 *Single-issue publics* – active on one issue in a specific area. These people might have decided to put all their energies into one cause, such as supporting refugees and asylum seekers for example, and to be very active but just in this one area.

4 *Hot-issue publics* – active on one issue that has a high profile and broad societal application (such as domestic violence). Often, these people seize on a theme that is receiving attention in the media (for example, the rights of fathers in cases of family separation and divorce) and will be very active on this one area, but only for a relatively short period of time.

This was refined by Grunig and Hunt (1984) who proposed a typology based on problem recognition rather than engagement with issues. In their situational theory, *latent* publics are people who face a similar problem but do not recognise it; *aware* publics recognise a common issue; and *active* publics are those who recognise the problem and organise to do something about it. The theory of situational publics has been criticised on a number of grounds. Sriramesh, Moghan and Wei (2007) highlight the ethnocentric development of the model using an empirical study of Singaporean publics to illustrate their point. They argue that the theory needs to incorporate culture as a 'referent criterion' – a variable that affects people's communication behaviour. Other researchers have criticised the theory for its limited acknowledgement of diversity among audiences, the fact that it ignores the power dimensions of the relationship between audiences and organisations (Leitch and Neilson 2001), the multidimensional

Mini Case Study 3.2
Using the web to understand users

One website that recognises the multiple interests of its users and successfully presents an 'electronic meeting place' for them is www.nzgirl.co.nz. The site offers its users a sense of community, the opportunity to participate in multiple publics, and thereby builds multiple relationships with them. Electronic communications are producing a shift towards individual, interactive, relationship-based PR strategies.

Source: Motion 2001

Think about 3.2   Multiple images of organisations

If you work part time, what is your image of the company you work for *from the point of view of an employee*? How do you feel about the company *as a customer*? And what do your friends say about the company? Does their opinion affect the way you feel about the company when you are talking to them?

Now think about how your company thinks about its audiences. Does it treat them as one group or does it differentiate between smaller groups or individuals?

What criteria does it use to do that? How effective is that differentiation?

Feedback

How do you reconcile contradictions in the way you think about the company? Do you expect to have a different relationship with it once you are 'in the door' as compared to when you are not working? If so, why? If not, why not?

---

nature of the relationships that audiences have with organisations (Moffitt 1994) and the factors that impinge on that relationship (Cozier and Witmer 2001). Hallahan (2000) offers an alternative typology that pays more attention to the role played by inactive publics, instead of privileging only active publics in an organisation's communications strategy.

Open systems

Acknowledging the importance of publics and their actions, Cutlip et al. (2000) have proposed an open systems theory of PR. Open systems are systems that take their environment into account and change their business activities accordingly. Closed systems do not adapt to external conditions. Cutlip and his colleagues suggest that PR should view itself as part of an open system. It should

help the organisation to monitor relevant environmental influences and adapt its activities accordingly, as well as encouraging changes in the external environment that will help the organisation. In this model, two-way symmetric communications and strategic monitoring of the environment are fundamental to good PR practice.

This approach has distinct advantages for practitioners:

■ It positions them as strategic advisors to the organisation and therefore gives them access to senior managers and more power to influence organisational activities.

■ It limits the potential for crises, since environmental scanning allows the practitioner to anticipate difficulties and take early corrective action.

■ It also ensures that PR makes a significant contribution to organisational effectiveness.

See Mini case study 3.3.

Mini Case Study 3.3
Greenpeace – an open system

For environmental activists, clear communication with the right people at the right time is essential for getting their message across. An organisation like Greenpeace is a classic example of an open-system organisation. Campaign planners have to take into account views from external parties in order to ensure that they develop appropriate and effective communications for the cause they serve. These are just some of the people whose views Greenpeace needs to take into account when deciding which campaigns to execute and how to execute them:

■ *biologists and environmental scientists* – to determine which plants, animals or environmental features

are in most need of help, as well as to gather useful facts and figures for campaigns

■ *its membership* – to determine which causes will generate most support, based on audience interests, as well as which causes would alienate members and therefore need to be avoided

■ *public opinion polls* – in order to establish what the public already knows about current or planned Greenpeace campaigns and where more education is required

■ *government and policy makers* – to understand what kind of information, in terms of content and presentation, they need to take Greenpeace's position into account when making policy

■ *people who are directly affected by Greenpeace campaigns* – for example, whaling communities that might lose their livelihoods if whaling were completely banned. The strongest campaigns need to present alternative options for such people to survive and maintain their living standards.

Extending the systemic view

Public relations as relationship management

An important emerging perspective in the systems family of approaches puts the actual relationship of an organisation with its publics at the centre of PR activity (Ledingham and Bruning 2000). Maintaining and improving that relationship is the objective of PR. This means that strategies and tactics should always be assessed in terms of their effect on the relationship between an organisation and its publics, rather than, for example, the benefits they provide for the organisation.

The focus on relationships broadens the perspectives used to formulate PR strategies and tactics, but also by definition requires greater involvement from organisations. This is not as simple as it sounds – involvement means genuine dialogue, which in itself can be challenging. For example, Kent and Taylor (2002) point out that dialogue in practice frequently fails to meet the expectations of those taking part. The outcomes of dialogue may not be what was desired, and dialogue itself requires disclosure of information that may make the owner of that information vulnerable. Practitioners pressing for greater interaction with publics must recognise, explain and manage these potential risks for organisations as well as for the publics they interact with. See Box 3.1.

Ledingham (2003: 190) proposed the following theory of relationship management for PR:

Effectively managing organisational–public relationships around common interests and shared goals, over time, results in mutual understanding and benefit for interacting organisations and publics.

Broom et al. (2000) drew together the most useful findings from relationship management theory and proposed the following principles for this type of approach to PR:

■ Relationships are characterised by *interdependence*: parties to the relationship adapt in order to pursue a particular function in the relationship.

■ Relationships represent *exchanges or transfers* of information, energy or resources; the attributes of these exchanges represent and define the relationship.

■ Relationships have *antecedents and consequences* that must be taken into account when analysing them; organisation–public relationships therefore have specific antecedents (histories) and consequences (effects or results).

Because communication is so central to relationship management, the communication process should therefore be the starting point for an analysis of organisation–public relationships and a relationship view of PR offers many different perspectives from which to examine the discipline. Factors that affect all relationships, such as their history, the background of the people or organisations involved and the social context of the relationship, to name just three, can be analysed in a PR context. For example, Ledingham et al. (1999) investigated the effect of time on organisation–public relationships using a survey of 404

Box 3.1

Theory in practice

Putting relationships first

The relationship perspective of PR does not require an organisation to give up its interests when deciding how to conduct its PR. But it does mean that wider thinking is required about how those objectives might be achieved. For example, if a computer manufacturer is faced with price increases from its suppliers, ultimately it is going to have to pass on some of those costs to its customers. Without a relationship perspective of communications, the company might decide to increase the cost of its products at short notice, announce it in a press release on the day of the increase and explain little about the conditions that led to the need to raise prices. This could alienate customers, who might feel that their needs and interests are being ignored by the company – after all, they might also be facing a tough economic climate.

A relationship perspective would prompt practitioners to moderate the impact of the price rise on customer opinions by working out what needs to be done to ensure they do not feel aggrieved. The resulting strategy might give six months' notice of the price rise, a full explanation of the reasons behind it, and perhaps offer a senior member of staff for interviews on the topic, rather than just sending out a dry press release that is open to misinterpretation. Customers would then have more complete information and better understand the company's position. They could assess and plan for the change more effectively and would feel that the company had taken their situation into account in its decision.

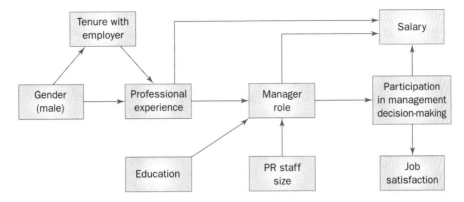

Figure 3.2 Interaction between gender, experience, education and managerial role (*source*: Dozier and Broom 1995: 16)

residential telephone customers. They found that it was a significant factor in respondents' perceptions of trust, openness, involvement, investment and commitment to the relationship on the part of the organisation and also influenced the propensity of the customer to stay in or leave the relationship.

To support practitioners trying to measure the health of their relationships, Huang (2001) developed a cross-cultural scale for measuring public perceptions of organisations based on five dimensions of relationships:

- control mutuality
- trust
- relational satisfaction and relational commitment
- **renqing** ('favour')
- **mianzi** ('face').

Practitioner roles

Practitioner roles have been a major focus for theory development within the systemic perspective. Broom and Smith (1979) proposed five practitioner role models: problem-solving process facilitators; expert prescribers; communication process facilitators; technical services providers; and acceptant legitimisers. These were later simplified by Broom and Dozier (1986), who defined two basic roles for the PR practitioner:

- the communications *technician*, who focuses on tactical matters such as writing, event management and media management
- the communications *manager*, who has a more strategic perspective and will normally create overall strategy, take and analyse client briefings and deal with issues and crises.

These roles have been confirmed in subsequent research (e.g. Terry 2001; Kelleher 2001) and a hierarchy has

emerged between the two types of role, with managerial roles generally enjoying greater perceived value and status (Grunig 1992; Grunig et al. 2002). However, Dozier and Broom (1995) showed that gender indirectly affected the role of practitioners and subsequent career success (Figure 3.2). Thus, men are more likely to have been longer with the organisation (tenure) and have more professional experience. The longer the tenure: the greater the professional experience; the longer the professional experience, the more likely it is that a practitioner has a managerial rather than a technician role; and the higher the salary. Feminists also argue that women are disadvantaged because the technician role has become 'women's work' and been devalued because of social stereotypes associated with professions dominated by women, even though it holds significant value in itself (Creedon 1991; Fröhlich and Peters 2007). Studies of the communications manager role have revealed a number of factors affecting it, including the variability of the communications environment and an open systems-orientated organisation making it more likely that practitioners execute a managerial role, while close links to marketing made a technical role more likely (Lauzen and Dozier 1992, 1994). Moss et al. (2000) also found that a managerial role was more likely if the organisation valued its stakeholders, the PR function could demonstrate their value to the organisation, and had a strong understanding of general business principles and practices that shaped their input. They found that senior managers divided up their roles into five main areas (Moss et al. 2004):

- *monitor and evaluator* – organising and tracking PR work
- *troubleshooting/problem solver* – handling a range of internal and external challenges to the organisation
- *key policy and strategy advisor* – contributing to top management, including contributions to and advice given in regular briefings and senior management meetings

■ *issues management expert* – intelligence gathering and analysis, monitoring external trends and recommending responses

■ *communication technician* – executing technical tasks associated with the PR role (e.g. writing press releases for financial reporting periods).

Beyond North America: cultural contexts

Researchers outside North America have tested Grunig and Hunt's typologies and found that country culture has a significant impact on the practice of PR. Practitioners use cultural norms and expectations to shape their approach to communication and these play a large part in determining the effectiveness of tactics and strategies. The ability of PR practitioners to target their audiences effectively is influenced by factors such as:

■ extent of technology use, such as the Internet, and its availability to individuals at home or work

■ preference for face-to-face or electronic communication

■ importance of hierarchy and power

■ demographics

■ split between urban and rural populations.

Sriramesh and Verčič (1995) developed a model for investigating international public relations (IPR) practices, taking into account environmental variables, including:

■ infrastructure (political, economic, legal, activism)

■ culture (societal and organisational)

■ media characteristics (mass media, level of control, media outreach, media access).

Most international studies have taken at least some of these variables into account (see, e.g. Sriramesh 1992; Bardhan 2003; Rhee 2002; Holtzhausen et al. 2003; Grunig et al. 1995; Sriramesh et al. 1999). The *Global Public Relations Handbook* (Sriramesh and Verčič 2003) offers a summary of PR practice in a wide range of countries elaborating on cultural, social, economic and political contexts and their implications for PR practice. In this way, normative understandings of PR are being developed across a broader range of cultural contexts than ever before.

Other studies have found region-specific characteristics associated with practice. Molleda (2000) found that economic, social and political circumstances in Latin America resulted in expectations that organisations would contribute to the development of society; consequently, the PR practitioner has a strong role as both change agent and

conscience of the organisation. In Europe, van Ruler et al. (2004) identified four characteristics of European PR: managerial, operational, reflective and educational, of which the reflective and educational characteristics were specific to Europe. Reflective characteristics are concerned with 'organisational standards, values and views and aimed at the development of mission and organisational strategies'. This is done through analysing relevant societal values, views and standpoints and discussing their implications with members of the organisation. Educational characteristics are concerned with 'the mentality and behaviour of the members of the organisation by facilitating them to communicate, and aimed at internal public groups'. This is done by helping all members of the organisation to communicate with, and respond effectively to, society (van Ruler et al. 2004: 54).

Developing theory: alternative approaches

The normative theories outlined in the first part of this chapter describe how a profession ought to behave and improve the understanding of PR practice. In more recent years, a concern with the social implications and effects of PR, combined with the emergence of postmodernism, has given rise to different schools of theory development. These new approaches to PR have cast the profession in a different light and challenged both academics and professionals to think beyond the nature of practice to its impact on audiences, society and the public sphere.

Critical theory

Critical theory has its origins in Marxist analyses of society and the economy, and focus in particular on power as a dynamic produced through relations of production. Critical theorists take objects, systems and events in PR to go beyond the immediate practice of PR and examine the effect of practice on its social and economic context.

Generally, critical theorists argue that PR practitioners perpetuate the ability of both corporations and government to maintain a privileged position in society, usually by dominating the news agenda and excluding minority voices from public debate. They have highlighted the dominance of corporate and government communications in the industry and the industry's dependence on these clients for its survival (Miller and Dinan 2000; Davis 2000; Mickey 2002; L'Etang and Pieczka 2006). In their analyses, they help to clarify a major aspect of the reality of PR – it exists to serve those who use it. If corporate and government organisations are the most frequent users of its services, then the industry is bound to generate social and economic effects that favour those institutions.

In addition, critical theorists propose two basic arguments about the relationship between media and PR that reinforce the power of PR. First, the 'resource imbalance' perspective emphasises the pressure on journalists to manage decreasing amounts of resource with increasing demands for copy. Such pressures, combined with the improved skills of PR practitioners and the increasing amount of resource invested in PR, lead directly to journalists becoming more dependent on PR practitioners and more willing to use their stories (Stauber and Rampton 1995; Moloney 2000; Pitcher 2003). Second, the 'structural' argument demonstrates that corporate patterns of media ownership result in internal censorship of news stories within media organisations and a news agenda that hesitates to challenge received wisdom, for fear of stepping on owners' and advertisers' toes (McChesney 1999; Croteau and Hoynes 2001). (See Think about 3.3.)

Think about 3.3

External pressures on journalists

If you were a journalist working for a TV news channel owned by Company A, and one of its main advertisers is Company B, how would you handle a report that criticised Company A's treatment of employees or problems with Company B's new product launch?

Feedback

Critical theorists would argue that you would be under pressure to downplay the story, with some suggesting that self-censorship means the story never even goes to the news editor.

Picture 3.2 Worldwide protest against alleged human rights abuses in China was led by Amnesty International in the run-up to the 2008 Beijing Olympics. Critical theorists argue that PR practitioners perpetuate the ability of both corporations and government to maintain a privileged position in society, usually by dominating the news agenda and excluding minority voices, such as campaigning groups, from public debate (*source*: Corbis)

From a different perspective, Pal and Dutta (2008) argue for a critical modernist theoretical view of PR. With its roots in critical theory and postmodernism, this perspective proposes that the discourses produced by PR form a mechanism through which power is distributed across social structures, because of the way they use language and affect daily life. For example, in social contexts that are already defined by hierarchies between different groups of people, PR work determines which of those groups are defined as 'important' or worthwhile 'audiences' for a particular organisation and which groups can be ignored or excluded. Critical modernism allows practitioners and researchers to examine these effects of PR work as they change depending on the campaign being conducted, the organisations or individuals employing PR tactics and the audiences being targeted.

Rhetorical perspectives

For the purposes of PR, rhetoric may be defined as 'persuasive strategies and argumentative discourse' (L'Etang 1996b: 106). The concept of rhetoric was originally closely aligned with the development of democracy, and the early Greek philosophers Plato and Aristotle focused in particular on the ability of rhetoricians to persuade an audience through effective debate and argumentation. Thus, rhetoric is a two-way discussion between parties that has a particular end goal in mind. It takes place, as Heath (1992) puts it, as part of a 'wrangle' of voices and not in isolation. Truth is necessary in order to engender trust in the rhetor (speaker), but individual perspectives must be brought to bear on the discussion in order to generate interpretation and debate. The ultimate outcome is assumed to be agreement between the two parties involved – the process of dialogue resulting in a meeting of minds somewhere in the middle of two extremes. As Heath (1992: 19) puts it:

> [The] ability to create opinions that influence how people live is the focal aspect of the rhetoric of public relations. In the process of establishing product, service or organizational identity . . . public relations practitioners help establish key terms – especially slogans, **axioms** and metaphors – by which people think about their society and organizations. These terms shape the way people view themselves as consumers, members of a community, contributors to the arts, and myriad other ways.

Scholars taking a rhetorical view of PR focus on ethics, power, influence and access to communication in the process of PR practice as part of their analysis of the broader impact of the practice on society (L'Etang 1996b). Rhetorical analysis of PR includes not just the spoken or written word, but other non-verbal and visual cues used by organ-

isations in the process of persuasion. Thus, the symbolic nature of PR is also incorporated into rhetorical studies.

Cheney and Dionisopoulos (1989) argue that PR is inherently political, rhetorical and symbolic; PR practitioners should be aware they exercise power in the interests of their 'bosses', in the process of creating realities and identities through their work. On the other hand, L'Etang (1996b) emphasises the importance of acknowledging organisations as key rhetors in society, rather than reducing analysis to the level of the individual, in order to detect structural influences on the power of the rhetorical process (see also Skerlep 2001). Both authors would agree that PR practice should be moderated by considerations of ethics, consistency and balance between the interests of the internal audiences, such as employees or management, and external audiences such as customers or shareholders (Moffitt 1992). For those on the receiving end of PR rhetoric, the challenge is to acknowledge those messages while facilitating their own advocacy through participation in relevant groups, engaging with companies where the

Activity 3.1

What's the *real* story?

Examine a party political press conference or broadcast (examples, including videos, from the 2005 UK election can be found at http://news.bbc.co.uk/1/hi/uk_politics/vote_2005/default.stm).

■ What message is the speaker communicating about their party's activities and what 'picture' are they presenting of their organisation?

■ What symbols are they using to tell the story (e.g. positive use of babies, technology, schoolchildren, nurses or negative stories about wasted resources, irresponsible management or lack of security)?

■ How do they want me to react to their 'story'?

■ What perspectives could have been included in the story but are not mentioned?

■ What issues is the person refusing to answer or avoiding? Why?

Feedback

Consider in your answers what fundamental view of the world the party is presenting – is it one that questions the principles of business or political process, or assumes they are inherently correct? Does it assume we all think the same way? Does it present 'families' or 'immigration' in a different way from other parties?

Think about 3.4

Your university or college

Do you passively accept what your university says to you about your course? Or do your experience, your opinions, the views of other students and other sources of information all act on their message to create a specific interpretation that is yours alone?

Feedback

Only you can create meaning in light of your own experience. What you tell other people about the university and the course you are on reflects this process of dialogue between what the university says and what you actually experience.

them in rhetorical terms (e.g. Crable and Vibbert 1983; Cheney and Dionisopoulos 1989; Livesey 2001). More recently, Heath (2006) applies rhetorical theory to issues management and outlines a number of ways in which rhetoric can help the understanding of issues management processes, including a focus on content and evaluation, on the narratives produced, on the relations between speaker and audience, and the notion of social exchange as inherent in the communications process.

Feminist views of public relations

Feminist analyses of PR emerged in the late 1980s, as the number of women in the profession exceeded the number of men for the first time. Today, approximately 70% of PR practitioners in most western nations are women. Despite the fact that this is a predominantly female profession, studies have repeatedly found gender inequalities in salaries, salary expectations, hiring perceptions and representation at management level (Grunig et al. 2001; Aldoory and Toth 2002).

opportunity arises and ensuring their reading of PR rhetoric is fully informed. (See Activity 3.1 and Think about 3.4.)

Brown (2006) argues that PR has four historically-determined rhetorical styles or 'cultures' that are evident in its discourses:

- activist PR (centred around unquestioning belief and action)

- oratorical PR (focused on discourse and speech)

- narrative PR (dealing with story-telling and numbers)

- performance PR (prioritising image and theatricality).

Brown suggests that close examination of how PR uses rhetoric to explain its own role can inform understandings of its effects and integration into society. Finally, a number of researchers have looked at PR initiatives and explained

Feminist analyses of the profession have focused in particular on the reasons for this imbalance as well as on feminist interpretations of PR activity. Findings have emphasised the role of stereotypes shaping perceptions of both female practitioners and PR as a feminised profession, the role of most women as technicians and the relatively low status of that role in the organisation structure; more limited support for women and more limited access to informal organisational networks and a lack of mentors (Choi and Hon 2002; O'Neil 2003; Creedon 1991; Grunig et al. 2001; Fröhlich 2004). See Mini case study 3.4.

Mini Case Study 3.4
A female public relations manager

To put these findings into context, take the example of a female PR manager with four staff in her team, managing a budget of £100,000. She might develop and manage PR campaigns primarily linked to marketing and product launches. These can be particularly high pressure and so when the volume of work gets too much for her team she might 'muck in' and help them

with the day-to-day tactical jobs like ringing the media or writing press releases. This doubling up of tasks (plus any family commitments) may prevent her from taking part in informal networking activities (such as drinks after work or sporting activities). She therefore has fewer opportunities to influence or impress senior managers and may find it hard to move up the management hierarchy as a result. As a manager, she might be on the management team alongside marketing, HR, finance and other business functions, but if she is the only woman – and working in an area that is seen to be subordinate to marketing – her opinions might not be valued as much as the other managers and decisions are unlikely to reflect her input.

Table 3.1 Four levels of change to address women's position in public relations (*source*: based on Hon 1995: 65–79)

Societal	Organisational	Professional	Individual
■ Raise levels of awareness about sexism	■ Establish family-friendly policies	■ Devise specific strategies for overcoming the marginalisation of the function	■ Monitor behaviour
■ Elect women to high government posts	■ Rethink the masculine ethic dominating most organisations	■ Reassess undergraduate education	■ Create a persona of promotability
■ Introduce legislation to support working parents	■ Value feminine attributes	■ Incorporate women's perspectives in the curriculum	■ Join professional associations
■ Outlaw sexual harassment	■ Make recruitment, hiring and promotion criteria and processes more objective		■ Help other women
■ Ensure affirmative action is effective			■ Become your own boss
■ Ensure equal representation for women in governmental organisations			
■ Eradicate sexism in education			
■ Break down gender stereotypes			

Based on these patterns, several feminist researchers have created the beginnings of feminist theories of PR. Hon (1995) provides a comprehensive feminist view of the field and a summary of antecedents (background/history) for, and strategies to improve, women's position in the profession. Acknowledging the effects of institutionalised sexism and organisational stereotypes, she argues for change at four levels:

■ society
■ organisation
■ profession
■ individual.

See Table 3.1.

The role of values and attitudes traditionally associated with women in PR practice has also been examined. Aldoory (1998) studied leadership styles of 10 female practitioners and found that they tended to have a personal, interactive approach to their role, using **transformational** or **interactional** leadership styles, adapting their approach and the language they used according to the situation they were in and aiming to motivate and inspire followers through cooperation and consultation. Grunig et al. (2000) compared feminist values with PR practice and suggested that **inclusivity**, respect, caring, cooperation, equity, self-determination and interconnection could enhance the ethical and effective practice of PR.

However, Fröhlich (2004) points out that this type of pigeonholing may end up being detrimental to female practitioners trying to break into management, where such skills might be seen as disadvantages rather than advantages. Fröhlich and Peters (2007) draw on psychological studies to suggest that in fact differences between men and women's roles in PR may be a function of preferences for different types of organisational culture. This, combined with the social barriers to promotion for women (the work–home conflict, for example), results in women choosing not to pursue managerial roles and self-selecting certain task- or work-environments over others. Wrigley (2002) suggests the concept of *negotiated resignation* to describe the manner in which women practitioners come to terms with the existence of discrimination in the workplace in a way that enables them to validate both their own position and organisational and professional structures and processes that perpetuate that discrimination. Processes of selection which favour masculine values worsen the existing imbalance between men and women at managerial level. Fröhlich and Peters (2007) found that the interaction between structural and individual characteristics did indeed affect career progressions. Perhaps more importantly, they found that women's own incorporation of the 'PR Bunny' stereotype into their own self-image and their descriptions of other practitioners was potentially a significant threat to both their own career and the regard for the profession as a whole. However, O'Neil (2003) found that, for those women who do reach senior management level, there were no significant gender differences in organisational influence. This is consistent with the findings of Moss et al. (2004) who studied senior managers and found no significant gender differences in work patterns, either in terms of the amount of involvement they had with senior management or the amount of tech-

nical tasks executed as a proportion of the overall role. They argue that female practitioners in the UK may have surmounted the glass ceiling in terms of the responsibilities they take on, but their study did not address other inequities including salary rates, perceived competence or expectations of the managers themselves. These are important areas where research so far is unanimous in its assessment of the relatively disadvantageous situation for women in PR.

Activity 3.3

Women in public relations

Why do you think so many women work in PR? Ask fellow students and any practitioners:

- What attracted them to the profession?
- What might make them leave?
- Where do they see themselves in 5, 10 and 20 years' time?
- Do they think being female makes a difference to their career opportunities?

Picture 3.3 An anti-smoking campaign aimed at minority ethnic groups in the UK. PR practitioners are trying to reach an increasingly diverse range of publics.

Diversity in public relations

There are two main diversity-related strands of thought in PR scholarship. The first relates to the increasing variety of audiences that PR practitioners are trying to reach. From this starting point, modifications of the symmetrical communication model have been proposed for non-US cultures and recognition of the diversity and autonomy of publics has been advocated (e.g. Holtzhausen 2000; Leitch and Neilson 2001). The reality of multicultural audiences has also resulted in calls for greater diversity within the profession, using the logic of 'requisite variety' (matching the diversity in audiences with diversity in the practitioner body, in order to communicate effectively). This approach to diversity has been criticised for prioritising the organisation's needs over those of the diverse groups and individuals (e.g. McKie and Munshi 2007; Munshi and McKie 2001). Munshi (1999) argues that the profession needs to acknowledge the benefit of integrating different values, approaches to communication and understandings of the world from a range of groups, because the quality of this input has the potential to change and enrich communications practice in ways that extend beyond simple economic benefit.

Very little research has been conducted on the position of minority groups within the PR profession, an omission that seems incomprehensible given the increasing diversity among both audiences and practitioners. Most research carried out so far has been done in the United States, focusing on ethnic minority practitioners (Kern-Foxworth et al. 1994; Zerbinos and Clanton 1993; Len-Rios 1998). Findings reveal that while practitioners were generally satisfied with their roles and found them meaningful, they regularly experience overt or covert discrimination. Barriers to advancement for practitioners of colour included stereotyping, pigeonholing, positive and negative discrimination on the basis of race or colour, and having

Think about 3.5

Connecting with publics

How many students on your course are female? How many from ethnic minorities? What is the situation at PR offices you know from placement or part-time work? What problems do you think there might be in conducting a PR campaign to encourage Asian women to use the public swimming baths if no one in the office understands the cultural factors that might prevent some of them from taking part in mixed events? What about language problems?

a role as 'the minority representative'. Researchers emphasised the need to attract more minorities into the profession by increasing the visibility of existing minority practitioners and educating career advisors on PR and the opportunities it offered to minorities. Kern-Foxworth et al. (1994) emphasised that their study was an initial examination of the roles occupied by black practitioners and called for more research into the area. Unfortunately, this call has gone largely unheeded, particularly in the UK. As the range of ethnic groups entering the profession increases, greater understanding of their experiences in the profession, as well as a recognition of the new perspectives that they might bring to communication, would enrich the body of knowledge both in this area as well as in the field of PR as a whole.

Postmodernism

Postmodernist views of PR (see **postmodernism**) challenge the very foundations of theory building in the field. PR originates in the modernist paradigm in that most frameworks attempt to create single explanations, or **metanarratives**, that define the social environment. By definition, modernists using metanarratives ignore (or label as 'wrong') variability and phenomena that do not fit with their model. In contrast, postmodernists acknowledge variability and welcome the multiplicity of voices and views of reality that exist in society. Postmodernists do not reject **modernism** but argue that metanarratives have no inherent claim to superiority over other views. Instead, they should be integrated as one of many perspectives available.

Holtzhausen (2002) argues that the profession is facing a future characterised by ever greater fluidity and diversity in its audiences; if practitioners continue to try and present metanarratives to a fragmented world, they will simply fail. A *postmodern* approach to PR can accommodate differences in culture, gender, ethnicity and society more effectively. Like critical theorists, postmodernists also recognise that PR can perpetuate the existing system of power relations by creating and sustaining 'realities' for their audiences, indirectly communicating principles that support the organisations for which they work in a culturally acceptable manner via the media and other channels. They also argue that, because of their existing power, businesses and government will always enjoy a more profitable outcome than their publics when the two are in dialogue. This has specific ethical implications for PR practice (Holtzhausen 2002; Mickey 1997). For example, PR practitioners have a duty to act ethically in acknowledging other voices and pointing them out to the organisation when the need arises. As boundary-spanners between an organisation and its publics, practitioners must work reflexively, regularly reviewing how broad the range of perspectives is that they include in their strategies.

Holtzhausen (2000) also reformulates the PR role to one of the organisational activist: someone who brings about fundamental change within the organisation. She presents three types of activism. First, practitioners acting as *community activists* integrate alternative views from the organisation's publics into communications strategies and make management aware of their significance. *Organisational activists* change the status quo from within, for example, through working with the human resources department to create inclusive internal communications principles and practices. Finally, Holtzhausen calls *PR activities themselves a form of activism*, when strategies are designed to instigate change in societal norms or dominant policies.

In sum, postmodernists recognise that PR practitioners face significant challenges from fragmented audiences, greater access to uncontrolled media, a more aggressive media, frequent challenges to government policies and to the principles of capitalism and globalisation, and a greater number of active publics. A postmodern perspective integrates this fragmentation and diversity into approaches to PR.

The public sphere and public relations

While US researchers conceptualise PR as an organisational function, relating to individual publics as determined by the interests of the organisation, European academics more frequently examine the profession at the societal level – often using the public sphere as a starting point for understanding how both companies and the PR profession contribute to the development of social norms and values. The public sphere was first conceptualised by Jürgen Habermas (1989) as a social space that mediates between the political sphere and the private sphere by providing space for discussion and negotiation. There are two types of public sphere: the *literary public sphere*, where individuals engage with various forms of the arts and culture in order to enhance their self-development and understanding; and the *political public sphere*, which constrains and influences the political sphere through free and open public discussion of government and legislative issues. The views that emerge from the political public sphere are understood to influence the development of the political sphere in democratic societies. Jensen (2001: 135) articulates some of the characteristics of the public sphere:

Thus, although the public sphere was originally thought of as being an assembly of citizens at a certain location or the population in general, it is not so today; yet it is dependent on freedom of assembly, association and speech. The public sphere is not the media; yet it is dependent on freedom of press and prevention of media monopolisation. The public sphere is not a set of common values, norms or opinions; neither is it the statistical result of opinion polls; yet it can influence institutionalised opinion – and will-formation in society. The public sphere is not the sum or aggregation of individual, private preferences, values and beliefs, although it depends on protection of 'privacy', the integrity of private life spheres: rights of personality, freedom of belief and of conscience. The public sphere is not obliged or normally able to come to an agreement or a decision; yet it can influence decisions made by individuals, institutionalised associations and government.

Habermas suggests that the *ideals* of the public sphere – free and open rational discussion among equals – should be a characteristic of modern democracies. However, he suggests the commercialisation of the public sphere has distorted communication to the extent that discussions are driven by vested interests rather than being open, rational arguments – to the detriment of democracy (Habermas 1989). Reviewing the public sphere in relation to PR, Jensen (2001) suggests that the public sphere be treated as an 'analytical concept, referring to the discursive processes in a complex network of persons, institutionalised associations and organisations' (2001: 136). Because these various discourses compete, the public sphere is characterised by disagreement rather than agreement. She also suggests an addition to the literary and political public spheres already introduced by Habermas: namely, the public sphere processes of *organisational legitimacy and identity*. It is here that PR is particularly relevant, since it plays a key role in engaging organisations both to promote and to justify particular organisational identities and 'ways of being'.

Jensen implies that social expectations change over time as a result of the interaction between **discourses** in the public sphere. In terms of the development of organisational legitimacy and identity, for example, social expectations of organisational behaviour will influence which discourses are acceptable, while discourses about responsible organisations reduce the number of political public sphere arguments for regulation of company activities through legislation. This is most obvious in the areas of corporate social responsibility (see Chapter 7), where economically successful and legally legitimate companies may still be subject to public wrath because they have not taken into account social expectations of corporate responsibility. Economic and legal arguments are of little use when competing against morality.

Integration of the public sphere as an analytical perspective for PR also modifies the concepts of publics traditionally used in normative PR theories. Both Jensen (2001) and Ihlen (2004) argue that traditional conceptions of stakeholder and publics neglect the interactive, discursive processes that characterise PR activities in the public sphere and fail to explain why particular organisational discourses become a matter for public interest. They therefore omit an important understanding of the operation and effect of PR activities on such groups. Raupp (2004) argues that PR should recognise that the different publics dealt with by organisations also form part of the public sphere and therefore take part in other, competing discourses – as well as participating in the same discourse on different levels.

Moloney (2006), in contrast, suggests a redefinition of the public sphere, given the fact that the utopian ideal proposed by Habermas does not exist, and suggests we now live in a *persuasive* sphere, where citizens must make sense of myriad messages about the merits of a vast range of products, policies and issues. He argues that PR practitioners who set out to persuade should do so in a way that ensures balance between the views that they represent and others who do not have the advantage of membership in the dominant coalition. He also highlights the responsibility of those on the receiving end of persuasive communications, who must actively, not passively, 'read' messages and judge them on the basis of their origins and context.

For PR, the ethics of practice and content therefore become an important focus. However, ethics and the nature of ethics in PR is itself a widely debated area and the institution of common norms has not been successful in the past (see Chapter 13 for a discussion of ethics). Moreover, the ability and awareness of different members of the public to 'actively read' persuasive messages will differ widely; those who are already socially disadvantaged (for example, by lower levels of education) may be unable or unwilling to engage at this level. While Moloney may well be correct in that we live in a more persuasive than public sphere, the ability to counter this persuasion with greater responsibility from all parties may be easier to achieve in theory than in reality.

Despite this, some scholars have attempted to apply Habermas's principles of communicative action to PR practice as a source of ethical guidance (Leeper 1996; Meisenach 2006). This would prioritise understanding as the ultimate PR goal, ensure practitioners stood by their claims of comprehensibility, truth, rightness and sincerity, and target equal participation in the discursive process for all stakeholders, in line with Habermas's conceptualisation of the ideal speech situation (Leeper 1996). More practically, Burkart (2007) focuses on Habermas's notion of understanding as the main objective of communication and proposes a model of Consensus-Oriented Public Relations (COPR) for planning and evaluating PR. Using Habermas's analysis of the ideal type of communication process (Burkart 2007: 250–251), the COPR model prompts PR practitioners to anticipate criticism of their practice and modify that practice in order to eliminate doubts about its sincerity or veracity, or other sources of validity. He argues that Habermas's differentiation between types of validity claims in the communicative process gives practitioners a more fine-tuned instrument for understanding the potential reactions of publics to their activities (Burkart 2007: 252). See discussion in Chapter 9.

Complexity, ecology and public relations

Several scholars have argued that the modernist paradigm that shapes most PR research is inadequate to cope with the emerging world of the twenty-first century, not simply because of the increasing diversity among audiences, but also because the environment in which organisations have to operate is itself marked by ever-growing complexity. Genuine engagement with the outside world also requires scholars to recognise issues that concern publics, and accommodate them in PR research in order to develop a way of integrating them into practice. McKie and Munshi (2007) argue that PR should play a key role in helping businesses meet their social responsibilities to the communities in which they operate, but suggest it is poorly equipped to meet 'the demand for a learning orientation, for experimentation, for discovery, for acknowledging uncertainty and for embracing ambiguity' (McKie and Munshi 2007: 21). They offer a wide-ranging discussion of three themes crucial to PR: ecology, equity and enterprise (see also McKie and Galloway 2007). In their view, PR is uniquely placed to address three major challenges faced by businesses in the twenty-first century. These are:

■ environmental and climate change

■ the decline of western dominance and the increasing importance of non-western cultural, social and economic contexts

■ the need for enterprise to be used responsibly to make commerce more socially and ecologically sustainable.

However, they argue that the narrow focus on managerial and organisational paradigms in both PR practice and scholarship is crippling the profession's ability to realise this potential. Only by accepting the reality of ambiguity and uncertainty, embracing a constant search for understanding and integrating insights from other understandings of enterprise and organisation, can PR really be a force for the public good.

Encouragingly, McKie and Munshi are not alone in their desire to make the context of PR more visible in practice and scholarship. Elmer (2007) calls for a perspective on PR scholarship and practice that is more culturally and socially embedded than is currently the case in mainstream work, while Toledano and McKie (2007) situate their analysis of Israeli PR practice in the cultural context of social integration as an unequivocal political and social goal. Specifically in relation to crisis management, Gilpin and Murphy (2006) use complexity theory to formulate new understandings of crisis situations. Complexity theory can be defined as the study of 'the (simple) interactions of many things (often repeated) leading to higher level patterns' (Goldberg and Markozy 1998: 4, cited in Gilpin and Murphy 2006: 380). Drawing on literature from the natural sciences and organisational studies, they suggest that complexity theory, which anticipates uncertainty and dynamism in complex systems, is a more productive way of understanding crises. A complexity-based approach to crisis management has implications for the whole of an organisation's practices, since it emphasises the reality of unpredictable and unknowable events that the organisation must absorb and react to in the manner of Weick's *enacting organisations*, which actively engage with an indeterminate world, rather than simply passively reacting to it (Gilpin and Murphy 2006: 386). In the light of this, skills such as improvisation, information gathering, ongoing reflective practice, situation awareness, risk assessment and problem-solving, are all crucial to effective crisis management practice. One might argue that Gilpin and Murphy (2006) could extend this application to other areas of PR scholarship, since much normative practice and research treats change as abnormal and stability as the holy grail, when any cursory examination of the 'real world' demonstrates that stability is the exception, rather than the rule – if it exists at all.

Sociological approaches to public relations: Giddens, Bourdieu and Foucault

A range of scholars have attempted to reframe PR using sociological perspectives. Witmer (2006) and Cozier and Witmer (2001), for example, adopt the lens of Anthony Giddens' (1984) structuration theory to examine the profession and practice. Structuration theory attempts to connect human action with the social structures in which it takes place, and argues that social life and social structures emerge through patterns of interaction that become embedded over time. This approach addresses some areas of PR that systems theories simply sidestep. For example, structurationist approaches open up avenues for research to focus on the interaction of organisations and practi

tioners with their environments and the manner in which they shape each other's activities and formation over time. They examine the importance of organisational culture and the role played by practitioners in both shaping it and existing within its constraints. Finally, they reformulate 'organisational publics' as multifaceted, fluid discursive communities – an analysis that presents new challenges for organisations seeking to connect and communicate with their stakeholders (Witmer 2006).

Falkheimer (2007) draws on this work and suggests that structuration prompts a focus on shared meanings, sensemaking and ideology in PR work. He also points out that Giddens' notion of late modernity (Giddens 1990), defined as societies characterised by risk, uncertainty and reflexivity as a consequence of the social dynamics of modernity, fits well with PR as a means of managing risk and uncertainty through communicative acts that influence symbolic spaces in society, build relationships and generate trust.

Edwards (2006, 2008a, 2008b) and Ihlen (2005, 2007) have adopted Pierre Bourdieu's framework of fields, capital and habitus to examine PR practice in organisational contexts. Bourdieu argues that individuals struggle for power in the context of fields, defined as specific areas of action in which they compete for four types of resources: economic capital, social capital, cultural capital and symbolic capital. Actions within the field are determined by habitus, the set of 'durable dispositions' that shape and are shaped by our view of the world (Bourdieu and Wacquant 1992). The volume and composition of the capital obtained by an individual or group determines whether they dominate or are dominated in that particular field. This hierarchy is reinforced by discourses that promote the symbolic power of those already in dominant positions, reinforcing and perpetuating their status (Bourdieu 1991).

Ihlen (2005, 2007) applies this view of the world to PR, arguing that organisations can be viewed as groups struggling for dominance in particular fields and that PR practitioners help them in this process. He suggests that social capital – the resources associated with the networks that agents are part of – is fundamental to understanding an organisation's relative position in its field and that PR practitioners enable organisations to extend and develop their networks. More importantly, he argues that the importance Bourdieu allocates to discourse, as a means of developing and maintaining power, fits well with a discipline like PR which uses communications for exactly this purpose.

Edwards (2008a, 2008b) takes a different tack using Bourdieu's ideas to investigate practitioners. Her exploratory survey of UK practitioners (Edwards 2008a) revealed a homogenous group of individuals with high levels of cultural and economic capital, squarely positioned among powerful groups in society. Bourdieu argues that dominant individuals have absorbed the habitus that promotes their own social position and are likely to reproduce this through their own actions – which suggests that PR practitioners only ever enhance the power of governments and big business. However, Edwards (2008a) points out that, while practitioners in corporate and government organisations may feel very comfortable communicating messages that shore up their employers' power, the social and cultural capital that practitioners have in non-mainstream organisations may also benefit them because it may give them access to sources of influence from which their organisations could otherwise be excluded.

Edwards (2008b) also applied Bourdieu's ideas to PR practitioners' activities within organisations. She studied a PR department in a large UK transport company, focusing on how they generated symbolic power for themselves within the organisation. Her findings showed that symbolic power was dependent on social capital derived from the practitioners' extensive networks within the organisation. This power was reinforced by the discourses that the department promoted about the organisation and was contingent on practitioners being seen to be competent and delivering effectively on senior management's expectations.

The final major strand of sociological work emerging in PR scholarship has been driven by Judy Motion and Shirley Leitch, who integrate the work of Michel Foucault into their analyses of PR practice. Motion and Leitch (2007) propose that Foucault's emphasis on discourse,

truth, power and knowledge can be fruitfully used to deconstruct PR work and reveal the more complex effects of this work on society. From this perspective, PR practitioners develop and transform discourses and in the process change socio-cultural practices as they affect the normalisation of 'truths' and the distribution of power in society. They have applied this thinking to PR work on personal and organisational identities (Motion 1999; Motion and Leitch 2002), to government consultation processes (Motion 2005), and – theoretically – to the notion and examination of truth in PR practice (Motion and Leitch 2007).

Public relations as a cultural phenomenon

While investigations of PR in different cultural contexts attempt to explain how the practice changes depending on cultural norms, they are generally normatively determined in that they focus on determining principles of 'best' or 'common' practice. In contrast, other studies look at the interaction between culture and PR, positioning the profession as both a determining force in culture (Curtin and Gaither 2005; Hodges 2006) and determined by culture. Included in this are examinations of the history of PR in different countries, where historical dynamics are understood to have been an active force shaping the profession.

Curtin and Gaither (2005, 2007) emphasise the importance of culture as a defining element in professional practice, industry and social structures and social expecta-

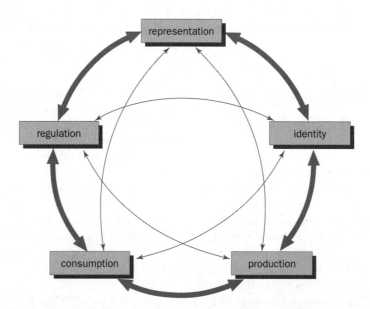

Figure 3.3 The Circuit of Culture. Applying this model to public relations, Curtin and Gaither (2005) explain public relations as a practice of socio-cultural representation, meaning production and identity in its specific presentations of organisations and audiences in particular socio-cultural roles (*source*: Du Gay et al. 1997: 3)

tions of the PR profession. In the context of international PR, they argue that PR practice is never neutral, because it implicitly or explicitly promotes specific cultural values and assumptions. They use the model of the circuit of culture (Du Gay et al. 1997) to create an understanding of how PR as a cultural practice also generates meaning and power in society. The model (see Figure 3.3) illustrates how five different 'moments' of meaning construction interact and overlap to create points of 'articulation', where meanings are renegotiated.

Applying the model to PR, Curtin and Gaither (2005) explain PR as a practice of socio-cultural representation (primarily discursive), of meaning production (in the practice of producing messages, stories, releases, images for a particular purpose) and of identity in its specific presentations of organisations and audiences in particular socio-cultural roles. PR is also relevant to the moments of consumption and regulation; it shapes consumption practices and is in turn shaped by them as products and services are consumed in particular ways. It is also a source of regulation in that it attempts to define what is and is not acceptable in specific cultural contexts. In all these moments, the PR profession and its practitioners can either enhance existing power structures or liberate subordinate voices; its position is always in flux, but power is always implicated in its practice. The model enables an understanding of PR as a cultural practice and challenges practitioners in their role as 'cultural intermediaries' (Curtin and Gaither 2005: 107) – conduits for cultural norms and values that are constantly renegotiated between organisations, individuals and social institutions through the articulations of the five moments of the circuit of culture.

Hodges (2006) echoes this call for an understanding of PR practitioners as cultural intermediaries, 'an occupational group which mediates between organisations and groups within wider society, seeking to communicate meanings through influential communicative practice' (Hodges 2006: 88). This leads to a focus on public relations practitioners (PRP) and their cultures as a means of understanding the profession in its social context. Hodges suggests that PRP culture has two basic components: first, practitioners' 'lifeworlds', defined as 'the totality of practitioners' thoughts, concepts, values and assumptions about their occupation (referred to collectively as "habitus") and their occupational experiences and identities that guide their behaviour. These will evolve through contact with other practitioners (occupational socialisation) and with wider social and cultural influences' (Hodges 2006: 85). Second, 'a system of occupational practices involving actions which "make a difference" to the world in some way' (Hodges 2006: 85). This approach allows a deconstruction of PRP culture into its component influences, which include formal and informal rules, professional and cultural

knowledge, socialisation, socio-cultural influences, political, economic and legal structures and historical contexts (Hodges 2006: 86–87).

On a different tack, but also positioning PR as an active force in the socio-cultural environment, Merten (2004) offers a *constructivist* interpretation of PR. The constructivist perspective underpins postmodernism as well as rhetorical theory and argues that PR constructs 'realities' through the promotion of particular discourses (for example, consumerism), particularly in the media. Merten points out that journalists used to present representations of reality, which were trusted because journalists were usually present at the event being described. However, news outlets and coverage options have widened considerably and journalists can no longer be present for each and every news story. PR acts as an intermediary, providing content to fill the space. However, these third-hand stories are never differentiated. They carry the same kudos as original news stories and are treated as equally real. From the constructivist perspective then, reality has in fact become a combination of authentic reality (observed first hand) and the representations, or fictions, produced by PR practitioners – among others – which appear in the news. Obviously, the power of PR is significant since it is now in a position to both provide a selection of realities from which journalists can choose to create a story, and/or define which events are in the public interest by providing representations and discourses that are only relevant to these events.

Summary

PR sits at the intersection of a wide range of both academic and practical disciplines. It is therefore appropriate that we learn more about our own area by integrating other understandings into our body of knowledge. By developing theory in this way, it can and will be of genuine help to PR practice.

Bibliography

Aldoory, L. (1998). 'The language of leadership for female public relations professionals'. *Journal of Public Relations Research* **10**(2): 73–101.

Aldoory, L. and E. Toth (2002). 'Gender discrepancies in a gendered profession: A developing theory for public relations'. *Journal of Public Relations Research* **14**(2): 103–126.

Bardhan, N. (2003). 'Rupturing public relations metanarratives: the example of India'. *Journal of Public Relations Research* **15**(3): 225–248.

Bourdieu, P. (1991). *Language and symbolic power* (G. Raymond and M. Adamson, Trans.). Cambridge, UK: Polity Press.

Bourdieu, P. and L. Wacquant (1992). *An invitation to reflexive sociology*. Chicago: Polity Press.

Broom, G.M. and D.M. Dozier (1986). 'Advancement for public relations role models'. *Public Relations Review* **12**(1): 37–56.

Broom, G.M. and G.D. Smith (1979). 'Testing the practitioner's impact on clients'. *Public Relations Review* **5**(3): 47–59.

Broom, G.M., S. Casey and J. Ritchey (2000). 'Concept and theory of organization–public relationships' in *Public Relations as Relationship Management*. L.A. Ledingham and S.D. Bruning. Mahwah, NJ: Lawrence Erlbaum Associates.

Brown, R. (2006). 'Myth of symmetry: Public relations as cultural styles'. *Public Relations Review* **32**: 206–212.

Burkart, R. (2007). 'On Jurgen Habermas and Public Relations'. *Public Relations Review* **33**(3): 249–254.

Cheney, G. and L.T. Christensen (2001). 'Public relations as contested terrain: A critical response' in *Handbook of Public Relations*. R. Heath (ed.). Thousand Oaks, CA: Sage.

Cheney, G. and G.N. Dionisopoulos (1989). 'Public relations? No, relations with publics: A rhetorical-organizational approach to contemporary corporate communications' in *Public Relations Theory*. C.H. Botan and V. Hazelton. Hillsdale, NJ: Lawrence Erlbaum Associates.

Choi, Y. and L.C. Hon (2002). 'The influence of gender composition in powerful positions on public relations practitioners' gender-related perceptions'. *Journal of Public Relations Research* **14**(3): 229–263.

Cozier, Z.R. and D.F. Witmer (2001). 'The development of a structuration analysis of new publics in an electronic environment' in *Handbook of Public Relations*. R. Heath (ed.). Thousand Oaks, CA: Sage.

Crable, R.L. and S.L. Vibbert (1983). 'Mobil's epideictic advocacy: "Observations" of Prometheus-bound'. *Communication Monographs* **50**: 380–394.

Creedon, P. (1991). 'Public relations and "women's work": Toward a feminist analysis of public relations roles'. *Public Relations Research Annual* **3**: 67–84.

Croteau, D. and W. Hoynes (2001). *The Business of Media: Corporate media and the public interest*. Thousand Oaks, CA: Pine Forge Press.

Curtin, P.A. and T.K. Gaither (2005). 'Privileging identity, difference and power: The circuit of culture as a basis for public relations theory'. *Journal of Public Relations Research* **17**(2): 91–115.

Curtin, P.A. and T.K. Gaither (2007). *International public relations: Negotiating culture, identity and power*. London: Sage.

Cutlip, S.M., A.H. Center and G.M. Broom (2000). *Effective Public Relations*, 8th edition. Upper Saddle River, NJ: Prentice Hall.

Davis, A. (2000). 'Public relations, business news and the reproduction of corporate power'. *Journalism* **1**(3): 282–304.

Dozier, D.M. and G.M. Broom (1995). 'Evolution of the manager role in public relations practice'. *Journal of Public Relations Research* **7**(1): 3–26.

Dozier, D.M., J.E. Grunig and L.A. Gruning (1995). *Manager's Guide to Excellence in Public Relations and Communication Management*. Mahwah, NJ: Lawrence Erlbaum Associates.

Du Gay, P., S. Hall, L. Janes, H. Mackay and K. Negus (1997). *Doing cultural studies: The story of the Sony Walkman (Vol. 1)*. London: Sage/The Open University.

Edwards, L. (2006). 'Rethinking power in public relations'. *Public Relations Review* **32**: 229–231.

Edwards, L. (2008a). 'PR practitioners' cultural capital: An initial study and implications for research and practice'. *Public Relations Review* **34**(4): 367–372.

Edwards, L. (2008b). 'The Social Impact of Public Relations Practice: Locating Practitioners in their Social Context'. 58th Annual International Communications Association Conference, 22–26 May, Montreal.

Edwards, L. (2009). 'Symbolic power and public relations practice: Locating individual practitioners in their social context'. *Journal of Public Relations Research* **21**(3).

Elmer, P. (2007). 'Unmanaging public relations: Reclaiming complex practice in pursuit of global consent'. *Public Relations Review* **33**(4): 360–367.

Falkheimer, J. (2007). 'Anthony Giddens and public relations: A third way perspective'. *Public Relations Review* **33**(3): 287–293.

Fröhlich, R. (2004). 'Feminine and feminist values in communication professions: Exceptional skills and expertise or "friendliness trap"?' in *Gender and newsroom cultures: Identities at work*. M. de Bruin and K. Ross (eds). Cresskill, NJ: Hampton.

Fröhlich, R. and S.B. Peters (2007). 'PR bunnies caught in the agency ghetto? Gender stereotypes, organizational factors, and women's careers in PR agencies'. *Journal of Public Relations Research* **19**(3) May: 229–254.

Giddens, A. (1984). *The constitution of society: Outline of a theory of structuration*. Berkeley, CA: University of California Press.

Giddens, A. (1990). *The consequences of modernity.* Cambridge: Polity Press

Gilpin, D. and P. Murphy (2006). 'Reframing crisis management through complexity' in *Public Relations Theory II.* C.H. Botan and V. Hazelton (eds). Mahwah, NJ: Lawrence Erlbaum Associates, pp. 375–392.

Grunig, J.E. (1983). 'Communications behaviors and attitudes of environmental publics: two studies'. *Journalism Monographs* 81.

Grunig, J.E. (1992). *Excellence in Public Relations and Communication Management.* Hillsdale, NJ: Lawrence Erlbaum Associates.

Grunig, J.E. (2001). 'Two-way symmetrical public relations: Past, present and future' in *Handbook of Public Relations.* R. Heath (ed.). Thousand Oaks, CA: Sage.

Grunig, J.E. and T. Hunt (1984). *Managing Public Relations.* New York: Holt, Rinehart & Winston.

Grunig, J.E. and F.C. Repper (1992). 'Strategic management, publics and issues' in *Excellence in Public Relations and Communication Management.* J.E. Grunig. Hillsdale, NJ: Lawrence Erlbaum Associates.

Grunig, J.E., L. Grunig, K. Sriramesh, Y.H. Huang and A. Lyra (1995). 'Models of public relations in an international setting'. *Journal of Public Relations Research* 7(3): 163–186.

Grunig, L.A., J.E. Grunig and D.M. Dozier (2002). *Excellent Public Relations and Effective Organizations.* Mahwah, NJ: Lawrence Erlbaum Associates.

Grunig, L.A., E.L. Toth and L.C. Hon (2000). 'Feminist values in public relations'. *Journal of Public Relations Research* 12(1): 49–68.

Grunig, L.A., E.L. Toth and L.C. Hon (2001). *Women in Public Relations.* New York: Guilford Press.

Habermas, J. (1989). *The Structural Transformation of the Public Sphere: An inquiry into a category of bourgeois society.* Cambridge, UK: Polity Press.

Hallahan, K. (2000). 'Inactive publics: The forgotten publics in public relations'. *Public Relations Review* 26(4): 499–515.

Heath, R. (1992). 'The wrangle in the marketplace: A rhetorical perspective of public relations' in *Rhetorical and Critical Approaches to Public Relations.* E. Toth and R. Heath. Hillsdale, NJ: Lawrence Erlbaum Associates.

Heath, R. (2006). 'A rhetorical theory approach to issues management' in *Public Relations Theory II.* C.H. Botan and V. Hazelton (eds). Mahwah, NJ: Lawrence Erlbaum Associates

Hodges, C. (2006). 'PRP culture: A framework for exploring public relations practitioners as cultural intermediaries'. *Journal of Communication Management* 10(1): 80–93.

Holtzhausen, D.R. (2000). 'Postmodern values in public relations'. *Journal of Public Relations Research* 12(1): 93–114.

Holtzhausen, D.R. (2002). 'Towards a postmodern research agenda for public relations'. *Public Relations Review* 28: 251–264.

Holtzhausen, D.R., B.K. Petersen and N.J. Tindall (2003). 'Exploding the myth of the symmetrical/asymmetrical dichotomy: public relations models in the new South Africa'. *Journal of Public Relations Research* 15(4): 305–341.

Hon, L.C. (1995). 'Toward a feminist theory of public relations'. *Journal of Public Relations Research* 7(1): 27–88.

Huang, Y-H. (2001). 'OPRA: A cross-cultural, multiple-item scale for measuring organization–public relationships'. *Journal of Public Relations Research* 13(1): 61–90.

Ihlen, O. (2004). 'Mapping the environment for corporate social responsibility: Stakeholders, publics and the public sphere'. Paper presented at the EUPRERA International Conference on Public Relations and the Public Sphere: (New) theoretical approaches and empirical studies, Leipzig.

Ihlen, O. (2005). 'The power of social capital: Adapting Bourdieu to the study of public relations'. *Public Relations Review* 31(4): 492–496.

Ihlen, O. (2007). 'Building on Bourdieu: A sociological grasp of public relations'. *Public Relations Review* 33(4): 269–274.

Jensen, I. (2001). 'Public relations and emerging functions of the public sphere: An analytical framework'. *Journal of Communication Management* 6(2): 133–147.

Kelleher, T. (2001). 'Public relations roles and media choice'. *Journal of Public Relations Research* 13(4): 303–320.

Kent, M.L. and M. Taylor (2002). 'Toward a dialogic theory of public relations'. *Public Relations Review* 28: 21–37.

Kern-Foxworth, M., O. Gandy, B. Hines and D. Miller (1994). 'Assessing the managerial roles of black female public relations practitioners using individual and organizational discriminants'. *Journal of Black Studies* 24(4): 416–434.

Lauzen, M.M. and D.M. Dozier (1992). 'The missing link: The public relations manager role as mediator of organisational environments and power consequences for the function'. *Journal of Public Relations Research* 4(4): 205–220.

Lauzen, M.M. and D.M. Dozier (1994). 'Issues management mediation of linkages between environmental complexity and management of the public relations function'. *Journal of Public Relations Research* 6(3): 163–184.

Ledingham, J.A. (2003). 'Explicating relationship management as a general theory of public relations'. *Journal of Public Relations Research* 15(2): 181–198.

Ledingham, J.A. and S.D. Bruning (2000). *Public Relations as Relationship Management: A relational approach to the study and practice of public relations.* Mahwah, NJ: Lawrence Erlbaum Associates.

Ledingham, J.A., S.D. Bruning and L.J. Wilson (1999). 'Time as an indicator of the perceptions and behavior of members of a key public: Monitoring and predicting organization–public relationships'. *Journal of Public Relations Research* 11(2): 167–183.

Leeper, R.V. (1996). 'Moral objectivity, Jurgen Habermas' discourse ethics and public relations'. *Public Relations Review* 22(2): 133–150.

Leitch, S. and D. Neilson (2001). 'Bringing publics into public relations: New theoretical frameworks for practice' in *Handbook of Public Relations*. R. Heath (ed.). Thousand Oaks, CA: Sage.

Len-Rios, M. (1998). 'Minority public relations practitioner perceptions'. *Public Relations Review* 24(4): 535–555.

L'Etang, J. (1996a). 'Corporate responsibility and public relations ethics' in *Critical Perspectives in Public Relations*. J. L'Etang and M. Piezcka. London: International Thomson Business Press.

L'Etang, J. (1996b). 'Public relations and rhetoric' in *Critical Perspectives in Public Relations*. J. L'Etang and M. Pieczka. London: International Thomson Business Press.

L'Etang, J. (1996c). 'Public relations as diplomacy' in *Critical Perspectives in Public Relations*. J. L'Etang and M. Pieczka. London: International Thomson Business Press.

L'Etang, J. and M. Pieczka (1996). *Critical Perspectives in Public Relations*. London: International Thomson Business Press.

L'Etang, J. and M. Pieczka (2006). *Public Relations: Critical debates and contemporary practice.* Mahwah, NJ. Lawrence Erlbaum Associates.

Livesey, S.M. (2001). 'Eco-identity as discursive struggle: Royal Dutch/Shell, Brent Spar, and Nigeria'. *Journal of Business Communication* 38(1): 58–91.

McChesney, R.W. (1999). *Rich Media, Poor Democracy: Communication politics in dubious times.* Chicago, IL: University of Illinois Press.

McKie, D. and C. Galloway (2007). 'Climate change after denial: Global reach, global responsibilities and public relations'. *Public Relations Review* 33(4): 368–376.

McKie, D. and D. Munshi (2007). *Reconfiguring public relations: ecology, equity and enterprise.* London: Routledge.

Meisenbach, R.J. (2006). 'Habermas's Discourse Ethics and Principle of Universalization as a Moral Framework for Organizational Communication'. *Management Communication Quarterly* 20(1): 39–62.

Merten, K. (2004). 'A constructivist approach to public relations' in *Public Relations and Communication Management in Europe*. B. van Ruler and D. Verčič. Berlin: Mouton de Gruyter.

Mickey, T.J. (2002). *Deconstructing Public Relations: Public relations criticism.* Mahwah, NJ: Lawrence Erlbaum Associates.

Mickey, T.J. (1997). 'A postmodern view of public relations: sign and reality'. *Public Relations Review* 23: 271–285.

Miller, D. and W. Dinan (2000). 'The rise of the PR industry in Britain 1979–98'. *European Journal of Communication* 15(1): 5–35.

Moffitt, M.A. (1992). 'Bringing critical theory and ethical considerations to definitions of a "public"'. *Public Relations Review* 18(1): 17–29.

Moffitt, M.A. (1994). 'Collapsing and integrating concepts of public and image into a new theory'. *Public Relations Review* 20(2): 159–170.

Molleda, J.C. (2000). 'International paradigms: The Latin American school of public relations'. *Journalism Studies* 2(4): 513–530.

Moloney, K. (2000). *Rethinking Public Relations: The spin and the substance.* London: Routledge.

Moloney, K. (2006). *Rethinking public relations: PR propaganda and democracy* (2nd edition). Oxford: Routledge.

Moss, D., G. Warnaby and A. Newman (2000). 'Public relations practitioner role enactment at the senior management level within UK companies'. *Journal of Public Relations Research* 12(4): 277–307.

Moss, D., A. Newman and B. DeSanto (2004). 'Defining and redefining the core elements of management in public relations/corporate communications context: What do communication managers do?' Paper presented at the 11th International Public Relations Research Symposium, Lake Bled, Slovenia.

Motion, J. (1999). 'Personal public relations: Identity as a public relations commodity'. *Public Relations Review* 25(4): 465–479.

Motion, J. (2001). 'Electronic relationships: Interactivity, internet branding and the public sphere'. *Journal of Communication Management* 5(3): 217–230.

Motion, J. (2005). 'Participative public relations: Power to the people or legitimacy for government discourse?'. *Public Relations Review* 31: 505–512.

Motion, J. and S. Leitch (2002). 'The technologies of corporate identity'. *International Studies of Management and Organization* 32(3): 45–64.

Motion, J. and S. Leitch (2007). 'A toolbox for public relations: The oeuvre of Michel Foucault'. *Public Relations Review* 33(3): 263–268.

Munshi, D. (1999). 'Requisitioning variety: Photographic metaphors, ethnocentric lenses, and the divided colours of public relations'. *Asia Pacific Public Relations Journal* 1(1): 39–51.

Munshi, D. and D. McKie (2001). 'Different bodies of knowledge: Diversity and diversification in Public Relations'. *Australian Journal of Communication* 28(3): 11–22.

Murphy, P. (1991). 'The limits of symmetry: A game theory approach to symmetric and asymmetric public relations' in *Public Relations Research Annual*. J.E. Grunig and L.A. Grunig. Hillsdale, NJ: Lawrence Erlbaum Associates.

O'Neil, J. (2003). 'An analysis of the relationships among structure, influence and gender: Helping to build a feminist theory of public relations practice'. *Journal of Public Relations Research* 15(2): 151–179.

Pal, M. and M.J. Dutta (2008). 'Public relations in a global context: The relevance of critical modernism as a theoretical lens'. *Journal of Public Relations Research* 20(2): 159–179.

Pieczka, M. (1996). 'Paradigms, systems theory and public relations' in *Critical Perspectives in Public Relations*. J. L'Etang and M. Pieczka. London: International Thomson Business Press.

Pitcher, G. (2003). *The Death of Spin*. Chichester: John Wiley & Sons.

Plowman, K.D. (1998). 'Power in conflict for public relations'. *Journal of Public Relations Research* 10(4): 237–261.

Raupp, J. (2004). 'Public sphere as a central concept of public relations' in *Public Relations and Communication Management in Europe*. B. van Ruler and D. Verčič. Berlin: Mouton de Gruyter.

Rhee, Y. (2002). 'Global public relations: A cross-cultural study of the excellence theory in South Korea'. *Journal of Public Relations Research* 14(3): 159–184.

Skerlep, A. (2001). 'Re-evaluating the role of rhetoric in public relations theory and in strategies of corporate discourse'. *Journal of Communication Management* 6(2): 176–187.

Sriramesh, K. (1992). 'Societal culture and public relations: Ethnographic evidence from India'. *Public Relations Review* 18(2): 201–211.

Sriramesh, K. and D. Verčič (1995). 'International public relations: A framework for future research'. *Journal of Communication Management* 6(2): 103–117.

Sriramesh, K., Y. Kim and M. Takasaki (1999). 'Public relations in three Asian cultures: An analysis'. *Journal of Public Relations Research* 11(4): 271–292.

Sriramesh, K. and D. Verčič (2003). (eds) *The Global Public Relations Handbook: theory, research and practice*. Mahwah, NJ: Lawrence Erlbaum Associates Inc.

Sriramesh, K., S. Moghan and D.L.K. Wei (2007). 'The situational theory of publics in a different cultural setting: consumer publics in Singapore'. *Journal of Public Relations Research* 19(4): 307–332.

Stauber, J. and S. Rampton (1995). *Toxic Sludge is Good for You: Lies, damn lies and the public relations industry*. Monroe, ME: Common Courage.

Terry, V. (2001). 'Lobbyists and their stories: Classic PR practitioner role models as functions of Burkean human motivations'. *Journal of Public Relations Research* 13(3): 235–264.

Toledano, M. and D. McKie (2007). 'Social integration and Public Relations: Global lessons from an Israeli experience'. *Public Relations Review* 33(4): 387–397.

van Ruler, B., D. Verčič, G. Butschi and B. Flodin (2004). 'A first look for parameters of public relations in Europe'. *Journal of Public Relations Research* 16(1): 35–63.

Witmer, D. (2006). 'Overcoming system and culture boundaries: Public relations from a structuration perspective', in *Public Relations Theory II*. C.H. Botan and V. Hazelton (eds). Mahwah, NJ: Lawrence Erlbaum Associates.

Wrigley, B. (2002). 'Glass ceiling? What glass ceiling? A qualitative study of how women view the glass ceiling in public relations and communications management'. *Journal of Public Relations Research* 14(1): 27–55.

Zerbinos, E. and G.A. Clanton (1993). 'Minority practitioners: Career influences, job satisfaction, and discrimination'. *Public Relations Review* 19(1): 75–91.

CHAPTER 4

Robert L. Heath

A rhetorical theory approach to issues management*

* Chapter 3 in *Public Relations Theory II*, edited by Carl H. Botan and Vincent Hazleton. Copyright © 2006 by Lawrence Erlbaum Associates, Inc. Reproduced with permission.

A rhetorical theory approach to issues management

Issues management has grown as an applied and research discipline to compensate for what some believed was an insufficient approach to the practice of public relations in the mid-1970s. The inadequacy of the then state-of-the art approach to activist criticism was repeatedly demonstrated by strategic responses to corporate critics through counter publicity efforts, rather than solid issues engagement and corporate strategic planning adjustments. Instead of taking more sound responses to such criticism, many organizations engaged in stonewalling, expressed outrage at what were alleged to be presumptuous outbursts by critics of big business, and blamed the problems of society on the persons who were trying to call attention to and offer ways to solve those problems. This reactionary response, which often tried to blame the messenger, seemed to imply that no civil-rights, consumer-rights, or environmental-rights problems would exist if the critics would cease their clamor.

To formulate new ways to meet this challenge to the prerogatives of corporate governance, leading practitioners, academics, and business leaders developed issues management through many heated discussions at the senior executive level. Tradition has it that W. Howard Chase (1977) drew on his experience at American Can Company to develop the concept: a means of strengthening large organizations' ability to monitor, analyze, and respond to challenges voiced by myriad critics of private sector practices and policies. His efforts were supported by others, such as John E. O'Toole (1975a, 1975b), O'Toole may have coined the term *advocacy advertising* which was offered to strengthen the corporate voice in response to strident challenges by critics.

The turbulent 1960s and 1970s had caught America's private sector leadership off guard. At the start of that era, public relations was a feel-good discipline devoted to media relations, publicity, promotion, and integrated marketing communication. In partial response to this narrowness of response options, public affairs had grown as a substitute for public relations. Public affairs quickly achieved substantial popularity with the managements of larger corporations. Today the Public Affairs Council and the Public Relations Society of America see proactive strategic response to marketplace and public policy issues as a vital and central challenge to corporate leadership.

Issues management was not the brainchild of any one person. Several academics, corporate leaders, public affairs/public relations practitioners, and even some advertising persons decided that a new or renewed array of strategic options was needed to respond to and even combat the broad and resilient challenges to corporate America and the U.S. government that were voiced during the activist era of the 1970s. To review the leadership of this movement, Heath and Cousino (1990) examined several hundred articles and other publications to better understand leaders' analysis and responses to deficiencies in organizations' preparedness to respond to their critics.

Critics of government and business eventually reshaped the culture and ideology of society on civil rights, environmental rights, consumer rights, worker rights – and the list continues. New sociopolitical dynamics began in the 1960s to guide government policies and private sector practices. Businesses lost much of their public policy clout as the result of four dramatic changes: (a) Activists claimed that natural resources, found to be limited and rhetorically defined as the property of the citizens of the nation, and even the world, were to be managed in the collective interest. (b) Society became sensitive to the increasing heterogeneity of values, attitudes, beliefs, interests, and cultures, which destroyed the business-first policy consensus that prevailed at the start of the 1960s. (c) Citizens became less willing to act with deference toward business and government; they lost confidence in the ability of large institutions, such as government, media, and business, to recognize and solve problems. Citizens placed their confidence in activist groups and called on them to exert their collective power. (d) Standards of corporate responsibility changed (Pfeffer, 1981). This fertile ground fed the growth of business criticism and issues management.

Building out of this perspective, the purpose of this chapter is to provide a comprehensive survey of the leading commentary on issues management and to investigate its theoretical underpinnings. In broad measures, this chapter features three topic areas: the definition and theoretical underpinnings of issues and issues management; the implications of these underpinnings for future research and theory development; and a discussion of the implications of the theory and research for the practice of issues management in conjunction with public relations and public affairs.

This review is designed to explore in specific the rhetorical implications for issues management. Given that latitude, this author elects to draw on Western Civilization's rhetorical heritage, in particular the works of teachers in the golden age of Greece and Rome, the writings of Kenneth Burke, and the implications of the narrative view of rhetoric. Also, a couple of social scientific underpinnings are valuable to this discussion as well – social exchange theory and information integration theory. The central theme extracted from this literature can lead one to conclude that the rhetoric of issues management examines the rationale, motives, processes, and outcomes of advocacy discourse on public policy matters that influence the relationships between corporate entities and their stakeholders/stakeseekers. The ultimate effort of this rhetoric is to create enough concurrence that interested members of the general public, business, government, media, and non-profit sectors can forge mutually beneficial policies. The upshot of this dialogue is a constant revision of citizens' expectations as to how business, government, media, and nonprofit organizations should conduct their business.

Literature review

Defining issues management and issues: the legitimacy gap

How we study issues management, and especially the rhetoric of issues management, depends on how we define the practice. How one defines issues management also reflects one's definition of public relations. Some see public relations as the umbrella concept under which issues management is one of many specialty functions. This view of the discipline would assume that public relations was always interested in public policy issues and routinely engaged in identifying, monitoring, analyzing, and strategically responding to them. To date, no definition of issues management has achieved consensus, nor has the discipline achieved its potential (Gaunt & Ollenburger, 1995).

Persons who see issues management as embracing but going beyond public relations and even public affairs are likely to conclude that especially during the activism of the 1960s, public relations practitioners were primarily interested in marketing publicity and promotion and simply dropped the ball when asked for advice on how to deal with activist critics. Advocates of a broader view of issues management are likely to ask whether public relations is seriously engaged in top-level organizational planning, development and implementation of standards of corporate responsibility, and advocacy – dialogue and collaborative decision making – that defends the interests of each organization by building effective relationships with its critical publics.

Any reasonable definition must acknowledge the challenge put down by Sethi (1977), one of the contributors to the research legacy of issues management. He believed that issues arise when large organizations suffer a legitimacy gap between what they do and what their markets and publics expect (prefer) them to do. The gap can result from differences of fact, value, and policy (Heath, 1997). It can foster division instead of merger. It can result in the enactment of competing narratives. It can strain the resource balances between organizations and the persons they affect. It can result in conflicting attitudes and behaviors between organizations and those of the persons whose goodwill they need. These strains can be managed rhetorically, but are more than differences of opinion. They often entail battles for power resource management. Activists learned to use power resources to force change that businesses would not make voluntarily.

Some who discuss this topic may argue that issues management entails only spirited defense and symbolic protection of the actions, rights, policies, and prerogatives of an organization – a stonewall approach to issues management, which presumes that the organization is always correct and critics are inherently wrong. This view of issues management urges that the symbolic boundaries of the organization should be defended by convincing critics that their challenges are unwarranted, unsubstantiated, and unmerited. A 'purely rhetorical approach' to issues management can presume that the organization is correct and does not need to change itself to abate the challenges of its critics. Such views of issues managements can lead to tactical victories, but are likely to lose the strategic battles and eventually the war of public policy. They simply do not address the root causes of the friction between organizations and their critics.

Strategic options: denying the legitimacy gap or stewarding change

On the one end of a spectrum we have the symbolic view of issues management. On the other end rests the operational approach, which suggests that executive managements of organizations need to constantly adjust their policies to please and appease their external critics. Between these two polar extremes, one can find variations and a blend of the positions: a stewardship commitment to communication, to the extent that rhetorical stances can solve the legitimacy gap, with the proviso that the organization may also need to make small or even dramatic policy and management changes to reduce that gap.

The rhetorical principles of issues management can and probably do have a strong persuasive element. Critics advocate change. The organization can defend current actions and the new policy positions it proposes that may be adopted to end the criticism. This dialogue can be strident. It can be cordial, an honest effort to engage in collaborative decision making. The process entails multiple stakeholder (and stakeseeker) publics. Some of these publics may agree with the issue positions and management policy changes advocated by the organization; others may oppose them. The rhetorical enactment of issues management entails multiple and varied voices who advocate various issues and policy positions – who challenge the best efforts to achieve consensus. Some stakeholders are likely to praise corporate policy changes at the same time other stakeholders oppose and are even outraged by them.

Given these dynamics, the rhetoric of issues management is best conceived of as dialogue. Both – sides have views they express and preferences they advocate. This dialogue is the product of statement and counter statement, voiced expressions of what organizations do and what they should do, what they prefer as ideology and policy principles.

The optimal outcome of such advocacy is the resolution of some or all of the differences, which can foster social harmony. To do so requires, from an organization's point of view, that it reduce the legitimacy gap by moving closer to the expectations of its stakeholders, or that it must convince the stakeholders that their expectations are incorrect or unwise.

In a limited sense, a rhetorical view of issues management can assume that the organization is always correct and that a variety of rhetorical strategies can win the day. As Cheney and Dionisopoulos (1989) have observed, the ultimate struggle is for 'control over the (value) premises that shape basic and applied policy decisions. In essence, corporate discourse seeks to establish public frames of reference for interpreting information concerning issues deemed important by Corporate America' (p. 144).

At one end of the rhetorical continuum, Sproule (1989) reasoned, 'Organizations try to privatize public space by privatizing public opinions; that is, skillfully (one-sidedly) turning opinion in directions favorable to the corporation' (p. 264). At the other end, critics seek to impose public policy controls on the private decisions of corporate leaders. Both sides devote their efforts to deciding which actions and policies are best and to defining the value premises of society that privilege some actions and prohibit others. Stressing this view of issues management, Ewing (1987) concluded that it 'developed within the business community as an educational task aimed at preserving the proper balance between the legitimate goals and rights of the free enterprise system and those of society' (p. 5). The battle over public policy and value principle hegemony is best when it seeks and achieves a mutually beneficial middle ground between interested parties.

Without doubt, the organization can be correct in the opinions it holds and the policies it implements. Thus, it can be expected to shoulder the stewardship responsibility of defending itself and the policy positions it prefers through strategic communication. Likewise, the organiza-

tion can be incorrect and therefore need to change its policies, actions, and missions to adopt new and better standards of corporate responsibility or to be more effective in implementing the standards that its critics have become convinced are the most acceptable. The requirement is to reduce the legitimacy gap between the organization and its stakeholders and stakeseekers. Following this logic, issues-oriented communication is best when it aspires to be collaborative rather than combative.

This section has argued that the battle over the legitimacy gap is the heart and soul of the issues management process. People and organizations can be at peace or at war with one another. Such battles are the rationale for issues management rhetoric.

Defining issues management and issues: organizational program or public relations function

What we carve out as the theory of issues management rhetoric depends on how we define the discipline. Several corporate executives, academics, and communication professionals working in the 1970s observed that the standard practice of public relations left corporations without an adequate rationale and set of strategies to counter allegations that eventually eroded much of the privilege the private sector had enjoyed. New public policies grew from a culture that had come to reflect increased sensitivities about myriad issues: civil rights, environmental quality standards, working conditions, consumer rights, women's rights, and the 'beat goes on.'

In its efforts to respond to these tensions, issues management was recommended to be an early issues detection system, a means for creating less contentious corporate policy and planning, a device for better meeting key publics' standards of corporate responsibility, and a function assigned the responsibility to create rhetorical responses to the organization's critics. Proponents of the discipline tend to feature issues management as performing some or all of these functions. They tend either to view the discipline as larger than public relations – often a senior-level management or staff function – or a strategic option or function of public relations.

Topics of this kind became more widely discussed and relevant to corporate success in the 1970s. In that decade, companies were brought to task for their actions and policies. They suffered public condemnation for the same policies that many corporate and governmental leaders believed were effective in ending the Great Depression and winning the Second World War. The heady feeling of those successes had been increased by a new sense of postwar consumer prosperity. Corporations could do no wrong. Then, activist challenges came fast and furious. Every part of society was reevaluated. The undergirding of business was assaulted.

Although the term was new – a product of the 1970s – the concept and practice of issues management were not. As Heath (1997) has documented, the origins of contemporary issues management can be traced back to the battles by corporate leaders to forge favorable public policy even before the turn of the 20th century. The clearest instance of that tradition was the evolution of state and federal policy that tolerated and even supported ever larger industrial complexes. Issues management efforts were brought onto the public policy battlefield by industry leaders who a century later would be household names: Edison and Westinghouse. One of the great issues management efforts was the 'battle of the currents,' in which these titans of the electric generating industry fought over industry standards, pitting direct and alternating currents against one another.

Evidence such as this can support the conclusion that issues management has long been a tool of corporations, labor, government, and even activists. Labor – the great era of labor organization around the turn of the 20th century – adopted the device of organizational advocacy to champion better working conditions. The Populist Farmers and the Progressive young professionals fought serious battles to oppose the threats to health, safety, and the public welfare brought about by the economic tyranny of burgeoning industrial combines formed by executives who had come to bear the name Robber Barons. All of this turmoil and struggle to forge corporate and public policy has become part of the legacy of the rhetoric of issues management.

At the rhetorical level, public policy contests of this sort entail the public examination of facts, evaluations, and policies. Symbolic positioning results in the creation and dissolution of identifications. It results in the creation of one set of narratives that subsequently is challenged by a competing set of narratives. Burke (1969) called this clash of voices 'the Scramble, the Wrangle of the Marketplace, the flurries and flare-ups of the Human Barnyard, Give and Take, the wavering line of pressure and counter pressure, the Logomachy, the onus of ownership, the War of Nerves, the War' (p. 23).

Competing voices produce new standards with which to define and evaluate 'the good organization.' Privileges seem to go to the 'good organization that communicates effectively.' Although the paradigm of the public spokesperson has been the corporate entity defining and protecting its symbolic boundaries (Cheney, 1992; Cheney & Dionisopoulos, 1989) for the better part of a century,

the conception of the effective corporate citizen is as ancient as the prescriptive preferences of Quintilian (1951), who reasoned that the paradigm of the effective citizen was the good person who could speak well.

Thus, one element of the paradigm of the rhetoric of issues management is the organization that seeks and achieves concurrence as to the best standards of corporate social responsibility. Another factor in that paradigm is that the organization must be capable of the stewardship of promoting and defending the sound policies and principles that support corporate operations in the mutual best interest of society.

To be an effective advocate for such standards requires the effective speaker to be above moral reproach. The next requirement is to communicate effectively. Advocates for higher moral standards must be able to demonstrate that they have met the challenges that they advocate for others. To examine the relationship between issues management and public relations assumes that we start with Quintilian's challenge. Can a bad organization communicate effectively? If it can do so in the near term, can such an organization sustain its privilege in the dialogue over the long haul?

The requirements of a rhetorical theory of issues management

To address that question drives us to the heart of what issues management is, and what its relationship to public relations is. Here we can explore the requirements for issues management rhetoric.

This analysis results in a clash of perspectives – a challenge of definitions that become institutionalized public and marketplace policies. Thus we can ask, is issues management a subfunction of public relations or an umbrella that encompasses it? How does issues management relate to strategic business planning? Is the function expected to reactively justify strategic planning, or is it vital to proactive strategic planning? In either case, the function cannot succeed without executive-level authority and budgetary support (Lukasik, 1981; Spitzer, 1979; Zraket, 1981).

Is issues management merely public relations revisited (Ehling & Hesse, 1983; Fox, 1983), and in that way more or less a subfunction of public relations (Cutlip, Center, & Broom, 2000; J. Grunig & Repper, 1992)? The Special Committee on Terminology of the Public Relations Society of America defined as 'issues management systematic identification and action regarding public policy matters of concern to an organization' (Public Relations Society of America, 1987, p. 9).

Is it a program to help companies enjoy more effective involvement in the public policy process (Public Affairs Council, 1978)? Is it an executive-level staff function and community-oriented sense of organizational culture that empower public relations by giving it greater involvement in corporate strategic business planning and management (Heath, 1988, 1997; Lauzen, 1994; Lauzen & Dozier, 1994; Nelson & Heath, 1986)? Is it a new organizational discipline that features 'public policy foresight and planning for an organization' (Ewing, 1987, p. 1)?

If public relations is limited to media relations and publicity and promotion – even integrated marketing communication, then it simply does not enjoy a corporate-level perspective and does not see and constructively deal with the big picture of the quality of fit between the organization and its stakeholders. In that case, public relations is not defined and implemented in a way that can even have issues management as a subfunction.

How issues management is defined depends not only on its organizational status but also on the functions that it performs. If issues management is only issues identification and response, it could be a public relations and public affairs function, if these disciplines engage in customer relations, community relations, government relations, and other efforts to adjust the relationship between the organization and its key publics and markets. If issues management is invested into the strategic planning and management of the organization – if the organization's executives want to position it so that it can affect as well as strategically adapt to its public policy arena and marketplace – then public relations simply may not be up to the challenge. However, as this discussion suggests, it's all in the definition.

In that regard, the turbulent 1970s demonstrated to many leaders – planning and operations executives as well as communication executives – that if public relations was not engaged in issues management – planning, monitoring, becoming a better organization, and responding to the voices of change – then the new discipline Chase, Ewing, and other corporate leaders had proposed could add value to the organization. Such challenges called on many if not most practitioners to increase the array of skills and strategic options that they needed to master. Under this challenge, many public relations and public affairs departments learned to take an issues management perspective.

Participants in this challenge engaged in 'old hat' and 'new stuff' debates. Some leading organizations created issues management teams and even departments that drew together personnel from the public relations department as well as from planning and operational departments. Those committees reported to executive management, not to the manager of public relations.

Putting a new face on an old challenge

One way to examine the nature of issues management is to explore the incentives that led important thinkers in the 1970s to believe they needed new corporate strategies to deal with turbulence created by critics. This turmoil went beyond what these leaders had experienced and seemed to challenge the very foundations of the private sector.

Witnessing these trends, Bateman (1975) advised companies 'to move from an information base to an advocacy position' in their responses to their critics and to build relationships with key publics (p. 5). This stance, he rationalized, was needed because 'companies should not be the silent children-of society' (p. 3). Taking a cautious step to advise companies to make more bold responses to their critics, the International Association of Advertising (IAA), in its global study of issues communication, urged adoption of the less contentious term *controversy advertising* (Barnet, 1975). By 1976, terms such as *issue advertising* and *advocacy advertising* were being used in business publication discussions of the aggressive op-ed campaign made famous by Mobil Oil Corporation (Ross, 1976). Making the connection between advertising and issues, Dinsmore (1978) contended that 'ideas could be sold like soap' (p. 16), but only if their presentation was complete and truthful. Advertising sought to provide the answer (Pincus, 1980).

Nevertheless, corporate leaders were convinced that they needed substantial revisions in the practice of advertising and public relations. Perhaps a new discipline was needed. Corporate executives and senior practitioners worked to define effective and ethical strategic responses their companies needed to take to counter their critics. In September 1978, Kalman B. Druck, Chairman, Harshe-Rotman & Druck, Inc. told the Houston Chapter of the Public Relations Society of America that 'enormous opportunities await those who are willing to make the commitment, to apply professional management and public relations skills to the bitter confrontations industry is now facing' (p. 114).

Some proponents of issues management were communication specialists who worked for executives guided by the assumption that critics of business could be shouted down. This organizational function exhibited a business-is-sacred bias that featured issues advertising, a concept that produced a backlash (Ehrbar, 1978). Corporate leaders and their communication specialists had taken the status of their organizations for granted, heady with the accomplishments of victory over the Great Depression and the foes defeated by Allied forces in World War II. Without realizing the trend, they had slowly become politicized.

In 1979, *BusinessWeek* commented on this trend, featuring the political challenge facing the private sector with its governmental allies and speculating on the communication options that would solve this problem: 'The corporation is being politicized and has assumed another dimension in our society that it did not have as recently as 10 years ago.' What was needed, the publication asked? Featuring public relations, it concluded that a new breed of practitioners was required to defend business by 'articulating its positions more clearly and urgently to government agencies, legislators, shareholders, employees, customers, financial institutions, and critical audiences' ('The Corporate Image,' 1979, p. 47).

The rhetorical paradigm of the good organization communicating well

What was needed, some thought, was not more articulate advocates, but advocates who had achieved higher standards of corporate responsibility. Thus, in the spirit of Quintilian (1951), the ancient Roman teacher of speakers, critics called for the organization to be good as a first step to becoming more articulate. One such critic, management professor S. Prakesh Sethi (1976a, 1976b, 1977) strenuously argued that merely explaining the corporate point of view could never be efficacious. Companies that shout loudest often may deserve regulation most. Sensitive to the limitations of a communication bias, some companies, such as Prudential Insurance Company of America (MacNaughton, 1976), institutionalized standards of corporate responsibility, especially in their governmental relations programs (Bradt, 1972).

Although a communication perspective dominated discussions of how companies could handle their critics, some executives recognized that issues analysis must be incorporated into strategic business planning. William S. Sneath, President of Union Carbide Corporation, said in 1977 that his company was using 'scenario evaluation' to project its business planning efforts 20 years into the future. Public policy issues, such as environmentalism, were a vital part of the planning effort at Union Carbide. Sneath said that only time could judge 'our legacy not only in terms of the economic accuracy of our business planning but in the way we committed our best minds and our best intentions to meet the needs and aspirations of a free society in an increasingly interdependent world' (p. 199). Corporate leaders who supported the innovation of issues management recognized that slick issue advertising could not manipulate opinion and thereby 'manage issues.'

Giving substance to this sort of preference, Archie R. Boe (1979), CEO of Allstate Insurance Companies (1972–

1982) and later President of Sears (1982–1984), created a Strategic Planning Committee in 1977 and an Issues Management Committee in 1978. The two groups had interlocking memberships. The vice president who chaired the Issues Management Committee was also a member of the Strategic Planning Committee. Supported by this level of corporate leadership, issues management's struggle for prominence did not rely exclusively on communication options. Leaders in the formation of this new discipline recognized the need for a well-integrated mix of strategic business planning, public policy analysis, and business ethics, along with advocacy communication.

Meeting challenges through multilevel responses

One of the strongest and most well-developed statements supporting issues management was published in 1978 by the Public Affairs Council. In a pamphlet titled *The Fundamentals of Issue Management*, the Council explained, 'Issues management is a program which a company uses to increase its knowledge of the public policy process and enhance the sophistication and effectiveness of its involvement in that process' (p. 1). Rather than relying only on communication as the savior of corporate privilege, the Council featured the need for several interlocking functions: 'Identifying issues and trends, evaluating their impact and setting priorities, establishing a company position, designing company action and response to help achieve the position (e.g., communication, lobbying, lawsuits, and advertising, etc.), and implementing the plans' (p. 2). Communication was the heart of issues management, the Council believed. It proclaimed, 'Public affairs has increasingly come to mean not merely a response to change, but a positive role in the management of change itself – in the shaping of public policies and programs, and in the development of corporate activities to implement change constructively' (p. 2).

Sponsored by The Conference Board's Public Affairs Research Council, James K. Brown (1979) conducted a research project to determine how public affairs practitioners and corporate executives defined issues management. The study's findings could be used to help public affairs practitioners 'and their colleagues in top management do a better job of planning' (p. ii). Rather than being limited to concerns regarding how issues mature into legislation or regulation, the study argued that issues management must be integrated into all management planning and be focused on the central task of helping the company – through its strategic management. What functions were needed for effective issues management? Brown advocated planning, monitoring, analyzing, and communicating.

What principle guides this activity? Strategic planning personnel need to spot, analyze, and know what can and cannot (should and should not) be done to communicate on public policy issues and how to adjust products and services to hostile environments as well as to take advantage of favorable ones. Brown (1979) reasoned that 'if management should accustom itself routinely to ask the full range of questions that ought to be asked about vital corporate decisions, taking into account all the relevant external environments as well as the internal environment, this business of issues would become, properly, a non-issue' (p. 74). No single issues management function can accomplish that goal. Thus, any commitment to issues management rhetoric that lacks substantial management planning and issues analysis support could render corporate responses hollow outbursts of moral outrage.

Recognition of such limitations led issues management innovators to recognize the virtue of subtle but firm integration of strategic business planning and issues monitoring. Strategic business planning and environmental scanning become partners – at least in the literature, if not in practice. In 1979, *BusinessWeek* reported on the fledgling trend by some companies to use environmental scanning to improve strategic business plans and to alert line managers to changes in public sentiments regarding operating procedures ('Capitalizing on social change;' 1979).

Proponents of new approaches to corporate positioning often associated themselves with public affairs. In this way, one attempt to identify the key functions of issues management reasoned that it involved three activities: 'issue identification, corporate proaction, and the inclusion of public affairs issues in established decision-making processes and managerial functions' (Fleming, 1980, p. 35). Business professors such as Fleming led this innovation by advising executives to realize that when corporate planning and public policy issues were on a collision trajectory, the company was likely to lose or waste valuable resources. Other business faculty, in particular Post (1978, 1979) and Buchholz (1982, 1985), produced seminal studies to expose the important role public policy plays in corporate planning and operation.

Reflecting on this trend, Renfro (1993), a pioneer in the theory and practice of issues management, stressed the need to identify and monitor issues as a preliminary to strategic planning. He made this case as he reflected on the history of the discipline: 'The field of issues management emerged as public relations or public affairs officers included more and more forecasting and futures research in their planning and analysis of policy' (Renfro, 1993, p. 23). In this sense, 'issues management is an intelligence function that does not get involved in the "operations side" unless specifically directed to do so' (Renfro, 1993, p. 89).

The rhetoric of issues management: internal and external dialogues

As it has emerged, issues management is a reaction to activism and the increasing intra- and interindustry pressures by corporations to define and implement higher standards of corporate responsibility – as well as debate in public what those standards should be. Issues management encompasses all efforts corporations must make to create harmony with key players in their public policy arena – by sensing changing standards of the norms of business practice preferred by key publics, especially those who have become activists. Corporate leaders and business college faculty led the discussion of corporate responsibility. Leaders in the discipline recognized the need to integrate strategic planning, public policy analysis, and communication (Marx, 1986). One of those leaders, Monsanto Corporation, has used issues management to determine which product lines are advisable in light of public policy trends (Fleming, 1980; Stroup, 1988). Describing Monsanto's contingency approach, Stroup (1988) observed: 'Early knowledge of these trends would give the company more time to change negative attitudes toward business or to adapt business practices proactively if attitudes and expectations could not be swayed from the identified path' (p. 89).

This brief review of literature about the definition and functions of issues management demonstrates that even though no perspective prevails, several functions recur in the discussion. To some, issues management is 'the organized activity of identifying emerging trends, concerns, or issues likely to affect an organization in the next few years and developing a wider and more positive range of organizational responses toward that future' (Coates, Coates, Jarratt, & Heinz, 1986, p. ix). Chase (1984) and Coates et al. (1986) were leaders in the efforts to increase management's awareness of issues while they were emerging. The assumption was that more leverage could be exerted on issues if responses could be made at the earliest stages of each issue's development. As Hainsworth and Meng (1988) contended, doing so gives 'senior management the means to intelligently participate in the public policy process' (p. 28). Authors such as Crable and Vibbert (1985) developed models of the issues emergence process trying to demonstrate how early detection and response could be achieved.

Thus, corporate social responsibility and issues development awareness seem vital for effective strategic business planning and communication. But issues awareness, identification, and analysis alone do no good. At some point actions are needed, whether they are refinements of the organization's strategic business plan, its standards of corporate responsibility, its public policy plans, or its communication plan.

Issues management can link the public relations function and the management function to help the organization be outer directed and to have a participative organizational culture. Blending these functions is vital for organizations that seek harmonious relationships in an environment that is complex because of the number of publics and the variety of issues to be considered. Astute public relations practitioners used issues management to 'expand the role of public relations beyond media relations and product publicity to a senior management problem-solving function critical to the survival of an organization' (Tucker, Broom, & Caywood, 1993, p. 38). The new discipline appealed to management as a 'process whose goal is to help preserve markets, reduce risk, create opportunities and manage image as an organization asset for the benefit of both an organization and its primary shareholders' (Tucker et al., 1993, p. 38).

As long ago as the late 1970s, astute observers noted that issues management is an amalgamation of several disciplines and specialty functions. It includes identifying, monitoring, and analyzing trends in key publics' opinions that can mature into public policy and regulatory or legislative constraint of the private sector. It involves a staff function that, along with technical and managerial personnel support, can develop a corporate or industry stance to be executed through strategic business plans and communication campaigns. No other corporate function more completely stresses the inseparability of ethical corporate behavior, public judgment, responsible production and delivery of goods and services, and internal and external attempts to inform and persuade targeted constituencies to gain their support. Issues management goes beyond communication with various constituencies. It can penetrate all operations. The underpinning principle of issues management is not to shield an organization against emerging legislation or regulation, but to balance the interests of all segments of the community, so that each enjoys the proper amount of reward or benefit in proportion to the cost of allowing industry free rein to impose its own operating standards.

Issues management as four functions

Taking one of the earliest and most comprehensive views of issues management, the Public Affairs Council (1978) described it as 'a program which a company uses to increase its knowledge of the public policy process and enhance the sophistication and effectiveness of its involvement in that process' (p. 1). The Council endorsed an issues management model that consists of (a) monitoring the public policy arena to determine which trends will demand a reorientation of corporate policy and communication process, (b) identifying those issues of greatest potential importance to the organization, (c) evaluating their operational and financial impact through issues analysis, (d) prioritizing and establishing company policy positions by coordinating and assisting senior management decision making, (e) creating the company response from among a range of issue change strategy options, and (f) implementing the plans through issue action programming.

Through the years, four functions have come to define issues management (Heath, 1997; Heath & Cousino, 1990):

- Engage in strategic planning in ways that consider the threats and opportunities of public policy changes

- Embrace and implement the highest standards of corporate responsibility to achieve credibility, to be above reproach, and thereby to earn the right to be a public policy steward

- Identify, analyze, and monitor issues to constantly understand the public policy formation processes to be able to exert influence as well as avoid collisions

- Voice facts, opinions, and policy positions that support collaborative decision making and foster an ever more sound society, create and sustain identification, and ensure that the narratives enacted by the dominant forces of society correspond rather than compete in ways that lead to disharmony.

However various proponents view the discipline, they realize that the product of its efforts must be an executive-level staff effort that can create harmony between the sponsoring entity and its key stakeholder publics. That is the challenge, by whatever name. This view of issues management assumes that no entity can wisely or rightfully think that it can manage issues, but can engage in the collective efforts of society to manage issues. Also, this view of the discipline knows that the management of issues is not synonymous with the manipulation of issues. The term *issues management* assumes that savvy organizations take a management approach to issues to reduce friction and maximize harmony. They do so because conflict – unproductive conflict – is an unnecessary cost and therefore not a position that wise management would support.

Speaking as chairperson of the Issues Management Association, W. Howard Chase (1982) offered a widely quoted definition: 'Issues management is the capacity to understand, mobilize, coordinate, and direct all strategic and policy planning functions, and all public affairs/public relations skills, toward achievement of one objective: meaningful participation in creation of public policy that affects personal and institutional destiny' (p. 1). Although wise supporters of the discipline realize that a bad organization cannot be defended by articulate communication, Chase stressed the proactive aspect of issues management, which 'rejects the hypothesis that any institution must be the pawn of the public policy determined solely by others' (p. 2). To be a major player in the public policy arena, the organization must strive to meet or exceed the ethical standards expected by its constituents and critics. Once it has a strong moral center, it can be the good organization communicating well.

Stressing outcomes deliverable by issues management, former Allstate Insurance Company executive for public affairs Raymond Ewing (1987) defined it as 'simply public policy research, foresight, and planning for an organization in the private sector impacted by decisions made by others in the public sector' (p. 18). Issues management can help fill 'the policy hole in the center of corporate management, making it possible for the CEO and senior management to strategically manage their enterprise as a whole, as a complete entity capable of helping create the future and 'grow' their company into it' (p. 18). The greatest contribution of issues management is gained by early and proactive efforts 'to intervene consciously and effectively and participate early in the process, instead of waiting passively until the organization finds itself a victim at the tail end of the process' (p. 19).

Issues management entails efforts to achieve understanding and increase satisfaction between parties and to negotiate their exchange of stakes. It engages interlocking cultures that are in various states of compatibility and similarity. It fosters the interests of the stakeholders by helping an organization achieve its goals in a community of complementary and competing interests.

To achieve its potential, issues management must add value by allocating, defining, and distributing resources: human, financial, and material. It serves its sponsoring organization by engaging in a field in which each player seeks its own advantage. Although these competing and conflicting interests are such that not all can be equally satisfied, issues management serves best when it assists in the planning, analysis, communication, and coalition-building efforts by which mutual interests are sought and appropriate resource allocation is achieved.

Learning from three decades of thinking about issues management

Before this chapter can explore in detail the topic of the rhetorical theory of issues management, we must understand the literature that has struggled to define issues management. One reasonable version of the discipline is that it is *the management of organizational and community resources through the public policy process to advance organizational interests and rights by striking a mutual balance with those of stakeholders.* This view of issues management adopts the underpinning rationale that is provided by social exchange theory. Any person in a relationship – or an organization in a relationship – will suffer the consequences of constraints if that relationship is seen as causing greater social, health, safety, environmental quality, political, and economic costs than it delivers. Activist and other public policy initiatives seek to employ power resources – including the rhetorical redefinitions of the value premises of society – to challenge and constrain organizational prerogatives.

Any sound view of issues management rhetoric requires an understanding that the limits of one set of actions is a counter, opposing set. Likewise, the limits on the statement advocated by one entity is the counter advocacy of many other voices. Any rhetorical statement is only as strong as its ability to sustain itself in the public debate and achieve concurrence.

This line of analysis features a view that issues management supports strategic business planning and management by understanding public policy, meeting standards of corporate responsibility expected by key stakeholders, and using two-way communication to foster understanding and minimize conflict. It adapts products, services, or operations to policy or seeks to change policy to support products, services, or operations. It is not limited to media relations, customer relations, or government relations. It is engaged in strategic business planning options that may change operations, products, or services as well as communicate to establish mutual interests and achieve harmony with stakeholders. It is expected to keep the firm ethically attuned to its community and positioned to exploit, mitigate, and foster public policy changes as they relate to the corporate mission.

Defining issues management and issues: rhetorical underpinnings

As Burke (1973b) said, democracy institutionalizes 'the dialectic process, by setting up a political structure that gives full opportunity for the use of competition to a cooperative end' (p. 444). This view of the rhetorical process can suggest that some organizational relationship problems require issues management rhetoric. Thus, to adopt the proper perspective for understanding issues management rhetoric, we should examine key issues that are central to the heritage of rhetoric in order to grasp the relevant assumptions and theoretical underpinnings.

Many views of rhetoric can be found. They range from the conception of rhetoric as the dialogue of assertion and counter assertion, focused on careful analysis of fact and value, to a sharply contrasting view of discourse based on statements devoid of a basis in fact and value. This range of views on rhetoric is between one devoted to a search for the best available truth to one dedicated to the self-serving expedience of deception and manipulation that is associated with the popular conception of 'spin.'

Examining the rhetorical heritage, Campbell (1996) championed this form of discourse as 'the study of what is persuasive. The issues it examines are social truths, addressed to others, justified by reasons that reflect cultural values. It is a humanistic study that examines all the symbolic means by which influence occurs' (p. 8). Although some critics of rhetoric might not agree, it is certainly acceptable to reason that ideas are likely to become better when subjected to public scrutiny through statement and counter statement. Defending that process, Lentz (1996) reasoned: 'Truth should prevail in a market-like struggle where superior ideas vanquish their inferiors and achieve audience acceptance' (p. 1).

On the one hand, many rhetorical theorists have argued that one of the assumptions of rhetoric is that even though we cannot know reality absolutely (because of that reality), we must be willing to accept relative truth as a standard of rhetoric. Thus, people can concur and share beliefs on various issues until more agreeable and accurate views on those issues become available. At one end of the continuum, the purview of rhetoric is the search for truth through discourse that engages the best analytical efforts of interested parties. In the spectrum of rhetorical opinions, we have a symbolic view of rhetoric, which suggests that people create attachments and bridge natural estrangements through a variety of strategic identifications. People identify because they share symbolic substance that reflects their shared identity and mutual interest.

At the purely symbolic end of the continuum, rhetoric can be manipulative: Say what is acceptable to the audience and what needs to be said to win the issue without regard to the truth or some higher order of virtue or integrity. A company can take a stand that symbolically states its agreement with a public, even if that stance is not honest or genuine. Symbolic rhetoric can resort to plays on tricky definitions and attempts to shift the burden of responsibility or reframe the issue so that it becomes distorted. This manipulative approach to rhetoric can ascertain what people believe and then falsely position the organization as though it agreed with them.

The best form of rhetoric, in sharp contrast to those symbolic and manipulative ones, is devoted to using discourse to seek the best available truth and set of value priorities to help the community of interested parties to make sound and principled decisions. These decisions advance the interests of the entire community, rather than more narrowly privileging the advocate of the position. The purely symbolic end of the continuum of rhetorical options is fraught with deceit and is committed to winning advantage for one side of a controversy by tricking the other side. It is often devoted to using any of a list of logical fallacies such as turning the tables, reframing the issue to the advantage of the advocate rather than in the mutual interest of the involved parties. This view advises the use of apology, even if it is not genuine, in order to make the offending organization appear to be the victim deserving of sympathy. It allows for stalling tactics that postpone a thoughtful and timely discussion of issues. Such strategies not only are morally repugnant, but are also likely to increase the legitimacy gap because they foster distrust over the long haul.

One central premise of the Western rhetorical heritage is that communicators design statements to address an important issue and thereby seek to solve a rhetorical problem shared by a community of interested persons. Rhetorical problems arise from needs or problems – exigencies – that can be solved by strategically developed and contextually meaningful actions and discourse (Bitzer, 1968). Customers' class action complaints may be a legal or public relations rhetorical problem. Activists' challenge to environmental emissions levels is a rhetorical problem. Consumers' complaints about foods being less nutritious than advertised is a rhetorical problem. Critics' appeal for companies to be forced to pay more taxes or create safer working conditions is a rhetorical problem. Whether these issues are of such magnitude that they require rhetorical response is part of issues management rhetoric.

Not all problems that an organization faces are rhetorical problems. A rhetorical problem is one that can be solved through discourse – essentially the dynamics of advocacy and counter advocacy. Some organizational problems require more savvy and sophisticated strategic planning and improved standards of corporate responsibility hence the need for issues management. If the leaderships of organizations encounter some isolated complaints and minor differences of opinions, they hardly need a sophisticated issues management program. As issues become more likely to damage the planning and operational preferences of the organization, its leadership needs to implement programs for identifying, analyzing, and tracking them (Dutton, 1993; Dutton & Ashford, 1993; Dutton & Duncan, 1987; Dutton & Jackson, 1987; Dutton & Ottensmeyer, 1987).

A rhetorical definition of issues

An *issue*, a rhetorical problem, is a contestable matter of fact, evaluation, or policy. It is a difference of opinion that can result from or lead to a legitimacy gap. An emerging public policy issue attracts significant attention to the way an organization plans and operates. It can result from marketplace practices, such as the sale of hazardous materials (asbestos) or products (tobacco). It may arise as the value premises of various publics become more persuasive in the public policy arena. An issue can mature into substantial changes in the public policy or market arenas that have serious implications for the operating standards and practices of an organization.

Issues that are part of the purview of issues management rhetoric fall into the following categories:

◾ Issues of fact, value, and policy that can have implications for the development and implementation of regulation or legislation (perhaps even adjudication), as well as collaborative decision making. Thus, if genetic engineering results in actual health hazards, or even leads to substantial concerns, this documentation can be used by critics of genetic engineering to argue for specific legislative and regulatory guidelines. If genetic engineering is alleged to cause such problems, that claim is contestable as an issue of fact and may even be an issue of evaluation. Perhaps the gains achieved by genetic engineering offset the risks. But that balance is likely to be an issue that some voices in society contest as fact, evaluation, and policy.

◾ Issues of fact, value, and policy that can have implications for the development of the organization's reputation. For instance, an automobile company that has a corporate mission to be seen as the technological leader in its industry can legitimately be expected to challenge claims by critics that its technology is not as good as it claims. The issues arise from the claims of critics. The organization needs to defend its reputation by challenging those claims to demonstrate where they are inaccurate.

◾ Issues of identification that can lead to merger or division that has implications for the development and implementation of regulation or legislation (perhaps even adjudication), as well as collaborative decision making. A wise organization seeks to create identifications by fostering shared identity and social reality with its stakeholders and stakeseekers. The assumption, which will be expanded later, is that identification leads to *merger* – a sharing of interests. The opposite of identification is division. Environmentalists may divide themselves from organizations that they believe harm the environment. They identify or merge with organization that they believe improve the environment. Thus, issues management rhetoric can be a contest of identifications.

◾ Issues of identification that can lead to merger or division that has implications for the development and enactment of the organization's reputation. People are variously attracted to certain organizational personae. These personae can feature issues that have public policy or marketplace positioning implications. In both senses, issues managers should be interested in the differentiations that can be created because of issues stances their organizations take. They can strategically seek to foster association (and even dissociation) merger rather than division. The persona of the organization is vital to persons' coming to see it as a good organization, one they want to associate with, as differentiated from organizations they want to dissociate from. The persona can be enacted through its identity including its goodwill (Heath, 1997).

◾ Issues of narrative interpretations that can position the organization to be a moral leader, one of many that have adopted acceptable narratives to guide their corporate responsibility; a moral follower; or a violator of moral standards. One of the key narrative themes is the morality of the personae (the characters in a story). One of the standards narrative – stakeholder of the mind (Mitroff, 1983) – is constant improvement of the quality of goods and services as well as advocate of better public policies.

◾ Issues of narrative interpretations where claims of fact, value, policy, and identification are interpreted as exhibiting fidelity and probability.

◾ Issues of stakeholder relationships where the social exchange is balanced so that mutually beneficial relationships occur rather than legitimacy gaps in which organizations violate the expectations held by their key publics.

Themes that give rise to issues management typically have been those that are at play and become resolved in the public policy arena. However, some organizations are coupling an issues management perspective with their marketing and reputation management strategies. For instance, if an automobile company wants to be known as the technological leader of its industry, it may also use an issues management approach to manage its reputation. In that regard, if an automobile editorialist or even a technical reporter doubts this company's technological superiority, the corporation can engage in dialogue to present, bolster, and even win its case on the specific issues. These responses involve the presentation and examination of fact and the advocacy and counter advocacy of evaluative claims. This is the essence – form and substance – of issues management rhetoric.

Given this review, we can pause to examine the rhetoric of issues management. It needs to address facts, values, and policies. It creates and adapts to identifications. It fosters and applies narratives. The savvy issues manager becomes an advocate externally seeking to engage in the dialogues of these kinds that have an impact on the policies – public arena and marketplace – that shape the destiny of organizations and affect their relationships with markets, audiences, and publics. Issues managers do more than communicate to external audiences. They communicate through dialogic advocacy. They advocate changes to key internal stakeholder audiences as well as support specific interpretations of fact or policy for the consideration of external stakeholder audiences. This engagement is the essence of issues management rhetoric.

Directions for research and theory development

Given this overview that has helped to define the rhetorical context of issues management, we shift attention to the rhetorical options that are essential to reducing the legitimacy gaps that plague the planning and operations of organizations. One option is to use rhetorical positioning to convince management to alter policies that result in abrasive relationships with their stakeholders. Another option is to rhetorically manage differences by advocating that critics should take on more accurate perspectives.

The venues of this discussion can vary from public advocacy, through issues advertising, to collaborative decision-making sessions in which persons who have vested interests come together to work for the best solutions to shared problems. Several lines of rhetorical analysis help define the directions that research and theory development can take to improve the quality of issues management rhetoric. These themes are discussed in the following sections.

Issues management rhetoric: a rational process

With some literature on rhetoric shunning attempts to deal constructively with the difficulties of analyzing propositions of fact, value, and policy, we could adopt an extreme relativism and simply conclude that issues management rhetoric is purely symbolic. Extreme relativism suggests that rational efforts to generate and interpret facts and seek better evaluations and policies becomes meaningless. All truth and knowledge are relevant. Cynicism is the outcome of any rhetorical process that is not founded on good reasoning or good reasons (Wallace, 1963; Weaver, 1953, 1970). At its worst, symbolic rhetoric

becomes nothing more than a form of facile impression management. For this reason, the research challenge is to improve the ability of issue management rhetors to link analytical and rhetorical processes to achieve better conclusions of fact, value, and policy.

If issues management cannot help people to obtain a better, more accurate, and more useful view of the problems they confront, then it is likely to lead them to be ever more cynical about the role that the search for truth plays in the rhetorical process. If public policy and marketplace policy are driven by image without efforts to get and refine substance, then cynicism can become the standard approach to problem solving.

A substantial body of literature in rhetoric and philosophy asks that we guard against a naive approach to the nature of fact and the role that interpretations of fact plays in the rhetorical process. Does issues management have a privileged means to discover and reveal the truth? The answer to this epistemic question is, probably not (Rorty, 1979; see also Bernstein, 1983; and Brummett, 1990; and Cherwitz & Hikins, 1986, who contended 'all ways of knowing are inherently rhetorical' p. 92). But like the rhetorical tradition, issues management rhetoric is best when it engages in the refinement of knowledge, values, and truth to the mutual good of interested parties.

Relativism is a timeless issue. It cannot be solved here. But one cannot reasonably ignore the relevance of fact for policy or market decisions. It is the crux of the rhetorical process in the minds of many. Taking a perspective on this issue, Campbell (1996) compared scientists for whom 'the most important concern is the discovery and testing of certain kinds of truths,' to 'rhetoricians (who study rhetoric and take a rhetorical perspective) [and who] would say, "Truths cannot walk on their own legs. They must be carried by people to other people. They must be explained, defended, and spread through language, argument, and appeal"' (p. 3). From this foundation, Campbell reasoned, rhetoricians take the position 'that unacknowledged and unaccepted truths are of no use at all' (p. 3).

The rhetoric of issues management, toward these ends, must begin with a consideration of the quality of facts, values/evaluations, and policy positions that are advocated and eventually enacted. As difficult as it is to achieve certain knowledge and truth, those outcomes need to be the constant goal of issues management rhetoric. Without a commitment to better facts, evaluations, and policies, the discipline devolves into the worst of 'spin.' The public will not tolerate a callous commitment to relativity. Relativity carried to its ultimate extreme suggests that because no truth or knowledge is superior, people are legitimately justified in taking a cynical commitment to abandon the pursuit of truth and knowledge. Nihilism or the power grab thus become alternative strategies. The preferred option is a good-faith effort to use the dialogue of rhetoric to produce and refine facts, evaluations, and policies in the public view through the processes of advocacy and counter advocacy. This is the essence of the rational approach to issues management rhetoric.

The substance of the rational approach to issues management rhetoric centers on the quality of information (fact), the sense that some principles are superior to others (evaluation), and the proposition that some policies bring better business, nonprofit, and governmental practices, products, and services. This search is in keeping with Kenneth Burke's (1966) observation that humans are rotten with perfection (p. 16). Burke noted the human propensity to seek the perfect identification, perfect values, perfect enemy, perfect identity, and so forth. As Burke continued:

> There is a kind of 'terministic compulsion' to carry out the implications of one's terminology, quite as, if an astronomer discovered by his [or her] observations and computations that a certain wandering body was likely to hit the earth and destroy us, he [she] would nonetheless feel compelled to argue for the correctness of his [her] computations, despite the ominousness of the outcome (p. 19).

The incentive toward perfection assumes the perfect fact, perfect evaluation, and perfect policy. That rhetorical incentive translates into the perfect challenges launched by activists to motivate improved operating and planning principles on the part of businesses, nonprofits, and governmental organizations.

The process of issues management rhetoric assumes that better conclusions can be derived if issues of fact, evaluation, and policy are subject to public and private debate. The range of communication options and tools is substantial. It can include comments made to customers or activists as well as to reporters and legislators. Such communication can entail collaborative decision making, within the context of a conference room, a senate chamber, or public discussion in media or on the Internet. Venues change. Best practices suggest many options where ideas have the best opportunity for scrutiny.

Short of consensus, the process can at least achieve concurrence. From each step in the process additional steps are possible. This approach to decision making can result not only in better solutions and policy positions but also in ones that the participants are more committed to support because of their participation in the process. This process is likely to be unending as the dialogue continues and new problems, issues, facts, evaluations, and policy positions give motive to advocates to offer their views.

Viewed from the vantage point of issues management rhetoric, a strategic issue 'is anything that may substantially impact your organization. Other ways to think of strategic issues are: all major questions needing answers; decisions needing to be made; things about the organization that need to be changed, corrected, or improved; or the primary challenges the organization faces' (Bandrowski, 1990, p. 18). In short, an issue is a contestable proposition of fact, evaluation, and policy that is of mutual concern to two or more parties.

The magnitude of issues can range from one reporter's statement about the quality of a company's product all the way to controversy about global warming. Matters of fact are judged within the analytical context of what observations of phenomena are more or less true. Evaluations are likely to be founded on fact, but extend to issues of preference. For instance, a timber company may clear-cut (fact) and science may show that clear-cutting has some detrimental effects on the environment. The real issue, however, may be the evaluations – perhaps pitting corporate financial interests against environmental aesthetics – of whether the damage is tolerable. Policy matters are stated as preferences, as *oughts* in debate and *shalls* and *shoulds* in operation. This operation can include matters of issue enacted by government or the private preferences of customers based on demonstrable claims about the quality of products, services, and organizational reputation.

In this case, issues count. For that reason, they need to be subjected to dialogue. They can affect the future of individuals, corporate entities, and society. The research and theory challenge is to improve the quality of analytical dialogue, which can sustain and foster the search for the value truths, knowledge, and policy positions in the interest of the community.

Issues management rhetoric: courtship battles for identification

Organizations invite individuals as well as other organizations to identify with them. Members of an industry, such as agriculture, have reason to identify with one another. They share interests, needs, wants, values, policy preferences, goals, and opinions. Even then, differences of opinion can occur. Such differences, however, are likely to be greater when there is less apparent justification for individuals to identify with one another, where estrangement exists. Burke (1969) suggested that courtship is the essence of the rhetoric of identification. If we have estrangement, then we can have motives and appeals to come together. This coming together in an interpersonal sense is courtship. That premise can extend to the rhetorical appeals of issues management. The research challenge for the rhetoric of issues management is to improve the understanding of the substance and forms of appeal to end estrangement through courtship.

The rhetoric of issues management entails appeals to share substance and thereby to engage in the courtship of identification. Organizations position themselves as being different. People think of themselves as being different. In this sense, they are estranged.

Society cannot operate with total estrangement. Communication must bridge estrangement. But it cannot succeed for long in creating bridges that are asymmetrical. The essence of courtship is people's need to join, cooperate, with others. As much as it implies cooperation, it also entails competition. Recognizing this phenomenon, Burke (1969) built his rhetorical theory around the dialectic of merger and division, between cooperative competition. Herein lies a rationale for issues management rhetoric founded on the dialectics of identification.

Although many competing versions of reality (social reality) exist, groups share enough social knowledge and a common identity that they can coordinate their efforts toward mutually beneficial ends. These give them the ability to live and work in varying degrees of cooperation and competition. Identification through a shared social knowledge allows them to band together, even if that banding puts them at odds with other groups.

Rhetoric deals with 'the ways in which the symbols of appeal are stolen back and forth by rival camps' (Burke, 1937, p. 365). Burke (1965) cautioned, 'Let the system of cooperation become impaired, and the communicative equipment is correspondingly impaired, while this impairment of the communicative medium in turn threatens the structure of rationality itself' (p. 163). The dialectic goes like this. Environmentalists argue that green is good, including green products, to create that identification. Extending that logic, manufacturers of consumer products appeal for identification based on claims that their products are green and environmentally sound. Thus, we have competing calls for identification.

At the organizational level, people identify through a commitment to their modes of production. 'Modes of cooperation,' wrote Burke (1973a), '(production and distribution) give form to modes of communication. The modes of communication thus refer back to the modes of cooperation' (p. 312). In this sense, for Burke, *cooperation* is a means by which individuals form a group with its own identity. To sustain that group is some common mission of the members of the group. They collaborate. They conspire. They compete.

Through competitive competition, people engage in self-governance. Through the rhetoric of identification, they engage in the dialectic of merger and division. They unite with some people and polarize against others. What facilitates this movement? It results from the sharing of symbolic substance by which the identities of individuals can become the basis for their identifications.

Burke (1966) featured that logic in the development of his definition of *rhetoric* as 'identification.' Rhetoric, he reasoned, is 'the use of language as a symbolic means of inducing cooperation in beings that by nature respond to symbols' (p. 43).

By this logic, the environmentalist challenges the business or industry to share the substance of environmental responsibility (identify with that substance) or to be at odds with that substance. In addition, the environmentalist seeks to define this substance. The company can respond to these definitions. It can contest these definitions. It can contest the extent to which its actions meet or exceed those definitions.

Such definitions and the enactment of those definitions can lead an organization to position itself in public policy or marketplace debates. Several personae can be the basis of the positioning an organization (corporate, nonprofit, and governmental) takes in its issues management. These strategic options include its differentiation – setting itself out as being unique because of its persona on issues; its association – coupling its symbolic substance to that preferred by those stakeholders it courts; and its identity – taking on one of several archetypal persona such as bold advocate or technically expert adviser (Heath, 1997).

All of those strategic options are part of issues management rhetoric derived from the rhetoric of identification. Two interesting and valuable contributions to the issues management literature help to demonstrate these principles. Mobil Oil Company is the focal point of the analysis of both discussions. Crable and Vibbert (1983) interpreted the 1970s issue positioning of Mobil as fitting the Prometheus icon. It sought to identify with persons who were convinced that a strong corporate voice – a bold advocate – was needed to counter the false claims by reporters who were eroding public confidence in business decision makers. Simons (1983) saw the Mobil issue advertising campaign from a different perspective. He claimed that Mobil, like the male bower bird (bold corporate advocate), was using its anti-media appeals to lure the unsuspecting female bower bird (passive follower who preferred pro-corporation to more democratic interpretations of corporate criticism) into his lair to take advantage of it.

These appeals elicit different courtship identifications. Schmertz (1986), one of the designers of the Mobil campaign, concluded that it had positive marketplace and public opinion impact. People like to identify with a company that takes aggressive stances on public policy issues that support its business practices. This aggressive stance – bold advocate – Schmertz concluded, even leads some consumers to prefer doing business with such companies.

Thus, issues management rhetoric can be understood as courtship appeals to build and bolster cooperation through shared symbolic substance and social knowledge. It can build on this foundation to call for additional perspectives and actions because of shared symbolic substance. As Kruckeberg and Starck (1988) have argued, the ultimate identification is the community – the shared interests of persons who have a common identification. Caution, however, is expressed by Brummett (1995), who suggests that one rhetorical stance used by the defenders of the status quo is to challenge counter advocates – typically critics of some prevailing point of view – as taking stances that threaten the sense of community. Can we better understand the dynamics of the rhetoric of courtship and identification? To do so is likely to entail better understanding of the ways in which critics can challenge the assumptions of the community in the name of improving the community. These are research challenges of the issues management rhetoric of identification.

Issues management rhetoric: corporate narrans

Another research challenge is to improve our understanding of the dynamics of rhetorical use of narratives. Establishing the intellectual rationale for this approach to rhetoric, Fisher (1985, 1987, 1989) characterized humans as storytellers – *Homo narrans*. By extension, we can frame issues management rhetoric as 'corporate narrans' – the organization as storyteller (Heath, 1994). Stories are the eternal and compelling substance of human communication. They help people to achieve shared knowledge, identity, and practices that allow for a workable society. People not only tell stories, but also frame their actions, opinions, and lives in narrative form and substance. They frame one set of stories in terms of other stories. Those stories either agree with and complement or compete with and challenge one another.

Stories, Fisher (1987) concluded, become more compelling rhetorically if they exhibit *fidelity* – if they fit the facts that others know or believe to be true. If the story presents facts that differ from those others know or believe to be true, then the storyteller is handicapped rhetorically. If a corporate narrative lacks fidelity, it is less persuasive.

Stories also need to be *probable* (Fisher, 1987): They must present details that are internally and thematically consistent. Part of the interpretative frame of probability is the likelihood that the specific story is sustained by a specific account of details and actions.

We can suggest, as well, that stories are lived experience (Mangham & Overington, 1987) that take on different levels of generality or universality. Thus, there are societal-level narratives, such as those representing and justifying the free market system (Narrative1). Each company (non-profit activist group or governmental agency) constitutes a narrative variation of that societal narrative (Narrative2). Units within organizations are a third level of narrative; persons in these units enact narratives that take their substance from the two more embracing narratives (Narrative3). Individual actions constitute the fourth level of narrative (Narrative4).

Such narratives can be contested rhetorically in terms of their fidelity and probability. They can be challenged by other narratives. Thus, the free market narrative that features corporate efficiency and productivity at the expense of environmental quality can be challenged by the environmental responsibility narrative that suggests that the outcome of the free market narrative is a world unfit for human existence.

Issues management rhetoric, in this way, can capture perspectives of fact, value, and policy and express them in narrative form and substance. Narratives have personae (enactors of the story), plots, themes, and scripts. People – individually and on behalf of organizations – communicate to define the scene. A scene defines which acts are appropriate and inappropriate given the nature of the scene. Issues management rhetoric can consist of contests of narrative fidelity and probability, as well as clashes of narratives.

Narrative analysis fits comfortably with news gathering and reporting protocols. News is narrative. Even more specific, this line of analysis supports the issues management rhetoric of crisis response. Each crisis is a story. Persons engaged in the crisis tell stories. Crisis response teams can rhetorically respond to and participate in the generation of stories. The public seeks the resolution of a story in 'happily ever after' terms. The public does not like stories that fail to demonstrate fidelity and probability as well as to achieve resolution. Thus, one research challenge of issues management rhetoric is to continue to refine our understanding of the competing narratives that offer form and substance by which people contest mutually agreeable outcomes.

Issues management rhetoric: social exchange

Part of the challenge of issues management rhetoric is to strike a balance between competing and conflicting interests. This aspect of issues management rhetoric assumes that relationships that balance interests and tend toward mutual benefit are empowering and therefore more desirable. When the position advocated or the values enacted privilege the interest of one party at the expense of one or more others, then frictions are likely to occur and become the motives for issues management debates and collaborative decision making. The research challenge of this aspect of issues management rhetoric is to better understand how power resource management and mutual benefit can be achieved through collaborative decision making.

To explain these dynamics, we can briefly turn to social exchange theory. Prior-Miller (1989) has offered a compatible rationale for issues management issues, as has Heath (1997). This perspective suggests that as one party violates the obligations for a balanced and mutually beneficial relationship, a legitimacy gap can occur (Sethi, 1977). Imbalance exists in a relationship, leading competing interests to advocate issues positions, when the actions of one entity aggrieve the interests and standards of one or more other parties.

To balance this equation – to achieve or restore harmony – requires a change in the way the organization behaves or performs, a new standard or approach to corporate responsibility. It may entail a rhetorical stance that can persuade the critic that the standards preferred by the organization are best and do not constitute an imbalance in the relationship. It may require that the ostensibly offending party not do what is thought to be offensive.

In this way, we have a rationale for issues management rhetoric that centers on the issues of mutually beneficial interests and the balance of relational outcomes. Thus, we introduce the issues management rhetorical implications of power, control, cognitive involvement, problem recognition, trust, knowledge, and support/opposition. Participants can rhetorically contest the norms and social exchange ratios that lead to the achievement of mutually beneficial relationships and the resolution of conflict. This rationale can challenge us to better understand the efforts to use collaborative decision making to resolve differences and achieve win-win outcomes.

Issues management rhetoric: information integration/expectancy value

In addition to the more humanistic approaches, issues management rhetoric is enriched with the more social scientific theory and research of information integration/expectancy value. Ajzen and Fishbein (1980; Fishbein & Ajzen, 1975, 1981) are instrumental researchers and theorists in the effort to explain the connections between beliefs as subjective probabilities, evaluations, subjective norms, and behavioral intentions. The assumption, relevant to issues management rhetoric, is that people create attitudes (including yielding to persuasive messages they

encounter) in an effort to achieve rewarding outcomes and avoid or prevent unrewarding ones.

This line of analysis fits nicely with the principles of the rational approach to rhetoric, the Greek and Roman rhetorical heritage. It supports the interest of public relations theorists in estimating the influence that people's opinions and preferences have on one another (subjective norms), and on decisions to take some actions in preference to others. This line of analysis has also been used to describe and evaluate the opinions of policy makers and publics (Thomas, Swaton, Fishbein, & Otway, 1980), a key theme in issues management rhetoric.

In essence, this line of analysis is comfortable with the reasoning that information affects beliefs – subjective probabilities. Evaluations result from many sources, including the influence of significant others. Based on attitudes (beliefs coupled to evaluations) and subjective norms, people create and even execute their behavioral attentions. In this way, we have empirical means of assessing some of the rhetorical principles implied in the humanistic approaches discussed earlier.

This line of analysis can also be used to measure and estimate the goodness of fit between the opinion positions of organizations, stakeholders, and stakeseekers. In this way, we can measure the legitimacy gap and imagine the shifts in opinion that increase or decrease the gap.

Conclusion

Issues management rhetoric can take its foundations from the lines of analysis outlined in this section, and even go beyond them. Key themes have been selected from the rhetorical heritage to offer underpinnings for issues management rhetoric.

Analysis has stressed the essential role that information, facts, and evaluations play in public-arena and marketplace policy discussions. Policy that is devoid of a sensitivity to fact and evaluation as preferences is likely not to last and may even result in cynicism. The search for order (Heath, 1997) constitutes a need for vigilant attention to the data that can bring about a sharper, clearer, and better view of reality. The policies, narratives, and identifications that surround, influence, and result from this policy are assumed to become better when subjected to the processes featured in the rhetorical tradition. This tradition, concluded Bryant (1953), consists of the processes and substance by which people are adjusted to ideas and ideas are adjusted to people. Issues management rhetoric is a process in which key participants voice their preferences, on behalf of organizations and as individuals – to create a social dialogue that can lead to a higher sense of value and a refined sense of social order.

Theory and research in practice

The practice of issues management entails coupling issues analysis, a continually refined sense of corporate responsibility, and communicative strategies – directed internally and externally – to achieve each organization's strategic business plan. The limits of this planning process are set by the abilities of corporate rhetors to define and delimit the standards of acceptance that reduce rather than enlarge the legitimacy gap. This line of analysis assumes that people cannot continue to operate organizations in ways that offend the limits set by the larger community.

In practice, therefore, we are likely to be interested in the rhetorical processes, message content, and delivery tools. These topics are developed in this section.

Rhetorical processes

Rhetoric at heart is the process of advocacy and counter advocacy. It is the rationale for suasive discourse. Rhetoric assumes that ideas appropriately framed and presented can affect strategic and ethical changes. It assumes that the symmetry of relationships is best defined by the ability of ideas to sustain themselves under the scrutiny of public discourse.

Starting from this premise, we can explore some of the practices of issues management rhetoric. Some of these applications have been implied in previous sections. They are presented here in outline form rather than with full rationale, based on the assumption that they draw their rationale, from the analysis presented in earlier sections.

This line of analysis needs to be undertaken with sensitivity to the challenges of functionalism by scholars of the critical theory and cultural studies perspective. Crass functionalism trivializes the rhetorical process and can lead users to believe that it can be reduced to its functionalist extremes: Load a message, lock the strategy, fire, and hit the target. The process is more complex than this. A strongly functionalist's approach is paternalistic, assuming that a strong source of influence can, perhaps even should, dominate a passive persuadee. The practices that follow feature functions that should be taken in the most embracing manner.

To demonstrate: Since the age of Aristotle (1952), rhetoricians have recognized the ethical responsibility rhetors have to produce information in support of the conclusions they advocate. If ideas count, they do so because of their ability to achieve concurrence for a preferred, more accurate and detailed understanding of some issue.

To evaluate: Rhetoric is more than description. It is not limited to achieving understanding. It presumes the ability of humans to convince one another that something is better or worse than something else. It deals with evaluations and preferences.

To recommend: Policy statements traditionally are framed as *oughts*, *shoulds*, and *shalls*. They are the culmination of the evaluative examination of facts and values. They are designed and employed to discriminate between good outcomes and negative outcomes.

To identify through courtship: In one sense, any thing is no more than what people believe it to be. An organization, in this case, is what others perceive it to be. If in actuality it is inaccurately perceived, then communication must put this right. If the organization wants to achieve identification, it begins by understanding the essence of the substance available for it to share in identification with others. In this sense, it must demonstrate that others can and should identify with it – merge with it in interest and symbolic action. It can differentiate itself from some members of society as a means of demonstrating a higher commitment to the good of the community.

To narrate: Each narrative exists as part of the shared social reality of a people at a time and place. Issues management rhetoric can be used to convince management that it must adopt a story that is shared with those with whom it wants to achieve mutually beneficial relationships. This story needs to be enacted by the organization. The story can be shaped through statements as it evolves and changes through social discourse.

To foster community through social exchange: Interests can be narrow or those which embrace the good of the community. Such interests are definable rhetorically. They are subject to evaluation and the development of policy that guides choices – preferring positive to negative outcomes. The rhetorical effort consists of the constant search for the essence of community, which leads to mutual benefits for its members. In this social exchange ratio, an organization cannot legitimately expect to achieve rewards that are disproportionate to the costs it creates and the rewards it provides to the other interested parties in the community.

Message content

Issues management rhetoric can be reduced to organizations saying what they think others will believe. Messages can be scientifically adjusted to appear to address issues and manipulate opinions without truly addressing the issues that are on the minds of the stakeholders of society.

The rhetorical tradition suggests that message content can be evaluated in terms of positions preferred by advocates. However, such messages are vetted for their informativeness and the evaluative preferences they contain in terms of the larger interests of the community. In this case we can ask whether the messages add value to discussions that frame, negotiate, and foster the interests of the community.

Message content can voice the interests of the dominant members of society. To the extent that it does this to the exclusion of other voices, the community is asymmetrical and resources are out of balance. Messages gain strength to the extent that they capture the interests of even the silent voices of society. As previously silent voices emerge, they may support and express reservations to the voice and dominant messages of society; they become part of the dialogue as others are willing to listen to them.

Message content consists of information, evaluation, preferences, courtship, and narrative. Through this content, not only do members of society learn and evaluate the ideas that are best, but they also have the opportunity to accommodate themselves and their interests to these ideas. People use rhetoric to adjust ideas to people and people to ideas.

Tools

The tools employed for issues management rhetoric cover the gamut. In the 1970s, issues management was often associated with issue advertising. This is a narrow, and likely dysfunctional, view of the range of options for the dialogue of issues management rhetoric.

Tools include the gamut of mediated communication options: books, articles, talk show appearances, videos, movies (for instance. *The Insider*, which criticized the tobacco industry, or *China Syndrome*, which challenged practices of nuclear power generation), and billboards. Advertising, news releases, congressional hearings, lawsuits, and Web site debates as town meetings (Coombs, 1998; Heath, 1998) – all of these and many more are the tools of issues management rhetoric.

Organizations have also discovered the value of other communication tools that are more specifically devoted to collaborative decision making. They can invite critics to engage in planning and positioning dialogues. They can create and sustain public decision-making sessions. They can listen. They can protest. They can demonstrate. They can boycott.

This list suggests the arsenal of tools available to the advocates who engage in public and private discourse as a means of reconciling differences, and achieving concurrence, as good people and organizations work to communicate effectively with one another.

Conclusion

Rhetoric may be thought of as manipulative, or invitational. Advocating an invitational view of rhetoric, Foss and Griffin (1995) argued against persuasive strategies that 'constitute a kind of trespassing on the personal integrity of others when they convey the rhetor's belief that audience members have inadequacies that in some way can be corrected if they adhere to the viewpoint of the rhetor' (p. 3). The trespass view of persuasion is patriarchal; it enacts the values of source-centered change, competition, and domination. The invitational approach to rhetoric can temper the privileging of an advocate's point of view. Any arena where multiple advocates compete is healthier by definition and more likely to engage in invitation than patriarchy.

References

Ajzen, I., & Fishbein, M. (1980). *Understanding attitudes and predicting social behavior.* Englewood Cliffs, NJ: Prentice Hall.

Aristotle. (1952). Rhetoric. (Trans. by W. R. Roberts). In R. M. Hutchins, (Series ed.), *Great books* (Vol. 2, pp. 593–675). Chicago: Encyclopaedia Briticannica.

Bandrowski, J. F. (1990). *Corporate imagination – plus.* New York: The Free Press.

Barnet, S. M., Jr. (1975). A global look at advocacy. *Public Relations Journal,* 31(11), 17–21.

Bateman, D. N. (1975). Corporate communications of advocacy: Practical perspectives and procedures. *Journal of Business Communication,* 13(1), 3–11.

Bitzer, L. (1968). The rhetorical situation. *Philosophy and Rhetoric,* 1, 1–15.

Bernstein, R. J. (1983). *Beyond objectivism and relativism: Science, hermeneutics and praxis.* Philadelphia: University of Pennsylvania Press.

Boe, A. R. (1972, October). The good hands of Allstate: A Spectator exclusive interview with Archie Boe, Allstate's Chairman of the Board. *Spectator,* pp. 1–3.

Bradt, W. R. (1972). *Current trends in public affairs.* New York: The Conference Board.

Brown, J. K. (1979). *The business of issues: Coping with the company's environments.* New York: Conference Board.

Brummett, B. (1990). Relativism and rhetoric. In R. A. Cherwitz (ed.), *Rhetoric and philosophy* (pp. 79–103). Hillsdale, NJ: Lawrence Erlbaum Associates.

Brummett, B. (1995). Scandalous rhetorics. In W. N. Elwood (ed.), *Public relations inquiry as rhetorical criticism: Case studies of corporate discourse and social influence* (pp. 13–23). Westport, CT: Praeger.

Bryant, D. C. (1953). Rhetoric: Its function and its scope. *Quarterly Journal of Speech, 39*, 401–424.

Buchholz, R. A. (1982). Education for public issues management: Key insights from a survey of top practitioners. *Public Affairs Review, 3*, 65–76.

Buchholz, R. A. (1985). *The essentials of public policy for management.* Englewood Cliffs, NJ: Prentice Hall.

Burke, K. (1937, January 20). Synthetic freedom. *New Republic, 89*, 365.

Burke, K. (1965). *Permanence and change* (2nd. revised ed.). Indianapolis: Bobbs-Merrill.

Burke, K. (1966). *Language as symbolic action.* Berkeley, CA: University of California Press.

Burke, K. (1969). *A rhetoric of motives.* Berkeley, CA: University of California Press.

Burke, K. (1973a). *The philosophy of literary form* (3rd. ed.) Berkeley, CA: University of California Press.

Burke, K. (1973b). The rhetorical situation. In L. Thayer (ed.), *Communication: Ethical and moral issues* (pp. 263–275). New York: Gordon and Breach.

Campbell, K. K. (1996). *The rhetorical act* (2nd. ed.). Belmont, CA: Wadsworth Publishing Company.

Capitalizing on social change. (1979, October 29). *BusinessWeek*, 105–106.

Chase, W. H. (1977). Public issue management: The new science. *Public Relations Journal, 32*(10), 25–26.

Chase, W. H. (1982, December 1). Issue management conference – a special report. *Corporate Public Issues and Their Management, 7*, pp. 1–2.

Chase, W. H. (1984). *Issue management: Origins of the future.* Stamford, CT: Issue Action Publications.

Cheney, G. (1992). The corporate person (re)presents itself. In E. L. Toth & R. L. Heath (eds), *Rhetorical and critical approaches to public relations* (pp. 165–183). Hillsdale, NJ: Lawrence Erlbaum Associates.

Cheney, G., & Dionisopoulos, G. N. (1989). Public relations? No, relations with publics: A rhetorical-organizational approach to contemporary corporate communications. In C. H. Botan & V. T. Hazleton, Jr. (eds), *Public*

relations theory* (pp. 135–157), Hillsdale, NJ: Lawrence Erlbaum Associates.

Cherwitz, R. A., & Hikins, J. W. (1986). *Communication and knowledge: An investigation in rhetorical epistemology.* Columbia, SC: University of South Carolina Press.

Coates, J. F., Coates, V. T., Jarratt, J., & Heinz, L. (1986). *Issues management: How you can plan, organize and manage for the future.* Mt. Airy, MD: Lomond.

Coombs, W. T. (1998). The Internet as potential equalizer: New leverage for confronting social irresponsibility. *Public Relations Review, 24*, 289–303.

Crable, R. E., & Vibbert, S. L. (1983). Mobil's epideictic advocacy: 'Observations' of Prometheus-Bound. *Communication Monographs, 50*, 380–394.

Crable, R. E., & Vibbert. S. L. (1985). Managing issues and influencing public policy. *Public Relations Review, 11*(2), 3–16.

Cutlip, S. M., Center, A. H., & Broom, G. M. (2000). *Effective public relations* (8th ed.). Upper Saddle River, NJ: Prentice Hall.

Dinsmore, W. H. (1978). Can ideas be sold like soap? *Public Relations Quarterly, 23*(3), 16–18.

Druck, K. B. (1978). Dealing with exploding social and political forces. *Vital Speeches, 45*(4), 110–114.

Dutton, J. E. (1993). Interpretations on automatic: A different view of strategic issue diagnosis. *Journal of Management Studies, 30*, 339–357.

Dutton, J. E., & Ashford, S. J. (1993). Selling issues to top management. *Academy of Management Review, 18*, 397–428.

Dutton, J. E., & Duncan, R. B. (1987). The creation of momentum for change through the process of strategic issue diagnosis. *Strategic Management Journal, 8*, 279–295.

Dutton, J. E., & Jackson, S. E. (1987). Categorizing strategic issues: Links to organizational action. *Academy of Management Review, 12*(1), 76–90.

Dutton, J. E., & Ottensmeyer, E. (1987). Strategic issue management systems: Forms, functions, and contexts. *Academy of Management Review, 12*(2), 355–365.

Ehling, W. P., & Hesse, M. B. (1983). Use of 'issue management' in public relations. *Public Relations Review, 9*(2), 18–35.

Ehrbar, A. F. (1978). The backlash against business advocacy. *Fortune, 98*(4), 62–64; 68.

Ewing, R. P. (1987). *Managing the new bottom line: Issues management for senior executives.* Homewood, IL: Dow Jones-Irwin.

Fishbein, M., & Ajzen, I. (1975). *Belief, attitude, intention, and behavior.* Reading, MA: Addison-Wesley.

Fishbein, M., & Ajzen, I. (1981). Acceptance, yielding and impact: Cognitive processes in persuasion. In R. E. Petty, T. M. Ostrom, & T. C. Brock (eds), *Cognitive responses in persuasion* (pp. 339–359). Hillsdale, NJ: Lawrence Erlbaum Associates.

Fisher, W. R. (1985). The narrative paradigm: An elaboration. *Communication Monographs,* 52, 347–367.

Fisher, W. R. (1987). *Human communication as narration: Toward a philosophy of reason, value, and action.* Columbia, SC: University of South Carolina Press.

Fisher, W. R. (1989). Clarifying the narrative paradigm. *Communication Monographs,* 56, 55–58.

Fleming, J. E. (1980). Linking public affairs with corporate planning. *California Management Review,* 23(2), 35–43.

Foss, S. J., & Griffin, C. L. (1995). Beyond persuasion: A proposal for an invitational rhetoric. *Communication Monographs,* 62, 1995.

Fox, J. F. (1983). Communicating on issues: The CEO's changing role. *Public Relations Review,* 9(11), 11–23.

Gaunt, P., & Ollenburger, J. (1995). Issues management revisited: A tool that deserves another look. *Public Relations Review,* 21, 199–210.

Grunig, J. E., & Repper, F. C. (1992). Strategic management, publics, and issues. In J. E. Grunig (ed.), *Excellence in public relations and communication management* (pp. 117–157). Hillsdale, NJ: Lawrence Erlbaum Associates.

Hainsworth, B., & Meng, M. (1988). How corporations define issue management. *Public Relations Review,* 14(4), 18–30.

Heath, R. L. (ed.). (1988). *Strategic issues management: How organizations influence and respond to public interests and policies.* San Francisco: Jossey-Bass Publishers.

Heath, R. L. (1994). *Management of corporate communication: From interpersonal contacts to external affairs.* Hillsdale, NJ: Lawrence Erlbaum Publishers.

Heath, R. L. (1997). *Strategic issues management: organizations and public policy challenges.* Thousand Oaks, CA: Sage Publications.

Heath, R. L. (1998). New communication technologies: An issues management point of view. *Public Relations Review,* 24, 273–288.

Heath, R. L., & Cousino, K. R. (1990). Issues management: End of first decade progress report. *Public Relations Review,* 17(1), 6–18.

Kruckeberg, D., & Starck, K. (1988). *Public relations and community: A reconstructed theory.* New York: Praeger.

Lauzen, M. M. (1994). Public relations practitioner role enactment in issues management. *Journalism Quarterly,* 71, 356–369.

Lauzen, M. M., & Dozier, D. M. (1994). Issues management mediation of linkages between environmental complexity and management of public relations function. *Journal of Public Relations Research,* 6, 163–184.

Lentz, C. S. (1996). The fairness in broadcasting doctrine and the Constitution: Forced one-stop shopping in the 'marketplace of ideas.' *University of Illinois Law Review,* 271, 1–39.

Lukasik, S. J. (1981). Information for decision making. *Public Relations Quarterly,* 26(3), 19–22.

MacNaughton, D. S. (1976, December). Managing social responsiveness. *Business Horizons,* 19, 19–24.

Mangham, I. L., & Overington, M. A. (1987). *Organizations as theatre: A social psychology of dramatic appearances.* New York: Wiley.

Marx, T. G. (1986). Integrating public affairs and strategic planning. *California Management Review,* 29(1), 141–147.

Mitroff, I. I. (1983). *Stakeholders of the organizational mind: Toward a new view of organizational policy making.* San Francisco: Jossey-Bass.

Nelson, R. A., & Heath, R. L. (1986). A systems model for corporate issues management. *Public Relations Quarterly,* 31(3), 20–24.

O'Toole, J. E. (1975a). Advocacy advertising – act II. *Cross Currents in Corporate Communications,* No. 2, pp. 33–37.

O'Toole, J. E. (1975b). Advocacy advertising shows the flag. *Public Relations Journal,* 31(11), 14–16.

Pfeffer, J. (1981). *Power in organizations.* Boston: Pitman.

Pincus, J. D. (1980). Taking a stand on the issues through advertising. *Association Management,* 32(12), 58–63.

Post, J. E. (1978). *Corporate behavior and social change.* Reston, VA: Reston.

Post, J. E. (1979). Corporate response models and public affairs management. *Public Relations Quarterly,* 24(4), 27–32.

Prior-Miller, M. (1989). Four major social scientific theories and their value to the public relations researcher. In C. H. Botan & V. Hazleton, Jr. (eds), *Public relations theory* (pp. 67–81). Hillsdale, NJ: Lawrence Erlbaum Associates.

Public Affairs Council. (1978). *The fundamentals of issue management.* Washington, DC: Public Affairs Council.

Public Relations Society of America. (1987). Report of Special Committee on Terminology. *International Public Relations Review,* 11(2), 6–11.

Quintilian, M. F. (1951). *The institutio oratoria of Marcus Fabius Quintilianus* (C. E. Little, Trans.). Nashville, TN: George Peabody College for Teachers.

Renfro, W. L. (1993). *Issues management in strategic planning.* Westport, CT: Quorum Books.

Rorty, R. (1979). *Philosophy and the mirror of nature.* Princeton, NJ: Princeton University Press.

Ross, I. (1976). Public relations isn't kid glove stuff at Mobil. *Fortune,* **94**(9), 106–111: 196–202.

Schmertz, H. (1986). *Good-bye to the low profile: The art of creative confrontation.* Boston: Little, Brown.

Sethi, S. P. (1976a). Dangers of advocacy advertising. *Public Relations Journal,* **32**(11), 42, 46–47.

Sethi, S. P. (1976b, Summer). Management fiddles while public affairs flops. *Business and Society Review,* No. 18, pp. 9–11.

Sethi, S. P. (1977). *Advocacy advertising and large corporations: Social conflict, big business image, the news media, and public policy.* Lexington, MA: D. C. Heath.

Simons, H. W. (1983). Mobil's system-oriented conflict rhetoric: A generic analysis. *Southern Speech Communication Journal,* **48**, 243–254.

Sneath, W. S. (1977). Managing for an uncertain future. *Vital Speeches,* **43**(7), 196–199.

Spitzer, C. E. (1979). Where are we getting all this information and what are we doing with it? *Public Relations Journal,* **35**(2), 8–11.

Sproule, J. M. (1989). Organizational rhetoric and the public sphere. *Communication Studies,* **40**, 258–265.

Stroup, M. A. (1988). Identifying critical issues for better corporate planning. In R. L. Heath (ed.), *Strategic issues management: How organizations influence and respond to public interests and policies* (pp. 87–97). San Francisco: Jossey-Bass.

The corporate image: PR to the rescue. (1979, January 22). *BusinessWeek,* pp. 47–61.

Thomas, K., Swaton, E., Fishbein, M., & Otway, H. J. (1980). Nuclear energy: The accuracy of policy makers' perceptions of public beliefs. *Behavioral Science,* **25**, 332–344.

Tucker, K., Broom, G., & Caywood, C. (1993). Managing issues acts as bridge to strategic planning. *Public Relations Journal,* **49**(11), 38–40.

Wallace, K. R. (1963). The substance of rhetoric: Good reasons. *Quarterly Journal of Speech,* **49**, 239–249.

Weaver, R. M. (1953). *The ethics of rhetoric.* Chicago: Henry Regnery Company.

Weaver, R. M. (1970). *Language it sermonic* (ed. by R. L. Johannesen. R. Strickland, & R. T. Eubanks). Baton Rouge, LA: Louisiana State University Press.

Zraket, C. A. (1981). New challenges of the information society. *Public Relations Quarterly,* **26**(3), 12–15.

CHAPTER 5

Robert L. Heath

Shifting foundations:
public relations as relationship building*

Heath's Introduction to Section 1 of *Handbook of Public Relations* is reproduced below. Naturally it relates to that particular collection of various authors' articles, but his Introduction is of considerable value in itself, touching as it does on issues that are relevant to the debate on public relations. See Sue Wolstenholme's Introduction to this Digest on p. ix.

Section 1 of the handbook addresses the very broad question: What is public relations – how *do* we define the discipline? Academics delight in using that question to initiate the first class session of an academic semester. It is asked during job interviews and appears on internship and scholarship applications. Although some definitions persist, even a casual review of the professional and academic literature of public relations suggests that answers to the question change over time.

Authors who have contributed to this section of the handbook were not specifically charged with the task of answering that question. Nevertheless, the themes they addressed are sufficiently basic that their answers to the question are implied in their contributions to this section. The section is intended to press each reader to rethink his or her definition of the field. Reading this section might lead each of us to come away believing that our definition – the answer to the question – has become more blurred than clarified. Each chapter raises issues ignored and slighted in the previous chapters. Like a good mystery, just as we think we have the clues sorted out, a new one is revealed in each chapter in this section.

Worth noting is the fact that very little discussion in this section addresses the use of public relations to promote and protect the image or reputation of an organization relevant to product or service publicity or promotion. This section focuses more on the rationale for using public relations to reduce the cost of conflict than for increasing awareness of an organization's products or services or for motivating buyers to purchase them, donors to contribute to nonprofit projects, or lawmakers to fund governmental projects. Academic discussions tend to address public policy issues relevant to advancing harmony between organizations and publics, whereas practitioners spend the bulk of their time dealing with other dynamics of the marketplace. Most professionals base their practice on attracting buyers, protecting or promoting image, promoting donations, and/or attracting tax funding to various governmental agencies and projects. An evening spent at an awards banquet of the Public Relations Society of America or the International Association of Business Communicators gives a much different view of the field than is reflected in this section.

Scholars are more interested in conflict reduction as the rationale for public relations than in the ability of public relations to help organizations generate market share and income – revenue, donations, or funding. Scholars who have contributed to this section might defend this bias by offering a *cost* reduction paradigm as the foundation for a *revenue generation* paradigm. Proponents of this line of reasoning might suggest that people (markets, audiences, publics, stakeholders, stakeseekers, and constituents) like to do 'business' with organizations (for-profit, nonprofit,

and governmental) that meet (do not violate) their expectations and that also create and maintain harmonious, mutually beneficial relationships. Therefore, a relationship development rationale for public relations can justify a revenue enhancement paradigm, but probably more indirectly than is assumed by many practitioners who devote attention to media relations, publicity, and promotion.

Concerns and intellectual or professional choices force us to think about the rationale for public relations – the definition of the discipline. How do practitioners justify their staff and line functions in organizations? What roles do they play in society? Do they add material value to organizations while, or perhaps because of, adding value to society? Are they more than flack masters and spin doctors?

To address those questions, many considerations must be made. One consideration centers on where we have come from and where we are going. In the simplest sense, we have come from mass communication (often limited to journalism) origins and are becoming something much more than that, both in terms of communication tools and in terms of the intellectual rationale for the discipline.

The mass media rationale can limit the vision of the discipline to an interest in message design and dissemination to achieve awareness (publicity and promotion at their best), to inform, and to persuade – even manipulate. Carried to its extreme, that mass communication view embraces the engineering of consent and other narrowly self-interested utilitarian, functional outcomes as the underpinning principles of the discipline. Indeed, a case can be made that each of the chapters in this section reacts to and rejects that rationale of public relations. One underpinning assumption in this section is that corporations tend to be bad and engage in public relations either to mask that evil nature or to be responsive to community expectations of a better vision of corporate performance.

If the chapters in this section indicate future directions that the discipline should and will take, then one can conclude that engineering of consent is the past, probably in practice as well as in theory. Shifting foundations for the discipline suggest that a new set of terms is the heart and soul of current intellectual ferment. The emerging vocabulary of the new definition of the discipline includes the following: relationships, shared control, trust, social capital, shared meaning, argumentativeness, listening, openness, mutually beneficial relationships, multiple publics (stakeholders and stakeseekers), epistemological issues of fact, axiological issues of value, ontological issues of choice-based actions, chaos in place in linearity, cognitive involvement, legitimacy gap, problem recognition, constraint, power, and collaborative decision making. The heart of the new view of the practice of public relations is the mutually beneficial relationships that an organization needs to enjoy a license to operate. Instead of engineering acceptance of a product or service, the new view of public relations assumes that markets are attracted to and kept by organizations that can create mutually beneficial relationships. Likewise, activists are less likely, as is government, to punish organizations that establish mutually beneficial relationships with them.

For this reason, no term is more important to understanding relationships than is *community*. Many of the chapters in this section stress the role that community plays as independent and dependent variables in the practice, theory, and research of public relations. Despite its positive implications, we know that 'community' can become a hegemonic tool that an advocate uses to claim a privileged definition of community (e.g., 'You cannot seek to protect owls because this community needs the jobs provided by the timber industry,' 'You cannot attack tobacco because this community needs its revenue').

And so, we turn our attention to themes that feature relationships. J. Grunig recaps and expands his interest in the ethical practice of public relations. Centering attention on publics as the basis for stakeholder relations, his analysis relies on principles of systems theory to offer solutions to the problems that organizations – primarily commercial ones – create for their publics. Grunig has searched for an approach that is capable of recognizing, or even empowering, the publics who are seeking to influence the actions, statements, and policies of organizations.

The key to creating and maintaining beneficial and harmonious relationships, Grunig reasons, is high-quality communication processes – more symmetrical than asymmetrical. So long as some part of a system is out of balance with another of its parts, corrective forces are going to be at work. Thus, public relations needs to be one, if not the major, corrective force. In the latest advance of this perspective on public relations, Grunig opts for mixed-motive responses by organizations to their publics. The quality of these responses should constitute the rationale for the practice and pedagogy of public relations by excellent organizations. An excellent organization exhibits characteristics that make it a more positive part of its larger system.

Thus, to achieve harmony, the organization might constantly adapt itself to the ethical preferences of its publics. Awareness that critics doubt the wisdom of asking organizations to sacrifice their interests for those of their publics has led Grunig to modify his theoretical perspective to champion a mixed-motive approach to reconciling interests in conflict. This advance in theory recognizes the reality that public relations practitioners are expected to advance the interests of their organizations rather than easily abandon them in deference to the interests of its publics. In this sense, public relations is a professional practice that helps organizations and publics to

understand each other's interests. Once these interests are understood, efforts can be made to blend them or at least reduce the conflict by helping the publics and the organizations to be less antagonistic toward each other. We have the predicate that the win-win approach to conflict resolution is preferred. Thus, a systems approach supplies a process rationale for public relations, but it does not explain the roles that ideas and words play in ethical harmony-building activities.

To establish a more embracing rationale for public relations, Heath draws on the rhetorical heritage, which in Western thought reaches back to the golden age of Greece and the Roman Empire to draw on the works of Plato, Aristotle, and other thinkers who followed their leadership. These rhetorical theorists pondered how being a good and articulate spokesperson is essential to society – the community. In that way, a rhetorical perspective strengthens or even replaces some aspects of the systems theory underpinnings of public relations. Rhetorical theory can explain and guide the actions and discourse tactics that key players use to strategically maneuver to be in harmony with one another. A rhetorical foundation for public relations can explain how statements count in the dialogue by which individual and collective ideas are formed. By this logic, we can explain the constructive roles that facts, values, and policies play in the marketplace and public policy arena.

A rhetorical approach to public relations justifies the proposition that organizations build effective relationships when they adhere to the best values – those most admired by the community of interest – as a first step toward being effective communicators. Once they meet ethical standards – defined through dialogue with other members of their community – organizations can more effectively advocate their interests, which never are separate from or indifferent to the interests of their markets, audiences, and publics. A rhetorical rationale for public relations reasons that the limit of one ethical perspective is the presence of a more compelling one. The limits of the accuracy of one set of facts is the presence of a more compelling set. The limits of commercial and public policy is the presence of a more compelling policy. Thus, rhetoric is dialogic. Ideas and ethical positions are not privileged. Manipulation cannot sustain itself because others will disclose and vilify the manipulator. Selfish interests cannot prevail because advocates will persuasively advance their countervailing interests.

Rhetoric is the rationale of suasive discourse. It presumes that ideas are better for having been debated. Interests are clarified and protected through advocacy. Such advocacy is the stuff of public policy discourse, but once we find a rationale for this process by connecting the rhetorical heritage and enactment theory, we have an even stronger underpinning for the need for public relations as well as the rationale for its practice. Rhetorical enactment theory reasons that all of what an organization does and says is a statement. It is a statement that is interpreted idiosyncratically by each market, audience, and public. Whether in public or merely in the privacy of personal thought, individuals and collective publics can agree with, respond to, reject, or even ignore the statement enacted by the organization. Thus, public relations can draw on the claim that each organization makes statements that can build better relationships when they are agreeable to those markets, audiences, and publics whose interests are at stake because of the actions and statements of the organization. This theoretical perspective views rhetoric not as hollow talk or the strategy of merely telling people what they want to hear – either of which is manipulative. The rhetorical enactment approach to public relations reminds us that ideas count epistemologically, axiologically, and ontologically. By helping to discover and bring to bear the best facts, values, and policies, public relations can help to build mutually beneficial relationships that foster the well-being of community through the creation of social capital.

This rationale for using public relations to build community is advanced by Starck and Kruckeberg. Their attention focuses on the constructive or destructive roles that corporations play in domestic and international communities. This line of reasoning, Starck and Kruckeberg contend, is even more important as the new century gives us reason to reflect on the extent to which the actions and policies of corporations narrowly advance their own interests or more fully add value to the communities in which they operate. Do corporations seek to work cooperatively with communities, or do they dominate those communities? How that question is answered defines the quality of the communities in which they operate and challenges public relations practitioners to defend the quality of communities. Setting high standards for the ethical operation of businesses and the responsible practice of public relations, Starck and Kruckeberg end their chapter with a challenge: 'Corporations must recognize that the greatest stakeholder – the ultimate environmental constituency – is society itself, to which such corporations are ultimately and irrefutably answerable' (p. 59). Public relations practitioners are charged with learning how to communicate *with*, rather than *to*, their publics. Organizations operate by consent of communities, their ultimate stakeholders.

To better respond to community interests, practitioners need to know what those interests are. They need to be able to hear society – to understand and appreciate the opinions that are on the minds of people whose goodwill is vital for the mandates of their organizations. These principles grow out of rhetoric, systems, and community. To address issues central to these concerns, Leichty and Warner reason that the thoughts of society break into

cultural topoi. Topoi is a concept that was used by classical rhetoricians to express the collective and embracing thoughts that lead people to draw one set of conclusions as opposed to another. People arrive at different conclusions because they subscribe to different cultural topoi.

To adjust organizations to society and to adjust society to organizations require an understanding of how the substance of both agrees or is in conflict. Cultural topoi are zones of meaning. Some are shared, and others are in conflict – or at least appear to be. One of the daunting challenges of public relations practitioners is to find points of agreement and to work toward consensus by increasing agreement and reducing disagreement. Understanding these topoi can help practitioners to understand where the opinions of organizations can be adjusted to society and where society can be adjusted to organizations. Thus, practitioners are prudent to take perspectives – to see their organizations' statements, policies, and actions from the perspectives of the cultural topoi held dear by their publics. Careful examination and prudent strategic use of cultural topoi can help practitioners to build agreement and reduce disagreement. This approach to public relations features the reality that organizations are in dialogue with their publics. This dialogue consists of a complex set of arguments that people – individually or collectively – use to achieve social capital. Social capital increases when organizations and people work to add value to society rather than expecting society to conform to their narrow self-interests.

This line of analysis is advanced by McKie, who asks scholars and practitioners to abandon a linear, 'old scientific' approach to the study and practice of public relations. A linear, old scientific approach is narrowly self-interested, and for that reason, it decenters society and destroys the quality of relationships. McKie calls for practitioners and scholars to become interested in the 'new science,' which he believes enriches thought and strategic choices because it acknowledges the diversity of complexity and the nonlinearity of chaos. The weakness of the old linear science of public relations, McKie contends, is a false sense that the skilled practitioner can understand and control the process. That approach to public relations was epitomized by Edward Bernays' belief that practitioners could and should engineer consent. Such incentives are driven by the dysfunctional desire to control rather than adjust to opinions, a desire that is frustrated by the complexity of diverse opinions, values, and interests. The inherently weak linear approach assumes that opinions and actions of key publics can be known and controlled. Instead of taking that dysfunctional approach, practitioners and scholars need to embrace 'continuous adaptation to unexpected changes in circumstances and timetables' (p. 90) – the principles of complexity and chaos.

Instead of seeking to control publics, the paradigm of the discipline has come to feature strategies that foster trust and build community. As R. Leeper demonstrates, society is stronger when individual interests are melded into community interests. Used manipulatively, community can stifle individualism through prescriptions of the following type: Do this or do not do this in the 'name of community.' Community can be a tyranny manipulated to the interests of some through language. The ideology of sound collectivism, communitarianism, reasons that society becomes stronger when individuals and organizations shoulder the responsibility of blending their visions with other visions to define the ends of society. Individual responsibilities and rights are made real and whole by blending into community. 'Community is seen as necessary to the development of the individual' (p. 97), reasons Leeper. Thus, public relations is challenged to define itself as a professional practice that stresses 'commitment to and the quality of relationships, a sense of social cohesion, the importance of core values and beliefs, balancing rights and responsibilities, citizen empowerment, and a broadening of perspective so as to reduce social fragmentation' (p. 99). If such a challenge is valuable for the practice of public relations in any community (including the community of each country), then it is even more important as we seek to forge a global community. Communitarianism is a challenge not for organizations to expect communities to accept them or for communities to demand unreasonable contributions by organizations. The challenge of public relations is to use rights and responsibilities to balance interests and resolve conflicts so that communities become better places for the individuals – human or corporate.

Adding his voice to those advocating a relationship approach to public relations, Coombs challenges scholars and practitioners to search for variables that define the quality of relationships and also can predict qualitative changes in such relationships. Coombs wants scholars and practitioners to look beyond the principles of mass communication as the rationale for defining the discipline. Rather than relying on the mass dissemination of information and influence, building relationships stresses the virtue of harmony and the blending of stakes and stakeholders into mutually beneficial arrangements. Coombs reasons that 'excellence suggests that communication helps the organization not only to understand but also to negotiate expectations' (p. 112). Thus, the dominant model of public relations based on interpersonal communication theory sees the practice as chat, conversation, and accommodation to build mutual benefit between the engaged parties. This paradigm moves us beyond a linear mass communication approach. Dialogue replaces monologue in the advancement of public relations theory and practice.

At times, scholars and practitioners might err by thinking that the practice is defined by dialogue between one organization and one public. Some leading research and theory might even make that mistake. Addressing the need for a multipublic approach to public relations, Springston and Keyton draw on the literature of group dynamics. A group is a composite of individuals, each of whom has ideas, facts, values, and policy preferences that may agree or disagree with those of others in the group. Recognizing this dynamic principle of groups, theorists have worked to explain how groups can achieve consensus despite these types of differences. That line of research and analysis is vital to the practice of public relations. The organization using public relations often is confronted by the prospect that two or more publics vital to its future do not agree with each other and might agree or disagree with the organization on key points.

The call for community as the dominant paradigm of public relations must acknowledge that community exists through the comanagement of agreement and disagreement of multiple complementary and competing perspectives. Springston and Keyton discuss how such agreement and disagreement can be identified and used to work toward mutually beneficial outcomes. The authors demonstrate how field dynamics theory complements and refines other theories to better understand a contingency-based negotiation perspective of public relations. Calling for community is easy. Understanding how to achieve it is more difficult. Positions need to be blended and compromised. Stakes need to be exchanged. Interests need to be advanced, as well as sacrificed, in a steady march toward the forging of mutually beneficial relationships.

Such relationships result from dialogue between organizations and publics. This is a well-established theme in the definition of the discipline. What is less well understood is the nature of publics and the dynamics of their relationships with key organizations. According to Leitch and Neilson, publics demonstrate unique (relatively minor to dramatically different) lifeworlds, and they accomplish different amounts of internal and external network positioning. For this reason, publics seek to define who they are, what they believe, and the role they play in the dynamic process of policy formation in society. Leitch and Neilson reason that researchers make mistakes if they assume that publics are defined only by the organizations that are responding to them. Prudent public relations practice and theory acknowledge the unique defining efforts of publics to advocate important lifeworld perspectives and to play power roles in public policy formation.

Publics influence the practice of public relations. They support or criticize organizations on their own terms and with their own power dynamics. Consequently, they must be enjoined in dialogue based on who they are rather than merely on who the organizations (which are under attack) define them to be. In this way, Leitch and Neilson advocate that theory and practice of the discipline can be enriched by developing a public-centered view of the practice rather than looking essentially at organizations (which are under attack) and taking an organization-centered view of the practice. The interests of the organization and of community may be advanced if the practitioner can prudently understand, appreciate, and champion the perspectives and interests being asserted by each public. The interests of the organization and community at large can be enhanced if each public is embraced and its structure is incorporated into the larger power and decision-making structure of the community. Public relations is most constructive when practitioners approach each public from its unique point of view rather than from that of the organization or the community at large. Public relations is a means for fostering dialogue so that the players come into meaningful contact to resolve differences and advance individual and collective interests.

Joining the discussion of publics, Vasquez and Taylor review the origins of that concept as the foundation for better understanding what publics are and the role that they play in the rhetorical dialogue of society. A rhetorical rationale for public relations is supported by the view that a public is a 'rhetorical community that develops a group consciousness around a problematic situation' (p. 151). In this process, members of the public function as 'homo narrans' – people who share a narrative view of life and who enact that view in concert (conflict and cooperation) with others who enact similar or competing narratives. Thus, the substance of each public – what it believes and says – reflects its narrative view of reality that it creates through discussions that help members recognize that they have had similar experiences and so share narratives and the opinions that make those narratives unique. Whereas Leichty and Warner focus on cultural topoi, Vasquez and Taylor use homo narrans theory to explain how individuals use communication to 'first become and then function as a public' (p. 146). The rhetoric of public relations is a dynamic clash of narratives that can require that negotiation occurs to resolve differences and achieve mutually beneficial outcomes.

As McKie suggests, the dynamics of public relations can occur in a chaotic environment fraught with complexity. Chaos and complexity are key concepts that help us to understand the dynamics of crises. Practitioners who are responsible for making comments during a crisis are wise to understand and attempt to accommodate to the chaos and complexity that they cannot manage but might be able to mitigate. Seeger, Sellnow, and Ulmer set themselves to the task of defining the discipline from a crisis response mode. Crises can occur. They can be poorly managed and

thereby become issues. Issues can be poorly managed and, consequently, become crises. Thus, public relations seeks orderly responses to a disorderly environment. Rather than embracing a manipulative information and opinion control model of crisis response, Seeger et al. suggest that an organization experiencing a crisis is prudent to make open, timely, informed, and consistent responses. Public relations needs to help the community interested in the crisis to form a narrative – homo narrans – that allows interested parties to understand the crisis and to foretell its happy conclusion – '. . . all lived happily ever after.'

The positions taken in this section dramatically change the paradigm of public relations. The underpinning assumption is that public relations is a relationship-building professional activity that adds value to organizations because it increases the willingness of markets, audiences, and publics to support them rather than to oppose their efforts. Will this view of public relations sustain itself and live up to its promise? In one sense, only time will tell. Scholarship and practice grow as individuals put their minds to the task of improving the discipline. To assess how well the practice is going, the editors of the handbook invited Cheney and Christiansen to reflect on the chapters that were devoted to defining the discipline. This gives our diagnosis and prescription the benefit of a 'second opinion.' Just as patients are prudent to request a second opinion, scholars also can benefit from independent review of the evidence. So, we ask of Cheney and Christiansen: Are we healthy, and what prescriptions are necessary for recovery and good health?

This section of the handbook is devoted to defining the field of public relations. Cheney and Christiansen believe that this section largely accomplishes that goal but also falls short in several key ways. Their diagnosis and prescriptions are likely to help jar academics and leading practitioners to continue to refine their thinking on several key challenges. Thus, they argue that public relations theory and research need to address, rather than gloss over or dismiss, issues of power and influence that is exerted by and against corporations. This body of literature also needs to differentiate more clearly the roles and responsibilities of marketing, advertising, and public relations. The discussion would be enriched by close analysis of the role of public relations in the struggle for democracy in cultures that are dominated by, or at least largely biased toward, corporatism. The authors caution against limiting public relations definitions to principles that feature a Western rationalist set of assumptions. Can we take a nonmanagerial approach to public relations and thereby discover a research agenda that features public relations as a discipline that helps to liberate and foster the human spirit and identity? That is a daunting challenge. It might shape the agenda of the next generation of scholarly output.

Audiences, stakeholders, publics*

Learning outcomes

By the end of this chapter you should be able to:

■ describe and compare various concepts of the audience

■ evaluate and compare theories of stakeholders and publics

■ evaluate and contrast competing versions of these concepts, as used in public relations campaigns.

Structure

■ The passive audience

■ The active audience

■ Stakeholders and publics

■ New thinking on publics

* Chapter 11 in *Exploring Public Relations* Second Edition, edited by Ralph Tench and Liz Yeomans (2009).

Introduction

How we plan and do public relations (PR) depends on our understanding of the nature of audiences, stakeholders or publics, i.e. the theories of audiences, stakeholders or publics that we hold. These in turn are an integral part of our understanding, or theories, of PR and communication. People working in PR, whether academics or practitioners, understand these objects or phenomena in different ways. Some of these different theories may be complementary or perhaps even contradictory.

Theories, concepts and models of audiences, stakeholders or publics, PR and communication are important because they help us understand and explain our PR campaigns and the situations these campaigns address. They determine how we plan and conduct PR. Different ways of understanding lead to different ways of planning and practising PR.

The way communicators imagine their audience affects the way they communicate with that audience; it changes the relationship.

This chapter contrasts the concepts of passive and active audiences before considering stakeholder theory and the situational theory of publics. A case study is presented which reflects on how publics have been or could be regarded. The chapter concludes by considering some new thinking about publics and their role in communication campaigns.

The passive audience

Communication and PR are directed at audiences and stakeholders or publics, often via the mass media. Mass media have traditionally been seen as having a mass audience. The concept 'mass' has been understood not merely as large in terms of numbers but rather as a large mass of isolated, anonymous and unorganised individuals. The negative connotations implied by the concept of 'mass' included the mass being seen to be unintelligent, having poor taste and lacking in judgement. Hence the mass was passive, and easily influenced and manipulated (Ang 1995).

European and American social theorists of the late nineteenth and early twentieth centuries saw mass society, mass culture and the mass audience as arising from industrialisation and urbanisation. Social change and the shift of populations from rural villages to industrial cities were believed to have brought about social disintegration and the breakdown of traditional ties (McQuail 2000: 37). Emile Durkheim (1893–1972), one of the nineteenth-century founding fathers of sociology, defined *anomie* as the condition prevalent in societies undergoing transformation, in which individuals suffered from a lack of standards or values, and an associated feeling of alienation and purposelessness. Thus the individual was isolated from their fellow men, unorganised and hence susceptible to negative influence and manipulation.

The masses thus had to be protected – as much from their own vulgarity as anything else. On the one hand, the development of industrial capitalist society had given rise to the vulnerable masses and the passive audience in need of protection. On the other hand, despite their vulgarity, lack of intelligence, taste and judgement, sheer numbers meant that the masses would take part in the transforma-

tion of a society undergoing structural change. In fact, the masses constituted much of society as workers, consumers and, after the establishment of universal suffrage in 1928 in the UK, as voters. Given their vulgarity and susceptibility to manipulation, this influence would inevitably be negative.

Matthew Arnold, the Victorian poet and literary critic, believed that high culture – i.e. the culture that was most highly valued by the elite and which he defined as 'the best which has been thought and said in the world' (1882) – had to be protected from vulgar, popular culture. Thus, traditional society had to be preserved from both the vulgar masses and the radical social changes that had produced these masses. The passivity and vulnerability that made protection of the masses necessary also meant that the masses could be both protected and protected against, by virtue of that very same passivity. The practice of PR in the UK in the early twentieth century sought to ensure and communicate the stability and continuity of traditional culture and society. The masses, their opinions and behaviour, had to be managed through education and propaganda (Moloney 2000). The then British Broadcasting Company was founded in 1922 on a public service broadcasting ethos of educating, informing and entertaining – i.e. the propagation of high culture to the mass audience. It reflects the view of the audience as passive, as both capable of being, and needing to be, influenced. John Reith, the first Director-General of the BBC, declared: 'It is occasionally indicated to us that we are setting out to give the public what we think they need – and not what they want – but very few people know what they want and very few what they need' (cited in Cain 1992: 40).

Similarly, John Grierson, the father of the documentary film, wrote:

The British documentary group began not so much in affection for film per se as in affection for national education . . . its origins lay in sociological rather than aesthetic aims . . . We . . . turned to the new wide-reaching instruments of radio and cinema as necessary instruments in both the practice of government and the enjoyment of citizenship. (Grierson 1946/1979: 78)

Thus John Reith and the BBC, as much as Stephen Tallents, John Grierson and the Empire Marketing Board, are key players in early twentieth-century PR in the UK, despite the myths of PR being distinct from the media it seeks to influence, and of the objectivity and impartiality of the BBC. Reith secretly wrote propaganda for the Conservative Baldwin government during the General Strike of 1926 and noted in his diaries that impartiality was a principle to be suspended whenever the established order and its consensus were threatened (cited in Pilger 2003). The object of the attention of this early twentieth century PR was an audience seen to be passive and thus both needing to be, and capable of being, influenced.

Defining the audience as passive

How can we understand the passiveness of the audience? The 'passive' audience (or at least the audience that is seen as being passive) passively responds to and accepts media content, rather than actively engaging intellectually and emotionally with it. Thus this passivity is defined primarily in terms of the strong effects that media communication is believed to have on the audience and the corresponding role assigned to the audience in communication. An example of contemporary concern surrounding strong **media effects** is the perceived ability of violent scenes shown on television or in film to incite violent acts among vulnerable audiences such as children and teenagers.

The development of the mass media, from newspapers to film and radio, was accompanied by both (a) the fear that the media would have powerful effects on audiences that would be detrimental to both audiences and society, and (b) the desire to use these media for propaganda to, and PR with, these audiences.

The *hypodermic model* or 'magic bullet theory' of media effects posits not only that the media have strong effects but that the effects of messages 'injected into' or 'shot at' passive, mass audiences would be uniform; much as the physical effects of being injected or shot at are uniform. Although perhaps no one, or at least not academics, actually believed in the hypodermic model – at least with respect to themselves – nonetheless in some sense the media are thought to have strong effects on audiences on account of their passivity. Thus governments, businesses and other elite interests communicate through the mass media to influence audiences. While at the same time, '*moral panics*' have arisen about the alleged effects of media aggravating crime and violence (Cumberbatch 2002).

The passivity of the audience, and the strong effects that media communication has on the audience, imply a correspondingly subordinate role assigned to the audience in communication. This understanding of media effects, the audience and communication is represented in the *linear* (also called the *transport, transmission* or *process) model* of communication, of which Shannon and Weaver's model (1949) is an example.

The linear model portrays the messages and meanings in communication as if they were physical things to be transported, much as the hypodermic model portrays media effects as physical effects mechanically inflicted. Carey (1989) writes that in the nineteenth century the word 'communication' referred both to the communication of messages as well as the transportation of people and goods by road, rail or ship. Thus the transport of the physical medium that messages were transcribed on, such as letters and books, was easily confused with the communication of messages and the meanings that were read into these messages.

The linear model of communication portrays messages and their meanings as being transported intact from sender to receiver like physical things (Schirato and Yell 2000). The sender is privileged in that they communicate and decide what the correct message and its meaning is. The receiver can merely passively accept what the sender says. Any difference in interpretation and opinion is taken to be misinterpretation and misunderstanding, as 'noise', a concept Weaver adapted from Shannon's original description of signal loss in telecommunications. The audience is limited to feedback, a concept from cybernetics merely describing a test of the success or failure of the sender's communication in order to allow adaptation of subsequent communication to ensure future success (Rogers 1994).

Raymond Williams, the father of media and cultural studies in the UK, wrote that 'there are in fact no "masses", but only ways of seeing people as masses' (1961: 281). The mass was either the elitist and moralistic way in which high culture saw popular culture in others or a way of seeing others in the formation and management of audiences to serve the interests of government, business and other elites. As such, we include others rather than ourselves in the mass audience. In the same way, strong media effects are often seen as third-person effects: they occur to others rather than ourselves. We personally are more sophisticated and less passive and vulnerable (Davison 1983).

Hermes (2002) states that academic research is conducted into how media influence works in order that we

Picture 6.1 A Moonie wedding: is this a passive audience? (*source*: © Gideon Mendel/Corbis)

may guard against it. Often enough, however, mass communications research has been motivated just as much, if not more so, to enable government, media and other businesses and their PR and advertising practitioners to take advantage of media influence over audiences. In fact, mass communication and market research share common roots in the work of Paul Lazarsfeld, at Princeton and then Columbia University in the USA in the 1930s and 1940s (Rogers 1994). Rather than reflect communication realistically, linear models were adopted to serve the strategic and political needs of political and business communication (Schirato and Yell 2000). (See Think about 6.1.)

The active audience

If audiences are neither mass nor, as Cutlip et al. (2000) claim, passive, what would an 'active' audience be? Hermes (2002) asks in what sense are audiences 'active', what is the nature of this audience activity? *Uses and gratifications theory* focuses attention not on what media do to audiences but rather, what *audiences do with media*. Media audiences are active in their choice of media. Media

choice is selective and motivated (i.e. rational and goal directed). Audiences use media in expectation of gratification of their individual social and psychological needs. Thus audience activity is seen not in the taking or making of meaning, but in the active and intentional selection of media to be used to satisfy individual needs. Audiences are formed on the basis of common needs for which satisfaction

Think about 6.2   Media consumption

■ How do you make your choice of media to consume? What motivates your choice?

■ Is your selection and use of media casual or motivated by a particular interest? How do you feel when your expectation of a medium – that this magazine will be entertaining, for example – is disappointed?

■ Finding out about party platforms to decide how to vote in the elections, picking out adult DVDs at your

local store, channel surfing on cable TV, browsing through magazines at your friend's house – are these active and motivated selection and use of media?

Feedback

Does selection and use of media describe the extent of your activity as an audience?

---

is sought. Such gratifications sought may include the need for information, the formation of personal identity, achieving social integration and interaction, and the desire for entertainment (Katz et al. 1974).

McQuail (1984) criticises uses and gratifications theory in that it does not reflect much media use, which tends to be circumstantial and weakly motivated, and also for its behaviourist and functionalist assumptions, i.e. it ignores what lies behind behaviour and functions. For example, uses and gratifications theory sees media use in terms of the individual and ignores the fact that media use is social; it also ignores media content and how audiences understand these and it implicitly acts as justification of media as it is, i.e. the media are seen as responsive to audience needs (Ang 1995). (See Think about 6.2.)

Understanding audience activity

Uses and gratifications theory limits audience activity to the selection of media to be used to satisfy needs. It does not engage with the role of audiences in understanding and creating meanings. However, a richer understanding of the audience and its activity needs to reflect the different and complex ways in which the media are used and what the media mean for users as a social and cultural activity (Ang 1995). Thus audience activity needs to be defined in terms of the active role audiences play in the construction of meaning that takes place in communication. The concept of the active audience rejects the privileging of the sender as the authority that decides the meaning of the message that is found in the linear model of communication.

Reception analysis is the study of audience activity in making or producing, not merely taking or consuming, meanings from media communication. The meaning of media messages is not fixed by the sender in the media text. Rather, meaning is constructed or negotiated by audiences when they interpret what they see, hear and read in

media communication. This active reading and interpretation of media content takes place within the social and cultural environments that audiences live in. The context of meaning production includes the social power relations that audiences are in. Thus the construction of meaning and the audience use of media takes place within, and is integrated into, the circumstances of everyday life (Ang 1995; Schirato and Yell 2000).

This understanding of the active audience and communication is represented in the cultural model of communication, or the idea of communication as culture (Carey 1989; Schirato and Yell 2000). Culture is understood as systems of meaning consisting of rules, conventions that constitute communication practices. Communication is the practice of producing and negotiating meanings. The particular social and cultural contexts that audiences live in depend on factors such as class, ethnicity, age, gender, sexual preference, etc. and the power relations that these imply.

In contrast to the unique meanings that messages are supposed to have in the linear model of communication, communication as culture asserts the *polysemy of communication*, i.e. messages are always open to different possible interpretations. Stuart Hall's (1973/1980) encoding/decoding model classifies these different possible meanings that can be read into a message into preferred, negotiated and oppositional 'readings':

■ Preferred or dominant readings are in agreement with the sender's intentions.

■ Oppositional readings disagree with and reject the sender's message.

■ Negotiated readings represent a compromise in partial agreement with the sender's meanings.

Thus the understanding of communication as culture distinguishes between the audience misunderstanding the intentions of the sender, on the one hand, and the audience understanding but choosing to read the message in

Think about 6.3　　Alternative readings

In the 2005 general election campaign, the then prime minister of Britain, Tony Blair, wrote an open letter to *Daily Mirror* readers (6 April 2005). He wrote that those who voted for Labour were the people who ended Conservative party rule in 1997 and 2001. He asserted that Labour had since built a more prosperous and fairer Britain, with low inflation, mortgage rates and unemployment, better public services and lower crime. Blair wanted to further extend opportunity and continue to protect Britain from security threats. There may have been big disagreements, e.g. over Iraq, but voters who wanted Britain to continue moving forward rather than go back to the Conservatives should vote Labour:

■ What was Blair's message? Who (different possible groups) might accept the preferred reading of Blair's message?

■ What would oppositional and negotiated readings of Blair's message look like? Who might hold these oppositional and negotiated readings?

■ Would anyone or any group that may have suffered as a result of Blair's policies, e.g. parents/spouses/children who have lost children/spouses/parents who served in Iraq subscribe to Blair's preferred reading?

■ Would anyone or any group that may have benefited as a result of Blair's policies, e.g. people who have seen the kind of improvements described in his letter, not subscribe to Blair's preferred reading?

---

opposition to the sender's interpretation on the other. It does not assume that audience readings different from the sender's are in fact misunderstandings and miscommunication, i.e. 'noise'. On the contrary, the very nature of communication as culture means that messages will inevitably be, at least to some extent, read and interpreted differently by different people because of each person's specific contexts. Not only is there no necessary correspondence between the sender's and the audience's meanings, there is, of necessity, at least some difference in meanings offered and accepted. The problem presented by the linear model is turned on its head – what needs to be explained is not so much difference but rather agreement in the construction of meaning. For if the preferred or dominant reading prevails, it does so through the limits and constraints imposed by power (Ang 1996; Schirato and Yell 2000). (See Think about 6.3.)

Audience activity and media effects

The long history of research into media effects has not resulted in a consensus among media scholars on the strength or nature of the influence that the media may have over audiences. Perhaps Schramm et al. (1961: 13) sum up media effects research best:

For some children under some conditions, some television is harmful. For other children under the same conditions, or for the same children under other conditions, it may be beneficial. For most children under most conditions television is probably neither harmful nor particularly beneficial.

The failure to find powerful effects could be down to the complexity of the processes and the inadequacy of research designs and methods. This might mean not that media are without effects or influence but that these effects or influence are not of a direct causal nature along the lines of mechanical effects. McQuail (2000) believes that what he calls the 'no effect' myth arises from the undue concentration in the research undertaken on a limited range of effects, especially short-term effects on violent behaviour, instead of broader social and institutional effects. Thus research still seeks to identify potential effects of the media but conceptions of the social and media processes involved have been revised. There has been a shift of attention to long-term change in cognitions rather than attitudes and affect (feelings) and to collective phenomena such as climates of opinion, structures of beliefs, ideologies, cultural patterns and institutional forms of media provision and intervening variables of context, disposition and motivation. In other words, the potential effect of the media depends on an individual's circumstances and how these interact with complex social and cultural conditions.

Kitzinger (2002) suggests that rather than the narrow conception of media effects found in mass communications theory, the 'new effects research' on how the world is represented in the media, and the ideology and discourse that lie behind these representations, has proved more fruitful in understanding how the media affects audiences. Media representations of the world can influence how audiences understand and engage with that world they live in. Language and meaning structures and shapes our perception of reality, and how we define, understand and value the world around us.

Think about 6.4   The role of the media in everyday life

How do you understand and interpret fashion; the way you and others dress and look?

Is your understanding of fashion related to fashion magazines, television programmes and films? Is your understanding of fashion forged in negotiation with the

fashion ideas you are exposed to by the media? Do you modify the fashion messages you see (latest designs, this season's look, for example) in terms of your peer group (what others are wearing around you), your family (to shock or please them), your religion, national culture or other factors (as well as your budget)?

Understanding 'communication as culture' recognises that the media are influential. However, rather than strong media effects that affect a passive audience in a mechanical way, media influence is seen to involve audience participation and is negotiated. The most significant media effect is seen to be the role that media play in an audience's social construction of meaning. The media offer their messages and meanings to audiences. It is then up to the audience how they read these messages and the extent to which they incorporate these into their understanding or sense of reality of the world they live in (McQuail 2000). (See Think about 6.4.)

Stakeholders and publics

The concept of the stakeholder originates in political theory. Interest in the concept of the corporate stakeholder arose in the debate on corporate governance during the 1980s' climate of corporate takeovers in the USA (Freeman 1984). The debate was about making companies responsive to shareholders' interests but stakeholding ideas emerged as an alternative way of understanding the interests at stake. Stakeholders are those who have a stake or interest in a particular organisation, i.e. 'they depend on the organisation to fulfil their own goals and on whom, in turn, the organisation depends' (Johnson and Scholes 2002: 206). Thus stakeholders are those who influence or can influence the organisation, as well as those affected by it. An organisation's stakeholders would include its employees and their trade unions, financial investors, customers, suppliers, distributors, the local community, local and central government, industry groups and the media (see Figure 6.1).

The distinction between stakeholders and publics is not a sharp one. Sometimes both terms are used interchangeably. Others, like Grunig and Hunt (1984: 145) for instance, distinguish publics as stakeholders that face a problem or have an issue with the organisation. (See also Chapter 3.)

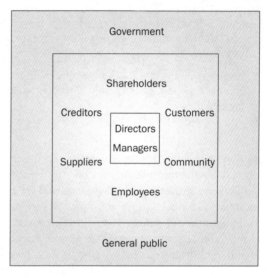

Figure 6.1 Stakeholders (*source*: Letza et al. 2004: 243)

Thus stakeholders are potential publics, the critical factor being the arrival of a problem or issue. The risk to the organisation is that when such a problem or issue arises, stakeholders organise to become publics and are able to affect the interests of the organisation. Some of McDonald's customers become a public when they become concerned about their diet and obesity, and organise to campaign for more healthy menus and government regulation of food advertising on television targeted at children. Rover workers at Longbridge, the UK car manufacturing plant, become a public when they organise to protest at the loss of their jobs.

Stakeholder mapping

Stakeholders should be considered at the first stage of strategic management, in environmental scanning and situation analysis to identify the consequences of the organisation's behaviour on the stakeholders and vice versa, to anticipate any possible issues and problems. Grunig and Repper (1992) see communication at the stakeholder stage as helping to develop the stable, long-term relationships that an organisation needs to build support and to manage conflict when issues and problems arise.

Relevant factors that are considered in the mapping of stakeholders include their possible impact on the organisation and hence their interests, expectations, needs and power. Individuals may belong to more than one stakeholder group. Employees often live in the local community where their employers are located and also own shares in the company.

Johnson and Scholes (2002), writing on corporate strategy, consider how likely stakeholders are to press their expectations on the organisation to suggest strategies to contain or manage stakeholders. They consider how much interest stakeholders have in potential issues and problems with the organisation, whether they have the means to push their interests and how predictable they would be.

They map the power of the stakeholders against both their level of interest in the issue and the predictability of their behaviour.

If the stakeholders have both a high level of power and interest, then they are key players crucial to the welfare of the organisation. If they are powerful but have merely low interest in the issue, the organisation would do well to keep things that way by keeping them satisfied as that would not require much effort. If they are highly interested but lack power, then all the organisation needs to do is merely to keep them informed. Likewise, powerful but unpredictable stakeholders present the greatest opportunity and threat to the organisation's interests. Thus in situation analysis, stakeholders are mapped and their importance weighted accordingly. (See Mini case study 6.1.)

Mini Case Study 6.1
Applying stakeholder mapping

Fast food companies and the obesity issue

In the past few years, government departments and agencies, MPs, non-governmental organisations (NGOs) and the health professions have raised concern about the growing obesity problem in the UK and the role of fast food companies such as hamburger chains. Concern has centred not just on the nature of the food products sold but how they have been promoted, particularly in television advertising.

How would a fast food company map and decide the relative importance of its various stakeholders in the obesity issue? What aims and objectives, and strategies and tactics did fast food companies adopt?

Stakeholders relevant to the obesity issue can be grouped into government departments and agencies, customers and potential customers, NGOs such as the Food Commission and the British Medical Association, other companies and trade bodies in the food and advertising industry (such as the Advertising Association and its Food Advertising Unit) and members of the public who were not customers.

These stakeholders are mapped in the matrix below according to their levels of power and interest. In addi-

tion, a '+' indicates that the stakeholder is broadly supportive of the fast food company on the issue, while a '−' indicates the opposite. One of the issues for fast food companies was the House of Commons' Health Select Committee's recommendation of a ban on the advertising of junk food to children being adopted in the government's White Paper on health and then subsequently becoming law. Both the Department of Health and government agencies such as the Food Standards Agency were in favour of stricter government regulation of junk food advertising. These were stakeholders that were both powerful and interested, but not supportive of the position of fast food companies.

Members of the food industry, i.e. other food companies, and industry bodies such as the Advertising Association were powerful and interested stakeholders that shared common interests with fast food companies on this issue. These were also supported by other powerful and interested stakeholders in government. The Department of Culture, Media and Sport was concerned about the impact of a junk food advertising ban on the revenues of the commercial television industry. Tessa Jowell, the then Culture Secretary, dismissed calls for restrictions early in the debate and called instead for the advertising industry and their clients in the food industry to use their creativity to help in anti-obesity campaigns. In particular, McDonald's responded with the Yum Chums, cartoon characters exhorting children to have a healthy diet and to exercise.

McDonald's also implemented changes to its menu. It reduced the salt in its fries, stopped the practice of *mini case study 6.1 (continued)*

super-sizing meals, and introduced a new menu including salads and fruits in March 2004. It introduced a new breakfast menu including oat porridge and bagels in October 2004. It also ran campaigns, such as 'McDonalds, but not as you know it', to promote these changes.

Such changes in the policies and products of fast food companies tell interested stakeholders, such as the government, NGOs, and the health and diet-conscious members of the public who may be customers, potential customers or potential activists, that some fast food companies offer a healthy menu (at least now, if not in the past), promote their food responsibly, are worthy of their custom and can be trusted to self-regulate their promotional activities.

		Level of interest	
		Low	High
Power	Low	Non-customers not conscious about health and diet	Health and diet-conscious non-customers (–) NGOs such as the Food Commission (–)
	High	(Potential) customers not conscious about health and diet	Other food companies and the food industry (+) Department of Culture, Media and Sport and government media agencies such as Ofcom (+) Department of Health and government health and food agencies such as the Food Standards Agency (–) Commons Health Select Committee (–) Health and diet-conscious (potential) customers (–)

The White Paper on health was published in November 2004. There was no ban on junk food advertising, just a promise to consult on working out a strategy on food promotion in the next few years. This outcome would have been the result of lobbying by those sympathetic to the food industry, both within and outside the government. However, the campaigns conducted by fast food companies consisting of both their actions and communications would have helped the case of the food industry.

Situational theory of publics

Stakeholders are contained, or at least relationships with them are managed, in order to prevent them developing into publics that may organise against the organisation. Grunig and Hunt's situational theory of publics (1984) examines why and when publics are formed and most likely to communicate, how their predicted communication and behaviour can be used to segment publics in order to provide a basis for deciding what strategy is most likely to achieve cognitive, attitudinal and behavioural effects in the publics (see Table 6.1). The theory sees stakeholders developing into publics when they recognise that an issue or problem affecting them exists and they see it as worth their while getting involved with the issue or problem. Latent publics do not as yet recognise the issue or problem they are facing with the organisation. Aware publics recognise that the issue or problem exists and active publics organise to discuss and respond to the issue

Latent publics	Groups that face a particular problem as a result of an organisation's action, but fail to recognise it.
Aware publics	Groups that recognise that a problem exists.
Active publics	Groups that organise to discuss and do something about the problem.

Table 6.1 The situational theory of publics (*source*: adapted from Grunig and Hunt 1984: 145)

or problem. Thus fast food customers who face obesity and health problems but who do not see it as a problem would constitute a latent public. It is only customers who are not only aware of the problem but also organise to act on the problem, e.g. changing their diet, campaigning for menu changes and regulation of advertising, that make an active public. It would thus be in the company's interests to address the issue while most of its customers are still latent or aware publics, rather than wait until the active public has reached sizeable numbers.

The situational theory further classifies publics on the basis of the range of issues to which they are responsive:

- Apathetic publics disregard all issues/problems.

- Single-issue publics are active on a small set of issues/ problems that has limited popular appeal (i.e. fringe activist groups).

- Hot-issue publics are active on a single issue that has significant appeal (e.g. the anti-war movement).

- All-issue publics are active across a wide range of issues/problems.

Both Johnson and Scholes' (2002) stakeholder mapping and Grunig and Hunt's (1984) situational theory of publics are classification or segmentation tools in the execution of strategy to manage and contain the impact of publics on organisations – they are practical techniques for realising publics as subjects that PR practitioners do things to. However, looked at another way, theories of publics and stakeholder analysis are vulnerable to Raymond Williams' charge that 'there are no masses, only ways of seeing people as masses' (1961: 281). (See Box 6.1 and Think about 6.5, overleaf.)

Mini case study 6.2 (overleaf) illustrates and summarises the various conceptions of audiences and stakeholders or publics that we have considered so far in this chapter. We then go on to look at new, alternative ways of thinking about publics.

New thinking on publics

The different ways of understanding audiences, stakeholders and publics – i.e. passive or active, nature of activity, their importance to and ability to affect the organisation – affect our understanding of communication and PR and hence the way we plan and conduct PR.

The starting point for alternative thinking on publics, different from the way Shell frames its publics as incompetent and hence ignorant (See Mini case study 6.2), has to be Williams' 'there are no masses, only ways of seeing people as masses' (1961: 281). Ways of seeing involve the exercise of power in the social construction of reality, i.e. that human beings make the world they live in. Karlberg (1996) and Moffitt (1994) claim that organisations see publics from the narrow perspective of their own interests rather than that of their publics.

To move away from this narrow perspective, and like Holtzhausen (2000), Chay-Nemeth (2001) asserts that the ethical practice of PR should focus on empowering and

Box 6.1

Stakeholders or publics?

Sometimes the words stakeholders and publics are used interchangeably, so what is the difference?

Grunig and Repper (1992: 125) describe the difference thus: 'People are stakeholders because they are in a category affected by decisions of an organisation or if their decision affects the organisation. Many people in a category of stakeholders – such as employees or residents of a community – are passive. The stakeholders who are or become more aware and active can be described as publics.'

'Publics form when stakeholders recognise one or more of the consequences (of the behaviour of the organisation) as a problem and organise to do something about it or them' (1992: 124).

As Davis (2004: 59) points out, 'publics sound more important than stakeholders'. However, he goes on to

say that some groups, for example pressure and cause-related groups, do not form out of a stakeholder mass: they exist as publics immediately because, by definition, they are active. Furthermore, it is clear that not all publics are active (Grunig himself recognises apathetic publics – Grunig and Repper 1992) and they are not always adversarial. Davis (2004: 59) defines the groups thus: 'Publics have an importance attached to them because of their specific interest and power, current and potential, while for stakeholders the levels of interest and influence are relatively lower and more generalised.'

The person regarded as largely responsible for stakeholder theory, Freeman (1984), accepts that 'the term means different things to different people' (Phillips et al. 2003: 479), but goes on to say that it encompasses a particular and close relationship between an organisation. His co-author Phillips (Phillips et al. 2003) differentiates between normative stakeholders (to whom an organisation has a direct moral obligation to look after their well-being, for example financers, employees and customers), and derivative stakeholders (who can harm or benefit the organisation, but to whom there is no direct moral obligation – for example, competitors, activists and the media).

Think about 6.5   Publics

Consider a recent PR campaign that you have come across, organised or been the target of.

■ How did the campaign view the publics involved? As latent, aware or active publics?

■ What publics do you belong to? How active are you in these roles?

Feedback

Does stakeholder mapping and/or the situational theory of publics view audiences and/or stakeholders/

publics as passive subjects that PR practitioners do things to? Or as active and hence needing to be managed and contained in the organisation's interests?

You might be a member of the following publics: student body, course member, group or society member, resident in an area near your place of study, ex-member of your school, place you grew up in, and so on. What factors affect your activity in these publics?

Mini Case Study 6.2
Shell's publics

How does Shell understand its publics, particularly in the Brent Spar case and the corporate recovery strategy Shell embarked on after Brent Spar?

In 1995, Shell's plans to dispose of the Brent Spar oil platform by sinking it 150 miles west of the Hebrides met with fierce opposition from Greenpeace Germany. The Greenpeace campaign attracted much attention and support from the media, European governments, Shell's customers and the public. Shell backed down and reversed its decision. It commissioned an independent survey by the Norwegian ship classification society, Den Norske Veritas, and looked at 200 possible options. It subsequently dismantled and recycled the platform, in part as a roll-on, roll-off ship quay in Norway (Varey 1997; Henderson and Williams 2001).

Varey asserts that Shell had made a perfectly rational decision and chosen the best, most practical option of sinking the platform on the basis of cost–benefit analysis of business, technical and environmental considerations. Various onshore and offshore abandonment options were considered. Rudall Blanchard Associates Ltd, an environmental consultancy, was commissioned to report on the environmental impacts of sinking the platform.

In contrast to Shell's scientific and technical rigour and objectivity, Varey describes the Greenpeace campaign as manipulation of both the media and 'people's feelings about . . . apparent injustice'. Nonetheless, public outcry driven by emotions and a lack of understanding of Shell's 'rational, scientifically sound decision' led to the reversal of that well-made decision (Varey 1997: 104–105). Similarly, Henderson and Williams (2001: 13), who have both been involved in PR for Shell, write of Shell's 'knowledge gap' problem in its corporate recovery

campaign. Its publics just did not understand Shell's values and approach, i.e. how good Shell really was, particularly on the environment and human rights. Further, facts alone were not enough and Shell had to engage the emotions of its publics.

Before you continue reading this case, answer the questions in Think about 6.6.

How justified is Varey's and Shell's view of Shell's publics? Varey praises Shell's analysis as 'apparently very thorough. Over four years was spent in getting DTI [i.e. British government's] approval for the plan.' But read between the lines and you will see that this was not an objective, scientific Shell against an emotional, irrational public. Shell spent four years lobbying the DTI, while Rudall Blanchard's environmental report was published only six months before the planned sinking. Thus what Shell lobbied for could not have been based on the technical evidence that might have justified its plans.

Varey tells us that Shell commissioned an independent survey, by the Norwegian ship classification society, Den Norske Veritas, only after the Greenpeace campaign. Instead of the several options considered earlier in its scientifically sound analysis, Shell was now looking at 200 possible options.

We can understand what Varey considers to be Shell's 'rational, scientifically sound decision' when he writes that Shell's analysis 'dealt only with whether the environmental measure was worth pursuing and deciding this on cost in a cost–benefit analysis'. In other words, it was not worthwhile for Shell to bear the costs when the benefits of an environmentally sound disposal did not accrue to, and environmental damage to the northwest Atlantic was not borne by, Shell.

Thus perhaps the publics' active and oppositional reading of Shell's actions was not simply misunderstanding and ignorance of Shell, nor simply to be dismissed as just so much 'noise' preventing Shell from being heard.

Think about 6.6 Shell's publics

How do Varey and Shell view Shell's publics?

■ Are these publics seen to be active or passive?

■ Are they seen to be intelligent, capable of rational, scientific reasoning?

■ Are they seen as easily influenced and manipulated by emotions?

■ Can they be rational and, at the same time, guided by their emotions?

■ Do these publics hold preferred, negotiated or oppositional readings of Shell on the environment?

■ Have these publics got the power and interest to affect Shell's fortunes?

■ How do Varey and Shell evaluate the competency of these publics to judge Shell?

giving voice to disempowered and silent publics. She goes on to suggest how this may be done in practical terms by a typology based not on the power, interest or actions of a public to affect the organisation, but on the ability of the public to participate in the issues in which they have a stake.

She conceives of a public as a political space or site where power plays out, material resources and discourses (i.e. ideas, concepts, language and assumptions) are produced and reproduced, exchanged and appropriated, to achieve social and political change or to maintain the status quo. Communication is not simply about information exchange but a practice of power relations. Hence publics are not merely senders or receivers of information but also producers and reproducers of meaning.

In her conception of publics and power, she applies Foucault's (1991) concept of governmentality, where people are disciplined through everyday discourses and practices that they perform voluntarily and take for granted as obvious and natural. Governmental discipline produces docile and passive publics.

She considers three historical conditions as the basis for a typology of publics:

Picture 6.2 A critical public is dissatisfied with the status quo. Here, Greenpeace's 'Save the Climate' balloon floats above a coal-fired power station (*source*: Corbis)

1 *resource dependency* – the extent to which a public depends on others for resources such as funds, information, training, education, the media and publicity

2 *discursive connectivity* – the extent to which one public shares in the discourse, ideas, concepts, language and assumptions of others and hence the potential for negotiation and competition with these others

3 *legitimacy* – the extent to which each public has the right to speak and act within its given role in the community.

She applies these conditions to publics in the HIV/AIDS issue in Thailand, to derive a typology of four publics: circumscribed, co-opted, critical, and circumventing publics. However, she states different cultural and historical conditions will yield different historical criteria for categorising publics.

A *circumscribed public* is highly dependent on others for resources. They find it difficult to enter into mainstream discourses. Their legitimacy to speak or act is limited by how others see their roles. Thai Buddhist monks involved in AIDS hospice work are a circumscribed public. They depend on the community and the state for their livelihood, and hence are pressured to conform to these interests. Hospice monks may be circumscribed because they lack funds to finance AIDS-related projects and have little access to the media. Their lack of education and training in science and counselling, and the framing of their spiritual training and knowledge as parochial is used by the state, the medical profession and non-governmental organisations (NGOs) in competition with the hospice monks, to justify their circumscription. Some community groups also maintain that monks should not be involved with AIDS as sexual conduct should be taboo to monks. Thus the limited legitimacy of the hospice monks to speak and act freely in the discourses of modern medicine and sexuality is related to how others see their role as monks.

A circumscribed public may remain so, or become a co-opted, critical or circumventing public if conditions are appropriate, e.g. a redistribution of resources and the cooperation of others.

A *co-opted public* behaves within limits prescribed by powerful others and hence has access to resources. They accept the legitimacy of the status quo and are not considered subversive or dangerous. Governmental organisations, non-governmental organisations and community groups may be examples of co-opted publics. Monks may be co-opted in confining themselves to teaching Buddhist meditation. They are awarded funds by the government, whereas monks who do hospice work are denied funding.

NGOs may be co-opted to agree with the circumscription of the monks from the medical sphere as they are competing with hospice monks for funds or legitimacy from medical quarters for their own projects. The need to secure state funding and legitimacy may compel NGOs to circumscribe less favoured publics. The legitimacy of co-opted groups is seldom disputed because they help to reproduce dominant discourses and practices. For example, the Thai government appealed to NGOs for endorsement to improve Thailand's international image in tourism.

A *critical public* is dissatisfied with the status quo. They may include medical staff, NGOs, AIDS patients opting for indigenous herbal treatments instead of modern medicine, communities who blame the government's tourism-orientated development policies for the thriving sex industry and monks resisting the roles set for them by the state and society. Critical publics face constraints such as dependency or competition with others for funding. Many critical publics rely on government or foreign funding.

There are many points of contention between critical publics and the state. They contend that state strategies on HIV/AIDS are misguided and budgets are poorly managed. Community activists have criticised the government's industrialisation and tourism policies. The confluence of rural migration, consumerism, the sex industry and tourism has aggravated the spread of AIDS to rural villages.

Legitimacy varies for each critical public. NGOs, community groups and AIDS patients have more legitimacy in their AIDS work than do the monks in hospice care. Critical publics compete not only for a redistribution of resources but also for the expansion of their discourse, and seek to establish their legitimacy. Co-option into state domination is one response to circumscription, the resistance of critical publics is another.

A *circumventing public* follows a critical public in resistance to governmentality. The docile citizen sacrifices their desired sexuality to the discipline of the norms and conventions of being a healthy citizen. A circumventing public resists this discipline by consciously or unconsciously engaging in behaviours considered deviant. However, their engagement behaviour is the result of material constraints such as economic poverty (e.g. prostitution to provide for the family).

Circumventing publics may include commercial sex workers, intravenous drug users and homosexuals. They seek out public resources only when absolutely necessary. Some AIDS patients prefer to use indigenous medicine rather than use state hospitals where disclosure of AIDS status is necessary. Others prefer to suffer in silence. Because of their high resource dependency, circumventing publics possess little legitimacy to speak for themselves. (See Think about 6.7.)

Think about 6.7

Rethinking publics

Consider a recent PR campaign that you have come across, organised or been the target of.

Would resource dependency, discursive connectivity and legitimacy be useful criteria on which to classify the publics in this campaign? What other factors might be useful criteria?

Would circumscription, co-option, critique and circumvention be a useful typology of these publics? What other types of public might be useful to map the campaign?

Feedback

Would such a different conception and classification of publics lead to a different kind of PR? How so?

Summary

In this chapter we have considered ideas of the passive and active audience and the nature of this passivity and activity. We then considered stakeholder theory, stakeholder mapping and Grunig and Hunt's situational theory of publics. We considered how these concepts are understood in practice by examining two cases.

We concluded by looking at how a different typology of publics may be useful for a different kind of PR that considers the interests of the publics that are the subjects of PR campaigns.

Bibliography

Ang, I. (1995). 'The nature of the audience' in *Questioning the Media: A critical introduction*, 2nd edition. J. Downing, A. Mohammadi and A. Sreberny-Mohammadi (eds). Thousand Oaks, CA: Sage.

Ang, I. (1996). *Living Room Wars: Rethinking media audiences for a postmodern world*. London: Routledge.

Arnold, M. (1882). *Culture and Anarchy: An essay in political and social criticism*, 3rd edition. London: Smith, Elder & Co.

Branston, G. and R. Stafford (2003). *The Media Student's Book*, 3rd edition. London: Routledge.

Branston, G. and R. Stafford (2006). *The Media Student's Book*, 4th edition. London: Routledge.

Cain, J. (1992). *The BBC: 70 years of broadcasting*. London: BBC.

Carey, J.W. (1989). *Communication as Culture: Essays on media and society*. London: Unwin Hyman.

Chay-Nemeth, C. (2001). 'Revisiting publics: A critical archaeology of publics in the Thai HIV/AIDS issue'. *Journal of Public Relations Research* 13(2).

Cohen, S. (1972). *Folk Devils and Moral Panics*. London: MacGibbon and Kee.

Cumberbatch, G. (2002). 'Media effects: Continuing controversies' in *The Media: An Introduction*, 2nd edition. A. Briggs and P. Cobley (eds). Harlow: Longman.

Cutlip, S.M., A.H. Center, and G.M. Broom (2000). *Effective Public Relations*, 8th edition. Upper Saddle River, NJ: Prentice Hall.

Davis, A. (2004). *Mastering Public Relations*. London: Palgrave.

Davison, W.P. (1983). 'The third-person effect in communication'. *Public Opinion Quarterly* **47**: 1–15.

Durkheim, E. (1893/1972). 'The division of labour in society'. Excerpts reprinted in *Selected Writings*. A. Giddens (transl. ed.). London: Cambridge University Press.

Foucault, M. (1991). 'Governmentality' in *The Foucault effect: Studies in governmentality*. G. Burchell, C. Gordon and P. Miller (eds). Chicago: University of Chicago Press.

Freeman, R.E. (1984). *Strategic Management: A stakeholder approach*. Boston: Pitman.

Grierson, J. (1946/1979). *Grierson on Documentary*. London: Faber & Faber.

Grunig, J.E. and T. Hunt (1984). *Managing Public Relations*. New York: Holt, Rinehart & Winston.

Grunig, J.E. and F.C. Repper (1992). 'Strategic management, publics and issues' in *Excellence in Public Relations and Communication Management*. Hillsdale, NJ: Lawrence Erlbaum Associates.

Hall, S. (1973/1980). 'Encoding/decoding' in *Culture, Media, Language: Working Papers in Cultural Studies, 1972–79*. Centre for Contemporary Cultural Studies (ed.). London: Hutchinson.

Henderson, T. and J. Williams (2001). 'Shell: Managing a corporate reputation globally' in *Public Relations Cases: International perspectives*. D. Moss and B. DeSanto (eds). London: Routledge.

Hermes, J. (2002). 'The active audience' in *The Media: An introduction*, 2nd edition. A. Briggs and P. Cobley (eds). Harlow: Longman.

Holtzhausen, D.R. (2000). 'Postmodern values in public rela-tions'. *Journal of Public Relations Research* **12**(1): 93–114.

Johnson, G. and K. Scholes (2002). *Exploring Corporate Strategy*, 6th edition. Harlow: Pearson Education.

Karlberg, M. (1996). 'Remembering the public in public relations research: From theoretical to operational sym-metry'. *Journal of Public Relations Research*, **8**(4): 263–278.

Katz, E., J.G. Blumler and M. Gurevitch (1974). 'Utilization of mass communication by the individual' in *The Uses of Mass Communication*. J.G. Blumler and E. Katz (eds). Newbury Park, CA: Sage.

Kitzinger, J. (2002). 'Media influence revisited: An intro-duction to the new effects research' in *The Media: An introduction*, 2nd edition. A. Briggs and P. Cobley (eds). Harlow: Longman.

Leitch, S. and D. Neilson (2001). 'Bringing publics into public relations: New theoretical frameworks for practice' in *Handbook of Public Relations*. R. Heath (ed.). Thousand Oaks, CA: Sage.

L'Etang, J. (1998). 'State propaganda and bureaucratic intel-ligence: The creation of public relations in 20th century Britain'. *Public Relations Review* **4**: 413–441.

Letza, S., X. Sun and J. Kirkbride (2004). 'Shareholding versus stakeholding: A critical review of corporate governance'. *Corporate Governance* **12**(3): 246–262.

McQuail, D. (1984). 'With the benefit of hindsight: Reflec-tions on uses and gratifications research'. *Critical Studies in Mass Communication* **1**: 177–193.

McQuail, D. (2000). *McQuail's Mass Communication Theory*, 4th edition. London: Sage.

McQuail, D. (2005). *McQuail's Mass Communication Theory*, 5th edition. London: Sage.

Moffitt, M.A. (1994). 'Collapsing and integrating concepts of public and image into a new theory'. *Public Relations Review* **20**(2): 159–170.

Moloney, K. (2000). *Rethinking Public Relations: The spin and the substance*. London: Routledge.

Moloney, K. (2006). *Rethinking Public Relations: PR pro-paganda and democracy*, 2nd edition. London: Routledge.

Phillips, R.A., R.E. Freeman and A.C. Wicks (2003). 'What stakeholder theory is not'. *Business Ethics Quarterly* **13**(4): 479–502.

Pilger, J. (2003). 'The BBC and Iraq: Myth and reality'. *New Statesman*, 5 December.

Rogers, E.M. (1994). *A History of Communication Study: A biographical approach*. New York: Free Press.

Schirato, T. and S. Yell (2000). *Communication and Culture: An introduction*. London: Sage.

Schramm, W., J. Lyle and E.B. Parker (1961). *Television in the Lives of Our Children*. Stanford, CA: Stanford University Press.

Shannon, C.E. and W. Weaver (1949). *The Mathematical Theory of Communication*. Urbana, IL: University of Illinois Press.

Varey, R. (1997). 'Public relations: the external publics con-text' in *Public Relations: Principles and Practice*. P. Kitchen (ed.). London: International Thomson Business.

Williams, R. (1961). *Culture and Society*. Harmondsworth: Penguin.

CHAPTER 7

Ralph Tench

Community and society: corporate social responsibility (CSR)*

Learning outcomes

By the end of this chapter you should be able to:

■ critically evaluate the role of organisations in their society/societies
■ define the concept of corporate social responsibility in the context of relevant regulatory frameworks
■ define and critically evaluate the role of ethics in business policy and practice
■ diagnose ethical problems and identify strategies for making ethical decisions in organisational/cultural contexts
■ appreciate the environmental complexities that influence organisational communication and public relations strategies.

Structure

■ Social and economic change
■ Sustainable business: corporate social responsibility (CSR)
■ Business case for corporate social responsibility: why be socially responsible?
■ Organisational responsibilities to stakeholders
■ Organisational responsibilities to society
■ Corporate responsibility and irresponsibility
■ Regulatory frameworks
■ Ethics and business practice

* Chapter 6 in *Exploring Public Relations* Second Edition, edited by Ralph Tench and Liz Yeomans (2009).

Introduction

Enron, Shell UK, Union Carbide, Wal-Mart and Exxon Corporation are just a few of the major international corporations that have been under the worldwide media spotlight for their corporate actions and activities. Executives from these companies have at varying times over the past 20 years been vilified by the media, attacked by shareholders and customers and in some instances imprisoned. Why? Because the organisations they represent have had a major impact on the social and physical environments in which they operate (e.g. oil and chemical leaks). This chapter will explore the role of organisations in society and how, irrespective of the profit or not-for-profit imperatives, many are taking a critical view of their roles and responsibilities. In many instances (including some of the companies above), this has involved a radical repositioning of the organisation's **vision and values** that are impacting on the operational as well as the public relations (communication) strategies they employ.

Concern for the environment in which a business operates is not a new phenomenon but its prevalence in Anglo-American business policy is growing and, due to the internationalisation of markets and business practice, this is influencing corporate strategy for large PLCs and small to medium-sized enterprises (SMEs) throughout the world. These corporate policy changes are encouraging organisations to increase their awareness and concern for the society/societies in which they operate. An additional development is in the more sophisticated business use of the societal relationship as part of the corporate strategy and as a marketing tool. This has been demonstrated through the expansion of sponsorship programmes and more recently with the development of cause-related marketing (CRM) – associating companies or brands with charitable causes. This chapter will describe in detail the relationships between an organisation and the community within which it operates. It will explore the complex issue of business ethics with guidelines on how to promote ethical decision making in practice. Public relations (PR) is responding to an increasingly CSR-conscious business environment through the development of communications programmes (see Case study 7.1).

Social and economic change

All our societies are continually changing and evolving. Factors such as economic and financial performance have a significant influence on our standards of living and manifest themselves in day-to-day measures such as inflation, taxation, fuel and food prices. These issues are increasingly being highlighted and recognised as the world comes to terms with the significant changes in economic power as North America and Europe move in and out of more regular economic downturns. (Note the impact worldwide of the US originated 'credit crunch' in 2008/9 where the ability for banks to lend money to businesses and individuals had a major rippling effect on established economies and even brought down some major companies e.g. Lehman Brothers in September 2008.) As some national economies have experienced a slowdown in growth, others such as India and China continued to expand rapidly. The role of business is therefore put into the spotlight as we witness patterns of change in the climate and the environment more generally. Issues such as global warming have, as a consequence, been brought into sharp focus by a range of campaign and interest groups as well as by senior public and political figures (Kofi Anan with the United Nations and former US presidential candidate Al Gore).

Al Gore's seminal book (2007) and film (2006) *An Inconvenient Truth* (www.climatecrisis.net) focused on and highlighted the environmental damage being caused by modern, consumptive societies/businesses. Although a debated concept, Gore's work did raise the level at which such discussions were being held in nation states. It is not directly as a consequence but in line with this increased awareness that there are now many more and powerful organisations asking questions about the role and responsibilities of business in a global society (see the Global Responsible Leadership Initiative (www.grli.org) and the UN Global Compact established in 2000 (www.unglobalcompact.org).

Sustainable business: corporate social responsibility (CSR)

Individual members and groups in the community in which an organisation operates are increasingly being recognised as important **stakeholders** in the long-term security and success of large and small enterprises. Building relationships with these community groups is, therefore, an important

Case Study 7.1
BBC World Service Trust – international impact

The aim of the BBC's World Service Trust is to help developing countries and countries in transition to build media expertise for the benefit of the population.

Following over 30 years of conflict in Afghanistan, the country is now looking to the future and the Afghan media have a major role to play in uniting the nation, rebuilding its culture and changing the population's mindset from one of war to peace.

The BBC's role has been to help develop the media infrastructure. The work of the BBC World Service Trust has been focused on helping the Afghanistan media to rebuild themselves and ensure they have the necessary broadcasting skills and principles.

The BBC World Service Trust has helped set up a new public service broadcasting body, a strong and independent media network that may reassure the Afghan people that action is being taken to recreate a democratic society. The BBC World Service Trust claims the programme has gone far beyond its remit to rebuild Afghanistan's media infrastructure.

According to the BBC World Service Trust, the impact is as follows:

- increased audience – now estimated at 85% of the population – and improved profile for the BBC as a social broadcaster
- staff development opportunities and enhanced motivation for staff from different BBC divisions – including developing skills for BBC journalists working on news gathering
- increased trust – as a result of the BBC's long-term commitment to Afghanistan and production of education programmes, covering human rights, civil society, voter education, women's rights and minority rights
- establishment of an independent media – with a robust infrastructure that allows the reconstruction process to be communicated to even the most isolated communities
- training for Afghan journalists – of whom 20% are women (who were denied employment and education under the Taliban regime)
- media resources and training to use radio and studio equipment.

This example demonstrates how an organisation can get involved with a section of society and make real improvements. In this example, the BBC is using its experience as a broadcaster to help improve the media landscape in a specific country. The engagement with the issues is, however, more than just a practical one; other outputs relate to the communications impact in Afghanistan, staff development, perceptions of the BBC and an ability to meet the corporate objectives/mission of the BBC.

Source: www.bbc.co.uk/www.bitc.org.uk

issue in corporate and communications strategy. In order to understand how this can be achieved it is essential to understand in more detail the complexities of the relationships between a business and its community/communities. It is also important to define some of the business terminology that is frequently used when analysing businesses in their societal contexts.

Corporate social responsibility

A well-used business and management term, corporate social responsibility (CSR), is often associated with the phrase 'enlightened self-interest' – how organisations plan and manage their relationships with key stakeholders. CSR is, therefore, an organisation's defined responsibility to its society(ies) and stakeholders. Although organisations are not a state, country or region, they are part of the

infrastructure of society and as such they must consider their impact on it. A simple analogy for the impact organisations have on their community has been presented by Peach (1987; see Figure 7.1, overleaf), which shows the ripples from a stone thrown into a pond to represent the impact of a business on its environment. There are three levels of impact ranging from the *basic* in which a company adheres to society's rules and regulations to the *societal* where a company makes significant contributions towards improving the society in which it operates. In the middle level, companies are perceived to manage their activities so they adhere to the level and go beyond it. For example, this might be a company obeying legal requirements on employment rights as a foundation and then providing more generous interpretations of these legal rulings. Also the company may seek to reduce the negative impact of the organisation on its society without necessarily

Picture 7.1 Being corporately responsible should mean taking steps to avoid having a negative impact on the society in which an organisation operates (*source*: © Reuters/Corbis)

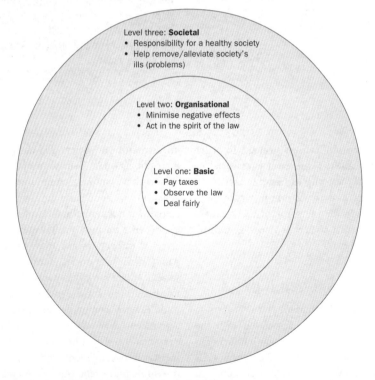

Figure 7.1 Impact of a business on its environment (*source*: after Peach 1987: 191–193)

Peach model in action

Some clear examples at the *basic* level might be a company in the supermarket retail sector that is profitable, pays its taxes and maintains minimum terms and conditions for its employees. At the highest, *societal*, level you could describe a supermarket retailer that conforms to society's rules and laws but also contributes to its society by funding community initiatives (e.g. holidays for disadvantaged children, investments in school facilities, transport for elderly people, lobbying for improved treatment of waste by local companies in line with its initiatives, contributing to positive legislation change in support of society, surpassing national and international employment rights and conditions, innovation in childcare or part-time mothers' conditions of work, etc.).

Activity 7.1

Business impact on society

Identify, name and describe a company or organisation that fits into each of the levels in the 'stone in the pond' analogy.

What would those organisations in levels one and two need to do to move towards the third, societal level?

Feedback

You need to consider what changes in ethical business policy or practice would make a difference to society. It is not enough just to make statements of intent.

taking positive action to make improvements that would take it to level three. (See also Box 7.1.)

Companies operating at the highest level, *societal*, do exist: companies are increasingly obtaining public recognition and visibility for their positive corporate actions. For example, in the UK, Business in the Community (BITC) has a PerCent Standard (formerly the Per Cent Club, started in 1986), which is awarded as a voluntary benchmark to companies donating at least 1% of pre-tax profits to community/social benefits. In 2002, 122 companies reporting to the standard invested a total of £854.7m. This demonstrated a significant increase from £303.37m in 1999. Box 7.2 gives the full details from the BITC survey for 2004. From 2007 the PerCent Standard, which has run for over 20 years, was replaced with a new measure by BITC: the CommunityMark. The CommunityMark was launched with an initial 21 member companies which met the 5 principles (see www.bitc.org.uk/communitymark/five_communitymark.html). See also Box 7.2. It is important to note that in the UK there is a legal requirement that any donation over £200 has to be recorded in a company's end of year annual report and accounts (the financial statement to shareholders).

When considering CSR it is important to make a distinction between corporate activities that are intended to contribute to the society and charitable acts or philanthropy (see Activity 7.1).

Philanthropy

One simple definition of **philanthropy** is that 'corporations perform charitable actions'. This is very different from CSR, with philanthropy being a charitable act not necessarily linked to the expectations of society. Philanthropy did occur in large industrial firms in the UK during the nineteenth century (such as Joseph Rowntree, Titus Salt) through the donation of money and amenities such as schools, hospitals or housing for employees and their communities. **Corporate philanthropy** can be perceived as a short-term one-way relationship, which is unpredictable on behalf of the recipient and therefore more difficult to manage and strategically plan for. For example, during the dotcom boom (during the late 1990s when the financial performance and market impact of web-based businesses and technology companies in general were seriously exaggerated), technology company directors commonly gave large sums in charitable donations. The Slate 60 is an annual list of US charitable gifts and pledges that has reported since 1996: in 2008 the top pledge was for a single gift of $4bn. (See www.slate.com). Depending on the general and sector-specific economic performance, individuals go on or off the list, reinforcing the unpredictable nature of this type of activity. For example, Bill Gates (the world's richest man and Microsoft's founder) was on the list in 2001 with $2bn in gifts. In 2005 Gates made the largest ever private donation of £400m ($750m) to the child health charity he set up with his wife, Melinda, the Bill and Melinda Gates Foundation (www.gatesfoundation.org). In 2008 Bill Gates relinquished his management of Microsoft to become non-executive chairman to concentrate on

Box 7.2

PerCent Standard results for 2004

In 2004, 152 companies reported their community investment through to the PerCent Standard. Submissions were received from companies in the FTSE 250 and Business in the Community's membership. The results found that:

116 companies achieved the 1% Standard
109 companies are members of Business in the Community
 56 companies are members of the FTSE100
 58 are members of the London Benchmarking Group
  6 companies still contributed to their community but made pre-tax losses
 35 companies reported for the first time.

2004 total reported community investment was £934,327,608. This is broken down between:

Cash contribution:	£604,509,460 (2003 – £496,623,319; 2001/02 – £381,280,998; 2000 – £244,126,127; 1999 – £200,755,733)
Employee time:	£60,618,041 (2003 – £44,819,158; 2001/02 – £38,641,240; 2000 – £28,754,690; 1999 – £25,500,729)
Gifts in kind:	£195,848,025 (2003 – £263,204,495; 2001/02 – £101,625,924; 2000 – £41,798,114; 1999 – £35,032,923)
Management costs:	£73,351,282 (2003 – £50,086,509; 2001/02 – £42,020,316; 2000 – £28,777,488; 1999 – £22,332,603).

The 2004 top 10 UK givers were:

Allen & Overy – £12,600,000
Vodafone in the UK – £10,514,160
Co-operative Group – £8,124,661
Procter & Gamble – £6,628,933
Sainsbury's – £6,069,143
Allied Domecq – £5,761,900
BSkyB – £5,054,631
GWR Group – £5,033,145
KPMG – £4,270,234
John Lewis Partnership – £4,166,803

The top 10 in absolute terms were:

GlaxoSmithKline – £144,290,400
Altria – £128,150,272
BP – £50,123,223
Unilever – £45,780,905
Royal Bank of Scotland – £40,100,000
Lloyds TSB – £36,680,000
Barclays – £32,821,803
HBOS – £29,392,310
BHP Billiton – £25,941,192
Anglo-American – £24,158,000

The 21 initial businesses to achieve the CommunityMark at the launch in September 2008 were:

Axis, Barclays, Blackburn Rovers Football & Athletic Club, BT, Contract Scotland, Deloitte, Design Links, Elementus, Ernst & Young, GlaxoSmithKline, HBOS, Heart of Midlothian Football, KPMG, Marks and Spencer, PricewaterhouseCoopers, Rangers Football Club, RWE npower, Sainsbury's, Tesco, The Town House Collection, Zurich Financial Services (UK).

Source: Business in the Community (www.bitc.org.uk)

working with his foundation, which to date has given grants and donations totalling $16.4bn (audited financial accounts for 2008).

Although gifts can be turned on and off by the donor, like a tap, there are some benefactors who donate through trusts, which enable the act to be sustained over longer periods of time (e.g. the Rowntree Foundation or the Wellcome Trust in the UK, the John D. Rockefeller Foundation or the Bill and Melinda Gates Foundation). (See Activity 7.2.)

In recognition of the interest shown by various stakeholder groups – employees, customers and particularly the financial community and investors – it is now common business practice for large and small to medium-sized enterprises (SMEs) to publish corporate literature and brochures giving details of their community activities and CSR. Non-financial reporting on corporate responsibility in annual reports became prevalent in the mid-1990s. In the UK, for example, BT's annual review and summary financial statement (1996/7), included a section called

'Why we are helping the community: we're all part of the same team'. Within the report BT stated that:

> It is increasingly clear that businesses cannot regard themselves as in some way separate from the communities in which they operate. Besides, research has shown that the decision to purchase from one company rather than another is not a decision about price alone.

The practice has evolved to such a degree that companies now produce specific corporate responsibility reports. For example, O2 (formerly part of BT) is a Europe-wide mobile telephone company that launched its first corporate responsibility report in 2003.

Business case for corporate social responsibility: why be socially responsible?

Organisations in developed economies are today influenced by public opinion, shareholders, stakeholders (who can be shareholders, consumers and members of campaign groups) and the political process. Consequently, organisations that ignore their operational environment are susceptible to restrictive legislation and regulation. This is a particular issue in Europe with the increasing power and influence of the European Union, the single currency and the European parliamentary process. Representative bodies for business such as Business in the Community (BITC), CSR Europe, Institute of Business Ethics, Business for Social Responsibility, and the Prince of Wales International Business Leaders Forum (IBLF) have formed

to help senior managers deal with the demands of varied stakeholder groups. Outside the EU, influencers such as the United Nations (UN Global Compact) are making an impact on business and political decision making.

Is CSR good business practice? On the one hand, many companies profited from unethical practices in the early part of the twentieth century, as demonstrated by the success of textile and mining industries and more recently with companies manufacturing chemical-based products such as asbestos. Furthermore, Milton Friedman has been the consistent business voice stating that the business of business is simply to increase profits and enhance shareholder value. Friedman (1970) wrote key articles arguing these views in the 1960s and 1970s. Although there are few contemporary academic papers supporting his views, they are frequently cited as the opposing arguments to CSR.

On the other hand, in contrast to Friedman's views, there are the examples of both old and new companies benefiting themselves, their stakeholders and employees through more ethically based practice. Worldwide examples include Cadbury, Lever's, IBM, Co-operative Bank and Coca-Cola. Even before corporate responsibility became a boardroom agenda item around the turn of the millennium, there is evidence of its commercial value. For example, Johnson & Johnson's chief executive officer, James Burke, demonstrates that companies with a reputation for ethics and social responsibility grew at a rate of 11.3% annually from 1959 to 1990 while the growth rate for similar companies without the same ethical approach was 6.2% (Labich 1992). Furthermore, arguments and evidence are emerging to support CSR's contribution to the financial performance of organisations (Little and Little 2000; Moore 2003).

CSR can contribute to corporate image and reputation (Lewis 2003; Sagar and Singla 2004). The importance of a good reputation can include the following:

- Others are more willing to consider the organisation's point of view.

- It helps to strengthen the organisation's information structure with society and therefore improve resources in all areas.

- It makes it easier for the organisation to motivate and recruit employees – and to promote increased employee morale (Lines 2004).

- It will enhance and add value to the organisation's products and services.

A socially responsible reputation is also a way of differentiating organisations and providing competitive advantage. This is supported by announcements from companies such as McDonald's and BT in the UK that they would be investing more time and resources into socially responsible activities. BT was influenced by a MORI report, which stated that 80% of respondents believed it was important to know about an organisation's socially responsible activities in order to form a positive opinion about them. CEOs worldwide are starting to recognise that CSR is an important agenda item. Research by the India Partnership Forum (2003) shows that nearly 70% of CEOs say that CSR is 'vital' to profitability and that, irrespective of economic climate, it will remain a high priority for 60% of CEOs across the globe.

A company with an acknowledged strategy change on corporate responsibility and environmental engagement is oil firm Royal Dutch/Shell. During 1998, Shell had its first meeting with institutional shareholders (major company investors, e.g. on behalf of pension funds) to explain the company's new policies on environmental and social responsibilities. This initiative came following criticism of the company's action in high-profile environmental issues (e.g. when Shell was challenged by campaign groups over its decision to dismantle the Brent Spar oil platform at sea rather than on land owing to the supposed environmental impact) and human rights cases (execution of human rights activist Ken Sara Wiwo, in Ogoniland, where Shell had a dominant interest).

Picture 7.2 Ken Saro-Wiwa was a human rights activist from the Ogoniland where Shell had a dominant interest (*source*: AFP/Getty Images)

At the meeting with shareholders, Mark Moody Stuart of Shell Transport and Trading (the company's UK arm) stated that he did not agree with arguments that institutional shareholders were not interested in issues such as social responsibility: 'I don't think there is a fundamental conflict between financial performance and "soft" issues. Many shareholders want outstanding financial returns in a way they can feel proud of or comfortable with.' (See Think abouts 7.1 and 7.2.)

Think about 7.1

Shell Europe

During both the Brent Spar and Ogoniland crises, Shell faced a Europe-wide consumer boycott of its fuel products as well as significant media criticism (see above, www.shell.co.uk, www. greenpeace.org.uk). Why do you think Shell took the potentially risky strategy of reopening debate about environmental and societal issues after such high-profile vilification by the two important stakeholder groups (consumers of their products and the media)?

Feedback

This initiative by Shell clearly demonstrates the company directors' desire to tackle key issues head on but also to make the company more accountable to its publics and specifically to the communities (and therefore stakeholder groups) in which it operates.

Think about 7.2

Business effects of CSR

Does CSR stretch an organisation's relationship with, and activities of, its supply chains (companies that supply products and services)? Can you think of suppliers for a company that it should not be associated with?

Feedback

Some companies have developed supplier policies that define the requirements for supplier organisations. For example, it would not be socially responsible for a furniture retailer that operates a 'green' purchasing policy to buy its raw materials from suppliers who purchase their wood from unsustainable sources.

Organisational responsibilities to stakeholders

Stakeholder analysis is a clear way of defining those groups and individuals who have a significant relationship with an organisation (see also Chapter 6). Stakeholders can be described as those with a vested interest in the organisation's operations. Figure 7.2 simply demonstrates the most common stakeholders in for-profit organisations.

These are simplified stakeholder groups which can be expanded and broken down into subgroups. In order for an organisation to act with social responsibility it is necessary to understand the fundamental elements of the organisation's operations and its relationships with stakeholders. To achieve this it can be helpful to ask and analyse the following questions:

1 How is the organisation financed, e.g. shareholders, private ownership, loans, etc.?

2 Who are the customers for the products and services, e.g. agents, distributors, traders, operators, end users, etc.?

3 What are the employee conditions and terms, including status, contracts and hierarchical structures?

4 Are there community interactions at local, regional, national and international levels?

5 Are there governmental, environmental or legislative actions that impact on the organisation?

6 What are the competitor influences on the organisation, e.g. markets, agents, distributors, customers, suppliers?

7 What are the supplier influences on the organisation, e.g. other creditors, financial supporters, competitors?

8 Are there any issues or potential risks that may be affected by local, national or international pressure groups or interests?

CSR from a stakeholder perspective may bring the organisation closer to its stakeholders and importantly improve the two-way flow (Grunig and Hunt 1984) of information and subsequently understanding.

Once stakeholders are identified, you need to define the responsibilities you have towards them and then define and develop strategies to manage these relationships (see Activity 7.3).

Figure 7.2 Typical for-profit organisational stakeholders

Activity 7.3

Defining organisational stakeholders

(a) Choose an organisation and define its stakeholders.

(b) How would you prioritise these stakeholders in terms of their importance to financial performance for the organisation?

Feedback

Financial performance is important for all organisations but this prioritised list may look different if instead it were arranged according to CSR performance towards stakeholders.

Organisational responsibilities to society

Business ethics writer Carroll (1991) argues there are four kinds of social responsibility: economic, legal, ethical, and philanthropic; demonstrated through the CSR pyramid in Figure 7.3.

To aid managers in the evaluation of an organisation's social responsibilities and to help them plan how to fulfil the legal, ethical, economic and philanthropic obligations, Carroll designed a 'stakeholder responsibility matrix' (see Table 7.1, overleaf). Carroll makes the clear distinction that social responsibility does not begin with good intentions but with stakeholder actions.

Carroll's matrix is proposed as an analytical tool or framework to help company managers make sense of their ideas about what the firm should be doing – economically, legally, ethically and philanthropically – with respect to

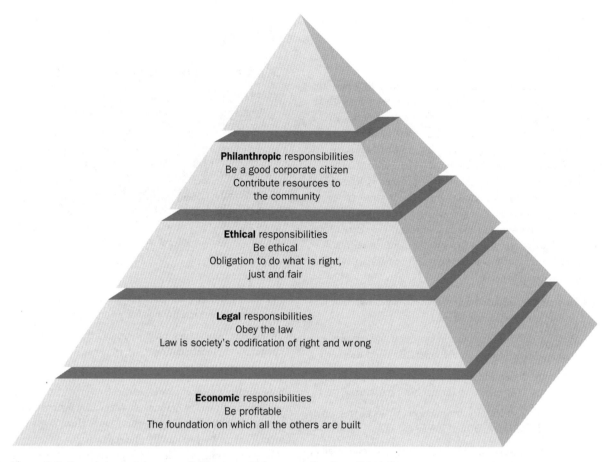

Figure 7.3 Corporate social responsibility pyramid (*source*: after Carroll 1991)

Table 7.1
Stakeholder
responsibility matrix
(*source*: after Carroll
1991)

Stakeholders:	Economic	Legal	Ethical	Philanthropic
Providers of capital				
Customers				
Employees				
Community				
Competitors				
Suppliers				
Pressure groups				
General public				

its defined stakeholder groups. In practice, the matrix is effective as it encourages the manager to record both descriptive (qualitative) and statistical data to manage each stakeholder. This information is then useful when iden-tifying priorities in long- and short-term business decision making that involves the multiple stakeholder groups that influence most organisations. It enables these decisions to be made in the context of the company's or organisation's value

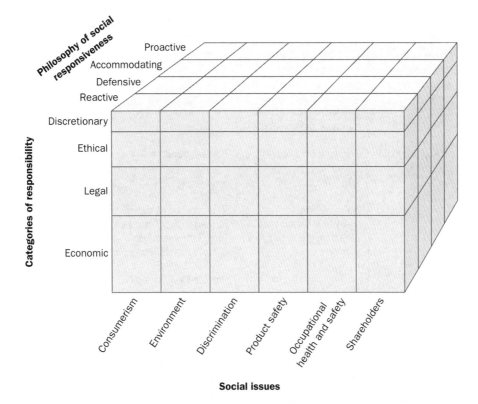

Figure 7.4 Carroll's responsibility matrix (*source*: adapted from Carroll 1991)

systems – what it stands for – as well as accommodating economic, social and environmental factors. To express this simply, the manager is able to make decisions in a more informed way with a clear map of the numerous factors that will impact on these decisions. It is a detailed approach to stakeholder management but is one way of providing informed foundations about stakeholders to enable strategies, actions or decisions to be taken that reflect the complex environment in which most organisations operate (see also Figure 7.4).

Table 7.2 (overleaf) provides an example of the matrix applied to one stakeholder group and the types of recorded data required. The organisation is a small clothing manufacturing business. The stakeholder group used for the analysis is customers. Each social responsibility cell has been considered in the context of this stakeholder group and data input currently available about the responsibility the firm acknowledges towards this group. Clearly the data included are not exhaustive and further records could be sought or gaps in information identified and subsequently commissioned by the PR or communications team.

This information will help managers when the organisation is defining corporate strategies for long- and short-term decisions to ensure they accommodate the multiple stakeholder interests.

Corporate responsibility and irresponsibility

Tench, Bowd and Jones (2007), Jones, Bowd and Tench (2009 pending) build on and critique some of Carroll's early work to discuss alternative interpretations. The main conclusions of this discussion are in the exploration of Corporate Social Irresponsibility (CSI) as a concept in contrast to Corporate Social Responsibility and the consequences of this dichotomy for corporate communications. The CSI–CSR model is described, explained, analysed and used as a conceptual tool to make the theoretical move from a pyramid or level-based approach (Carroll) to a more dynamic corporate framework for communication.

Figure 7.5 serves to show that internal and external variables as well as mixing with and affecting each other also interact and impact on the CSI–CSR continuum. The model is a rotating sphere intersected by its axis, the continuum. The need of business to make profit can, and does at times, coincide as well as conflict with its stated ethical aims and objectives. Competing stakeholders with differing needs, rights and obligations have to be managed to ensure conflict is minimised, the business survives, grows and is able to meet its commitments to CSR.

Stakeholders	Economic	Legal	Ethical	Philanthropic
Customers	Financially well-managed company	Conform to consumer health and safety product guidelines (e.g. quality controls and standards for fire safety of garments, etc.)	Fairly priced products	Give waste products to needy organisations
	Clear financial reporting	Correct labelling	Highest quality	Give unsold products to customers' preferred charities or homeless groups
		National and transnational product labelling, e.g. European standards	Products are designed for and fit for purpose (e.g. if for specialist sector such as workwear)	Support other employee and customer initiatives
			Provide best products with the highest standards of care for employers and suppliers	
			Transparent sourcing of materials (no use of child labour or low-paid employees)	
			Do not abuse our suppliers or workers	

Table 7.2 An application of the stakeholder responsibility matrix to a small clothing manufacturer

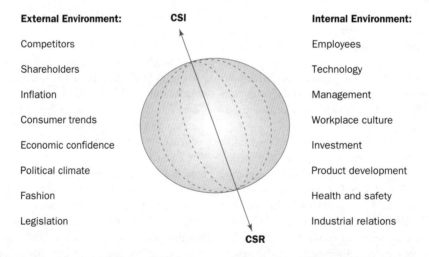

Figure 7.5 CSI–CSR Environmental Dynamic model (*source*: Jones, Bowd and Tench 2009 pending)

The model moves away from a definition, explanation and analysis of CSR as a staged hierarchy, as espoused by Carroll (1991) in his pyramid of corporate social responsibility. Here, an alternative conceptualisation is suggested based on the notion that CSI should be separated out from CSR to facilitate greater understanding of the terms, their meaning, nature and purpose. Issues interspersed and feeding into the CSI–CSR continuum are affected by internal and external environmental factors. Such factors give shape, form and context to corporate governance and

CSR. Placing Carroll's (1991) pyramid, of corporate social responsibility metaphorically in the sphere recognises that the levels of responsibility are intrinsic to the way in which CSR is conceived. However, in suggesting that the pyramid, and by implication the levels, can be rotated the inference is that the levels are neither hierarchical nor static but fluid and necessary to each other. By introducing the concept of CSI it counteracts the tendency to treat the concept of CSR as a one-dimensional single entity and unpacks the terms to reveal multi-faceted layers of complexity that are shaped by context.

The majority of companies are keen to embrace CSR issues and of their own volition go beyond legal minimum requirements. Not only do companies want to do well by doing good, but also some want to do good because they believe it to be the right and proper thing to do. Not all businesses are communicating what it is they do in regards to CSR to best effect. Regarding their social responsibility practices, a CSI–CSR audit can help businesses identify areas of strength and areas for improvement. In itself such an exercise can act as a useful vehicle of and for communication. As discussed, it is increasingly recognised that adopting a CSR approach can be both an ethical and profitable way to manage a business. Ethics and profit are not mutually exclusive terms but have a symbiotic relationship in the form of CSR. Though, nevertheless, at the end of the day and as Friedman (1962) rightly noted, the purpose of business is to make profit.

Regulatory frameworks

As consumers we have product choice – do we go for brand, price or even ethical or corporate responsibility performance? Companies such as Shell, Nike and Nestlé have experienced the threat and financial effects of global boycotts and are realising that greater mobility of stakeholders and globalisation of communication mean that reputation management is increasingly important. One manifestation of this is the speed of communication and in particular news distribution globally via new technology, satellite and the emergence of 24-hour news channels. The process of news gathering has been speeded up as has the news production cycle – all of which is crucial for PR when managing reputation and communication for organisations. Research by the World Economic Forum in 2003 revealed that 48% of people express 'little or no trust' in global companies. Consequently, even large and powerful corporations must adopt more ethical working practices in order to reduce risk and maintain favourable reputation. The growth of organisations such as Business in the Community in the UK and CSR Europe is helping to place

CSR in the mainstream of business thinking and encourage more organisations to leverage the opportunities of CSR. This has a number of implications, including the increased need for guidance for companies. Subsequently the past few years have seen the emergence of an increasing number of standards and guidelines in the areas of CSR and sustainable development. These include:

- Dow Jones Sustainability Index
- FTSE 4 Good Index
- Business in the Community's Corporate Responsibility Index
- Global Reporting Initiative's (GRI) Reporting Guidelines.

Public and business attitudes are changing and in 1999 a global poll of 25,000 citizens (MORI 1999) showed that perceptions of companies are more strongly aligned with corporate citizenship (56%) than either brand quality (40%) or the perception of the business management (34%). In essence public attitude has changed from the 1970s when it is said that more people in Britain believed the profits of large companies were also benefiting customers. Following a range of public scandals and financial collapses – even before the dramatic financial meltdown of 2008 and 2009 – the public are much more cynical and keen to challenge the dominance and perceived greed of corporates and their executives. This attitude change is reiterated by Fombrum and Shanley (1990) who found in earlier studies that a business that demonstrates responsiveness to social concerns and gives proportionately more to charity than other firms receives higher reputation ratings by its publics. There is a range of research that demonstrates consumers' willingness to reward socially responsible companies, with far-reaching effects. One such effect is the changing focus of investment decisions. This has resulted in the emergence of '**triple bottom-line' reporting** whereby social and environmental performance hold equal importance to financial performance. It can therefore be argued that, in the eyes of consumers, the media, legislators and investors, social and environmental responsibilities are increasingly powerful drivers of reputation. (See Case study 7.2.)

Ethics and business practice

Before looking in detail at the techniques for operating a business in society (and for implementing CSR programmes), we need to consider the important issue of **ethics** and ethical business practice. **Business ethics** is a substantial issue and an important part of understanding what is called corporate governance. It ranges from high-profile issues about equal opportunities, 'glass ceilings'

Case Study 7.2

European campaign – GlaxoSmithKline – Barretstown

Therapeutic recreation for children with serious illness

GlaxoSmithKline (GSK) is one of the world's largest pharmaceutical companies. The company's partnership with Barretstown in Ireland began in 1994 to kick start their European Community Partnership Programme focusing on children's health.

Barretstown was established as the first 'hole in the wall' camp in Europe, building on the success of the first North American camp to enable children with serious illnesses to experience 'summer camp' by providing first-class medical facilities on the site of the camps. Barretstown Castle was donated by the Irish government to provide a similar facility and additional facilities were constructed to adapt to the children's special needs.

Through a programme of activities and adventure in a safe and medically supported environment, children meet and develop friendships with other children. Many paediatricians see their patients' participation in Barretstown as an integral part of clinical treatment. As well as helping children feel better through greater confidence and self-esteem, their experience at Barretstown helps them do more than they ever thought they could. Being involved with the programme helps GSK volunteers learn how to deal sensitively with issues relating to disability.

As Barretstown involves children from countries where GSK has a business operation, it reflects their regional structure and draws different GSK businesses together to work on a shared programme. GSK employees from these countries participate as volunteer carers (helpers) and GSK businesses provide practical support locally, for example funding children's flights to Ireland. GSK's funding has been focused on establishing the 'European Liaison Network', an important interface between Barretstown and children's hospitals. The network provides a framework across 19 countries for raising awareness about the camp among doctors, parents and children, as well as recruiting children to participate. More than 110 hospitals across Europe nominate children to participate. According to GlaxoSmithKline, the impact is as follows:

- Barretstown provides volunteers with opportunities for personal development, in particular for developing creativity, teamwork and diversity awareness. GSK volunteers learn how to deal sensitively with issues relating to disability, especially the way those children feel about their appearance and body image.

- GSK Barretstown has created a model for other GSK businesses to adapt to local programmes. Several of GSK's businesses have adopted 'therapeutic recreation' as a focus in developing their own community programmes. GSK supports smaller-scale programmes with local children's hospitals in Hungary, Portugal and Romania.

- Early data show that the main benefits of the programme are that the children regain self-esteem, develop confidence and have some of their independence restored after what may be long periods of isolation and hospitalisation.

- From serving 124 children in 1994, Barretstown has grown and now supports over 10,000 children drawn from 110 hospitals in 19 European countries.

- The partnership with Barretstown has been key in contributing to building GSK's reputation as a good corporate citizen among internal and external stakeholders.

Source: www.gsk.com/www.bitc.org.uk

for women in work, whistleblowing (employees reporting on unethical or illegal activities by their employers), whether large PLCs pay their SME suppliers or contractor on time down to whether it is all right for a director or senior manager to take a ream of paper home for a computer printer, when this is a sackable offence for an office junior!

Business ethics is therefore about us as individual members of society, as part of the community or as part of organisations (whether these are work or leisure/interest organisations). For example, we may be an employee of a national supermarket chain and a trustee for a local school or scout group. We make decisions within these environments that have ethical implications and societal impact (see Peach 1987; Figure 7.1). Ethics is an important part of business reality, as managers make decisions that affect a large range of stakeholder groups and communities from the employees of the organisation to the residents who live close to its business sites. (See Think abouts 7.3, 7.4 and 7.5; see also Box 7.3.)

Think about 7.3   Ethical dilemmas

Ethical dilemmas occur when we are faced with decisions that cause dissonance (conflict) in our loyalty (taken from Festinger's theory of cognitive dissonance). Take the example of a cheating colleague who is extracting small amounts of money from the organisation through false expenses claims. If we know about their actions, should we show loyalty to them or to our organisation? We are left with an 'ethical decision'. What do you think you would say or do if it were a director or management colleague in this case? How would you manage the ethical dilemma?

Feedback

'Ethical problems are not caused entirely by "bad apples". They're also the product of organisational systems that either encourage unethical behaviour or, at least, allow it to occur,' Trevino and Nelson (1995: 13).

You need to gather all the facts and also consider the impact of your decisions/actions on the organisation as a whole. See the section on ethical decision making.

Think about 7.4

Good apples and bad apples

The 'good' and 'bad apple' analogy is frequently used in the context of ethics. Apply this analogy to your own experience and think of an example of unethical conduct. Was it the responsibility of the individual (apple) or the organisation (barrel) or was it a combination of the two?

Feedback

Arguably, we are born amoral, not moral or immoral. Psychologists have argued that ethics, as such, are not innate. They are culturally bound and influenced by the social environment we grow up in. We develop and change our personalities throughout our lives – including during our adult life – and research (Rest and Thoma 1986) has found that adults in their 30s who are in moral development programmes develop more than young people.

Box 7.3

Example of ethical guidelines

Unilever has published its ethical guidelines – or ethical principles – as follows: 'Unilever believe that economic growth must go hand in hand with sound environmental management, equal opportunities world-wide and the highest standards of health and safety in factories and offices.'

Its code of business principles covers sensitive issues such as bribery: 'Unilever does not give or receive bribes in order to retain business or financial advantages. Unilever employees are directed that any demand or offer of such a bribe must be immediately rejected.'

Source: www.unilever.com

Think about 7.5

Individual and corporate ethics

Dissonance or conflict is what causes individual problems with corporate ethics and there are stark examples such as a religious person working for a pharmaceutical company that decides to market an abortion product, or an environmentally conscious employee working for a high-polluting company. What should these individuals do to manage the conflict? What should their management do?

Ethical decision making: theory and practice

Business ethics author Snell (1997) argues that there are two approaches to the teaching and understanding of business ethics by practitioners. One of these is termed 'systematic modernism', which is the more explanatory, conservative voice of business leaders and political leaders on societal issues. The explanations are more functional and seek resolutions in the short to medium term, i.e. through legislation, the use of law and order and reliance

Issue	Typical systematic modern narrative	Typical critical modern narrative
Corruption: bribery and extortion	Bad because it dents local or national pride, deters inward investment and is a sign of backwardness	Bad because it is inherently unfair, disadvantaging the politically and economically weak
Protection of the environment	Our sons and daughters will suffer or perish unless we adopt proper controls	Indigenous (native) peoples, rare animal species and future citizens are entitled to a habitable environment
Inflated executive salaries	One should set up systems of corporate governance overseen by non-executive directors to safeguard minority shareholders' interests	One should campaign for wider social justice, including action to help the poor and reduce unemployment
Function of codes of ethics	They are tools for inspiring the confidence of customers and investors, and a means of controlling staff	They are a starting point only. People should be encouraged to develop their own personal moral code
Preferred Kohlberg stages	Conventional reasoning: preserving stability, the rule of law and order and social respectability	Postconventional reasoning: concern for social welfare, justice and universal ethical principles

Table 7.3 Competing modern narratives on business ethics (*source*: adapted from Snell 1997: 185)

on individual's social responsibility. In contrast, 'critical modernism' is the current 'underdog' yet this has been influenced more by theoretical ethical debates. It is argued therefore that the critical approach takes business ethics a stage further than just face-value explanations of why something is right or wrong.

Table 7.3 highlights how the two schools of thought operate and interpret different ethical issues. (See Activity 7.4.)

Activity 7.4

Ethics in everyday life

Think about how you act in different situations. How would you react if a college friend started telling jokes about people with physical disabilities? Would you smile in an embarrassed way, laugh and hope they wouldn't carry on, confront the speaker and ask them to stop, or what?

Feedback

It is often useful to reflect on our codes of ethics, what we see as right and wrong, and on whether we act on our beliefs or are more interested in how others perceive or see us.

Philosophers have studied ethical decision making for centuries and tend to focus on decision-making tools that describe what should be done in particular situations (see also Chapter 13). The most well-known philosophical theories are categorised as consequentialist, regarding the consequences of actions, with utilitarianism being the best known and associated with the 'greatest happiness' principle (i.e. the greatest happiness for the greatest number of people). Trevino and Nelson (1995: 67) state that a utilitarian approach to ethical decision making should 'maximise benefits to society and minimise harms. What matters is the net balance of good consequences over bad.'

Generally, utilitarian ethical decision making is therefore focused on what we do and what are the consequences of our actions, i.e. who will be harmed or affected. In a business context, this means which stakeholders will be affected. One method of testing this approach is to ask if everyone acted in the same way, what sort of environment would be created? Just imagine what the impact would be if each of us dropped our lunch wrappers and leftovers onto the floor every day! Extend this out to all businesses draining their waste water/fluids into the nearest river/ocean outlet. This theory does underlie a lot of business writing and thinking and people's approaches to ethical decision making.

A second strand of philosophical thinking is categorised under deontological theories which focus on motives and intentions through duties or the action itself rather than the outcome or results. German philosopher Emmanuel Kant wrote about the 'categorical imperative', which asks whether your ethical choice is sound enough to become universally accepted as a law of action that everyone should follow (see Kant 1964). The obvious example is whether telling lies is ever acceptable. Imagine a company context where it was perceived that telling a lie for the good of the company was to its benefit. Kant would argue against this case unless the company is prepared to accept that from that point forward all employees were permitted to lie – a 'categorical imperative'. You need only consider the case of Enron in the USA to appreciate where such an ethical management system will lead with regard to telling mistruths and lies to a range of stakeholders.

Another ethical approach that is popular with business ethics academics and fits into the business context is virtue ethics, which is also founded in traditional philosophical theory. It focuses on the integrity of the actor or individual more than on the act itself. Within this approach it is important to consider the relative importance of communities or stakeholder groups. For example, in a professional context you may be bound by community standards or practical codes of conduct. This can help the individual make ethical decisions because it gives them boundaries to work within.

Changing the culture and changing organisational ethics

Any attempt to change ethical practice within an organisation must be based on a simple assumption that all human beings are essentially good and capable of development and change. Changing ethical practice through changing the culture of an organisation is not a quick fix; it takes time as you have to address the formal and informal organisational subcultures. The culture of an organisation clearly affects what is appropriate or inappropriate behaviour. To understand the culture an audit is necessary and can be carried out through surveys, interviews and observations.

Having completed an audit, the next stage is to write a culture change intervention plan that includes targeting the formal and informal systems.

The formal systems are more transparent and easier to change, as follows:

- draw up new codes of conduct
- change structure to encourage individuals to take responsibility for their behaviour
- design reward systems to punish unethical behaviour
- encourage **whistleblowers** and provide them with appropriate communications channels and confidentiality
- change decision-making processes to incorporate attention to ethical issues.

For the informal system, the following may be important:

- re-mythologise the organisation – revive old myths and stories about foundations, etc. that guide organisational behaviour (revived myths must, however, fit with reality).

See Activity 7.5 and Case study 7.3, overleaf.

Activity 7.5

Ethics in practice

To conclude this chapter on business and its role in communities and society, think about the following.

Managers are the key to ethical business practice as they are the potential role models for all employees, customers, suppliers, etc. and also the endorsers of ethical policies. Due to changes in management practice, business process reengineering and the downsizing of western companies, many modern businesses have fewer managers today – yet each manager has more staff to control:

1 How should organisations be ethical? Identify three or four reasons. Divide these reasons into those that are linked to financial gain and those that are societally sympathetic.

2 Are employees attracted to ethical employers? Give reasons why you believe they may or may not be.

3 List those companies you would be proud to work for and those that you would be ashamed to be employed by or represent. What are the key features of each? What are the similarities and differences?

Case Study 7.3

Co-operative Bank case study

At the Co-operative Bank they have brought it all together extremely well. Established in 1872, it was always a small bank. But in the late 1980s a new managing director asked the bank's few but loyal customers why they were there. From a significant minority, the answer came back that they thought the bank was ethical. The bank then asked 30,000 of them what else they would like. (Most national opinion polls in the UK ask about 2,000 people.) The questions were based on the simple premise that a person will only knowingly lend money for something they approve of and as putting money into a bank is indirectly lending it to others it has the same effect. In 1992 this led to the first ethical policy where the bank promised never to invest in areas not approved of by its customers. The results were as follows: 90% only wanted to support governments or businesses supporting human rights; 87% would not fund companies manufacturing or trading in armaments to oppressive regimes; 80% were against animal exploitation; 70% wanted to reduce environmental damage; 66% rejected the fur trade; and 60% did not want to support the production or sale of tobacco products. (See the company website for the current policy.)

The bank also produces reports indicating how well it is doing against the often challenging measures set by its customers, which can also be seen at its website. The policy has worked. During a time of severe economic downturn for most, the bank's profitability almost tripled, from £45.5m in 1996 to £122.5m in 2002.

As the sector grows the research will continue to add to our knowledge or its value. Those expressing values-led decisions are moving up to overtake the profit led – or you could say that people are beginning to ask the true cost of products and services rather than just what is on the price ticket. In a MORI poll for the Co-operative Bank it was found that 25% have actively sought products from companies with a responsible reputation. Interestingly, where they had the facts, 50% have chosen the responsible and 50% have boycotted the irresponsible.

CSR policies have to be well researched and managed as shown here and they have to go deep and for the long term – there are a lot of pressure groups watching very closely and testing claims.

Source: Co-operative Bank (www.co-operativebankcasestudy. org.uk; www.co-operativebank.co.uk)

Summary

Milton Friedman's perception that the business of business is simply to increase profits and enhance shareholder value has less credibility in the twenty-first century. Also, the public is increasingly sophisticated on environmental and ethical issues such as: global warming; worldwide natural disasters such as the Asian tsunami and businesses' responses; animal testing; hunting with dogs in the UK; or whale hunting. There is rising power for the consumer in national and international contexts as demonstrated by Shell and Body Shop. The influence of corporate image and reputation on an organisation's business success (Andersen; McDonald's/McLibel) is increasingly recognised, as is the use of business ethics to create competitive advantage (Co-operative Bank; The Body Shop). Enhanced communication (the Internet) for and with stakeholders and interest groups, media expansion and global influence (24-hour news), and the mobilisation of national and international issue and pressure groups (such as Greenpeace; the Anti Iraq War lobby; UN Global Compact; or influential figures such as Al Gore) can all separately and together affect any business today.

This chapter has focused on the role organisations play in their society(ies) and how the understanding of business ethics and CSR may improve business performance and enhance reputation through more effective use of PR and communication to build understanding and awareness. CSR is being incorporated into many organisations' strategic planning and public relations is being used to support this.

Discussion in this chapter has focused on:

■ stakeholder influences

■ ethical decision making

■ changing cultural and organisational ethics.

Bibliography

Adams, R., J. Carruthers and S. Hamil (1991). *Changing Corporate Values*. London: Kogan Page.

Cannon, T. (1992). *Corporate Responsibility*. London, Pitman.

Carroll, A.B. (1991). 'The pyramid of corporate social responsibility: toward the moral management of organizational stakeholders'. *Business Horizons* **34**(4): 39–48.

Clutterbuck, D., D. Dearlove and D. Snow (1992). *Actions Speak Louder: A management guide to corporate social responsibility*. London: Kogan Page.

Concise Oxford English Dictionary, 8th edition (1995). Oxford: Clarendon Press.

Cutlip, S.M., A.H. Center and G.M. Broom (2000). *Effective Public Relations*, 8th edition. Upper Saddle River, NJ: Prentice Hall.

Davies, P.W.F. (ed.) (1997). *Current Issues in Business Ethics*. London: Routledge.

Fombrum, C. and M. Shanley (1990). 'What's in a name? Reputation building and corporate strategy'. *Academy of Management Journal* **33**: 233–258.

Friedman, M. (1962). *Capitalism and Freedom*. Chicago, IL: Chicago University Press.

Friedman, M. (1970). 'The social responsibility of business is to increase its profits'. *New York Times Magazine* 13 September: 32.

Gore, A. (2006) *An Inconvenient Truth*. Director, David Guggenheim: Paramount.

Gore, A. (2007) *An Inconvenient Truth*. New York: Penguin (Viking Press).

Grunig, J. and T. Hunt (1984). *Managing Public Relations*. New York: Holt, Rinehart & Winston.

India Partnership Forum (2003). www.ipfndia.org/home, accessed 30 September 2008.

Jones, B., R. Bowd and R. Tench (2009 pending). 'Corporate irresponsibility and corporate social responsibility: competing realities'. *Social Resposbility Journal*.

Kant, I. (1964). *Groundwork of the Metaphysic of Morals*. London: Harper & Row.

Klein, N. (2000). *No Logo: Taking aim at the brand bullies*. London: Flamingo.

Labich, K. (1992). 'The new crisis in business ethics'. *Fortune* 20 April: 167–176.

Lewis, S. (2003). 'Reputation and corporate social responsibility'. *Journal of Communication Management* **7**(4): 356–364.

Lines, V.L. (2004). 'Corporate reputation in Asia: Looking beyond the bottom line performance'. *Journal of Communication Management* **8**(3): 233–245.

Little, P.L. and B.L. Little (2000). 'Do perceptions of corporate social responsibility contribute to explaining differences in corporate price-earnings ratios? A research note'. *Corporate Reputation Review* **3**(2): 137–142.

Moore, G. (2003). 'Hives and horseshoes, Mintzberg or MacIntyre: What future for corporate social responsibility?'. *Business Ethics: A European Review* **12**(1): 41–53.

MORI (1999). 'Winning with integrity'. London: MORI.

Peach, L. (1987). 'Corporate responsibility' in *Effective Corporate Relations*. N. Hart (ed.). Maidenhead: McGraw-Hill.

Rest, J.R. and S.J. Thoma (1986). 'Educational programs and interventions' in *Moral Development: Advances in research and theory*. J. Rest (ed.). New York: Praeger.

Sagar, P. and A. Singla (2004). 'Trust and corporate social responsibility: Lessons from India'. *Journal of Communication Management* **8**(3): 282–290.

Schwartz, P. and B. Gibb (1999). *When Good Companies Do Bad Things: Responsibility and risk in an age of globalization*. New York: John Wiley & Sons.

Skooglund, C. (1992). 'Ethics in the face of competitive pressures'. *Business Ethics Resource*. Fall: 4.

Snell, R. (1997). 'Management learning perspectives on business ethics' in *Management Learning*. J. Burgoyne and M. Reynolds (eds). London: Sage.

Tench, R. Bowd, R. and Jones, B (2007) 'Perceptions and perspectives: corporate social responsibility and the media'. *Journal of Communication Management* **11**(4): 348–370.

Thomson, S. (2000). *The Social Democratic Dilemma: Ideology, governance and globalization*. London: Macmillan

Trevino, L.K. and K.A. Nelson (1995). *Managing Business Ethics: Straight talk about how to do it right*. New York: Wiley & Sons.

Vandenberg, A. (2000). *Citizenship and Democracy in a Global Era*. London: Macmillan.

Wolstenholme, S. (2004). 'An issues management approach to corporate social responsibility'. Paper presented at the Vilnius Conference, 23 April.

World Economic Forum (2003). www.weforum.com, accessed 26 March 2005.

Websites

BBC: www.bbc.co.uk

Bill and Melinda Gates Foundation: www.gatesfoundation.org

British Society of Rheology: www.bsr.org.uk

Business in the Community: www.bitc.org.uk

Cadbury: www.Cadbury.com

Chartered Institute of Public Relations: www.cipr.co.uk

Co-operative Bank: www.co-operativebank.co.uk

CSR Europe: www.csreurope.org

The Gap: www.gap.com

GlaxoSmithKline: www.gsk.com

Global Responsible Leadership Initiative (GRLI): www.grli.org

Greenpeace: www.greenpeace.org.uk

Institute of Business Ethics: www.ibe.org.uk

Nike: www.nike.com

O2: http://www.O2.co.uk/

The Shell Group: www.shell.com

Slate 60: www.slate.com

United Nations Global Compact: www.unglobalcompact.org

Unilever: www.unilever.co.uk

CHAPTER 8

Martin Langford

Crisis public relations management*

Learning outcomes

By the end of this chapter you should be able to:

■ define and describe crisis public relations

■ recognise how crises occur

■ identify the key principles of crisis public relations planning and management

■ apply this understanding to simple, personally meaningful scenarios

■ apply crisis public relations planning and management principles to real-life scenarios.

Structure

■ Crisis public relations management: the context

■ Crisis public relations management vs operational effectiveness

■ Where do crises come from?

■ Communicating *during* a crisis

■ The Internet and public relations crisis management

■ How to prepare for a crisis

■ Key principles in crisis management

* Chapter 19 in *Exploring Public Relations* Second Edition, edited by Ralph Tench and Liz Yeomans (2009).

Introduction

Crisis public relations (PR) management is one of the most critical aspects of modern communications. Effective crisis management protects companies, their reputations and, at times, can salvage their very existence. A crisis is an event that disrupts normal operations of a company or organisation and, if badly managed, can ruin hard-won reputations in just days and even, in some cases, destroy companies (note the disastrous effects in 2008 of the 'credit crunch' on established banks and businesses e.g. Lehman Brothers, Halifax Bank of Scotland (HBOS), AIG and others). The list of companies whose share price and market capitalisation have nose-dived because of badly managed crises would fill this entire book, let alone this chapter. In a crisis, there is always more than the immediate issue at stake.

This chapter will look at examples of effectively managed crisis situations as well as some of those badly handled crises. We will explore, in some detail, the characteristics of a crisis.

The key to PR crisis management is preparedness. It is vital to effective crisis management that a crisis is identified *before it happens* and, when it does, that it does not get out of control. In this 'information and communications' age, when a crisis does happen, it is crucial to understand the role communication plays and particularly the role of the Internet. In this chapter we will examine the key principles for managing *any* crisis situation using a variety of case studies of both good and bad practice.

Mini Case Study 8.1
Crisis snapshot – Andersen

In 2001 Andersen was one of the best known and respected auditing companies in the world. It was an established and trusted brand. As it became caught up in, and associated with, the problems arising from the Enron energy company crisis (Enron executives had been mismanaging the business and falsifying its financial performance), it saw its business and client base rapidly and drastically reduced. More than just being associated with Enron's mismanagement, Andersen was implicated in an attempted cover-up with reports of coded instructions to employees to 'clean out' Enron-related documents as US federal investigators prepared to launch an investigation. Andersen's board were quickly into a situation of 'last ditch rescue talks' seeking a merger with rival firms. Eventually, Andersen as a brand and as a commercially operating company was destroyed as a consequence of a poorly managed crisis.

Crisis public relations management: the context

PR crisis management literature is filled with lists of 'dos' and 'don'ts' together with countless checklists, for example Howard and Mathews (1985) include a 17-point crisis plan in their media relations book. All these are helpful in describing and dissecting crises. Some of this planning relates to the preparations before a crisis has happened, but generally the lists and guidelines concern coping with the situation in a practical sense after a crisis has happened. Issues management is often closely associated with the crisis planning or preparation phase, i.e. defining and understanding the issues. Heath (1997) supports the link to crisis management and highlights how managing issues can help prevent a crisis. He states (1997: 289): 'If a company is engaged in issues management before, during, and after a crisis (in other words, ongoing), it can mitigate – perhaps prevent – the crisis from becoming an issue by working quickly and responsibly to establish or re-establish the level of control desired by relevant stakeholders.' In this chapter we will aim to build understanding by applying theoretical and practical models to crisis scenarios.

As a starting point it is important to define the area. Cornelissen (2008) describes crisis management as a point of great difficulty or danger to an organisation, possibly threatening its existence and continuity, that requires decisive change.

Seymour and Moore (2000: 10) use a snake metaphor to argue that crises come in two forms:

> The cobra – the 'sudden' crisis – this is a disaster that hits suddenly and takes the company completely by surprise and leaves it in a crisis situation.
>
> The python – the 'slow-burning' crisis or 'crisis creep' – a collection of issues that steal up on the company one by one and slowly crush it.

In 1989 Sam Black broke crises down into the 'known unknown' and the 'unknown unknown'. The former

Activity 8.1

Cobras and pythons

Spend some time thinking about (and researching) crises that have affected organisations and list them under the headings of cobras and pythons as described by Seymour and Moore.

Feedback

Now refer to Lerbinger's eight types of crisis (below) and classify your list under one of them.

includes mishaps owing to the nature of the organisation and its activities, e.g. manufacturing or processing and potential for spillage. The 'unknown unknowns' are events that cannot be predicted and that can come about from employees' behaviour, unconnected events or circumstances that are unpredictable. Before reading further, see Activity 8.1.

Lerbinger (1997) categorised eight types of crisis that he attributed to two causes: management failures or environmental forces. The eight categories are:

1 *natural* (for example, the Asian tsunami, which affected nations, governments, corporations, businesses and the lives and social infrastructure of millions)

2 *technological* (Mercedes 'A' Class car had a design fault and 'rolled over')

3 *confrontation* (Shell Oil whose petrol stations suffered a consumer boycott after the company wanted to sink an oil platform in the North Sea – the Brent Spar, see also Chapter 7)

4 **malevolence** (product tampering by a private citizen, like the Tylenol case detailed later, or direct action by animal rights campaigners, such as placing bombs under the cars of executives whose stores sell cosmetics tested on animals)

5 *skewed management values* (Barings Bank went out of business after managers were accused of turning a blind eye to 'rogue' trader Nick Leeson who hid details of his massive financial losses in the currency markets. An act repeated in 2008 by Jérôme Kervie when working for the French bank, Société Générale. See later in the chapter)

6 *deception* (examples include deceiving employees about the amount of money in pension funds after it has been used by executives to support the business, a UK case being that of Robert Maxwell and the Mirror Group of national newspapers)

7 *management misconduct* (Enron is one of the most shocking examples of this with both illegal and unethical practices rife in the senior management of the practice – see also Andersen, Mini case study 8.1)

8 *business and economic* (the late 1990s boom/bust in numerous small IT/technology companies is an example of how economic cycles can impact an organisation).

Fearn-Banks (2006) defines five stages of a crisis, outlined in Table 8.1.

Table 8.1
Fearn-Banks' five stages of a crisis (*source*: adapted from Fearn-Banks 2006)

	Stage	Features
1	Detection	The organisation is watching for warning signs or what Barton (1993) calls *prodromes* (warning signs)
2	Preparation/prevention	The organisation takes note of the warning signs and prepares plans proactively to avoid the crisis, or reactive ones to cope with the crisis if it comes
3	Containment	Taking steps to limit the length of the crisis or its effects
4	Recovery	This is the stage where effort is made to get back to the 'normal' operational conditions or effectiveness of the organisation
5	Learning	This is when the organisation reflects and evaluates the experience to consider the negative impacts for the organisation and any possible positive benefits for the future

Crisis public relations management vs operational effectiveness

However well a crisis is managed from an operational perspective, it is how an organisation communicates about the crisis that makes the real difference. There is evidence that good communication in a crisis situation can support or increase a company's reputation (British Midland, Tylenol, discussed later). Poor management or a lack of communication skills can have a powerful negative effect on a company's business.

Let us examine the case of the *Exxon Valdez* oil spill in March 1989. The spill took place in Alaska, one of the few true wildernesses in the world, and received a considerable amount of global media coverage. Even though the accident site was appropriately cleaned up (*operational effectiveness*), Exxon took far too long to address its stakeholders (see Chapter 6 for a definition of stakeholders) and, particularly, the media. As a result of this failure of communication, its reputation was substantially tarnished. Insult was added to injury when the CEO finally did talk to the media as he blamed them for exaggerating 'the public relations disaster' that was created around the spill. Exxon's stock market capitalisation dropped $3 billion in the two weeks after the *Exxon Valdez* oil spill in Alaska. (Seymour and Moore 2000: 157)

Seymour and Moore (2000) describe the 'association' or 'parenthesis' factor that lingers on after a crisis. In discussing the mass poisoning of Minimata Bay in Japan, caused by Chisso Corporation, when mercury was dumped into the sea over several decades, poisoning thousands of consumers who ate polluted fish, Seymour and Moore (2000: 157) write:

> For Chisso the hundreds of deaths and thousands of injuries represented a financial burden, aside from the fact that it would be linked with Minimata. The 'association factor' lingers on over other companies; Union Carbide and Bhopal; Exxon, the Exxon Valdez and oil spills; the Herald of Free Enterprise, ferry safety, and P&O.

Now, consider the frequently discussed case at Johnson & Johnson. Over 25 years ago Johnson & Johnson faced a potentially devastating crisis. Tylenol, the company's trusted and leading analgesic (pain reliever) was contaminated with cyanide by a member of the public. This action directly caused the deaths of six people in the Chicago area. Could anything worse happen to an over-the-counter product? Johnson & Johnson did not hesitate to

act and act quickly. For the first time in the history of any product, it issued a comprehensive product recall. It literally pulled off the shelves *all* the capsules throughout the USA – not just in the Chicago area where the deaths occurred. The potential financial consequences of losing a leading product, and the subsequent damage to its brand, could not be exaggerated. But, at the same time, it communicated exactly what it was doing, in a timely manner to *all* stakeholders – shareholders, employees, regulators, the police, press and consumers. How would it act next? How would it re-establish confidence in the product and the brand? How was anyone to trust a Johnson & Johnson product again? Could anyone with a grievance or grudge or another random 'madman' claim to have poisoned the product and effectively blackmail them?

Johnson & Johnson's next response was both direct and decisive. It introduced tamper-evident packaging. It was, in many ways, a very simple operational 'addition' in terms of production – a metal foil to visibly 'seal' the product plus two more physical barriers to entry. Its simplicity was its key. Now, without any doubt, all stakeholders could actually see that the product was safe. Johnson & Johnson acted swiftly and effectively both in terms of operation and communication. Even today Tylenol is seen as one of the best-managed crises and the brand (appropriately) is still a success around the world. This crisis was so well handled that Johnson & Johnson's reputation has actually benefited in the long term – Johnson & Johnson's words *and* actions were seen to be in accord. (See Activity 8.2.)

Activity 8.2

Crisis lessons

What could Exxon have done better in its situation – think in terms of actions and words? If you were an environmentalist, what would you want to know? If you had shares in the company, how would you react? If you were a news reporter, what would your agenda be?

The good . . .

What do you think are the key lessons from the Tylenol case that make this crisis, from over 25 years ago, still discussed so favourably? What do you feel the company got right? How did the company get it right?

Picture 8.1 Protests against Union Carbide following the Bhopal chemical plant disaster (*source*: © Reuters/Corbis)

Where do crises come from?

A spoonful of sugar

Leading crisis counsellors argue that over 50% of crises occur with products that are either ingested or swallowed – including food, drink and oral pharmaceuticals. We all eat and get ill – it is easy to understand how a damaged or defective foodstuff or pharmaceutical can be a major cause for concern. But the source of a crisis might not always be so subtle. A crisis can hit any organisation regardless of what or whom it represents. Whatever manufacturing process is employed or whatever information is disseminated, things can and will go wrong. The food dye scandals that hit the UK in early 2005 showed the extent of impending crisis, when potentially cancer-causing additives resulted in the recall of nearly 500 products (see Food Standards Agency, www.food.gov.uk/news/newsarchive/2005/ for further information).

It's not what you know, but who knows it

This is the information and communications age when highly confidential information somehow always escapes the bounds of its host organisation. Strictly confidential, paper-based hospital records have been found on rubbish dumps, and the hard drives of second-user computers have been found to contain sensitive company or even government information. On 18 October, 2007 HM Revenue and Customs (HMRC) sent via unregistered mail two unencrypted CDs containing the entire child benefit database to the National Audit Office, but they did not arrive. The data on the disks included name, address, date of birth, National Insurance number and bank details of 25 million people. HMRC chairman Paul Gray resigned as a consequence of the crisis. Police believed the CDs were thrown out as rubbish, but over 7 million UK families were asked to remain alert to fraudulent use of their details.

In today's climate it is nearly impossible to keep confidential information confidential. Any organisation should expect that what is known on the *inside* is just as well known on the *outside*.

You won't believe what so-and-so just told me

According to the Institute of Crisis Management, around a quarter of global crises are caused or triggered by employees/members of an organisation. Employees are a company's best asset when they are effectively motivated, remunerated and appreciated. But loyalty may turn – often when least expected. The disaffected employee or former employee taking some form of revenge can trigger a crisis – and when feelings are running high, their negative impact can be huge. One disaffected employee brought down the stock price of a leading healthcare firm by 35% by giving incorrect research information to a leading newspaper; how can we forget the one-man crisis caused by Nick Leeson who brought down the merchant bank Barings through his overzealous financial actions! These actions were well chronicled in a 1998 film, *Rogue Trader*.

On 24 January 2008 French bank Société Générale reported it had fallen victim to the activities of another rogue trading fraud and as a result lost almost €5 billion. The bank stated that these fraudulent transactions were conducted by Jérôme Kerviel, a trader with the company. After the initial investigation police stated they lacked evidence to charge him with fraud and charged him with abuse of confidence and illegal access to computers. Kerviel stated that his actions were known to his superiors as the transactions had been going on for over two years.

Seymour and Moore (2000: 142) outline the characteristics of rumours under crisis conditions:

■ Accept that rumours always generate interest and are often more attractive than the facts.

■ Silence – or a vacuum caused by lack of communication – will always be filled by rumour and speculation.

■ Any organisation of 10 or more people will always have a series of rumours circulating.

Under these circumstances, rumour can contribute to and exacerbate already serious problems. Thus monitoring and **pickup systems** are required, especially when a company is facing or handling a crisis situation.

What are the real costs of a crisis?

With any crisis there are, as we have seen, clear financial costs involved in withdrawing a product, cleaning up after an industrial accident, oil spill, etc. However, compared to the damage that can be done to a reputation, these costs are minimal. Let's take a look at the *real* costs of a crisis.

Management distraction

Even when a crisis is handled well, key leaders or the leadership team are preoccupied for periods that can last from several days to several weeks and cannot manage the daily business. When a crisis hits, the people running an organisation have a crisis to handle!

Labour/employee concern

Employees will naturally be concerned about their own welfare, jobs and financial security. Too few companies communicate effectively with their employees during a crisis. Employees who are both well informed and motivated can be a powerful force in times of crisis. Without them, an organisation will not exist. With them, most things are possible.

Political backlash

Whether at country, EU or global level, crises sow discontent among regulators and 'the authorities' and the chances of regulatory or political pressure on or against an organisation are high. This may be driven by public reaction to the crisis.

Legal actions

We live in a 'do or sue' world. Crises encourage litigious behaviour in individuals, and injury or other compensation claims can inflict huge financial demands. In terms of litigation, an organisation must plan for the worst – and particularly so in the area of product liability.

Customer reactions

It is reassuring how forgiving customers can be, but only if they feel their concerns have been adequately addressed. When an organisation fails to communicate effectively with consumers, it is likely to see its support disintegrate and market share plummet often irretrievably.

Market confidence and reputation

This is the most significant cost of all. Rebuilding a reputation with stakeholders, such as shareholders, consumers and regulators, is not only costly, it can also take years to achieve. Again effective communication is key to reinforcing both public and market confidence. (See Activity 8.3 and Box 8.1.)

Communicating *during* a crisis

The examples and experiences described so far in this chapter dramatically demonstrate that today it is more and more evident why a company or organisation should

Activity 8.3

Crisis and reputation

In 2004 Shell was overoptimistic about its global oil reserves (oil stocks). This miscalculation resulted in the resignations of the head of exploration and the chairman. These revelations plus the two resignations had a substantial impact on share price and reputation for Shell. Think about the points just examined – how would you, as a trainee PR crisis manager, begin to piece together the full impact on Shell of its crisis? What should you be thinking about? Whom should you be thinking about? How does the future look? How has your reputation suffered? What is the way forward?

Feedback

You need systematically to research and answer questions such as these to build an accurate picture.

Box 8.1

Crises in action – What *actually* happens and how does it feel?

The following description of a crisis is based on the experiences of a senior crisis consultant who describes what happens and how it feels.

There is a distinct pattern of events and behaviour that occurs during a crisis. Let's take a look at them.

Surprise!

Crises happen at the most inopportune times – Easter, Christmas, bank holidays or 8 o'clock on a Friday night after a week of hell, when you're enjoying a 'good night out'. It's almost guaranteed that if a crisis were to happen in Japan it will be during the Golden Week holiday, in China it will happen during Chinese New Year or over Thanksgiving in the USA. And the company is usually unaware of the situation until the issue is raised by someone else – be it a regulator, 'authority', key customer or media. Your mobile phone rings. You don't recognise the number, but it's a work phone, so you answer it. What next?

You're on your toes and you can guarantee that your briefcase is not where you left it and you can't find the number for the out-of-hours PR officer. You think you know what to say and the caller tells you they've got a deadline and whatever you say is going to be quoted. As you are thinking on your feet, so your organisation may feel they don't have enough information to deal with the crisis. What are the facts? Who has that information and how is it best understood and represented? Both you and your organisation feel there is an escalating flow of events. Within what may feel like moments, the media are talking about the situation, investment analysts are asking awkward questions and NGOs are getting involved. Everyone seems to be looking in on the organisation – you are in a goldfish bowl and everyone is peering in. It's highly probable that you and your organisation will feel a loss of control over the situation – there are so many different stakeholders and they want to know *right now* what has actually happened and what's being done, or going to be done, and said about it.

Roll down the shutters – crisis leads to drama

There is immense and intense scrutiny from outside the company. This can lead to a siege mentality where individuals feel everyone is *against them* and their organisation. This reaction invariably and rapidly leads to panic. 'I don't know what you're on about!' you tell the caller. 'I don't believe a word of it – you're just after a story. I suggest you go and pick on someone less gullible.' Once panic sets in rational decision making goes out of the window. But applying *rational* thinking to *irrational* events is exactly what's called for. 'Those are very serious allegations. It is not appropriate for me to comment immediately. I will return your call within 15 minutes. Before this time, I'm afraid I'm unable to comment.' What happens next?

communicate effectively at the onset of a crisis. Yet many companies argue against it. Preparing for a crisis costs time, money and energy – and crisis preparedness training is often seen as an unnecessary luxury. Even when an organisation is urged to communicate about its situation by experienced crisis management counsellors, there is often a list of reasons why it cannot communicate, such as:

Think about 8.1

'No comment'– what happens when companies will not respond

If a company spokesperson refuses to comment, what is your reaction? What would you think if you were the journalist asking the question? or a customer of the company?

Feedback

The sequence of events may go something like this:

- The company chooses to say: 'No comment.'

- The media say: 'The company was unwilling to take part in this programme.'

- Consumers think: 'No smoke without fire.'
  'They're hiding something.'
  'Guilty!'

When an organisation does not take control of a crisis situation and fails to communicate immediately, the media will go to a whole range of *other* sources to get the information they need. Take a look at the following list – they are all readily available sources of information and 'expert' opinion in a crisis situation: the company website; the Internet; emergency services – police, ambulance, fire, coast guard, mountain rescue, etc.; hospital authorities; medical, scientific and other experts; former employees; directors; local authorities; government departments; government ministers and

other politicians; social services; neighbouring businesses, security, business and other analysts; academics; your customers and clients; charities and aid organisations; psychologists and 'disaster' counsellors; specialist writers and correspondents; freelance journalists; newspaper cuttings; film; picture libraries; public records; annual and other reports and directories; members of the public and 'eye witnesses'; competitor companies and organisations; trade unions and professional bodies and pressure groups and other NGOs.

The media will also talk to the company receptionist – the friendly face who's been on the front desk representing the organisation for the last 25 years. They'll speak to the night security officer or the person in company overalls who keeps the boiler going and is seen leaving the plant at 6 o'clock in the morning. They're loyal and dependable; they are the face of the company . . . But how much do they really know? How much do you think they know? Maybe they know more than you think. Have they been prepared for crisis situations – for the leading questions of journalists who might appear to be their best friend? They have a voice and the media will let them speak for themselves. If they are prepared appropriately, they too are an invaluable resource to a company.

- The need to assemble all the facts before it communicates.

- The desire to avoid panic, for instance it fears that by mentioning the individual brand, people will think the corporate brand is 'infected' as well.

- It does not have a trained spokesperson and is not going to put anyone up against a seasoned television interviewer such as Jeremy Paxman on the BBC's *Newsnight* (a late-evening 'hard' news programme).

- It has had other problems recently and cannot talk about this problem because it will impact on its overall corporate reputation.

- The issue of how to solve the crises – no one knows how to solve the problem at the outbreak of the crisis; every single crisis situation companies face, and their solutions, will be substantially different.

- The fear of revealing proprietary information or revealing competitive information that may give the company new competitive problems.

See Think about 8.1.

Talking to the media

The way a company communicates to the media is critical. Selecting a spokesperson or spokespeople is one of the most important decisions in the effective management of any crisis. Whoever acts as spokesperson should follow the proposed 5Cs model (Figure 8.1) to be effective. This is based on consultancy experience of senior crisis managers.

Concern
Clarity
Control
Confidence
Competence

Figure 8.1 The 5Cs effective communication model

The sections of the 5Cs model in Figure 8.1 can be explained as follows.

Concern

Not to be confused with legal liability, concern is a simple human emotion. The organisation's spokesperson needs to show true concern about the problem, concern about what has happened and concern for the people affected now and in the future – including potential customers/service users.

Clarity

Organisations need to talk with clarity. Starting from the early hours of the crisis, they need to have very clear messages. What the spokesperson says at the outset will be repeated throughout the duration of the crisis.

Control

When talking to the media, spokespeople must take control of the messages, the situation, the environment and the venue.

Confidence

The spokesperson must get the key messages across with confidence, but without appearing complacent or arrogant.

Competence

They must also demonstrate competence and reflect how, as the representative of the organisation, they will handle the crisis.

How will the media react?

In the first instance, the media will want to know the facts. Their first questions are likely to be those in Box 8.2.

Box 8.2

Typical first questions from the media

- What happened?
- What went wrong? Why?
- Who is to blame/accountable?
- What is happening right now?
- What are you doing to prevent it from happening again?

While these initial questions are generally predictable, how the media will act and how they will report a crisis should never be assumed. Everyone asks questions from 'their own perspective' and everyone, especially the news-hungry media, will have their 'own take' on the crisis situation. As well as general reporters, there may also be very well-informed specialist correspondents to consider. (See Activity 8.4.)

Activity 8.4

A crisis from a journalist's perspective

Put yourself in the position of a journalist being asked to report on a crisis scenario, say a major rail crash. How might you react as a journalist in a crisis? What might you want to know if you were in their situation? To whom would you want to speak? What do you need to get your story on the front page? How different would your questions be if you worked for the local paper or a transport publication?

Feedback

If you were in this situation, what kind of media coverage should you expect? You *could* experience the following:

- The initial media reports will be speculative, wrong, exaggerated, sensationalised, often very personalised, spiteful or hurtful – and possibly, even, right! Expect the media to 'round up' the scale of the problem simply because it makes for a better story. Expect the media to make a drama out of your crisis.

- Experts will be called in to comment on the problem. These 'specialists' in various 'fields of expertise' will discuss ideas of what went wrong and how it happened.

- An exclusive article, containing sensitive information that, of course, the organisation did not want to have made known.

- Someone will say this disaster has been waiting to happen.

- The timing will be wrong, the crisis team will be out of town, their deputies abroad or the spokesperson's mobile phone will have been stolen!

- Opinions and rumours will dominate media reporting – especially if the organisation does not respond effectively. Expect rumours to become fact and expect rumour to chase rumour.

The Internet and public relations crisis management

Since the days of the Tylenol crisis referred to earlier in this chapter, the media environment has changed dramatically. The once limited media market has become global and highly sophisticated. The impact the Internet has on crisis management today is enormous. The speed with which communications can be delivered is phenomenal and available to so many people – from home computers, via Internet cafés, through to corporate communications infrastructure. If something happens, someone somewhere will be giving their own, often live, version of events. From individuals, through online communities, adversarial organisations and NGOs, the Internet is very effective in putting a message out. It is impossible to censor the Internet – which is both its strength and its weakness – but it is a highly effective vehicle for the dissemination of information and opinion that may masquerade as information.

Seymour and Edelman (2004) describe the new challenges posed by the Internet:

> But when considering how to turn around a crisis today, management teams must accept that the media represent only part of an array of communication channels – albeit one of the most noisy and demanding. In a world dominated by low trust and the corrosive effects of cynicism, corporate voices can quickly be ignored, distorted or drowned out by the incessant noise that characterizes each and every crisis situation . . . Over the last ten years, crisis management and communications have been forced to develop in response to a series of technology and IT-driven changes. . . . At the same time single-issue groups and NGOs were recognizing the potential of the internet. Now it is possible for a small group to drive campaigns across the internet, while at the same time empowering individuals to express their opinions at the click of a mouse.

(See Box 8.3.)

The totally unregulated nature of the Internet thus gives organisations huge cause for concern. The Internet has become the new rumour mill where people can say anything they want or create websites that criticise specific organisations, companies and specific industries (see, for example, www.untied.com, which is dedicated to problems with United Airlines, or www.mercedes-benz-usa.com/, a site whose agenda is obvious!). On a basic level, we see viruses crippling so many of our computer systems, from worms to Trojans, and the average user gets increasingly concerned about losing control of their own com-

Box 8.3

Speed of the Internet in a crisis

The speed of spread of information and news in the new communication era is well illustrated by the Paddington/Ladbroke Grove accident in London on 5 October 1999.

At 08.06, Michael Hodder, the Thames Train driver, pulled out of the platform at Paddington Station.

At 08.11, having gone through three warning and stop signals, the Thames Train ploughed into the front of inbound GNER express train.

It took until 08.32 for the operational staff at Reading to establish from the controlling signal box at Slough that a serious accident had taken place involving one of their trains, that a serious fire had broken out (most unusual in train crash incidents) and that there were probably many injuries and even fatalities.

But if anyone had been on the Internet at 08.21 they would have been able to read 'breaking news' reports of a rail accident at Ladbroke Grove involving deaths, serious injuries and a severe fire.

puter. As technologies advance, so these viruses and the impact they have on our day-to-day lives become more apparent – they are, at best, an annoyance.

At a corporate level, there are a host of both technical and security issues that affect the operation and effectiveness of an organisation. Consider website tampering – where individuals can gain access to a company's website – a malicious individual or organisation can enter their views, enforce some new policies or give spurious comments, interfere with email and raise all manner of hoaxes. This costs a considerable amount of time and money and can become unmanageable. In September 2004, UK telephone company NTL had its systems sabotaged when a hacker changed the outgoing message on its customer service phone number to tell callers that NTL did not care about their problem and they should just get a life! One need only think back to the resources deployed for preparations for the 2000 new year (Y2K, the new millennium, when there was a fear that all computer systems would crash) to see how many companies chose to spend large sums of money on IT, rather than take any chances. The Gartner Group estimates that global spending on Y2K totalled $600 billion.

Direct face-to-face communication generally, and particularly during a time of crisis, is therefore a positive advantage – whether that be two individuals face to face in a TV interview or the CEO of a 'mega corp' (major multinational organisation) addressing their staff directly at a meeting.

How to prepare for a crisis

Crises do come as a surprise and at unexpected times, but any organisation – commercial or public sector – can prepare itself for the inevitable and every company should. Methods such as research in the form of crisis audits, preparing a crisis manual and conducting crisis simulations or training will ensure that organisations are better equipped to handle any crisis. (See Box 8.4.)

Crisis audit

The first step in preparation is to conduct an audit that assesses the current vulnerabilities and strengths of the company or organisation. The audit will research key areas, such as operations, marketing, employee relations, safety experts, environmental experts, government, legal and communications people. It will ask tough questions to determine the most likely scenario that could happen, assess how well prepared the company is to deal with it and whether it has all the necessary resources.

Box 8.4

Actions to prepare for a crisis

- Conduct a crisis audit.
- Prepare a crisis manual.
- Conduct regular crisis simulation training.

Activity 8.5

Doing a crisis audit

If you were conducting a crisis audit for your place of study or work, what would you need to know? Make a list of the key areas where something might go wrong. How could you find out whether your organisation has a crisis plan? What would you expect it to contain?

Feedback

The audit often shows companies a need for change. It might be an operational change, a change in how a product is labelled or how the company is marketed, or a change in what research is openly discussed with the regulator.

An educational organisation, for example, would have to consider potential problems originating from staff or students, such as scandals, court cases, exam results, protests. Some colleges and universities have also had crises due to outbreaks of meningitis, for example, which have led to clearer guidance to new students about symptoms and proper actions to take.

The audit results can then be used to identify the key trouble spots, identify which stakeholders would be affected and help management build scenarios to train a key crisis team with the techniques of effective crisis management. In addition to being able to train a crisis team, the assessment can help build a comprehensive system for managing crisis communications. (See Activity 8.5.)

Crisis manual

Another means of preparation is a crisis manual. A good crisis manual contains a simple system of rapid communications, basic messages and audience identification and should not be more than 10 pages long. Anything longer will not be used in a crisis. A well-prepared crisis manual can serve as a guide for many of the basic tasks, such as activating the crisis team and facilities, and allows more time for the crisis team to focus on the more critical issues (see Figure 8.2).

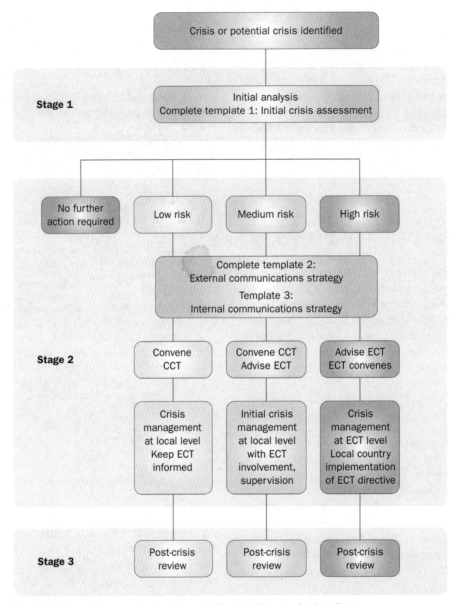

Key: ECT – External Communications Team; CCT – Crisis Communications Team

Figure 8.2 Crisis communications action plan

Crisis simulation and training

The final step in crisis planning is to conduct simulation training. Crisis simulation training is designed to create a real atmosphere of crisis. It integrates group and individual exercises, tests the skills of the spokesperson or spokespeople, tests the crisis plan and finally examines and evaluates the communications tools to find weak spots. Such exercises range from desktop exercises to full-blown global tests of the team. Repetition of crisis simulation and exercises are crucial to ensure that any weaknesses are addressed.

A useful method that can also help prepare a company is to incorporate debriefing sessions into the communications plan to make sure the team understands the emerging issues, what they are doing in terms of community relations and how they are working with the newest techniques in crisis management. They should also be aware of the importance of community and employee relations.

Today in the UK, just over one-quarter of companies (27%) research possible vulnerabilities but only 16% conduct regular crisis preparedness workshops (Webserve Solutions Ltd, www.webservesolutions.net). Those companies who have not prepared or trained will be rehearsing their crisis strategy in the middle of their first major crisis!

Ambassador L. Paul Bremer, former Chairman of the US National Terrorism Commission before he was assigned to his mission in Iraq, stated in an article in the *Harvard Business Review* April 2002:

> *Before 9/11, a poll of CEOs in the US showed that 85% expected to manage a crisis during their time in office but only 50% admitted to having a plan. However 97% were confident that they could handle a crisis. This sounds to me like over-confidence. I hope that more businesses are taking a hard look at their plans.*

There is no doubt that physical and IT aspects of plans – contingency plans, business continuity, security and business interruption – have come under closer scrutiny since the **9/11** tragedy. However, the main focus has been on operational factors and often the key aspects of communication readiness and planning have been neglected.

One of the hallmarks of a well-managed crisis is knowledge. A company is better prepared when it knows what its stakeholders think about the product, the brand and the corporation. Both Mattessons Walls (see the Peperami case, Case study 8.1) and Johnson & Johnson (in the Tylenol crisis covered earlier in the chapter) commissioned research throughout their situation to find out precisely what their key audiences were thinking. There is often a tendency to judge what the audience thinks on the basis of media headlines, which can lead to overreaction and mismanagement of a crisis.

Key principles in crisis management

To draw this chapter together and support students in understanding how to manage crisis PR situations, the following 10 key principles have been identified. These are based on the experience of leading crisis consultants (counsellors) over three decades and influenced by the analysis of crises in a range of international settings, with various commercial and non-commercial situations. These principles are summarised in Box 8.5 and described in further detail below.

Crisis management principles

Define the real problem

This is the most critical aspect of effective PR crisis management. Define both the short-term problem – address

---

Box 8.5

Ten key principles in public relations crisis management

1   Define the real problem.
2   Centralise or at least control information flow.
3   Isolate a crisis team from daily business concerns.
4   Assume a worst-case planning position.
5   Do not fully depend on one individual.
6   Always resist the combative instinct.
7   Understand why the media are there.
8   Remember all constituents (stakeholders).
9   Contain the problem.
10 Recognise the value of short-term sacrifice.

---

the situation right now – and the long-term problem to ensure the brand/corporation recovers in terms of both market share and reputation.

Centralise or at least control information flow

This applies to items of information both coming in and going out. If there is a multi-country issue, have one 'central place' as the focus. This, in very practical terms, will make communication within the organisation easier. If it is not feasible to have one centre, then all spokespeople must be rigorously trained so as to communicate the same message. Be aware of language sensitivities and terms of reference that may not translate readily from one language to another.

Isolate a crisis team from daily business concerns

Crises, as we have seen, are by their very nature all enveloping. While managing a crisis, the day job has to be put on hold. In the case of Tylenol, Jim Burke, Johnson & Johnson CEO, insisted he became the brand manager for Tylenol. He was able to delegate his many leadership tasks and this enabled him to focus on doing the right thing for Johnson & Johnson while relieving him of his day-to-day responsibilities.

Mini Case Study 8.2
Coca-Cola Belgium

Coca-cola representatives in 1999 acknowledged that the crisis described below was bigger than any worst-case scenario they could have imagined. They also publicly admitted that perhaps they had lost control.

Philippe L'Enfant, a senior executive with Coca-Cola Enterprises in 1999, in an interview on Belgian television said: 'Perhaps [we] lost control of the situation to a certain extent.'

The population of Belgium was still reeling from fears about mad cow disease and the presence of the carcinogen dioxin in animal feed when reports of schoolchildren being hospitalised after drinking Coca-Cola surfaced. More cases from other parts of Europe were found and Coca-Cola products were banned in several countries. While the public speculated as to the cause, ranging from rat poison to extortion, the company delayed full apologies and tried to deny the problem and its responsibility.

Coca-Cola sources speculated that the problem could be due to contaminated CO_2 and creosote-tinged pallets and were quoted as saying: 'It may make you feel sick, but it is not harmful.' Meanwhile, Coca-Cola was losing an estimated $3.4 million in revenue each day and 19% of consumers had 'reservations' about drinking Coke.

Coca-Cola most definitely had a crisis management strategy but it still found itself losing control.

Box 8.6

Key learning points from the Coca-Cola case

- Facts do not always rule – emotions, speculations/rumours are strong complicating factors.
- Think 'outside in' – plan messages and actions based on stakeholders' perspectives. Here, Coca-Cola was caught out by a combination of extremely sensitive regulatory authorities and parents keen to protect their children.
- The CEO must be visible.
- Do not let other stakeholders shape your reputation.
- Call on your allies (these could be other producers or suppliers of materials or packaging).
- Message alignment and internal communications are key (to maintain consistency in messages circulating inside and outside the organisation).
- Regret, resolution and reform (demonstrate regret, find a resolution to the problem and how to reform what the company is doing).
- Be better prepared – think 'worst case', not just precedent.

Assume a worst-case planning position

Ensure the crisis team thinks about the worst-case scenario in terms of what could happen to the brand and to the organisation. More often than not, people estimate the worst from their own perspective, or what they are able to handle, rather than a true worst case. It is, therefore, important to brainstorm and get as much input from others as possible. (See Mini case study 8.2 and Box 8.6.)

Do not fully depend on one individual

The person managing the crisis must depend on the whole team for information, but never rely on information from just one individual. Some team members may have a vested interest in a particular area and want to protect their own or their department's reputation. It is important that the messages put out during a crisis are not subverted by the influence of one department over another. These subtleties can be worked out at a later date. There is usually more than one department's internal reputation on the line when a crisis hits.

Always resist the combative instinct

Do not go into battle with the media, NGOs, competitors or suppliers. An organisation must demonstrate it is in control during the crisis. The outcome of being combative could well destroy the brand or reputation. Words said in anger, or defence, may be temporarily satisfying, but they may not represent the best position for the crisis PR manager or the organisation. When Ronald Li, Chairman of the Hong Kong Stock Exchange suspended trading in 1987 in an attempt to defuse a run on the exchange, the

Activity 8.6

Stakeholders (publics)

Think of an organisation you know well or are interested in and note down all the stakeholders (publics). See also Chapter 6 for further information about stakeholders. You could think about the university or college you considered in Activity 8.5.

Feedback

It can be useful to break stakeholders down into internal and external as follows.

Internal stakeholders

Employees and their families, medical department, security, supervisors, managers and corporate managers and unions if applicable. In a university, there would be employees – academics, administrators and service workers, each group with its own hierarchies and unions, as well as students and their unions.

External stakeholders

The online community, local authorities, factories or facilities (in the local community), community residents and leaders, regulator(s), government, contractors, suppliers, customers, distributors, shippers, technical experts, the financial community and relevant NGOs. A university is accountable to the government, research bodies, grant-making bodies, suppliers, students' parents and local authorities, as well as the local community.

Activity 8.7

Consumer reaction to a crisis

Consider these questions related to the Peperami case (Case study 8.1).

Why did consumers react so positively to Mattessons Walls' handling of this crisis?

The market share of the product increased by 14% post-relaunch – why do you think this happened?

Feedback

Now think about companies and products you experience every day.

As a consumer, what do you want to know about the products you buy? Make a list and try to organise the issues you are interested in. Put them in themes or categories, e.g. safety, the manufacturing process, location of production, who owns the company, etc.

relate to. A firm can assert the facts as it sees them and thus defuse an 'on-the-face-of-it' story.

Remember all constituents (stakeholders)

It is not just the media that need fast and relevant responses during a crisis. The crisis plan has to take all the stakeholders into consideration. (See Activity 8.6.)

Contain the problem

Reduce the problem to as small a geographical area as possible to prevent it becoming a bigger problem – from local to national or national to international. In these days of the international media and the Internet, localising an issue is a major challenge. However, it should be an objective. For example, in the Peperami case (Case study 8.1), the affected batch was only being sold in the UK. Efforts to focus the problem led to the subsequent recall being limited to just the UK despite the product being widely available throughout Europe.

Recognise the value of short-term sacrifice

This might involve recalling the product or dismissing the person responsible for causing the problem.

The value of short-term sacrifice can be well illustrated by Case study 8.1 on Peperami (see also Case study 8.2).

crisis was made worse when he lost his cool with a journalist at the subsequent press conference. The journalist suggested that closing the exchange was outside Mr Li's legal powers. Mr Li responded by demanding his name and threatening to sue him. He actually ended up in prison himself (for unrelated charges of insider trading).

During the 2001 general election campaign in the UK, the Deputy Prime Minister John Prescott found out only too well the impact of a violent reaction from someone in the public eye. When a heckler threw an egg at Mr Prescott, it was not particularly newsworthy. But when Mr Prescott replied with a left-hook punch, it was in all the papers for days.

Understand why the media are there

The media are searching for a good story. They need focus, a 'cause and effect' – something that their audience will

Case Study 8.1
Peperami

In 1987 the UK Department of Health linked Peperami to an outbreak of salmonella poisoning, a notifiable illness in the UK. The decision was taken to recall affected products, but due to the packaging used for the product, the affected batch could not be precisely identified by consumers from the bar code. The recall was therefore extended to the whole of the UK.

Peperami dominated the salami-style meat snacks market, with 80% of market share and widespread product distribution across 40,000 outlets. Peperami could be found in a huge range of retail outlets, including supermarkets, corner stores, clubs and pubs.

Strategy

Peperami is just one of many meat products produced by Mattessons Walls and a key early priority was to limit the impact of the salmonella problem to the Peperami brand. Mattessons Walls was positioned as an importer and not a manufacturer, distancing Peperami from the parent company to stop a product problem becoming a major corporate problem. Meanwhile, it was crucial to share the facts in the case and communicate fully to all stakeholders.

Actions

A media control centre was set up, manned by experienced media relations people 24 hours a day, 7 days a week. A consumer telephone centre was also established with telephone operators given daily updates/briefings. Tracking research was initiated to determine exactly how consumers thought the crisis was being handled and analyse their perceptions of the Peperami brand, giving the management team crucial information on the impact it was having beyond the media reactions.

Employee statements were prepared for all Mattessons Walls employees and regular updates were given to Unilever, Mattessons Walls' parent company, to keep it up to date with developments.

During the recall and the time the product was off the market, each media relations executive worked with an individual health editor from each national newspaper and a member of the team was appointed to liaise with the Department of Health.

Result

Mattessons Walls received public commendation from the Department of Health for the way it had handled the situation, and research showed that more than 90% of consumers were impressed with the way the withdrawal was handled. Within three months of relaunch, Peperami's share of the salami snack foods market stood at 94%, a 14% increase, despite the introduction of a competitive product from a national supermarket's (Sainsbury) own label. (See Activity 8.7.)

Case Study 8.2
Melbourne Gas crisis

Finally, let us take a look at a crisis that puts all these key principles into perspective: the Melbourne Gas crisis that threw the entire state of Victoria, Australia, into chaos for a fortnight, but is remembered for being one of the best managed crises in Australian history.

Event

A major explosion at the Exxon refinery at Longford, Melbourne, on Friday 25 September 1998 destroyed part of the plant, killing two and injuring eight refinery workers and cutting gas supplies to factories, businesses and private homes across the state.

Effects

The state of Victoria was highly dependent on cheap gas and its population of more than 3 million was almost totally dependent on this one plant. Ninety-eight per cent of Victoria's gas customers would have no gas supply for the foreseeable future. Manufacturing industries stood down 150,000 employees and the estimated cost to industry was $A100 million a day. VENCorp, the distributor of gas for Victoria, invoked emergency powers to restrict gas use, and media reporting highlighted that millions of people faced the prospect of cold showers.

case study 8.2 (continued)

Strategy

Gas would only be available to emergency services and both VENCorp and the state government stressed in all communications that jobs were the first priority, not hot showers!

When the gas supply was ready to be restored, it constituted the biggest single gas relight programme in the world and both consumers and the system needed to be prepared to be protected from relighting accidents. The crisis team made editorial content and a multi-language brochure the focus of a safe relight communications programme. Operationally, when the supply was ready to be reintroduced, the odd/even house numbers would be used to phase gas supply in safely and particularly to protect the gas network.

Actions

Four thousand emergency service volunteers were used to turn off gas meters, and call centres were established which, at the crisis peak, received 131,561 calls a day. There was in-house coordination and development of call centre scripts and the top 10 frequently asked questions from the call centres were advertised daily in major media.

To ensure seamless communication, the communications team sat on the government gas supply emergency coordination committee and critical services working group, established a 24-hour media response centre manned by a team of 15 people and arranged twice-daily media briefings at 10am and 3pm. Key spokespersons were given media training.

A responsive and pre-emptive issues management programme was developed and as a key element of a safe relight programme, 2.3 million brochures were sent to all households and small businesses alongside a major print and television ad campaign.

Communicating with the ethnic communities was identified early as a challenge in Victoria; the brochure was translated into 20 languages and distributed, and an information line was set up offering interpreter services in 100 languages.

Assessment

When the gas supply was restored there were only 9 relight accidents and 12,000 appliance repairs. Alan Stockdale, Treasurer of Victoria, said at a government press briefing on Friday 9 October 1998:

I think every Victorian can take pride in the fact that our community has responded so well, and that the reconnection program, on the massive scale, is taking place in such a safe and orderly manner.

We estimate that 1.1 million domestic customers, out of a total of 1.35 million, have been reconnected to the gas supply now.

Eighty-five percent of domestic customers have been able to reconnect without assistance, indicating that the wide-ranging safety program has been very successful.

I consider this to be the best-handled issue that I have seen since I have been interested in public affairs issues in this state.

I have been told by many, including my wife, that this [holding up the brochure] was the first document of the kind that they have read and clearly understood what they needed to do and what they shouldn't do.

This incident has been managed as well as it could have possibly been done – there is no higher praise than that.

David Guthrie-Jones, Manager Communications VENCorp, said at an Australian Gas Association meeting on 16 November 1998:

So we called in communications experts, who sent an excellent team of experience and enthusiasm to help with our crisis communication strategy and implementation.

I can tell you this. Having back-up communication or public relations consultants experienced in crisis management is absolutely crucial to the success of handling large scale emergencies . . . this is what helped make the difference between success and failure for us at the end of the day.

Summary

There is no guaranteed recipe for successful crisis management but there are key ingredients: knowledge, preparation, calmness, control and communication will see an organisation secure the best possible outcome from a crisis. They may even help to find the opportunity that can come from a crisis (the characters that represent 'crisis management' in both Chinese and Japanese actually mean 'danger' and 'opportunity'). Preparing for the unexpected but inevitable ensures that any organisation can take the drama out of a crisis.

Bibliography

Baker, G.F. (2000). 'Race and reputation: Restoring image beyond the crisis' in *Handbook of Public Relations*. R.L. Heath (ed.). London: Sage.

Barton, L. (1993). *Crisis in Organisations: Managing communications in the heart of chaos*. Cincinati, OH: South Western.

Baskin, O. and C. Aronoff (1997). *Public Relations: The profession and the practice*. London: Brown & Benchmark.

Black, S. (1989). *Introduction to Public Relations*. London: Modino Press.

Bland, M. (1998). *Communicating Out of a Crisis*. London: Macmillan.

Bremer, P.L. (2002). 'Doing business in a dangerous world'. *Harvard Business Review* 80(4), April: 22.

Cornelissen, J. (2008). *Corporate Communications: A guide to theory and practice*, 2nd edition. London: Sage.

Daniels, T., B. Spiker and M. Papa (1997). *Perspectives on Organizational Communication*, 4th edition. London: Brown & Benchmark.

Fearn-Banks, K. (2000). 'Crisis communication: A review of some best practices' in *Handbook of Public Relations*. R.L. Heath (ed.). London: Sage.

Fearn-Banks, K. (2006). *Crisis Communications: A casebook approach*, 3rd edition. Mahwah, NJ: Lawrence Erlbaum Associates.

Fearn-Banks, K. (2008). *Crisis Communication Student Workbook*, 3rd edition. London: Routledge.

Food Standards Agency (2005). www.food.gov.uk/news/newsarchive/2005, accessed 26 September 2008.

Harrison, S. (2000). *Public Relations – An Introduction*, 2nd edition. London: Thompson Business Press.

Hearit, K.M. (2000). 'Corporate apologia: When an organization speaks in defense of itself' in *Handbook of Public Relations*. R.L. Heath (ed.). London: Sage.

Heath, R.L. (1997). *Strategic Issues Management: Organizations and public policy challenges*. Thousand Oaks, CA: Sage.

Heath, R. L. (2004). *Handbook of Public Relations*. London, Sage.

Howard, C. and W. Matthews (1985). *On Deadline: Managing media relations*. Prospect Height, IL: Waveland Press.

Laune, J. (1990). 'Corporate issues management: An international view'. *Public Relations Review* XVI(1), Spring.

Laville, L. (2008). 'A crisis case study: The London Bombings 2005', unpublished. Leeds Metropolitan University

Lerbinger, O. (1997). *The Crisis Manager: Facing risks and responsibility*. Mahwah, NJ: Lawrence Erlbaum Associates.

Olaniran, B.A. and D.E. Williams (2000). 'Anticipatory model of crisis management: A vigilant response to technological crises' in *Handbook of Public Relations*. R.L. Heath (ed.). London: Sage.

O'Rourke, R. and B. Marsteller (1998). 'Managing in times of crisis'. *Corporate Reputation Review* 2(1).

Regester, M. and J. Larkin (1997). *Risk Issues and Crisis Management*. London: Kogan Page.

Regester, M. and J. Larkin (2008). *Risk Issues and Crisis Management in Public Relations*. London: Kogan Page.

Reynolds, C. (1997). 'Issues management and the Australian gun debate'. *Public Relations Review* 23(4), Winter.

Seitel, F. (2006). *The Practice of Public Relations*, 10th edition. London: Prentice Hall.

Seymour, M. and D.J. Edelman (2004). 'Fighting on all fronts'. *CEO Magazine* September.

Seymour, M. and S. Moore (2000). *Effective Crisis Management: Worldwide principles and practice*. London: Cassell.

Thill, J. and C. Bovee (1996). *Business Communication Today*, 4th edition. New York: McGraw-Hill.

Young, D. (1996). *Building Your Company's Good Name: How to create and protect the reputation your organization deserves.* New York: Amacon.

Zyglidopoulos, S. (1999). 'Responding to reputational crisis: A stakeholder perspective'. *Corporate Reputation Review* 2(4).

Websites

Food Standards Agency: www.food.gov.uk
The *Daily Telegraph:* www.dailytelegraph.co.uk
The *Guardian:* www.guardianunlimited.co.uk

CHAPTER 9

Sue Wolstenholme

Campaigning organisations and pressure groups*

Learning outcomes

By the end of this chapter you should be able to:

■ analyse how campaigning organisations and pressure groups are motivated and formed and how they grow

■ avoid the risks of publicity for its own sake

■ recognise the use that is made of the Internet for campaigning, recruiting and disrupting

■ analyse the public relations roles on all sides and the use of two-way communication and consensus

■ plan a campaign for a pressure group

■ evaluate the development of consensus or dissensus using research to inform the co-orientation model.

Structure

■ Types of campaigning organisation

■ Key issues for public relations practitioners in organisations and campaigning groups

■ Campaign tactics

■ People, politics and globalisation

■ Building and evaluating consensus

■ Practical guidelines for campaigning public relations

* Chapter 28 in *Exploring Public Relations* Second Edition, edited by Ralph Tench and Liz Yeomans (2009).

Introduction

Campaigning organisations and pressure groups (or activist groups as they are also known) are the embodiment of active publics (Grunig and Hunt 1984). They are groups of people who share a common interest or concern and have come together to do something about it – whether to march, raise funds, change public policy, prevent something from happening (such as an airport extension or the damming of a valley), make something happen (such as winning the vote for black people in South Africa) or just to raise awareness about an issue.

This chapter explores some of the motivations for these groups and some of the activities and tactics employed by them. It also examines the role of public relations (PR), both within the activist groups and in the organisations or companies that might have inspired their development.

Types of campaigning organisation

When talking about campaigning organisations, the PR literature frequently refers to 'activists'. Activists are regarded as a challenge to PR practitioners working for corporations but it should also be borne in mind that activist organisations employ PR practitioners too. Activists include 'special interest groups, pressure groups, issue groups, grassroots organizations, or social movement organizations' (Smith 1996).

Trade unions

Trade unions were formed on a mass scale in Britain at the end of the nineteenth century to represent the workers employed in major industries such as cotton, mining, metallurgy and shipping. Elsewhere in Europe, the trade union movement grew up around ports and other forms of transport such as railways. Later, especially in France, public service unions were formed to represent employees of the state. What united these very different groups of workers was the growing influence of socialist ideology, particularly the idea that the working classes could be organised politically and did not have to put up with social injustice (Hobsbawn 1987).

Today, trade unions exist across the globe to protect workers' rights and to campaign for improved pay and conditions for their members. These groups have become very formalised with written constitutions and a clear set of objectives and rules. However, in some countries, such as Burma and Equatorial Guinea, it is illegal to belong to a union. In other countries, it is positively dangerous. The most dangerous place in 2000 was Colombia, where 153 trade unionists were assassinated or 'disappeared'. According to the International Confederation of Free Trade Unions' annual survey of violations of trade union rights (www.globalpolicy.org), there are 108 countries that put up legal obstacles to union membership. In most democracies, union membership is optional. However, in the USA, some employers hire professional 'union busters' to break up any unions at their workplaces. The different unions often have to work hard to win members. Also many countries have introduced legislation to curb the power of trade unions, often making it impossible or very difficult for workers to withdraw their labour by striking, thereby taking from them their most effective tool of protest or persuasion. (See Think about 9.1.)

Non-governmental organisations (NGOs)

Nearly one-fifth of the world's 37,000 non-governmental organisations (NGOs) were formed in the 1990s (McGann and Johnston 2006). Some NGOs play an official international role in ensuring that countries work together to support peace, better education and health – the United Nations and its associated bodies, UNESCO and the World Health Organisation, being the main examples. However, the activities of NGOs as campaigning and pressure groups are on the increase in response to a wide range of global issues concerned with the effects of human consumption and resources: the food we eat, the energy we use, the environment we inhabit and the ways in which resources are distributed among nations and societies; as well as the ways in which human rights are dealt with. Well-known examples of activist NGOs (also known 'grassroots' campaigners) include Amnesty International and Greenpeace.

Charities

Some NGO organisations in the UK can become registered charities as long as their purpose and function fit the rules of the Charity Commission for England and Wales. The 'essential requirement of charities is that they operate for

Think about 9.1 — Employees' freedom of expression

As a PR officer in a company, you might be responsible for internal communication and helping to maintain staff morale. How important do you think it is for staff to be able to express their views without fear of reprisal? How might you go about gauging staff views and morale?

You might like to consider the following quotes about the significance of good employee relationships. 'Recognition of the efficient use of human resources for business success, together with advances in social democracy have highlighted the increasing importance of employee involvement and industrial partnership including the role played by trade unions' (Coupar 1994: 45–50 in Mullins 1999).

'No organisation can perform at its best unless each employee is committed to the corporate objectives and works as an effective team member. That is not going to happen if the employee's views are not listened to within an open two-way dialogue' (Mullins 1999: 651).

Feedback

You would need to consider organisational culture and to what extent this 'allows' views to be expressed, either formally through trade union representation or through upward communication channels. Bear in mind that formal representations by trade unions are made to the human resources function, not to the PR function. However, strike action can be damaging to an organisation's reputation and therefore trade unions are a significant public.

To gauge staff views and morale in a culture where upward communication channels are encouraged, you could carry out a communications audit.

---

the public benefit and independently of government or commercial interests' (Charity Commission 2005). The Charity Commission regulates the activities of charities through regular visits and checks, and maintains a register of charities that anyone can inspect. This registration gives the benefit of certain financial advantages (those making donations can have the amount of their gift increased by the tax they would have paid had they kept the money for themselves) and the credibility of having been recognised as a properly run organisation.

Registered charities exist: to alleviate suffering for people or animals; work to develop or educate in particular ways or to do good works in society. Their campaigning is mainly to raise funds for the causes that they exist to help and to raise awareness about their work. However, not all campaigning groups would be acceptable to the Charity Commission, as these groups often engage in overtly political activities and persuasion. For example, Amnesty International is a human rights organisation and its main campaigning work is to free prisoners of conscience (those imprisoned anywhere in the world because of their beliefs and attitudes) and abolish the death penalty. This is not acceptable to the Charity Commission. However, Amnesty has established an educational section, which prepares packs for school projects and publishes research, which *is* a registered charity. (See Think about 9.2.)

Think about 9.2

Role of charities

In 1994 Oxfam entered into the public debate about the situation in Rwanda, where mass killings together with the resultant refugee crisis had led to the deaths of millions. They pointed to the failure of governments to act decisively to prevent these deaths and were criticised severely by then UK Prime Minister, Margaret Thatcher, who called on the Charity Commission to check their rulebook. Rather than have its charitable status revoked, Oxfam retreated.

What do you think about this situation? Should charities just deal with the problems *after* the event or should they be free to make political statements that might embarrass the very governments who have given them financial help through the taxation system?

Feedback

Charities in the UK are free to set up campaigning sections that do not have the same financial benefits as charitable status but that do share the same positioning as the umbrella brand.

Picture 9.1 'Each time a person stands up for an idea, or strikes out against injustice, he sends forth a tiny ripple of hope; and crossing each other from a million different centres of energy and daring, those ripples build a current which can sweep down the mightiest web of oppression and resistance', Robert F. Kennedy, speaking in South Africa, 1966 (*source*: Stuart Franklin/Magnum Photos)

Most campaigning organisations and pressure groups depend on attracting members to create an income stream and swell the ranks of supporters who will take part in and generate activities to achieve their objectives. This puts them in competition with other groups, including others with the same or very similar objectives.

Within less than 10 years of the AIDS crisis coming to the public's attention, there were 107 organisations in the UK that had been set up to raise funds for research and alleviate the problems of sufferers. The current Terrance Higgins Trust is an amalgamation of five organisations based in five different cities, which merged in the late 1990s.

As its Chief Executive, Nick Partridge, said: 'This decision by trustees and agencies of all those involved sets a precedent for the voluntary sector, where mergers are still relatively rare' (BBC News website, 27 January 1999). (See Mini case study 9.1 and Think about 9.3.) By 2008 there were 84 HIV/AIDs organisations and there had been no more mergers.

Mini Case Study 9.1
Merging interests – Cancer Research UK

Until February 2002 those wanting to support research into causes of and cures for cancer had a choice between the two leading charities – the Cancer Research Campaign and the Imperial Cancer Research Fund – as well as many smaller others, often focused on specific types of cancer. The two big ones have now joined together, as Cancer Research UK, to combine their efforts and impact.

Think about 9.3

How charities spend their money

Some campaign groups and charities have become so big that they need to raise large sums of money to maintain their own survival before they can spend anything on the cause for which they were first established.

After establishing Surfers Against Sewage (see Case study 9.1) and beginning to succeed, Chris Hines was approached by other environmental groups offering him jobs. His main condition was that he did not want to work in London or for an organisation that paid out the sums necessary to have offices there. He now works as an independent consultant in Cornwall in south-west England.

Do you think he has a point? Check some campaigning organisations' websites for their annual report, see how their money is spent and consider their mission and messages. Are there any inconsistencies?

Pressure groups

In this chapter we talk about pressure groups. In US PR literature, these groups are referred to as activist groups whose 'primary purpose is to influence public policy, organizational action, or social norms and values' (Smith and Ferguson 2001: 292). Drawing on studies in political science, sociology, communication and PR, three perspectives are put forward on how pressure or activist organisations are formed:

■ the macro-level perspective

■ the publics perspective

■ the developmental perspective (Smith and Ferguson 2001).

The *macro-level perspective* is concerned with the political, economic and cultural conditions within a particular country that may encourage activism. It has been assumed that democratic values, such as the freedom of expression, provide the basis for activism and particularly economic activism arising from class inequalities. However, activism today embraces publics across educational and economic strata, giving rise to the idea of *interest* groups that are interested in securing benefits for themselves and *issue* groups that are more motivated by their moral convictions about policies.

The *publics perspective* is concerned with the communication process whereby people identify shared problems and argue for change in resolving those problems. In the situational theory of publics, Grunig developed Dewey's theories on publics to consider their behaviour in various situations. Important to this perspective is the notion that publics are categorised according to their responses to issues. Publics are categorised as all-issue, apathetic, single-issue and hot-issue publics. According to situational theory, publics become active publics when an issue they face is seen as a problem, are highly involved in that issue and recognise few constraints in doing something about the problem (Grunig and Hunt 1984).

Single-issue publics, which are often associated with activism, are defined as being: 'Active in one or a small subset of the issues that concerns only a small part of the population. Such issues have included the slaughter of whales or the controversy over the sale of infant formula in developing countries' (Grunig and Repper 1992: 139).

Many big campaigning organisations started out as pressure or activist groups spurred on by a specific issue or concern. They begin in bars, coffee shops, people's homes or at school gates – wherever a group of people might gather and move from being an aware to an active public because someone says: 'What are we going to do about it?' The zeal and fervour that moves small groups to become wider movements has to be strong. One determinant may be charismatic individuals who found the group, hold the vision and protect it, often fiercely.

The *developmental perspective* examines the movement from problem recognition to action. The idea of a 'lifecycle' of activism assumes that there are separate stages that require different communication activities. The five stages identified by Heath (1997) are:

■ *strain* – publics recognise issues, define them and seek to gain legitimacy

■ *mobilisation* – activists form organisations, establish communication systems and start to mobilise resources to pursue their goals

■ *confrontation* – activists push corporations and/or the government to resolve problems

■ *negotiation* – various sides in the dispute exchange messages designed to reach a compromise

■ *resolution* – the controversy is solved (possibly in part only).

See Think about 9.3 and Activity 9.1.

Activity 9.1

Leaders and causes

Can you match the following well-known charismatic activists with their causes and can you think of others?

1	Martin Luther King	a	Banning landmines
2	Gandhi	b	Drop the (world) debt
3	Nelson Mandela	c	Saving rainforests
4	Aung San Suu Kyi	d	Equal rights in the USA
5	Dalai Lama	e	Votes for black South Africans
6	Sting	f	Democracy in Burma
7	Princess Diana	g	Independence for India
8	Bono	h	World peace

What qualities do these and other leaders have in common?

Feedback

Their campaigns have all depended on 'the **oxygen of publicity**' to create sympathy, generate further actions and develop an identity with the millions that became their followers or members. In other words, like any campaigning organisation, they have needed effective PR to deliver their messages, build relationships with supporters and persuade people (and sometimes governments) to change their behaviour.

(**Answers:** 1d, 2g, 3e, 4f, 5h, 6c, 7a, 8b)

Activity 9.2

Being true to the vision

Examine the following list of invented vision statements and decide which of the relevant events in the second list would generate the most publicity:

1   To eradicate world poverty

2   To reduce harmful emissions

3   To stop the export of live animals

4   To stop whaling

5   Fox hunting is good for the countryside

a   Blow up a whaling ship in Reykjavik harbour

b   Hold a 4 × 4 driving rally in Hyde Park, London

c   Blockade all ports for a bank holiday weekend

d   Celebrity 'pie eating 'til they're sick' competition

e   Block all city streets with bicycles

Feedback

This short exercise demonstrates the risk of gaining publicity at the expense of the values of the organisation and contradictory to its aims. Of the statements and events, only b and e could be done in the spirit of 5 and 2 (respectively). All the others have the potential to cause so much nuisance and offence that they could severely damage the cause that they have been staged to help. (Versions of all of them have, however, been done!)

Key issues for public relations practitioners in organisations and campaigning groups

Campaigning organisations and pressure or activist groups have several PR advantages over many public and private sector organisations and companies. They have a clear vision; they are able to define their objectives simply; they are often controversial and therefore newsworthy and that, in turn, means that they can attract the support of personalities and other organisations who want to share the media spotlight. Of course, some campaigning organisations also take up unfashionable or unpopular causes and have to work very hard to generate media coverage.

As in any in-house or consultancy role, the PR person has a duty to ensure that all campaigns, events, sponsorships or tie-ins with others reflect and remain true to the original vision on which the organisation was founded. (See Activity 9.2.)

Is all publicity good publicity?

Lavish celebrity dinners in the name of world poverty are often held in the wealthier cities around the world as successful fundraisers but the publicity value of them is questionable. PR people need to take great care when balancing the fundraising, publicity, awareness and sympathy needs of the campaigning or pressure groups that they represent.

The irreverent British sense of humour is enjoyed in most of Europe and respected. However, when Amnesty International first staged its *Secret Policeman's Ball* comedy shows, in which famous comedians appeared in sketches about torture, Amnesty's German national office nearly split

Think about 9.4

Turning 'bad' money to good use

If an organisation with a strongly held vision is short of the funding it needs to promote its work, should it take money from (and thereby give credibility to) a company that makes that money from the very thing that it stands against? Many charities and organisations do so in the belief that they are turning bad money to good use. In PR terms, what conflicts might this generate in people's perception of both the sponsors and the recipients of the money?

Feedback

For the sponsors, payments to an organisation whose ethical standing is greater than its own can be extremely beneficial in reputation terms. It can be seen to share the 'halo' of the recipient of funds, especially if the organisation carries the sponsor's branding. However, for the PR practitioner working on behalf of a charity or campaign group, there is a need to be aware of the risks involved in taking funds from an organisation that is a target for pressure groups.

Activity 9.3

Pressure group targets

Examine two campaigning websites, www.breastfeeding.com and www.babymilkaction.org, and consider the risks for the charities Help the Aged and Kids' Club in receiving sponsorship funds from Nestlé.

pressure or activist groups. Their causes are often prejudicial to the well-being of large corporate interest groups which cannot afford for them to have their say too loudly. PR consultancies are sometimes hired to discredit pressure groups in the interest of the survival of the companies under attack. Compared to those companies, most campaigning or activist groups are under-resourced financially as well as in terms of experience and skills. Many do not survive their attempts at denting corporate power bases. However, modern communication technology and Internet campaigning techniques have given poorly resourced and disparate interest groups the power to sway policy and inflict serious corporate damage.

away from the organisation as it felt unable to be associated with the use of humour about such a serious matter.

The same principle can apply to sponsorship or support of any kind. Companies often use corporate social responsibility (see Chapter 7) to balance the negative aspects of some of their activities. For example, an oil company that has been breaking sanctions and trading with an oppressive regime might appear to be interested in human rights by offering money to Medicins Sans Frontières (a non-partisan charity, based in France, that sends medical help into areas of conflict and war to help the wounded on all sides). (See Think about 9.4 and Activity 9.3.)

It is not only companies that like to align themselves with organisations or pressure groups that are generating a lot of media interest. Successful campaigning groups are often approached by would-be or once-were celebrities asking if there is anything they can do for the group. At high-profile events such as Live Aid in the 1980s, organised by Bob Geldof to raise money for the starving peoples of Africa (repeated as Live 8 in 2005 to put pressure on the G8), many of the musicians who had long before disappeared shot back to fame. There are also disadvantages in PR terms to working with campaigning organisations and

Campaign tactics

Using the World Wide Web

There are various methods by which pressure groups can use the World Wide Web to conduct effective campaigns and some are discussed here.

Site attack

Software has been designed that will bombard a site with requests for facts or information to such an extent that the whole site becomes non-functional to other users. The World Trade Organisation and Starbucks have both suffered in this way (Thomas 2003).

In May 2007 the whole of Estonia suffered from a co-ordinated attack by 'hacktivists' that is thought to have involved, unknown to their owners, a million computers worldwide. Following the removal of a bronze memorial statue to a World War Two Soviet soldier in Tallinn, the country's websites were so heavily bombarded with data that its largest bank had to close down its online service. Estonia's defence minister, Jaak Aaviskoo, said in an interview: 'It turned out to be a national security situation. It can effectively be compared to when your ports are shut to the sea.' The culprits were never found although many Internet sites were found with instructions for the disruptive action written in Russian (Landler and Markoff, 2007).

Hacking

Hackers can access an organisation's email system; for example, in the case of Samsung, threats were sent out, apparently from Samsung, to large numbers of customers, resulting in 10,000 complaining emails being sent back during the busiest time of the protest, costing Samsung millions of dollars (Thomas 2003). One almost successful activist campaign was fought by animal rights activists trying to shut down the Huntingdon Life Sciences laboratories in the UK because it tests products on animals. The company nearly went bankrupt after its shareholders were barraged with often threatening emails advising them to withdraw their investments.

Parody sites

These sites can be even more dangerous than hacking as they can confuse publics. The Internet is undoubtedly a very good medium for bringing together like-minded groups, making publics aware, creating dialogues and giving publics opportunities to become active. Shell set up a useful site to build dialogues with its publics entitled 'Tell Shell'. This was quickly parodied into 'Tells Hell', which search engines would find for the unsuspecting Internet surfer who would then learn negative things about Shell's activities, particularly in Nigeria (Thomas 2003). Companies are learning too late that when they register a site, they have to think of all the possible derivations of spelling and register those too at the same time – or someone else will! (See Mini case study 9.2.)

Online humour

One of the most useful tools in the campaign kit of the under-resourced organisation or group is humour (see Surfers Against Sewage, Case Study 9.1, p. 165, for some examples). Corporations often fail to deal with humorous attacks well and fall into the trap of appearing like bullies, which role is then quickly publicised around the world. For example, Nike created a clever online ordering service on which buyers could request a pair of personally customised trainers. It had been ignoring quite vocal protests about its use of low-paid workers in factories with poor employment conditions, known as 'sweatshop labour'. Nike defended its position stating that it was their subcontractors whose employment conditions contravened basic human rights. When it declined Junah Perretti's order for a pair of trainers embroidered with the word 'sweatshop', its defensive and humourless response was quickly emailed around the world.

Mini Case Study 9.2
Activism in action: 'McLibel'

Most global net campaigns are environmental, human or animal rights based. A very successful tactic in the global arena is to create a corporate bully. The most famous example of this is what became known as the 'McLibel' case. McDonald's sued an unemployed postal worker, Dave Morris, and a community gardener, Helen Steel, for libel in a trial that ran for 313 days in court. The case was brought against the pair following their publication of a pamphlet in 1986 that took McDonald's to task on almost all aspects of its work, from third world poverty to the depletion of the rainforest. During the four years of the case McDonald's offered to pay money to a cause of the defendants' choice in exchange for a promise that all criticism would end, but Steel and Morris chose to go on. As Naomi Klein, in *No Logo* states: 'They saw no reason to give up now. The trial, which

had been designed to stem the flow of negative publicity – and to gag and bankrupt Steel and Morris – had been an epic public relations disaster for McDonald's' (Klein 2000: 387). Although McDonald's won the case, as aspects in the pamphlet pertaining to food poisoning, cancer and world poverty were not proved, it did not collect the $61,300 that was awarded. By now the pamphlet had been distributed worldwide, with three million copies circulating in the UK alone. The *Guardian* (20 June 1997) reported: 'Not since Pyrrhus has a victor emerged so bedraggled. As PR fiascos go, this action takes the prize for ill-judged and disproportionate response to public criticism.'

The case also gave rise to the McSpotlight website, where the leaflet and trial transcript can be found, along with a debating room where other McDonald's 'horror stories' are exchanged. Klein reported in *No Logo* that by her publication date in 2000 there had already been 65 million visits to the site. This case was revisited in 2004 with an appeal by Morris and Steel to the European Court of Human Rights in Strasbourg claiming that they should have received help with legal costs. In February 2005 they won that appeal.

Picture 9.2 A McDonald's protest in New Zealand. Activists push corporations to resolve problems (*source*: Getty Images)

seemed real and imminent. The campaign was opposed to all nuclear weapons worldwide and endorsed all forms of non-violent protest. It gained publicity and attracted members by writing letters to newspapers and members of the UK Parliament, writing and distributing leaflets and organising petitions, debates and huge marches and demonstrations. Early marches took three days to walk from a nuclear base at Aldermaston to central London. Later, campaigners all over the UK carried briefcases (in the late 1960s this would have been far more noticeable than today) to remind people that the US president took one wherever he went, enabling him to launch a nuclear attack at any time.

On 24 March 2008, 50 years after the first CND march, an estimated 5,000 protestors were back at Aldermaston to protest against the British Government's funding proposals for new Trident missiles. The UK's *Guardian* newspaper reported that '102-year-old Hetty Bower, a life-long socialist who first marched to Aldermaston in 1959 and still goes on anti-war marches despite sight and hearing problems, was holding court from a foldout chair. "I feel sad to be here today," she said. "I hope the young will get into the peace movement and strengthen the UN wherever they can. My message is peace to mankind. Until we have it we are not civilised." ' (Williams 2008).

Another simple idea was the Methodists' refusal to take sugar in hot drinks – this started as a protest against the slave trade and has been handed down, often unwittingly, through families ever since.

Laura Illia's winning EUPRERA Jos Willems Award entry in 2002 entitled 'Cyberactivism and public relations strategy: new dynamics and relationship rules' detailed a disturbing array of cheap to inflict but seriously damaging ways for groups or individuals to attack their targets. It also made some useful suggestions for PR people faced with cyberactivists, observing that the Internet had changed the dynamics of activism into a new form of pressure and that this had come about as the result of different pressures on corporations. Illia concluded that: 'Each communication medium had to be considered as a relationship medium instead of a communication medium' (Illia 2002).

The simplest of ideas

The simplest of ideas are often the best. For example, one of the largest single protest movements of the second half of the twentieth century was the Campaign for Nuclear Disarmament (CND). It started in the 1950s when the threat of nuclear war between the USA and the USSR

People, politics and globalisation

John and Thomson (2003) state in the first line of the introduction to their book entitled *New Activism and the Corporate Response*: 'Capitalism and corporations are under more pressure now than at any time since the Great Depression' (2003: 1).

Although politicians in all democracies complain that apathy is killing the political process (more people voted in reality TV shows than in the European elections in many EU member states in 2004), they overlook the fact that large numbers of people are becoming politically active in other ways.

Ethical shopping guides are published and sold in large numbers to inform people who only want to spend their money with companies that will not invest in production or other systems that hurt others or the environment. Naomi Klein's *No Logo* has become an international best seller and an influence on readers' buying habits that is doing real financial harm to major global corporations.

In Britain there are roughly a million members of all the political parties put together but the environmental organisations have about 5 million paid-up members. On 15 February 2003, more than 10 million people marched in cities around the world, with only a few days' notice to organise their protest, expressing their opposition to the war in Iraq. This action also contradicts the concept of political voting apathy.

The interesting thing for politicians is that, in the main, their power is limited to geographical boundaries whereas big corporations now act globally, as do campaigning organisations and pressure groups, because this is where differences can be made.

So although globalisation integrates along one dimension (the economic or private), it fragments along another (the political or public) (Reinicke 1998) and that fragmentation is changing people's interaction with political systems.

Campaigning and pressure groups have gone global. When the **World Trade Organisation** or the **G8** meet now – whether in Seattle, Davos or Toronto – there will be a large, well-informed and very vocal body of protesters. They attract international publicity and often embarrass world leaders with their presentation of issues. These protesters have often come from once fragmented single-issue organisations concerning, for example, animal rights or child poverty, to form a global alliance against corporate globalisation.

PricewaterhouseCoopers' 2002 Global Chief Executive Officers' survey (involving over 1,100 CEOs drawn from 33 countries) showed that 33% thought that the anti-globalisation movement was a threat to them while in an era of economic downturn in 2008, concerns about technology disruption persisted (www.pwc.com). So, returning to Grunig's situational theory of publics discussed earlier, anti-globalisation campaigners can be seen as active publics who: have formed around an issue that they recognise as a problem; are highly involved in the issue; and recognise few constraints in demonstrating about the problem. (See Think about 9.5.)

Picture 9.3 Although these campaigns have not yet dealt major final blows for companies, they have had big impacts and changed the direction of policy in a great many boardrooms (*source*: Nick Cobbing/Panos Pictures)

Building and evaluating consensus

So what can companies do to fend off threats to their future profitability? As we discussed earlier, the answer is effective PR. Campaigning and pressure groups have become some of the most important publics with whom companies need to have open dialogues. If conducted effectively, this can lead to genuine working relationships, which will mean changes and compromises on both sides

Think about 9.5

Activism

Have you ever been asked to sign an email petition to support a cause? If you signed it and sent it on to others you are an activist. In fact, if you have ever resisted buying a product or service on your own moral grounds, you have become part of a pressure group.

At the end of this chapter there is a far from exhaustive list of websites informing and encouraging activism. Many of them will make you aware of things that you did not know before – will any of them make you active?

– just like all relationships! Consensus and co-orientation are two of the terms used in PR that best describe what is needed.

Consensus-oriented public relations (COPR), as formulated by Burkart (1993), is a communication theory based on the theories of communicative action by Habermas (1984). It develops aspects of mutual understanding as described in Grunig and Hunt's 'two-way symmetrical model' (1984), where communication can flow equally back and forth between sender and receiver. (See Chapter 3 for a fuller exploration of these theories.)

The co-orientation process seeks to establish understanding based on truth. The system was developed to deal with situations where there was a conflict between groups. In Burkart's study the conflict was between those who managed landfill and waste disposal and the population local to the proposed sites. When considering the basis for communicative action theory, Habermas presumes the acceptability of certain claims, namely:

- *intelligibility* – the message must be understandable

- *truth* – the message must be factual and accepted as being factual

- *trustworthiness* – the bearer of the message must be honest and accepted as being honest

- *rightness* or *legitimacy* – the messages must be acceptable on the basis of mutually recognised values.

As well as the claims, which must be accepted by both partners in the communication process, Habermas also refers to three dimensions (the *objective*, the *subjective* and the *social* dimensions) of reality to which both parties in a communication relate. As Burkart (1993) summarises, the aim of such a process of understanding is the agreement of both communication partners. Mutual understanding is reached when speaker and listener agree on the truth of assertions (which is the objective dimension of reality), on their truthfulness (the subjective dimension of reality) and on the rightness of their expressed interests (the social dimension of reality). Therefore COPR, according to the conditions just described, requires that careful analysis be carried out to plan the communication with specific publics and the specific information to be communicated, as shown in Figure 9.1.

Understanding and agreement occur when all that is asserted within these dimensions is not doubted. However, most communication processes do not start and finish here: there is usually at least one area of disagreement and therefore a discourse becomes necessary in which all sides have the same chance to tell their point of view and their arguments. The task of COPR is the creation of the conditions for such a discourse. In other words, all the involved persons must have the opportunity to doubt the

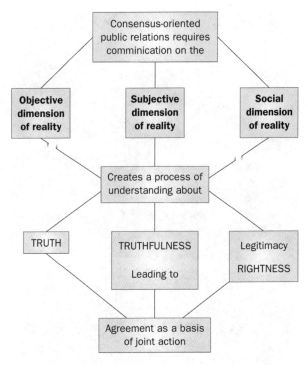

Figure 9.1 Consensus-oriented public relations (*source*: adapted from Burkart 1993, 'Conflict communication – an important part of public relations'. Paper presented at the CERP meeting, Strasbourg.)

truth of assertions, the truthfulness of expressions and the rightness of interests.

There must be a predetermined willingness for compromise with the communicator being open to adapt according to the interests of the publics involved and thereby giving the publics some power over the situation. This occurs in the third stage of the process of COPR.

Burkart breaks the process down in stages to indicate the care that is needed as the goals are gradually reached. The first stage is based on information concerning which rational judgement can be formed. It does not require the active involvement of a public as it is a one-way process creating the basis for dialogue.

The aims of the second stage are to create dialogue with as great a part of the segment – or public – concerned as possible. The third stage can only work if the second is successful as it is there for discourse to deal with areas of disagreement. The fourth stage exists for an assessment to take place to consider the situation and decide whether further discourse is necessary (see Table 9.1).

Burkart shows how the COPR model is applied where a community plans to build a waste disposal site. In this case, a citizens' group may be formed with the aim of

	Communication		
	Issues/facts	**Organisation/institution persons**	**Legitimacy of interest**
PR stages	Objective dimension of reality	Subjective dimension of reality	Social dimension of reality
Information	Determination/definition of relevant facts and terms and explanation of consequences	Explanation of self-interest and intentions, announcement of publics for communication	Justification of interest by reasoning and arguments
Discussion	Relevant facts and terms	Cannot be discussed	Adequacy of arguments
Discourse	Agreement on the rules for evaluation of judgements on relevant facts	Cannot be subject of a discourse	Agreement on rules for the evaluation of judgements on legitimacy
Definition of situation	Agreement on judgements	Agreement on trustworthiness	Agreement on judgements

Table 9.1 Communication process of COPR (*source*: Burkart 1993, 'Conflict communication – an important part of public relations'. Paper presented at the CERP meeting, Strasbourg)

preventing the project going ahead. The local media are likely to support the group and create a conflict situation. Burkart advises that on the basis of the COPR model, PR managers of the landfill company should consider the following:

- any assertion they make will be examined concerning its truth – e.g. whether figures about the quantity of waste to be deposited are correct
- the persons, companies and organisations involved will be confronted with distrust – e.g. representatives of companies might be taken as biased, or experts/consultants as incompetent or corrupt
- their intention for building the landfill will be doubted in principle – either because the basic strategy for waste disposal is questioned or because the choice of the site for landfill is seen as unjustified on the basis of developing tourism, for example.

If such doubts can be eliminated or prevented from the beginning, then the flow of communication will remain undisturbed (Burkart 2004: 463).

Several companies are going to these lengths to bring groups in to work with them towards consensus (Stafford et al. 2000 contains several examples). Some of the groups involved risk losing members for sitting down to discuss terms with their former enemies, so they too need to move into these new situations with great care and must not be seen to let up the pressure.

Care is also needed when either side in the process feels the need to celebrate some small victory or influence

change in direction. Corporations' shareholders could become uncomfortable and pressure groups' members will also be watching closely but it is in the interest of all sides to keep moving towards consensus.

All work of professional standard needs mechanisms with which practitioners can evaluate progress and make informed changes to ongoing strategies. Consensus development is no exception to this and a model has been devised in recognition of the need for PR people who are practising two-way communication to be tracking both sides of the relationship around an issue at the same time.

Broom and Dozier's co-orientation model (1990) evaluates the progress in a relationship where there is a topic of mutual concern or interest (See Figure 9.2). One of their examples is the relationship between a paper products company and a conservation group concerned about the effects on habitats of certain logging processes.

They discuss how the research into the relationship, to discover how each perceives the other, needs to ask the following questions:

- 'What are the organization's views on the issue?
- What is the dominant view within the organization of the public's view?
- What are the public's actual views on the issue?
- What is the dominant view within the public of the organization's view?' (Broom and Dozier 1990: 37)

The aim of these questions is to calculate the three co-orientation variables – agreement, accuracy and perceived agreement.

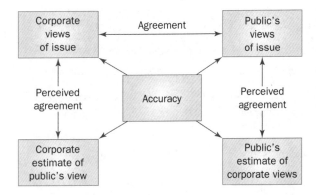

Figure 9.2 Co-orientational model of relationships (*source*: Broom, Glen M. and Dozier, D.M. *Using Research in Public Relations: Applications to Program Management, 1st Edition* (c) 1990. Adapted by Permission of Pearson Education, Inc, Upper Saddle River, NJ)

Accuracy indicates the extent to which one side's estimate of the other's views is similar to the other's actual views. Perceived agreement represents the extent to which one side's views are similar to their estimate of the other's views. Unlike agreement and accuracy, however, perceived agreement does not describe the relationship between the organization and the public. Rather it describes how one side views the relationship and no doubt affects how it deals with the other side in the relationship. (Broom and Dozier 1990: 38).

If a consensus is to be reached there must be research to establish the distance that has to be travelled by both sides to make it happen. As Broom and Dozier go on to say: 'If two sides hold accurate views of each other's positions on an issue two types of relationships are possible. True consensus occurs when both the organization and the public actually agree and accurately perceive that agreement' (1990: 38). Clearly, the opposite case is also a possibility – where a disagreement is accurately perceived and this state is referred to as *dissensus*.

Greenwood (2003) states in an essay on trade associations and activism : 'Trust is the cement in the relationship between institutions and civil society. When trust breaks down, civil society either withdraws from participation or expresses protest outside the mainstream channels of participation' (2003: 49).

It is the role of the PR practitioner, on whatever side of a debate, to build and maintain that trust by being open, transparent and fully accountable to publics, not only in words but also in actions. It is essential to build common ground at every stage of a relationship that might be going to work.

Practical guidelines for campaigning public relations

To summarise the key points arising from this chapter for would-be PR practitioners in campaigning organisations or pressure groups, here is a quick checklist:

1 Agree and state your purpose clearly and simply (vision or mission statement).

2 Establish measurable objectives to give the campaign achievable milestones.

3 Develop your legitimacy – attract third-party endorsement from opinion formers, celebrities, academics, MPs and journalists – and provide them with useful materials like fact sheets.

4 Create a calendar of newsworthy events, meetings, reports and stunts (but remember not to conflict with your stated purpose!).

5 Try to employ humour and always stay within the law (maybe only just sometimes but always definitely on the right side of the line!).

6 Avoid technical jargon and be very clear, with human/animal/environmental examples to show the need for the changes you are seeking.

7 Make sure that those who might join you or follow you know why they should, how they can and what they can do to help.

8 Make good use of technology – set up a website and use email, blogs, wikis, webcasts and social networks such as Facebook.

9 Provide as many opportunities for your key publics to meet your people, discuss your issues, hear your message and become active – from the stand at the village fête to the international demonstration.

10 Set up a membership scheme and when the budgets allow, create a range of merchandise – T-shirts, badges, caps, pens, etc. People will want to show that they identify with you and these things can be a great source of income.

11 Service your members well with newsletters, online discussion boards, parties, etc.

12 Make them feel welcome and involved.

Activity 9.4

Surfers Against Sewage

From the history of Surfers Against Sewage in Case study 9.1, identify the elements of good campaigning practice that helped it towards success.

Case Study 9.1
Surfers Against Sewage

In the UK, in December 1989 a wave of national disquiet followed the privatisation of the water companies, arising from a belief that these new companies would prioritise profits over environmental concerns. The issue that gave impetus to the campaign was known as 'the panty liner effect' – surfers making duck-dives were emerging on the other side of a wave with a panty liner stuck to their head: the beaches were strewn with panty liners, condoms, human excrement and sometimes even hypodermic needles.

Early in 1990, 10 surfers met at Martin Mynne's house to discuss the pollution on the beaches and in the sea, and decided to call a public meeting (four people put £10 on the table and it was decided to charge £2 membership).

A press release was produced, which was reviewed in the local media. The public meeting that followed overflowed with 200 people in attendance.

The vision of the new group, Surfers Against Sewage (SAS), was clear and they resolved to campaign on the following demands:

- all sewage to be treated before discharge
- complete cessation of toxic discharge
- sewage and water content to be regarded as a resource rather than as waste
- ensure that the newly privatised water companies' money would be well spent.

The vision united a wide range of beach users, from the cliff walker who witnessed a seal pup surface through a sewage slick, through to the parents who feared for their children's safety on the beach and swimmers who were getting ill.

During the summer of 1990 a campaign of voluntary work to clean beaches was well publicised. The first SAS chairman, Andrew Kingsley-Tubbs, introduced some military tactics to get the attention of the authorities and the gasmask was adopted as a symbol. A national newspaper, the *Daily Mirror*, featured surfers wearing gasmasks, and *Sky News* also ran the story.

SAS researched alternative sewage discharge methods and bought shares in South West Water to secure a voice at the company's annual general meeting (AGM). In September it went to South West Water's AGM

in wetsuits and gasmasks. Mike Hendy, the SAS shareholder, held the floor for 20 minutes resulting in full national news media coverage. Channel 4 made a documentary on the issue entitled *Our Backyard*.

In addition, surfing magazines gave free advertising space and by the end of the first summer SAS had £10,000 in the bank. SAS members Chris Hines and Gareth Kent were paid for six weeks to run the campaign office. Six weeks eventually became 10 years and the telephones were always answered.

In the summer of 1991 SAS members decided to take their cause to the heart of government and they appeared at the House of Commons in wetsuits, gasmasks and with a large inflatable turd (excrement) which generated a lot of national news coverage.

Chris Hines began to build up a national profile through roadshows. Facts and figures were produced clearly and kept up to date – for example, it was discovered that Jersey, in the Channel Islands, used ultraviolet sewage treatment and that its pollution count was 50 times lower than on most UK beaches.

Academics came forward to offer research and further legitimise the campaign. SAS recognised that it had a high level of responsibility as 10,000 people paid their fees and invested their money in the campaign. However, all the claims made by SAS were reasonable and achievable.

SAS as a brand became increasingly successful through its appeal to young surfers and its use of British toilet humour.

SAS engaged with the political system – at a House of Lords select committee, Chris Hines announced that he would feel 50 times safer putting his head in Jersey's outfall pipe than bathing on many of the UK's beaches. One month later, at the invitation of the island, he did just that, generating further national news media coverage.

In 1991, while maintaining grassroots involvement with surfers, windsurfers were also invited to join SAS resulting in a 400% increase in members. Co-operative Bank's Customers Who Care campaign brought in £20,000 overnight, which was invested in campaigns almost as quickly – members still liked to see demonstrations, and the use of the Internet was established to save paper and postage costs.

case study 9.1 (continued)

Evidence that SAS was now becoming 'accepted' by the establishment was demonstrated when Glyn Ford, MEP, invited wetsuited surfers to meet the President of the European Parliament. Further evidence came in 1994, when Welsh Water came 'on side' following a customer consultation. Despite marginally higher costs, Welsh Water launched a policy of full treatment for all coastal discharges. This gave the Welsh company a way to stand out and SAS opened the new sewage works.

Merchandise started to become a major earner for SAS, which by now was developing a cult following with its 'must-have' clothing range, badges and car stickers.

SAS, however, resisted the danger of becoming too linked to the establishment, while being careful to maintain negotiations with all parties and understand the pressures on all sides. For example, it took advantage of the five-yearly periodic review of environmental spend that had been introduced by the UK Parliament.

By 1994 SAS messages had stopped being a threat and for many they became an opportunity – Wessex Water was next to adopt the full treatment policy. However, members complained that SAS was not visible enough on the beaches and spent too much time in boardrooms. Some members only understood one way of campaigning and had to be given projects to keep them interested.

Campaigners researched and took advantage of events, such as anniversaries of laws passed to improve sewage treatment, which provided them with hooks for the news media. Always light on their feet, SAS campaigners travelled to Brussels from Cornwall (in south-west England) to take advantage of a speaking opportunity to influence the bathing water directive, alongside partners in the European Water Alliance.

SAS also advised the Labour MP Michael Meacher while he was opposition environment spokesman. Once Labour came to power in 1997, Chris Hines was invited to become a special advisor, and sewage treatment went further up the political agenda. Seats in parliament were won on the basis of the campaign messages. Pressure was kept up, resulting in levies against all utilities (including the water companies) to pay for environmental clean-ups.

SAS had learned to plan over a long period to put the right pressure on at the right time. By 1999 it had won agreement that all sewage discharges should have at least secondary treatment and a large percentage would have tertiary treatment.

By now there was pressure from European groups to widen the campaign internationally. However, a members' survey in 2000 showed that they wanted to keep the campaign for the UK but take in wider environmental issues.

SAS runs on a £20,000 annual budget but has a £400,000 turnover, nearly all of which is invested in the campaign.

Key points from the campaign to date include:

- avoiding the temptation to take sponsorship from companies whose ethics conflicted with its own, but they happily took part in an education tour with Quiksilver, the leisure goods company
- keeping to a strong image, supplying a regular diet of good imagery for the news media – always being ready with tight soundbites
- being very disciplined; never breaking the law; keeping it humorous whenever possible and becoming skilled opportunists
- working with scientists
- ensuring representation in each TV region
- maintaining a three-strong campaigns team at headquarters to keep up the pressure.

SAS is now led by Richard Hardy, who has an animal welfare and environmental campaigning background. He too is driven by conscience.

The *Independent on Sunday* newspaper called SAS 'Britain's coolest pressure group' (23 July 1995); the BBC described its members as 'some of the government's most sophisticated environmental critics'.

The UK population still wastes drinking water by flushing toilets with it, there is still a massive pollution problem in rivers and at sea and too many people are still not listening. There is plenty still to be done by campaigners like SAS.

Source: www.sas.org.uk; www.edenproject.com; interview with Chris Hines (www.chrishines.org) and Richard Hardy

Summary

In this chapter we have discussed the motivations of campaigning organisations and how they form and grow. We have argued that in today's global media environment, campaigning organisations have many advantages over big business and that the Internet facilitates debate on issues, helps to recruit members and provides the means for disrupting business.

Furthermore, we have argued that campaigning groups may help to reinvigorate political debate, albeit on single issues. We have critically analysed the PR roles on all sides and the use of two-way communication and consensus in achieving mutual goals. We concluded by presenting key principles of campaigning and demonstrating successful campaigning through a case study.

The author would like to thank Rachael Clayton for her work in tracking down material for this chapter.

Bibliography

Broom, G.M. and D.M. Dozier (1990). *Using Research in Public Relations: Applications to program management.* Upper Saddle River, NJ: Prentice Hall.

Burkart, R. (1993). 'Conflict communication – an important part of public relations'. Paper presented at the CERP meeting, Strasbourg, France.

Burkart, R. (2004). 'Consensus-orientated public relations (COPR)' in *Public Relations and Communication Management in Europe.* B. van Ruler and D. Verčič (eds). Berlin: Walter de Gruyter.

Charity Commission (2005). www.charity-commission.gov.uk, accessed 5 May 2005.

Cutlip, S.M., A.H. Center and G.M. Broom (eds) (2000). *Effective Public Relations,* 8th edition. Upper Saddle River, NJ: Prentice Hall.

Greenwood, J. (2003). 'Trade associations, change and the new activism' in *New Activism and the Corporate Response.* S. John and S. Thomson (eds). Basingstoke: Palgrave Macmillan.

Grunig, J.E. (ed.). (1992). *Excellence in Public Relations and Communication Management.* Mahwah, NJ: Lawrence Erlbaum Associates.

Grunig, J.E. and T. Hunt (1984). *Managing Public Relations.* New York and London: Holt, Rinehart & Winston Inc.

Grunig, J.E. and F.C. Repper (1992). 'Strategic management, publics and issues' in *Excellence in Public Relations and Communication Management.* J.E. Grunig (ed.). Mahwah, NJ: Lawrence Erlbaum Associates.

Habermas, J. (1984). *Theory of Communicative Action: Reason and the rationalization of society.* London: Heinemann.

Heath, R.L. (1997). *Strategic Issues Management: Organizations and public policy challenges.* Thousand Oaks, CA: Sage.

Heath, R.L. (ed.) (2001). *Handbook of Public Relations.* Thousand Oaks, CA: Sage.

Hobsbawm, E. (1987). *The Age of Empire 1875–1914.* London: Weidenfeld & Nicolson.

Illia, L. (2002). 'Cyberactivism and public relations strategy: new dynamics and relationship rules'. www.euprera.org.

John, S. and S. Thomson (eds) (2003). *New Activism and the Corporate Response.* Basingstoke: Palgrave Macmillan.

Klein, N. (2000). *No Logo.* London: Flamingo.

Landler, M. and J. Markoff (2007). 'War fears turn digital after data siege in Estonia'. *The New York Times.* www.nytimes.com/2007/05/29/technology/29estonia.html, accessed 22 August 2008.

McGann, J. and M. Johnston (2006). 'The power shift and the NGO credibility crisis'. *The International Journal of Not-for-Profit Law* 8(2), found at http://www.icnl.org/knowledge/ijnl/vol8iss2/art_4.htm, accessed 23 October 2008.

Monbiot, G. (2003). 'The corporate takeover' in *New Activism and the Corporate Response.* S. John and S. Thomson (eds). Basingstoke: Palgrave Macmillan.

Mullins, L.J. (1999). *Management and Organisational Behaviour,* 5th edition. Hemel Hempstead: Pearson Education.

Raymond, D. (2003). 'Activism – beyond the banners' in *New Activism and the Corporate Response.* S. John and S. Thomson (eds). Basingstoke: Palgrave Macmillan.

Reinicke, W. (1998). *Global Public Policy: Governing without government?* Washington, DC: Brookings Institution Press.

Smith, M.F. (1996). 'Public relations as a locus for workplace democracy'. Paper presented at the meeting of the National Communication Association, San Diego, CA.

Smith, M.F. and D. Ferguson (2001). 'Activism' in *Handbook of Public Relations.* R.L. Heath (ed.). Thousand Oaks, CA: Sage.

Stafford, E., M. Polonsky and C. Hartman (2000). 'Environmental NGO-business collaboration and strategic bridge building: A case analysis of the Greenpeace–Foron Alliance. *Business Strategy and the Environment* (9): 122–135.

Thomas, C. (2003). 'Cyberactivism and corporations: new strategies for new media' in *New Activism and the Corporate Response*. S. John and S. Thomson (eds). Basingstoke: Palgrave Macmillan.

Williams, R. (2008). '5,000 take peace message to Aldermaston, 50 years on', The *Guardian*, www.guardian.co.uk/uk/2008/mar/25/antiwar.military, accessed 22 August 2008.

Wilson, D. and A. Leighton (1993). *Campaigning: The A–Z of public advocacy*. London: Hawkesmere.

Websites

Journal of the mental environment – started Reclaim the Streets and Buy Nothing Day: www.adbusters.org
AlterNet: www.alternet.org
e-fluentials: www.efluentials.com
FOX News: www.foxnews.com
Get Ethical – consumer magazine created by *The Big Issue* and *Red Pepper*: www.getethical.com
Ilisu Dam Campaign: www.ilisu.org.uk
Independent Media Center (IMC): www.indymedia.org
McSpotlight: www.mcspotlight.org
PricewaterhouseCoopers – including the annual Global CEO Survey on global risk: www.pwc.com
Teaching Values.com: www.teaching-values.com/goldenrule.html
The Yes Men: www.theyesmen.org
Transnational Institute: www.tni.org/george/articles/dissent.html

Parody sites
Murder King – PETA campaign against Burger King: www.muderking.com
Tells Hell: www.tellshell.com

Campaign sites
Baby Milk Action: www.babymilkaction.org
Amsterdam-based NGO that monitors European multinationals: www.ceo.org
CorpWatch: www.corpwatch.org
USA-based research and activist centre: www.globalexchange.org
Greenpeace: www.greenpeace.org.uk
Pressure group working to change US foreign and domestic policy for sustainability: www.ips-dc.org
Oxfam: www.oxfam.org
Against unsustainability – big study on Enron: www.seen.org
The Petition Site: www.thepetitionsite.com

World social forum
World Social Forum: www.forumsocialmundial.org.br
Global Policy Forum – information on the repression of trade unions around the world: www.globalpolicy.org/socecon/inequal/labor/1010union.htm

CHAPTER 10

Lyn M. Zoch and Juan-Carlos Molleda

Building a theoretical model of media relations using framing, information subsidies and agenda-building*

* Chapter 10 in *Public Relations Theory II* edited by Carl H. Botan and Vincent Hazleton. Copyright © 2006 by Lawrence Erlbaum Associates, Inc. Reproduced with permission.

This chapter focuses on an area of public relations that many nonpractitioners see as the *only* function of public relations – that of media or press relations. The vision of the practitioner as the press agent, the 'mouthpiece' who tells the organization's good-news-only story or the TV-camera-blinded company spokesperson, has a long history.

Scott Cutlip (1994) traces the roots of today's public relations practitioners to the press agentry used by those promoting settlements on the East Coast of the United States in the 1600s. Modern public relations' use of media relations can be traced to the founding of The Publicity Bureau in mid-1900, and the firm's subsequent work for Harvard University, the railroads, and AT&T (Cutlip, 1994). The early careers of practitioners such as Ivy Lee, Edward Bernays, John Hill, and Carl Byoir were based on what was then called press agentry and today has evolved into media relations.

Although the public relations field has expanded well beyond the concept of one-way press agentry, no public relations textbook is complete without a chapter on media relations. Some textbooks use simple titles such as 'Media Relations' (Baskin, Aronoff & Lattimore, 1997), 'Publicity and Media' (Seitel, 1998), or 'Media and Media Relations' (Cutlip, Center, & Broom, 2000), whereas others attempt to draw the focus away from the media by placing relationships with the media within a broader context such as two-chapter packages titled 'Written Tactics' and 'Spoken Tactics' (Wilcox, Ault, & Agee, 1998) or 'Communication Channels and Media' and 'Tactics and Techniques' (Newsom, Turk, & Kruckeberg, 2000). In whatever way it is presented, media relations is considered to be an important tool in the practitioner's skill set.

Knowing this, it was then surprising for us to discover in reviewing literature for this chapter that when the key words 'media relations' were used to search the Communication Institute for Online Scholarship (CIOS) database, which covers the past 25 years of academic research in the field of communication, there were no matches. It was even more surprising that when we used 'press relations' as the key words, only eight articles were cited, and six of those articles actually referred to the relationships between the 'press' and various organizations or government bodies.

This, of course, does not mean that no research has been done in the area of public relations effect on the media coverage of organizations, issues, or events (see References). What it does mean is that the work being done may be hard to access through a simple search by a public relations student or practitioner interested in finding out which theories or models inform the practice of media relations.

To simplify the search for a theory with which to underpin media relations, in this chapter we attempt to create a theoretical framework, composed of three currently popular paradigms, through which the practice of media relations can be viewed. We describe it as an active process in which the public relations practitioner has, at the least, a modicum of control over the message she wishes to reach the public, its timing, the source of that information, and the effect on the media agenda of the issue presented.

The three areas we discuss, and from which we construct the theoretical framework, are framing theory, the concept of information subsidies, and the agenda-building paradigm. In this chapter we (1) discuss each of the three theoretical areas individually, (2) make interconnections between the areas, (3) discuss implications of the three paradigms for practice, (4) develop a model of media relations using the three theoretical areas, and (5) end by discussing the model's implications for theory and research.

Framing

The concept of framing has been variously attributed to sociologist Erving Goffman (1974) and anthropologist Gregory Bateson (1955). Although Goffman credits Bateson with the first use of the word 'frame' in the sense of a frame of interpretation or metamessage about what is going on in a particular situation, it is Goffman himself who carries the concept into the linguistic analysis of face-to-face interactions.

A number of elements are necessary to understand the concept of the 'frame' or message 'framing.' Goffman (1974) defines a *frame* as a 'schemata of interpretation' through which individuals organize and make sense of information or an occurrence (p. 21), whereas Reese (1997) notes that '[f]rames are organizing principles that are socially shared and persistent over time, that work symbolically to meaningfully structure the social world' (p. 5).

'Frames select and call attention to particular aspects of the reality described, which logically means that frames simultaneously direct attention away from other aspects' writes Entman (1993, p. 54). Here the metaphor of a window frame comes to mind. The message framer has the choice of what is to be emphasized in the message, as the view through a window is emphasized by where the carpenter frames, or places, the window. If the window had been placed, or framed, on a different wall, the view would be different.

Because framing involves selecting a particular viewpoint to bring to the fore as well as communicating some aspect of the whole to make it the salient point or points of the frame, it quickly becomes apparent that framing can take place in several locations along the path of any communication transaction. Entman (1993) identifies four locations where frames can occur in the communication transaction, and there serve their function of selecting and emphasizing, in the communication process: the communicator, the receiver, the text, and the cultural framework.

Frames or schemata of interpretation are present in both the communicator and the receiver from which they either build the message or the interpretation of the message. 'The *text* [italics in original] contains frames, which are manifested by the presence or absence of certain keywords, stock phrases, stereotyped images, sources of information, and sentences that provide thematically reinforcing clusters of facts or judgments' (Entman, 1993, p. 52). Culture or a social grouping is the origin for many commonly accepted frames that are present in the thinking of a particular group of people. A good example of this is the issue of flying the Confederate battle flag over the state house in South Carolina. The frame of one social grouping might be that the flag embodies the history and culture of the South and should be flown out of respect for the heritage of the state. Another social grouping works with the collective frame that the flag represents a repressive society and the enslavement of an entire race of people. Goffman (1974) separates frames into two broad classes – natural and social. Natural frames identify occurrences that are purely physical, such as the weather as given in a report. As public relations practitioners we are more concerned with social frames, which Goffman describes as 'guided doings' where there is motive and intent to present a particular viewpoint, much like a public relations practitioner presenting information to the media about a particular issue or event. 'Social frameworks . . . provide background understanding for events that incorporate the will, aim, and controlling effort of an intelligence, a live agency, . . . the human being' (Goffman, 1974, p. 22). Thus framing is critical to the construction of social reality – the way people view the world.

In his exhaustive literature review of framing and its relationship to public relations, Hallahan (1999) makes this connection to the practitioner:

> *Implicitly, framing plays an integral role in public relations. If public relations is defined as the process of establishing and maintaining mutually beneficial relations between an organization and publics on whom it depends (Cutlip, Center, & Broom, 1995)(sic) the establishment of common frames of reference [italics in original] about topics or issues of mutual concern is a necessary condition for effective relations to be established (p. 207).*

In terms of a public relations practitioner's use of framing to get out her organization's message, frames have four functions: (1) They define problems, or 'determine what a causal agent is doing with what costs and benefits,' in this case the organization; (2) they diagnose causes or identify what is causing the problem, either within or outside the organization; (3) they make moral judgments about the situation causing the problem; and (4) they suggest remedies or 'offer and justify treatments for the problems' (Entman, 1993, p. 52).

A frame can also be viewed as an idea or central story line that organizes and provides meaning (Gamson & Modigliani, 1987) to the events related to a story or issue. Those looking for such frames can identify them through the use of five common devices: catchphrases, depictions, metaphors, exemplars, and visual images (Gamson & Modigliani, 1989).

From the media's perspective, frames allow journalists to work with large amounts of information quickly, assign that information to its place in the scheme of the story, and package it for the audience so that they too see where the information fits into the issue (Gitlin, 1980). Media framing thus takes into account not just the topic, but how the journalist or media in general cover and package an issue. By focusing attention on the language and defining the issue under consideration, 'framing goes well beyond the traditional agenda-setting model, which tends to take issues as givens' (Kosicki, 1993, p. 113). Media can also affect the way issues are framed through the choices of journalists who cover a story, and those who may be chosen as sources (Kosicki & Pan, 1996). For public relations practitioners engaged in working with the media, this is an important point. As is discussed later in this chapter under information subsidies, positioning yourself as an accurate, dependable, and readily available source goes a long way toward getting your message into the media outlets.

A great deal of research has been done on how various topics are framed by both the media and what researchers often term *organizational policy actors*. Andsager and Smiley (1998) write, 'Policy actors are entities – such as government agencies, large corporations, elite professional organizations and even citizen-activists – who are outside the media but, because of their size and influence, also possess the ability to intervene in the production of news. Policy actors employ public information officers to communicate their frames' (p. 185).

The largest body of framing research is based around how these policy actors attempt to frame their particular issue or event for the media. Health issues (Andsager & Smiley, 1998; Shriver, White & Kebede, 1998), race (Gandy, Kopp, Hands, Frazer & Phillips, 1997), the environment (Liebler & Bendix, 1996), political campaigns (Domke, Shah, & Wackman, 1998; Miller, Andsager & Riechert, 1998; Missika & Bregman, 1987; Rhee, 1997; Sullivan, 1989), nuclear issues (Entman & Rojecki, 1993;

Meyer, 1995), war (German, 1995; Iyengar & Simon, 1993; Reese & Buckalew, 1995; Tankard & Israel, 1997), the government (Jasperson, Shah, Watts, Faber, & Fan, 1998), and political issues (Hanson, 1995; Iorio & Huxman, 1996; Norris, 1995; Woo, 1996) have each lent credence to the idea that the ability to frame the news is an exercise in power.

This chapter posits that along with the media's framing of events and issues, public relations practitioners who act as sources, whether or not they are public information officers for policy actors, also contribute to the framing of a story as presented in the media. They do this by highlighting or withholding specific information about a subject or issue from those covering the story.

The work done by Entman and by Gamson and Modigliani perhaps best inform the conscious framing by public relations practitioners. By using one or more of the five devices noted earlier, and creating a storyline to organize the message (Gamson & Modigliani, 1989), the practitioner can better emphasize her frame to the media. The work of Entman can help the practitioner best determine when use of a frame may be most effective – when defining problems, diagnosing causes or identifying what is causing the problem, making moral judgments about the situation causing the problem, or suggesting remedies for the problems (Entman, 1993, p. 52).

Those engaging in media relations must daily construct and process the information about their organization before releasing that information to the media. Pan and Kosicki (1993) state that framing may be considered a 'strategy of constructing and processing news discourse or as a characteristic of the discourse itself' (p. 57). Another responsibility of those practicing media relations is to help the media outlet develop what Gamson (1984, 1989) calls media packages that arrange the assorted facts of a situation or event concerning an organization into a meaningful, organized whole.

Information subsidies

Public relations practitioners generate prepackaged information to promote their organizations' viewpoints on issues, and to communicate aspects of interest within those issues, to their internal and external publics. Publicity and public information strategies also assist organizations to meet legal demands of financial disclosure, to influence legislation, and, among other purposes, to publicize organizational actions and operations that could have an impact on their publics or could add to the formation of positive organizational images in the minds of their

publics. Gandy (1982) describes the packaged information generated by public relations professionals as *information subsidies*, or the 'efforts to reduce the prices faced by others for certain information in order to increase its consumption' (p. 8).[1]

The generation of information by media relations practitioners not only facilitates organizations to freely contribute to the marketplace of ideas, but also facilitates the newsgathering process of media organizations. Newsom et al. (2000) explain:

> *Publicity is supposed to facilitate the newsgathering process. PR people expect news people to regard news releases critically, and to use or not use the news release at their own discretion. The release can be rewritten, incorporated with other materials, or not used at the time and used at a later date, sometimes in an unflattering way that is not helpful. That is part of the risk in being a source (p. 238).*

The facilitation of the newsgathering process by public relations sources has economic implications for both the practitioners' organizations and media organizations. Organizations of all kinds invest human and monetary resources in producing information that expresses their viewpoints. Media organizations save these resources when they receive packaged information for free or significantly below the cost of production.

The belief that 'information is power' is applicable to the implicit value of information subsidies and their control. Turk (1986) writes, 'Who has access to information and to what sources of information they have access, seems an important determinant of whose opinion and participation has the potential for influencing organizational life' (p. 1).

Information is seen as a commodity that has a value for those who provide and use it. Gandy (1982) states:

> *Sources enter into an exchange of value with journalists in which (1) they reduce the costs of news work to increase their control over news content; (2) they reduce the costs of scientific research to increase their control over scientific and technical information; and (3) they even reduce the costs of writing and producing television fiction to increase their control over the cultural background against which social policy questions are generally framed. (p. 15)*

Turk (1986) adds that 'sources who make information quickly and inexpensively available to journalists through . . . "information subsidies" increase the likelihood that the information will be consumed by the journalists and used in media content' (p. 3).

According to Gandy (1982), subsidized information could decrease or increase its value depending on how well disguised the quality of self-interest of the information is, how credible the sources are, and how diverse the available competing information is. Moreover, the value of an information subsidy increases in relation to its quality as perceived by reporters and editors. Editors who believe the authors of news releases share with them a similar education and training in news values are more likely to see the news release as more informational and less promotional (Kopenhaver, 1985, p. 41).

Scholars have studied information subsidies' effectiveness – mainly the generation and publication of news releases – in different types of organizations, such as state appellate courts (Hale, 1978), state agencies (Martin & Singletary, 1981; Turk, 1985, 1986, 1991; Walters & Walters, 1992), a comparison of U.S. and U.K. state agencies (Turk and Franklin, 1987), educational institutions (Bollinger 1999; Morton, 1988; Morton & Warren, 1992a, 1992b, 1992c; Rings, 1971), interest groups (Griffin & Dunwoody, 1995), and the scientific community (Walters & Walters, 1996). Other scholars have focused on wire service delivery of subsidized information (Morton and Ramsey, 1994) and the news media screening process of subsidized materials (Abbott & Brassfield, 1989; Berkowitz & Adams, 1990; Cameron & Blount, 1996).

Scholars have also focused on the information subsidy itself, exploring different characteristics of news releases that appear to contribute to their success in entering the media agenda. For instance, Hale (1978) explains that there seems to be a positive correlation between the length of new releases and the length of coverage. Nevertheless, most research has determined that although public relations practitioners do not have complete control over the outcome of their information subsidies, they can increase their value and chances for success if they focus on certain news values, such as thoroughness and accuracy. Martin and Singletary (1981) state, 'Thoroughness and accuracy can be interpreted to mean that, when a reporter receives a news release, the facts should be checked with the news source. The reporter should be alert both to what it said and what it didn't say. It is further assumed that news releases are sometimes self-serving and hence should be rewritten' (p. 93).

News releases distributed through wire services appear to have a high rate of acceptance by newspapers (Gandy, 1992; Martin & Singletary, 1981; Walters & Walters, 1992). Not surprising to most public relations practitioners dealing with the media, releases of a negative or critical nature generate more published stories (Martin & Singletary, 1981). Newspapers, which because of competition increasingly focus mainly on local events, are more receptive to news releases generated by local sources than to releases issued by sources located in other cities or states (Martin & Singletary, 1981; Morton & Warren, 1992a). Similarly, both

newspapers and television stations identified local focus, angle or relevance (Abbott & Brassfield, 1989; Berkowitz & Adams, 1990; Morton & Warren, 1992b; Turk, 1985), and timeliness (Abbott & Brassfield, 1989; Rings, 1971; Walters & Walters, 1992) as important factors for saving or rejecting a news release. In addition to standard news value, television stations place special emphasis on the visual possibilities for news releases.

Other aspects of a news release that are considered important by editors are accuracy (Kopenhaver, 1985), readers interests or benefit (Abbott & Brassfield, 1989; Kopenhaver, 1985; Turk, 1991), newsworthiness (Turk, 1991; Walters & Walters, 1992), avoidance of persuasive tactics or objectivity (Rings, 1971; Turk, 1991) and impact (Turk 1991; Griffin & Dunwoody, 1995). In contrast, Morton and Warren (1992a) note that there are three news elements that are difficult for the public relations practitioners to utilize despite the value those news elements have for journalists and editors: oddity, magnitude, and known principals.

The distinction between direct and indirect subsidies is explained by Gandy (1982): 'The journalist receives a *direct* [italics in original] information subsidy, and the target in government receives an *indirect* subsidy when the information is read in the paper or heard on the news' (p. 62). When subsidized information is filtered through the media before it reaches its intended audience, usually the government, it becomes an indirect subsidy. Gandy (1992) further elaborates this concept of indirect subsidies:

Policy actors provide indirect subsidies through a variety of means, most of which have to do with using a credible source to deliver a persuasive message. Journalists are blessed with a self-generated cloak of objectivity. Thus, material perceived as news, rather than as opinion, has a higher value to the decision maker. Indirect subsidies are therefore regularly provided through journalists and editors of print and electronic news media (p. 143).

Indirect subsidies are also delivered through the use of experts, grassroots lobbying, wire services, and satellite distribution (Gandy, 1992). Lobbyists combine subsidized information from their clients and data from their own research and expertise to influence legislation. Legislators use the indirect subsidy for decision making, and media report the development and outcome of this decision making process, which is a second use of that indirect subsidy provided by lobbyists.

By using the methods of direct and indirect subsidies, public relations practitioners wise in the ways of media, and aware of the needs of policy actors to obtain 'objective' information about a particular issue, can make every effort to influence decision making for the benefit of their organizations. We also contend that when media outlets are provided a carefully framed message, perhaps even arranged into an organized media package to help facilitate their newsgathering, the benefits to a practitioner's organization increase geometrically. Following is the final piece necessary to build a complete model of active media relations.

Agenda-building process

McCombs and Shaw (1972) introduced the concept of agenda setting to explain the impact of the news media in public opinion formation. The authors explained that the decisions made by editors, reporters, and broadcasters in choosing and reporting news plays an important part in shaping political reality. The findings of the first agenda-setting study, which was based on a political campaign, suggested a very strong relationship between the emphasis placed on different campaign issues by the media and the judgments of voters as to the salience and importance of various campaign topics.

In 1985, Weaver and Elliot asked the question, 'Who sets the agenda for the media?' They argued that 'it is not quite accurate to speak of the press *setting* [italics in the original] agendas if it is mainly passing on priorities set by other actors and institutions in the society' (p. 87). Earlier discussion in this chapter points out how a media relations practitioner can contribute to *building* the media agenda. For the purposes of our discussion the switch from a discussion of agenda setting to that of agenda building is perhaps most accurate.

This question of who builds media agendas was discussed by Cobb and Elder (1972) and Lang and Lang (1981) early in the development of the agenda-setting paradigm. On the one hand, Cobb and Elder explain that politicians act as opinion leaders and publicize particular issues creating a systematic and formal agenda through symbolic crusades. On the other hand, Lang and Lang (1981) suggest that the agenda-building is a collective and reciprocal process. More specifically, they state that the agenda-building process 'is a continuous one, involving a number of feedback loops, most important among which are the way political figures see their own image mirrored in the media, the pooling of information within the press corps, and the various indicators of the public response' (p. 466).

Max McCombs has spent almost 30 years developing and tracking the agenda-setting paradigm (See for example: Brewer & McCombs, 1996; Lopez-Escobar, Llamas, McCombs & Lennon, 1998; McCombs, 1992; McCombs & Masel-Walters, 1976; McCombs & Shaw, 1972; McCombs

& Shaw, 1993; Stone & McCombs, 1981; Wanta, Stephenson, Turk & McCombs, 1989). During that time he has presented and watched many changes in the way we view agenda setting. He has come to see agenda setting as a series of levels or phases and now writes of it in that way. Recently he has written that the currently evolving phase of agenda-setting research transformed the news agenda from independent variable to dependent variable, and that means the exploration of the sources that set the agenda to the media (McCombs, 1992; Roberts and McCombs, 1994). According to McCombs, 'The outermost layer is the array of sources routinely used by journalists to obtain news. New agenda setting studies linked the interests of public relations researchers with work in the sociology of news. Other work expanded the scope of presidential studies to explore the agenda-setting influence of the nation's number one newsmaker' (1992, p. 816).

Johnson et al., (1996) explain that the collective and reciprocal agenda-building process means that the press, the public, and public officials influence one another and, at the same time, are influenced by one another. They conducted path analysis research and concluded with a model of agenda building that includes at least four stages: (1) real-world conditions set into motion the agenda-building process; (2) the news media increases coverage of the issue; (3) the public picks up salience cues from both real-world conditions and media coverage; and finally (4) the opinion leader (the president in this study) reacts to public concern.

In a similar attempt to explain a model of the agenda building process, Corbett and Mori (1999) point out how issues first arise in society (e.g., a disease epidemic); then interest groups become involved and take positions regarding those issues; third, those interest groups' positions influence the news media and the public; and finally, the news media's coverage influences interest groups that originally became involved in addressing the issue from their particular perspectives. Media coverage also influences the public and politicians.

Walters and Gray (1996) identify another starting point for the agenda-building process when studying how politicians match the agenda of issues important to voters. They argue that voters first set the agenda of issues for political candidates, then voters and candidates simultaneously or separately set the agenda for the news media, and finally the news media organize the agenda of issues of different candidates and groups or voters.

The different stages of the media agenda-building process summarized in Table 10.1 have implications for public relations practitioners in charge of media relations, as well as for the development of a theoretical framework and future research in the area. These implications will be discussed later in this chapter.

Researchers	Lang & Lang (1981)	Walters & Gray (1996)	Johnson et al. (1996)	Corbett & Mori (1999)
Process' label	Collective and Reciprocal	Matching Voters' Agenda	Reciprocal Agenda	Circular Relationship
Starting stage	▶ News media highlight events, activities, groups, and personalities	▶ Voters set the agenda of issues to candidates	▶ Real-world conditions set into motion the agenda-building process	▶ Issues arise in society (epidemic disease)
Second stage	▶ The object focus of attention is framed	▶ Both voters and candidates set the agenda to the news media	▶ The news media increase coverage of the issue	▶ Interest groups become involved and take positions regarding those issues
Third stage	▶ The buildup step links the object or event to secondary symbols and it becomes a continuing story	▶ News media organize the agenda of different candidates and sectors in society	▶ The public picks up salience cues from both real-world conditions and media coverage	▶ Interest groups influence the news media and the public
Final stage	▶ Spokespeople articulate demands and command media attention		▶ Opinion leaders react to public concerns	▶ The news media's coverage influences the public, interest groups, and politicians

Table 10.1 Dynamic agenda-building process

Interconnections between the concepts

Framing and information subsidies are just tools media relations practitioners can use to participate in the building process of the media agenda. After more than two decades of research regarding the effectiveness of news releases and other subsidized information, findings and implications clearly point to two additional factors that help determine the effectiveness of an information subsidy to influence the media agenda. Although information subsidies may set the stage for the presentation of particular viewpoints, they must be reinforced and complemented by interpersonal interaction and a variety of communication channels. Taking the news release as an example of a subsidy, Ohl, Pincus, Rimmer, and Harrison (1995) argue that it must 'be considered more a "stage setter" than a self-contained news package; that is, it provides basic facts and presents the sponsor's perspective, both of which hopefully whet reporters' appetites to seek further clarification and/or additional information from company sources' (p. 100).

In a previous section we discussed what seems to be a positive relationship between the quality of an information subsidy and the news media's rate of acceptance of it. The ideal outcome of information subsidies' efforts will be that the coverage reflects a similar viewpoint to the one presented in the subsidies. For instance, as early as 1978, Hale found that newspapers emphasized the same characteristics as the court-prepared and subsidized news releases on which the articles were based.

Researchers also have found that when sources of information (in this case public relations practitioners), reporters, and editors cultivate personal relationships with a high level of interpersonal contact based on similar approaches to news values, professional standards, and education level, the impact of those sources on the agenda-building process is greater (Berkowitz & Adams, 1990; Lipschultz, 1991).

Berkowitz (1987), too, argues that the literature regarding sources also facilitates the understanding of the agenda-building process. Some sources, because of their nature and placement within an organization, are seen as more believable than others. An understanding of media needs also helps a source to get information published or to get air play. A number of studies present high-ranking government officials and corporate executives as sources who dominate the agenda-building process by successfully providing their subsidized information to the news media (Berkowitz, 1987; Cameron & Blount 1996; Corbett, 1998; McCombs, Einsiedel & Weaver, 1991; Sachsman, 1976; Weaver & Elliot, 1985). Other sources that researchers find seem to grasp the attention of the media and, therefore, actively participate in building the media agenda are public relations practitioners and spokespersons (Duhé & Zoch, 1994–95; Kopenhaver, 1985; Ohl et al., 1995; Rings, 1971), the U.S. president (McCartney, 1994; Wanta, 1991; Wanta, Stephenson, Turk & McCombs, 1989), celebrities (Corbett & Mori, 1999; Denham, 1999), interest groups (Chang, 1999; Huckins, 1999), scientists (Dunwoody & Ryan, 1983), and court lawyers (Hale, 1978; Lipschultz, 1991).

A number of researchers have made a direct connection between information subsidies and agenda building, starting with Gandy (1982), although he does not use the words *agenda building*, choosing rather to use *agenda setting*. Turk (1986), in her study of public relations influence on the news, was the first to view the connection positively for media relations practitioners. While admitting that the agenda-building process is a complicated one, Berkowitz and Adams (1990) write, 'The importance of studying the role of information subsidies in the agenda-building process is that it helps assess the magnitude of news source power' (p. 723). They conclude that the most powerful sources in local televisions news are those who both create news events and cultivate interpersonal relationships with reporters.

Framing also has a connection to agenda building. McCombs has designated it the 'emerging second level of agenda setting' (McCombs, Llamas, Lopez-Escobar & Rey, 1997, p. 704) because rather than looking at issues, or what the authors call 'objects,' framing is involved with describing '*attributes*, [italics in original] those characteristics and properties that fill out the picture of each object' (p. 704). They contend that both the selection of objects and that of attributes are powerful agenda-setting roles. This is a role that the practitioner often plays while attempting to frame her organization's issue in such a way as to make it of interest to the media, because framing a message involves active decisions about the information to include or exclude, to emphasize or elaborate on, to evaluate or interpret. As McCombs et al. (1997) write, 'In the language of the second level of agenda setting, framing is the selection of a small number of attributes for inclusion on the media agenda when a particular object is discussed' (p. 704).

As early as 1972 in their article about agenda building in politics, Cobb and Elder write about another aspect of

framing. 'The symbols, or language, in which an issue is phrased' will affect those who become aware of the issue (p. 162). The decisional aspect of choosing the right words or symbols to convey a particular meaning is part of a conscious effort to frame an issue in a certain way.

Few researchers discuss the use of message framing by sources in their attempt to provide information subsidies, perhaps because it seems too obvious to note. In one study that looked at presidential primaries and developed frames for the candidates based on press releases, the authors noted that these frames were transmitted by public relations practitioners. 'This public relations function is referred to as providing information subsidies' (Miller et al., 1998, p. 313).

While no one researcher has previously interconnected the three concepts we have set out here – framing, information subsidies, and agenda building – it became obvious to us in our reading that each of the areas overlaps the other in informing the practice of media relations. We therefore decided to attempt to develop a theoretical model that would have practical implications for the media relations practitioner.

Implications of the three paradigms

The quality and value of information subsidies to the originating source depend on numerous factors: the quality of the information provided in terms of traditional news values, how carefully the issue is framed to get across a particular issue, the relationship between the source and the reporter or editor, the media organization's news gathering and production process, the conditions present in the social environment, the individual judgment of the journalist, and organizational pressures within the newsroom. These factors affect each other and interact in multiple directions.

Because of these multiple interacting factors, there is also more than one direction or time sequence that can be used to describe the media agenda-building process. Characteristics of the news, where the information used was originally generated – a private organization, government, or a community group, for example – or who first detects an issue and generates the initial story determine which factors play the initial role in the agenda-building process.

Not every issue, or the consequences reported about it, evolves following the same pattern. An issue could arise from society, be produced by an organization, or be uncovered by a news medium. Following are descriptions of the different types of issue development that determine who initiates the media agenda building process.

1. The media agenda-building process could be initiated by the staff of an organization that knows an action or operation could affect one of its publics. This organization would take a proactive approach and design a communication plan to deal with the consequences of its actions or operations on that primary public. An example here would be a pharmaceutical company that developed and tested a new drug to reduce the potential for strokes in people over 65. The drug, as with any strong medication taken by a possibly fragile population, does have the potential to cause life-threatening side effects in a very few people.

   The plan could include the production of subsidized information to facilitate the news-gathering process for the news media, and the organization would take the lead in releasing the organization's viewpoint on the issue. The message would be framed that the drug is safe if taken as directed, and the number of strokes it prevents far outweigh any risks of side effects from the medication. Here the organization could initially control the situation, and media would depend on the organization for original information.

   Once the information is released to the media, new actors will participate in the media agenda-building process, including journalists, editors, interest groups such as the American Association of Retired Persons (AARP), the Food and Drug Administration, and any others affected by the issue. The agenda-building process is a dynamic one, and if the media relations practitioner's responsibility is to gain control of the situation for the benefit of the organization she advocates, she needs to also understand how a public forms and evolves and how media follow interest or issue trends. Walters and Gray (1996) explain the dynamic agenda building process with a marketing approach in mind:

   > [T]he public relations practitioners recognized, as do all good marketers, that bands of virtual publics linked not by proximity, but by interests and attitudes, define the marketplace. . . . The marketed public perspective not only recognizes that the agenda building process changes in harmony with the media business, it also changes in concert with society. Just as the concept of a homogeneous melting pot has given way to the view of a socially diverse salad bowl, and as the marketplace of ideas has become the menu of ideas, so too are there changes in the public and its power (p. 14).

2. In contrast, the actions and operations of an organization could affect one of the organization's publics

without the organizations having forecast it. Continuing with the example used above, a drug produced by the pharmaceutical company could have side effects on a group of people with certain unusual characteristics, and those side effects never showed up in drug trials because none of those in the test group had those characteristics (being more than 50% over healthy body weight for example). In this scenario the issue arises from society when a lobbying organization and/or interest group such as the AARP brings the issue to media and public awareness by staging events, taking the issue to the media, or publicly denouncing the company in some other way. Only at this point will the affected organization, the government, opinion leaders, and the news media have influence on the agenda-building they process, and thus they will not have initial control over how the issue is initially framed.

3. Finally, the news media could become interested in an issue created by an organization or affecting a group in society, but one that has not yet reached the public agenda. To follow with our example, doctors may have contacted the pharmaceutical company about problems their severely overweight patients are having with the drug. The company is working with the FDA to include stronger warnings when the drug is dispensed. In this situation a news organization could initiate the agenda-building process by uncovering and reporting the issue before the organization releases information on the situation along with the steps it is taking to alleviate the problem.

   Depending on the prominence and impact of the issue on society, and the activism of special interest groups such as the AARP, other news media will also follow suit in covering the issue. The organization and affected stakeholders will eventually be approached as sources of information or will attempt to provide information subsidies to reporters with whom they have previously worked, and only at that point will they become part of the media agenda-building process.

No matter who originates the coverage of an issue or in what stage of the agenda-building process that entity starts to participate, there are certain characteristics of issues as well as the corporate, media, or societal environments that could determine how information subsidies should be produced and handled. Griffin and Dunwoody (1995) explain that when information about health risks or related topics, such as the release of a new drug and its attendant side effects, is released, this type of information will be treated carefully by the organizations and news media involved in its dissemination. Subsidized information on these topics is valued by news organizations. The greater the impact on individuals or society, the more valuable is the subsidy; the greater the information scarcity, the better the chance that sources who control that information can influence the media agenda.

In both routine and crisis situations, journalists seek information from official sources. Nevertheless, the choices for the selection of sources in crisis situations could vary depending on the availability of the people knowledgeable about the situation. In these cases, organizations could be proactive and provide subsidized information to the news media so their positions are included in the coverage. In routine situations, reporters have more sources available, and so news organizations have more control over who and what is presented in the coverage. This implies that when only a few sources control the submission of information subsidies, these sources could produce subsidies according to the journalists' needs and still frame the information according to their organization's interest. The framing of the news should be done carefully to avoid the devaluation of the subsidy due to heavily self-serving content. Whatever the case, crisis or routine situations, a highly credible source has a greater chance to shape what enters the media agenda.

A model of media relations and its implications for practice

What we are about to discuss is an ideal vision of the process of media relations from an organizational viewpoint. The model was developed from the perspective of the public relations or media relations practitioner and takes into account all we have learned about positively affecting media coverage and the media agenda from our study of framing, information subsidies, and agenda building. In this section we are attempting to provide the practitioner with a theoretical and practical base from which to communicate with the media and other publics when an organizational issue arises.

The proposed model of media relations (Table 10.2) illustrates how the theoretical framework discussed in this chapter could be applied in the day-to-day production of framed information subsidies, the attempt by the media relations practitioner to participate in building the news media agenda, and ultimately inclusion on the public's agenda of issues. This model of media relations will also help in focusing future research on each of the stages of the process in an attempt to build a meta-theory that fully explains the complexity of media-public agenda building.

Information management

Successfully conducting media relations starts long before the media ever become involved. The successful practitioner is constantly involved in a proactive internal information management process. The best position from which to do this, of course, is that of an upper-level manager, a person who participates in the management level decision making of an organization. The IABC Excellence Study, which produced the book *Excellence in Public Relations and Communication Management* (1992), found in its study of 321 organizations that only those organizations in which public relations functions as an integral part of the management team could truly be considered excellent.

Although the media relations practitioner may not, herself, be part of an upper management team, she must have open access to those in upper management and keep direct communication open with important organizational sources such as the CEO, CFO, president, or vice presidents of important divisions or functions within the organization. Although every organization has its hierarchy and chain of command, employees such as media relations practitioners who are expected to interact quickly and accurately with important external publics must be accorded direct access to the sources they need to accurately explain the organization's stand on issues of concern.

In addition to direct access to important sources, public relations practitioners must engage in constant environmental scanning and issue identification. Environmental scanning is simply gathering information about an organization's publics and external environment in order to identify potential problems. Environmental scanning can be as simple and technical an activity as reading newspapers and journals relevant to an organization and clipping articles that relate to the organization or issues affecting it. It is also 'ideally suited for a number of qualitative research techniques, including focus-group studies' (Dozier & Repper, 1992, p. 187). Other methods for such scanning include exploratory surveys and simple case studies.

If organizations deal with arising problems with publics when they are first identified through environmental scanning, public relations practitioners will never find themselves dealing with issues. Unfortunately, that is not usually the case, and a public will make an 'issue' out of a situation that hasn't been resolved, thus attracting media coverage of the situation. Examples of common issues are consumer or neighborhood safety concerns, environmental problems involving clean air or water, community development or involvement concerns, and the financial health of the organization.

Proactive *information management* and issues tracking entail . . .

▸ Direct communication with organizational sources.
▸ Identify management positions regarding current or potential issues.

Need to generate an *information subsidy* starts the process . . .

1. Actions or operations will affect a public
2. A public reacts before the organization, which failed in tracking an issue/crisis
3. A real-world event produces consequences for the organization
4. The news media report an issue that involves the organization and publics

Proceed with the Internal/external *news-gathering* process . . .

• *Internal:* use information file/Intranet-Web site/organizational sources.
• *External:* use professional/industry associations, opinion leaders, experts, etc.
▸ Identify/seek authorization to express organizational viewpoint/position statement
▸ Produce information subsidy using traditional news values
▸ Carefully including organizational viewpoint through framing

Provide news media, interest/grassroots groups with subsidized information . . .

▸ Be ready/available with framed viewpoint for clarification/further inquiries from the news media.
▸ Monitor news media and audiences' responses/reactions.
▸ Follow up responses/possible generation of a sequence of information subsidies.
▸ Pay attention to competing sources – The more competing sources, the more difficult is to be heard.

Evaluate the process and outcome to improve the media relations' efforts.

▸ Be sure to assess final interpretations/reactions of affected publics regarding organizational viewpoint.

Table 10.2 A model of media relations

Need to generate information subsidy

The need to generate an information subsidy starts the media relations portion of the process. We have identified four situations, based to some degree on research in agenda building, in which a practitioner would recognize the need to become involved with the media.

1. The first situation is a case where the organization recognizes that its actions or operations will affect one of its publics.

2. The second situation is when a public reacts before the organization, which has failed to track an emerging issue or situation, reacts. This situation, although in our case involving an organization, parallels the research done by Walters and Gray (1996) involving political candidates. In their study, voters set the

agenda of issues for a candidate before the candidate publicly stated the issues he intended to focus on.

3. The third situation is a case where a real-world event produces consequences for an organization. For an organization this could mean the sudden death of a CEO, a natural disaster, or a coup in a country in which the organization operates. Research by Johnson et al. (1996) and Corbett and Mori (1999) (as described in Table 10.1) sets out the agenda-building process in cases where issues first arise in society or 'the real world.'

4. The final situation is one in which the news media report an issue that involves the organization and at least one of its publics, without the organization first initiating the information subsidy. Lang and Lang (1981), in an early agenda-building article, clearly describe the stages in the process when the media initiate a story or issue.

In the first three situations, the media relations practitioner can be proactive in contacting the news media, providing information subsidies, and carefully framing the organization's stand or viewpoint. In the fourth situation, the best a practitioner can do initially is to promptly attend to media requests for information, provide the organization's viewpoint as quickly and accurately as possible, provide properly prepared upper management spokespersons as required, and frame answers to the information requested as carefully and positively as possible.

Information-gathering process

Once it becomes obvious that there is a need to provide an information subsidy, the practitioner proceeds with internal and external information gathering. This is a time to carefully review the organization's file of articles published about the organization, the issue in question, or related issues; conduct Internet searches for information about similar issues that may have affected competitors; call the relevant internal department, division, or individual to obtain the latest information available about the situation; interview upper management to cull good quotes; and begin to develop the frame with which the organization will discuss the issue. Developing a frame means deciding which information to include or exclude, particular words to use or avoid, visuals to provide, etc. Areas to consider when framing an issue will be discussed in more depth in the following section.

Producing the information subsidy

As we discussed earlier in this chapter, in the section on information subsidies, there are specific ways a media relations practitioner can improve her chances of getting the organization's viewpoint out to the ultimate target audience – the public – intact. Table 10.3 is a compilation of the important qualities of an information subsidy in order for it to be usable by the media, along with the researchers who identified those qualities. It is also important to remember that a solid interpersonal relationship established over time between a practitioner and a reporter goes a long way toward getting an information subsidy a reading or hearing. Research also has shown that reporters repeatedly go to sources who are like themselves, and that they tend not to select sources who refute their own ideas (Powers & Fico, 1994). A media relations practitioner would do well to cultivate relationships with reporters who have shown themselves supportive, or at the least objective, about the sorts of issues that affect her organization.

Table 10.3 Quality of information subsidy

Components of News	Author(s)
▶ **Impact** on the local community or business sector	Griffin & Dunwoody, 1995
▶ **Prominence** of the news source (This may emphasize to the media relations practitioner the importance of using a manager at the highest possible level from whom to extract quotes)	Weaver & Elliot, 1985
▶ **Credibility** of the news source (A source is more credible when he or she has no obvious interest in the outcome of an issue, so finding a credible, disinterested source may become a priority with some issues)	Gandy, 1982
▶ **Attractiveness** of the news source to the targeted public	Wanta, 1991
▶ Shape the information to fill the **journalists' needs**	Berkowitz & Adams, 1990
▶ **Access** to company executives may affect story length, point of view, and publication of lead paragraphs	Ohl et al., 1995
▶ Inclusion of **traditional news values**, such as thoroughness, accuracy, local focus, timeliness, visual possibilities (television-Internet), newsworthiness, readers' interests or benefit, avoidance of persuasive tactics, and impact	See pages 285 and 286 for a complete list of authors.
▶ **Quotability** of source	Culbertson & Stempel, 1984

Table 10.4 Elements of framing

Media Relations Practitioner's Actions or Thought Process	Adapted From
▶ **Interpret** what is going on in a particular situation.	Bateson, 1954
▶ **Select and call attention** to particular aspects of the described issue or situation, which logically means directing attention away from other aspects.	Entman, 1993
▶ **Include or exclude** certain keywords, stock phrases, stereotyped images, and sources of information that thematically reinforce clusters of facts or judgments.	Entman, 1993
▶ **Establish** common *frames of reference* about topics or issues of mutual concern.	Hallahan, 1999
▶ **A frame has four functions**: (**1**) to define the problem, or state what the organization is doing with what costs and benefits; (**2**) they identify what is causing the problem, either within or outside the organization; (**3**) they make moral judgments about causing the problem; and (**4**) they suggest or justify solutions to the problem.	Entman, 1993
▶ **Use examples**, visual images or metaphors.	Gamson & Modigliani, 1989
▶ **Frames can be affected** by the journalist who covers a story, and sources used in providing the subsidy.	Kosicki & Pan, 1996

Careful framing of the organization's position or stand on the issue is also an important step in preparing an information subsidy for the media. Table 10.4 reviews aspects of framing that should be considered by the media relations practitioners when constructing an information subsidy of any kind.

Organizational authorization

Once the media relations practitioner has gathered all the information she considers relevant to the situation, and carefully framed the information to present the organization's viewpoint in an accurate yet positive way, she needs to verify the statement and collateral information she will present to the media. This is the time for the practitioner to recontact those individuals who were interviewed in the information-gathering process. This may also, depending on the issue, be the time to contact the legal or other regulatory departments within the organization.

In all situations, but especially in a situation where the organization is reacting to a media report, it is essential for the media relations practitioner to seek as high a level of authorization as possible to express the organizational viewpoint or position. This is a case where a public relations practitioner having unquestioned access to upper levels of management is essential to the organization.

Once the position statement has been authorized, and the information to be released to the media agreed upon, the media relations practitioner can move to the next step.

Contact the news media

The message is framed, the subsidy prepared, and necessary authorizations received. If this is a situation in which the organization can be proactive, the media relations practitioner contacts the news media to provide the subsidy. In cases where the organization has not been the first to report an issue, and it has been reported first by the media, the public relations practitioner must be ready and available to talk with the media to clarify the organization's position on the issue and to answer any further inquiries. In such a case, the subsidy must be prepared and framed as carefully, if not more carefully, than if the organization had contacted the news media first.

Monitor coverage and responses

When the information subsidy is accepted by the news media and coverage starts appearing in various news outlets, the media relations practitioner begins to monitor this media coverage for accurate reporting of the organization's stand, completeness of information, how organizational sources are presented, and the media framing of the issue. It is important to remember that framing of an issue can be at the level of the source, the media, or the ultimate audience, and monitoring the media will only identify the first two levels.

The practitioner also monitors the reactions and responses not only of the general media audience (the newspaper reader or television viewer) but also of targeted publics and particular interest groups that themselves are affected by the issue at hand. Do the publics themselves respond in the media, or do they communicate directly with the organization? How close do the positions of the organization and the affected public or interest group appear to be, as reported in the media? From this monitoring, the media relations practitioner decides how any follow-up information should be framed and goes through the process of preparing further subsidies, as noted earlier.

Follow up as necessary

All responses from affected publics or interest groups must be noted and responded to. The practitioner should also prepare for possible generation of a sequence of information subsidies as the agenda on the issue is building in the media and the organization's environment. Continue to monitor media coverage of the issue, and pay particular attention to competing sources such as interest groups, community opinion leaders, politicians, or other organizations as they 'weigh in' on the issue in the media. The more competing sources there are commenting on the issue, the more difficult it is to be heard, and the small amount of control the media practitioner has over the message the public is receiving through the media becomes even less.

It is at times like these, when the media are rife with competing viewpoints, that the practitioner must remember there are other ways to reach the organization's publics and stakeholders than through the mass media. Although the purposes of this chapter are to discuss media relations, how to frame messages targeted to the media, and how to produce information subsidies with the goal of building the media agenda, it would be remiss of us not to remind the reader that messages can be relayed and reinforced by means other than mass media.

Evaluate

The final step is to evaluate both the process of producing the subsidy and the outcome of media coverage in order to improve the media relations' efforts in the future. It is important to identify and assess the final interpretations

and reactions of affected publics regarding the organizational viewpoint in this situation. It is also important to determine whether your theoretical framework – producing a carefully framed information subsidy in order to attempt to build the media agenda – for the media relations effort was effective.

Did the organization's position, as framed and provided through information subsidies, reach the publics? Did the publics understand the position? Were they swayed in their viewpoint? Does further communication activity, perhaps reaching beyond the media, need to take place with this public or interest group? Has the organization reached understanding with the affected groups?

The proposed model of media relations presents different stages on which researchers should focus. . . . Each stage has implications for the next. The output from one stage will be the input for the next, and a cycle develops. Even though we are presenting this model as linear, it is not linear in the world. According to the type of issue, crisis or noncrisis situations, the number of competing sources, and the quality of the relationships between media and source, the process will change.

Implications for research and theory

Becoming proficient in media relations is a complex process involving a deep understanding of media routines, interpersonal relations, and message construction; a savvy regard for timing, organizational factors, and news values; good research, both internal and external; awareness of current and potential environmental and public issues; and familiarity with organizational stakeholders, publics, and interest groups. Each of these areas holds potential for further research into the media relations process.

Much of the research we have quoted here has been undertaken from the viewpoint of the reporter or the media organization, a common problem also faced by other public relations researchers attempting to write about the relationship between public relations practitioners and the media. Cameron, Sallot, and Curtin, in their 1997 article on public relations and the production of news, write that although a 'significant portion of the media sociology literature is devoted to source-reporter relations . . . most of this literature focuses on the routines and values of the reporter, not of the source' (p. 112).

Researchers would add significantly to the public relations body of knowledge simply by focusing their studies from the standpoint of the source rather than the receiver of information. Although some scholars complain that most public relations research is simply descriptive, we believe that with the dearth of research in this area, even descriptive studies will contribute if they are theoretically based. The areas discussed in this chapter – framing, information subsidies, and agenda building – offer the framework for three theories on which research studies can be built. Theories can also be pulled from management, interpersonal relations, sociology, and psychology to underpin further studies on organizational culture and its relationship to media relations, message construction, source-reporter and organization-public relationships, and the types of information subsidies that are most effective.

More work needs to focus on how framing theory is used by public relations practitioners, or sources in general, to influence not only media coverage, but the building of media agendas on particular issues. To date most mass communication research has focused on media use of framing in presenting issues to their audiences.[2]

Historically, in agenda-setting research, most studies have compared 'Time One' to 'Time Two' in order to assess the influence of the media agenda over the public agenda, and vice versa. Research undertaken to test the model introduced in the chapter, in which a media relations practitioner attempts to influence the agenda-building process through the use of carefully prepared and framed information subsidies, requires a multistage research process using both quantitative and qualitative methods.

For example, a story or issue could be the unit of analysis in a time sequence.

1. Measurement at Time 1 would be the production of the information subsidy. The researcher might study the influence of organizational, professional, and personal variables in the production of the subsidy. Specific framing techniques might also be quantified so they could be followed through the process to measure their inclusion in the other stages.

2. Time 2 would involve measuring the inclusion of the story or issue on the media agenda. The researcher would identify broadcast or print stories that identified, included, or followed the issue. Additional variables to study might be the influence of relationship quality between the source and reporter, competing sources, and media organization variables.

3. The final measurement at Time 3 in this example would be public understanding of the organization's framed position or viewpoint. Members of the ultimate target public who received the framed subsidy through the mass media could be studied. In this case, variables of interest might be the influence of competing sources and the quality of the indirect subsidy provided by the news media.

It would be appropriate to use a combination of research methods to conduct the proposed multistage research that is required to study the variables affecting the effectiveness of information subsidies in entering the media and public agendas of issues. Examples of possible methods are content analysis, interviews, survey research, focus groups, and path analysis.

Of course, other questions regarding information subsidies remain. A great deal of research has been done with regard to making the direct media subsidy as effective as possible, with researchers looking at timing, method of transmission, commonality of the source with the receiver, self-interest of the information, credibility of the source, and availability of competing information. Most research, however, has been conducted with a focus on media releases, or direct media subsidies. No work has been done to date to compare direct to indirect subsidies, or to even attempt to determine the efficacy of indirect subsidies, since Gandy's 1992 theoretical explication of the concept.

What we have done in this chapter is to review three existing theories or concepts in the communication literature in light of the potential impact of organizations and media for setting the agenda for the public. This allowed us to describe the media relations process based on theory, and thus to provide an example of the usefulness of combining theories or concepts to explain a phenomenon, in this case the media relations process.

The three concepts discussed here complement and inform each other and the practice of media relations. Not only do they provide a model of the practice of media relations, but we found this to be an excellent way to see the evolution of a theoretical approach such as agenda setting. After the first question – how do the media set the agenda of public issues? – we looked at who set the agenda for media. The third step was to identify how information is relayed (subsidies) and communicated (framing), and the final step was to pull together how practitioners can use all of this to better do their jobs.

In the case of two of the theories used in this chapter – framing and agenda building – we have taken concepts that have been used to explain the process from the media perspective and now here are being used to explain the process from the practitioner's perspective. Agenda building developed from agenda setting – the study of how the media act to identify issues the public needs to be concerned with. Agenda building takes the concept back one step to the source of the information used by the media. In the mass communication use of framing, framing theory was used to describe how media organizations presented information to the public. In this use, issues or stories were seen in certain ways by the reader or viewer because of the words and visuals used by reporters – how they 'framed' the story. In this chapter we discuss how practitioners 'frame' information to be presented to media representatives.

The same process of taking theories used in other contexts and applying them to pubic relations can be used to explain other aspects of practitioners' jobs. Perhaps to us the most exciting part about this type of exercise is the potential to generate new ways to conduct research and to combine theories from different fields into interdisciplinary explanations that can be used by public relations practitioners.

Notes

1. Gandy derived this definition from Randall Bartlett's (1973) book *Economic Foundations of Political Power*.

2. Framing theory's original focus was on interpersonal communication.

References

Abbott, E. A., & Brassfield, L. T. (1989). Comparing decisions on releases by TV and newspapers gatekeepers. *Journalism Quarterly*, **66**, 853–856.

Andsager, J., & Smiley, L. (1998). Evaluating the public information: Shaping news coverage of the silicone implant controversy. *Public Relations Review*, **24**, 183–201.

Bartlett, R. (1973). *Economic foundations of political power*. New York: Free Press.

Baskin, O., Aronoff, C., & Lattimore, D. (1997). *Public relations: The profession – the practice (4th ed.)*. Brown, Benhmaks & Dubuque.

Bateson, G. (1954). A theory of play and phantasy. *Psychiatric Research Reports*, **2**, 39–51.

Berkowitz, D. (1987). TV news sources and new channels: A study in agenda-building. *Journalism Quarterly*, **64**, 508–513.

Berkowitz, D., & Adams, D. B. (1990). Information subsidy and agenda-building in local television news. *Journalism Quarterly*, **67**, 723–731.

Bollinger, L. (1999). *Exploring the relationship between the media relations writer and the press: An analysis of the perceptions, goals and climate of communication*. Unpublished doctoral dissertation, University of South Carolina, Columbia.

Brewer, Marcus, & McCombs, Maxwell. (1996). Setting the community agenda. *Journalism and Mass Communication Quarterly*, **73**, (1, Spring), 7–16.

Cameron, G. T., & Blount, D. (1996). VNRs and air checks: A content analysis of the use of video news releases in television newscasts. *Journalism and Mass Communication Quarterly*, **73**, 890–904.

Cameron, G. T., Sallot, L. M., & Curtin, P. A. (1997). Public relations and the production of news: A critical review and theoretical framework. *Communication Yearbook*, **20**, 111–155.

Chang, K. (1999). Auto trade policy and the press: Auto elite as a source of the media agenda. *Journalism and Mass Communication Quarterly*, **76**, 312–324.

Cobb, R. W., & Elder, C. D. (1972). *Participation in American politics: The dynamics of agenda-building*. Baltimore: Johns Hopkins University Press.

Culbertson, Hugh M., & Stempel, Guido H., III. (1994). The prominence and dominance of news sources in newspaper medical coverage. *Journalism Quarterly*, **61**(3, Autumn), 671–676.

Corbett, J. B. (1998). The environment as theme and package on a local television newscast. *Science Communication*, **19**, 222–237.

Corbett, J. B., & Mori, M. (1999). Medicine, media, and celebrities: News coverage of breast cancer, 1960–1995. *Journalism and Mass Communication Quarterly*, **76**, 229–249.

Cutlip, S. M. (1994). *The unseen power: Public relations – a history*. Hillsdale, NJ: Lawrence Erlbaum Associates.

Cutlip, S. M., Center, A. H., & Broom, G. M. (1994). *Effective public relations (7th ed.)* (p. 6). Englewood Cliffs, NJ: Prentice Hall.

Cutlip, S. M., Center, A. H., & Broom, G. M. (2000). *Effective public relations (8th ed.)*. Upper Saddle River, NJ: Prentice Hall.

Denham, B. E. (1999). Building the agenda and adjusting the frame: How the dramatic revelations of Lyle Alzado impacted mainstream press coverage of anabolic steroid use. *Sociolofy of Sport Journal*, **16**, 1–15.

Domke, D., Shah, D. V., & Wackman, D. B. (1998). Media priming effects: Accessibility, association and activation. *International Journal of Public Opinion Research*, **10**, 51–74.

Dozier, D. M., & Repper, F. C. (1992). Research firms and public relations practices. In J. E. Grunig (ed.), *Excellence in public relations and communication management* (pp. 185–215). Hillsdale, NJ: Lawrence Erlbaum Associates.

Duhé, S. F., & Zoch, L. M. (1994–95). Framing the media's agenda during a crisis. *Public Relations Quarterly*, **39**, 42–45.

Dunwoody, S., & Ryan, M. (1983). Public information persons as mediators between scientists and journalists. *Journalism Quarterly*, **59**, 647–656.

Entman, R. M. (1993). Framing: Toward a clarification of a fractured paradigm. *Journal of Communication*, **43**, 51–58.

Entman, R. M., & Rojecki, A. (1993). Freezing out the public: Elite and media framing of the U.S. anti-nuclear movement. *Political Communication*, **10**, 155–173.

Gamson, W. A. (1984). *What's news: A game simulation of TV news*. New York: Free Press.

Gamson, W. A. (1989). News as framing. *American Behavioral Scientist*, **33**, 157–161.

Gamson, W. A., & Modigliani, A. (1987). The changing culture of affirmative action. In R. G. Braungart & M. M. Braungart (eds), *Research in political sociology* (vol. 3, pp. 137–177). Greenwich, CT: JAI Press.

Gamson, W. A., & Modigliani, A. (1989). Media discourse and public opinion: A constructionist approach. *American Journal of Sociology*, **95**, 1–37.

Gandy, O. H., Jr. (1982). *Beyond agenda setting: Information subsidies and public policy*. Norwood, NJ: Ablex.

Gandy, O. H., Jr. (1992). Public relations and public policy: The structuration of dominance in the information age. In E. L. Toth and R. L. Heath (eds), *Rhetorical and critical approaches to public relations* (pp. 131–163). Hillsdale, NJ: Lawrence Erlbaum Associates.

Gandy, O. H. Jr., Kopp, K., Hands, T., Frazer, K., & Phillips, D. (1997). Rice and risk: Factors affecting the framing of stories about inequality, discrimination and just plain back luck. *Public Opinion Quarterly*, **6**, 158–182.

German, K. M. (1995). Invoking the glorious war: Framing the Persian Gulf conflict through directive language. *Southern Communication Journal*, **60**, 292–302.

Gitlin, T. (1980). *The whole world is watching: Mass media and the making and unmaking of the new left*. Berkeley: University of California Press.

Goffman, E. (1974). *Frame analysis: An essay on the organization of experience*. Cambridge, MA: Harvard University Press.

Griffin, R. J., & Dunwoody, S. (1995). Impacts of information subsidies and community structure on local press coverage of environmental contamination. *Journalism and Mass Communication Quarterly*, **72**, 271–284.

Grunig, J. E. (ed.). (1992). *Excellence in public relations and communication management*. Hillsdale, NJ: Lawrence Erlbaum Associates.

Hale, F. D. (1978). Press releases vs. newspaper coverage of California Supreme Court decisions. *Journalism Quarterly*, **55**, 696–702/710.

Hallahan, K. (1999). Seven models of framing: Implications for public relations. *Journal of Public Relations Research*, **11**, 205–242.

Hanson, E. C. (1995). Framing the world news: *The Times of India* in changing times. *Political Communication*, **12**, 371–393.

Huckins, K. (1999). Interest-group influence on the media agenda: A case study. *Journalism and Mass Communication Quarterly*, **76**, 76–86.

Iorio, S. H., & Huxman, S. S. (1996). Media coverage of political issues and the framing of personal concerns. *Journal of Communication*, **46**, 97–115.

Iyengar, S., & Simon, A. (1993). News coverage of the gulf crisis and public opinion: A study of agenda-setting, priming, and framing. *Communication Research*, **20**, 365–383.

Jasperson, A. E., Shah, D. V., Watts, M., Faber, R. J., & Fan, D. P. (1998). Framing and the public agenda: Media effects on the importance of the federal budget deficit. *Political Communication*, **15**, 205–224.

Johnson, T. J., Wanta, W., Boudreau, T., Blank-Libra, J., Schaffer, K., & Turner, S. (1996). Influence dealers: A path analysis model of agenda building during Richard Nixon's war on drugs. *Journalism and Mass Communication Quarterly*, **73**, 181–194.

Kopenhaver, L. L. (1985). Aligning values of practitioners and journalists. *Public Relations Review*, **11**, 34–42.

Kosicki, G. M. (1993). Problems and opportunities in agenda-setting research. *Journal of Communication*, **43**, 100–127.

Kosicki, G. M., & Pan, Z. (1996, May). *Framing analysis: An approach to media effects*. Remarks presented to the annual meeting of the International Communication Association, Chicago.

Lang, G. E., & Lang, K. (1981). Watergate: An exploration of the agenda-building process. *Mass Communication Review Yearbook*, **2**, 447–469.

Liebler, C. M., & Bendix, J. (1996). Old-growth forest on network news: News sources and the framing of an environmental controversy. *Journalism & Mass Communication Quarterly*, **73**, 53–65.

Lipschultz, J. H. (1991). A comparison of trial lawyer and news reporter attitudes about courthouse communication. *Journalism Quarterly*, **68**, 750–763.

Lopez-Escobar, E., Llamas, J. P., McCombs, M., & Lennon, F. R. (1998). Two levels of agenda setting among advertising and news in the 1995 Spanish elections. *Political Communication*, **15**, 225–238.

Martin, W. P., & Singletary, M. W. (1981). Newspaper treatment of state government releases. *Journalism Quarterly*, **58**, 93–96.

McCartney, J. (1994, September). Rallying around the flag. *American Journalism Review*, 40–46.

McCombs, M. (1992). Explorers and surveyors: Expanding strategies for agenda-setting research. *Journalism Quarterly*, **69**, 813–824.

McCombs, M., Einsiedel, E., & Weaver, D. (1991). *Contemporary public opinion*. Hillsdale, NJ: Lawrence Erlbaum Associates.

McCombs, M., Llamas, J. P., Lopez-Escobar, E., & Rey, F. (1997). Candidate images in Spanish elections: Second level agenda-setting effects. *Journalism and Mass Communication Quarterly*, **74**, 703–717.

McCombs, M., & Masel-Walters, L. (1976). Agenda-setting: A new perspective on mass communication. *Mass Communication Review*, **3**, 3–7.

McCombs, M. E., & Shaw, D. L. (1972). The agenda setting function of mass media. *Public Opinion Quarterly*, **36**, 176–187.

McCombs, M. E., & Shaw, D. L. (1993). The evolution of agenda-setting research: Twenty-five years in the marketplace of ideas. *Journal of Communication*, **43**, 58–67.

Meyer, D. S. (1995). Framing national security: Elite public discourse on nuclear weapons during the cold war. *Political Communication*, **12**, 173–192.

Miller, M. M., Andsager, J. L., & Riechert, B. P. (1998). Framing the candidates in presidential primaries: issues and images in press releases and news coverage. *Journalism and Mass Communication Quarterly*, **75**, 312–324.

Missika, J. L., & Bregman, D. (1987). On framing the campaign: Mass media roles in negotiating the meaning of the vote. *European Journal of Communication*, **2**, 289–309.

Morton, L. P. (1988). Effectiveness of camera-ready copy in press releases. *Public Relations Review*, **14**, 45–49.

Morton, L. P., & Ramsey, S. (1994). A benchmark study of the PR News Wire. *Public Relations Review*, **20**, 171–182.

Morton, L. P., & Warren, J. (1992a). News elements and editors' choices. *Public Relations Review*, **18**, 47–52.

Morton, L. P., & Warren, J. (1992b). Proximity: Localization vs. distance in PR news releases. *Journalism Quarterly*, **69**, 1023–1028.

Morton, L. P., & Warren, J. (1992c). Acceptance characteristics of hometown press releases. *Public Relations Review*, **18**, 385–390.

Newsom, D., Turk, J. V., & Kruckeberg, D. (2000). *This is PR: The realities of public relations (7th ed.)*. Belmont, CA: Wadsworth.

Norris, P. (1995). The restless searchlight: Network news framing of the post-cold war world. *Political Communication*, **12**, 357–370.

Ohl, C. M., Pincus, J. D., Rimmer, T., & Harrison, D. (1995). Agenda building role of news releases in corporate takeovers. *Public Relations Review*, **21**, 89–101.

Pan, Z., & Kosicki, G. (1993). Framing analysis: An approach to news discourse. *Political Communication*, **10**, 55–75.

Powers, A., & Fico, F. (1994). Influences on use of sources at large U.S. newspapers. *Newspaper Research Journal*, **15**, 87–97.

Reese, S. D., & Buckalew, B. (1995). The militarism of local television: The routine framing of the Persian Gulf War. *Critical Studies in Mass Communication*, **12**, 40–59.

Reese, S. D. (1997). *Framing public life: A bridging model for media study*. A synthesis keynote review presented at the inaugural conference of the Center for Mass Communications Research, College of Journalism and Mass Communications of the University of South Carolina, Columbia, SC.

Rhee, J. W. (1997). Strategy and issue frames in election campaign coverage: A social cognitive account of framing effects. *Journal of Communication*, **47**, 26–48.

Rings, R. L. (1971). Public school news coverage with and without PR directors. *Journalism Quarterly*, **48**, 62–72.

Roberts, M., & McCombs, M. (1994). Agenda setting and political advertising: Origins of the news agenda. *Political Communication*, **11**, 249–262.

Sachsman, D. B. (1976). Public relations influence on coverage of environment in San Francisco area. *Journalism Quarterly*, **53**, 54–60.

Seitel, F. P. (1998). *The practice of public relations (7th ed.)*. Upper Saddle River, NJ: Prentice Hall.

Shah, D. V., Domke, D., & Wackman, D. B. (1996). 'To thine own self be true': Values, framing, and voter decision-making strategies. *Communication Research*, **23**, 509–560.

Shriver, T. E., White, D. A., & Kebede, A. (1998). Power, politics, and the framing of environmental illness. *Sociological Inquiry*, **68**, 458–475.

Stone, G. C., & McCombs, M. E. (1981). Tracing the time lag in agenda-setting. *Journalism Quarterly*, **58**, 51–55.

Sullivan, P. A. (1989). The 1984 vice-presidential debate: A case study of female and male framing in political campaigns. *Communication Quarterly*, **37**, 329–343.

Tankard, J. W. Jr., & Israel, B. (1997). *PR goes to war: The effects of public relations campaigns on media framing of the Kuwaiti and Bosnian crises*. Paper presented at the annual convention of the Association for Education in Journalism and Mass Communication, Chicago, IL.

Turk, J. V. (1985). Information subsidies and influence. *Public Relations Review*, **11**, 10–25.

Turk, J. V. (1986). Information subsidies and media content: A study of public relations influence on the news. *Journalism Monographs*, **100**, 1–29.

Turk, J. V. (1991). Public relations' influence on the news. In D. L. Protess and M. McCombs (eds), *Agenda setting:*

Readings on media, public opinion, and policymaking (pp. 211–222). Hillsdale, NJ: Lawrence Erlbaum Associates.

Turk, J. V., & Franklin, B. (1987). Information subsidies' Agenda-setting traditions. *Public Relations Review*, **13**, 29–41.

Walters, L. M., & Gray, R. (1996). Agenda building in the 1992 presidential campaign. *Public Relations Review*, **22**, 9–24.

Walters, L. M., & Walters, T. N. (1992). Environment of confidence: Daily newspaper use of press releases. *Public Relations Review*, **18**, 31–46.

Walters, L. M., & Walters, T. N. (1996). It loses something in the translation: Syntax and survival of key words in science and nonscience press releases. *Science Communication*, **18**, 165–180.

Wanta, W. (1991). Presidential rating as a variable in the agenda-building process. *Journalism Quarterly*, **68**, 672–679.

Wanta, W., Stephenson, M. A., Turk, J. V., & McCombs, M. E. (1989). How president's State of Union talk influenced news media agendas. *Journalism Quarterly*, **66**, 537–541.

Weaver, D., & Elliot, S. M. (1985). Who sets the agenda for the media? A study of local agenda-building. *Journalism Quarterly*, **62**, 87–94.

Wilcox, D. L., Ault, P. H., & Agee, W. K. (1998). *Public relations strategies and tactics (5th ed.)*. New York: Longman.

Woo, J. (1996). Television news discourse in political transition: Framing the 1987 and 1992 Korean presidential elections. *Political Communication*, **13**, 63–80.

CHAPTER 11

Michael Pfau and Hua-Hsin Wan

Persuasion:
an intrinsic function of public relations*

* Chapter 4 in *Public Relations Theory II* edited by Carl H. Botan and Vincent Hazleton. Copyright © 2006 by Lawrence Erlbaum Associates, Inc. Reproduced with permission.

The role of persuasion in public relations is the focus of considerable controversy. Edward Bernays (1955) initially posited that persuasion was integral to public relations. Bernays defined the function of public relations in terms of using 'information, persuasion, and adjustment to engineer public support for an activity, cause, movement, or institution' (1955, pp. 3–4). He and Ivy Ledbetter Lee viewed the role of the public relations practitioner as an advocate in the arena of public opinion, much as a lawyer is an advocate in the courtroom: as 'pleader to the public of a point of view' (Bernays, 1923, p. 57). Unlike Lee, however, Bernays was the first to view public relations as in the modern vernacular of strategic communication. He argued that the public relations practitioner 'engineers consent' by 'creating symbols which the public will respond to, analyzing the responses of the public, finding strategies that resonate with receivers, and adapting communication to receivers' (1923, p. 173). In Bernays' vision of public relations, persuasion is an integral function of public relations and, given the essential role that he envisioned public relations would play in democratic society, 'persuasion . . . is an inseparable part of a democratic way of life' (1955, p. 8).

More recently, James Grunig proposed an alternative vision of the nature of public relations. Grunig maintains that Bernays' perspective is based on 'manipulating publics for the benefit of organizations' (1989b, p. 18), which results in ineffective and/or unethical practices. Grunig led the way for the many public relations scholars, and a more limited number of public relations practitioners, who sought to distance themselves from persuasion. He maintains that a two-way symmetrical approach to public relations, which is grounded more in shared interests and dialogue involving communicator and receiver, is superior to the Bernays persuasion-based model, which Grunig characterized as a 'two-way asymmetrical approach.'

This chapter argues that, although both 'asymmetrical' and 'symmetrical' approaches are needed, depending on the circumstances, persuasion continues to be an essential function of contemporary public relations, especially in campaigns designed to establish, change, and/or reinforce an organization's image and in the role that public relations plays in an organization's commercial or social marketing efforts. In addition, the chapter maintains that the controversy over whether public relations should operate from an asymmetrical or symmetrical model is misguided; that public relations is best viewed as a form of strategic communication, in which persuasion plays an integral role; and that the controversy over optimal approach has stunted public relations scholarship. Finally, the chapter explores potential applications of select theories of persuasion in public relations, as exemplars of how future scholarship might inform both persuasion theory and public relations practices.

Nature and role of persuasion in public relations

Persuasion, which we define as the use of communication in an attempt to shape, change, and/or reinforce perception, affect (feelings), cognition (thinking), and/or behavior, plays a pivotal role in many public relations activities, particularly in those dealing with external publics. Many of the core functions of public relations, such as community relations, media relations, crisis communication, and others, manifest an implicit, if not explicit, goal of cultivating or maintaining a positive organizational image. Persuasion is intrinsic to this process. Other functions of public relations, including fundraising, lobbying, commercial or social marketing, and others, embody explicit suasory goals.

As a result, public relations scholars and educators have long acknowledged the central role that persuasion plays in public relations. The late Gerald Miller, in the first edition of *Public Relations Theory* (1989, p. 45) referred to persuasion and public relations as 'two "ps" in a pod.' This is because 'public relations [at least in its functions that involve external publics] is, in practice, advocacy' (Jones, 1955, p. 156). Barney and Black (1994) explain: 'The public relations professional finds herself wearing the mantle of single-minded advocate in the arena of public opinion. This requires the tools of persuasion' (p. 240). Even the Grunigs, who champion an alternative model that downplays the role of persuasion, acknowledge, 'Many, if not most, practitioners consider themselves to be advocates for or defenders of their organizations and cite the advocacy system in law as an analogy' (J. Grunig & L. Grunigs, 1990, p. 32). Thus, Pavlik (1987) acknowledges that 'public relations has traditionally been viewed as a form of persuasive communication' (p. 26).

Public relations texts have traditionally recognized a key role for persuasion in public relations. Marston (1979) describes public relations as 'the use of planned persuasive communication designed to influence significant publics' (p. 3). Moore and Canfield (1977) characterize the nature of public relations work as 'the development of favorable public opinion' (p. 5), thereby placing attitude formation and maintenance at the forefront of public relations practice. Cutlip, Center, and Broom (1985) argue that the work of public relations involves 'ethically and effectively plead[ing] the cause of a client or organization in the forum of public debate' (pp. 450–451). Center and Jackson

(1995) describe the goal of 'effective public relations' as eliciting 'mutually favorable behavior from the organization and its publics': such behaviors as getting publics to act or not act, or winning their consent to let the organization act (p. 3). Robinson (1969) adds, 'The goal of nearly all PR problem situations is to change attitudes and behaviors' (p. x).

Controversy over models

Despite the obvious role that persuasion plays in public relations, Grunig led an effort to reconceptualize public relations in terms of his two-way symmetrical model. His model assumes a more level playing field involving organizations and publics and implies use of communication practices based on shared interests and dialogue involving communicators and receivers (Grunig & Grunig, 1992). Grunig posits that two-way symmetrical public relations constitutes the ideal approach: a minority, but an emerging view of public relations (Grunig, 1989b). Grunig claims that his model is superior to the traditional press agentry and public information approaches because it is scientific, it is grounded in research as to what publics think, and it is superior to a two-way asymmetrical paradigm because it is not manipulative and, therefore, is more ethical. Advocates of two-way symmetrical model believe 'understanding . . . is the principal objective of public relations rather than persuasion' (Grunig & Grunig, 1992, p. 289).

Grunig's two-way symmetrical model has received a great deal of attention in public relations scholarship. The search for an alternative to a persuasion-based model of public relations has intrigued academics, in part because of the desire to carve out a distinctive niche for a fledgling discipline, and in part as a result of a queasiness over the ethical basis of public relations work. Grunig's alternative model has appeal to many academics because it is distinctly rooted in public relations domain – in contrast to persuasion, whose conceptual and empirical foundations are not even located in the broad terrain of journalism, which gave birth to public relations as an academic domain, but rather are firmly rooted in the disciplines of communication and social psychology. The ethical question has proven particularly troublesome to many academics and practitioners, prompting the recent retreat from use of the name of 'public relations' in job titles, replaced by what Seitel (1998) terms 'euphemisms,' such as corporate communications, public affairs, and other titles (p. 3). Barney and Black (1994) observe that 'public relations practitioners . . . often appear uneasy, and somewhat defensive, about the moral basis of their profession' (p. 236).

We take issue with Grunig's model on two grounds. First, the model presumes goal compatibility and a relatively even playing field between organizations and their external publics. Vasquez (1996) terms the assumption of goal compatibility as an 'idealistic presupposition about the role of public relations in society' (p. 62). In fact, organizations and publics often manifest disparate goals. An oil company proposes offshore drilling that environmental groups oppose; a manufacturing firm wants to locate a plant on a site that community groups oppose; tobacco, alcohol, or gun manufacturers seek unfettered marketing of their products, which opponents deem harmful to the public health: a company disputes the news media's claims that question the safety or the performance of its products; and so on. Zealous advocates of the symmetrical model argue that, in those circumstances in which goals appear disparate, public relations can serve as the vehicle for a compromise solution that benefits the organization, all interested publics, and even society as a whole (Grunig & Grunig, 1992). Vasquez (1996) terms this line of reasoning as 'tautological,' since incompatible goals are, by their very nature, often intractable and defy magical transformation into compatible goals by virtue of the use of public relations processes. Not surprisingly, one study of the approach that 31 organizations used in dealing with activist groups espousing different goals than the organization reported that none of them employed two-way symmetrical methods (Grunig, 1986). The fact is that public relations frequently involves conflicting goals, in which the interests of an organization and interested publics inherently clash (Murphy, 1991; Tuleja, 1985; Vasquez, 1996). In those situations involving mixed motives, the process of negotiation may yield compromise through accommodation (Dozier, Grunig, & Grunig, 1995). [Ironically, persuasion plays a critical role in negotiation (Heath, 1993).] Often, however, such situations 'are adversarial in their essence' and defy solution (Leichty, 1997; Murphy, 1991; Tuleja. 1985; Vasquez, 1996).

In addition, the communications playing field is more often than not uneven, especially in the corporate arena. A corporation, which possesses an enormous resource advantage over most publics with which it deals, is in a position to bring to bear tremendous power in achieving its goals. Yet, Pavlik's game theory results (1989) reveal that, because organizations can optimize their interests by practicing asymmetrical communication, two-way symmetrical communication simply won't happen until publics gain equal power. Given an uneven playing field, Barney and Black's (1994) admonition is right on target: 'The unstructured public relations marketplace offers no guarantees of equity in public discussion' (p. 241).

The truth is that the continuing controversy over whether public relations should operate from a two-way symmetrical or asymmetrical model is a classic 'straw man,' which has stunted public relations scholarship. There is no single best approach, and attempts to suggest otherwise fly in the face of reality. Research indicates that most public relations practitioners use both approaches, depending on the circumstances (Katzman, 1993). Long (1987), Hellweg (1989), Murphy (1991), and Cancel, Cameron, Sallot, and Mitrook (1997) have argued that the public relations practitioner is first and foremost a problem solver, who 'must typically choose, either consciously or by default, a stance somewhere between pure advocacy and pure accommodation' (Cancel et al., 1997, p. 37). They view most situations as involving considerable nuance, with strategic decisions made using either the perspective of a continuum that ranges at the poles from circumstances requiring either pure advocacy or pure cooperation (Dozier et al., 1995; Hellweg, 1989; Murphy, 1991), or the perspective that diagnoses situations in terms of 'clusters of activities, techniques, and strategies.' In either case, the professional operates from the maxim 'What is going to be the most effective method at a given time' (Cancel et al., 1997, p. 35). Sometimes the best approach involves use of cooperation and dialogue between communicator and receiver, but at other times, especially in dealing with external publics, the optimal approach requires influence. Even the Excellence study, which equates excellence and symmetrical practices, acknowledges that 'In the rough and tumble, everyday world . . . communicators alternately negotiate and persuade, depending on the situation. The excellent communicator . . . knows how to use both . . . symmetrical and asymmetrical models of communication' (Dozier et al., 1995, pp. 13–14).

The second reason we take issue with Grunig's model is that it is based on erroneous assumptions about the nature of persuasion. Grunig (1989b) maintains that the 'Bernay's paradigm,' which emphasizes persuasion, has 'steered research and theory in the field in a direction that I consider to be both ineffective and ethically questionable' (p. 18). This position is echoed by Grunig and White (1992), who maintain that the 'asymmetrical worldview steers public relations practitioners toward actions that are unethical . . . and ineffective' (p. 40). Is the use of persuasion in public relations ineffective? The many successes organizations have achieved in promoting and maintaining positive image, fundraising, lobbying, or marketing products, services, and causes provide a resounding rebuttal to this claim.

We suspect that the charge of ineffectiveness is based on two erroneous assumptions. The first is that persuasion is, at times, an inappropriate response to a public relations problem. We concur. In those situations that require simple information or use of cooperation and dialogue,

an asymmetrical approach would be inappropriate and, if utilized, would probably prove to be ineffective. It is not our position that persuasion is the sine qua non of public relations practices, but rather that persuasion plays an important role in many public relations activities. Clearly, the professional's choice of approaches requires an insightful diagnosis of the situation.

The second assumption is that persuasion seeks conversation or attitude change, and that this is problematic. Grunig (1992) asserts that an asymmetrical view 'suggest[s] that organizations can achieve powerful effects with communication.' However, 'these effects seldom occur, . . . and thus asymmetrical public relations programs usually fail' (1992, p. 10). This view of persuasion is simply outdated. It was once in vogue. It was referred to as the 'change' or 'conversion' model, and it assumed that the process of influence is unidirectional, in which an active communicator works his/her magic on a passive receiver (Miller, 1989). Based on this view of persuasion, Grunig is correct that most attempts at influence are destined to fail. This was the prevailing view at the time classic studies were conducted that subsequently ushered in the limited effects view of the influence of the mass media (Berelson, Lazarsfeld, & McPhee, 1954; Katz & Lazarsfeld, 1955; Klapper, 1960; Lazarsfeld, Berelson, & Gaudet, 1948). However, persuasion scholars long ago abandoned this linear view and, along with it, the conversion model of influence.

Most contemporary persuasion scholars view persuasion from a transactional paradigm, involving the dynamic interplay of all elements in the communication's process (Pfau & Parrott, 1993) and view the process of persuasion as incremental, in which communicators seek specific objectives chosen from a broad spectrum of influence possibilities (Miller & Burgoon, 1973). Operating from this perspective, single persuasive messages seek small movements in receivers: initially forming or shaping thoughts, feelings, or behaviors where none existed before; reducing hostility levels in opponents; winning over apathetic, uninformed, or conflicted receivers; or intensifying thoughts, feelings, and/or behaviors among supporters. In the context of public relations, attaining these outcomes is only possible via persuasive campaigns, fully integrated and sustained communication efforts, which consist of multiple messages that seek clearly defined objectives (Pfau & Parrott, 1993).

The charge that persuasion is 'ethically questionable' is grounded on the assumption that Bernays' perspective of public relations is based on 'manipulating publics for the benefit of organizations' (in Grunigs 1989b, p. 18). This argument is somewhat more intricate.

Is persuasion inherently manipulative, as Grunig claims? Yes! Persuasive communication in all forms either explicitly or implicitly seeks to frame messages for optimal effectiveness and, thereby, affect receivers. Subsequently, all persuaders, whether operating in the realm of public relations, social marketing, commercial advertising, or politics, 'rationalize their persuasive efforts in terms of the public interest' (Salmon, 1989, p. 47). As a result, effective persuasion is inherently manipulative. Is manipulation, de facto, unethical? No! It isn't manipulation, per se, that is ethically suspect. 'The persuasive ethic is defensible and laudable, in a participatory democracy' (Barney & Black, 1994, p. 233).

As Gerald Miller (1989) reasons, persuasion is a means or vehicle that is designed to accomplish specific ends. There is nothing inherently unethical about means or ends. Rather, both means and ends require scrutiny for their ethical appropriateness. Miller (1989) explains, 'Ethical issues . . . are . . . relevant to *particular* political, policy, or product ends and to the *specific* persuasive means used to pursue these ends' (p. 48). Concerning means, it is ethically proper to employ legitimate tools of persuasion in the pursuit of legitimate ends. However, it is ethically wrong to employ 'deceptive or dishonest message strategies' (p. 48), no matter how laudable an end, such as making up information in order to make a claim appear even more compelling, a practice that has become all too common (Crossen, 1994). In terms of ends, it is ethically wrong to use persuasion to market products that harm workers, consumers, or the environment, or to use persuasion to deny or conceal these outcomes.

In assailing persuasion as 'manipulation,' Grunig is placing the ethical onus on means as opposed to ends. However, instead of examining means for ethical appropriateness, he offers a blanket indictment of all persuasion as ethically suspect because it involves manipulation. In doing so, he believes his symmetrical model resolves the ethical quagmire because 'it defines ethics as a process of public relations rather than as an outcome' (Grunig & Grunig, 1992, p. 308). As we will argue shortly, symmetrical public relations does not resolve what critics term the 'marked relativism [which] . . . undergirds public relations work' (Jackall, 1995, p. 380). Indeed, in providing a blanket panacea for ethical nuances involved in process or means, Grunig oversimplifies what is an intricate problem area.

The public relations profession should ensure that practitioners employ appropriate means, but in doing so, it should concentrate its efforts on what most experts would agree are actual ethical violations. This is precisely what the profession is attempting to do.

Public relations professionals have acted to provide ethical standards for the profession. Their canons of appropriate conduct focus on means, attempting to regulate the way that public relations' practitioners conduct themselves. For example, the profession requires honesty

in public relations communications. Both the Code of Professional Standards for the Practice of Public Relations, authored by the Public Relations Society of America (PRSA), and the Code of the International Association of Business Communicators (IABC) focus on honesty. The fifth article of the PRSA Code states: 'A member shall not knowingly disseminate false or misleading information and shall act promptly to correct erroneous communication for which he or she is responsible.' The second article of the IABC Code prescribes that 'Professional communicators disseminate accurate information,' and admonishes that they act 'promptly' to 'correct any erroneous communications for which they may be responsible.'

Of course, efforts to regulate conduct, even obvious cases involving dishonesty, are difficult. Indeed, both the PRSA and IABC codes lack effective enforcement mechanisms, which renders them little more than prescriptive. However, even if such codes could be enforced, they would not quell ethical criticisms of the public relations profession because the real ethical battleground in contemporary public relations, one that can't be resolved via professional codes of conduct, is over ends.

The most serious ethical issues in public relations today concern ends, not means. When critics assail public relations as 'flackery,' 'manipulation,' 'coverup,' and 'spin,' they address what public relations does, more than how it does it. Some go so far as to argue that all public relations is ethically suspect (Ewen, 1996; Gandy, 1982; Herman & Chomsky, 1988; Jackall, 1995; Olasky, 1987; Stauber & Rampton, 1995). What public relations does is to tip the balance of power in favor of large corporate interests. Greider (1992) argues that large corporations employ public relations, coupled with ease of media access and use of campaign contributions and lobbying, to influence politicians at all levels, and that this unbridled use of power has undermined American democracy.

> At the highest levels of government, the power to decide things has . . . gravitated from the many to the few . . . Instead of popular will, the government now responds more often to narrow webs of power – the interests of major economic organizations and concentrated wealth and the influential elites surrounding them (p. 12).

Stauber and Rampton (1995), among the most unabashed critics of the profession, indict public relations for usurping democratic values: for harnessing the power of public relations 'on behalf of wealthy special interests,' thereby enabling corporate interests to dominate debate, discussion, and decision-making (p. 205). As a result, they charge that public relations often has been used for unsavory ends: to promote unhealthy and/or unsafe products, to damage the environment, and to silence individuals and groups who are critical of these practices.

The net result of this distortion of process is that public relations has contributed to the elevation of corporate values, as manifested in individual acquisitiveness, and the undermining of public values. Stauber and Rampton (1995) claim that 'The values that dominate our lives today are corporate, not democratic values' (p. 203). Ewen (1996) argues that, public relations has 'played a critical role' in demeaning public institutions (e.g., public housing, education, broadcasting, assistance, and health) (p. 407). Ewen charges that since the 1970s, corporate interests have taken the initiative in the effort to 'dismantle' public policies: in essence, to transform people's perception of public services into something undesirable (p. 407).

These ethical issues concern what public relations does, not so much how it does it. They are about ends, as opposed to means. Those of us who are interested in the ethics of public relations must address these core issues, which have practically nothing to do with whether the profession employs a two-way asymmetrical or symmetrical approach.

Public relations as strategic communication

As we indicated at the outset of this chapter, neither the asymmetrical nor the symmetrical model offers a single optimal approach to the practice of public relations, and the dispute over approaches is misguided. The public relations professional inevitably confronts unique circumstances: organizations vary in their size, function, and culture, which McElreath (1997) posits affects response options; furthermore, the nature of problems to be confronted are often unique.

We echo Bernays, who maintains that public relations should be viewed as a form of strategic communication, in which persuasion plays an integral role. Early in the century, Bernays advised that the public relations council affects public opinion 'by creating symbols which the public will respond to, analyzing the responses of the public, finding strategies that resonate with receivers, and adapting communication to receivers' (1923, p. 173). Bernays viewed strategic communication as putting the receiver first and, through research, devising communication to achieve specific objectives with targeted receivers.

Strategic communication views the public relations person as problem solver who, when confronted with a situation, researches it, determines what needs to be done, and selects, implements, and monitors strategies that are designed to achieve predetermined objectives. If objectives are suasory, as will often be the case in dealing with external publics, communication approach can and should feature persuasion. Within ethical parameters, strategic communicators are principally concerned with 'what is going to be the most effective method at a given time' (Cancel et al., 1997, p. 35).

Critical elements in strategic communication include use of environmental scanning to examine the organization's overarching goals, discern relevant publics, and identify potential problems or opportunities. In terms of a specific campaign, it uses formative research to set overall goals, segment audiences, set specific communication objectives for each audience, and devise optimal communication strategies for attaining these objectives; then, it implements the campaign and employs impact studies to monitor its progress and summative evaluation to assess effectiveness. Strategic communication, at its core, relies on quality research to determine both direction and strategy. Unfortunately, most public relations practitioners continue to view their work in technician terms, disdaining research and, with it, strategic communication (Dozier, 1990; Dozier & Repper, 1992; Gronstedt, 1997; Pavlik, 1987). We agree with the Excellence study (1995), which calls for a strategic approach to public relations (Grunig & Repper, 1992), but we disagree with the conclusion that excellence should be operationalized as symmetrical practices that, in essence, eschew the role of persuasion in public relations (Grunig, 1992).

The role of theory in public relations

The unfortunate downside to the controversy concerning two-way symmetrical versus asymmetrical approaches is that it has stunted public relations scholarship. The search for an alternative to a persuasion-based model of public relations fascinates academics, in part, because of the desire to locate a theoretical base for the fledgling discipline within the confines of public relations, instead of relying on theory and research in the more established disciplines. Grunig (1989b) advanced precisely this argument as the rationale for his two-way symmetrical model in the first edition of *Public Relations Theory*. In his essay addressing 'symmetrical presuppositions,' he acknowledged that 'public relations is an infant scholarly field' (p. 18). The abstract of the essay provides a blueprint for the field's maturation:

Public relations theorists have borrowed theories from communication science and other social sciences, but few have developed unique theories of public relations. Scientific disciplines always have borrowed from one another, but they do not advance unless they build original theories from the borrowed concepts. (p. 17)

He is quite correct about the absence of theory in public relations scholarship. In the opening essay in the same edition, Hazleton and Botan (1989) lament that, 'there has been little of public relations research that is theory driven' (p. 14). Botan (1989) adds that 'public relations has not systematically addressed the development of theory or the relationship of practice to research and theory building' (p. 101). Instead, what has been the emphasis in public relations scholarship? Pavlik observed more than a decade ago that 'almost all research on public relations is limited to description' (1987, p. 41).

We hasten to add that very little has changed since Pavlik's characterization. Many public relations scholars continue to add to the litany of case studies in public relations, settling for what amounts to anecdotal evidence. Others, preoccupied with the mission of carving out a distinct niche for the discipline, have focused their efforts on the two-way symmetrical model, ignoring relevant theories in other disciplines. The downside of both of these approaches is that they mire public relations scholarship in a narrow niche, in what amounts to a scholarly ghetto. Scholarly output appears in public relations books or journals, which are read by public relations academics and practitioners, but are of interest to no one else, particularly in the academy. The price public relations pays for this tunnel vision is steep: It is extracted in the form of diminished credibility of public relations scholars and the discipline, both in academic units where public relations is housed and across the university. This in evident in growing pedagogical debate in journalism programs, in particular, over 'the fit' of public relations study (Habermann, Kupenhauer, & Martinson, 1988), and in the difficulty many scholars, who publish almost exclusively in public relations outlets, experience in tenure and promotion processes at Tier I research universities.

The contextual approach to public relations scholarship has accelerated in recent years, during the same period that public relations academics abandoned persuasion. Today, most academics define public relations as building and maintaining mutually beneficial relationships between an organization and its publics (e.g., Caywood, 1997; Crable & Vibert, 1986; Cutlip et al., 1985; Grunig & Hunt, 1984; McElreath, 1997; Seitel, 1992; Wilcox, Ault, & Agee, 1992). Although this definition provides a good start in describing what public relations is, it doesn't go far enough. The definition ignores the many functions of public relations, above and beyond building and maintaining relationships, which contribute to organizational effectiveness (e.g., fundraising, lobbying, promoting organizational image, marketing). These functions are largely suasory. Further, the definition says nothing about how public relations works. How does public relations build and maintain relationships or perform the other functions identified earlier? We maintain that communication, more often than not persuasive communication, is the essential means/vehicle in this process. Thus, we agree with Botan and Hazleton's (1989) position in the preface to the first edition of *Public Relations Theory* that the primary emphasis in public relations scholarship should focus on communication.

Public relations can be best understood as a specialized kind of communication . . . [and, therefore, that] it should be possible to study public relations as an instance of applied communication. We should be able to apply communication theory to explain and predict public relations practice, and use public relations practice as a site for the development of communication theory. (p. xiii)

The choice for scholars interested in public relations or other applied communications domain (e.g., health communication, political communication) is simple: They can address core functional issues, usually dealing with communication processes, or they can focus narrowly on context. Functional questions deal with theoretical content about communication. Although research on functional questions is set in a specific context and its results inform communication practices in that context, the results of research on functional questions also carry important theoretical implications that cross contexts and, therefore, are of interest to a broad array of communication scholars. We urge scholars to make communication theory, and not context, the engine that propels their research.

Theories of persuasion: select exemplars

This chapter has argued that persuasion continues to be an integral function of public relations. As a result, theory and research in persuasion constitute fruitful ground in the search for functional questions, which are theoretically important in their own right and which may inform public relations practices. This section explores the potential applications of theories of persuasion in public relations, in the form of select exemplars, including involvement and information processing, affect, medium theory, functional theory, and inoculation. The exemplars chosen are intended to be illustrative, not exhaustive.

Involvement and information processing

Until the 1970s, scholars and practitioners operated on the assumption that receivers process messages actively. The active message processing model assumes that thinking *is* information processing (Lodge & Stroh, 1993, p. 231). In order to persuade, communicators are advised to employ good arguments and evidence, operating on the premise that well-crafted messages force attention, affect beliefs and, ultimately, exert influence. The active model elevates messages to center stage.

Today, the active approach guides many, perhaps most, public relations practitioners. They operate from an implicit premise that information is the key: that it triggers cognitive responses in people, thereby affecting attitudes and behaviors. Most social action messages, which seek to affect thinking and behavior about using child restraints, protecting against crime, or avoiding various deleterious behaviors (e.g., smoking, drug use, excessive drinking), rely heavily on specific content. Wallack (1989, p. 366) summarized the dominant message approach employed in the health area: 'We tend to define fundamental health problems as a basic lack of information and then to rely on the mass media to provide the right information in the right way to the right people at the right time.' Traditional public relations messages manifest a similar bias. A number of content analyses of organizations' communication in community relations, crisis communication, and other contexts reported heavy reliance on information appeals grounded in argument (see Heath, 1994).

During the 1960s and 1970s, theorists and practitioners began questioning the underlying assumptions of the active model. They were founders of what came to be known as the passive, heuristic, or low-elaborative message processing model. Krugman (1965, 1971) was one of the first to articulate a low-involvement perspective of message processing. Krugman reasoned that most contemporary influence attempts occur in low-involvement circumstances, where there is little, if any, active cognition. Krugman reasoned that this was true of most television content, whether it takes the form of news, advertising, or entertainment. Krugman argued that receiver involvement dictated how people process communication. Although Krugman's thesis was the first major step in formulating an alternative conceptualization of message processing, his view of involvement was subsequently challenged for generalizing about media while not taking into consideration differences in message content (Salmon, 1986).

Today, most scholars accept the thesis of Krugman's position that receiver involvement determines whether people will seek out and actively process public relations messages (see Grunig, 1980, 1989a; Heath, Seshadri, & Lee,

1998), and that there are distinct methods of message processing and, therefore, 'two different *'*routes' to attitude change' (Batra & Ray, 1985, p. 15). Passive or heuristic message processing bypasses active cognition. It assumes a more mindless processing. As Chaiken (1987) describes, 'Opinion change in response to persuasive communications is often the outcome of only a minimal amount of information processing' (p. 3).

During the 1980s, the dual explanations for the process of influence were combined in two processing explanations that sought to predict circumstances when one or the other would prove predominant. The explanations, the Elaboration Likelihood Model (ELM) developed by Petty and Cacioppo (1986) and the Heuristic Systematic Model (HSM) articulated by Chaiken (1987), are similar, although there are subtle differences between them.

The ELM and HSM feature two distinct paths in influence: one that is active and thoughtful, termed *central* in the ELM and *systematic* in the HSM, and another that is more passive and less thoughtful. This route is called *peripheral* in the ELM and features such cues as source factors, the number of arguments contained in a message, or the feelings triggered by a message, any one of which may be responsible influence in low-elaboration conditions (Alba & Marmorstein, 1987; Axsom, Yates, & Chaiken, 1987; Maheswaran & Chaiken, 1991; Petty & Cacioppo, 1979, 1984a, 1984b, 1986; Petty, Cacioppo, & Kasmer, 1988; Wood, Kellgren, & Preisler, 1985). The more passive and less thoughtful route in the HSM is termed *heuristic*. It is more narrowly conceptualized than peripheral processing in the ELM. Heuristic cues constitute decision rules that people employ, such as (Chaiken, 1987, p. 4) 'experts are always right'; 'people I like usually have correct opinions on issues'; 'more arguments' are indicative of stronger positions; 'arguments based on expert opinions are valid'; and so forth.

Heuristics are learned decision rules that people acquire over time. People employ heuristics because, in those situations when they are not motivated to attend communication, which is a frequent circumstance for public relations messages, they become 'minimalist' information processors, expending only the minimum effort needed to get the job done (Chaiken, 1980, 1987; Chaiken, Liberman & Eagly, 1989). Research supports the basic logic of the HSM, particularly for the heuristic cues of consensus (Hazlewood & Chaiken, 1990) and communicator likability (Chaiken, 1980, 1987; Chaiken & Eagly, 1983; Roskos-Ewoldson & Fazio, 1992).

The main difference with the ELM, and one that makes the HSM an attractive alternative, is that it accommodates use of parallel or complementary processing (Stiff, 1994). To date, however, the HSM has not received the same level of scrutiny or extent of empirical support as the ELM.

Because of its theoretical promise, and because the HSM has not been researched as extensively as the ELM, it is a fruitful area for further research. What should render the HSM attractive for public relations scholars is the fact that heuristic message processing is, in all likelihood, the dominant processing mode for most public relations content. The information age probably has not produced more informed decisions, but it most certainly has caused information overload (Patterson, 1993). Furthermore, an organization's internal or external communication, regardless of its intended purpose, is not particularly involving, at least not for most people in most circumstances. So, are people likely to process an organization's communication actively or passively? We suspect that people typically employ information shortcuts to draw inferences. These shortcuts consist of decision rules, or heuristics.

Exploring circumstances in which an organization's messages result in systematic or heuristic processing carries important implications for public relations professionals. Where heuristic processing dominates, determining what shortcuts are more likely to be employed by specific receiver groups in what circumstances would inform public relations practices. Results of research that addresses these issues should be of interest to academics and practitioners: offering additional nuance about the HSM, and providing invaluable guidelines for strategic communicators, who strive to make informed decisions about message design, sources, communication outlets, and so on.

Affect

Affect is an umbrella term that encompasses a variety of states, including reflex, drive, feeling, emotion, mood, and personality trait (Izard, 1993). Affect is positive or negative valence of an emotional experience (Clore, Schwartz, & Conway, 1994). Batra (1986) refers to it as 'feelings toward a stimulus that lead to relative preferences toward that stimulus out of a class of similar stimuli,' and thus involve preferences as opposed to emotional states (p. 54). Affect tends to be subjective and consists of assertions that can be viewed as points on two independent continua, ranging from bad to good (Eagly & Chaiken, 1993) and negative to positive (Dillard, 1998). Affect can enter the communication process at one or more of three points: it may precede, perhaps induce, communication; communication, itself, can manifest emotion; and communication may elicit an emotional response (Dillard, 1998).

The role and influence of affect in persuasion, especially in applied social influence, has not received as much attention as is warranted (Ottati & Wyer, 1993). Jorgensen

(1998) characterizes the overemphasis in persuasion research on message design and source considerations, and the resulting dearth of studies on affect, as 'lamentable' (p. 404). Social psychologists led early research on affect, but there is growing appreciation of the integral role that emotion plays in influence (Arnold, 1985; Dillard & Wilson, 1993; Jorgensen, 1998).

Advertisers have long had 'an intuitive understanding of the importance of affect' in consumer behavior (Peterson, Hoyer, & Wilson, 1986, p. 151). More recently, the results of preliminary advertising research suggest that affect can play a 'major role' in consumer decisions (p. 143). Public relations scholars have yet to acknowledge the role and influence of affect in people's decision processes (Scott & O'Hair, 1989).

Early research indicates that affect, above and beyond mere cognition, exerts sizable impact on human perception. As Zajonc (1980) observes, 'In nearly all cases . . . feeling is not free of thought, nor is thought free of feelings . . . thoughts enter feelings at various stages of the affective sequence, and the converse is true for cognitions' (p. 154). Affect and cognition often have an impact on people's attitudes independently of one other (Edell & Burke, 1987; Zajonc, 1984). The fact that affect can function wholly independent of conscious thought (Wilson, 1979; Zajonc, 1984) makes it a useful tool in the arsenal of influence. Affect can even manifest itself absent *any* stimulus recognition (see Fink, Monahan & Kaplowitz, 1989; Moreland & Zajonc, 1977; Zajonc, 1980, 1984; Zajonc & Markus, 1982). Most of the time, however, feeling and thinking occur conjointly (Lazarus, 1982; Zajonc, 1980; Zuwerink & Devine, 1996) but, even then, extant research indicates that affect precedes cognition (Zajonc, 1980, 1981, 1984), suggesting that it may be the more instrumental of the two (Edell & Burke, 1987; Holbrook & Batra, 1987).

Affect is actively employed in commercial advertising and public relations campaigns. One strategy involves directly eliciting affect in receivers. Such messages stress 'emotional quotient,' seeking to trigger happiness, pleasure, warmth, or other feelings. In public relations, feel-good, image-oriented corporate campaigns are common. Spurred, in part, by the success of General Electric's 'We bring good things to life' campaign, total spending on corporate advertising tripled between 1975 and 1984, exceeding $1 billion (Pavlik, 1987). Greider (1992) argues that corporations that are the most active in these image-based promotional campaigns are those with known substantive problems, including Chevron, Dow, General Electric, and Northrup. Research in commercial advertising indicates that messages that utilize affect are quite effective in eliciting emotional response, often during the first seconds of a message, which produces a positive impact on consumer behavior (Aaker, Stayman, & Hagarty, 1986; Holbrook & Batra, 1987). No comparable data are available for corporate image campaigns.

A second strategy involves association of a corporation or its products with stimuli that elicit positive emotions. This is the basis of the classical conditioning model, which posits that, following pairing over time of an unconditioned stimulus, capable on its own of eliciting a response, with a conditioned stimulus, normally not capable of eliciting the response, the conditioned stimulus alone becomes capable of eliciting the response (Watson, 1925). This strategy is prevalent in contemporary commercial television advertising, in which brands are paired with pleasant emotional stimuli, often elicited by 'scenes of good times and beautiful surroundings' (Breckler, 1993; Pechman & Stewart, 1989; Peterson et al., 1986, p. 151; Pfau & Parrott, 1993). Research indicates that such advertising appeals are capable of eliciting the desired emotional response quickly (Stuart, Shimp, & Engle, 1987), and that they contribute to positive attitudes toward the advertised brand and to purchase intention (Edell & Burke, 1987; Hitchon & Thorson, 1995).

It is also a frequent strategy in public relations efforts. Organizations try to associate themselves with popular activities (e.g., extensive corporate sponsorship of the arts and sporting events), special events (e.g., the Olympics), and popular causes (e.g., missing children or the environment). These associations constitute more than an opportunity for corporations to be seen. They enable sponsors to establish linkages based on affect. These linkages function as image enhancers for sponsors, which boost public perceptions of a corporation or its products/services. One executive explained that, 'You attach yourself to . . . events, piggybacking on them' (in Harris, 1991). Research suggests that an organization's image can be enhanced through association with positive events and causes (Denbow & Culbertson, 1985; Young, 1996; Zbar, 1993). Jackall (1995) claims that such 'indirect methods' of promoting corporate image or persona 'are thought to be particularly effective' (p. 368).

Despite extensive use of affect in corporate advertising campaigns that seek to enhance image and the use of corporate sponsorships to establish perceptual linkages based on affect, public relations scholars have largely ignored this domain. Scott and O'Hair (1989) call attention to 'the paucity of emotional assessment in public relations' (p. 212), speculating that the seeming lack of interest may stem from the perception that 'the concept of emotion is rather arbitrary and elusive' and defies clear conceptualization (p. 212). It is true that affect is 'a messy construct to investigate either theoretically and empirically' (Lazarus, 1999; Peterson et al., 1986, p. 144). Nonetheless, it has generated a growing interest among social psycho-

logy and communication scholars during the past decade (Dalgleish & Power, 1999).

Although affect is an integral element in persuasion and, therefore, relevant to applied persuasion contexts such as public relations, there is much to be learned about its use and impact in persuasion (Jorgensen, 1998). Jorgensen argues that study of the types of messages that are most effective in eliciting specific emotional responses is 'perhaps the single greatest contribution that communication scholars can make to the study of emotion' (p. 417). Other unresolved questions include the relationship involving affective appeal, communication form, and elicited emotional response; how specific affective appeals work, both alone and in conjunction with other emotional and cognitive appeals; and optimal sequencing of emotional appeals (Jorgensen, 1998).

Dillard (1998) recommends that emotion should be studied in the context of the process of persuasion, and Dalgleish and Power (1999) call for further research dealing with the role and impact of cognition and emotion, especially studies that apply findings in basic research to 'real-life' contexts. Scholars interested in investigating influence in the context of public relations should heed their call.

Medium theory

One implication of theories involving dual processing models and affect is that individual mass media vary in the way in which they exercise influence. Thus is the underlying premise of *medium theory*, which posits that, independent of the particular content communicated, media forms manifest unique symbol systems that shape both what is communicated and how it is received (Chesebro, 1984; McLuhan, 1964; Meyrowitz, 1985; Salomon, 1987). Television, because it relies significantly on a 'pictorial symbol system' (Salomon, 1981, p. 205), communicates a different message than other media; and, because its visually laden messages require less active processing (Chesebro, 1984; Graber, 1987; Krugman, 1971; Salomon, 1987, 1981; Wright, 1974), television exercises influence differently. Receiver involvement level dictates the appropriate medium which, in turn, determines how receivers are likely to respond to messages. Chaudhuri and Buck (1995) report that television is the optimal medium for advertising appeals on behalf of low-involving products. Their research indicates that television, since it can transport emotions, is uniquely able to 'create an emotional bond with the brand' (p. 122). In all likelihood, the same rationale applies to the communication of messages about organizations, although the thesis hasn't been investigated in a public relations context.

Meyrowitz (1985) contrasts television and print messages. Television, as a result of the primacy of the visual channel, is expressive, stressing images and impressions, whereas print is communicative, grounded in symbols and, consequently, ideally suited to the presentation of arguments and facts. Television is presentational, emphasizing visual images, while print is more discursive, featuring more abstract messages. Finally, television is analogic, stressing more intimate relational messages, whereas print is digital, emphasizing content.

Messages communicated via each communication form manifest unique possibilities. The distinctions drawn by Meyrowitz between television and print communication can by distilled to a single overarching difference: Television is more about the source of messages and print is about the content of messages. The primacy of source over content is further magnified by differences in message processing. Because television is less involving, it is much more likely to elicit peripheral (ELM) or heuristic (HSM) message processing, in which influence can be accomplished 'with only a minimal amount of information processing' (Chaiken, 1987, p. 3; Chaiken & Eagly, 1976, 1983; Graber, 1987; Markus & Zajonc, 1985; Salomon, 1981). In the dual processing models, source cues function as peripheral or heuristic devices, thus suggesting an elevated role in the process of influence.

This rationale is supported in research which points to an accented role for source cues in television influence (Andreoli & Worchel, 1978; Chaiken, 1987; Chaiken & Eagly, 1983; Gold, 1988). Pfau (1990) compared the relative influence of five communication modalities, including print, television, and radio media, plus public address and interpersonal communication. Results indicated that all communication forms were persuasive, as compared with a control condition, but there were no differences in influence between modalities. However, results revealed that the factors responsible for influence varied across modalities. The contribution of source overwhelmed content with television and interpersonal modalities, but content dominated source in print and public address forms.

Television's emphasis on communicator expressiveness and more intimate relational messages suggests greater emphasis on affect in influence. Relational messages consist of how people perceive their relationship with a communicator (Burgoon & Hale, 1984) and derive from what Watzlawick, Beavin, and Jackson (1967) termed the 'command' dimension of messages. Relational messages have been reported to exert considerable impact in the process of persuasion in those instances where communication form facilitates real or perceived personal contact between a source and a receiver, as is obvious in the example of interpersonal communication (Burgoon, 1980; Burgoon & Hale, 1987), but just as real, although less apparent, in

the case of television (Pfau, 1990). Television creates the perception of contact (Levy, 1979; Rubin & McHugh, 1987). It fosters the illusion of interpersonal contact, even a sense of intimacy (Beniger, 1987; Jamieson, 1988; Horton & Wohl, 1956; Keating & Latane, 1976; Perse & Rubin, 1989).

As a result of the primacy of source over content, coupled with a heightened sense of intimacy, the video modality rewards a warmer, much more casual communication style (Jamieson, 1988; Keating & Latane, 1976; Meyrowitz, 1985; Pfau, 1990), similar to what is required in effective interpersonal communication (Levy, 1979). This manifests itself in terms of more positive relational messages. Relational messages communicate the way people perceive their relationship with another (Burgoon & Hale, 1984, p. 193).

Pfau's (1990) study of factors that facilitate influence across communication modalities found that relational messages exerted much more influence than content in television, whereas the reverse was true for print communication. The dimensions of relational communication that have proven most influential in studies focusing specifically on television communication are those that manifest positive affect: receptivity/trust, which involves perception of source interest in the receiver, honesty, and sincerity; immediacy/affection, which includes perceptions of enthusiasm, warmth, and involvement; and similarity/depth, which features perceptions of friendliness, similarity, caring, and getting to know another better (Pfau, 1990; Pfau, Diedrich, Larson, & Van Winkle, 1993; Pfau & Kang, 1991).

As indicated previously, medium theory hasn't been studied in the context of public relations. Yet, the same logic applies, indicating that different media manifest unique message features, which contribute to influence. Because public relations expands the range of media options available to communicators, it would be an ideal domain to study medium theory.

Holbert (2002) calls for systematic empirical assessment of media form in persuasion. He advocates a shift in the focus of medium theory, from a macro emphasis (e.g., Meyrowitz, 1994), as in the examples above, to more of a micro orientation, based on human sensorial involvement. The approach applies basic tenets of medium theory to recent work on cognitive function in the fields of communication and psychology. Holbert (in press) argues that the next generation of empirical studies of medium theory should stress the way particular media forms impact the construction and development of human schematic structures (e.g., Markus & Zajonc, 1985). Studies that address such theoretical content within the context of public relations provide an opportunity to contribute both to further understanding of persuasion and to public relations practices.

Functional theory

In a general sense, functional theory constitutes a family of theories with their origins in sociology, which trace their philosophical roots to Emile Dirkheim. The functional approach is unique in that it focuses on why people hold attitudes, as opposed to how their attitudes are structured or whether they may change (Eagly & Chaiken, 1993, p. 479). People's behaviors are grounded in attitudes, which in turn serve functions, which are based on psychological motives. Functions are perceived as psychologically useful, which implies that attitudes are both active and mindful. Functional theory suggests that, in order to understand people's attitudes and the way that communication might affect them, communicators must understand the individual's motivation for holding an attitude (Kiesler, Collins, & Miller, 1969).

Although functional theory constitutes a family of theories, Katz's psychological need theory is particularly representative. Katz (1960) posits that attitudes may serve one or more functions for people.

First, attitudes serve a utilitarian function. Katz (1960) refers to this function as 'instrumental' or 'adjustment' function. The utilitarian function 'recognizes the fact that "people strive to maximize rewards in their external environment and to minimize the penalties" ' (Katz, 1960, p. 171). For example, people develop and maintain favorable attitudes toward those organizations that facilitate their goals and negative attitudes toward those that impede their goals.

In order to create or to maintain attitudes, communicators attempt to link an attitude object with personal goal attainment. Many public relations campaigns are designed to help people to achieve personal goals. This is a common technique in community relations efforts. For example, hospitals offer information about diet, exercise, blood pressure, and other health concerns. Banks and insurance companies conduct seminars about personal finance, investing, and retirement. This approach also is characteristic of many internal public relations efforts. For instance, firms conduct sessions for employees to explain their health insurance options, or to preview retirement conditions.

To change utilitarian attitudes, communicators may create new needs, shift the balance of benefits and costs associated with needs, or provide superior vehicles for need satisfaction. Because needs are difficult to create or change, Katz (1960) advocates that communicators focus on the latter strategies. 'The area of freedom for changing utilitarian attitudes is ... much greater in dealing with methods of satisfying needs than with the needs themselves' (p. 178).

A second function that attitudes serve is value expressive. Katz (1960) maintains that some attitudes serve the main purpose of expressing to other people the kind of person we think we are, or that we want to be. Such attitudes express people's sense of self, including their core values. They signal to others who we are: our moral values, religious beliefs, group attachments and affiliations, political philosophy, and tastes; and they allow us to verify and confirm our self-concept (Greenwald, 1989). This function stresses expression, which implies that those attitudes that serve this function will manifest a very strong behavioral component. The main approach used in attempting to modify value expressive attitudes is for a communicator to demonstrate 'the inappropriateness of their present ways of expressing their values' (Katz, 1960, p. 189).

Communication based on value expressive attitudes is common in public relations. It manifests itself in a variety of ways. Stockholder relations stress the organization's contribution to the environment. Corporations sponsor those sporting or cultural events that reflect their public image. Companies in the United States during the early 1990s were spending about $1.5 billion per year sponsoring major sporting events plus $1 billion sponsoring the arts (Harris, 1993). Furthermore, total spending on sponsorships doubled between the late 1980s and the middle 1990s (Cornwell & Maignan, 1998). In addition to sponsorships, many companies also employ corporate advertising designed to promote a public image, or engage in advocacy advertising to speak out on controversial issues not directly relevant to the company's mission, thus fostering the perception of corporate citizenship.

A third function attitudes serve is knowledge. This doesn't imply a pure quest for knowledge per se, but rather a desire for order in the face of ambiguity. Katz (1960) notes, 'People are not avid seekers after knowledge as judged by what the educator or social reformer would desire. But they do want to understand the events that impinge directly on their own life' (p. 176). What this means is that attitudes serve to clarify and simplify events for people. Attitudes serve as schemas, providing a useful 'frame of reference' (Katz, 1960, p. 175) for the purpose of 'organizing and simplifying ... perceptions of an often complex or ambiguous information environment' (Eagly & Chaiken, 1993, p. 480). Katz (1960) recommends that, in order to change knowledge-based attitudes, communicators should stress 'inadequacies of existing attitudes to deal with new and changing situations.... People's intolerance for ambiguity exerts pressure to 'either modify his beliefs to impose structure or accept some new formula presented by others' (pp. 190–191).

The knowledge function explains people's desire for simple answers for complicated issues. Communicators who can simplify complicated content for receivers can be very effective. However, it also explains people's vulnerability to negative political and issue advocacy advertising, such as when the nation's health care providers launched an extensive advertising campaign in 1993 in response to the proposed Clinton health care proposal. More than half of the spots, which attempted to boil the Clinton plan down to a few essentials that then could be the focus of attack, were judged by Jamieson and colleagues to be 'unfair, misleading, or false' (Annenberg School, 1994).

The fourth function that attitudes serve is ego-defensive. Attitudes protect people's self-image or ego (Katz, 1960). This function is less relevant to public relations.

Functional theory is heuristically provocative. The theory provides a new way of thinking about attitudes, placing emphasis on underlying motivations for attitudes (Eagly & Himmelfarb, 1974). As a result, functional theory initially sparked a great deal of scholarly interest following its introduction. However, interest soon waned. The main reason was the dearth of empirical data in support of the theory (Kiesler et al., 1969). Functional theory poses special challenges for researchers. The problem is that it is difficult to operationalize in advance the functions served by attitudes, which makes it impossible to conduct a fair test the theory (Eagly & Chaiken, 1993). As Snyder and DeBono (1987) observe, '[R]esearchers need to know the functional underpinnings of people's attitudes before . . . persuasive messages are delivered, in order to choose the message appropriate to an attitude serving that function' (p. 110). Inability to identify functions in advance renders functional theory nonfalsifiable, which Synder and DeBono claim was the primary cause of reduced interest in the theory. This problem is compounded by subsequent research indicating that, not only do attitudes serve different functions for different people, but they often serve multiple functions for any one individual (Eagly & Chaiken, 1993). As a result, Kiesler and colleagues (1969) conclude, 'Functional theories leave us powerless to predict' (p. 326).

To overcome this problem, Snyder and DeBono (1987) suggest a 'global strategy,' based on 'identifying categories of people for whom attitudes may be serving different functions' (p. 110). The authors suggest that the attitudes of people who are 'high self-monitors' may serve an adjustment or utilitarian function, whereas those of people who are 'low self-monitors' may serve a value expressive function. Research by Herek (1987) has developed improved techniques for measuring attitude functions.

More recently scholars have shown renewed interest in the functions which underpin attitudes (Eagly & Chaiken, 1993; Shah, Domke, & Wackman, 1996). Contemporary perspectives continue to explore the original functions, but they accept that attitudes typically serve multiple functions for people (Eagly & Chaiken, 1993). One new wrinkle in recent work on functional theory is the assumption that, irrespective of the traditional functions that attitudes

may serve, they provide a schematic function, offering a frame of reference for understanding and ordering attitude objects (Fazio, 1986, 1989; Shaw et al., 1996), although 'the schematic function may be limited to strong, well established attitudes' (Eagly & Chaiken, 1993, p. 483).

Another recent development involves reconceptualization of attitude functions. Some researchers recommend recategorization of the basic functions into two. The first function focuses on the attitude object itself and is utilitarian or evaluative, stressing the benefits/rewards and costs/punishments associated with object (Herek, 1986). 'In this scheme, the utilitarian function emerges as the *evaluative* function of attitudes' (Eagly & Chaiken, 1993, p. 483). The second function stresses attitude expression and is termed 'value expressive' (Herek, 1986). This category would subsume the original social adjustment and ego-defensive functions (Eagly & Chaiken, 1993). Other researchers suggest the presence of three functions: social identity, which is a composite of adjustment and value expressive; self-esteem; and knowledge (Shavitt, 1989, 1990).

Functional theory is a viable potential domain for scholars in public relations. It has generated renewed interest, and yet manifests as-yet-unresolved theoretical and measurement issues (Abelson & Prentice, 1989; Shavitt, 1989). Further, utilitarian, value expressive, and knowledge functions, in particular, may undergird people's attitudes in a wide array of public relations contexts, as the examples just given demonstrate.

Inoculation theory

In contemporary society, tremendous emphasis is placed on influencing others. The irony is that, given all the emphasis in contemporary society on influencing people, there has been little emphasis on conferring resistance to – defending people against – influence. However, this is changing. As Eagly and Chaiken (1993) observe: 'Despite the obvious importance of studying mechanisms of resistance, few formal theories of attitudinal resistance have flourished.' The exception, they argue, is inoculation theory, whose purpose is specifically intended 'to explain resistance to influence' (p. 560).

Inoculation is a strategy designed to strengthen existing opinion against change. It is a resistance theory. The theory posits that refutational treatments, which introduce challenges to existing attitudes while simultaneously offering preemptive refutation of those challenges, threaten the individual, which triggers the person's motivation to bolster attitudes against change and, as a result, confers resistance to counterarguments which a person might be exposed to (Papageorgis & McGuire, 1961).

Inoculation stands as an alternative to a supportive, bolstering approach to strengthening attitudes. McGuire (1964) explains that the supportive defense is nonthreatening since it consists solely of bolstering content. Because it doesn't expose receivers to challenges against attitudes, it tends to make them overconfident and, therefore, vulnerable. The supportive defense leaves the individual unaware of potential weaknesses in his or her position and both unmotivated to, and unpracticed in, defending his or her attitudes (Wyer, 1974). Subsequent studies confirmed that refutational defenses are superior to supportive in protecting attitudes against subsequent influence (Anderson & McGuire, 1965; Crane, 1962; McGuire, 1962, 1964, 1966; McGuire & Papageorgis, 1961, 1962; Papageorgis & McGuire, 1961; Suedfeld & Borrie, 1978; Tannenbaum, McCaulay, & Norris, 1966; Tannenbaum & Norris, 1965), although a combination of both is superior to either approach alone (McGuire, 1961, 1962; Tannenbaum & Norris, 1965).

Although early research on inoculation was limited to laboratory studies and conducted using noncontroversial topics, recent studies have returned to inoculation's core logic in an effort to further refine the workings of the theory. The results confirm McGuire's thesis that threat and refutational preemption function as critical ingredients in inoculation (Pfau et al., 1997, 1999). Threat involves the forewarning of impending challenges to attitudes. It is designed to get individuals to acknowledge the vulnerability of their attitudes to potential attack and, as a result, to trigger the internal process of cognitive reinforcement. Threat operates in tandem with refutational preemption. Refutational preemption consists of systematically raising, and then answering, one or more specific challenges to existing attitudes. Threat motivates the individual to bolster attitudes, and refutational preemption provides both the specific cognitive content to use in answering potential challenges and rehearsal of the process used to strengthen attitudes. These studies indicate that inoculation elicits both threat and counterarguing, that threat functions to immediately strengthen initial attitudes and further contributes to counterarguing and elicited anger, and that counterarguing and anger promote resistance. In addition, refutational preemption directly fosters resistance (Pfau et al., 1997, 1999).

Inoculation has received considerable attention in applied influence settings. It has been found to confer resistance to the influence of comparative advertising appeals (Hunt, 1973; Pfau, 1992), social marketing messages (Bither, Dolich, & Nell, 1971; Szybillo & Heslin, 1973); political campaign attacks (Pfau & Burgoon, 1988; Pfau, Kenski, Nitz, & Sorenson, 1990), and to the counterattitudinal pressures on younger adolescents to initiate cigarette smoking (Pfau, Van Bockern, 1994; Pfau, Van

Bockern, & Kang, 1992). In a public relations context, Burgoon, Pfau, and Birk (1995) reported that Mobil Oil Corporation's extensive issue advocacy advertising campaign functions to inoculate. When faced with counterattitudinal issue attacks, the company's advertorials inoculate readers against attitude slippage and protect Mobil's overall credibility rating.

One promising application of inoculation in public relations is as a preemptive, proactive approach in crisis communication. The crisis communication literature recommends use of preemptive, proactive strategies because of the inevitability of crises. As Coombs (1999) advises, 'It is a mistake to believe that an organization can avoid or prevent all possible crises. Eventually, a crisis will befall an organization' (p. 126). Therefore, Coombs and others recommend strategies to prevent crises from occurring in the first place, which is obviously the ideal. However, acknowledging the inevitability of crises, many scholars and professionals advise the use of proactive strategies designed to soften their impact (Druckenmiller, 1993).

The latter strategies typically involve establishing a base of goodwill that might serve to partially deflect the damage to an organization's image that typically accompanies a crisis. This approach operates on the assumption that accumulation of 'image credits,' earned via positive performance, can serve to 'offset the reputational damage generated by the crisis' (Coombs, 1998, p. 182). This approach makes intuitive sense, and there is some anecdotal evidence suggesting that it works. However, there are no hard data documenting efficacy; instead 'untested assumptions' prevail in crisis communication, at both proactive and reactive levels (Coombs, 1999, p. 126). This proactive preemptive approach is conceptually similar to a supportive, or bolstering, message in inoculation theory and research. In inoculation, supportive treatments provide positive arguments designed to bolster original attitudes, thus protecting against attitude slippage in the face of subsequent challenges, much as good deeds enhance attitudes toward an organization, thereby protecting against the erosion of attitudes in the event of a crisis.

Inoculation provides an untested, but promising, alternative proactive approach in crisis communication. Inoculation, which would raise an organization's potential vulnerabilities and the specter of crisis, and then preemptively refute them, delineating what the organization is doing to address these vulnerabilities, may prove to provide greater protection once a crisis occurs than prior efforts to enhance positive image, much as refutational defenses confer greater resistance than supportive defenses (Anderson & McGuire, 1965; Crane, 1962; McGuire, 1962, 1964, 1966; McGuire & Papageorgis, 1961, 1962; Papageorgis & McGuire, 1961; Suedfeld & Borrie, 1978; Tannenbaum, McCaulay, & Norris, 1966; Tannenbaum &

Norris, 1965). Or, use of inoculation in conjunction with an image-enhancing strategy may provide the optimal protection for an organization in a crisis, safeguarding its image better than either approach alone, much as extant research reveals that the use of a combined bolstering and inoculation strategy confers more resistance than either defense alone (McGuire, 1961, 1962; Tannenbaum & Norris, 1965).

Hua-Hsin Wan (2000) has launched an investigation that compares the efficacy of image-enhancing and inoculation proactive approaches in crisis communication. In addition, Wan's investigation probes whether use of inoculation, because organizations would expose their vulnerabilities, carries the intrinsic risk of undermining an organization's image absent a crisis.

Inoculation is a source of potential applications in public relations. It has demonstrated efficacy in advocacy advertising to strengthen public attitudes consonant with the organization's position on issues, and may offer a viable proactive strategy to protect an organization's image in event of a crisis. These and other applications warrant further investigation. In addition, there are unresolved theoretical questions in inoculation that additional research needs to address. For example, in addition to the mechanisms of threat and counterarguing, which have been proven to play an active role in conferring resistance (Pfau et al., 1997, 2003), what process might explain the direct impact of refutational preemption in resistance? One possibility is that inoculation treatments make attitudes more accessible for the receiver, perhaps by priming them (Szabo & Pfau, 2002). Other questions also require resolution (Pfau, 1997; Szabo & Pfau, 2002). What is the most appropriate message approach: use of content-oriented or peripheral or systematic messages? What is the best community modality for delivering inoculation messages? What is the ideal timing of inoculation treatments and booster messages in relation to subsequent attacks?

Conclusion

We have argued in this chapter that persuasion continues to be an integral function of public relations. It is intrinsic to public relations activities aimed at external publics. Persuasion plays an implicit role in community relations, media relations, crisis communication, and other public relations tasks. Persuasion is more explicit in such endeavors as fundraising, lobbying, and commercial and social marketing. We also argued that the controversy over whether public relations should operate from an asymmetrical or symmetrical model is misguided; that public

relations is a form of strategic communication in which persuasion plays an intrinsic role.

Finally, we explored potential applications of theories of persuasion in the context of public relations in the form of select exemplars. These exemplars, all drawn from the extant literature in persuasion, illustrate how persuasion theory and research offer fruitful ground for public relations scholars. If scholars make functional issues, many of which are grounded in persuasion, the focus of their research, the results of their efforts can simultaneously enhance understanding of persuasion and inform public relations practices. This approach would enable public relations scholars, and the discipline as a whole, to rise above the limitations inherent in the present preoccupation with context.

References

Aaker, D. A., Stayman, D. M., & Hagarty, M. R. (1986). Warmth in advertising: Measurement, impact, and sequence effects. *Journal in Consumer Research*, **12**, 365–381.

Abelson, R. P., & Prentice, D. A. (1989). In A. R. Pratkanis, S. J. Breckler, & A. G. Greenwald (eds), *Attitude structure and function* (pp. 361–381). Columbus: Ohio State University Press.

Alba, J. W., & Marmorstein, H. (1987). The effects of frequency knowledge on consumer decision making. *Journal of Consumer Research*, **14**, 14–25.

Anderson, L. R., & McGuire, W. J. (1965). Prior reassurance of group consensus as a factor in producing resistance to persuasion. *Sociometry*, **28**, 44–56.

Andreoli, V., & Worchel, S. (1978). Effects of media, communicator, and message position on attitude change. *Public Opinion Quarterly*, **42**, 59–70.

Annenberg School for Communication, University of Pennsylvania (1994, Fall). Advertising and the health care debate. *News Link*, **4**(3), p. 6.

Arnold, V. D. (1985). The importance of pathos in persuasive appeals. *The Bulletin*, 26–27.

Axsom, D., Yates, S. M., & Chaiken, S. (1987). Audience response as a heuristic cue in persuasion. *Journal of Personality and Social Psychology*, **53**, 30–40.

Barney, R. D., & Black, J. (1994). Ethics and professional persuasive communications. *Public Relations Review*, **20**, 233–248.

Batra, R. (1986). Affective advertising: Role, process, and measurement. In R. A. Peterson, W. D. Hoyer, & W. R. Wilson (eds), *The role of affect in consumer behavior:*

Emerging theories and applications (pp. 53–85). Lexington, MA: Lexington Books.

Batra, R., & Ray, M. L. (1985). How advertising works at contact. In L. F. Alwitt & A. A. Mitchell (eds), *Psychological processes and advertising effects: Theory, research, and applications* (pp. 13–43). Hillsdale, NJ: Lawrence Erlbaum Associates.

Beniger, J. R. (1987). Personalization of mass media and the growth of pseudo-community. *Communication Research,* **14**, 352–370.

Berelson, B., Lazarsfeld, P., & McPhee, W. (1954). *Voting: A study of opinion formation in a presidential campaign.* Chicago: University of Chicago Press.

Bernays, E. L. (1923). *Crystallizing public opinion.* New York: Boni and Liveright.

Bernays, E. L. (1955). The theory and practice of public relations: A resume. In E. L. Bernays (ed.), *The engineering of consent* (pp. 3–25). Norman: University of Oklahoma Press.

Bither, S. W., Dolich, I. J., & Nell, E. B. (1971). The application of attitude immunization techniques in marketing. *Journal of Marketing Research,* **18**, 56–61.

Botan, C. H. (1989). Theory development in public relations. In C. H. Botan and V. Hazleton, Jr. (eds), *Public relations theory* (pp. 99–110). Hillsdale, NJ: Lawrence Erlbaum Associates.

Breckler, S. J. (1993). Emotion and attitude change. In M. Lewis & J. Haviland (eds), *Handbook of emotions* (pp. 461–473). New York: Guilford.

Broom, G. M., & Dozier, D. M. (1990). *Using research in public relations: Applications to program management.* Englewood Cliffs, NJ: Prentice Hall.

Burgoon, J. K. (1980). Nonverbal communication research on the 1970s: An overview. In D. Nimmo (ed.), *Communication yearbook 4* (pp. 179–197). New Brunswick, NJ: Transaction Books.

Burgoon, J. K., & Hale, J. L. (1984). The fundamental topoi of relational communication. *Communication Monographs,* **51**, 193–214.

Burgoon, J. K., & Hale, J. L. (1987). Validation and measurement of the fundamental themes of relational communication. *Communication Monographs,* **54**, 19–41.

Burgoon, M., Pfau, M., & Birk, T. (1995). An inoculation theory explanation for the effects of corporate issue/advocacy advertising campaigns. *Communication Research,* **22**, 485–505.

Cancel, A. E., Cameron, G. T., Sallot, L. M., & Mitrook, M. A. (1997). It depends: A contingency theory of accommodation in public relations. *Journal of Public Relations Research,* **9**, 31–63.

Caywood, C. L. (1997). Twenty-first century public relations: The strategic stages of integrated communications. In C. L. Caywood (ed.), *The handbook of strategic public relations & integrated communications* (pp. xi–xxvi). New York: McGraw-Hill.

Center, A. H., & Jackson, P. (1995). *Public relations practices: Managerial case studies & problems* (5th ed.). Englewood Cliffs, NJ: Prentice Hall.

Chaiken, S. (1980). Heuristic versus systematic information processing and the use of source versus message cues in persuasion. *Journal of Personality and Social Psychology,* **39**, 752–766.

Chaiken, S. (1987). The heuristic model of persuasion. In M. P. Zanna & C. P. Herman (eds), *Social influence: The Ontario symposium* (Vol. 5, pp. 3–39). Hillsdale, NJ: Lawrence Erlbaum Associates.

Chaiken, S., & Eagly, A. H. (1976). Communication modality as a determinant of message persuasiveness and message comprehensibility. *Journal of Personality and Social Psychology,* **34**, 605–614.

Chaiken, S., & Eagly, A. H. (1983). Communication modality as a determinant of persuasion: The role of communicator silence. *Journal of Personality and Social Psychology,* **45**, 241–256.

Chaiken, S., Liberman, A., & Eagly, A. H. (1989). Heuristic and systematic processing within and beyond the persuasion context. In J. S. Uleman & J. A. Bargh (eds), *Unintended thought* (pp. 212–252). New York: Guilford.

Chaudhuri, A., & Buck, R. (1995). Media differences in rational and emotional responses to advertising. *Journal of Broadcasting & Electronic Media,* **39**, 109–125.

Chesebro, J. W. (1984). The media reality: Epistemological functions of media in cultural systems. *Critical Studies in Mass Communication,* **1**, 111–130.

Clore, G. L., Schwartz, N., & Conway, M. (1994). Affective causes and consequences of social information processing. In R. S. Wyer & T. K. Srull (eds), *Handbook of social cognition* (Vol. 1, pp. 323–417). Hillsdale, NJ: Lawrence Erlbaum Associates.

Coombs, W. T. (1998). An analytic framework for crisis situations: Better responses from a better understanding of the situation. *Journal of Public Relations Research,* **10**, 177–191.

Coombs, W. T. (1999). Information and compassion in crisis responses: A test of their effects. *Journal of Public Relations Research,* **11**, 125–142.

Cornwell, T. B., & Maignan, I. (1998). An international review of sponsorship research. *Journal of Advertising,* **27**(1), 15–21.

Crable, R. E., & Vibert, S. L. (1986). *Public relations as communication management.* Edina, MN: Bellwether Press.

Crane, E. (1962). Immunization – with and without use of counterarguments. *Journalism Quarterly*, 39, 445–450.

Crossen, C. (1994). *Tainted truth: The manipulation of fact in America.* New York: Simon & Schuster.

Cutlip, S. M., Center, A. H., & Broom, G. M. (1985). *Effective public relations* (6th ed.). Englewood Cliffs, NJ: Prentice Hall.

Dalgleish, T., & Power, M. J. (1999). Cognition and emotion: Future directions. In T. Dalgleish & M. J. Power (eds), *Handbook of cognition and emotion* (pp. 799–805). New York: Wiley.

Denbow, C. H., & Culbertson, H. M. (1985). Linking beliefs and diagnosing an image. *Public Relations Review*, 11, 29–37.

Dillard, J. P. (1998). Foreword: The role of affect in communication, biology, and social relationships. In P. A. Andersen & L. K. Guerrero (eds), *Handbook of communication and emotion: Research, theory, applications, and contexts* (pp. xvii–xxxii). San Diego, CA: Academic Press.

Dillard, J. P., & Wilson, B. J. (1993). Communication and affect: Thoughts, feelings, and issues for the future. *Communication Research*, 20, 637–646.

Dozier, D. M. (1990). The innovation of research in public relations practice: Review of a program of studies. In L. A. Grunig & J. E. Grunig (eds), *Public relations research annual* (vol. 2, pp. 3–28). Hillsdale, NJ: Lawrence Erlbaum Associates.

Dozier, D. M., Grunig, L., & Grunig, J. (1995). *Manager's guide to excellence in public relations and communication management.* Hillsdale, NJ: Lawrence Erlbaum Associates.

Dozier, D. M., & Repper, F. C. (1992). Research firms and public relations practices. In J. E Grunig, D. M. Dozier, W. P. Ehling, L. A. Grunig, F. C. Repper, & J. White (eds), *Excellence in public relations and communication management* (pp. 185–215). Hillsdale, NJ: Lawrence Erlbaum Associates.

Druckenmiller, B. (1993). Crises provide insights on image. *Business Marketing*, 78, 40.

Eagly, A. H., & Chaiken, S. (1993). *The psychology of attitudes.* Orlando, FL: Harcourt Brace Jovanovich.

Eagly, A. H., & Himmelfarb, S. (1974). Current trends in attitude theory and research. In S. Himmelfarb & A. H. Eagly (eds), *Readings in attitude change* (pp. 594–610). New York: Wiley.

Edell, J. A., & Burke, M. C. (1987). The power of feelings in understanding advertising effects. *Journal of Consumer Research*, 14, 421–433.

Ewen, S. (1996). *PR! A social history of spin.* New York: Basic Books.

Fazio, R. H. (1986). How do attitudes guide behavior? In R. M. Sorrentino & E. T. Higgins (eds). *Handbook of motivation and cognition: Foundations of social behavior* (pp. 204–243). New York: Guilford.

Fazio, R. H. (1989). On the power and functionality of attitudes: The role of attitude accessibility. In A. R. Pratkanis, S. J. Breckler, & A. G. Greenwald (eds), *Attitude structure and function* (pp. 153–179). Hillsdale, NJ: Lawrence Erlbaum Associates.

Fink, E. L., Monahan, J. L., & Kaplowitz, S. A. (1989). A spatial model of the mere exposure effect. *Communication Research*, 16, 746–769.

Gandy, O. H., Jr. (1982). *Beyond agenda setting: Information subsidies and public policy.* Norwood, NJ: Ablex.

Gold, E. R. (1988). Ronald Reagan and the oral tradition. *Central States Speech Journal*, 39, 159–176.

Graber, D. A. (1987). Television news without pictures? *Critical Studies in Mass Communication*, 4, 74–78.

Greenwald, A. G. (1989). Why attitudes are important: Defining attitudes and attitude theory 20 years later. In A. R. Pratkanis & S. J. Breckler (eds), *Attitude structure and function* (pp. 429–440). Hillsdale, NJ: Lawrence Erlbaum Associates.

Greider, W. M. (1992). *Who will tell the people: The betrayal of American democracy.* New York: Simon & Schuster.

Gronstedt, A. (1997). The role of research in public relations strategy and planning. In C. L. Caywood (ed.), *The handbook of strategic public relations & integrated communications* (pp. 34–59). New York: McGraw-Hill.

Grunig, J. E. (1980). Communication of scientific information to nonscientists. In B. Dervin & M. J. Voight (eds), *Progress in communication sciences* (Vol. 2, pp. 167–214). Norwood, NJ: Ablex.

Grunig, J. E. (1989a). Sierra Club study shows who become activists. *Public Relations Review*, 15, 3–24.

Grunig, J. E. (1989b). Symmetrical presuppositions as a framework for public relations theory. In C. H. Botan and V. Hazleton, Jr. (eds), *Public relations theory* (pp. 17–44). Hillsdale, NJ: Lawrence Erlbaum Associates.

Grunig, J. E. (1992). Communication, public relations, and effective organizations: An overview. In J. E. Grunig, D. M. Dozier, W. P. Ehling, L. A. Grunig, F. C. Repper, & J. White (eds), *Excellence in public relations and communication management* (pp. 1–28). Hillsdale, NJ: Lawrence Erlbaum Associates.

Grunig, J. E., & Grunig, L. A. (1990, August). *Models of public relations: A review and reconceptualization.* Paper presented at the annual meeting of the Association for Education in Journalism and Mass Communication, Minneapolis, MN.

Grunig, J. E., & Grunig, L. A. (1992). Models of public relations and communication. In J. E. Grunig, D. M. Dozier, W. P. Ehling, L. A. Grunig, F. C. Repper, & J. White (eds), *Excellence in public relations and communication management* (pp. 285–326). Hillsdale, NJ: Lawrence Erlbaum Associates.

Grunig, J. E., & Hunt, T. (1984). *Managing public relations.* New York: Holt, Rinehart & Winston.

Grunig, J. E., & Repper, F. C. (1992). Strategic management, publics, and issues. In J. E. Grunig, D. M. Dozier, W. P. Ehling, L. A. Grunig, F. C. Repper, & J. White (eds), *Excellence in public relations and communication management* (pp. 117–157). Hillsdale, NJ: Lawrence Erlbaum Associates.

Grunig, J. E., & White, J. (1992). The effect of worldviews on public relations theory and practice. In J. E. Grunig, D. M. Dozier, W. P. Ehling, L. A. Grunig, F. C. Repper, & J. White (eds), *Excellence in public relations and communication management* (pp. 31–64). Hillsdale, NJ: Lawrence Erlbaum Associates.

Grunig, L. A. (1986, August). *Activism and organizational response: contemporary cases of collective behavior.* Paper presented at the annual meeting of the Association for Education in Journalism and Mass Communication, Norman, OK.

Habermann, P., Kupenhauer, L. L., & Martinson, D. L. (1988). Sequence faculty divided over PR value, status, and news orientation. *Journalism Quarterly*, 65, 490–496.

Harris, T. L. (1991). *The marketer's guide to public relations: How today's top companies are using the new PR to gain a competitive advantage.* New York: Wiley.

Hazleton, V., Jr., & Botan, C. G. (1989). The role of theory in public relations. In C. H. Botan and V. Hazleton, Jr. (eds), *Public relations theory* (pp. 3–15). Hillsdale, NJ: Lawrence Erlbaum Associates.

Hazlewood, J. D., & Chaiken, S. (1990, August). *Personal relevance, majority influence, and the law of large numbers.* Paper presented at the annual meeting of the American Psychological Association, Boston.

Heath, R. L. (1993). A rhetorical approach to zones of meaning and organizational prerogatives. *Public Relations Review*, 19, 141–155.

Heath, R. L. (1994). *Management of corporate communication: From interpersonal contacts to external affairs.* Hillsdale, NJ: Lawrence Erlbaum Associates.

Heath, R. L., Seshadri, S., & Lee, J. (1998). Risk communication: A two-community analysis of proximity, dread, trust/involvement, uncertainty, openness/accessibility, and knowledge on support/opposition toward chemical companies. *Journal of Public Relations Research*, 10, 35–56.

Hellweg, S. A. (1989, May). *The application of Grunig's symmetry-asymmetry public relations models to internal communications systems.* Paper presented at the annual meeting of the International Communication Association, San Francisco.

Herek, G. M. (1986). The instrumentality of attitudes: Towards a neo-functional theory. *Journal of Social Issues*, 42, 99–114.

Herek, G. N. (1987). Can functions be measured? A new perspective on the functional approach to attitudes. *Social Psychology Quarterly*, 50, 285–303.

Herman, E. S., & Chomsky, N. (1988). *Manufacturing consent: The political economy of the mass media.* New York: Pantheon Books.

Hitchon, J. C., & Thorson, E. (1995). Effects of emotion and product involvement on the experience of repeated commercial viewing. *Journal of Broadcasting & Electronic Media*, 39, 376–389.

Holbert, R. L. (in press). The embodied meaning of media form. In J. P. Dillard & M. Pfau (eds). *The persuasion handbook: Theory and practice.* (pp. 749–763). Newbury Park. CA: Sage.

Holbrook, M. B., & Batra, R. (1987). Assessing the role of emotions as mediators of consumer responses to advertising. *Journal of Consumer Research*, 14, 404–420.

Horton, D., & Wohl, R. R. (1956). Mass communication and parasocial interaction: Observations on intimacy at a distance. *Psychiatry*, 19, 215–229.

Hunt, H. K. (1973). Effects of corrective advertising. *Journal of Advertising Research*, 13, 15–22.

Izard, C. E. (1993). Four systems for emotion activation: Cognitive and noncognitive processes. *Psychological Review*, 100, 68–90.

Jackall, R. (1995). The magic lantern: The world of public relations. In R. Jackall, *Propaganda* (pp. 351–399). New York: New York University Press.

Jamieson, K. H. (1988). *Eloquence in an electronic age: The transformation of political speech-making.* New York: Oxford University Press.

Jones, J. P. (1955). Organization for public relations. In E. L. Bernays (ed.), *The engineering of consent* (pp. 156–184). Norman: University of Oklahoma Press.

Jorgensen, P. F. (1988). Affect, persuasion, and communication processes. In P. A. Andersen & L. K. Guerrero (eds), *Handbook of communication and emotion: Research, theory, applications, and contexts* (pp. 403–422). San Diego, CA: Academic Press.

Katz, D. (1960). The functional approach to the study of attitudes. *Public Opinion Quarterly*, 24, 163–204.

Katz, E., & Lazarsfeld, P. F. (1955). *Personal influence: The part played by people in the flow of mass communications.* New York: The Free Press.

Katzman, J. B. (1993). What's the role of public relations? *Public Relations Journal,* **49**(4), 11–16.

Keating, J. P., & Latane, B. (1976). Politicians on TV: The image is the message. *Journal of Social Issues,* **32**, 116–132.

Kiesler, C. A., Collins, B. E., & Miller, N. (1969). *Attitude change: A critical analysis of theoretical approaches.* New York: Wiley.

Klapper, J. T. (1960). *The effects of mass communication.* New York: The Free Press.

Krugman, H. E. (1965). The impact of television advertising: Learning without involvement. *Public Opinion Quarterly,* **29**, 349–356.

Krugman, H. E. (1971). Brain wave measures of media involvement. *Journal of Advertising Research,* **11**, 3–9.

Lazarsfeld, P., Berelson, B., & Gaudet, H. (1948). *The people's choice.* New York: Columbia University Press.

Lazarus, R. S. (1982). Thoughts on the relations between emotion and cognition. *American Psychologist,* **37**, 1019–1024.

Lazarus, R. S. (1999). The cognition-emotion debate: A bit of history. In T. Dalgleish & M. J. Power (eds), *Handbook of cognition and emotion* (pp. 3–19). New York: Wiley.

Leichty, G. (1997). The limits of collaboration. *Public Relations Review,* **23**, 47–55.

Levy, M. R. (1979). Watching TV as parasocial interaction. *Journal of Broadcasting,* **23**, 69–80.

Lodge, M., & Stroh, P. (1993). Inside the mental voting booth: An impression-driven process model of candidate evaluation. In S. Iyengar & W. J. McGuire (eds), *Explorations in political psychology* (pp. 225–263). Durham, NC: Duke University Press.

Long, R. K. (1987). Comments on 'Professional advocacy in public relations.' *Business and Professional Ethics Journal,* **6**, 91–93.

Maheswaran, D., & Chaiken, S. (1991). Promoting systematic processing in low motivation settings: Effect of incongruent information on processing and judgment. *Journal of Personality and Social Psychology,* **61**, 13–25.

Markus, H., & Zajonc, R. B. (1985). The cognitive perspective in social psychology. In G. Lindzey & E. Aronson (eds), *Handbook of social psychology* (Vol. 1, pp. 137–230). New York: Random House.

Marston, J. E. (1979). *Modern public relations.* New York: McGraw-Hill.

McLuhan, M. (1964). *Understanding media: The extensions of man.* New York: McGraw-Hill.

McElreath, M. P. (1997). *Managing systematic and ethical public relations campaigns* (2nd ed.). Dubuque, IA: Brown & Benchmark.

McGuire, W. J. (1961). The effectiveness of supportive and refutational defenses in immunizing and restoring beliefs against persuasion. *Sociometry,* **24**, 184–197.

McGuire, W. J. (1962). Persistence of the resistance to persuasion induced by various types of prior belief defenses. *Journal of Abnormal and Social Psychology,* **64**, 241–248.

McGuire, W. J. (1964). Inducing resistance to persuasion. Some contemporary approaches. In L. Berkowitz (ed.), *Advances in experimental social psychology* (Vol. 1, pp. 191–229). New York: Academic Press.

McGuire, W. J. (1966). Persistence of the resistance to persuasion induced by various types of prior belief defenses. In C. W. Backman & P. F. Secord (eds), *Problems in social psychology* (pp. 128–135). New York: McGraw-Hill.

McGuire, W. J., & Papageorgis, D. (1961). The relative efficacy of various types of prior belief-defense in producing immunity against persuasion. *Journal of Abnormal and Social Psychology,* **62**, 327–337.

McGuire, W. J., & Papageorgis, D. (1962). Effectiveness of forewarning in developing resistance to persuasion. *Public Opinion Quarterly,* **26**, 24–34.

Meyrowitz, J. (1985). *No sense of place.* New York: Oxford University Press.

Meyrowitz, J. (1994). Medium theory. In D. Crowley & D. Mitchell (eds), *Communication theory today* (pp. 50–77). Stanford, CA: Stanford University Press.

Miller, G. R. (1989). Persuasion and public relations: Two 'ps' in a pod. In C. H. Botan and V. Hazleton, Jr. (eds), *Public relations theory* (pp. 45–66). Hillsdale, NJ: Lawrence Erlbaum Associates.

Miller, G. R., & Burgoon, M. (1973). *New techniques of persuasion.* New York: Harper & Row.

Moore, H. F., & Canfield, B. R. (1977). *Public relations: Principles, cases, and problems* (7th ed.). Homewood, IL: Richard D. Irwin.

Moreland, R. L., & Zajonc, R. B. (1977). Is stimulus recognition a necessary condition for the occurrence of exposure effects? *Journal of Personality and Social Psychology,* **35**, 191–199.

Murphy, P. (1991). The limits of symmetry: A game theory approach to symmetric and asymmetric public relations. In J. Grunig and L. Grunig (eds), *Public relations research annual* (Vol. 1, pp. 87–96). Hillsdale, NJ: Lawrence Erlbaum Associates.

Olasky, M. N. (1989). The aborted debate within public relations: An approach through Kuhn's paradigm. In J. E. Grunig & L. A. Grunig (eds), *Public relations research annual* (Vol. 1, pp. 87–96). Hillsdale, NJ: Lawrence Erlbaum Associates.

Ottati, V. C., & Wyer, Jr., R. S. (1993). Affect and political judgment. In S. Iyengar & W. J. McGuire (eds), *Explorations in political psychology* (pp. 296–315). Durham, NC: Duke University Press.

Papageorgis, D., & McGuire, W. J. (1961). The generality of immunity to persuasion produced by pre-exposure to weakened counterarguments. *Journal of Abnormal and Social Psychology*, **62**, 475–481.

Patterson, T. E. (1993). *Out of order*. New York: Alfred A. Knopf.

Pavlik, J. V. (1987). *Public relations: What research tells us*. Newbury Park, CA: Sage.

Pavlik, J. V. (1989). Public relations: Public relations research annual, vol. 1. *Journalism and Mass Communication Quarterly*, **66**, 759.

Pechmann, C., & Stewart, D. W. (1989). The multidimensionality of persuasive communications: Theoretical and empirical foundations. In P. Cafferata & A. M. Tybout (eds), *Cognitive and affective responses to advertising* (pp. 31–56). Lexington, MA: Lexington Books.

Perse, E. M., & Rubin, R. B. (1989). Attribution in social and parasocial relationships. *Communication Research*, **16**, 59–77.

Peterson, R. A., Hoyer, W. D., & Wilson, W. R. (1986). Reflections on the role of affect in consumer behavior. In R. A. Peterson, W. D. Hoyer, & W. R. Wilson (eds), *The role of affect in consumer behavior: Emerging theories and applications* (pp. 141–159). Lexington, KY: Lexington Books.

Petty, R. E., & Cacioppo, J. T. (1979). Issue involvement can increase or decrease persuasion by enhancing message-relevant cognitive responses. *Journal of Personality and Social Psychology*, **37**, 1915–1926.

Petty, R. E., & Cacioppo, J. T. (1984a). The effects of involvement on responses to argument quantity and quality: Central and peripheral routes to persuasion. *Journal of Personality and Social Psychology*, **46**, 69–81.

Petty, R. E., & Cacioppo, J. T. (1984b). Source factors and the elaboration likelihood model of persuasion. *Advances in Consumer Research*, **11**, 668–672.

Petty, R. E., & Cacioppo, J. T. (1986). *Communication and persuasion: Central and peripheral routes to attitude change*. New York: Springer-Verlag.

Petty, R. E., Cacioppo, J. T., & Kasmer, J. A. (1988). The role of affect in the elaboration likelihood model pf persuasion. In L. Donohew, H. E. Sypher, & E. T. Higgins (eds), *Communication, social cognition, and affect* (pp. 117–146). Hillsdale, NJ: Lawrence Erlbaum Associates.

Pfau, M. (1990). A channel approach to television influence. *Journal of Broadcasting & Electronic Media*, **34**, 195–214.

Pfau, M. (1992). The potential of inoculation in promoting resistance to the effectiveness of comparative advertising messages. *Communication Quarterly*, **40**, 26–44.

Pfau, M. (1997). The inoculation model of resistance to influence. In G. A. Barnett & F. J. Boster (eds), *Progress in communication sciences: Advances in persuasion* (Vol. 13, pp. 133–171). Greenwich, CT: Ablex.

Pfau, M., & Burgoon, M. (1988). Inoculation in political campaign communication. *Human Communication Research*, **15**, 91–111.

Pfau, M., Diedrich, T., Larson, K. M., & Van Winkle, K. M. (1993). Relational and competence perceptions of presidential candidates during primary election campaigns. *Journal of Broadcasting & Electronic Media*, **37**, 275–292.

Pfau, M., & Kang, J. G. (1991). The impact of relational messages on candidate influence in televised political debates. *Communication Studies*, **42**, 114–128.

Pfau, M., Kenski, H. C., Nitz, M., & Sorenson, J. (1990). Efficacy of inoculation strategies in promoting resistance to political attack messages: Application to direct mail. *Communication Monographs*, **57**, 1–12.

Pfau, M., & Parrott, R. (1993). *Persuasive communication campaigns*. Boston: Allyn & Bacon.

Pfau, M., Roskos-Ewoldsen, D., Wood, M., Yin, S., Cho, J., Lu, K.-S., & Shen, L. (2003). Attitude accessibility as an alternative explanation for how inoculation confers resistance. *Communication Monographs*, **70**, 39–51.

Pfau, M., Szabo, E. A., Anderson, J., Morrill, J., Zubric, J., & Wan, H.-H. (2001). The role and impact of affect in the process of resistance to provision. *Human Communication Research*, **27**, 216–252.

Pfau, M., Tusing, K. J., Koerner, A. F., Lee, W., Godbold, L. C., Penaloza, L. J., Yang, V. S., & Hong, Y. (1997). Enriching the inoculation construct: The role of critical components in the process of resistance. *Human Communication Research*, **24**, 187–215.

Pfau, M., & Van Bockern, S. (1994). The persistence of inoculation in conferring resistance to smoking initiation among adolescents: The second year. *Human Communication Research*, **20**, 413–430.

Pfau, M., Van Bockern, S., & Kang, J. G. (1992). Use of inoculation to promote resistance to smoking initiation among adolescents. *Communication Monographs*, **59**, 213–230.

Robinson, E. J. (1969). *Public relations and survey research: Achieving organizational goals in a communication context*. New York: Appleton-Century Crofts.

Roskos-Ewoldson, D. R., & Fazio, R. H. (1992). The accessibility of source likability as a determinant of persuasion. *Personality and Social Psychology Bulletin*, **18**, 19–25.

Rubin, R. B., & McHugh, M. P. (1987). Development of parasocial interaction relationships. *Journal of Broadcasting & Electronic Media*, **31**, 279–292.

Salmon, C. T. (1986). Perspectives on involvement in consumer and communication research. In B. Dervin & M. J. Voight (eds), *Progress in communication sciences* (Vol. 7, pp. 243–268). Norwood, NJ: Ablex Publishing Corporation.

Salmon, C. T. (1989). Campaigns for social 'improvement': An overview of values, rationales, and impacts. In C. T. Salmon (ed.), *Information campaigns: Balancing social values and social change* (pp. 19–53). Newbury Park, CA: Sage.

Salomon, G. (1981). *Communication and education: Social and psychological interactions*. Beverly Hills, CA: Sage.

Salomon, G. (1987). *Interactions of media, cognition, and learning: An exploration of how symbolic forms cultivate mental skills and affect knowledge acquisition*. San Francisco: Jossey-Bass.

Scott, J. C., Jr., & O'Hair, D. (1989). Expanding psychographic concepts in public relations: The composite audience profile. In C. H. Botan and V. Hazleton, Jr. (eds), *Public relations theory* (pp. 203–219). Hillsdale, NJ: Lawrence Erlbaum Associates.

Seitel, F. P. (1992). *The practice of public relations*. New York: Macmillan.

Seitel, F. P. (1998). *The practice of public relations* (7th ed.). Upper Saddle River, NJ: Prentice Hall.

Shavitt, S. (1989). Operationalizing functional theories of attitude. In A. R. Pratkanis, S. J. Breckler, & A. G. Greenwald (eds), *Attitude structure and function* (pp. 311–337). Columbus: Ohio State University Press.

Shavitt, S. (1990). The role of attitude objects in attitude functions. *Journal of Experimental Social Psychology*, **26**, 124–148.

Shah, D. V., Domke, D., & Wackmann, D. B. (1996). 'To thine own self be true': Values, framing, and voter decision-making strategies. *Communication Research*, **23**, 509–560.

Snyder, M., & DeBono, K. G. (1987). A functional approach to attitudes and persuasion. In M. P. Zanna, J. M. Olson, & C. P. Herman (eds), *Social influence: The Ontario symposium, Volume 5* (pp. 107–125). Hillsdale, NJ: Lawrence Erlbaum Associates.

Stauber, J., & Rampton, S. (1996). *Toxic sludge is good for you: Damn lies and the public relations industry*. Monroe, ME: Common Courage Press.

Stiff, J. B. (1994). *Persuasive communication*. New York: Guilford Press.

Stuart, E. W., Shimp, T. A., & Engle, R. W. (1987). Classical conditioning of consumer attitudes: Four experiments in an advertising context. *Journal of Consumer Research*, **14**, 334–349.

Suedfeld, P., & Borrie, R. A. (1978). Sensory deprivation, attitude change, and defense against persuasion. *Canadian Journal of Behavioral Science*, **10**, 16–27.

Szabo, E. A., & Pfau, M. (2002). Nuances in inoculation: Theory and applications. In J. P. Dillard & M. Pfau (eds), *The persuasion handbook: Theory and practice* (pp. 233–258). Newbury Park, CA: Sage.

Szybillo, G. J., & Heslin, R. (1973). Resistance to persuasion: Inoculation theory in a marketing context. *Journal of Marketing Research*, **10**, 396–403.

Tannenbaum, P. H., Macaulay, J. R., & Norris, E. L. (1966). Principle of congruity and reduction in persuasion. *Journal of Personality and Social Psychology*, **2**, 223–238.

Tannenbaum, P. H., & Norris, E. L. (1965). Effects of combining congruity principle strategies for the reduction of persuasion. *Sociometry*, **28**, 145–157.

Tuleja, T. (1985). *Beyond the bottom line*. New York: Facts on File Publications.

Vasquez, G. M. (1996). Public relations as negotiation: An issue development perspective. *Journal of Public Relations Research*, **8**, 57–77.

Wallack, L. (1989). Mass communication and health promotion: A critical perspective. In R. E. Rice & C. K. Atkin (eds), *Public communication campaigns* (2nd ed., pp. 353–367). Newbury Park, CA: Sage Publications.

Wan, H.-H. (2000). *Priming and inoculation in the context of crisis communication*. Unpublished doctoral dissertation, University of Wisconsin – Madison.

Watson, J. B. (1925). *Behaviorism*. New York: Norton.

Watzlawick, P., Beavin, J. H., & Jackson, D. D. (1967). *Pragmatics of human communication: A study of interactional patterns, pathologies, and paradoxes*. New York: W. W. Norton.

Wilcox, D. L., Ault, P. H., & Agee, W. K. (1992). *Public relations strategies and tactics*. New York: HarperCollins.

Wilson, W. R. (1979). Feeling more than we can know: Exposure effects without learning. *Journal of Personality and Social Psychology*, **37**, 811–821.

Wood, W., Kallgren, C. A., & Priesler, R. M. (1985). Access to attitude-relevant information in memory as a determinant of persuasion: The role of message attributes. *Journal of Experimental Social Psychology*, **21**, 73–85.

Wright, P. L. (1974). Analyzing media effects on advertising responses. *Public Opinion Quarterly*, **38**, 192–205.

Wyer, R. S., Jr. (1974). *Cognitive organization and change: An information processing approach*. New York: Wiley.

Young, D. (1996). *Building your company's good name: How to create and protect the reputation your organization wants & deserves.* New York: American Management Association.

Zajonc, R. B. (1980). Feeling and thinking: Preferences need no inferences. *American Psychologist,* **35,** 151–175.

Zajonc, R. B. (1981). A one-factor mind about mind and emotion. *American Psychologist,* **36,** 102–103.

Zajonc, R. B. (1984). On the primacy of affect. *American Psychologist,* **39,** 117–123.

Zajonc, R. B., & Markus, H. (1982). Affective and cognitive factors in preferences. *Journal of Consumer Research,* **9,** 123–131.

Zbar, J. D. (1993, June 28). Environmental marketing. *Advertising Age,* pp. S1–S3.

Zuwerink, J. R., & Devine, P. G. (1996). Attitude importance and resistance to persuasion: It's not just the thought that counts. *Journal of Personality and Social Psychology,* **70,** 931–944.

CHAPTER 12

C. Kay Weaver, Judy Motion and Juliet Roper

From propaganda to discourse (and back again):
truth, power, the public interest and public relations*

* Chapter 1 in *Public Relations: Critical Debates and Contemporary Practice*, edited by Jaquie L'Etang and Magda Pieczka (2006). Copyright © 2006 by Lawrence Erlbaum Associates, Inc. Reproduced with permission.

Since Edward Bernays first introduced the term 'public relations counsel' in his 1923 publication *Crystallizing Public Opinion*, public relations, although widely practised by corporations and governments alike, has monumentally failed to establish itself as of positive social utility and benefit. As L'Etang has stated, 'It is something of a truism that public relations needs more public relations to increase public understanding of its role in society' (1997, p. 34). Indeed, public relations rarely enjoys good press and is continually maligned as little more than an industry of propaganda and spin that trades in lies and deceit (see, for example, Carey, 1997; Collison, n.d; Beder, 1997; Hager & Burton, 1999; D. Miller, 2003; Michie, 1998; Stauber & Rampton, 1995). This dismissive perspective is particularly likely to be espoused where there is an attempt to expose and/or oppose the messages constructed to garner public support for, for example, corporate or governmental policies and initiatives. Those objecting to the position advocated by the message are especially likely to encourage its casting aside as 'propaganda' or 'spin.'

However, while public relations is popularly described as propaganda and spin, the 'looseness' of these critical descriptions of public relations are not helpful to the development of a sophisticated understanding and evaluation of public relations as a particular form of communicative practice which purportedly advocates for not only organisational interests but also the public interest. Moreover, such dismissive labelling of public relations fails to accurately reflect how it might actually comprise part of the legitimate information management machinery of democratic societies, and how it attempts to gain public support for particular corporate, government, or for that matter even non-government organisations and activist practices. A related problem is the fact that the dismissal of public relations as 'propaganda' and therefore 'bad' reflects a particularly pejorative view of the term 'propaganda' itself. As L'Etang (1997) has noted, it is a position that simplistically defines propaganda as lying which, by implication, places it in opposition to 'truth.' In reality, the practice of both propaganda and public relations is much more complex than is implied by the use of such black-and-white oppositional terms.

From a post-structuralist position, the notion that there is a 'truth' which propaganda stands in opposition to is highly problematic. Post-structuralism regards all 'truth' as socially constructed and contestable. As one of the key post-structuralist thinkers, Michel Foucault (1980), has argued: 'Each society has its regime of truth, its "general politics" of truth: that is, the types of discourse that it accepts and makes function as true' (p. 131). In these

terms it becomes very difficult, if not impossible, to argue that propaganda is necessarily a form of lying – or the promotion of 'untruths.' Instead, the issue has to be understood as a question of what is *accepted* as 'truthful.' How does this impact on our understanding of the role that public relations and, indeed, propaganda, plays in society and our ability to pass evaluative judgement on these communicative practices? Does this mean that we should simply regard the promotion of particular messages by public relations and propagandist practitioners as a legitimate part of the struggle in the effort to have society adopt a particular version of 'the facts,' or of one truth over another? And, what are the implications of adopting this position? These questions form the core concern of this chapter, wherein we draw on critical perspectives to theorise the similarities and differences between the communication practices of propaganda and public relations. By drawing on critical theory in this analysis, our aim is to explore how critical perspectives tend to position public relations and propaganda on a continuum, but also how they might provide pathways to theorise the role that public relations plays in the construction of knowledge and, therefore, notions of truth, power, and the public interest.

We begin the chapter with an exploration of how early 20th-century American public opinion theorists regarded propaganda and its allied occupation, public relations counsel, as vital to the effective working of democratic society. We then explore why 'propaganda' has become a pejoratively loaded term and why, consequently, contemporary public relations theorists attempt to construct strict demarcations between propaganda and 'ethical' public relations practice. After outlining how systems theorists argue that public relations can be practised ethically, we then examine these arguments in relation to Jürgen Habermas's theory of 'communicative action,' in which private interests and power relations are put aside in favour of open, informed discussion from which public interests will be determined. Although idealistic, the notion of communicative action is used as a benchmark for democratic processes, and ones which public relations practice are not necessarily in alignment with. Building on this critique of 'ethical public relations,' we then draw on the work of Michel Foucault and Norman Fairclough to outline how public relations can be understood as discourse practice that is utilised in efforts to legitimate or challenge social, cultural, political, and/or economic power. With this we are brought full circle back to the question of whether there is, in fact, any substantive difference between propaganda and public relations once public relations is conceived of as a discourse technology of social governance.

Propaganda and public society

The term propaganda has not always carried the negative connotations that it does today. Its origins lie with the 17th century Roman Catholic Church, which established the '*de Propaganda Fide*' to 'mobilize talented intellectuals of every sort into a vast social apparatus to persuade men and women all across the globe to believe in Christian doctrine or, if perchance they had fallen astray, to rekindle their faith' (Jackall, 1995, p. 1). Even in the secular society of the early 20th century, propaganda was still regarded as making an important contribution to the mobilization of public opinion. Indeed, early public opinion theorists, such as Harold Lasswell, Walter Lippman and the 'father of public relations,' Edward Bernays, regarded propaganda as vital to the workings of democracy through its advocating, for example, government and business policy developments to the 'mass public.'

For many American social theorists, this mass public was a cause for concern in the period after World War I when 'Victorian ideals of an ordered society no longer held much sway, nor did the religious principles of delayed gratification and presumed hierarchies. It was unclear what would take their place. Anarchy?' (Tye, 1998, p. 94). Certainly the threats posed by a 'burgeoning of militant working-class politics . . . fears of revolt from below' and 'middle-class hostility toward big business' (Ewen, 1996, p. 60) were regarded by progressive politicians as evidence of an increasing slide toward social disintegration and chaos. It was in this context that social psychologists, political scientists, politicians, and the corporate sector saw propaganda as providing a means of engineering public opinion, controlling the masses, and reinstating social order. As Ewen (1996) stated: 'The dexterity with which a new class of experts could learn to manipulate symbols appeared to be the fortress that would protect the forces of order from the mounting tide of chaos' (p. 143).

However, in the early decades of the 20th century American propaganda practice did not focus on appealing to public rationale for support of political and/or corporate causes. Far from it. As a consequence of Freud's influence on psychological theories of the human mind – which posited unconscious instincts as determining individual behaviour – propagandists and early public relations practitioners focused efforts on appealing to public *emotion* rather than critical reasoning (Ewen, 1996). Indeed, the 'public mind' was regarded as illogical and irrational and in need of governance from 'responsible men' trained in decision making and leadership (Lippman, 1995 [1925]). As Ewen (1996) detailed, for Lippman, 'The key

to leadership in the modern age would depend on the ability to manipulate 'symbols which assemble emotions after they have been detached from their ideas.' The public mind is mastered, [Lippman] continued, through an "intensification of feeling and degradation of significance"' (p. 335).

Those who regarded propaganda as a crucial tool in the maintenance of social order in the early 20th century were not advocates of participatory democracy. Lippman's (1995 [1925]) position on this is made abundantly clear in his statement that:

> When public opinion attempts to govern directly it is either a failure or a tyranny. It is not able to master the problem intellectually, nor to deal with it except by wholesale impact. The theory of democracy has not recognized this truth because it has identified the functioning of government with the will of the people. This is a fiction. (p. 51)

Lippman advocated a technocratic representative democracy where power resided in the hands of a small, intellectual elite (Ewen, 1996) and public consent to their rule was engineered. Harold Lasswell's position was very similar: 'Regard for men in the mass rests upon no democratic dogmatisms about men being the best judges of their own interest. The modern propagandist, like the modern psychologist, recognizes that men are often poor judges of their own interests, flitting from one alternative to the next without solid reason' (1995 [1934], p. 24). From this perspective public interest is not debated, determined, and governed by the public itself but by an elite group. In these terms, the real value of propaganda lies *not* in its dissemination and promotion of *ideas*, but in its ability to orchestrate public opinion and social action that supported the ruling elite: 'The propagandist is one who creates symbols that are not only popular but that bring about positive realignments of behaviour is no phrase-monger but a promoter of overt acts' (Lasswell 1995 [1934], p. 25). What is more, as McNair has previously pointed out, Lippman also advocated propaganda practices that 'obscure personal intention, neutralise discrimination, and obfuscate individual purpose' (cited in McNair, 1996, p. 43).

While Lasswell, Lippman, and Bernays conceived propaganda – or as Bernays phrased it, 'public relations counsel' – as essential to the management of information, the social engineering of consent, and as, therefore, a normative aspect of modern democratic society (Robins, Webster, & Pickering, 1987; see also Barsamian & Chomsky, 2001, chap. 6), their theories of the value of the propagandist psychological manipulation of people later fell into disrepute. This was largely as a consequence of the highly effective, and catastrophic, application and development of propaganda theory by Hitler and his Nazi propaganda chief Joseph Goebbels during the lead up to and during World War II. That there is a relationship between the American theories of propaganda and the Nazi propagandist practices is not denied. As Tye (1998; see also Bernays, 1965, p. 652) reported, Goebbels owned a copy of Bernays' *Crystallizing Public Opinion* and 'while scholars still debate the extent to which the Nazis used Bernays's works, Goebbels did employ techniques nearly identical to those used by Bernays' (p. 111). In particular Goebbels, like Bernays, used 'scientific' methods to psychologically manipulate the propaganda audience through means such as the constant repetition of a few relatively simplistic points.

Like the American political scientists and public opinion theorists, Hitler held a dim view of the general population's ability to make responsible rational decisions – describing them as a 'great stupid flock' (Thomson, 1977, p. 117). Along with Goebbels, Hitler also – and again like the Americans – assigned enormous importance to the ability to manipulate the public mind through the use of symbols and emotional language. Both men also valued how propaganda could turn established 'truths' on their heads through – as Goebbels is often quoted:

a carefully built up erection of statements, which whether true or false can be made to undermine quite rigidly held ideas and to construct new ones that will take their place. It would not be impossible to prove with sufficient repetition and psychological understanding of the people concerned that a square is in fact a circle. What after all are a square and a circle? They are mere words and words can be moulded until they clothe ideas in disguise. (cited in Thomson, 1977, p. 111)

Goebbels' statement indicates a clear understanding of the significance that language plays in the effectiveness of propaganda and the establishment of (relativist) understandings of truth – an issue that we explore further below in relation to discourse and public relations. But it is also worth briefly examining how this theory of effective propaganda techniques – in terms of the perceived outcome of the repetition of the message – is dependent on a behaviourist stimulus–response transmission model of communication.

Theorising the public: propaganda audiences

Within a transmission model of communication, communication is regarded as a one-way process in which an active 'sender' communicates a message to a passive 'receiver' whose behaviour is then affected by the message content. This model – closely linked to the popular use of propaganda techniques in the United States and Europe in the early decades of the 20th century and 'the enduring notion of "the public" as a vulnerable and persuadable lot 'at risk' from propaganda' (Brooker & Jermyn, 2003, p. 5) – has informed a large proportion of media effects research and theorizing. However, as Gauntlet (1995) explained, the model – often termed the 'hypodermic model of communication effects' – is closely associated with:

methods and assumptions which are inherited from the natural sciences, and are therefore of questionable applicability to the study of such complex systems as human psychology, behaviour and social life. Whilst natural scientists can generally hope to observe stable and verifiable effects of one object on another, similarly straightforward predictions about social action obviously cannot be made. (p. 9)

Nevertheless, in the 1920s this model held considerable sway in mass communication theory – as it would for several more decades. Indeed, Harold Lasswell argued that:

The strategy of propaganda . . . can readily be described in the language of stimulus response: the propagandist may be said to be concerned with the multiplication of these stimuli which are calculated to evoke the desired responses, and with the nullification of those stimuli which are likely to instigate the undesired responses. (cited in Robins et al., 1987, p. 3)

It is hardly surprising that there is a direct relationship between stimulus–response transmission theories of communication and the beliefs espoused by Lippman, Lasswell, and Bernays that propaganda makes an important contribution to democratic society given these theorists' perception of the public as a highly impressionable passive 'herd' (Jackall, 1995, p. 358). Passive and irrational publics were regarded as in need of 'responsible' direction. What is more surprising is that despite the discrediting of transmission stimulus–response models and their replacement by transaction models in which there is 'acknowledgement of the active receiver, the obstinate and recalcitrant audience' (Robins et al., 1987, p. 4) – a theoretical shift that began in the 1940s (Brooker & Jermyn, 2003), critiques of propaganda are still implicitly underpinned by the transmission model. Consequently, essentially behavioural models are used to cast propaganda as deliberate, manipulative, and, therefore, unethical persuasion. For example, Jowett and O'Donnell (1992) stated that the

purpose of propaganda is to send out an ideology with a related objective . . . [and] there is a careful and predetermined plan of prefabricated symbol manipulation to communicate to an audience in order to fulfill [the] objective. The objective that is sought requires the audience to reinforce or modify attitudes and/or behaviour. (pp. 2–3)

This explanation of propaganda clearly implies that the audience is a passive one, and that behaviour is open to modification by a message from what is constructed as a 'powerful' *ideologically motivated* message sender. By defining propaganda in this way, Jowett and O'Donnell constructed all ideologically motivated messages as 'bad', or at least ethically questionable, and in so doing imply that there are some forms of communication that are ('good' and) free from ideological underpinning. However, post-structural conceptions of culture contradict the argument that some communication can be 'ideologically free,' as *all* cultural activities, including communication, are 'always situated in specific social-historical contexts which are structured in certain ways' (Thompson, 1988, p. 361) and located within relations of power.

Jowett and O'Donnell (1992) also continually described propagandists as highly powerful and operating with conscious, deliberated self-interested intent. This notion is central to their definition of propaganda: 'Propaganda is the deliberate and systematic attempt to shape perceptions, manipulate cognitions, and direct behaviour to achieve a response that furthers the desired intent of the propagandist' (p. 4). It is in these terms that propaganda is primarily associated with unethical communication and totalitarian regimes. However, some social commentators argue for the need to extend the association of propaganda to the strategic communication practices of democratic governments – such as, for example, those of President George W. Bush and Prime Minister Tony Blair in their campaigns to gain public support for the 2003 war on Iraq (Hiebert, 2003; D. Miller, 2003). Others have suggested that the communication practices used in environmental activist campaigns (Anderson, 1997; J. Palmer, 2000) and by non-government organisations and charities (Hutson & Liddiard, 2000) also make use of propagandist type approaches where the intention is to directly affect the emotions, attitudes, and behaviours of audiences.

However, the discrediting of behaviourist stimulus–response models of communication makes it much more difficult to explain the mechanisms by which recipients of propaganda messages can be persuaded to accept ideas or policies that do not, in reality, support their individual or collective interests. Under transactional theories of communication, audiences rationally chose to align with the message content and its senders' subject position as a result of some perceived benefit – be it personal, political, economic, social, or even pleasurable gain, for example,

in doing so. This perspective becomes much less palatable, however, when used to explain the overwhelming effectiveness of the propaganda strategies deployed by the Nazis which mobilized public support for Hitler's dictatorship, the causes of nationalism, anti-Semitism, and mass genocide.

For many propaganda theorists, it is preferable to construct the public opinion that supported Nazi atrocities as the unwitting *victim* of an omnipotent monstrous power. Once pro-Nazi anti-Semitic opinion is theorised as anything less than the result of such extraordinary power, the astonishing intellectual legacy around propaganda left by Hitler and his Propaganda Minister Josef Goebbels has to be acknowledged. As Doob (1995) stressed: 'Whether or when parts of [this legacy of propaganda] should be utilized in a democratic society are profound and disturbing problems of a political and ethical nature' (p. 192).

However, why the German public was seemingly willing to accept Hitler's message has to be considered in the wider context of the crippling effects of the post-World War I Treaty of Versailles on the German economy and employment, which in turn led to a groundswell in German nationalism. A more complex explanation of how Hitler's propaganda was effective would be that he engaged with an active, not passive public and that his messages resonated with commonly held public sentiments and national aspirations. Of course, Hitler's message was also soon underpinned by the suppression and censorship of anti-Nazi voices, threats, coercion, and violence (Marlin, 2002). Yet, it is Hitler's deliberate and so effective use of language and symbols which ensured public support for his horrific atrocities that has resulted in the term 'propaganda' being associated with *unacceptable manipulation* of public opinion.

For the vast majority of propaganda and public relations theorists, certainly in the Western world, there is overt agreement that the type of propaganda practised by the Nazis has no place in a democracy. However, to simply say that propagandist practices are the prerogative of totalitarian regimes (see, for example, Jowett & O'Donnell, 1992) is indicative of a complete denial that propaganda could or, indeed, does play a part in democratic societies. This is a concern that Robins et al. (1987) raised when they asked: 'Just how distinct is information management in the cause of democracy from dictatorial propaganda and information control? If there are those . . . for whom the principles seem clear cut, there are others who perceive a more muddy and ambiguous reality' (p. 15).

In an attempt to acknowledge that information management, or influence, does have a legitimate role to play in, for example, social and political relations, Jowett and O'Donnell (1992) described an arena for *ethical* influence – which they term 'persuasion.' Having defined propaganda as the *self-interested* attempt to manipulate the behaviour of others, they contrast this with ethical persuasion, which they conceive of as an 'interactive or transactive' process:

> in which the recipient foresees the fulfillment of a personal or societal need or desire if the persuasive purpose is adopted. The persuader also has a need fulfilled if the persuadee accepts the persuasive purpose. Because both persuader and persuadee stand to have their needs fulfilled, persuasion is regarded as more mutually satisfying than propaganda. (p. 21)

Here Jowett and O'Donnell attempt to distinguish propaganda from legitimate practices of persuasion and influence. As we will discuss below, identifying what is ethical influence has come to play a major place in the development of public relations theory. However, we would argue that Jowett and O'Donnell's explanation of ethical persuasion could be seen at work in 1930s Germany, because supporters of Nazism viewed Hitler as potentially fulfilling societal needs by offering a way out of a crippling national economic depression. This suggests that propaganda in itself is not unethical. Rather, whether propaganda is ethical or not has to be assessed in relation to the context in which it is practised, the ends to which it is used, the quality of transparency in terms of the persuaders' openness about the 'ends' they are seeking to achieve, and, as far as one is able to judge, the consequences of those ends.

Legitimising public relations

As propaganda has become increasingly discredited as an unethical tool for the manipulation of public opinion, new models of supposedly ethical persuasion have been developed. These models have attempted to notionally distance public relations from propaganda (despite early public relations theorists regarding them as one and the same thing) and provide legitimacy for the public relations profession.

Four models of public relations practice evolved from Grunig and Hunt's (1984) use of functionalist systems theory in the development of a new conceptualisation of public relations. As Trujillo and Toth (1987) outlined, functionalists 'are usually concerned with organizational effectiveness and efficiency as they relate to the 'bottom-line' financial health of the organization' (p. 202). Working from within the functionalist approach, systems theory specifically regards public relations as a means by which organisations can better manage uncertainties within their environments and so adapt and grow (Trujillo & Toth, 1987, p. 208). The four models of public relations

that Grunig and Hunt (1984) developed are (a) press agentry/publicity, (b) public information, (c) two-way asymmetrical, and (d) two-way symmetrical public relations. It is the last of these, the two-way symmetrical model, that was deemed *ethical* and *best practice* public relations communication.

Although the term propaganda does not feature within Grunig and Hunt's outlining of the four models of public relations, there is certainly an acknowledgement that public relations is used in the attempt to manage information and public opinion to protect the self-interest of the client, organisations, or dominant coalition. For example, Grunig (2001) stated that:

> Practitioners of press agentry seek attention for their organisations in almost anyway possible, whereas public information practitioners are journalists-in-residence who disseminate accurate, but usually only favourable information about their organisations. With the two-way asymmetrical model, practitioners conduct scientific research to determine how to persuade publics to behave in the ways their client organisations wish *(pp. 11–12, our emphasis).*

Interestingly, research into public relations practice has found that 'the dominant world view in public relations – the asymmetrical view [is] that public relations is a way of getting what an organization wants without changing its behaviour or without compromising' (Grunig & White, 1992, p. 39). This suggests that not only are strategies associated with propaganda used in democratic nations, but also that public relations practitioners view their use as normative.

There is little question that modern public relations acts on the need to secure public acceptance of organisational policy, be it government, business, or not-for-profit. For some public relations and media theorists, the use of communication to persuade public opinion in this context is viewed as entirely acceptable practice. For example, McNair (1996) stated: 'The public relations function is a necessary dimension of the modern political process, which has overall become more democratic, and not less, in the course of the twentieth century' (p. 53). This view is very much like that of Lasswell (1995 [1934]) in that it accepts public relations as necessary in spite of its propagandistic underpinnings. Indeed, as McNair stated, 'As the producer and disseminator of symbols which can contribute to the building of unity and consent . . . the public relations worker is, of course, a propagandist' (p. 43).

Yet, as noted above, Grunig and Hunt (1984) promoted the notion of *symmetrical* communication as the model for *ethical* public relations, which, although never directly stated, could be construed as setting public relations apart from propaganda – especially in terms of its striving for a balancing of organisational and public interests (Grunig, 2001). Indeed, the process of symmetrical communication – which involves an organisation using public opinion research and engaging in public dialogue with stakeholders in the development of organisational objectives, clearly suggests a distinction from propaganda if we accept that propagandists are in the business of seeking to persuade, by one means or another, the public to buy into values or beliefs that benefit the interests of the propagandists over and above the interests of the public. As Grunig and White (1992) defined it, ethical public relations is, in contrast, 'a symmetrical process of compromise and negotiation and not a war for power' (p. 39).

The idea of the two-way symmetrical communication model is that an organisation will engage with the public to assess what courses of action will work to benefit *both* the organisation and the public. Responding to public opinion may require that substantive changes are made to decisions about organisational direction and objectives. Grunig and White (1992) argued that, 'In the long run the symmetrical view is more effective: organisations get more of what they want when they give up some of what they want' (p. 39). From this perspective, publics were perceived as active participants in dialogue leading to the formulation of organisational policy and goals. Consequentially, the public relations professional was positioned as aligned with a worldview that 'presupposes that public relations serves the public interest, develops mutual understanding between organisations and their publics, contributes to informed debate about issues in society, and facilitates a dialogue between organisations and their publics' (Grunig & White, 1992, p. 53). In these terms public relations was cast as playing a very different role in society than that of propaganda. Its role is that of facilitator of dialogue working for the mutual benefit of both the client organisation and the public good.

As it was originally developed by Grunig and Hunt (1984), the symmetrical model of public relations practice can be seen as an attempt to advance public relations as an acceptable and ethical profession built upon democratic ideals. As Pieczka (1996) has argued, those who advocate for the legitimacy of public relations have been involved in a long campaign to distance the industry from any links to the practice of 'manipulative' propaganda and promote it as ethical, civilised, and even socially responsible. Indeed, acceptance of the role of public relations in the formation of public opinion and policy through open, democratic processes would provide legitimacy not only to the outcomes but also to public relations itself.

For critics of the 'ethical' representation of public relations, predominantly insurmountable tensions exist between balancing the needs of public interest and self- or private interest within public relations practice, making the application of the dialogical symmetrical model an unlikely rarity and even something of a fantastical ideal (Leitch & Neilson, 1997; Weaver, 2001). Interestingly, these are the very same tensions identified by the German communication philosopher Jürgen Habermas in his attempt to theorise a public sphere – an ideal space in which citizens came together in a process he described as 'communicative action' to discuss issues of public importance and political consequence.

A student of the Frankfurt School of social research, which promoted Marxist critique of Western capitalism, Habermas sought to provide a theory of civil society in which public opinion was not an outcome of partisan lobbying and strategic persuasive influence, but a result of rational public debate about what constituted 'truth' and the collective good. The notion of 'the public sphere' – an 'open arena of debate' (Golding & Murdock, 1991, p. 22) accessible to the public in all of its diversity – was central to Habermas' theory of a just society. In this society, with full provision of information and with private interests put aside, public opinion was formed that in turn determined public policy.

Within Habermas' theory of the public sphere, a stable public consensus of opinion can only be derived from communicative action. In these terms the strategic intention of propagandists and even public relations practitioners can*not* be said to create true consensus, however effective they may be. As Mayhew (1997) stated:

> *For Habermas, communication has its own imperatives, and if attempts to communicate violate its intrinsic character, they are deformed and ineffective in producing actual and stable consensus. Communicative action cannot employ force. Indeed, any mode of persuasion that falls short of a strict standard of reciprocity is coercive, even if its persuasive sway is not directly based on force. (p. 36)*

It is through the process of communicative action, and the acceptance of a better argument based on claims to 'comprehensibility, truth, rightness and sincerity' (Mayhew, 1997, p. 36), that policy is legitimated by citizens in terms of their accepting it as acting in the public interest (Habermas, 1976, 1996).

Habermas (1996) did, however, point to tensions between facticity and validity inherent in his (ideal) theory of the process of communicative action. The tension arises because the validity of truth claims will be under constant scrutiny in the light of counterclaims. He stated that, under ideal conditions, 'the acceptance of validity claims, which generates and perpetuates social facts, rests on the context-dependent acceptability of reasons that are constantly exposed to the risk of being invalidated by better reasons and context-altering learning processes' (p. 36).

Thus, the determination of what constitutes 'the public interest' is contestable and context dependent, linked to the social norms of a given time and place.

As is evident, Habermas' theory of public interest as derived through communicative action is very similar to the theory of the formation of public interest within Grunig and Hunt's (1984) and Grunig and White's (1992) model of two-way symmetrical public relations. But to what extent do public relations practitioners genuinely engage in communicative action in the attempt to balance the requirements of legitimising the actions of the organisations that employ them with the public interest? One area of public relations in which this is a key strategic concern is in issues management, which is concerned with helping organisations to 'make adaptations needed to achieve harmony and foster mutual interests with the communities in which they operate' (Heath, 1997, p. 3).

Heath directly related the concept and practice of issues management to public policy through the proactive management of key issues. If such issues were ignored then public policies might be developed in response. These would necessarily limit the ability of business to regulate itself. He stated that:

> The underpinning principle of issues management is not to avoid legislation or regulation but to balance the interests of all segments of the community so that each enjoys the proper amount of reward or benefit in proportion to the cost of allowing industry free rein to impose its own operating standards. (1997, p. 6)

From this perspective, Heath (1997) argued that where differences exist between perceptions of what companies are doing, and the community's expectations of what they *ought* to be doing, a 'legitimacy gap' may be said to occur (see also Sethi, 1977). This gap results from, according to Heath (1997), differences of agreement over 'fact, value and policy' (p. 4). For those public relations practitioners who advocate a two-way symmetrical model of communication, this poses the challenge of how to align the organisations's perspective with social norms and the public interest. Essentially this requires a dialogic process.

However, at this point it has to be said that the term 'dialogue' itself is open to different interpretations of process and historicizing. For example, Habermas tracked the shift in dialogical processes from that of collaborative rational–critical dialogue where outcomes are jointly conceived to a negotiated compromise among interests from the period of the 18th through to the 20th centuries (Calhoun, 1992). Dialogue may thus be conceptualised on a continuum from collaboration – that is, working together to achieve a shared interest, to negotiated compromise where one or both parties make concessions. It is from the latter perspective that Heath (1997) suggested

that dialogue is a process of 'statement and counterstatement' (p. 365) where 'people influence and are influenced. Judgement and conclusions are forged on the anvil of debate, negotiation and collaboration. Opinions change. Compromise is achieved' (p. 366). This is a process in which 'reason takes the form of rhetorical rebuttal of rhetorical statement' (Mayhew, 1997, p. 48) and parties attempt to persuade one another of the validity of their perspective, protecting their own self-interest, and attempting to gain a position of power with, or over, others.

In these terms, however, two-way public relations practice does not accord with Habermas' theory of communicative action. Rather, public relations activity – especially in the context of the corporate and government sectors which are intrinsically connected to the concerns of economy and state, money, and power – falls under what Habermas defined as 'strategic action.' Strategic action is defined as that action which is 'designed to achieve ends at the expense of other people' (Mayhew, 1997, p. 36). Yet, what also has to be considered is the lack of fit between the conception of the public interest within Habermassian theory of the public sphere and communicative action, and the conception of the public interest in the two-way symmetrical model of public relations. As outlined above, in Habermas' model of the public sphere 'people collectively determine through a process of rational argument the way in which they want to see society develop' (Curran, 1991, p. 83) and, therefore, what is in the public good or interest. In contrast, as Mayhew (1997) has argued, public relations professionals draw in a very narrow conception of the public interest and can do so because in their role as advocates:

> They are no more bound by detached, disinterested approaches to the facts than attorneys who argue on behalf of clients in courts of law. Providing selected truths in support of clients is entirely appropriate; it is up to the other side to present its own truths. (p. 203)

In these liberal democratic, adversarial, 'market of ideas' terms, it is up to each party to bring to the debate points of argument which support their own position and which contest, challenge, or seek to modify the claims presented by the other party (Barney & Black, 1994). It is considered fair that you would not intentionally undermine your own cause by bringing to the discussion information that would work in the other party's favour and against your own interest. Rather, within the ideals of democratic liberal freedom of speech, each party is free to expose the weaknesses of the other in claiming their own moral authority, and it is up to them to do so.

This does raise the question of why the legal practice of advocating for the interest of clients is predominantly regarded as socially acceptable, whereas in the case of public relations such partisan advocacy is decried as unethical and propagandist. An important distinguishing feature of lawyers compared with public relations practitioners is, however, that the role of lawyers is to defend their clients' claim to innocence and their right to retain their life, liberty, and property until the state proves them guilty in the court of public opinion. This compares with public relations practitioners, who advocate for their clients, but not in a situation of protecting that client against accusation and punishment by the state and, moreover, not in a situation where clients' claims are thoroughly examined by an advocate appointed to work for the public interest. This is because, as Habermas and other media and communication scholars have argued, capitalist liberal democracy has failed to deliver a public sphere in which, through genuine public dialogue, rational consensus about what is in the public interest can be achieved. As Mayhew (1997) has stated, 'Reason can only be realised in dialogue, and dialogue can only be institutionalised in society by providing strategically located public forums for expression and response, in which citizens speak freely about their socially located experience' (p. 48). Indeed, the professional communication industries of public relations, advertising, and marketing research have only further contributed to the erosion of the ideal possibility of the public sphere; and communication between citizens, governments, and corporations has become strategically invested with relationships of money, private interest, and, therefore, power. James Grunig (2001) acknowledged precisely this when he stated:

> Symmetrical public relations does not take place in an ideal situation where competing interests come together with good will to resolve their differences because they share a goal of social equilibrium and harmony. Rather, it takes place in situations where groups come together to protect and enhance their self-interest. (p. 18)

Consequently, public relations communication can be understood as the strategic attempt to control the agenda of public discussion and the terms in which discussion takes place. In these terms, public relations practitioners are complicit in the attempt to gain, and maintain, social, political, and/or economic power for the organisations that they represent. They do this by asserting the 'common sense' truth value of what they stand for and communicate.

Considering public relations from this perspective, the concept of hegemony (Gramsci, 1971) provides a means of understanding how social power or dominance (without coercion or violence) can be achieved. Because dominant truths based in ideas can be challenged at any time and from multiple perspectives, hegemony is never static but

must respond to such challenges through the making of concessions that will diffuse or absorb opposition (Hall, 1988). It is from this position that Roper (2005) argued that symmetrical communication, although conceived as a dialogic tool by which public relations can be practised *ethically*, is more likely to be utilised as a tool for the maintenance of hegemony. Certainly, dialogue can be undertaken in order to ascertain publics' concerns and responses to those concerns can be then negotiated. However, by making relatively small concessions in response to outside criticisms, organisations can undermine the arguments of their opponents and thereby strengthen their own positions. In this way power relations can be maintained rather than compromised. Thus, two-way symmetrical communication might involve the alteration of organisational practices in response to public dissent, but only insofar as it is necessary to maintain what is essentially 'business as usual.'

If, like Habermas, we are to argue that public relations practitioners play a key role in the maintenance of power without coercion and that their role is strategically invested, we need to examine the processes by which that strategy is effected. One key process is through construction and control of discourse.

Public relations as discourse

While Habermas was concerned with theorising issues of influence in civil society, he did not develop a theory of discourse, and neither did he theorise the relationship between discourse, influence, and power. The reason for this, certainly according to Mayhew (1997), is that Habermas sought to maintain a space for reason and 'true' rational consensus in society. This compares with Foucault, for whom the politics of truth, power, and knowledge were primary issues of concern. For Foucault, truth was not something that was 'arrived' at through public discussion, but something that is 'produced' through discourse.

From Foucault's perspective (1972), 'Discourses are composed of signs; but what they do is more than use these signs to designate things' – they are 'practices that systematically form the objects of which they speak' (p. 49). Thus, discourse structures how we know, understand, and speak about the world. Discourse is both a symbolic and constitutive system that structures knowledge and social practice. It is in these terms that Motion and Leitch (1996) argued that, 'Public relations practitioners . . . play a central role in the maintenance and transformation of discourse' (p. 298). This perspective shifts the role of public relations from information management and control to the production, contestation, and transformation of ideas and meanings that circulate in society.

The task for public relations practitioners is to ensure that certain ideas and practices become established and understood and thereby attempt to gain the hegemonic advantage for their client in this discursive struggle. This is what Motion and Leitch (1996) alluded to when they stated that, 'Public relations practitioners are involved in the maintenance and transformation of discourse primarily through the production and distribution of texts . . . strategically deploying texts that facilitate certain socio-cultural practices and not others' (p. 299). From this critical perspective public relations practitioners are theorised as working to (strategically) privilege particular discourses over others, in an attempt to construct what they hope will be accepted as in the public interest and legitimated as policy.

From this critical discourse perspective, public relations professionals are in the business of creating particular knowledge and identity positions which then influence the types of social relationships that are possible within and outside that discourse. Fairclough (1992) expressed these functions of discourse in the following terms: 'The identity function relates to the ways in which social identities are set up in discourse, the relational function to how social relationships between discourse participants are enacted and negotiated' (p. 64). In this context public relations is understood as explicitly concerned with constructing knowledge, identities, and relationships that will work to facilitate particular sociocultural practices – those that work for the needs and interests of the client organisation (see, for example, Motion & Leitch, 1996; Motion & Weaver, (2005); Weaver, 2001; Weaver & Motion, 2002). However, for any one discourse to dominate over others requires that it be sanctioned as 'the truth.' This is not to argue the case for an essential 'rational' truth of the kind that Habermas attempted to theoretically maintain. Rather, as Foucault (1980) has argued:

> There is a battle 'for truth' or at least 'around truth' – it being understood once again that by truth I do not mean 'the ensemble of truths which are to be discovered and accepted', but rather 'the ensemble of rules according to which the true and the false are separated and specific effects of power attached to the true', it being understood also that it's not a matter of a battle 'on behalf' of the truth, but of a battle about the status of truth and the economic and political role it plays. (p. 132)

Foucault is not interested in whether a discourse is true or real; he is concerned with the mechanics whereby one discourse becomes produced as the dominant discourse (Mills, 1997, p. 19). In order to maintain or transform social norms through discourse, a 'regime of truth' (Foucault, 1980, p. 131) must be established through relations of power.

The establishment of a regime of truth is 'linked in a circular relation with systems of power which produce and sustain it, and to effects of power which it induces and which extend it' (Foucault, 1980, p. 131). Truth and power, therefore, are inextricably linked and serve to reinforce one another. The struggle to establish a regime of truth is 'about the status of truth and the economic political role it plays' (Foucault, 1980, p. 132). What Foucault is arguing here, and what is key to a discursive theory of public relations, is that truth is, in fact, not itself the ultimate goal of a discourse struggle. Rather, establishing truth is a means of legitimising, or normalizing, material practices. As Fairclough (1995) explained, 'The power to control discourse is seen as the power to sustain particular discursive practices with particular ideological investments in dominance over other alternative (including oppositional) practices' (p. 2). This makes clear the intrinsic connection between discourse and power.

Foucault conceptualised power as both organised and hierarchical within the context of clusters of relationships. He also conceptualised power as relational in that both domination and resistance are strategically coordinated (McHoul & Grace, 1993). That is, Foucault (1980) saw individuals and organisations as deploying various discourse strategies to conform with, circumvent, or contest existing power relations. In this context he argued that:

> We must make allowances for the complex and unstable process whereby discourse can be both an instrument and an effect of power, but also a hindrance, a stumbling block, a point of resistance and also a starting point for an opposing strategy. Discourse transmits and produces power; it reinforces it, but also undermines it and exposes it, renders it fragile and makes it possible to thwart it. (Foucault, 1978, vol. 1, p. 101)

Although the term 'power' is traditionally associated with pejorative connotations of domination (just like propaganda), and is indeed even a much (mis)used concept in critical scholarship where it has itself become associated with the essentialising and fetishising of 'oppressed' groups (Shugart, 2003), Foucault (1972) conceived of power as positive and productive. He stated: 'What makes power hold good, what makes it accepted, is simply the fact that it doesn't only weigh on us as a force that says no, but that it transverses and produces things, it induces pleasure, forms knowledge, produces discourse' (Foucault, 1972, p. 119). Discourse is the vehicle through which knowledge and truth circulate and the strategic mode by which social, political, and/or economic power is maintained or transformed. Key to the acceptance of these social meanings and interpretations of types of knowledge is the strategic linking of the dominance with self- or public interest – which in turn explains their social acceptance. In these terms public relations practitioners are involved in the strategic attempt to have particular social meanings and interpretations of events, activities, or behaviours, for example, adopted over others, meanings and interpretations which, in turn, affect 'social interaction, . . . political deliberation and decision making' (Fraser, 1989, p. 135).

This discursive hegemonic conceptualisation of public relations makes it difficult to argue that there is any essential and substantive difference between public relations practices and propaganda. The arguments about propaganda outlined above where the predominant concern of critics was to decry propaganda as psychological manipulation can equally be applied to public relations as discourse where hegemonic power is obtained by way of offering attractive discursive positions for the public to identify with and subject themselves to. However, as we have argued, the psychological model – especially since the discrediting of transmission theories of communication effects – can provide no explanation of why people accept propaganda messages.

Unlike the behaviourist models of propaganda and persuasion that fail to sufficiently explain public uptake of messages, the discourse model, 'because of its lack of alliance to a clear political agenda, offer[s] a way of thinking about hegemony – people's compliance in their own oppression – without assuming that individuals are necessarily passive victims of systems of thought' (Mills, 1997, p. 30). That is, Foucault's view of power assumes an active participation in discourse by the public, whereby their part in the *relationship* is determined by whether or not a discourse resonates with their individual or collective subjectivities and perceptions of reality. From this perspective, the public itself takes an active role in the construction of reality and the discourses associated with that reality. However, we would argue that public relations (and, indeed, the closely associated industries of advertising and marketing) is involved in the attempt to govern our discursive understanding of organisational practice, for example, by 'condition[ing] and delimit[ing] the field of discourse within which our public and private conversations take place' (Goldman, 1992, p. 2).

Yet, we would also argue from a discourse theory perspective that the theory holds additional value in that it allows for the possibility that public relations discursive strategies might fail. While we would agree that powerful organisations (in hegemonic and economic terms) have extensively more resources from which to draw when trying to protect and enhance their own self-interest than do marginalised groups, their success is not *necessarily* predetermined given that the discourses promoted by an organisation are open to contestation and challenge.

Again, unlike behavioural arguments, the post-structuralist Foucauldian discourse position argues that 'Power is always a discursive relation *rather than something which a person or group wields or bears*' (McHoul & Grace, 1993, p. 21, our emphasis).

However, while discourse practice may be somewhat participatory, the ideologies of the social and economic contexts play a significant role in predetermining which discourses will achieve ascendancy. Therefore, the potential for collaboration across competing discursive positions is limited. Indeed, Deetz (1992) suggested that:

> An adequate theory of communication dealing with participation has to be able to assess whether or not people are able to represent their competing interests within the various institutions that compose society . . . It also has to do with deeper issues of whether or not people are able to openly form their own interests and whether they are able to contribute to the formation of meaning that enables them to represent the interests that they might have. (p. 109)

For Deetz (1992), as for Habermas, the emergence of the corporation 'as the primary institution in modern society' (p. 109), and its whole machinery of promotion and publicity, has severely restrained the ability of the public to formulate alternative meanings and interests outside of those constructed and maintained by capitalism. This is due in part to the fact that the corporation has so successfully, in both discursive and material terms, constructed 'the public interest' as intrinsically connected to 'the corporate interest.' Of course, the recent rise of the anti-globalisation movement does bear testament to the fact that the possibility for participation and the representation of competing or alternative interests does still exist.

Conclusion

As we have outlined, theories of propaganda very often position propagandists as possessing and wielding power, and succeeding in determining behavioural outcomes on the part of their audiences. While we reject the behaviourist underpinnings of this theory of propaganda effects, a view of propagandists and even public relations practitioners as being able to affect audience behaviour – against the interests of that audience – is not incompatible with a discourse perspective. In a situation of there being only a single discourse on an issue available that, for one reason or another, goes uncontested – perhaps because competing discourses have been discredited or the channels of communication closed down – audiences are more likely to accept and act upon the propaganda/public relations message. Certainly in dictatorial regimes this is how propaganda as discourse can be understood to work.

This is not to say that in democratic societies organisations do not similarly strive to have their 'propaganda' – or singular discursive perspective – on an issue accepted by publics. The difference is that in the context of democracy other competing discourses (supposedly) also have avenues for expression and promotion. In these terms, discourse theory helps to move away from the notion of propaganda as deception and lying because it acknowledges the potential for competing discourses and competing truths in society. Multiple discourses circulate and compete with each other for hegemonic power and therefore there is a choice of meanings, identities, and realities available to audiences, not one all-powerful construction of reality. As is evident, discourse theory recognizes that power is present in all relationships, but that publics are able to choose to accept or reject a discourse according to whether it is perceived as being either in their own or the public interest. Yet we would also argue, in agreement with Deetz (1992) and Philo and Miller (2001), that Western corporate capitalism has succeeded in dominating the range of discourses, and indeed our material practices and notions of public interest, to such an extent that it is difficult for alternative discourses and practices to rise to any level of ascendancy without violence – as the 9/11 attacks on the World Trade Center demonstrate. Those attacks can be understood as an attempt to make America and Europe pay attention to accumulated Muslim resentments against a history of Western prejudice, exploitation, and anti-Muslim foreign policy in the Middle East. In effect, Al Qaeda's actions forced consideration, though not necessarily successfully, of how the West has crowded out alternative discursive meanings and visions of how societies can be managed socially, politically, economically, and religiously.

While the critical theory perspective drawn on here finds no substantive difference between propaganda and public relations, this is as a consequence of a rejection of the notions that propaganda *necessarily* operates counter to the public interest, and that public relations necessarily works *for* the public interest. As we have argued, the merits of propaganda and public relations practice can only be judged in terms of the contexts and ends to which they are used. This does not necessarily mean that because critical theorists might regard propaganda and public relations as part of a continuum, that we regard systems theorists constructions of symmetrical public relations as 'a utopian attempt to make an inherently evil practice good' (Grunig, 2001, p. 16). Rather, we would argue that the critical discourse theory view of public relations, and indeed propaganda, provides a means of understanding the significance of the public relations contribution to the formation of hegemonic power, constructions of knowledge, truth, and the public interest. Understood in these terms, public relations becomes a tool of social power and change for utilization by not only those who hold hegemonic power, but also those who seek to challenge and transform that power and reconfigure dominant perceptions of the public interest.

References

Anderson, A. (1997). *Media, culture and the environment.* London: UCL Press.

Barney, R. D., & Black, J. (1994). Ethics and professional persuasive communications. *Public Relations Review,* **20**(3), 233–248.

Barsamian, D., & Chomsky, N. (2001). *Propaganda and the public mind.* London: Pluto Press.

Beder, S. (1997). *Global spin: The corporate assault on environmentalism.* Melbourne: Scribe Publications.

Bernays, E. (1923). *Crystallizing public opinion.* New York: Boni & Liveright.

Bernays, E. L. (1965). *The biography of an idea: Memoirs of public relations counsel Edward L. Bernays.* New York: Simon & Schuster.

Brooker, W., & Jermyn, D. (2003). 'It's out there . . . somewhere': Locating the audience for the *Audience studies reader*. In W. Brooker & D. Jermyn (eds), *The audience studies reader* (pp. 1–11). London: Routledge.

Calhoun, C. (1992). Introduction: Habermas and the public sphere. In C. Calhoun (ed.), *Habermas and the public sphere* (pp. 1–50). Cambridge, MA: MIT Press.

Carey, A. (1997). *Taking the risk out of democracy: Corporate propaganda versus freedom and liberty.* University of Illinois Press.

Collison, D. (n.d). Corporate propaganda: Its implications for accounting and accountability. Unpublished paper, Department of Accountancy and Business Finance, University of Dundee, Scotland.

Curran, J. (1991). Mass media and democracy: A reappraisal. In J. Curran & M. Gurevitch (eds), *Mass media and society* (pp. 82–117). London: Edward Arnold.

Deetz, S. (1992). *Democracy in an age of corporate colonization.* New York: State University of New York Press.

Doob, L. W. (1997 [1950]). Goebbels' principles of propaganda. In R. Jackall (ed.), *Propaganda* (pp. 190–216). New York: New York University Press.

Ewen, S. (1996). *PR! A social history of spin.* New York: Basic Books.

Fairclough, N. (1992). *Discourse and social change.* Oxford, UK: Polity Press.

Fairclough, N. (1995). *Critical discourse analysis: The critical study of language.* London and New York: Longman.

Foucault, M. (1972). *The archaeology of knowledge.* London: Routledge.

Foucault, M. (1980). *Power/knowledge.* Brighton: Harvester Press.

Fraser, N. (1989). *Unruly practices: Power, discourse and gender in contemporary social theory.* Minneapolis: University of Minneapolis Press.

Gauntlet, D. (1995). *Moving experiences: Understanding television's influences and effects.* London: John Libbey.

Golding, P., & Murdock, G. (1991). Culture, communications, and political economy. In J. Curran & M. Gurevitch (eds), *Mass media and society,* (pp. 15–32). London: Edward Arnold.

Goldman, R. (1992). *Reading ads socially.* London and New York: Routledge.

Grunig, J. (2001). Two-way symmetrical public relations: Past, present and future. In R. L. Heath (ed.), *Handbook of public relations* (pp. 11–30). London: Sage.

Grunig, J., & Hunt, T. (1984). *Managing public relations.* New York: Holt, Rinehart & Winston.

Grunig, J. E., & White, J. (1992). The effect of worldviews in public relations theory and practice. In J. E. Grunig (ed.), *Excellence in public relations and communication management* (pp. 31–64). Hillsdale and Hove: Lawrence Erlbaum Associates.

Habermas, J. (1976). *Legitimation crisis* (trans. T. McCarthy). London: Heinemann.

Habermas, J. (1996). *Between facts and norms: Contributions to a discourse theory of law and democracy* (trans. W. Rehg). Cambridge, MA: MIT Press.

Hager, N., & Burton, B. (1999). *Secrets and lies: The anatomy of an anti-environmental PR campaign.* Nelson, NZ: Craig Potton.

Hall, S. (1988). *The hard road to renewal. Thatcherism and the crisis of the Left.* London: Verso.

Heath, R. L. (1997). *Strategic issues management organizations and public policy challenges.* London: Sage.

Hiebert, R. E. (2003). Public relations and propaganda in framing the Iraq war: A preliminary review. *Public Relations Review, 29,* 243–255.

Hutson, S., & Liddiard, M. (2000). Exclusionary environments: The media career of youth homelessness. In S. Allan, B. Adam, & C. Carter (eds), *Environmental risks and the media* (pp. 160–170). London & New York: Routledge.

Jackall, R. (1995). The magic lantern: The world of public relations. In R. Jackall (ed.), *Propaganda* (pp. 351–399). New York: New York University Press.

Jowett, G., & O'Donnell, V. (1992). *Propaganda and persuasion.* Newbury Park, CA: Sage.

L'Etang, J. (1997). Public relations and the rhetorical dilemma: Legitimate 'perspectives', persuasion, or pandering? *Australian Journal of Communication, 24*(2), 33–53.

Lasswell, H. D. (1934, 1995). Propaganda. In R. Jackall (ed.), *Propaganda* (pp. 13–35). New York: New York University Press.

Leitch, S., & Neilson, D. (1997). Reframing public relations: New directions for theory and practice. *Australian Journal of Communication, 24*(2), 17–32.

Lippman, W. (1925, 1995). The phantom public. In R. Jackall (ed.), *Propaganda* (pp. 351–399). New York: New York University Press.

Marlin, R. (2002). *Propaganda and the ethics of persuasion.* Ontario: Broadview.

Mayhew, L. (1997). *The new public. Professional communication and the means of social influence.* Cambridge, UK: Cambridge University Press.

McHoul, A., & Grace, W. (1993). *A Foucault primer: Discourse, power and the subject.* Carlton: Melbourne University Press.

McNair, B. (1996). Performance in politics and politics of performance: Public relations, the public sphere and democracy. In J. L'Etang & M. Pieczka (eds), *Critical perspectives in public relations* (pp. 35–53). London: International Thomson Business Press.

Michie, D. (1998). *Invisible persuaders: How Britain's spin doctors manipulate the media.* London: Bantam Press.

Miller, D. (ed.). (2003). *Tell me lies: Propaganda and media distortion in the attack on Iraq.* London: Pluto Press.

Mills, S. (1997). *Discourse.* London: Routledge.

Motion, J., & Leitch, S. (1996). A discursive perspective from New Zealand: Another world view. *Public Relations Review, 22*(3), 297–309.

Motion, J., & Weaver, C. K. (2005). A discourse model for critical public relations research: The Life Sciences Network and the battle for truth. *Journal of Public Relations Research, 17,* 1. 49–68.

Palmer, J. (2000). *Spinning into control: News values and source strategies.* London: Leicester University Press.

Philo, G., & Miller, D. (2001). Cultural compliance. In G. Philo & D. Miller (eds), *Market killing: What the free market does and what social scientists can do about it* (pp. 3–95). Harlow: Pearson Education.

Pieczka, M. (1996). Paradigms, systems theory and public relations. In J. L'Etang & M. Pieczka (eds), *Critical perspectives in public relations* (pp. 124–156). London: International Thomson Business Press.

Robins, K., Webster, F., & Pickering, M. (1987). Propaganda, information and social control. In J. Hawthorn (ed.), *Propaganda, persuasion and polemic* (pp. 1–17). London: Edward Arnold.

Roper, J. (2005). Symmetrical communication: Excellent public relations or a strategy for hegemony? *Journal of Public Relations Research*, 17, 1, 69–87.

Sethi, S. P. (1977). *Advocacy advertising and large corporations: Social conflict, big business image, the news media, and public policy.* Lexington, MA: D.C. Heath.

Shugart, H. A. (2003). An appropriating aesthetic: Reproducing power in the discourse of critical scholarship. *Communication Theory*, 13(3), 275–303.

Stauber, J., & Rampton, S. (1995). *Toxic sludge is good for you! Lies, damn lies and the public relations industry.* Monroe, ME: Common Courage Press.

Thompson, J. B. (1988). Mass communication and modern culture: Contribution to a critical theory of ideology. *Sociology*, 22(3), 359–383.

Thomson, O. (1977). *Mass persuasion in history: A historical analysis of the development of propaganda techniques.* Edinburgh: Paul Harris Publishing.

Trujillo, N., & Toth, E. L. (1987). Organizational perspectives for public relations research and practice. *Management Communication Quarterly*, 1(2), 199–281.

Tye, L. (1998). *The father of spin: Edward L. Bernays and the birth of public relations.* New York: Crown.

Weaver, C. K. (2001). Dressing for battle in the new global economy: Putting power, identity, and discourse into public relations theory. *Management Communication Quarterly*, 15(2), 279–288.

Weaver, C. K., & Motion, J. (2002). Sabotage and subterfuge: Public relations, democracy and genetic engineering in New Zealand. *Media Culture & Society*, 24(3), 325–343.

CHAPTER 13

Anne Gregory

Ethics and professionalism in public relations*

Learning outcomes

By the end of this chapter you should be able to:

■ articulate why ethical practice and professionalism are important

■ describe the various ethical traditions and theories and apply them to public relations situations

■ analyse the responsibilities that practitioners have to self, organisation, profession and society and identify potential conflicts

■ describe some of the typical public relations dilemmas facing practitioners and point to appropriate resolutions

■ construct principles on which to build an ethical framework based on 'current' theory and practice

■ choose and use ethical decision-making models.

Structure

■ Importance of ethics and professionalism in public relations

■ Definitions of ethics and morality

■ Ethical theories (traditions)

■ Duty to whom?

■ Ethical issues in public relations

■ Ethical decision-making models and their application

* Chapter 14 in *Exploring Public Relations* Second Edition, edited by Ralph Tench and Liz Yeomans (2009).

Introduction

Recent corporate and political scandals, such as Enron, the activities of Conrad Black, the UK and US governments' presentation of a case for war in Iraq, have brought ethics very much into the spotlight.

In recognition of this, fresh attention has been given to business ethics in general and corporate responsibility (CSR) in particular (see Chapter 7) and to the process and practice of government communication. At the same time, certain activities in the media have also come in for censure. For example, the quest for celebrity information (and the dubious means by which it is obtained) have called into question media ethics.

Communication is at the heart of all these issues. It is a matter of some concern that although professional communicators are frequently faced with ethical decisions or are asked to represent an organisation when there is an ethical problem, very few have had formal ethics training or can articulate the processes they go through when arriving at difficult ethical decisions. It is also worth noting that the media relish covering news stories that focus on corporate or public relations (PR) practitioner ethics and (un)ethical behaviour.

This chapter examines ethics and professionalism. It looks at the various ethical traditions and professional codes of conduct, at the responsibilities of communication professionals and it provides some models for sound ethical decision making.

Importance of ethics and professionalism in public relations

There are many reasons why ethics and professionalism should characterise PR practice, but just five are explored here.

Trust

PR is about building and maintaining relationships. Trust is the key to successful relationships. Dictionary definitions of trust usually include words like reliability, confidence, faith and integrity. Trust is a precious thing, given by one individual to another and once broken, it can rarely be fully restored. If a PR practitioner acts ethically and professionally they are likely to be trusted. They will be described as having integrity – there is something wholesome, honest and trustworthy about them. Being ethical and professional is core to having a good reputation.

It is important for an organisation to be represented by someone who is ethical and professional. It says something about the values and character of the organisation itself. Stakeholders are more likely to trust the organisation and believe what it says if the person representing it is regarded as trustworthy.

The ethical guardian

There is much debate about the role of the practitioner as the guardian of the organisation's ethics. For example, L'Etang (2003) does not see much evidence for this. However, others such as Heath and Ryan (1989) argue that a part of the role of PR practitioners is to monitor the environment to detect various publics' attitudes to certain values. They should then make company managers aware of external ethical standards and help companies implement CSR programmes or develop codes of ethics. Cutlip et al. (2005) argue that an organisation's conduct is improved when PR practitioners stress the need for public approval.

What cannot be denied is that PR people have to justify the decisions and actions of their organisation to a range of publics. They should have, therefore, an acute awareness of what their publics' likely reactions will be and whether there will be a sense of moral outrage or approval. They then need the courage to challenge potential decisions and actions as they are being made and before they become reality. For example, there is increasing disquiet about senior managers being given significant bonuses when their company is in difficulties, at the same time that other employees are being made redundant or having minimal pay increases. In such a situation, it is imperative that the PR professional challenges the decision on moral and ethical grounds – even if there are legal reasons why the payment may have to be made to senior managers.

Social responsibility

Gone are the days when organisations were regarded as just economic entities whose sole responsibility was to make profits (Friedman 1970). Organisations are regarded as having wider responsibilities to society, and the CSR movement has come about largely because organisations have recognised they have responsibilities towards all stakeholding groups, to the environment and to society as a whole. Ongoing Ipsos MORI research (Ipsos MORI

2007) demonstrates quite clearly that organisations increasingly have to respond to stakeholder demands that they fulfil their social responsibilities. Earlier research for the UK Chartered Institute of Public Relations (CIPR) (Ipsos MORI 2002) shows that PR practitioners are usually responsible for communicating CSR policies and activities; indeed, CSR is often placed within the PR remit (see Chapter 7).

Community building and conflict resolution

Linked to the idea of social responsibility is the notion of community building and conflict resolution. This debate around the ideal of community has been stimulated by the *communitarian* movement associated with the American sociologist Amitai Etzioni (see Glossary for definition of **communitarianism**). To function properly, democracy must reflect an open society that is constantly challenging and reappraising its assumptions and values. PR brings to the public debate all kinds of ideas and represents all shades of opinion. As a result of informed debate, collective decisions can be made, citizens accept the democratic will, and society and community is built. As Kruckeburg and Starck (1998: 53) say:

> *A community is achieved when people are aware of and interested in common ends and regulate their activity in view of those ends. Communication plays a vital role as people try to regulate their own activities and to participate in efforts to reach common ends.*

Furthermore, PR builds community by helping to resolve conflict. By engaging in dialogue, understandings can be reached and accommodations made that allow opposing factions to live together with a measure of tolerance. It is worth noting that PR practitioners have been involved in conflict resolution work in Northern Ireland for many years.

Power and obligation

As has been said, trust depends to a large extent on the integrity of individual practitioners. As Seib and Fitzpatrick (1995) assert, one of the reasons PR is subject to so much scrutiny is because it is so powerful and influential (Witherow 2008). The criticism is that it works too well!

With power and influence comes responsibility (Bivins 2006). There is an obligation on practitioners to be as professional as possible. That means taking education and training as seriously as other professions, such as accoun-

Box 13.1

Examples of public relations professional bodies

The following are examples of professional bodies for PR in different countries:

- FERPI in Italy
- MIPR in Malaysia
- PRISA in South Africa
- PRINZ in New Zealand
- PRSA in America
- CIPR in the UK

tancy, law, medicine, building surveying, pharmacy or architecture. Intellectual training, mastery of the technical aspects of the job, management knowledge and ethical training are all important. Practitioners should be members of the appropriate professional body (see Box 13.1), ascribe to its code of conduct and strive to go beyond the minimum requirements. That in itself is an indicator of the seriousness with which they take their own professional calling. It is right and proper that organisations expect the highest standards from their communicators, just as they would from their corporate lawyers or accountants. (See Think about 13.1.)

Think about 13.1

Ethics and professionalism

- Can you think of other reasons why ethics and professionalism are important in PR?
- Do you have an image of PR as an ethical profession? If not, why not?

Feedback

Ethical professionalism is important because it:

- minimises risk to individuals and organisation
- increases standing of the professional
- is right in itself.

Definitions of ethics and morality

So, having given some reasons why ethics and professionalism are important, it is now necessary to clarify some terms.

There is confusion about the words '**morals**' and '**ethics**'; indeed they are often used interchangeably. Strictly speaking, morals are to do with the individual. From being small children we become aware of what is good and what are regarded as right actions. Fairly quickly we get an impression of what it means to be a 'bad' person. That awareness comes from parents, our own thinking and feeling about a situation or person, and from the group and society we are based in. Morals are described simply as our personal **values** or principles. So we speak of people having their own moral code, which might be different from ours. For example, someone with religious beliefs may believe abortion is immoral; someone else in the same society or even the same family will not.

Ethics, on the other hand, means the formal study and codification of moral principles into systematic frameworks so that decisions can be made about what is right and wrong in a reasoned and structured way. Hence, certain parts of the law are obviously framed to support standards of behaviour that have a strong moral basis – for example, the laws on theft and murder.

Trevino and Nelson (2004: 15) make a very clear link between morals and business ethics within organisations (see Figure 13.1). They explain that ethical decision making in organisations comprises 'three basic steps: moral awareness (recognising the existence of an ethical dilemma),

moral judgement (deciding what's right), and ethical behaviour (taking action to do the right thing)'. These steps are influenced by the characteristics of both the individual and the organisation.

McElreath (1997) points out that ethics, as a branch of philosophy, is not just about right and wrong; it is about what is good and what is bad. He quotes PR Professor Don Wright (Wright 1982) who says that ethics is really about being good and that the practitioner's task is to determine what a good action is. Some actions such as honesty, sincerity and truthfulness are essentially good in themselves. Indeed, it was Aristotle who claimed that people can become virtuous by practising the virtues (or, in modern parlance, become good by practising goodness).

The purpose of learning about ethics – frameworks of principles – is so that situations can be evaluated systematically, which encourages consistent behaviour and responses to situations. This is important because consistency is also a key element in building relationships. Being able to explain how and why we have reached a particular decision makes it transparent and understandable, even if the decision itself is unpopular.

Ethical theories (traditions)

Having looked at the connection between morals and ethics, it is now appropriate to look at some of the main frameworks that seek to provide a rational basis for moral judgements and ethical behaviour and at the implication of some of these theories for PR.

Cognitivism and non-cognitivism

The most basic question that ethical theorists ask is, 'Is it possible to know right from wrong?'

The word used by philosophers to define the view that there are *actual* and *objective* moral truths and absolutes is **cognitivism**. Cognitivism enables us to make firm statements about whether an action or belief is good or bad, right or wrong. The opposing school of thought, **non-cognitivism**, states that morality is purely *subjective*, or is bound up with the specific cultural context of individuals. Non-cognitivists say that there are no moral absolutes, only beliefs, attitudes and opinions.

This later, non-cognitivist school of thought, which draws heavily on the work of Kenneth Burke (1969a; 1969b), is represented in the PR literature by rhetorical theorists such as Pearson (1989), Toth and Heath (1992) and Heath (2004). They argue that truths emerge from a process of dialogue, negotiation and debate where individuals even-

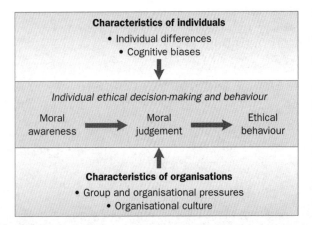

Figure 13.1 Ethical decision making in organisations (*source*: Trevino, L.K. and Nelson, K.A. (2004) *Managing Business Ethics, 3rd Edition*, p. 15 Copyright (c) 2004 John Wiley & Sons. Reprinted with permission of John Wiley & Sons, Inc.)

tually agree on a particular moral truth. They assert that the *process* by which the debate is conducted determines whether it is ethical or not. In this way, Pearson argues that PR 'plays a major role in managing the moral dimension of corporate conduct' (1989: 111). The equity of the process means that people reach a valid consensus, which then has moral authority.

Indeed, they place great stress on the rules for ethical dialogue to maintain its integrity and validity. Habermas (1984) has provided useful insights into what he calls an ideal communication situation. In essence, this requires that participants should test and probe ideas that are proposed, have equal freedom to initiate and continue dialogue, to set the discussion agenda and to challenge and/or explain. In order to do this properly, they must have freedom from manipulation and equality of power. In turn, all those that participate in dialogue become accountable for comprehensibility (ensuring they are understood), truth (factual accuracy), rightness (appropriate to those receiving the communication) and truthfulness (sincerity as well as factual accuracy). For rhetoricians there is almost agnosticism about who wins the argument eventually, as long as the process has integrity.

This view is regarded by many as an ideal to aspire to, but not grounded in reality. As Somerville (2001) points out, although the centrality of dialogue is an attractive proposition, power is a major issue. It is simply not the case that all participants in a dialogue are equal. In addition, dialogue cannot go on indefinitely and the resolution of the point under discussion may not have the agreement of everyone – it may suit the majority, but others may be profoundly opposed.

The value of Pearson's argument is that it promotes the notion that participants have equal value and they are not to be used as a means to an end. In other words, he does protect the 'rights' of individuals to have a voice and having a voice accords them some respect. Giving respect is itself a moral action.

Pearson's approach is supported by other PR academics in the rhetorical school, such as Heath. The point being made by them is that there are no absolute or objective standards of right and wrong. There are only subjective views of what is right and wrong and it is only through dialogue and agreement that moral rules can be arrived at. Communication therefore is a deeply ethical function because it is through it that agreement on right corporate behaviour is reached.

However, most people live their lives on the basis that there are objective standards of good and bad, right and wrong. Cognitivist ethical theories form the bulk of the literature and provide the foundation for most modern approaches to business and personal ethical frameworks. The following section outlines the main schools of thought in cognitivist theory.

Consequentialist theories

Consequentialist theories focus on the *results* or consequences of behaviour. This is often known as the teleological approach, deriving from the Greek words *telos* (end) and *logos* (the study of). Hence teleology is the study of ends. The best known consequentialist theory is *utilitarianism*, which holds that actions must be judged by the effects that they have, in other words, by their utility. Thus decision makers must consciously consider the impact of their actions. A right action is one that causes more benefit (or happiness) than harm. Indeed, ethical decisions should positively seek to maximise benefits and minimise harm in society.

However, there are three major problems with utilitarianism. The first is that it assumes you can predict the consequences of your actions accurately and then make a judgement. In reality this is often not the case: there are situations when just obtaining the facts is difficult enough.

Picture 13.1 Recent corporate and political scandals, such as Enron, have brought ethics very much into the spotlight (*source*: AFP/Getty Images)

For example, if you work for a construction company whose client wants to build a new road through an urban area, would you really know how everyone involved would be affected or what the long-term impact would be? Furthermore, PR practitioners are usually working under time pressures and it is simply not possible to find out. Pragmatic decisions within tight timescales have to be made.

The second major problem is that there can be conflicting benefits and the simple reality is that more weight is given to the views or interests of some stakeholders, whether they are in the majority or not, than others. So, for example, some managers may argue that corporate giving, which is good in itself, has to be limited in order to provide shareholders with a handsome dividend to retain their investment and loyalty.

The third argument against utilitarianism is that it leads to 'ends justifies means' thinking. So utilitarians would say it is acceptable to lie about the state of the company's research and development programme to preserve the jobs of thousands of employees. 'Ends justifies means' thinking can also lead to the sacrificing of individuals or groups for 'the greater good'. Therefore the displacement of indigenous groups so that land can be farmed is argued as ethical because the food produced is used to support the needs of larger communities who need food – the greater number benefit. (See Table 13.1 for a comparison of the theories.)

Non-consequential theories

The second set of cognitivist theories are *non-consequentialist*. This is often known as the deontological approach deriving from the Greek word *deontos* meaning duty.

Deontology is a duty-based ethic and focuses on obligation, principles and rights. It emphasises the duty of human beings to treat others with dignity and respect because they are human beings with rights. Deontologists believe that actions in and of themselves can be judged as right or wrong. They base their decision making on universal principles or values that transcend time or cultural perspectives. Josephson (1993) has identified 10 universal principles that form the basis of ethical life:

1   honesty
2   integrity
3   promise keeping
4   fidelity
5   fairness
6   caring for others
7   respect for others
8   responsible citizenship
9   pursuit of excellence
10 accountability.

Both the UN's (United Nations) Universal Declaration of Human Rights (http://www.un.org/Overview/rights.html) and the US Declaration of Independence (www.law.Indiana.edu/uslawdocs/declaration.html) subscribe to deontological principles by guaranteeing that individuals have certain rights that should not be violated, such as the right to life, liberty, security and equality before the law. It is the duty of society and of individuals to preserve these rights.

Some deontologists focus more on the duties that a person should discharge rather than their rights. They argue that rights can only be preserved when citizens take their duties seriously. Deontology is closely associated with eighteenth-century German philosopher Immanuel Kant, who devised the principle of the **categorical imperative**. This encouraged people to ask themselves if their action was suitable for translation into a universal law or principle that anyone faced with the same situation could follow. Thus, if you tell a lie to get yourself out of a difficult situation, the categorical imperative would demand you ask yourself 'is lying in these circumstances a principle everyone should adopt?' A deontologist decides what the moral law is by applying the universal principles such as those of Josephson quoted earlier. Many deontologists also adopt what is called 'the golden rule'. This is enshrined in many religions in phrases such as, 'Do unto others as you would have them do unto you.'

There are three main problems with deontological reasoning. The first concerns what happens if two moral laws clash. For example, you may have a moral duty to tell the truth, but you also have a moral duty to care for others. So what do you decide if a journalist names an employee and asks you to confirm whether they have had an accident at work before their family has been informed – which law do you obey?

The second is that Kant says you must fulfil your moral obligation irrespective of the consequences. So, for example, Kant would say that you must tell the truth, even if someone suffers as a result.

The third problem is that there is no agreement about what the moral law is. Societies develop and moral per-

Theory	Consequentialist (result of behaviour – the effect it has)	Non-consequentialist (duty – obligations, principles and rights)
Name	Teleological	Deontological
Theoretical example	Utilitarianism	Categorical imperative (Kant)

Table 13.1 Consequentialist vs non-consequentialist cognitivist theories

spectives change or differ from society to society. European culture would hold that executing a murderer is not acceptable. Mainstream North American culture believes that 'a life for a life' is a moral imperative.

Virtue ethics

Virtue ethics look more at the motivations of an individual rather than at their actions per se or the consequences of their actions. Character is all important. This does not mean that principles or consequences are unimportant, but they are considered in the light of the individual's character. For example, did the individual act honestly? Did they follow a principle, such as their professional code of conduct? Did they attempt to do no harm?

Character is, of course, difficult to define and it is intimately bound up with the community an individual inhabits. Bravery in one community may be regarded as barbarity in another. For PR practitioners this requires a detailed examination of the communities they inhabit. You may be a churchgoer, belong to a professional association or work in a company that has a business code of ethics. In any situation you should ask which community would have the highest standards and then apply those rules. Being a virtuous PR practitioner also means that you abide by the highest standards of the professional institute that represents the community of PR practitioners.

The value of virtue ethics is that it allows you to take on board appropriate standards without having to go through all the teleological or deontological arguments for yourself. The idea is that you draw on the wisdom of your peers who will have done the hard thinking on your behalf.

The two problems with virtue ethics are first that your 'community' might not have thought about your situation and, second, your 'community' might not have got it right. This can be a particular issue when PR practitioners are working overseas and they try to apply their ethnocentric principles in other cultures. However, a useful rule of thumb to apply when considering virtue ethics and the norms of a community is the 'disclosure rule'. That is, 'would I feel comfortable if my behaviour appeared on the front page of the local newspaper or if my family knew I'd done this?'

Situational ethics

There is one other school of thinking that is worth exploring and which, according to Pratt (1993), is prevalent in PR practice in the USA. Situational ethics asserts that no moral law or principle is absolute; indeed the situation itself alters the rules. Therefore, part of our moral responsibility is to put aside the rules for the greater good and do whatever the situation demands. At first this seems a sensible and pragmatic approach: modern life is so complex that it is difficult to come up with rules that can be applied across the board. However, it is not that easy. If a system of ethics depends on situations or contexts and each one is different, it loses the value of being systematic. We may as well say that ethics as such do not matter; everyone can run their life by merely considering what is happening in the current situation. However, there is a big difference between situational ethics and considering the situation when making ethical decisions. It is worth explaining this further as Martinson (1998) does (see Activity 13.1). Modern

Activity 13.1

Theory in practice

Martinson (1998) gives a case where circumstances do play a significant part. A college wants to dismiss a sports coach because of financial misjudgements. They 'allow' the coach to resign voluntarily and take another job in the college. The coach agrees to this. The college director tells the PR person to announce the resignation, but say nothing about the circumstances. How should the PR person respond when a local journalist asks for the 'real reason' for the resignation?

Take the same situation, but this time the problem is the coach has a drug addiction and he has been stealing funds to support his habit. What does the practitioner do now when asked for the 'real reasons'?

Feedback

In the first case, many people would say disclosure of additional facts is not appropriate. Promises have been made to the coach and there are limits to the public's 'right to know'. It is dubious that in this case the 'whole truth' is necessary. Some would argue that disclosure is the best policy and it is in the public interest that people know if public funds have been misused. In this context there is a genuine but reasoned argument for and against further disclosure to the press.

However, in the second example things are quite different. The coach's behaviour was illegal and his actions could endanger the well-being of others. In this circumstance it would be difficult to justify withholding the information.

The situations are different, but the ethical platform is clear – to communicate truthfully to those who have a right and a need to know and to act in the public interest. The principle can be universalised (deontological perspective) and the greater good for the greatest number (teleological perspective) is satisfied. This is very different from saying that moral principles do not apply and that the situation must dictate our response.

ethical theory states that three determinants must be considered to decide whether an action is ethical:

■ the act itself or what one does (the object)

■ the motives, why one does it (the end)

■ the circumstances, or how, where, when, etc. one does it.

So if a practitioner holds a press conference, the act (object) itself is morally neutral. If the motive is to provide accurate information then the act and the motive are ethical. If the motive is to mislead, then the entire action is unethical. In circumstances where the situation (or context) is also neutral, the discussion can end there.

Most people who work in PR have not been trained in moral philosophical systems and this has led Ryan and Martinson (1984: 27) to suggest that:

> If public relations has adopted any underlying principle, it is possibly the subjectivism (or individual relativism) theory that each individual must establish his or her own moral baseline . . . The only real constraint is that an individual be able to live with an action – at least for the short-term.

(See Think about 13.2.)

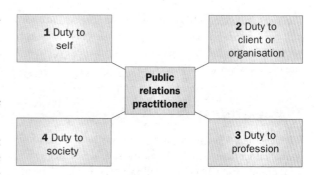

Figure 13.2 Loyalties and duties of practice (*source*: based on Seib and Fitzpatrick 1995)

Think about 13.2

Which philosophical approach

Which philosophical approach is most attractive to you? Utilitarianism, duty ethics, virtue ethics or situational ethics? List three reasons why.

Duty to whom?

Having considered various ethical frameworks, it is now time to look at the individual practitioner and examine the obligations that they have. One of the most difficult things for practitioners is reconciling the sometimes conflicting loyalties and duties that they have. Seib and Fitzpatrick (1995) identify four categories of duty (see Figure 13.2).

Duty to self

Practitioners should first look at their own value system and personal ethical codes. This requires detailed thought and is not always easy to do. Personal ethical codes will dictate whether they can work for certain organisations or undertake particular types of activity. In the final resort,

career choices and resignations are based on practitioners taking seriously their duty to maintain their own ethical standards.

Duty to client or organisation

Having decided to take the financial reward, many practitioners believe their primary duty is to their clients or organisations. Despite their own personal codes, they believe it to be their professional duty to represent their organisation to the best of their ability, rather like a lawyer represents a client or a doctor treats a person whose personal beliefs they oppose.

There are objections to the legal parallel. In the sphere of public debate there is no judge to oversee fair play and there is no trained opponent with a guaranteed voice who can marshal alternative views and interpretations. Big organisations have vast resources, are generally more powerful and sometimes act to suppress opposing voices. Furthermore, when lawyers defend clients they do not condone their client's crime. In the case of PR, organisational actions in themselves are defended and practitioners are directly associated with those actions because they are often employees or are retained specifically to defend the actions of an organisation (Martinson 1999). Lawyers are participating in the *process* of justice, which demands representation for the accused. In legal cases a defendant has a *right* to a defence; organisations do not have similar rights. They can *request* services from those willing to offer them.

Conversely, some practitioners regard it as their duty to bring all the facts to the public debate even if they may be under pressure not to do so. Regulated animal laboratories are legal enterprises and it is fair and proper that in open and democratic societies they should be able to put their case in a persuasive way. It is then up to the public to make up their own minds having had both sides of the argument explained to them. Democracy is about informed citizens making informed choices.

While there may be professional disagreements about whether a company should be represented, condoning activities that constitute a risk to others is not acceptable. Practitioners who knowingly support harmful activities violate their wider duty to society and this higher duty must take precedence. For example, defending the harvesting of scarce resources for profit alone is not acceptable.

Duty to profession

It can be assumed that a practitioner has a duty to support their profession and their professional colleagues. In this way common standards of behaviour can be agreed and the bounds of acceptable practice established. Very important here are the professional codes of conduct (see Appendices 1 and 2 for the UK Chartered Institute of Public Relations and the Global Alliance codes). These encapsulate principles of ethical practice and provide the basic standards for practitioners. It is a tough decision to argue with an insistent client or employer, but, at a minimum, the codes will alert them to the fact they are asking the practitioner to act unethically and will provide the practitioner with tangible support for an argument against taking a particular course of action.

Although it is often the case that organisations will *wish* their PR practitioners to be a member of a professional body, some organisations *require* those PR practitioners who contact them on behalf of others to ascribe to a code of conduct. Box 13.2 displays the EU Code, which applies to all public affairs practitioners who represent organisations or clients.

Box 13.2

Code of Conduct for Interest Representatives

Interest representation is a legitimate part of a democratic system. The European Commission, in its effort to enhance public confidence, has established a voluntary Register and adopted this Code of Conduct to bring more transparency to interest representation, its actors and their activities.

The present Code contains seven basic rules, specifying how interest representatives should behave when representing their interests. Registrants agree to abide by this Code or declare that they already abide by a professional code that has comparable rules. 'Interest representation' activities for which registration is expected are defined as 'activities carried out with the objective of influencing the policy formulation and decision-making processes of the European institutions'.

This definition does not include:

- Activities concerning legal and other professional advice, in so far as they relate to the exercise of the fundamental right to a fair trial of a client, including the right of defence in administrative proceedings, such as carried out by lawyers or by any other professionals involved therein;

- Activities of the social partners as actors in the social dialogue (trade unions, employers associations, etc.). However, when such actors engage in activities falling outside the role conferred on them

by the Treaties, they are expected to register in order to guarantee a level playing field between all the interests represented;

- Activities in response to the Commission's direct request, such as ad hoc or regular requests for factual information, data or expertise, invitations to public hearings, or participation in consultative committees or in any similar fora.

- The Commission recognises that the mission of most organisations engaged in interest representation is wider than the activities for which registration is expected. They engage in activities such as the production of studies, statistics and other information and documentation as well as the provision of training and capacity building for members or clients which fall outside the scope of this definition, if not related to activities of interest representation.

Principles

Interest representatives are expected to apply the principles of openness, transparency, honesty and integrity, as legitimately expected of them by citizens and other stakeholders.

Similarly, Members of the Commission and staff are bound by strict rules ensuring their impartiality. The relevant provisions are public and contained in the Treaty establishing the European Community, the Staff Regulations, the Code of Conduct for Commissioners and the Code of good administrative behaviour.

Rules

Interest representatives shall always:

(1) identify themselves by name and by the entity(ies) they work for or represent;

box 13.2 (continued)

(2) not misrepresent themselves as to the effect of registration to mislead third parties and/or EU staff;

(3) declare the interests, and where applicable the
clients or the members, which they represent;

(4) ensure that, to the best of their knowledge, information which they provide is unbiased, complete,
up-to-date and not misleading;

(5) not obtain or try to obtain information, or any
decision, dishonestly;

(6) not induce EU staff to contravene rules and standards of behaviour applicable to them;

(7) if employing former EU staff, respect their obligation
to abide by the rules and confidentiality requirements which apply to them.

Other Provisions

■ Breaches of the Code. Registered entities are informed and agree that breaches of the above rules

by their representatives may lead to suspension or
exclusion from the Register following a Commission
administrative process paying due respect to pro-
portionality and the right of defence.

■ Complaints. Registered entities are informed
that anyone can lodge a complaint with the Commission, substantiated by material facts, about a
suspected breach of the above rules.

■ Publication of contributions and other documents.
Registered entities are informed that their contributions to public consultations will be published
on the internet together with the identity of the contributor, unless the contributor objects to publication of the personal data on grounds that such
publication would harm his or her legitimate interests. The Commission may, upon request and subject to the provisions of Regulation (EC) No
1049/2001 on access to documents, have to disclose correspondence and other documents concerning the interest representatives' activities.

Duty to society

At the beginning of most PR codes of conduct is a statement
that the practitioner's primary responsibility is to society
or to the public interest. While this is a noble aspiration,
it is a complex one to unpack. First of all, what is society?
Is it local, national, international? What about the cultural
values and loyalty differences? And what does 'in the public
interest' mean? Clearly it is impossible to serve everyone's
interests all the time, and interests are sometimes in conflict.

Grunig and Hunt (1984), Bivins (1993) and the rhetorical school of PR (see Chapter 3) would argue that symmetric PR, or genuine dialogue, is at the heart of the public
interest. By engaging in dialogue, PR encourages public and
informed debate, clarity of argument is facilitated, good
democratic decisions can be made and communities are

reinforced. This is all in the public interest (Fitzpatrick 2006).

Another way to look at this in practical terms is to ask
if your actions harm anyone and, more positively, whether
you are making a valuable contribution that will enable
people to live more informed and/or better lives. (See
Think about 13.3.)

Ethical issues in public relations

Bearing in mind these various, and sometimes conflicting
duties, it is now appropriate to look at some of the areas
where PR practitioners encounter ethical problems.

Think about 13.3   Prioritising interests

Describe one example from recent news stories where
you think an organisation has put its own interests
above those of society.

Feedback

Examples of news stories where an organisation has
put its interests before those of society include:

■ dumping of toxic waste near residential areas

■ large increases in director salaries while closing
down factories in economically depressed areas

■ moving operations to countries where there are less
stringent employee safety regulations and putting
those employees at risk (e.g. stripping out dangerous toxins from recycled materials without adequate
protection).

Competence

If PR describes itself as a 'profession', then there are obligations laid on it to provide expert, objective advice of the highest possible standard. Seib and Fitzpatrick (1995) describe two areas of concern in the provision of professional services – *malfeasance* and *incompetence*. Malfeasance is providing services that should not be provided. So, for example, dentists should not, normally, remove healthy teeth. Similarly, PR people should not conduct campaigns they know will be ineffective or which are unnecessary. This is sometimes a tough call when there is money to be made or if another consultancy is willing to do this work, especially if the first consultancy wishes to protect the jobs of its employees.

Incompetence means that the practitioners undertaking the work do not have the necessary knowledge or experience to undertake it to the highest professional standards. It is tempting for consultancies to expand their business into areas where they have no expertise if a lucrative client has work to offer!

The UK CIPR Code of Conduct in its section on integrity, competence and maintaining professional standards is very clear that only work that is within the practitioner's competence should be undertaken.

Parsons (2004) suggests that the responsibility to be competent has three elements:

- Ensure you have the skills necessary to do the work assigned to you.
- Keep your knowledge, skills and expertise up to date.
- Ensure you do not give employers or clients the impression you can guarantee specific results.

This last point is an important one and raises an associated issue, namely 'overpromising', which seems endemic in the PR community. It is done for two main reasons, both of which are unacceptable. First, practitioners themselves have an unrealistic view of what can be achieved and, second, they will 'do what it takes' to obtain or retain the business.

Conflicts of interest

The UK CIPR Code of Conduct states that conflicts of interest (or circumstances that may give rise to them) must be declared in writing to clients, potential clients and employers as soon as they arise. It is then up to the client or employer to decide whether they consent to their work being continued. Usually conflicts of interest are easy to identify, for example, representing two supermarket chains is a case in point. However, situations are dynamic and something that did not originally create a conflict can

develop into one. For example, a consultancy may represent a supermarket chain and an optician chain. No conflict there – until the supermarket decides to open an in-store optician service. The consultancy should declare their interest to both clients and may even decide to take the initiative and resign one of the accounts. Mergers and acquisitions can sometimes present similar challenges as the environment and circumstances for the organisation(s) change.

Even if the clients decide that the consultancy can represent both organisations, there are operational difficulties: Will unintended favouritism develop? What about confidentiality? The CIPR code states ' "insider" information must not be disclosed'. What if this information is to the major benefit or disadvantage of the other client?

Conflicts of interest can also occur when individual interests clash with client interests. It could be very difficult for a consultancy employee to represent a tobacco company if a relative has a smoking-related disease. Many consultancies have 'conscience clauses' that allow employees to opt out of undertaking work that poses a conflict of interest or a particular moral dilemma.

'Whistleblowing'

PR people often know the most intimate details about organisations – warts and all. What happens if a practitioner discovers serious misconduct? For example, they may become aware that the company accountant is tipping off investment analysts that the company is about to be taken over. They have a responsibility to do something in the public interest (perhaps even become a **whistleblower**). In the UK there is a charity called Public Concern at Work (www.pcaw.co.uk), which will provide advice to anyone who believes they have unearthed unethical practice and is unsure how to proceed. In some countries, the law also provides some protection so that employees are not victimised for safeguarding the public interest.

The media

Seib and Fitzpatrick (1995) and Parsons (2004) point out the manifold ethical pitfalls of dealing with the media. The relationship is an important one because it is the core of much PR activity and because of the peculiar nature of the mutual dependencies that develop.

Accuracy and honesty should be an aspiration of both journalism and PR professions and there are issues that need to be confronted. When does cultivating journalists and providing them with hospitality and gifts turn effectively into bribery? What obligation does the free use of an expensive car put on a motoring journalist? What if some companies do not provide these things? Are they 'disadvantaged'?

Linked to truth telling is the issue of misleading by omission. It is perfectly possible to tell a partial story knowing that by omitting some key information the media (or any other receiver) will make assumptions that might be false. If a practitioner has clearly sought to mislead, this would be unethical.

Questions also arise over whether the whole truth should be told. Full disclosure is usually a good rule of thumb, but it is not always the right thing to do. Individuals need protecting in certain circumstances as the Kelly case (Mini case study 13.1) illustrates and it is debatable whether the revelation of his name was genuinely in the public interest.

Parsons (2004) suggests that four pillars support ethical media relations:

- honesty and accuracy
- judiciousness (e.g. knowing when and how to use the media)
- responsiveness
- respect.

(See Think about 13.4.)

Picture 13.2 Corporate bullying can put an individual under pressure and lead to ethical dilemmas (*source*: Getty Images)

Mini Case Study 13.1
Truth telling in practice

What does telling the truth entail? In 2003, the UK government Ministry of Defence communicators told the truth when confirming Dr David Kelly was the source for the BBC reporter, Andrew Gilligan. Gilligan had claimed, in a live radio broadcast, that according to his source the government had knowingly included false or 'sexed up' information about weapons of mass destruction in its dossier of evidence for going to war in Iraq. The consequences of being correctly named as the source were devastating for Dr Kelly personally – who committed suicide – and arguably for world affairs, which were significantly impacted by the events. While the subsequent Hutton Inquiry blamed the BBC more than the government for this series of events, there are still arguments about the truth of Gilligan's original report. However, this case shows that telling the truth can sometimes have devastating results. Truth on its own is not enough. Confidentiality, duty of care and judgement all need to come into the equation.

Think about 13.4

Ethical issues in public relations

Give three more examples of ethical issues in PR.

Feedback

Examples of other ethical issues include:

- personal relationships with suppliers, journalists, senior managers, etc.
- offering preferential treatment to certain media outlets, e.g. exclusives on a regular basis
- hospitality to key opinion formers
- payment to journalists for work, e.g. writing for customer magazine
- respecting intellectual property of suppliers/ potential suppliers, e.g. of consultants pitching for business
- use of 'off-the-record' briefings to gag or exploit media contacts.

Ethical decision-making models and their application

The next obvious question then is: how can practitioners make ethical decisions that are soundly based and which stand up to scrutiny?

We will now look at three aspects of the decision-making process: the individual, external guides and the decision-making process itself.

The individual

Ethical reasoning begins at home, with each individual. American psychologist Lawrence Kohlberg (1981) said that people go through three levels of moral development, each comprising two stages:

Level 1:
Stage 1: obey rules and avoid punishment
Stage 2: serve own needs, make fair deals

Level 2:
Stage 3: be loyal/good to others and positively conform to rules
Stage 4: do one's duty to society

Level 3:
Stage 5: uphold basic rights, values and contract of society
Stage 6: follow universal ethical principles

Kohlberg asserts that as children we do things to avoid punishment and seek to satisfy our own needs. For example, a child learns that if they behave as their parents want them to, they will escape punishment and get more of what they want. As we get older and more mature we are able to consider other people and act in self-restricting or even self-sacrificing ways because we believe that is the right thing to do. Of course, not everyone reaches that stage of development (some never get beyond level 1).

Whether or not you agree with Kohlberg, there are some important things here including an appreciation of yourself, a respect for others, a belief that you have certain obligations and duties and a value system that provides you with some guiding principles (Boynton 2006). This may be provided by a religious or philosophical code or by a self-constructed code of belief. In recent research, it was discovered that senior PR practitioners had a strong personal belief system that carried over into the way they behaved at work (Gregory 2008).

External guides

Having a personal set of values is a good starting point, but it is useful to have them validated by external and more objective sources.

The starting point is the law. Legally binding regulatory codes (in your country or society) such as the criminal law, rights legislation or financial regulations describe what is regarded as acceptable or ethical behaviour in society at large. However, the law has its limitations. What is legally acceptable is not always socially acceptable. CSR programmes usually go beyond what is required in law because minimum workers' rights or minimum environmental standards are not seen as being in the spirit of CSR which seeks not only to do no harm, but to make a positive contribution to society (see also Chapter 7).

Another external reference point is company and/or industry codes of practices. In the confectionery industry, many companies are now ensuring that their advertising is not targeted at younger children because of the issue of obesity. Cadbury is one such company with a strict code of practice on this – see marketing codes of conduct at http://www.cadbury.com/ourresponsibilities/consumer/ourmarketingcode/Pages/ourmarketingcode.aspx. Most companies have internal codes of conduct that cover things like conflicts of interest, the acceptance of gifts or what to do in cases of harassment, such as that operating at Coca-Cola, for example (see http://www.cokecorporateresponsibility.co.uk/marketplace/how_we_conduct_our_business.html).

Then there are the professional and business codes of conduct. The UK CIPR's Code of Conduct has already been mentioned, but it is useful to look at other professional codes for guidance. Useful sources of information are the Institute of Directors (www.IoD.co.uk), Business in the Community (www.bitc.org.uk), the Institute of Business Ethics (www.Ibe.org.uk) and the Global Reporting Initiative (www.globalreporting.org), which offers sound advice on how to put together CSR reports. The Global Alliance of Public Relations and Communication Management (www.globalalliancepr.org) offers advice on global PR ethics and how to practise in a wide range of countries.

Ethical decision-making models

Parsons (2004: 21) provides five 'pillars' that she claims 'carry the weight of ethical decision-making in public relations':

- veracity (tell the truth)
- non-malfeasance (do no harm)
- beneficence (do good)
- confidentiality (respect privacy)
- fairness (to be fair and socially responsible).

Using these pillars in the form of questions can help you recognise if there is an ethical issue (Parsons 2004: 142):

Mini Case Study 13.2
A financial services company

Financial Services plc has been downsizing because the increasingly competitive nature of the industry requires it to cut costs. It has been in discussions about a merger with Money Investment plc, which is in difficulties. Although rumours are rife, negotiations have not been completed. You are asked to issue a press release to respond to rumours, but senior management ask you to play things down and say discussions are at a very early stage. You know that discussions are well advanced and the company will make a formal announcement early next month. What do you do?

Using Potter's box, you first analyse the situation. You have been asked to put out misleading information on matters that are very important to some key stakeholders. When this is discovered you will be regarded as unethical and your reputation will be damaged. There may even be legal implications.

Second, you identify the values that are important; honesty and integrity may feature.

Third, you select the relevant ethical principles. What about Stock Exchange (legal) rules? Are there any issues with the financial services regulators? What about industry and company codes of conduct? What about the national public relations institute (e.g. in the UK the CIPR Code)? What about your personal ethics – don't lie, be loyal to your employer, do to others what you would want others to do to you?

Fourth, prioritise your stakeholders, who may include: Stock Exchange, regulators, shareholders, employees, customers, financial media, self, the industry.

This will be an uncomfortable business since it will force you to confront tough decisions about values and publics, but your decision (whatever it is), will be better and more consistent for it and you will have gone through a demonstrably rigorous process.

- Is there harm involved?
- Is there a missed opportunity to do something good?
- Could anyone be misled in any way?
- Will anyone's privacy be invaded?
- Is it unfair to assume?
- Does it feel wrong?

There are several ethical decision-making frameworks that can be used and a number are particularly applicable to PR. One of the more well known is that devised by Ralph Potter of Harvard Divinity School and known as the Potter box (see Figure 13.3, Seib and Fitzpatrick 1995).

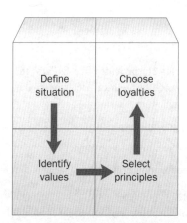

Figure 13.3 The Potter box (*source*: from *Public Relations Ethics*, 1st edition by Seib and Fitzpatrick © 1995)

Potter defined four steps in ethical decision making:

1. *Define situation*: get all the relevant facts. What led to the situation? What is it now? Who is involved? Are there different views? What is the context?
2. *Identify values*: what personal values apply here? (Remember Josephson's universal values.) What values can you draw from professional codes of practice? Are there legal guidelines?
3. *Select principles*: choose the decision-making framework that you and/or your company espouses, for example the virtue ethics approach.
4. *Choose loyalties*: prioritise all the stakeholders who demand your loyalty. Different situations will force you to choose your highest loyalty. For example, if your employer is doing something illegal, your loyalty to society must come first. If your company is being unjustly attacked, your loyalty to the company will come to the fore (see Mini case study 13.2).

Sims (1992) offers an equally useful model, which involves seven steps. He devised it specifically to help working practitioners who were faced with ethical dilemmas:

1. Recognise and clarify the dilemma.
2. Get all the possible facts, list *all* your options.
3. Test each option by asking is it legal? Is it right? Is it beneficial?
4. Make your decision.
5. Double-check your decision by asking: how would I feel if my family found out about this?

6   How would I feel if my decision was printed in the local newspaper?

7   Take action.

These models are, of course, only models, but they do show a pattern of thinking that can be useful to practitioners. They do not state which values or stakeholders should have priority – that is up to the practitioner to decide – but they do offer a useful framework to ensure that decision making is logical, rigorous, defendable and transparent, and that is critically important. They also help consistency of decision making, which helps build trust and credibility. (See Mini case study 13.3 and Activity 13.2.)

Mini Case Study 13.3
Global Alliance Protocol

The Global Alliance Ethics Protocol is given in Appendix 2. Here is an example from its website of its decision-making framework in action.

Scenario: Your consultancy represents the National Cement and Asphalt Contractors Association (NCACA) in Italy. You have been asked to organise the Livorno Citizens for Active Road Expansion (LCARE), sponsored by the Association.

You have been asked by the media about LCARE.

What do you tell them?

1   *Define specific ethical issues:*
    Is it ethical to omit sponsor information?
    Is it ethical to disseminate false information regarding LCARE?

2   *Identify internal/external factors that may influence the decision-making process:*
    Do local state or federal laws play a role?
    What are my consultancy's values policies or procedures?
    What action do I believe is in the public's best interest?

3   *Identify key values:*
    Honesty
    Fairness
    Independence

4   *Identify affected parties:*
    Livorno citizens
    Voters
    Government officials
    Media
    PR professions
    Colleagues/employees/self

5   *Select ethical principles:*
    Disclosure of information
    Open communication fosters informed decision making in democratic society

6   *Make a decision:*
    Responsible advocacy requires that those affected be given due consideration
    Appropriate action dictates a truthful response to the media disclosing your client as the sponsor of LCARE

Source: http://www.globalalliancepr.org/content/1/1/homepage

Activity 13.2

Public relations ethics

1   Draw up your own personal ethical code.

2   Do you think PR consultants should not represent any legally constituted organisation? List your reasons. Are there any organisations you would not work for? Why?

3   Look at the ethical decision-making models in McElreath (1997) and Seib and Fitzpatrick (1995). Which one do you think is most appropriate for PR practitioners? Why?

4   What are the key differences between 'putting a good, but fair gloss' on something and unacceptable 'spinning'?

5   If the press asked you to name an individual employee who was suspected of sexual harassment of young employees, how would you handle it? Articulate your decision-making process.

Feedback

■ For guidance on personal ethics codes, see Parsons 2004.

■ Decision-making models. Reasons why one model may be chosen over another might include: ease of use under pressure, simple to explain to others, aligns with my own moral stance, is similar to company code of ethics.

■ Key differences between a 'good gloss' and 'spinning'. The key issue is the intention to deceive. A good gloss should provide recipients of the information with a fair and truthful representation of a company, even if it is a positive representation. If other information is obtained, the recipient of the 'good gloss' should still recognise the representation as reflecting the facts. 'Spinning' implies that people will not receive a fair representation. Either the omissions of fact may be so great as to allow the recipients to draw false conclusions (and the information originator is aware of this), or misleading information may be included or implied.

Summary

This chapter has sought to provide some of the reasons why ethics in PR is important and why it is complex and challenging. However, just because something is difficult doesn't mean it should not be done. Reflecting deeply about your own personal values is hard. Reconciling all the conflicting demands on your loyalties is hard. Understanding all the various philosophical and theoretical frameworks that are designed to help you in the process is not easy. Despite all this, it is worth every bit of effort.

Being viewed by your peers and the people that you interact with as a person of judgement and integrity is a mark not only of your professionalism, but also of your personal character. People of integrity are most highly regarded; it is one of the keys to having a good reputation. For an individual of reputation to be in charge of an organisation's most precious asset, the relationships on which its own reputation is founded, is good news indeed. Furthermore, for people of high reputation to be involved in the profession of PR can only mean that, over time, the standing of the whole industry will improve.

Bibliography

Bivins, T.H. (1993). 'Public relations, professionalism, and the public interest'. *Journal of Business Ethics* 12: 117–126.

Bivins, T.H. (2006). 'Responsibility and accountability' in *Ethics in Public Relations: Responsible Advocacy*. K.R. Fitzpatrick and C.Bronstein (eds). Thousand Oaks, CA: Sage.

Boynton, L.A. (2006). 'A Delphi study to identify key values that guide ethical decision-making in public relations. *Public Relations Review* 4(32): 325–330.

Burke, K. (1969a). *A Grammar of Motives*. Berkeley, CA: University of California Press.

Burke, K. (1969b). *A Rhetoric of Motives*. Berkeley, CA: University of California Press.

Cutlip, S.M., A.H. Center and G.M. Broom (2005). *Effective Public Relations*, 9th edition. Upper Saddle River, NJ: Prentice Hall International.

Etzioni, A. (1995). *The Spirit of Community: Rights, responsibilities and the communitarian agenda*. London: Fontana.

Fitzpatrick, K. R. and C. Bronstein (2006). *Ethics in Public Relations*. Thousand Oaks, CA: Sage.

Fitzpatrick, K.R. (2006). 'Baselines for Ethical Advocacy' in *Ethics in Public Relations: Responsible Advocacy*. K.R. Fitzpatrick and C. Bronstein (eds). Thousand Oaks, CA: Sage.

Friedman, M. (1970). 'The social responsibility of business is to increase its profits'. *The New York Times Magazine*, 13 September.

Gregory, A. (2008). 'Competencies of senior communication practitioners in the UK: An initial study'. *Public Relations Review* 34(3): 215–223.

Grunig, J.E. and T. Hunt (1984). *Managing Public Relations*. New York: Holt, Rinehart & Winston.

Habermas, J. (1984). *The Theory of Communicative Action, Vol. 1: Reason and the rationalization of society*. (T. McCarthy, trans.). Boston, MA: Beacon.

Heath, R.L. (2004). 'Shifting foundations: Public relations as relationship building' in *Handbook of Public Relations*. R.L. Heath (ed.). Thousand Oaks, CA: Sage.

Heath, R. and M. Ryan (1989). 'Public relations role in defining corporate and social responsibility'. *Journal of Mass Media Ethics* 4(1): 21–38.

Ipsos MORI (2002). 'Operating and Financial Review'. Research study for the Institute of Public Relations 2002.

Ipsos MORI (2007). *Annual Corporate Social Responsibility Study*. London: Ipsos MORI.

Josephson, M. (1993). 'Teaching ethical decision making and principled reasoning'. *Business Ethics*, Annual edition 1993–1994. Guilford, CN: Daskin Publishing Group.

Kohlberg, L. (1981). *The Meaning and Measurement of Moral Development*. Worcester, MA: Clark University Press.

Kruckeburg, D. and K. Starck (1988). *Public Relations and Community: A reconstructed theory*. New York: Praeger.

L'Etang, J. (2003). 'The myth of the "ethical guardian"'. *Journal of Communication Management* 8(1): 22–25.

Martinson, D.C. (1998). 'Public relations practitioners must not confuse consideration of the situation with "situation ethics"'. *Public Relations Quarterly*, Winter 1997–98: 39–43.

Martinson, D.C. (1999). 'Is it ethical for practitioners to represent "bad" clients?' *Public Relations Quarterly* 44(4): 22–25.

McElreath, M. (1997). *Managing Systematic and Ethical Public Relations Campaigns*. Madison, WN: Brown & Benchmark.

Parsons, P. (2004). *Ethics in Public Relations*. London: Kogan Page.

Pearson, R. (1989). 'Business ethics as communication ethics: Public relations practice and the idea of dialogue' in *Public Relations Theory*. C.H. Botan and V. Hazelton (eds). Mahwah, NJ: Lawrence Erlbaum Associates.

Pratt, C.B. (1993). 'Critique of the classical theory of situational ethics in US public relations'. *Public Relations Review*, Fall.

Ryan, M. and D.L. Martinson (1984). 'Ethical values, the flow of journalistic information and public relations person'. *Journalism Quarterly*, Spring.

Seib, P. and K. Fitzpatrick (1995). *Public Relations Ethics*. Forth Worth, TX: Harcourt Brace.

Sims, R.R. (1992). 'The challenge of ethical behaviour in organisations'. *Journal of Business Ethics* 11.

Somerville, I. (2001). 'Business ethics, public relations and social responsibility' in *The Public Relations Handbook*. A. Theaker (ed.). London: Routledge.

Toth, E.L. and R.L. Heath (eds) (1992). *Rhetorical and Critical Approaches to Public Relations*. Hillsdale, NJ: Lawrence Erlbaum Associates.

Trevino, L.K. and K.A. Nelson (2004). *Managing Business Ethics*, 3rd edition. Hoboken, NJ: John Wiley & Sons.

Witherow, J. (2008). *The Sunday Programme*. BBC Radio 4. Broadcast 16 March.

Wright, D.K. (1982). 'The philosophy of ethical development in public relations' in *Managing Systematic and Ethical Public Relations Campaigns*. M. McElreath (1997). Madison, WN: Brown & Benchmark.

Appendix 1: Chartered Institute of Public Relations Code of Conduct

CIPR Principles

1. Members of the Chartered Institute of Public Relations agree to:

   i. Maintain the highest standards of professional endeavour, integrity, confidentiality, financial propriety and personal conduct;

   ii. Deal honestly and fairly in business with employers, employees, clients, fellow professionals, other professions and the public;

   iii. Respect the customs, practices and codes of clients, employers, colleagues, fellow professionals and other professions in all countries where they practise;

   iv. Take all reasonable care to ensure employment best practice including giving no cause for complaint of unfair discrimination on any grounds;

   v. Work within the legal and regulatory frameworks affecting the practice of public relations in all countries where they practise;

   vi. Encourage professional training and development among members of the profession;

   vii. Respect and abide by this Code and related Notes of Guidance issued by the Chartered Institute of Public Relations and encourage others to do the same.

Principles of Good Practice

2. Fundamental to good public relations practice are:

Integrity

- Honest and responsible regard for the public interest;
- Checking the reliability and accuracy of information before dissemination;
- Never knowingly misleading clients, employers, employees, colleagues and fellow professionals about the nature of representation or what can be competently delivered and achieved;
- Supporting the CIPR Principles by bringing to the attention of the CIPR examples of malpractice and unprofessional conduct.

Competence

- Being aware of the limitations of professional competence: without limiting realistic scope for development, being willing to accept or delegate only that work for which practitioners are suitably skilled and experienced;
- Where appropriate, collaborating on projects to ensure the necessary skill base.

Transparency and conflicts of interest

- Disclosing to employers, clients or potential clients any financial interest in a supplier being recommended or engaged;
- Declaring conflicts of interest (or circumstances which may give rise to them) in writing to clients, potential clients and employers as soon as they arise;
- Ensuring that services provided are costed and accounted for in a manner that conforms to accepted business practice and ethics.

Confidentiality

- Safeguarding the confidences of present and former clients and employers;
- Being careful to avoid using confidential and 'insider' information to the disadvantage or prejudice of clients and employers, or to self-advantage of any kind;
- Not disclosing confidential information unless specific permission has been granted or the public interest is at stake or if required by law.

Maintaining Professional Standards

3. CIPR members are encouraged to spread awareness and pride in the public relations profession where practicable by, for example:

   - Identifying and closing professional skills gaps through the Institute's Continuous Professional Development programme;

- Offering work experience to students interested in pursuing a career in public relations;

- Participating in the work of the Institute through the committee structure, special interest and vocational groups, training and networking events;

- Encouraging employees and colleagues to join and support the CIPR;

- Displaying the CIPR designatory letters on business stationery;

- Specifying a preference for CIPR applicants for staff positions advertised;

- Evaluating the practice of public relations through use of the CIPR Research & Evaluation Toolkit and other quality management and quality assurance systems (e.g. ISO standards); and constantly striving to improve the quality of business performance;

- Sharing information on good practice with members and, equally, referring perceived examples of poor practice to the Institute.

Appendix 2: Global Alliance Ethics Protocol

Declaration of Principles

A profession is distinguished by certain characteristics or attributes, including:

- Mastery of a particular intellectual skill through education and training

- Acceptance of duties to a broader society than merely one's clients/employers

- Objectivity

- High standards of conduct and performance

We base our professional principles therefore on the fundamental value and dignity of the individual. We believe in and support the free exercise of human rights, especially freedom of speech, freedom of assembly, and freedom of the media, which are essential to the practice of good public relations.

In serving the interest of clients and employers, we dedicate ourselves to the goals of better communication, understanding, and cooperation among diverse individuals, groups, and institutions of society. We also subscribe to and support equal opportunity of employment in the public relations profession and lifelong professional development.

We pledge

- To conduct ourselves professionally, with integrity, truth, accuracy, fairness, and responsibility to our clients, our client publics, and to an informed society;

- To improve our individual competence and advance the knowledge and proficiency of the profession through continuing education and research and where available, through the pursuit of professional accreditation;

- To adhere to the principles of the Global Protocol on Ethics in Public Relations.

Protocol Standards

We believe it is the duty of every association and every member within that association that is party to the Global Protocol on Ethics in Public Relations to:

- Acknowledge that there is an obligation to protect and enhance the profession.

- Keep informed and educated about practices in the profession that ensure ethical conduct.

- Actively pursue personal professional development.

- Accurately define what public relations activities can and cannot accomplish.

- Counsel its individual members in proper ethical decision-making generally and on a case specific basis.

- Require that individual members observe the ethical recommendations and behavioural requirements of the Protocol.

We are committed to ethical practices, preservation of public trust, and the pursuit of communication excellence with powerful standards of performance, professionalism, and ethical conduct.

Advocacy

We will serve our client and employer interests by acting as responsible advocates and by providing a voice in the market place of ideas, facts, and viewpoints to aid informed public debate.

Honesty

We will adhere to the highest standards of accuracy and truth in advancing the interests of clients and employers.

Integrity

We will conduct our business with integrity and observe the principles and spirit of the Code in such a way that our own personal reputation and that of our employer and the public relations profession in general is protected.

Expertise

We will encourage members to acquire and responsibly use specialised knowledge and experience to build understanding and client/employer credibility. Furthermore we will actively promote and advance the profession through continued professional development, research, and education.

Loyalty

We will insist that members are faithful to those they represent, while honouring their obligations to serve the interests of society and support the right of free expression.

Advancing the Protocol

We believe it is the responsibility of each member association to draw upon its own members' experiences to expand the number of examples of good and bad practice so as to better inform members' ethical practices. Experiences should be broadly shared with other members within the association and with the Global Alliance so as to build up case histories that may assist in individual cases throughout the world.

CHAPTER 14   Loraine Blaxter, Christina Hughes and Malcolm Tight

All at sea but learning to swim*

Structure

- Introduction
- The first time researcher
- Getting a flavour of possibilities
- Why am I doing this research?
- Will I have anything new to say?
- In whose interests is this research?
- At last, writing up
- Summary
- Exercises
- Further reading

* Chapter 1 in *How to Research* Third Edition, by Loraine Blaxter, Christina Hughes and Malcolm Tight (2008). Copyright © Loraine Blaxter, Christina Hughes and Malcolm Tight 2008. Reproduced with the kind permission of Open University Press. All rights reserved.

Introduction

This book focuses on the processes of research as well as research methods. It aims to demystify research, recognizing the everyday skills and techniques involved. It encourages you to think of research as a kind of spiral through which you revisit the various stages of the process, but always with different and developed insights. The book is multidisciplinary in scope. It is designed to be suitable for those undertaking research in the social sciences, as well as in related subjects such as education, business studies and health and social care.

Are you currently feeling *all at sea* and not knowing in which direction to turn with your research project? Or is your research *going swimmingly* and you are *steaming ahead* sure in the knowledge that you are doing a good job? Perhaps you are fluctuating between the ends of this spectrum. You have a sense of *drowning* at one moment in the size of the task ahead, and then *floating* serenely along at the next moment content with the work you have produced so far. Maybe you are *treading water* and feeling your work has come to a standstill. Or perhaps you are at the stage of *dipping your feet* into icy cold waters for a short *paddle* in order to test the water, before you *take the plunge* and begin your research.

As a new, or not so new, researcher, such feelings are common. Indeed, we could say that they go with the territory of research. There is excitement at the prospect of discovering new insights into a topic of interest. There is a sense of confusion over what you are meant to be doing and when. You are aware that you have the ability to build on your current skills and aptitudes to

complete the task ahead successfully. But this can be undermined by a hint of fear that maybe you are not really up to the mark of undertaking what is, after all, a major form of independent study.

Surviving and feeling that you are thriving across the period of your study is, therefore, an important goal, as this will enable you to maintain motivation when things get tough, and to develop a sense of competence and expertise in the conduct of your work. This book is about the practice and experience of doing research, and is designed to ensure that you survive and thrive. It is aimed at those, particularly the less experienced, who are involved in small-scale research projects. It is intended to be useful to both those doing research, whether for academic credit or not, and those responsible for teaching, supervising or managing new researchers.

However, to survive and thrive does not simply mean staying in *familiar seas*. As a person involved in learning, surviving as a research student is about accumulating knowledge and extending skills. Thriving as a research student can be helped by anticipating the sorts of skills, the different forms of knowledge and the resources that you will need. This involves looking ahead and doing some preparation. It means that you need to simulate *stormy seas* in order to begin to develop the *swimming* skills that you need to thrive.

With this in mind, this opening chapter is designed to encourage you to look ahead in several senses. Through a series of case studies, this chapter takes you through key aspects of the research process. These range from getting started to writing up. In addition, this chapter introduces you to a number

of common dilemmas and concerns facing research students. These include maintaining motivation, understanding the meanings of originality, and exploring issues of truth, power and values. Overall, this chapter is designed to encourage you to gain a sense of the route you are taking, because if you don't know the destination, how are you going to get there? Happy swimming!

The chapter is organized into the following sections:

- **The first time researcher.** Undertaking an audit of the skills, knowledge and resources you already possess, and developing a Personal Development Plan for the successful completion of your research.
- **Getting a flavour of possibilities.** Introducing some elements of research design and developing understandings of the varied nature of research.
- **Why am I doing this research?** Exploring your motivations for undertaking research.
- **Will I have anything new to say?** Debunking the idea of originality.
- **In whose interests is this research?** Issues of truth, power and values and the context of your research.
- **At last, writing up.** Planning ahead means ensuring you know the rules, regulations and audiences for your research.
- **How to use this book.** What you will find in it, and how to make your way through it.
- **What is different about this edition?** What has changed and what has been added since the second edition.

The chapter ends with a summary.

The first time researcher

Case Study 14.1

John has an appointment to see his dissertation supervisor. He is worried. He has no idea what topic he might research or even a clear idea about the different kinds of methodological techniques available to him. His assumption is that it is only great men, who have far more superior skills and knowledge than he might ever possess, who actually do 'real' research. But his intellectual anxieties are only one of his concerns. He also has doubts whether he will be organized enough to complete a piece of work that he will have to design and execute himself. To date, his only experiences of education have been on courses with set tasks and readings. This dissertation is really going to test him. 'Am I up to it?', he thinks, as he knocks on the supervisor's door.

In our experience, it doesn't really matter what level you are studying at, doing research usually provokes a series of anxieties. You might be asked to undertake research for an 'A' level module or as part of your undergraduate degree. You may be writing a dissertation for an MA or a PhD thesis. At the outset you may, therefore, be feeling all at sea, wondering what is expected and how you are going to cope. Indeed, it is often the case that these anxieties and worries occur *despite* other positive experiences of research. For example, you might be embarking on your undergraduate dissertation having already written methodological essays for a research methods module. Or you might be beginning your PhD having recently completed a 15,000 word MA dissertation. Whatever your situation, as a first time researcher or a not-quite-first-time researcher, you are likely to experience various concerns and worries. In such a situation, it is easy to forget that by the time you are required to undertake first-hand research, you already have a wide knowledge and sets of skills that have been developed to enable you to be successful.

Our intention in this book is to give you the skills and confidence that will take you successfully from the initial idea to a completed piece of research. With this in mind, there is no better time to start than now. Whatever your level, you will be beginning this particular research project with a host of skills, resources and knowledge derived from your education and life experiences to date. These skills will be technical (e.g. use of information retrieval

systems such as libraries and the Internet) and social (e.g. working collaboratively with fellow students, getting on with others). Resources will include social resources (e.g. family, friends, teachers), emotional resources (e.g. resilience) and material resources (e.g. time and money). And of course, you will have knowledge about your subject area (e.g. sociology, psychology, education, business studies, health, etc.).

One way of gaining a sense of the skills, resources and knowledge you already possess is to undertake an audit. You can do this by completing Exercise 14.1 at the end of the chapter. Exercise 14.1 should provide you with the base line you are working from. However, there is no doubt that undertaking first-hand research will require you – and indeed will enable you – to increase your skill and knowledge levels, to work more independently and to have a greater sense of self-direction.

The gap between the level you are working at now and the level required for successful completion of your research project represents your personal learning needs. In order to produce a development plan that will enable you to meet these learning needs, you will need to assess the adequacy of your current skills, resources and knowledge for the task you are now facing. Do you, for example, need to have a higher level of skill in searching for existing research relating to your topic using Internet search engines or specialist journal sources? Or are there specific knowledge areas relating to your topic that you need to be more familiar with? For example, if your research is concerned with the role of professionalism in nursing, are you required to have an understanding of the changing nature of professionalism in a range of employment fields? Moreover, do you need to have a better appreciation of the financial resources you will need for your research?

Some of the resources, skills and knowledge you possess will, though, be more than adequate for the task ahead. Exercise 14.2 is designed to help you work out where the specific gaps are, and to identify your learning needs. Exercise 14.2 should have highlighted four issues:

1. That you already possess some of the main elements that will contribute to you successfully completing your dissertation or project. When things get tough don't forget this.

2. That, in terms of skills and knowledge, you have some learning needs that need addressing in either the short or the long term.

3. That you have resource needs that need addressing.

4. That there are some areas of skill, knowledge and resources that you are unsure or unclear about and, in consequence, need to explore further.

Box 14.1

An example of a Personal Development Plan

Identified learning need?	How will I achieve this need?	What is my timescale?
Settle on a topic	Talk to friends and other students Work through Chapter 2 of this book	In the next week
Review existing research on my topic	Conduct a range of literature reviews	In the next 6 weeks
Questionnaire design	Consult textbooks and supervisor Look at examples in other research	In the next 2 weeks In the next 3 weeks
Qualitative data analysis	Attend a course	In the next 4 months

In terms of your learning needs, it is at this point that you should consider creating a Personal Development Plan. Such a plan can be relatively simple in that it records three aspects which will be central for the successful completion of your project: your identified learning needs; how they are going to be met; and the planned timescale for meeting these. An example is provided in Box 14.1.

For resource needs and areas where you are unclear or do not yet have sufficient information, it is worthwhile identifying the sources of help that will address these. Box 14.2 provides a list of some of the potential ones that we have identified.

So far, our aim has been to encourage you to recognize that you bring valuable skills, knowledge and resources to your research. You already possess many of the requirements that are necessary for success at this stage. We have also encouraged you to recognize that you can contribute to the likelihood of your being successful through developing an understanding of your learning and resource needs, both for the immediate future and in the longer term. This means that, as well as looking back at what you have learnt and understood, you also need to look forward to what will be required. Now is the time, therefore, to draft your Personal Development Plan (see Exercise 14.3).

Box 14.2

Some potential sources of help

- Your supervisor
- Your fellow students
- The departmental secretary
- University or college services (counselling, information technology, careers, library)
- Specialist departments (e.g. computing, English language support)
- Student union
- Your manager
- Other work colleagues, particularly those who have undertaken similar research projects recently
- Family
- Friends
- Lecturers/supervisors/teachers from previous courses of study
- The various handbooks that your department or school provide
- The various textbooks that have been written for research students (including, of course, this one)

Getting a flavour of possibilities

Case Study 14.2

'Well, that wasn't too bad', Samia thought, as she left her supervisor's office. I now know that all that reading I did on Malthusian economics might pay off for me. And my IT skills are in pretty good shape. I still don't really have a handle on the variety of different kinds of research though. My supervisor said I might think about what kinds of methodological approaches I prefer. Do I want to do numbers or do I want to talk to people? The only research I really know about is surveys and questionnaires. I hadn't given any thought to something like spending long periods of time with a small group of people and doing participant observation. But she said it was a possibility. And I never even knew that I could base the whole of the design of my project on library research. I had always thought that was just the literature review part of it. I will have to give some thought to the different types of research and see if any appeal or are possible.

It is often not fully appreciated that, at the very earliest stages of thinking about research, there are many ways in which this might proceed. For example, say your general topic was 'Asylum Seekers in the UK'. You might research this in any, and indeed all, of the following ways:

- By gathering together existing statistics
- Looking at policy at local and national level
- Exploring the responses of relevant charitable organizations
- Devising a questionnaire for various 'stakeholders' in this field
- Conducting interviews with asylum seekers
- Living among asylum seekers over a period of time
- Undertaking an analysis of media representations of asylum seekers

Your decision on how you might proceed clearly depends upon a number of factors. The most significant of these is what you are interested in finding out. For example, if your research questions whether the numbers of asylum seekers coming to the UK are increasing or decreasing, which countries they are travelling from, and what sex and age they are, then an analysis of existing statistics would be a very useful place to start. You would then be in a position to use percentages and bar charts to demonstrate your findings. Alternatively, if you are more interested in the experiences of asylum seekers once they have arrived in the UK, then you might consider interviews or even try to spend some time living among them as a form of participant observation. Your project or dissertation would then present the words of your research participants or extracts from your research diary detailing, for example, something of daily life for a particular group of asylum seekers.

In addition, your methodological decisions will depend upon how much time you have available, the expected word length of your project or dissertation, your research skills, the regulations and preferences of your department, school, examination board, manager and/or supervisor, what and whom you are able to access, the ethical parameters of your proposal and your own preferences. These represent some very practical concerns, and you would be well advised to consult with your supervisor or manager at the very outset.

For example, if you are thinking of conducting an interview-based study and you are completing a 10,000 word MA dissertation conducted over a 3 month period, you might plan to interview between six to eight people once only. By comparison, for a PhD of 80,000 words conducted over a 3 year period and using a qualitative research approach, you might be expected to have an in-depth knowledge of the lives of your research respondents, and be planning to spend an equivalent of 12 months conducting fieldwork. If you are planning to take a more quantitative approach and you are an undergraduate student undertaking a dissertation, you are unlikely to have the resources, in terms of time and money, available to conduct a large-scale survey. Secondary data analysis may, therefore, be a more fruitful strategy. Conversely, if you are conducting a quantitatively based PhD, then you should expect to have already, and to acquire further, a high level of statistical ability.

The ways in which your research questions and interests shape the possible design of your research combine with practical issues such as time, resources and abilities. Accordingly, they each contribute to the ways in which your project will proceed. With this in mind, take a look at the representations of research shown in Box 14.3. These diagrams give alternative views of the research process. The most standard understanding of research is that showing a linear design, where the research begins with a problem and proceeds through data collection and analysis to the written report. The other diagram shows a far more iterative approach. This design seeks to convey the interrelationship between data collection, analysis and report writing. These two representations

Box 14.3

Representations of the research process

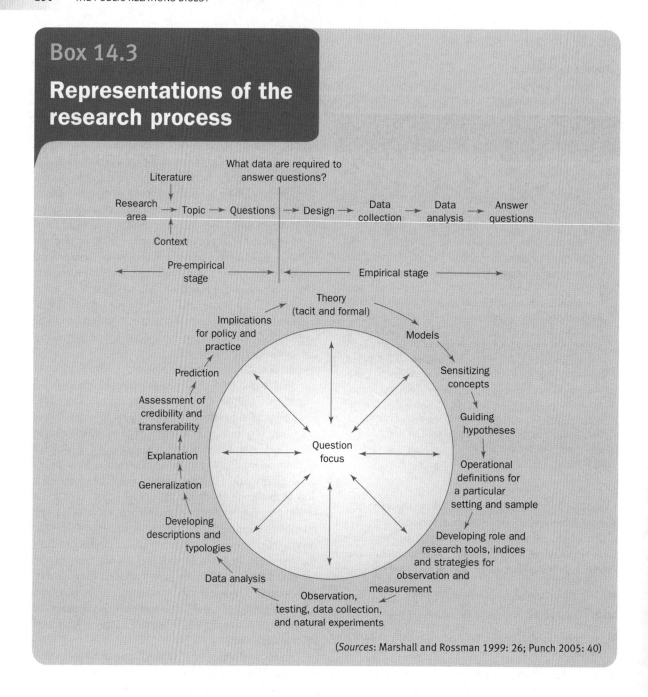

(*Sources*: Marshall and Rossman 1999: 26; Punch 2005: 40)

may be understood as lying towards the polar ends of a continuum where, between these points, there are many variations.

Indeed, there are at least four common viewpoints when it comes to conveying and understanding the various processes of research:

■ Research is often presented as a fixed, linear series of stages, with a clear start and end. This is the 'standard' view.

■ There are also somewhat more complicated representations of this linear view that allow for slightly different routes to be taken through the process at particular stages.

■ Another common representation portrays research as a circular process, analogous to the more general process of learning. Much the same set of stages is included, and in much the same order as in the linear view, but there is an implication both that the process

Box 14.4
The research spiral

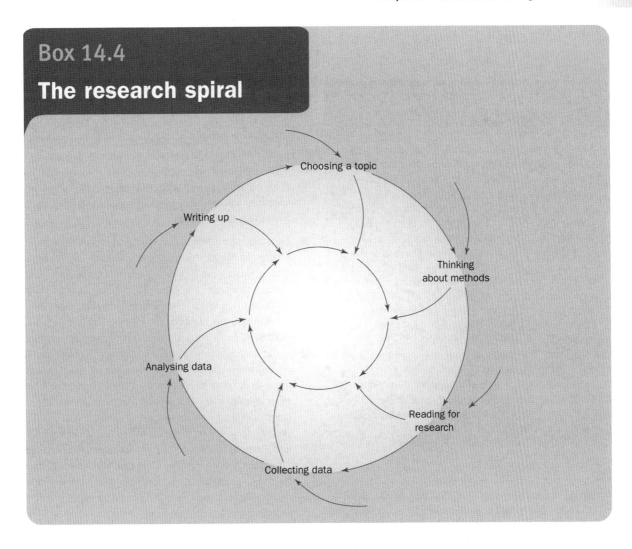

might be entered at a number of points, and that the experience of later stages might lead to a reinterpretation or revisiting of earlier stages.

■ There are also variants, often associated with action research, that see the research process as cyclical. Here, the process is shown as going through a number of cycles, the effects of each one impacting upon the way in which successive cycles are approached.

Our preferred view builds on these representations, seeing the research process as a spiral (see Box 14.4). Seen from this perspective, research: is cyclical; can be entered at almost any point; is a never ending process; will cause you to reconsider your practice; and will return you to a different starting place.

The nature of the cycle varies between research designs. For example, in most quantitative research projects, deci-

sions about analysis have to be taken before any fieldwork or data collection is undertaken. This is because the types of statistical techniques that are possible vary with the types of data collected. In the case of qualitative research, by contrast, data collection, sorting, analysis and reading can take place simultaneously. Getting a flavour of each of the possible – even ideal – ways your project might proceed is an important part of the initial stage. This will enable you to select the most appropriate research process for your needs and interests, and to develop a sense of the limitations of the one you do select. This will also enable you to develop an understanding of the implications of your research approach, in terms of when the different elements are staged and accomplished, and in terms of what you might expect about the process and your associated experiences.

Why am I doing this research?

Case Study 14.3

Helen is sitting in the library. She has several books on the desk in front of her. One is open but unread. The others are stacked in short piles giving the look of a stockade around her. Her notepad is open, the page already containing her first embryonic notes and several doodles. She has spent the best part of the morning searching for these texts, and counts herself lucky that at least some of those on her list were actually still on the shelves. And she had a breakthrough the other day as she had decided that her research design would be based on qualitative approaches. Yet now she's got herself organized to this stage, she is wondering why she's doing this research. Is it really going to be that interesting a topic? Isn't there too much (i.e. boring) preparatory work to do before she can really get going? She would much rather get out there talking to and interviewing people. But, actually, even that seems too much effort now. Maybe it's best to pack up. Start another day. Not do it at all . . .

While there are many highs when doing research, it also has to be acknowledged that there will be many moments when the task ahead appears daunting or tedious, or simply not worth the effort. It is important, therefore, to remind yourself, from time to time, of why you are undertaking, or interested in undertaking, research. Quite often professional researchers are initially motivated by hopes that their work will change the world in some way. There are also many researchers who reflect upon how their initial choice of topic was motivated by their personal circumstances or something that is close to their personal interests. For example, stepmothers may study stepfamilies, or non-traditional students may study the experiences of other non-traditional students. Of course, research is a job like any other. Researches, therefore, often undertake studies on topics that are not of their personal choosing, but because they pay the rent or may take them on to the next stage of their career. Think about your reasons for doing your project and try to complete Exercise 14.4.

As a researcher, you will find it useful to understand why you are involved in research. This will affect how you go about your research, and what you get out of it. If you are in doubt about your motivation, or reach a low spot when you feel that you want to give up, you might ask yourself the following questions:

- What are the personal rewards from completing this study? For example, how will the award of the qualification associated with your research enhance your career and employment prospects? What new skills will you have acquired? Will your research have enabled you to develop new contacts or visit new places? Will it have enabled you to demonstrate hitherto hidden competencies to significant others? What kinds of satisfaction will you experience once the last word is written on the last page?

- How will the knowledge you produce contribute to furthering understandings or changing lives? Most often this question is understood in terms of large-scale change through, for example, finding the ultimate solution to a perennial problem. However, most contributions from research tend to be smaller in scale, though no less significant in terms of their importance to the individuals involved. For example, your research respondents may feel that this is the first time anyone has ever taken a real interest in their concerns. After all, it is quite rare – outside of therapeutic encounters – for anyone to sit down, listen intently and record everything you say for an hour or so. Research can, therefore, be a very important validating experience for research respondents. The enthusiasm you garner from being involved in research can also be very persuasive for others who may develop insights from, or become more interested in, the issues arising from your research. This can create incremental and cascading changes that, while they may not rock the world immediately, nonetheless become significant in themselves.

But what might you do if you really feel you have no motivation at all? After all, if you aren't motivated, or are not motivated very strongly, this will affect your drive to finish the research project successfully. The obvious answer to the researcher with no motivation is to get some quickly or do something else! If the latter is not possible, you might seek motivation in one of the following ways:

- changing your research project to something you are more interested in;

- focusing on the skills you will develop through undertaking the research;

- incorporating within the research some knowledge acquisition of relevance to you;

- seeing the research project as part of a larger activity, which will have knock-on benefits for your work, your career, your social life or your life in general;

- finding someone who will support you and push you through until you finish;
- promising yourself a reward when it is successfully completed.

Will I have anything new to say?

Case Study 14.4

It's all been done before. Everything I was planning to do I can now see that other researchers have done before. What's the point, then, of carrying on? Hussain felt a strong sense of rising panic as the deadline for handing in his dissertation was fast approaching. He had completed all the data collection and had also completed quite a lot of the analysis. He realized that his findings were not terribly new to anyone who knew his research field. They also confirmed much of what he had previously thought was the case.

For many research projects, particularly those carried out for a university degree, there is often a need for some kind or level of originality. This will typically be expressed in regulations or guidance in very general terms: 'an original project', 'an original contribution' or 'evidence of original thinking'.

But what is originality? And where can you get some? If you are unsure, and it matters to you in your research, take a look at Box 14.5. Here you will find 15 definitions of originality, collected together by others. Have a look at them and consider if your research meets any of the criteria listed. As the definitions quoted indicate, it is possible to be original in terms of topic, approach or presentation. The element of originality in your own research is, realistically, likely to be very small. Highly original research is very unusual, and you are probably setting your sights far too high if you try aiming for it.

The corollary of this is that your research is almost certainly original in some way, always providing, that is, that you are not slavishly copying someone else's earlier research. So be reassured. Indeed, it is quite common for researchers to become so familiar with their topic that they forget that it was all new to them when they started. While good researchers need to be over-familiar with the relevant literature, their data and their findings, this can lead to a mistaken assumption that everyone else is as

Box 14.5

Fifteen definitions of originality

Here are 15 definitions of originality, as put together by Phillips and Pugh. The first six are derived from a previous author, Francis, while the other nine derive from interviews with Australian students, supervisors and examiners.

1 Setting down a major piece of new information in writing for the first time.

2 Continuing a previously original piece of work.

3 Carrying out original work designed by the supervisor.

4 Providing a single original technique, observation or result in an otherwise unoriginal but competent piece of research.

5 Having many original ideas, methods and interpretations all performed by others under the direction of the postgraduate.

6 Showing originality in testing somebody else's idea.

7 Carrying out empirical work that hasn't been done before.

8 Making a synthesis that hasn't been made before.

9 Using already known material but with a new interpretation.

10 Trying out something in this country that has previously only been done in other countries.

11 Taking a particular technique and applying it in a new area.

12 Bringing new evidence to bear on an old issue.

13 Being cross-disciplinary and using different methodologies.

14 Looking at areas that people in the discipline haven't looked at before.

15 Adding to knowledge in a way that hasn't previously been done before.

(*Source*: Phillips and Pugh 2005: 62; partly after Francis 1976)

knowledgeable as they are. Researchers therefore forget their initial excitement and interest in gaining new knowledge and, in consequence, they forget that what they have to say may well be novel and new to other audiences. But if you are in doubt, check it out with those who will judge the originality of your research as early as possible. This advice also applies if you fear that you may be being too original for comfort. If you want to complete a useful piece of research in a particular context, it would not be sensible to, for example, present it in a way which is unacceptable.

In whose interests is this research?

Case Study 14.5

Rishi thought his research was telling the facts of the case. He was very pleased that he had proven how poor the management was at Britwell and Company. He was shocked when his supervisor told him that all he could say was that 'such and such' was someone's perspective. Actually he said that Rishi needed to consider how much his values and experiences had impacted upon the selection of data and the analysis. It wasn't a perspective. Rishi raged, it was the truth. The management were lazy and inept. All of his research respondents told him so.

Many people coming to research for the first time have a tendency to think that they are in the business of establishing 'the truth' about a particular issue or subject. They want to find out 'the facts' or want to 'prove' (or perhaps disprove) a particular argument. They believe that they can be 'objective' in their research and that others will sit up and take notice when they present their findings. We shouldn't be surprised that this is the case because the 'standard' view of research is that of a detached scientist examining the facts of the case coolly and unemotionally. However, this standard view of research belies the extent to which, as we have suggested, research is a social activity that can be powerfully affected by the researcher's own motivations and values. It also takes place within a broader social context, within which politics and power relations influence what research is undertaken, how it is carried out and whether and how it is reported and acted upon. To examine how this effects the different forms of data that can be collected, its subsequent analysis and findings, try Exercise 14.5.

Exercise 14.5 suggests how politics, power and values may be important considerations for your research, especially if you carry it out within your own or another organization. Your contacts will affect your access to the subjects of your research, may require you to submit your research proposals for scrutiny, and to revise them, and may exercise some veto over what you can actually write up or publish. If your research requires ethical approval prior to proceeding, which is increasingly likely to be the case, you will be required to adhere to a broader set of values and ways of proceeding, regardless of whether your research is organizationally based or not. And, if you are unlucky, misread the organizational politics or irritate the researched, you may find cooperation withdrawn part way through your project.

It is important, therefore, to understand the perspectives and motivations of those who facilitate your access, or take part in, or who may be stakeholders in, your research. Preparatory time spent in learning about this is always well spent, as well as being valuable contextual research in its own right. Rather than expecting to 'find the truth', therefore, it is better to think of research work in terms of words like rigour, reliability, professionalism and systematization. No one research project can realistically aspire to do more than advance our understanding in some way. Most researchers have to compromise their practices to fit into the time and other resources available for their studies. Doing research is, therefore, about producing something that is 'good enough' rather than providing the last final word of truth on a particular topic.

This does not mean, of course, that such research cannot be pursued with drive, passion and commitment. These are important qualities that help maintain momentum and interest, and can impact beyond the research into dissemination. However, all researchers need to take care that their passion does not lead to dogma or an uncritical take on the views of research participants. Rather, researchers need to maintain their levels of critical reflection, and so ensure their research is conducted in as open and transparent a way as possible in terms of its intentions, methodology, analysis and findings.

At last, writing up

Case Study 14.6

The data had all been collected. The analysis was virtually complete. Now is the time to switch on the word file and begin to write it all up. But hang on, thought Becky, how do I do this? What is the format? I've never written a dissertation before. Do I need an index and chapters? Or do I just set it all down like an essay? How many references should I use? Do I have enough? Or maybe, lucky me, I have too many? Then again, I promised to give a copy to the manager of the call centre where I conducted the research. She was really keen to see it because she's hoping it will help her improve productivity. Will she want to read all this literature review stuff? Also, how is she going to take some of the things the staff had to say about her? Oh dear . . .

assessed according to academic criteria. It may be, however, that you are carrying out a research project for your employer, who will expect a concise report emphasizing the implications of your findings and recommending action. You may be balancing both of these roles. However, while the processes may be broadly similar, the outputs are likely to look very different.

Your audience may also include those you are researching, whether at work or within a community organization. If the latter, your approach may be to work from the bottom up, gaining consensus and support from all involved throughout the process; and the research may be as much about the change and development engendered in your audience as about any written output.

The important theme which runs through this discussion is your need, as a researcher, to be aware of the context in which you are researching. This manifests itself in rules, whether written or unwritten. You need to be aware of these rules and to follow them if you wish to succeed. You cannot hope just to muddle along and not run into problems.

It may seem that the writing up stage is a long way off, but it is important to consider the rules, regulations and expectations of the various audiences for your research early on. For example, if you are researching for a university degree or another form of formal qualification, you will have to produce a dissertation or a thesis that will be

Hint: Open a file on 'Regulations and Expectations'. Include copies of all the written regulations that apply to you research project and add notes on any unwritten expectations which you may find out about during your work.

Summary

Having read this chapter, you should:

■ have an awareness of the skills, knowledge and resources you already possess that will enable you to survive stormy waters ahead;

■ have an awareness of the skills, knowledge and resources that you need to enhance or acquire to enable you to thrive through your research work;

■ now recognize the need to produce a Personal Development Plan;

■ have some understanding of the variety of activities which may be considered as being 'research';

■ appreciate that the research process is not straightforward, predictable or linear;

■ have a clearer idea of your own motivations for engaging in research and of the context for your research;

■ be more confident about your own ability to carry out a small-scale research project.

Exercises

14.1 What skills, resources and knowledge do you already have? Identify as many of the following as you can that have contributed to your success in academic work in the past: skills (e.g. information technology, reading, writing, managing time); resources (e.g. time, money, support networks); knowledge (e.g. subject knowledge, research knowledge, knowledge of systems, processes); your personality/temperament.

14.2 Expanding on past successes. Using the list of skills, resources and knowledge that you have produced in Exercise 14.1, identify those areas that: you know are adequate for your current needs; you know need developing for your future needs; or where you are unsure whether you have a high enough level of a particular skill, resource or knowledge.

14.3 My Personal Development Plan. To produce a personal development plan, you should enter at least one item under each of the following headings: Identified learning need? How will I achieve this need? What is my timescale? Review your Plan periodically as your research progresses.

14.4 Reasons for undertaking research. List your reasons for your current or anticipated involvement in research. List as many as you can think of.

14.5 The context of your research. Imagine you are doing research on experiences of training at work, whether within your own company or another. Would your findings be different if you approached your interviewees through: the managing director, the personnel manager, the shop stewards' committee, the unemployment centre? How might they differ? How might this affect your conclusions? What if you had to write a report of your conclusions for each of these audiences? You can think about this as an exercise in finding out what is safe and what is risky in terms of expectations, theory, styles of writing, etc.

References

Francis, J. (1976) Supervision and examination of higher degree students, *Bulletin of the University of London*, **31**: 3–6.

Marshall, C. and Rossman, G. (1999) *Designing Qualitative Research*, 3rd edn. Thousand Oaks, CA: Sage.

Phillips, E. M. and Pugh, D. (2005) *How to Get a PhD: A Handbook for Students and their Supervisors*, 4th edn. Maidenhead: Open University Press.

Punch, M. (2005) *Introduction to Social Research: Quantitative and Qualitative Approaches*, 2nd edn. London: Sage.

CHAPTER 15

György Szondi and Rüdiger Theilmann

Public relations research and evaluation*

Learning outcomes

By the end of this chapter you should be able to:

■ identify the role of research and evaluation in public relations practice

■ define and describe both quantitative and qualitative research approaches

■ apply relevant research methods

■ understand the different theoretical and practical approaches to evaluation in public relations.

Structure

■ Context of research in public relations

■ Designing research

■ Qualitative vs quantitative research

■ Research methods

■ Designing research instruments

■ Research applications

■ Evaluation

* Chapter 10 in *Exploring Public Relations* Second Edition, edited by Ralph Tench and Liz Yeomans (2009).

Introduction

Research plays a crucial role for many different reasons in public relations (PR). First, it is an integral part of the PR planning process. Without research it is difficult to set communication objectives, identify publics or develop messages. Second, research is also undertaken to evaluate PR efforts. Evaluation has been one of the biggest and most talked about issues over many years for the entire PR industry. Evaluation helps practitioners understand and improve programme effectiveness through systematic measurement and proves the value of PR efforts to clients, management or other disciplines, such as marketing or integrated communications.

Research and evaluation can also reveal a lot about the current state of PR practice as well as contribute to the development of the PR theoretical knowledge base. Research findings have business benefits too and can facilitate attempts to show how PR can improve the bottom line. This chapter will explore the research process, the most commonly used research methods in PR and the theory and practice of evaluation. The principles of research approaches and methods would fill a book, therefore in this chapter only the basic principles will be discussed.

Context of research in public relations

Academic research aims to generate theories and models, to describe and analyse trends in PR. Academic journals, such as the *Journal of Public Relations Research* or *Public Relations Review,* are concerned with theory building and are among the major outlets of academic research. Another important contribution comes from students in the form of undergraduate and postgraduate dissertations and theses as part of a degree. The ability to understand and carry out systematic research highlights the importance of education. Practitioners with a degree in higher education are better equipped in the complex world of research as opposed to those who use only 'seat-of-the-pants' methods.

Research can have different purposes and origins. The primary purpose of research is to contribute to the existing body of knowledge in the field of PR, even if such research does not deal with the real problems of practice ('basic research'). But the purpose of research is also to answer questions that come out of practice or are imposed by a client ('applied research').

Nevertheless, if we use the term 'research' – either basic or applied – we always mean 'scientific' research, not 'informal, 'quick and dirty' or 'everyday-life research' – as it is often understood by practitioners. For example, Lindenmann (1990) reports results of a survey among PR professionals in which about 70% of the respondents thought that most research on the subject was informal rather than scientific (Cutlip et al. 2006; Gregory 2000).

In contrast to scientific research, informal research is based on subjective intuition or on the 'authority' of knowledge or 'tenacity', which refers to sticking to a practice because it has always been like that (Kerlinger 1986). It is subjective if information is gathered in an unsystematic way by talking to a couple of people, looking at guidelines ('Five Steps to do World Class Public Relations') or just based on feelings. Other examples of PR practice based on informal research are where:

- a practice might be considered as best practice because the senior manager of a well-known consultancy declares it to be the latest trend in PR (based on 'authority')

- an advisory committee, panel or board recommends it (based on 'authority')

- an organisation writes news releases in the same style they have used for the last 10 years ('tenacity' – 'it is the right way because we have always done it like that').

Scientific research is systematic and objective: it follows distinct steps and uses appropriate research design. In doing PR research we have to guide research by:

- defining the research problem (what to research)

- choosing a general research approach (qualitative or quantitative)

- deciding on research strategy (primary or secondary research)

- selecting the research method (survey, content analysis, focus group, etc.)

- deciding on the research instruments (questions in a questionnaire or categories in a content analysis)

- analysing the data (e.g. Wimmer and Dominick 2006).

See Think about 15.1.

Research and evaluation in public relations planning and management

Research is an integrated part of PR management, which means that it should be included in each step of the PR

Think about 15.1   SWOT and PEST – research or not?

To identify internal and external environmental factors, SWOT and PEST (or EPISTLE) analyses are often considered to be useful techniques. This might be conducted in a meeting in which practitioners of the in-house PR department gather and do a brainstorming session about the strengths, weaknesses, opportunities and threats of their organisation. But can this be considered as research? SWOT and PEST brainstorms may offer guidelines about what to research but they are not research in themselves. For example, to explore the weaknesses of an organisation, a focus group discussion might be conducted. Only by doing a SWOT or PEST analysis with proper research methods does it become research. Doing a SWOT or PEST analysis by subjective intuition might reveal interesting ideas but is not research.

planning process. This might sound controversial, since models such as the RACE model – research, action, communication and evaluation – suggest that research is only undertaken in the first and the last steps: 'research' and 'evaluation'. Nevertheless, this does not mean that research is limited to these steps; it is crucial in each step. The following four points refer to the four stages in the Cutlip et al. (2006) planning process:

- using research to define PR problems
- using research to assess PR plans and proposals
- using research during programme implementation
- using research for programme impact.

Using research to define PR problems

Research findings such as problem definitions or identifying publics are key inputs for programme planning. For example, an organisation might have a bad image in the media and turn to a PR consultancy to address this problem. The consultancy is very likely to use research to find the reasons for the image problem, before developing a strategy to address it. This process can be defined as *problem definition* and *situation analysis* and should address the following research questions:

- What are the internal and external environmental factors that affect the organisation?
- Who are the publics?
- What do they know? What do they think about key issues?
- How are public–organisation relationships characterised?
- What media do publics rely on or prefer for information?

Using research to assess PR plans and proposals

Before implementing a plan, its various elements can be tested through a variety of measures: expert assessment; using checklists as criteria; testing messages in focus group discussions; or in a survey among key publics. Initial identification of publics, messages, strategies or tactics included in the plan might be subject to assessment. The assessment might result in changes in the programme.

Using research during programme implementation

Process research aims at improving programme performance and takes place while the programme is in operation (in process). It is also referred to as *monitoring* or *formative* evaluation. It enables the PR practitioner to modify campaign elements, such as messages (too complicated, misunderstood, irrelevant), channels (inappropriate choice for delivering a particular message), or the chosen strategies and tactics. Research during implementation enables the practitioner to make corrections according to circumstances and issues that were not foreseen during the planning process, especially in the case of complex and long-term programmes. It can also document how the programme is being implemented, including the practitioner's own activity, resources allocated or timing of the programme.

Using research for programme impact

Finally, research is done to measure programme impact or effectiveness with respect to goals and objectives. Principles of programme evaluation will be discussed in the second half of the chapter.

Areas of research

Lerbinger (1977) offers a classification that defines areas of PR research less concerned with the process of programmes. He distinguishes four major categories of PR research as: environmental monitoring (or scanning); PR audits; communication audits; and social audits. Table 15.1 identifies these categories of research and defines the scope of each approach.

Table 15.1
Categories of
research and
their scope (*source*:
based on Lerbinger
1977: 11–14)

Categories of research	Scope of research
Environmental monitoring (scanning)	Issues and trends in public opinion Issues in mass media Social events which may have significant impact on an organisation Competitor communications analysis
Public relations audit	Assesses an organisation's public relations activities
Communication audits	All forms of internal and external communications are studied to assess their consistency with overall strategy as well as their internal consistency Narrower than a public relations audit
Social audits	Measures an organisation's social performance

Designing research

After identifying questions that help assess the initial situation, we have to decide how to research them. This demands a research plan that answers the following questions:

■ What types of data are of interest?

■ Which research approach should be followed: qualitative or quantitative research?

■ Which research methods are appropriate?

■ How should the research instruments be designed?

Type of data: primary or secondary research?

Information or data can be gathered in two basic ways: through primary or secondary research. Primary research generates data that are specific for the case under investigation. Primary data are directly retrieved ('in the field') from the research object through empirical research methods – interview, focus group, survey, content analysis or observation (Wimmer and Dominick 2006).

Secondary research or 'desk research', in contrast, uses data that have already been gathered, are available through different sources and can be analysed sitting at the desk as opposed to gathering data 'in the field' (Neumann 2003). The term 'secondary' implies that somebody else has already collected this information through primary research and documented the results in various sources. A specific type of secondary research is 'data mining', which is the explora-

tion and analysis of existing data with reference to a new or specific research problem.

Data about size and composition of media audiences such as newspaper readership or television audiences are available to the practitioners and are published regularly. Table 15.2 is an example from the *Guardian*'s media supplement.

Secondary data are available from many different sources like libraries, government records, trade and professional associations, as well as organisational files. The following list includes some of the large UK and European datasets:

■ Annual Employment Survey, which covers about 130,000 businesses (www.statistics.gov.uk)

■ British Social Attitudes survey (www.natcen.ac.uk)

■ Chartered Institute of Public Relations: posts useful resources of research on its website (www.cipr. co.uk)

■ Eurobarometer, which monitors public opinion in member states on a variety of issues (enlargement, social situation, health, culture, information technology, environment, the euro, defence policy, etc.)

■ Eurostat, the Statistical Office of the European Communities

■ online research services such as LexisNexis (www. lexisnexis.com)

■ population census, which is held every 10 years (www.census.ac.uk).

Caution must be taken when interpreting and using secondary research findings since they can reflect the views and interests of the sponsoring organisations. (See Activity 15.1.)

Table 15.2 UK national daily newspaper circulation excluding bulks, December 2007 (*source*: adapted from Guardian Unlimited, 1 April 2008, http://www.guardian.co.uk/media/table/2008/sep/05/abcs.pressandpublishing. Copyright Guardian Newspapers Limited 2008. Data from Audit Bureau of Circulations)

Title	Dec 2007	Dec 2006	% change
Daily Express	744,539	773,768	−3.78
Daily Mail	2,310,806	2,311,057	−0.01
Daily Mirror	1,494,114	1,540,917	−3.04
Daily Record	385,928	407,212	−5.23
Daily Star	726,465	750,374	−3.19
Daily Telegraph	873,523	899,493	−2.89
FT	449,187	437,720	2.62
Guardian	353,436	365,635	−3.34
Independent	228,400	238,756	−4.34
Sun	2,985,672	3,028,732	−1.42
Times	615,313	635,777	−3.22

Activity 15.1

Secondary research

You are commissioned by the Department of Health to design a PR campaign to raise awareness of obesity in the UK. You are interested in hard facts about this disease. What types of secondary sources would you turn to? Put together a small research report on the topic.

Feedback

Start with the following link: www.official-documents.co.uk.

Starting research

As a first step to start research in Case study 15.1, research questions must be developed. Key questions in the first stage of the planning process are:

1　What do residents know about the service?

2　What do residents think about recycling?

3　Are residents willing to recycle?

A next step is the question of which type of data to use to answer these questions. Primary or secondary research might be conducted. An example of secondary research would be to find and use research data that has been gathered by other city councils in the UK or use data from

Case Study 15.1

Research and evaluation: 'Bin There Done That'

The following case study on Westminster City Council's campaign about recycling will be used throughout the rest of the chapter.

Background

The improvement of doorstep recycling formed part of a new Westminster cleansing contract. Recycling was seen as a critical part of the cleansing service. Getting doorstep recycling right was seen as essential for the council to meet government targets by 2010. Large increases to landfill tax and costs of incineration also made the success of the new service vital.

Objectives

■ To change the behaviour of residents to increase take-up of service by one-quarter and thereby recycle a greater proportion of waste – from 30 tonnes per week to 50 tonnes per week

■ To position the authority as the leading recycling authority through raising the City Survey satisfaction rating from 43% to 60% for recycling

case study 15.1 (continued)

■ To increase awareness of recycling service among target audience to drive up usage to help us meet government targets for tonnage of recycled household waste by 2010

Planning and implementation

Audit

Westminster City Council's (WCC) in-house PR department examined its market extensively before committing to the final campaign. Quantitative research surveying 502 residents in July 2003 found that:

■ 60% of residents did not feel informed about the service

■ 98% said that recycling was important

■ 72% said they would recycle only if the council made it easier first.

To accurately target audience and message, WCC conducted two focus groups of Westminster residents drawn from across the borough in July 2003. One group recycled regularly and one had never recycled.

The focus group research found that there was a shocking lack of knowledge about WCC's recycling service, confusion over what materials could be recycled and an emphatic desire for the process to be made easy.

Two campaigns were market tested to the groups. Both groups unanimously opted for a 'we've made it easy, you make it happen' message.

Strategy

WCC had to vastly improve the information sent to households, providing clear, concise and accurate information about the types of material that could be recycled.

Its communications had to:

> Reinforce that the Council had made the service easier (a single bin for all goods), promote two way communications (a helpline and website were introduced), deliver strong messages that were easy to understand.

The Bin There Done That (BTDT) campaign was adopted after trialling a number of alternatives, as it met these criteria. The research had shown that messages must be clear, simple, easy and immediately recognisable as WCC. The campaign included:

■ a two-week teaser campaign (something's coming to your doorstep)

■ rollout of service information campaign (ways to recycle)

■ advertising campaign (Bin There Done That)

■ intensive field marketing follow-up campaign

■ follow-through information campaign.

Evaluation and measurement

Evaluation was ongoing. Trained council staff surveyed over 16,000 homes and as a result some new messages were adopted, e.g. how to order replacement bins that neighbours had stolen! Final evaluation compared the council's 2002/3 City Survey conducted by MORI with the 2003/4 MORI City Survey, a specially commissioned populus survey on communication messages and analysis of tonnages and rates of participation.

Results of analysis were then compared against objectives.

■ *Objective 1: change behaviour of residents to recycle a greater proportion of their waste – increase from 30 tonnes per week to 50 tonnes per week.* Tonnage for doorstep recycling increased from 30 tonnes per week to 85 tonnes per week.

After seeing the campaign, people were much more likely to recycle: 68% of those aware of the campaign now recycle whereas only 45% who were unaware chose to do so.

Of residents who were aware of the campaign, 73% thought that the council had made recycling easier for them. This is nearly twice as many (40%) as those who had not seen the campaign.

■ *Objective 2: position the authority as the leading recycling authority through raising City Survey satisfaction rating from 43% to 60% for recycling.* There was almost a 20% increase in satisfaction rating to 61% for the recycling service (City Survey 2002/3 to 2003/4). The Association of London Government Survey of Londoners 2003 found an increased satisfaction rating for recycling of only 7% across all London boroughs.

The City Survey 2003/4 found that residents felt more strongly about the importance of recycling. Recycling was the fourth most important service. In 2002/3 recycling did not even make an appearance in the list of top 10 services.

Residents also believed that recycling was the second 'elective' (voluntary) service that they most benefited from, behind libraries (53%) – recycling 35%. This shows an increase from 2002/3 of 25% (City Survey 2002/3 to 2003/4).

Of the public that were aware of the campaign, 84% thought it was a good idea to recycle compared with 70% who were unaware of the campaign (December 2003).

■ *Objective 3: increase take-up rate of service by one-quarter.* The increase in take-up for the doorstep recycling service has almost trebled – from 4,843 participants in May 2003 to 12,572 in December 2003.

Source: www.cipr.co.uk/member_area and Westminster City Council Communication Team research in other countries about the acceptance of recycling. Nevertheless, the validity of such data would be questionable since the local situation, awareness and traditions would not have been considered. Therefore, it is more appropriate to conduct primary research.

Qualitative vs quantitative research

The question of whether to use qualitative or quantitative research methods is widely discussed in the academic and professional community. However, the answer depends on each research question: **qualitative** approaches are often used to explore areas about which no knowledge exists yet and results are expressed in words ('qualities'); **quantitative** approaches are used to deliver comparable, generalisable results, expressed in numbers ('quantities').

Picture 15.1 Research 'in the field': data gathering for public relations can require working with diverse publics and therefore in a wide range of settings (*source*: Jack Sullivan/Alamy)

> ### Mini Case Study 15.1
> ## Qualitative or quantitative?
>
> The Inland Revenue (UK tax-gathering authority) is a public sector organisation that wants to research its image among employees, prior to developing a corporate identity programme. Since this is the first time that the internal image has been researched, not a lot of information is available about issues that are relevant in the eyes of the employees. Therefore, the first step might be to hold focus group discussions as a qualitative approach. The goal is to explore relevant features of the image. The second step would be to analyse the results of these focus groups to develop standardised questionnaires that are then distributed to all employees. The features of the image that were explored in the focus groups are assessed by the employees and provide a general view of the employees of their organisation.

Qualitative and quantitative research approaches are complementary and should be combined rather than used as alternatives. In research terms this is often described as the *mixed method* approach (Lindlof and Bryan 2002). Mini case study 15.1 gives an example.

Qualitative and quantitative approaches both have advantages and disadvantages, which are summarised in Table 15.3.

Westminster City Council's BTDT campaign is another good example of how qualitative and quantitative methods can be combined. The focus groups found that there was a lack of knowledge about the council's recycling service, confusion over what materials could be recycled and a huge motivation for the process to be made easy. Especially since the motivation of residents to recycle ('Are residents willing to recycle?', 'What might determine their willingness to recycle?') was rather an unexplored issue, it was appropriate to use a qualitative approach. The results of the focus groups could then be used in the survey that gave a representative overview of what Westminster residents know and think.

Research methods

The main research methods used in PR research and evaluation are:

Table 15.3
Advantages and disadvantages of quantitative and qualitative research techniques (*source*: adapted from Neumann 2003: 150)

	Potential advantages	Potential disadvantages
Quantitative approaches	Generate comparable results Results can be generalised Can be guided by less experienced researchers (e.g. interviewers) Higher acceptance by clients	Quantitative methods can only find out what is put in through prepared questions or categories Can guide respondents into a rather irrelevant direction Do not allow deeper analysis of reasons
Qualitative approaches	Provide insights into causes and motivations Explore information that is completely unknown or unpredicted	Time consuming and demand financial resources Demand qualified researchers Limited generalisation Results are influenced by researcher

- qualitative: intensive or in-depth interviews and focus groups
- quantitative: surveys and content analysis.

In the case of the BTDT campaign, focus groups or surveys were used as methods to research knowledge, attitudes and motivation of Westminster residents to behave in a certain way. But it is not always so obvious what the most appropriate method is, as Think about 15.2 demonstrates.

Intensive or in-depth interviews

Intensive interviews are a specific type of personal interview. Unlike surveys, they do not attempt to generalise answers. So when is it appropriate to use intensive interviews? Their main purpose is to explore attitudes and attitude-relevant contexts. The biggest advantage is the wealth of detail that they can provide. On the negative side, they are sensitive to interviewer bias. The answers might easily be influenced by the behaviour of the interviewer, so well-trained interviewers are needed to minimise the bias. Intensive interviews are characterised by:

- generally *smaller samples* of interviewees
- *open questions* that probe the reasons *why* respondents give specific answers: they elaborate on data concerning respondents' opinions, values, motivations, experiences and feelings
- being *customised* – or reactive – to individual respondents in so far as the order and/or wording of questions can be changed, or new questions added, during the interview depending on the answers given

---

Think about 15.2   Evaluation of a news release

After releasing a news story about new online services on behalf of its client, a large telecommunications provider, ABC PR consultancy discusses how to evaluate the outcome of this activity. Should it:

- measure the media coverage by monitoring media (newspapers, radio, TV, www) and analysing circulation numbers and readership figures using available media data, or
- conduct a representative survey among relevant publics?

Feedback

With the first suggestion, it can be very precisely tracked in which media the news has come up. Additionally, the media data provide figures on the number and type of reader (age, gender, education, income, etc.) who might have seen or read the news. But this is already the weak point in the evaluation: it remains unclear whether they have read the news, what they think about the news and whether they can recall the news.

Using a survey, in contrast, gives clear evidence of what people know and think about the online services of the telecommunications provider. But it remains rather vague as to where they have obtained their information. It might be that the information originates from sources other than the media coverage of the news release.

■ *non-verbal behaviour* of respondents being recorded and contributing to the results.

Focus groups

Focus group or group interviewing is like an intensive interview, with 6 to 10 respondents who interact with each other. Focus groups generate qualitative data. The interviewer plays the role of a moderator leading the respondents in a relatively free discussion about the topic. The interactions between the group members create a dynamic environment that gives respondents additional motivation to elaborate on their attitudes, experiences and feelings.

Main disadvantages are that groups can become dominated by a self-appointed group leader who monopolises the conversation. Focus groups depend heavily on the skills of the moderator who must know when to intervene to stop respondents from discussing irrelevant topics, probe for further information and ensure all respondents are involved in the discussion.

In the BTDT campaign, focus groups were not only conducted to explore attitudes of the residents; they were also used to test messages for the campaign. The use of focus groups helped the PR department to understand that the main criterion for residents doing recycling is convenience. If a survey were used as the only method, it could have provided misleading results. A survey would have measured positive attitudes of the residents about recycling. But why do only few practise it? The focus groups could explore and explain in-depth the gap between attitudes and behaviour: the inconvenience of recycling.

Box 15.1 gives some rules for conducting a focus group study.

Surveys

The survey among Westminster residents illustrates the kind of decisions that have to be taken when conducting a survey.

Which type of survey should be conducted?

Table 15.4 details the types of survey and their advantages and disadvantages. (See Activities 15.2 and 15.3.)

How many people should be interviewed and how will you select them?

Since most research cannot reach all members of a population (all units of consideration to be researched), a sample has to be drawn. There are various sampling designs that

---

Box 15.1

How to conduct a focus group study

There are 12 basic steps in focus group research:

1 Is a focus group study really appropriate?

2 Define the problem.

3 Decide who will moderate.

4 Determine the number of groups necessary.

5 Design a screening questionnaire for selecting a sample.

6 Recruit participants according to screening results.

7 Develop question guideline for the moderator.

8 Brief the moderator.

9 Select and brief focus group observers.

10 Prepare facilities and check catering arrangements.

11 Conduct the session.

12 Analyse the data and report findings.

Source: Broom and Dozier 1990;
Wimmer and Dominick 2006

---

can be used to select the units of research. For example, in our case of the BTDT campaign, the population consists of all residents of Westminster from which a sample is drawn. The sample consists of 502 residents, which is a sufficient sample size to ensure validity of the results.

What do you want to measure?

Before developing a survey questionnaire, you need to decide what you want to measure. A basic distinction is to research awareness/knowledge/beliefs (cognitions), attitudes, behaviour.

In the BTDT campaign the key research questions cover these aspects:

■ What do residents know about the service (knowledge)?

■ What do residents think about recycling (attitudes)?

■ Are residents willing to recycle or what prevents them from recycling (motivation/behaviour)?

Table 15.4 Types of survey

Method	Requirements	Advantages	Disadvantages
Mail survey – self-administered questionnaires (self-explanatory)	Mailing list Reply envelope Cover letter (separate) Incentives Follow-up mailings	Anonymity Specific mailing lists available Low cost, little time to prepare and conduct Respondent convenience	Response rate Slow data collection Only standardised questions Response: only motivated respondents – not representative
Telephone survey	Telephone numbers Interviewers Training and instruction (manner of speaking, what to say . . .)	Interviewers can clarify questions Speed, costs Control, probing complex answers High response rates, completeness of questionnaires	Reach of respondents Limited use of scales, visual materials
Personal interview (face to face)	Interviewers and training	Interviewers can clarify questions Use of scales and visual materials	No anonymity Expensive Interviewer bias
Online surveys	Website Email list	Inexpensive Respondent convenience Anonymity	No control who is contacted Only Internet users Not representative Low response rates

Activity 15.2

Types of survey

In the BTDT campaign the sample consisted of 502 residents. But which type of survey would be the most appropriate method to collect data?

Consider and write down:

- How will respondents be reached?
- What might be the response rate?
- Think about cost and time effectiveness, too.

Activity 15.3

Developing a questionnaire

One key question in the BTDT campaign was to find out the attitudes of Westminster residents about recycling. Develop a short questionnaire to measure this.

Which instruments do you use?

Do you measure them directly or indirectly?

What are you going to ask?

The next step is to develop 'instruments for measurement', that is, framing the right kind of questions. The key research questions in the BTDT campaign indicate 'what' is to be measured, but they are not yet the questions that are used in a questionnaire. In general, the objects of research – in this case, knowledge, attitudes, behaviour – can be measured with various types of question and scale. Developing questions means to develop instruments that measure knowledge, attitude, etc. These concepts are *operationalised* through the questions (Wimmer and Dominick 2006). (See Glossary for definition of **operationalisation**.)

Example 15.1	Item pairs

Please assess the Royal Mail according to the following terms:

Boring . . . . .Interesting
Honest . . . . .Dishonest

Are you going to measure attitudes or images?

Images or attitudes can be measured using a variety of different techniques and instruments. Instruments are the specific questions or scales with which attitudes are measured. The next section gives an idea about the instruments that can be used depending on the object (e.g. attitudes about fast food), the respondents and the situation. The instruments are either quantitative, with standardised scales, or qualitative, going more in depth and providing insights that are not generated by quantitative approaches.

Further instruments can be classified as direct or indirect. Direct instruments clearly reveal the purpose of the questioning, for example, 'Do you intend to recycle?' Indirect instruments are used when there is the danger that respondents might answer in a 'socially acceptable' manner or follow existing stereotypes in their answers, instead of revealing their real attitudes.

An example of the choice of the instrument influencing the results are surveys about fast food. Fast foods and restaurants serving them seem to have a rather negative 'image' among university students, according to many surveys, if they are directly asked about their attitudes. There seems, however, to be a gap between the results of surveys and the behaviour of the students, who constitute one of the biggest customer groups of fast food restaurants.

Designing research instruments

Quantitative instruments to measure attitudes or images

Semantic differential (Example 15.1) is one of the most frequently used instruments in image measurement. It consists of pairs of contrary items by which the object of interest (organisations, persons, advertisements, issues, etc.) is evaluated. This approach draws on semiotics, an approach to the study of words, signs and symbols, which

discovered that people tend to group objects in simple either/or categories. Cars, councils, celebrities, baked beans can all be assessed by asking people whether they think these things are either luxury or basic goods, for example. You can go on to ask if they are old/young, male/female, etc. These either/or polarities can be either descriptive-direct or metaphoric-indirect. Item pairs that are descriptive-direct are **denotative**, that is, they relate to the perceived functions of the subject. Metaphoric-indirect items are **connotative**, that is, they relate to the emotional or mental associations of the item being researched. It is useful to use either denotative or connotative items. For example, if you evaluate a car, then item pairs such as 'slow–fast', 'expensive–good value' are denotative. Pairs like 'female–male' or 'warm–cold' are rather connotative.

The advantage of semantic differentials is that it is a highly standardised instrument with which different objects can easily be compared. A disadvantage is that it might consist of items that are rather irrelevant to the respondent's attitude about an object. If the research object is new and unexplored, then the relevance of items can be unclear.

Likert scales (Example 15.2) ask how far a respondent agrees or disagrees with statements about an object. The statements should cover all relevant facets of the research object. Nevertheless, it remains open as to how relevant statements are for respondents in their attitude about the object.

In *rank ordering* (Example 15.3), respondents have to place research objects – often listed on separate cards – in order from best to worst. This can be combined with open, qualitative questions that ask what they most like/dislike about the objects. This explores which features are relevant for their assessment. A problem with rank orders is that each object is only evaluated in comparison with the others but not on an absolute scale. An advantage is that the object is assessed as a whole entity and leaves it to the respondents to decide which features determine their opinion.

The *Kunin scale* (Example 15.4) is an example of how to assess objects non-verbally, which is easy for children or elderly people to understand.

Example 15.2   **Likert scale**

How much do you agree with the following statement: 'BT is a progressive corporation'?
Please tick one box.

Strongly agree	Agree	Neither agree nor disagree	Disagree	Strongly disagree

---

Example 15.3   **Rank order**

In front of you there are 10 cards with telecommunications providers. Please put the card with the telecommunications provider you like the most in the first position, the one you like the second best in the second position, and so on.

Example 15.4   **Kunin scale**

Please mark how much you like Virgin Trains.

Example 15.5   **Free associations**

Question: Please write down everything that comes into your mind when you hear the words 'Royal Mail'.

Possible answers: post, expensive, conservative, reliable, etc.

Additionally, the respondents might be asked in a follow-up question to assess all their answers and state whether they consider them 'positive (+)', 'neutral (0)' or 'negative (–)'. This avoids subjective misinterpretations of the researcher:

Post (0), expensive (–), conservative (0), reliable (+)

Qualitative instruments to measure attitudes or images

Free associations (Example 15.5) are considered to be a qualitative instrument because the respondents are not guided by existing categories for their answers.

If there is a danger that respondents might not admit or even express their real opinions, it makes sense to use a *projective question technique* (Example 15.6). The respondent is asked to answer a question as if replying for somebody else. The respondent projects their real answers into that person.

In the *balloon test* (Example 15.7) as a *specific projective instrument* the respondent gets a drawing with two people and is asked to fill in the empty 'balloon'. The idea is that the respondent projects their thoughts into the person with the empty balloon.

Box 15.2 on page 269 provides an example of measuring relationships by surveys.

Example 15.6	**Projective question**

In your opinion, what do other people think about the Royal Mail?

Example 15.7	**Balloon test**

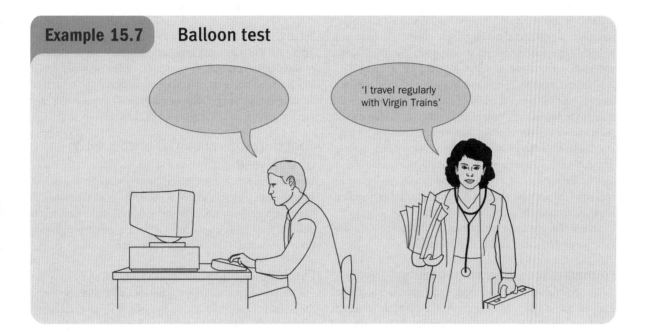

'I travel regularly with Virgin Trains'

Box 15.2

Using survey research to measure relationships

A typical research project for the study of relationships between an organisation and its publics is Hon and Grunig's (1999) measurement of relationships. So the research object is 'relationships'. Hon and Grunig specify 'successful relationships' as: control mutuality, trust, satisfaction, commitment, exchange relationship and communal relationship. The research method is conducting a survey.

In order to measure the concept 'relationship' they operationalise – 'make measurable' – the idea of relationship. They explore the six factors mentioned above by generating a list of statements for each factor, for respondents to agree or disagree with.

For example, the factor 'trust' is measured by statements:

- This organisation treats people like me fairly and justly.
- This organisation can be relied on to keep its promises.
- Whenever this organisation makes an important decision, I know it will be concerned about people like me.
- I feel very confident about this organisation's skills.
- I believe that this organisation takes the opinions of people like me into account when making decisions.

With these statements they conduct a survey among publics who evaluate their relationship with different organisations by how much they agree/disagree with each statement.

Source: Hon and Grunig 1999

Media content analysis

Media monitoring, collecting and counting press clippings, is widely used in public relations to track publicity. However, collecting data or output is only a first step in conducting a media content analysis. Only the systematic analysis of these materials according to a set of criteria can be considered as content analysis. 'Content analysis is a method to analyse media reality, verbal and visual output (content of newspapers, magazines, radio, television and web) which leads to inferences about the communicators and audience of these contents' (Merten 1995: 15).

Content analysis itself does not directly measure outcomes – for example, the image of an organisation in the mind of the audience – and might only be considered as an indicator of certain effects. Web logs, online newsgroups and chatrooms can be monitored, too. Computer-assisted content analysis uses specific software programs, which analyse frequencies of words or other categories. There are specialist research firms that offer services in this field (e.g. www.uk.cision.com).

In general, a content analysis is conducted in eight discrete steps (Wimmer and Dominick 2006).

Formulate the research question
Table 15.5 presents an overview of typical questions that can be answered by content analysis. The particular research question determines the further steps in the process of a content analysis.

Define a population
By defining the time period and the types of media (population) that will be analysed, the researcher sets the frame for the investigation.

For example, a content analysis might compare how fast food providers are covered in mass media. Since the general public might be considered a relevant audience, daily newspapers are defined as the population in question.

Select a sample from the population
As stated above, it is not possible to survey all members of a population all the time. So a smaller number of outlets and a specific period of time must be selected.

For example, the time period of the last half-year is the period in which the media coverage is analysed. Smaller newspapers reach fewer readers, so only the top five daily newspapers with the highest readership are selected.

Select and define a unit of analysis
There needs to be agreement about what exactly is being counted in the analysis. For example, each newspaper article in which the name of a fast food provider or the term 'fast food' is mentioned is a unit of analysis (in other words, not every mention of hamburger or of chips is counted).

Construct the categories of content to be analysed
The categories are determined by the research questions. In our example, this might be the rating of an article as 'positive/negative/neutral', the topic of the article, the sources quoted, etc. It is important to define indicators which determine what 'positive/negative/neutral' mean.

Establish a quantification system
The category system used to classify the media content is the actual measurement instrument. For each category, subcategories must be created. An example of a category might be 'corporate social responsibility'. Subcategories could be 'donations to charity', 'employee volunteering' and 'environmental policy'. The subcategories should be exhaustive, in that they cover all aspects of 'corporate social responsibility' that occur in the articles, and exclusive, which means that they should not overlap or denote the same.

Train coders and conduct a pilot study
To obtain valid results, different researchers, or coders, must assess the same article in the same way. A pilot study,

Table 15.5 Examples of questions researched through content analysis (*source*: adapted from Merten and Wienand 2004: 5)

Media	Issues and actors	Image
Which media/journalists dominate the media coverage?	Which issues dominate the media coverage?	Which image is portrayed?
How do media report about the organisation? (positive/negative/neutral)	Which actors dominate the media coverage?	Which factors dominate the image?
How many and which audiences are reached?	In the frame of which issues does the organisation and its representatives appear?	How is the organisation positioned in its sector?
		What do competitors do?

or trial run, can point out weaknesses in the categories or instructions for the coders. In practice, this will involve analysing a small sample of articles to test the instrument – the category system.

Code the content according to established definitions

Finally, all sample articles have to be assessed for each category and given a number for that assessment. The assessments are determined by the definitions associated with each category. For example, a mention of 'donations to charity' as a subcategory of 'corporate social responsibility' might be given a number code 1 to denote 'donations to charity'. Numbering like this helps with the data analysis, particularly across a wide range of categories and subcategories.

Research applications

Internet as a research tool and object

The Internet has become an increasingly important research object as well as a research tool. Research objects can be issues which are discussed in web logs or chatrooms. Another increasingly relevant issue is the measurement of the chatter and discussion about an organisation in cyberspace, which can be used to help understand an organisation's image or reputation. The same criteria used in analysing print and broadcast articles can be applied when analysing postings on the Internet, which is referred to as cyberspace analysis (Lindenmann 1997). Another output measure of cyberspace might be a review and analysis of website traffic patterns. For example, some of the variables that ought to be considered when designing and carrying out cyberspace analysis might include examining the requests for a file of website visitors, a review of click-throughs or flash-click streams, an assessment of home page visits, domain tracking and analysis and assessment of bytes transferred, a review of time spent per page, traffic times, browsers used and the number of people filling out and returning feedback forms (Lindenmann 1997).

The Internet also offers new opportunities to conduct research in online focus groups, online interviews or online surveys. Online focus groups can be conducted in 'real time' or in 'non-real time', or using a combination of both. It allows access to populations in disparate places and is highly cost effective. Nevertheless, the problem of participant verification (who is recruited as participant through the Internet) remains a problem in all forms of online research techniques (Mann and Stewart 2000).

Identifying publics: social network analysis

One tool that is used to identify relevant publics and opinion leaders, and to understand the communication flow and lines of influences within and between groups of people, is social network analysis (SNA) (Scott 2000). SNA is the mapping and measuring of relationships and flows between people, groups or organisations. It can be used for external and internal analysis (organisational network analysis) of relationships. But like a PEST (or EPISTLE) or SWOT analysis, the social network analysis is not a method itself. The network has to be explored, for example, through observation or interviews.

To understand the network, the location and context of the actors (people whose relationships are being observed) has to be evaluated first. For example, with whom does an actor interact? How many connections does an actor have? Is a person central in a network or peripheral? Is a person connected to well-connected or poorly connected people?

Of further interest in network analysis is:

- structural equivalence: which actors play similar roles in the network?
- cluster analysis: find cliques and densely connected clusters
- structural holes: find areas of no connection between actors that could be used for communication
- E/I ratio: find which groups in the network are open or closed to others (Scott 2000).

Communication audit

Communication audits assess the tangible and intangible communications resources of an organisation. A very formal and thorough audit may take months to complete. Communication audits examine:

- face-to-face communication
- written communication in the form of letters, memos and internal reports
- communication patterns among individuals, sections and departments
- communication channels and frequency of interaction
- communication content, its clarity and effectiveness
- information needs of individuals, sections or departments
- information technology
- informal communication, particularly as it affects motivation and performance

- non-verbal communication
- communication climate (Hamilton 1987: 4–5).

Evaluation

Importance of evaluation

Evaluation is the evergreen topic of the entire practice and one of the areas where both practitioners and academics have a vast common interest. In the UK, the Chartered Institute of Public Relations has initiated and coordinated research on evaluation and encouraged practitioners to evaluate their efforts in a systematic way by using a variety of methods.

Evaluating PR activities is essential for many reasons, including accountability, assessment of programme effectiveness and professionalism.

Evaluation is the systematic assessment of the impacts of PR activities. It is a purposeful process, carried out for a specific audience. Audiences include numerous parties that have an interest in the evaluation – the organisation, the PR practitioners involved, target publics and the evaluators themselves. (Sometimes an external agency, such as a media monitoring company, does media evaluation.) (See Activity 15.4.)

In a typical PR campaign, the following actors are present: the *organisation*, which can commission a *PR agency* to work on its behalf to reach and communicate with a variety of *publics* through the *media*. Figure 15.1 visualises the actors and their influences.

Out of these four actors, the emphasis has been on media, and print media evaluation still dominates the field of evaluation. Measuring effects on, and changes in, the targeted publics' knowledge, attitudes and behaviour in the form of outcome is also paramount. During the early

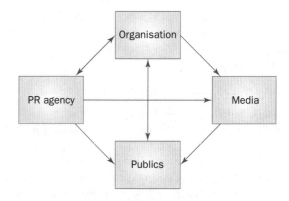

Figure 15.1 Actors and their influence

1990s the organisational dimension was emphasised, demonstrating how PR can add value to achieving organisational goals. Around the turn of the millennium a new dimension emerged, measuring relationship in the client/agency and client/publics contexts. Table 15.6 summarises the aims of evaluation according to orientations.

For an extensive evaluation, each of these orientations should be considered. However, the emphasis often remains on only one or two of these dimensions. Evaluation often serves as budget or action justification. In the media orientation approach the emphasis is on the quantity (how many articles were generated, how big is the circulation of the newspaper in which an article appeared) and quality of media coverage (negative, positive tone). (See Mini case study 15.2.)

PR practitioners overemphasise print media evaluation. Despite the fact that the world is moving more and more towards image-based communication, PR practice has been slow to embrace methods of evaluating TV and other types of image. Fathers4Justice is a pressure group in the UK whose aim is to highlight the problems of fathers separated from their children by divorce or relationship breakdown. They have performed 'stunts' to attract media attention to their issue by dressing up as children's or comic book characters. They have climbed government buildings, bridges and the Queen's London residence, Buckingham Palace, to create visually sensational, shocking images that can be easily transmitted into the living rooms of millions and grab attention. (See Activity 15.5.)

Dimensions of evaluation

PR evaluation can be:

- **formative**, **summative** or **goal-free evaluation**, depending on the time of intervention
- assessed at individual, programme, organisational and societal level, depending on the level of effectiveness.

Table 15.6
Orientations of public relations evaluation

Orientation	Aim of evaluation	Levels
Media	Quantity and quality of coverage	Programme, societal
Publics	Effects on publics, how they have changed their knowledge, attitudes or behaviour as a result of public relations activities	Programme
Organisation	To demonstrate how public relations can contribute to achieving organisational goals	Organisational
Persuasion	Demonstrates return on investment (ROI) to clients or management; value of public relations; accountability of public relations professionals or departments	Individual, programme
Relationship	Client/agency, organisation/publics	Individual, organisational

Mini Case Study 15.2

The IKEA story in the media

The media reported extensively the chaotic opening of London's Edmonton IKEA store in February 2005. Beyond the negative headlines was an undercurrent of hostility towards the company. The IKEA consumer experience, deemed to come a poor second to low prices, was singled out for particular criticism: 'IKEA treats its customers so badly, a riot is the least it might have expected' wrote the *Guardian* (10 February 2005), cataloguing an absence of Internet ordering, insufficient stock, poor customer service and lengthy queues. Others accused it of irresponsibly stimulating demand with heavy advertising and special offers in a deprived area: 'Does it pay to advertise?' (*The Times*, 10 February 2005).

Figure 15.2 is a typical example of evaluating media coverage, counting how many times certain types of messages occurred and assessing the tone of the coverage.

Source: www.echoresearch.com

Activity 15.5

Measuring media stunts

Examine the Fathers4Justice campaign (visit their website: www.fathers-4-justice.org). How would you conduct content analysis of TV coverage of one of their campaigns?

Feedback

Quantity: how many times was the name of the pressure group mentioned? How long was the entire coverage? Was it a leading piece of news?

Quality: What was the context of the coverage? Who was interviewed? How did the newsreader comment on their actions (favourably or unfavourably)? Do you now understand their demands more clearly?

As we saw earlier, formative evaluation (or process research) takes places while the programme is still in operation. Summative evaluation aims at assessing outcomes and impacts as they take place towards the end of a programme or after its conclusion. Summative research evaluates results against objectives. This can be feasible only if SMART objectives have been set: specific, measurable, achievable, realistic and timebound.

Evaluation purposes and circumstances dictate which type of evaluation (summative, formative or goal free) is most appropriate in a given case. Bissland's (1990: 25) definition illustrates that in PR literature evaluation is frequently used as a summative activity: 'Evaluation is the systematic assessment of a program and its results. It is a means for practitioners to offer accountability to clients – and to themselves.'

Messages by volume

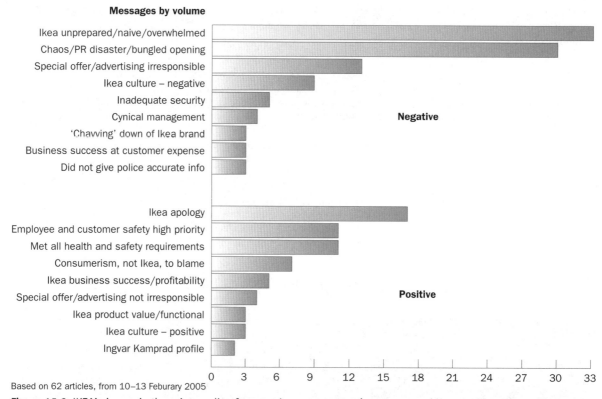

Based on 62 articles, from 10–13 Feburary 2005

Figure 15.2 IKEA's image in the print media after opening a new store (*source*: a weekly snapshot review of 'messages in the news' prepared by Echo Research for trade journal *PR Week*; Echo Research, http://www.echoresearch.com)

Picture 15.2 Fathers 4 Justice using media stunts to raise their campaign's media profile (see: http://www.fathers-4-justice.org) (*source*: Alisdair Macdonald/Rex)

Box 15.3

Four categories of performance measure

Input: background information and research that informs initial planning.

Output: measures the result of PR activity such as media coverage or publicity (exposure to messages, quantifiable features such as number of press releases sent out, consultation sessions scheduled, telephone calls answered or audience members at speech events). Output measures are short term, concentrate on visible results and do not say anything about audience response.

Outcome: the degree to which PR activities changed target public's knowledge, attitudes and behaviour. It may take weeks, months or even years for these changes to occur.

Outtake: describes an intermediate step between output and outcome. It refers to what people do with an output but what might not necessarily be a specific outcome as a set objective of a campaign. Whereas outtake is related to the output, outcome is to be seen with reference to the objectives set. For example, people might remember the message (outtake) of a communication campaign but might not change their behaviour (outcome).

Source: adapted from Gregory 2000: 169–71

Levels of effectiveness

According to Hon (1997) effective PR occurs when communication activities achieve communication goals. She conceptualised effectiveness at four levels.

Individual practitioners

The first level is that of individual practitioners, measuring how effective they are at achieving whatever is expected of them. This is closely related to performance measurement, partly because consultancy practitioners work on a fee basis. Depending on the positions and experience, the hourly rate of consultancy practitioners can vary. Another dimension of the individual level is the quality and nature of relationship between the consultant and the client. Client/agency relationship has become the focus of many evaluation studies, moving beyond the simple programme evaluation level.

Programme level

The second level is the programme level. Effectiveness in PR is quite often synonymous with effectiveness at the programme level and this level is usually the focus of evaluation. The results of PR activity can be further assessed by means of four categories of performance measures: input, output, outcome and outtake. Box 15.3 summarises these measures. (See Think about 15.3.)

Organisational level

The third level of effectiveness is organisational level. The typical question at this level is, 'How do PR activities and

efforts contribute to achieving organisational goals, such as being the market leader or increase sales figures?' Assessing effectiveness at organisational level also includes the aggregates of different PR activities, as in the case of a multinational organisation, which has regional or national offices with their own PR plans and programmes. If PR objectives are not in line with organisational goals, it might be difficult to evaluate the programme at this level. Another issue at this level may be the difficulty of separating PR effects from other effects (advertising, direct mails).

Think about 15.3

Output or outcome evaluation

Legoland Windsor is a family theme park aimed at three to twelve-year-olds. To help build excitement, the park attempted to build the world's tallest Lego tower over the May Day bank holiday 2008. The campaign objectives were to:

■ achieve national press and broadcast coverage

■ increase visitors to the museum

Source: *PR Week* 18 July 2008, campaigns section – 'Lego builds fanbase one brick at a time', p. 25

How do you evaluate the campaign?

What are the output and outcome measures?

Article mentions versus headlines
Press set: UK newspapers

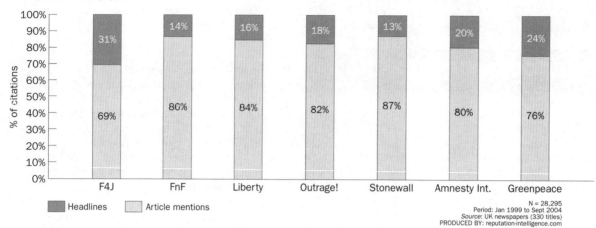

Figure 15.3 F4J grabbing headlines (*source*: Reputation Intelligence)

Societal level

As Hon noted, the final level of effectiveness is at the level of society. This level is usually examined from either a systems theory or a critical perspective (see Chapter 3). The systems theory approach asserts that PR plays a positive role in society; according to the critical perspective, PR activities have negative consequences on the society at large.

Evaluation methods

Earlier we discussed surveys, focus groups, interviews and content analysis as most frequently used methods to conduct research. They are used to evaluate PR programmes as well but there are other methods available for PR practitioners.

PR Week commissioned research in 1999 among 200 PR practitioners to gauge their attitudes and behaviour with regard to evaluation. About 60% of respondents said that they used media content analysis or press cuttings to evaluate their PR activities. The next most frequently used technique was opportunities to see (OTS), which is the number of occasions that an audience has the potential to view a message. The circulation numbers of the British daily newspapers presented in Table 15.2 includes these opportunities in the case of print media.

Surveys, focus groups and advertising value equivalents (AVEs) are also often used to evaluate PR programmes. AVE is the notional equivalent cost of buying editorial. It is a controversial method and practitioners are being discouraged from using this method because it compares advertising and PR (Watson and Noble 2005). However, national and international research confirms this method remains widely used by both in-house and consultancy practitioners. (See Box 15.4.)

Box 15.4

PR effects on societies

The effects and influences of PR practices on society at large can be broad and varied. PR can help to:

- Maintain the trust in the political system (western democracies)

- Integrate a society (after the collapse of the Soviet Union many Russians remained in the Baltic States and PR has been used to integrate Estonians, Latvians and Lithuanians with Russians)

- Transform a society (Latin America) or economy (Eastern Europe)

- Build nations (Malaysia, East Timor)

- Disintegrate countries, regimes (e.g. Yugoslavia, or Hill and Knowlton's infamous case about using alleged Iraqi atrocities to mobilise public opinion for a war against Iraq in 1991)

Source: Szondi 2006: 20

Box 15.5

Fathers4Justice (F4J) press coverage

On behalf of F4J, Reputation Intelligence, a research agency, analysed more than 10,000 articles from 330 UK newspapers published between 2000 and 2004. Media evaluation showed that:

- Articles on fathers' rights have increased by over 700% since F4J mounted its high-profile media campaign.
- F4J has engaged the politicians to speak on fathers' rights and encourage opposition parties to take up its fight.
- Compared to other political campaigning organisations, F4J is grabbing a high ratio of headlines to article mentions (see Figure 15.3, p. 276).
- F4J is well placed to turn this profile into clear messages on policy reform.

Source: Reputation Intelligence (2004)

Organisations do not always want to get publicity. In the case of a crisis, for example, the company may prefer minimal exposure to media. Nor is publicity the same as understanding – newspaper coverage may be extensive without clearly explaining the goals of those seeking publicity.

Evaluation guidelines

'Is it possible for those of us who work in the public relations field to ever develop generally accepted models or standards of public relations evaluation upon which everyone in the industry can agree?', asked Walter Lindenmann (1997: 391), a well-respected research specialist in the field.

The search for an objective, simple and effective methodology for evaluating PR programmes occupied much academic literature in the 1980s. Pavlik (1987: 65) commented that: 'Measuring the effectiveness of PR efforts has proved almost as elusive as finding the Holy Grail.' The search was over at the beginning of the 1990s, as Lindenmann (1993: 9) commented: 'There is no one simplistic method for measuring PR effectiveness . . . An array of different tools and techniques is needed to properly assess PR impact.'

Searching for a single and universal method was replaced by practitioners focusing on compiling an evaluation toolkit based on the best practice guidelines. In 1997 a 28-page booklet entitled *Guidelines and Standards for Measuring and Evaluating PR* was published by the

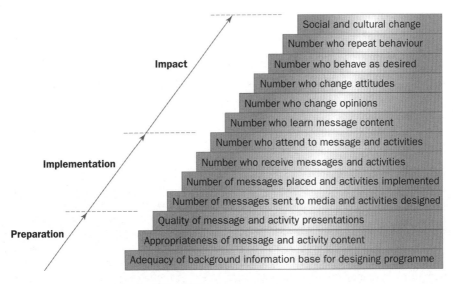

Figure 15.4 Stages and levels of public relations programme evaluation (*source*: Cutlip, Scott M., Center, Allen H., Broom, Glen M., *Effective Public Relations, 8th Edition*, © 2000, p. 437. Reprinted by permission of Pearson Education, Inc., Upper Saddle River, NJ)

Institute of Public Relations Research & Education in the USA. In Europe, two booklets were produced with a more focused purpose, covering how to prepare measurable goals and objectives prior to the launch of a campaign and how to measure PR outputs.

In the UK, a research and evaluation toolkit was compiled in 1999 utilising the findings of the above-mentioned *PR Week* survey on evaluation. This toolkit spells out the best reasons for employing research and evaluation in campaigns and gives guidance on how to set about it. The author of the toolkit argued that the UK is taking a leading position on research and evaluation. In 2003 the Institute of Public Relations published the 'IPR Toolkit: Media evaluation edition'.

Evaluation models

A number of evaluation models have been developed to serve as guidelines in terms of what to evaluate and how to evaluate. Most are three-stage models embracing a variety of techniques. Cutlip et al.'s 'stages and levels of public relations programme evaluation', represents different levels of a complete programme evaluation: preparation, implementation and impact (Figure 15.4). This first level assesses the information and planning, the implementation evaluation deals with tactics and activities while the impact evaluation provides feedback on the outcome.

Preparation evaluation assesses the quality and adequacy of information that was used to plan the programme. Some key publics might have been unidentified at the planning stage or some issues overlooked. This stage is very similar to the plan assessment we discussed earlier.

At the second level, implementation evaluation assesses the number of messages distribution and measures outputs. The final stage, the impact level, examines the extent to which the defined goals of the campaigns have been achieved. This level is primarily concerned with the changes in knowledge, attitudes and behaviour.

As the authors noted, the most common error in programme evaluation is substituting measures from one level for those at another (Cutlip et al. 2006).

Macnamara's (1992) model is similar but uses different terminology: inputs, outputs and results. (Output is usually the short-term or immediate results of a particular PR programme or activity.) This model lists evaluation methodologies that can be applied to each step, but for different steps different methodologies are required. The model is presented in a pyramidal form starting from inputs through outputs to results (see Figure 15.5; see also Activity 15.6).

Barriers and challenges to developing and using effective research in PR activities can be summarised as follows. Watson (1994) found that the barriers to evaluation uncovered in his survey were mirrored worldwide:

■ lack of time

■ lack of personnel

■ lack of budget

■ cost of evaluation

■ doubts about usefulness

■ lack of knowledge

■ can expose practitioner's performance to criticism

■ aversion to scientific methodology.

The challenge of the profession lies in overcoming these difficulties.

Activity 15.6

Macnamara's model

Review the evaluation of the Bin There Done That campaign. What are the inputs, outputs and results that are measured in this campaign? What does it tell you about the extent or depth of evaluation?

Summary

This chapter outlined the principles of research, which is a central activity in any PR programme. A variety of research methods have been presented that enable PR practitioners to conduct systematic and objective research, and scopes of research and evaluation have been outlined.

Since an organisation's public relations are related to other communication activities such as marketing communications, research must also be integrated with these areas. PR research and evaluation cannot be seen in isolation from an organisation's other communication research. If we talk about integrated communications, then we also have to talk about 'integrated communications research (and evaluation)'.

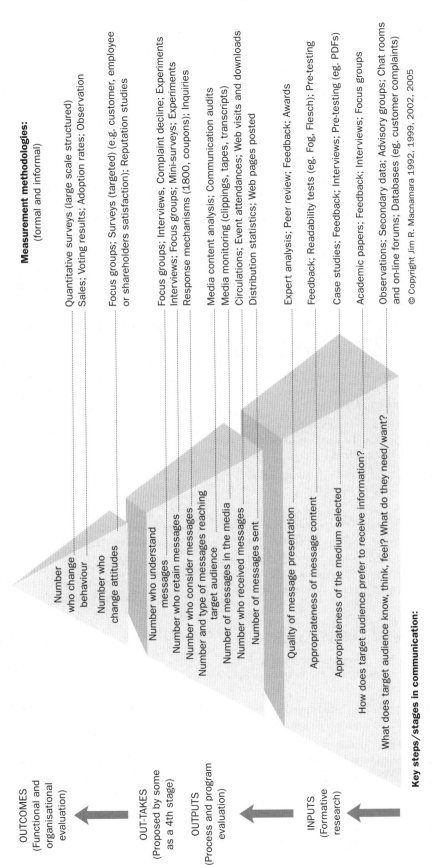

Figure 15.5 Macnamara's evaluation model (updated) (*source:* Macnamara 1992: 28)

Bibliography

Besson, N. (2008). *Strategische PR-Evaluation. Erfassung, Bewertung und Kontrolle von Öffentlichkeitsarbeit*, 3. Auflage. Wiesbaden: VS Verlag für Sozialwissenschaften.

Bissland, J.H. (1990). 'Accountability gap: evaluation practices show improvement'. *Public Relations Review* 16(2): 25–26.

Broom, G.M. and D.M. Dozier (1990). *Using Research in Public Relations: Applications to program management.* Englewood Cliffs, NJ: Prentice Hall.

Cutlip, S.M., A.H. Center, G.M. Broom (2000) *Effective Public Relations*, 8th edition, p. 437. Pearson Education, Inc., Upper Saddle River, NJ.

Cutlip, S.M., A.H. Center and G.M. Broom (2006). *Effective Public Relations*, 9th edition. Upper Saddle River, NJ: Prentice Hall International.

Gregory, A. (2000). *Planning and Managing Public Relations Campaigns*, 2nd edition. London: Kogan Page.

Hamilton, S. (1987). *A Communication Audit Handbook – Helping Organisations Communicate.* London: Pitman.

Hon, L.C. (1997). 'What have you done for me recently? Exploring effectiveness in public relations'. *Journal of Public Relations Research* 9(1): 1–30.

Hon, L.C. (1998). 'Demonstrating effectiveness in public relations: Goals, objectives, and evaluation'. *Journal of Public Relations Research* 10(2): 103–135.

Hon, L.C. and J.E. Grunig (1999). *Measuring Relationships in Public Relations.* Gainesville, FL: Institute for Public Relations.

Kerlinger, F.N. (1986). *Foundations of Behavioral Research*, 3rd edition. Fort Worth, TX: Holt, Rinehart & Winston.

Kim, Y., J. Kim, J. Park and Y. Choi (1999). 'Evaluating media exposure: An application of advertising methods to publicity measurement'. *Corporate Communications* 4(2): 98–105.

Lerbinger, O. (1977). 'Corporate uses of research in public relations'. *Public Relations Review* 3(4):11–20.

Lindenmann, W.K. (1990). 'Research, evaluation and measurement: A national perspective'. *Public Relations Review* 16: 3–15.

Lindenmann, W.K. (1993). 'An "effectiveness yardstick" to measure public relations success'. *PR Quarterly* 38(1): 7–9.

Lindenmann, W.K. (1997). 'Setting minimum standards for measuring public relations effectiveness'. *Public Relations Review* 23(4): 391–408.

Lindlof, T.R. and C.T. Bryan (2002). *Qualitative Communication Research Methods.* Thousand Oaks, CA: Sage.

Macnamara, J.R. (1992). 'Evaluation of public relations: The Achilles heel of the profession'. *International Public Relations Review* 15(4): 17–31.

Mann, C. and F. Stewart (2000). *Internet Communication and Qualitative Research: A handbook for researching online.* London: Sage.

Merten, K. (1995). *Inhaltsanalyse. Einführung in Theorie, Methode und Praxis.* Opladen: Westdeutscher Verlag.

Merten, K. and E. Wienand (2004). 'Medienresonazanalyse'. Paper presented at the Redaktion und wissenschaftlicher Beirat der Pressesprecher Conference, Berlin, 7 May.

Neumann, P. (2003). *Markt- und Werbepsychologie* Bd. 2. *Praxis.* Gräfelfing: Fachverlag Wirtschaftspsychologie, 2nd edition.

Pavlik, J.V. (1987). *Public Relations: What research tells us.* Newbury Park, NJ: Sage.

Reputation Intelligence (2004) 'F4J heralds a new era in political campaigning: Media Report', http://bten.co.uk/fathers-4-justice.org/pdf/ReputationIntelligence_MediaReport_14 Sept04_v4.pdf. accessed 25 September 2008.

Scott, J. (2000). *Social Network Analysis.* London: Sage.

Szondi, G. (2006). 'Re-Valuating Public Relations Evaluation – Putting Values at the Centre of Evaluation'. *Medien Journal* (4): 7–26.

Vos, M. and H. Schoemaker (2004). *Accountability of Communication Management – A Balanced Scorecard for Communication Quality.* Utrecht: Lemma Publishers.

Watson, T. (1994). 'Evaluating public relations: models of measurement for public relations practice'. Paper presented at the International Public Relations Symposium, Lake Bled, Slovenia.

Watson, T. (1997). 'Measuring the success rate: Evaluating the PR process and PR programmes' in *Public Relations Principles and Practice.* P. Kitchen (ed.). London: Thomson Business Press.

Watson, T. and P. Noble (2005). *Evaluating public relations.* London : Kogan Page.

Wimmer, R.D. and J.R. Dominick (2006). *Mass Media Research: An introduction*, 8th edition. Belmont, CA: Wadsworth.

Index